2016:
THE CAMPAIGN CHRONICLES

2016:
THE CAMPAIGN CHRONICLES
SECOND EDITION

JD FOSTER

Copyright © 2019 by JD Foster.

Library of Congress Control Number: 2019914545
ISBN: Hardcover 978-1-7960-6051-5
Softcover 978-1-7960-6050-8
eBook 978-1-7960-6049-2

All rights reserved. No part of this book may be reproduced or transmitted in any form or by any means, electronic or mechanical, including photocopying, recording, or by any information storage and retrieval system, without permission in writing from the copyright owner.

The views expressed in this work are solely those of the author and do not necessarily reflect the views of the publisher, and the publisher hereby disclaims any responsibility for them.

Any people depicted in stock imagery provided by Getty Images are models, and such images are being used for illustrative purposes only.
Certain stock imagery © Getty Images.

Print information available on the last page.

Rev. date: 10/08/2019

To order additional copies of this book, contact:
Xlibris
1-888-795-4274
www.Xlibris.com
Orders@Xlibris.com
800600

CONTENTS

Prologue xix

Chapter 1: The Gun Sounds 1
   Part of a Pattern? 2
   The Cycle Starts 4
   Essential Realities into the 2014 Election 7
   Opening the 2014 Can of Political Whoop Ass 10
   Follow the Money, 2014 Version 13
   What to Do about Obama 15
   The Timeline 16
   Wisdom from the National Pastime 18

Chapter 2: Initial Rumblings 21
   Obama Shapes the Terrain 22
   Losing Landrieu 24
   The Fires of December 25
   A Cajun Exclamation Point and the Senate's Balance of Power 26
   Sine Die 30
   The Hillary Factor 31
   The Clinton Snooze 33
   Warren's Calling 34
   Jeb Bush: Mr. Methodical 36
   Bush and the New Republican Party 39
   First Mover 42
   Viva, Cuba! 44

CHAPTER 3: NEW YEAR, NEXT CAMPAIGN 47
    Chris Christie's Bridge to Purgatory 48
    Peyton Manning as Mitt Portent? 51
    The First Mitt Waves 54
    A Quiet Little Chat 56
    If It Bleeds, It Leads 57
    Walker's Run 59

CHAPTER 4: THE FINE ART OF WASHINGTON POLITICAL THEATER 61
    The DHS Dance 61
    The Republican State of Play, End of February 65
    Cracks in the Clinton Foundation 66
    O'Malley Calling 70
    Trump and Carly 71
    Learn, Adapt, Overcome? 75

CHAPTER 5: THE PARADE STARTS 78
    First Casualty and Future Phoenix 81
    The Parade Continued 82
    Feeling the Bern? 88
    The Graham Cracker 91
    Stripping Away the Mask 93
    The Clinton (Campaign) Foundation Is Crumbling 96
    Hillary Speaks (Very) Softly but Scores a Big Payday 100
    An Immigration Detour to the Rescue 101
    A Few More Candidacy Footnotes for the Record 103
    Mike Huckabee, Curiosity 104
    The Difference between Intelligence and Experience 104
    Elections across the Pond an Omen for the United States? 105
    Unforced Errors, Big Time 107
    Rubio's Rub 112
    June and Breakfast at Bernie's 114

CHAPTER 6: THE BOYS AND GIRLS OF SUMMER 116
  A Republican Complex 118
  The Texas Two-Step 120
  The New York Times Sets a Rubio Speed Trap 121
  A Shakeup before Kickoff 122
  The Four Percent Fantasy 123
  Filling Out the Dance Card 125
  Walker on the Wild Side 127
  Kasich the Caboose 129
  Emanuel AME Here 130
  American Football, Duets, and Lessons about
  International Trade 135
  SCOTUScare 139
  Tale of Two Impossibles 141
  Cash Is King 146
  Hillary Continues to Stumble 146
  Joe B Stirs 150

CHAPTER 7: THE BIG CACOPHONY AND BEYOND 152
  The Clash in Cleveland 155
  After the Gab 157
  And the Winner Is? 158
  Bernie Continues His Ascent 160
  A Little Higher Ed Initiative 161
  Drip, Drip, Drip in Hillary's Kitchen 163
  The High Price of Loyalty 166
  Trump Gets Positional 169
  Joe's Getting Warmer 175
  No Tea, No Party 179

CHAPTER 8: GEARING UP: LABOR DAY TO DECEMBER 182
  Jim Gilmore's Stealth Campaign 185
  Hillary's Filet of Flounder 186
  Graham's Crackers II 187
  Tax Reform, Anyone? 188

- Democrats Do Taxes 191
- Fall Pruning 192
- Oh Crap! 194
- Backstage Talent 196
- Republicans Rumble in Reaganland 197
- Clinton's Pipeline 203

CHAPTER 9: FALL MANEUVERS 206
- Boehner Bows Out 208
- Krauthammer's Take 210
- Trump's Tax Tanks 211
- How Long Can This Last? 212
- The Market's View 213
- What Does Hillary Really Believe? 214
- The First Democratic Debate 215
- Speaking of Ryan and Benghazi 220
- CNBC's Debacle: The Third Republican Debate 222
- Jeb Can Fix It 228
- Early Winds of Change? 229
- Campaigns as Debating Societies 230
- ISIS Attacks, the Campaign Pivots 231
- A Sort of Cajun Bites the Dust 233
- Paris Echoes 233
- Taking Stock at Thanksgiving 234

CHAPTER 10: THE IOWA RUN-UP 237
- An Angry Nation 238
- Into the Next Debates 242
- The Speaker Speaks 245
- The Democrats Debate Again. Anyone Notice? 245
- Taking Stock for Christmas 247
- Rubio Tacks to Attack 249
- The National Picture 251
- Bye-Bye, Lindsey, We Hardly Knew You 252

Obama the Almost Invisible 252
The WaPo Stoops to a New Low.. 253
Bill Is Fair Game 254
Who Were These Trumpees? 256
Happy New Year (?) 257

Chapter 11: Give Iowa a Chance 258
A Nation Uneasy 259
The Polls to Start the Year 260
Hillary in Iowa 262
Iowa First—Why? 264
A Question of Balance 266
Iowa in Portrait, Politically 268
When Front-Runners Get Nervous 269
Obama's Last SOTU 270
Chelsea on the Attack 272
January 14 Republican Debate—Gloves Off 273
Campaign Strategery[294] 274
The Palin Drone 276
Superdelegates and Clinton's Institutional Advantage 279
Beyond Top Secret 280
Cats and Dogs 281
Pregame Gab 282

Chapter 12: Voters Vote, Finally 284
Pocketbook Issues 285
Too Top Secret to Release 286
A Five-Candidate Race 287
Iowa Votes, at Last 290
New Hampshire Awaits 292
At Liberty to Exit 294
Knowing When to Stop Punching 295
Ben's Not-So-Excellent Ted Adventure 296
A Nasty Tiff in New Hampshire 297
Who Are Your Friends? 298

The Republicans' New Hampshire Debate..................300
Going Ballistic..................302
Hillary's Speeches and Other Handicaps..................302
Secretary Mush..................304
New Hampshire Finally Has a Voice..................304
Too Little Winnowing..................308

CHAPTER 13: OF PALMETTOS AND DICE: SOUTH CAROLINA AND NEVADA..................311
New Hampshire Aftermath..................312
Down and Dirty in the Deep South..................313
Palmetto Polls to Start..................314
Bloomberg's News..................315
Hillary's Up, Down, and Sideways..................317
Debate as Debacle..................319
The Longest-Serving Supreme Falls..................321
Another Clinton Email Drip, with a Caddell Kicker..................324
Trump Fights with the Pope..................325
Nikki's Nod..................327
Trump Goes Lite on Policy..................328
Flaming Tongues of Fire..................329
Game Day for the Gamecocks..................330
Sanders's Roll of the Dice..................332
Republicans Try Their Luck..................333
The Texas Gang Fight..................334
Next Up, Dems in South Carolina..................338
Who's Got the Numbers?..................340
The Narrative Process..................340

CHAPTER 14: MARCH, THE SUPER MONTH..................342
An Odd Calm..................342
Super Tuesday by Design..................344
Super Tuesday Results..................346
The Kasich/Carson Effect..................347
Democrats on Super Tuesday..................348

Another, Ahem, Debate 349
A Steady Parade of Election Results 350
Drip, Drip, Drip—Immunity 351
Hopes for a Trump Virus Vaccine 352
Just When the Path Seemed Clear 353
Yet Another Flinty Debate 355
Tweener Tuesday 356
Hillary, Trade, and Another Kama Sutra 359
Staying in Character: The Rise and Fall of Marco Rubio 360
Two More Debates—Sigh 363
Religious Curiosities and Minor Contests 364
American Politics Takes a Decided Turn for the Worse 366
John Kasich's Own Little Fantasy 368
Super Tuesday II 370
Another Stage, Another Grind 374
Ryan—No! 375
An Army of One 377
Arizona, Utah, Idaho, American Samoa 377
Cruzian Realities 378
Cuba and Brussels 380
Gathering Forces in Self-Defense 382
Trump Sinks to a New Low 383
Enquiring Minds and the Lawyer's Offer 384
Hillary Cruisin', Bernie Bruisin' 384

CHAPTER 15: WISCONSIN CHEESE TO ACELA PRIMARY 386
Is You Is or Is You Ain't a Republican? 387
Wisconsin Cheese 388
Sanders Goes Super 389
Drip, Drip, Drip . . . Discovery 389
The Abortion Issue 391
Trump's NATO Air Strike 393
Trump's Independent Streak 395
Feinstein Trips on Accomplishments 396
Accomplishments a Nuisance, the FBI a Threat 397

Fiscal Fantasies of a Trumpian Dimension 398
Badger Votes 400
On to the Empire State 401
A Cycle Without Pause 402
Cruz the Delegate Master 404
Cruz and "New York" Values 408
What Is Paul Ryan Up To? 409
Black Lives Matter, Meet Bill. Bill, Meet Black Politics 410
Sanders's First Endorsement 413
Brooklyn's Electric Kool-Aid Acid Test 414
By the Numbers 415
RNC to Trump: Quit Your Kvetching 417
Ted Gives Donald More Grounds for Whining 418
Just How in the Tank Was the WaPo? 419
New York Votes 420
Next Up 422
A Flaky Alliance 425
Northeasterners Take the Acela Primary 426

Chapter 16: The Final Rounds of Two Epic Fights 428
It Ain't Over Till the Skinny Lady Sings 429
Trump Goes All Foreign 432
The Award for the Second-Limpest Endorsement Goes
to . . . Mike Pence, Governor of Indiana 433
Further Delegate Machinations 434
Getting Hairy at the Trump Rallies 437
"This Is Nuts" 437
Say Good Night, Ted 438
Indiana's Bernin' 441
Why Trump? 443
Drip, Drip, Drip in May 444
Unity? Bah, Humbug 446
Trump's Veepstakes Anew 448
The Ever-Varying Candidate 448
GOP's Existential Angst 451

The Democrats Were Still Battling 453
Why Can't We Be Friends? 454
Trump's Bummer Taxes 456
Predictions vs. Disruptive Forces 458
Drip, Drip, Drip, Mills Takes a Walk 460
Crossing the Line 461
Kentucky, Oregon, and Back to Nevada 464
Trump Goes into the Bridge-Building Business Big-Time 467
National Polls 469
A *WaPo* Day in the Life of Hillary 470
Drip, Drip, Drip, Brick Wall 472
Trump Gains a New Antagonist—Pocahontas 475
Trump's Take on the Press 476
The Era of Non-Ringing Endorsements 477
Three's a Crowd 479
Hillary Takes Her Best Shot 480
Violence Comes to Cali 481
A Climactic Finale 481

CHAPTER 17: THE STORM BEFORE THE STORM 483
Oh, Orlando 484
Drip, Drip, Drip Plus $18 Million 486
Vlad Hacks the DNC 487
Distinguishing Heart, Mind, and Muscle 488
First Rumble 490
What a Week! 493
Cleaning Up After Your Own Parade 495
ISIS Losing Ground, Winning the War 497
Drip, Oh Huma! 498
Drip, Drip, Phoenix 499
Drip, Drip, Drip … Walk 501
The Media Meets Its Match 505
A Bad Night in Baton Rouge, in Minneapolis, in Dallas,
in Chicago 507
Drip, Drip, Drip, DOJ Referral 510

Veeping...511
A Supreme Puts More Than a Toe over the Line......................512
The Midsummer Polls...513

CHAPTER 18: CONVENTIONAL WISDOM 516
The Two Shades of Bias...518
A World in Tumult 520
I Like, You Like 521
Unity..523
Republican Convention, First Night 524
Republicans, Days Two and Three 526
Republican Convention, Day Four 528
Running with a Kaine 530
Now, the Democrats 531
Michelle O Has Her Say..534
Do Democrats Even Know Islamic Terrorism Exists?............535
Bill Takes the Show..536
Tidbits Off the Floor..537
Day 3 Oratorical Notables 539
Hillary's Big Moment 541

CHAPTER 19: THE AUGUST LULL THAT WASN'T 543
The Wrath of Khan 544
Catching Up with the Polls..552
Trump's Very Bad Week 552
How Bad Did It Get?...555
The Tiger's Stripes..556
Hillary's Returns...557
What Campaigns in Trouble Do 558
Drip, Drip, Drip—FBI Dump...559
Manafort to the Ukraine 561
Drip, Drip, Drip . . . Surprise! More Emails..............................563
Trump Wobbles on Immigration 567
Trump the Surpriser in Chief..569
Into the Mud Pits, Dear Friends 570

Drip, Drip, Drip—Not Again!..571
Wheezing into Labor Day..572
A Labor Day Snapshot..574

CHAPTER 20: THE SEPTEMBER OF OUR DISCONTENT...............576
By the Slimmest of Margins..577
Drip, Drip, Drip—the FBI Reports...580
Drip, Drip, Drip . . . Bill's Excellent $17.6 Million
Education Adventure..582
Hillary's Health..583
They're Back!..585
The Ideological-Political Complex 587
The Candidates Go Intrepid and Get Defensive........................589
Stronger Together 590
Hillary's Basket of Deplorables 591
A Quick Look at the Polls...592
Trump Struggles Pretending to Be a Republican 593
Trump and Birthing..596
Events, Dear Boy..598
Hillary Sliding into the Debate..600
Trump Flaws, Foibles, and Fundamentals..................................602
Trump Advantages to Not Being Republican 604
Not Again! 605
Fundamental Differences: Growth vs. Redistributionism 607
Hillary between Two Ferns 608
Ted Cruz Returns and President Pseudonym...........................609
Clinton's Mounting Desperation 611
The First Debate..612
Drip, Drip, Drip—More Immunity... 619
Obama's Iraq, Hillary's Missed Fact Check 621

CHAPTER 21: THE LAST MILE..623
Trump's Bad Week..624
Catching Up with "Third Party" Candidates 627
Trump Foundation Foibles...628

Bill C: It's the Craziest Thing in the World 629
Kainus Interruptus 630
Oh, That Donald Trump 632
Hillary's Open Borders 634
The Second Debate: Hell Comes to St. Louis 636
A Contrast in Reactions 639
By George, They're All Corrupt 642
The WaPo Comes Clean, Jenny Gets Dirty 645
Donald Trump's Dodgy History 646
Clinton Continues to Wiki Leak 647
Signs of the Times 648
Trump Unleashed 649
A Campaign Dominated by Sex 650
Trump's Enemies Just as Bad 651
Melania and Ivanka Defend Donald 653
More Rigging 654
Trump's Tide Turns Tail 656
The Third Debate 657
    Supreme Court 658
    Gun Control 659
    The Economy 659
    Accepting Rigged Elections 661
    Immigration 661
    Pay to Play 663
    The Allegations 664
After the Debate 667

CHAPTER 22: THE COUNTDOWN 669
    E-Day Minus 14, Tuesday, October 25: The Din Gets Louder 669
    E Minus 13—"They Wanted to Get Away with It" 671
    E Minus 12—Bill Clinton Inc 671
    E Minus 11—FBI: Kaboom 674
    E Minus 10—Clinton's Smart Move 675
    E Minus 9—Weiner Strikes Again! 676
    E Minus 8—The FBI Investigates, the DOJ Stonewalls 679

 The Empire Strikes Back 680
 CNN Parts Company with Donna Brazile 681
 Mutually Very Unfavorable 682
 A Peak at the States 682
E Minus 7, Tuesday, November 1—Clinton Sinking 683
E Minus 6, Wednesday, November 2—Isn't That Rich! 684
 The FBI Gets a Little Jiggy 685
 Taking the Temperature 687
E Minus 5, Thursday, November 3—Drip, Drip, Drip,
the FBI Does the Foundation 688
E Minus 4, Friday, November 4—Clinton Holds a Lead,
Barely 691
E Minus 3, Saturday, November 5—Not Done Yet 693
E Minus 2, Sunday, November 6—The End Is Nigh, Indeed ... 694
 Comey's Second Letter 697
 Obama Encourages Illegal Residents to Vote 698
 The DOJ Has a Mole 699
E Minus One, Monday, November 7—Down to the Last 700
Clinton Leads, but Trump Contends 701

CHAPTER 23: DECISION AT JOURNEY'S END 704
 The Wait 706
 Stunning 707
 Final Results 708
 Two Americas, Revisited 709
 Into the Weeds a Bit 710
 Immediate Aftermath 712

ENDNOTES 717
INDEX 797

PROLOGUE

In politics, an absurdity is not a handicap.[1]
—Napoleon Bonaparte

I began this project the day after the 2014 midterm elections. The midterms produced some surprising results, and the stage seemed set for at least a moderately interesting 2016 presidential campaign. Pres. Obama wasn't particularly popular, but the Democratic Party seemed likely to nominate former Secretary of State Hillary Clinton, so one party at least would have a credible contender.

For their part, the Republicans were highly energized and optimistic. A great many credible names were holding their hats, ready to toss them into the ring to chase the Republican nomination. The Republican establishment would be well represented by former Florida Gov. Jeb Bush and maybe former Republican presidential nominee Mitt Romney. Various hard-right candidates were circling, and some seemed viable. Some governors of various political flavors also waited in the wings.

All in all, Republicans' optimism seemed well-founded and underscored by the weak performance of the U.S. economy. Pocketbook issues and domestic security would dominate the campaign it seemed; and on both counts, the Democratic nominee would have a difficult hill to climb, either running to carrying the unpopular Obama's legacy or striking out on a new path and risking Obama's wrath.

It seemed the nation was about to watch an interesting story play out, one worth recording as it happened. "Interesting," in hindsight, may not be the best word to describe the 2016 campaign; but whatever word one chooses, there can be little doubt the drama that unfolded over the following two years merited recording at length.

Many books have been written on past presidential campaigns, but rarely has a campaign's story been written explicitly as a chronicle of events. Looking back on events from the perspective of months or years has the great advantages of perspective and access to mountains of relevant information. However, with the passage of time, such efforts lose the flavor and intensity of the moment and can miss defining details.

The author can honestly attest to having no favorite in either the primaries or the general election. Fair warning: anyone believing Hillary Clinton walked on water or that Donald Trump was America's political messiah will find many sections of this book infuriating. If a reader supported a candidate "warts and all," then hopefully the warts and all will appear presented in proper proportion to the candidate's virtues. All the flaws that seemed noteworthy at the time are discussed as appropriate; but also, whenever a candidate of either party said or did something worthy of praise, same was duly noted.

As originally envisioned, the work would reflect a blending of national and world events, public policy, and, of course, campaign developments, all from a distinctly Washington perspective. After the fact, it became clear the original vision no longer fit the campaign as it unfolded. The vision would have been fine for a normal election but not for 2016. Thus, some significant editing became necessary to make the work more appropriate to the fact, hence, this second edition.

This chronicle of the 2016 presidential election is by no means the last word on the topic, but hopefully it will provide an interesting window to the reader and prove a useful starting point for those who in the future ask various forms of the question, "What the heck happened?"

Finally, I would like to thank my family for their patience. This project has been great fun for me but not always for them.

CHAPTER 1
THE GUN SOUNDS

November 8, 2016, the American people elected Donald Trump, final survivor of the most bizarre political campaign since the memory of man runneth not to the contrary. Incredibly, Trump would be the forty-fifth President of the United States of America. Against incalculably impossible odds, against sixteen opponents in the Republican primary season, against a seasoned, disciplined, and well-funded general election opponent, Trump had prevailed; and now the real work began. Elation, exhaustion, trepidation, panic, pride, and maybe even humility likely washed like a flashflood through his mind over the next few hours and days.

America had survived eight years of Barack Obama just as it had survived eight years of George W. Bush before. Surely, you'll do better, Trump must have thought to himself. Divine providence? Trump surely wondered. Lord knew the country needed if not a savior, then at least a minor prophet. What have I done? he surely asked himself in awe mixed with horror.

Two years prior, you were the shiny new CEO of a startup business of poor prospects in a frenetic industry. Slowly at first, and then steadily faster, the business grew. You built your campaign team, somehow overcame mistakes that should have ended your run, made a few particularly deft moves, watched your competition falter, and now your company dominated the industry. Congratulations!

Then, all at once, you sold the business and the very next day began to prepare to take over the biggest, most diverse, most complicated, often most opaque business known to man: the United States government. You have seventy-two days to get ready, and most of the business's top executives will leave as you arrive.

Such was Donald Trump's next journey. This is the story of the incredible journey that was the 2016 presidential campaign resulting in Trump's own personal brave new world. The campaign had been a whirlwind, but that was just a warm-up for the ordeal just begun. Welcome to the biggest of the big leagues, Mr. Trump.

This is the story not of running the world's most enormous enterprise but of running to run that enterprise. It is a chronicle of the campaign for the presidency of the United States, 2016 edition. The 2016 presidential campaign will spawn articles and analyses and books for years to come. Many such are written after modern campaigns—some by journalists, others by campaign operatives—full of stories of slights, missteps, personalities, foibles, and the occasional stroke of genius. These are then followed by deeper analyses by professional historians. These works are useful as they look back into history with the dual benefits of hindsight and new data. This telling differs in that it chronicles events as they happened, recording the impressions, assumptions, and common beliefs along the way.

This telling is different in another way. This telling chronicles the events through the lens of national and world events and of congressional machinations and federal policies influencing and influenced by the election. Elections don't happen in a vacuum.

Part of a Pattern?

Recent presidential elections had been increasingly bizarre. In 1992, a scrub former Arkansas Governor, Bill Clinton, a man of great charm and charisma and enough personal baggage to exhaust a small army of Sherpas, defeated the liked but hapless President George H. W. Bush. Clinton's reelection victory over the war hero and longtime Republican leader, Kansas Sen. Bob Dole, was fairly routine; but then

George W. Bush defeated Clinton's Vice President, Al Gore, in a hotly contested election.

The presidency then fell to a junior senator from Illinois bereft of accomplishments but blessed with an extraordinary oratory and a remarkable ability to connect with the voters and to convey the inspiration one seeks in a presidential candidate. Barack Obama also just happened to be African American. All ideology aside, the nation merits some hope when a black man can become president. For his reelection, Obama then dispatched yet another aging war hero, Arizona Sen. John McCain.

In the course of the 2016 campaign, former First Lady, former New York senator, and former Secretary of State Hillary Clinton had been forced into a surprising and lengthy primary against the cranky old Vermont Socialist, U.S. Sen. Bernie Sanders. Just as Barack Obama as a black man becoming president was cause for hope, so too the fact a major political party had nominated a woman, Hillary Clinton, to be its presidential nominee. America, it seemed, would before long have a woman president—just not Hillary Clinton.

On the Republican side, at the beginning, the field of seventeen candidates appeared diverse and strong. The Republicans ran a black man, minorities, and a woman. They ran moderates, moderate conservatives, Tea Party faves, and Donald Trump, at the time a Republican of convenience only. They ran governors and senators, a surgeon, and a businessman. For the eventual nominee, Donald Trump, claiming the Republican nomination seemed at the start simply preposterous.

The contest between Clinton and Trump was one for the ages. Never before had either political party nominated a candidate regarded so poorly by so many, and yet both parties had done so. In most campaigns, the key was to highlight the opponent's weaknesses and flaws and to emphasize your own strengths. In this campaign, the key was to let the other candidate flounder on their own, weighed down by past mistakes or current self-inflicted wounds. On whomever the spotlight shone brightest, that candidate's poll numbers fell.

In the end, Hillary Clinton won the popular vote because of enormous margins in highly populated states like California and New York while Donald Trump prevailed in the electoral college because he won many more states. Donald Trump better reflected the anger and frustration and fear in the nation. Hillary Clinton had little choice but to run for Barack Obama's third term, and Obama hadn't left the country in very good shape.

For all the ups and downs, in the end most voters voted the way they usually vote. What seemed to have made the difference was not the usual appeal to fickle-independent and undecided voters, often making a decision in the last minutes prior to voting. The decisive demographic seemed to be a bloc of traditional Democratic Party voters: middle-class white often union-card-carrying members who felt the party under Barack Obama had abandoned them. In large part by speaking a language these former Democratic voters understood, Trump refashioned the electoral college map, just as he had refashioned the Republican Party.

THE CYCLE STARTS

A suitable starting point for the campaign concluding November 8, 2016, occurred two years prior, on or about 8:00 a.m., November 5, 2014. Just another fall day for many, for serious politicos and politicians with images of the Oval Office dancing in their heads, this was the first workday of the upcoming American presidency marathon.

The day's mood was set by the shellacking the Democratic Party suffered the night before in congressional elections. Democrats had expected to claw back ground in the House of Representatives and to gain seats in the Senate, maybe enough to claim the majority. They failed—badly.

While most of the country breathed a ragged sigh of relief from the onslaught of political commercials, and while some candidates celebrated miraculous wins and others zombie walked in stunned defeat, the political class poured itself a collective cup of steaming java to begin the long slog ending 24 months later.

That 2014 morning gave no hint of the psychedelic adventure about to unfold. True, all presidential elections share certain trends and characteristics; yet every campaign truly is different, all part of the grand experiment that is the American political experience. Even so, 2016 was fundamentally different from any campaign in modern memory. This observation is obviously mundane, much as it is to observe the American Civil War wrought terrible carnage; yet the obvious must be stated to do justice to the story's telling.

Without their fully knowing it, or knowing their own frustrations were widely shared among their fellow citizens, vast swathes of the American people were fed up. They were angry. And their tolerance for the typical perceived BS from politicians had reached rock bottom. In this they were part of a widespread movement across the Western world of ordinary citizens no longer believing in the modern liberal (in the classic sense) structuring of society or in the elites long trusted to guide society.

Most presidents fade into the blur of history (anyone remember President Tyler?), yet we are told in all seriousness the upcoming presidential election is "critical" and "historic." And sometimes it would be for the country. But always these elections are historic at least for those immediately involved, those who will enjoy their moment in the sun, those who imagine themselves alongside Washington and Lincoln and Roosevelt, equally destined for great things.

In ways only the unfolding of history can reveal, the 2016 election would indeed stand out if only for its bizarre twists and turns and upending of modern traditions. This would be no repetition of past campaigns. Of course, there would be the usual differences in the political environment, in personalities, in the issues dominating and shaping the campaign, in campaign technology and strategy, and in consequences for the country. This campaign would present a grand surplus of personalities and consequences. Furthermore, this campaign would present a break, whether permanent or temporary, from the expected course of American political discourse into places low and base and yet very real.

The differences in this election revealed much about the state of American political culture and indeed much about the state of America herself. Elections provide snapshots of a nation along its journey. Where are we, really? Who are we, really? For what do we hope? What futures inspire us? What is the American dream as we progress through the twenty-first century? Elections don't always provide answers, but they always provide clues. This election provided many such clues, and they were rarely encouraging.

No campaign truly has a distinct starting point. Every political cycle in some ways continues those that went before. For years, every Democratic aspirant ran as the reincarnation of Franklin Delano Roosevelt and then of John F. Kennedy. While few Republicans ran as the next Eisenhower, and none emulated Richard Nixon, prior to 2016 every modern Republican sought Ronald Reagan's mystical mantle, however distant the memory and however well or poorly the mantle fit.

Every political cycle also builds on the trends of recent experience. The political makeup of key states and regions shifts, sometimes dramatically. California and the Deep South have swapped roles, for instance. California, once so reliably Republican, now equally reliably votes Democratic while the South presents just the reverse.

Many states once settled are now decidedly schizophrenic. Virginia, once bedrock Republican, now tends to Democrat when electing presidents, governors, and senators. Yet the state legislature tends toward Republicans.

The technology of campaigning evolves continuously in almost every respect except for the importance of a ground game. With every campaign, consultants and data wizards further refine the technology of identifying individual voters by political leaning. In 2012, for example, as Republican canvassers walked neighborhoods with 1980s vintage paper printouts of suspected likely supporters, Obama's intense grassroots machine went door to door with state-of-the-art electronics on par with those used by major delivery companies to track packages. Advantage Obama—big time.

So while political campaigning is perpetual, every story must have a start; and the natural starting point for this story is the day after the November 2014 election. To tell the story requires a nod to the state of play at the start, specifically

- the state of the foreign affairs and the domestic economy,
- the 2014 election outcome, and
- the margin of victory in the 2012 presidential election.

ESSENTIAL REALITIES INTO THE 2014 ELECTION

Pres. Obama's dismal approval ratings dominated the political landscape into the 2014 midterm elections, languishing around 42% for months. On any given subject, whatever Obama was selling, the American people weren't buying, making for a tough environment for Democrats. Like it or not, Obama was still the head of the party, Democrat #1, the top of the ticket. No Democrat could escape his shadow entirely.

In foreign affairs, the United States faced a diverse set of growing challenges and embarrassments:

- ISIS, which had claimed a substantial portion of Iraq and which Obama had to his own embarrassment previously labeled the "JV team."
- China, rising rapidly, delighted in demonstrating its disdain for all things America.
- Russian Pres. Putin's own blatant, obvious, and personal disdain for Pres. Obama on display as he harassed the Ukraine, having effortlessly absorbed the Crimean Peninsula.
- The winding down of the United States' role in the war in Afghanistan. Largely indifferent to U.S. wishes, the Afghani government negotiated with the Taliban for some kind of settlement. George W. Bush having thoroughly defeated the

Taliban, Barack Obama sat back as the Taliban crept back like kudzu on the bayou. And this was the war Obama had long supported.

- Iraq, where U.S.-fighting troops had left, but to refer to the territory as a country was overly generous by a mile. The Kurds were increasingly autonomous, the Shia and Sunni barely contained their sectarian feuds, while ISIS captured major towns as the United States' armed and trained Iraqi Army fled at the first shot.
- Pres. Obama's relationship with Israel, America's only real and enduring ally in the Middle East, regularly plumbed new lows. One could only hope it would improve. It didn't.

Even the oh-so-superior Europeans had tired of Obama's lecturing and waffling. How ironic after giving Obama the Nobel Peace Prize at the beginning of his administration for the sole accomplishment of succeeding George W. Bush as president.

To be fair, few of these developments were entirely Obama's fault:

- ISIS and the Taliban were problems for all civilized nations, not just the United States.
- China's rise and need to flex its muscles as it joined the first tier of nations was inevitable.
- Putin was a wannabe Tsar dreaming of restoring Russia's imperial glory before Russia succumbed to the sum total of its past mistakes.
- Apparently no force on earth could compel Iraq's political leaders to do what was necessary to secure their own country.
- Israel is, well, Israel.
- The European cognoscenti are inherently a fickle lot.

All in all, not entirely Obama's fault, but in 2014 one would be hard-pressed to identify a single Obama foreign policy moving the dial in the right direction. In any case, when you're president, fault doesn't matter. Blame ultimately affixes according to the calendar. Obama was president. He got the blame. This isn't tiddlywinks.

At home, the state of play appeared worse. The gross mishandling of the Ebola virus outbreak brought renewed attention to the apparent incompetency of the Obama administration, much as Hurricane Katrina's devastation of New Orleans had done for George W. Bush. Entirely unfair in both cases, but again, this isn't tiddlywinks.

Despite a steady stream of major presidential economic policy addresses, the U.S. recovery from the Great Global Recession of 2008–2009 crawled at a snail's pace. After six years, the economy still performed poorly and remained far from fully recovered, as evidenced by the fact the Federal Reserve maintained the most aggressively stimulative monetary policy in the nation's history.

True, the unemployment rate had come down dramatically, from a peak of 10% in October of 2009 to the mid-fives, but no one argued this was still a sensible gauge of labor market health. Too many workers had fled the workforce in frustration. Too many who wanted to work full-time were working part-time. For many who did have jobs, wage growth was essentially nonexistent.

The housing sector's recovery from the Great Recession certainly provided good news for most homeowners. Financial markets fared well, in part due to the central bank's aggressive policies. The revolution in energy markets thanks to fracking had fundamentally transformed global energy markets, but also in the U.S. economy, which had gone from being a massive net importer of energy to achieving essential balance in energy.

For all this, the economy continued to just muddle along; and no one knew for certain why. Some tried to "dumb down" growth, essentially saying "just get used to it," which is a lot like a C student capable of straight As telling his parents, "just get used to it." Add in Americans' increasing resentment of his sanctimonious lecturing, and the prevailing circumstances at home and abroad fully explained Pres. Obama's enduring dismal approval ratings.

Even so, despite the 2014 election's results detailed below, Republicans were not in great shape either, especially in Washington.

The situation was ultimately simple enough—a sustained schism between the old guard and a hearty if poorly led band of insurrectionists.

House Speaker John Boehner (R-OH) and Senate Majority Leader Mitch McConnell (R-KY), both highly capable and experienced legislators, faced near-constant revolt from large contingents of their own troops. Nothing highlighted this tension better than the 2014 defeat of House Majority Leader Eric Cantor of Virginia in the Republican primary by Tea Party favorite David Brat, an academic economist of no political experience or repute.

Simply put, while most congressional Republicans liked Boehner and McConnell personally, those more or less aligned with the Tea Party movement didn't trust their party leadership not to sell them out to cut a deal with Obama. These conservative rebels were passionate. They were principled. Contrary to the impressions carefully crafted by their ideological foes in the mainstream media, many were very smart and worked very hard. They loved America, and they hated what Obama was doing to America as they saw it.

Tea Party types in and out of Congress were also amateurs and, more often than not, first-class bumblers. They rarely bothered to master the subjects or the parliamentary rules controlling debate. They proved time and again passion and principles could not overcome the essential limits of one's political power. Despite repeated lessons on these points, the rebels just wallowed in their fury and most rarely learned their lessons. By election day 2014, many independent voters were just tired of it. But they were even more tired of the president.

OPENING THE 2014 CAN OF POLITICAL WHOOP ASS

The 1990s era entertainer/professional wrestler/actor Hulk Hogan developed the colorful expression of getting into the ring and "opening a can of whoop ass." Surprising to almost everyone, that's what Republicans did to Democrats on election day 2014. Republicans opened a big ol' can of political whoop ass.

Coming into the election upward of 10 Senate seats were thought to be hotly contested. The Republicans held forty-five seats, the

Democrats fifty-five, plus two "independents" who caucused with the Democrats, one being the soon-to-be-famous Vermont Socialist Bernie Sanders.

Despite Obama's dismal polls, Democrats believed they had legitimate cause for optimism. Polls consistently showed very tight races in the Georgia and Iowa contests for open seats, a Republican having retired in Georgia and a Democrat in Iowa. Polls were tight in Kentucky and Kansas, offering Democrats prime pickup opportunities. In Kentucky, crusty old Republican leader Mitch McConnell looked to have his hands full with the young and articulate Alison Lundergan Grimes.

Democrats were also defending four Senate seats in tight races in Alaska, Colorado, Louisiana, and Virginia where strong incumbents attempted to stave off equally strong Republican challengers. Under normal circumstances, the advantage in each race should have been with the incumbent. This time, not so much as three out of four fell.

When the dust settled election night, many of these supposedly close races had been blown wide open with Republicans romping. On election day, opinion polls showed McConnell with a nail-biting slight lead in Kentucky. Once the votes were tallied, Grimes had been thoroughly thumped, 56% to 41%. A similar pattern played out in state after state.

In the final tally, Republicans picked up eight Senate seats, with a December runoff strongly leaning Republican in Louisiana. Even Mark Warner, the very popular moderate Virginia Democrat, squeaked by with a mere 17,000-vote margin on nearly 2.2 million votes cast. (The Libertarian Robert Sarvis received 53,000 votes, demonstrating once again Libertarians, despite their intentions, truly are some of big government's best allies.)

In the House, Republicans also did quite well, expanding their majority by 17 seats to 247, a gain made all the more remarkable because Republicans had an apparent current ceiling of perhaps 250 seats counting all true red seats and all that were reasonably competitive between the parties. Republicans also gained three governorships on net, for a total of 31, and expanded their control over state legislatures from coast to coast.

What was on the license plate of the truck that had flattened the Democrats? It sure wasn't a universally strong opinion of Republicans, whose reputations continued to suffer from a series of embarrassing blunders in Congress relating primarily to fiscal policy and the debt limit. The story of the 2014 election was much less an embrace of Republicans than a wholesale shunning of anyone even vaguely associated with Barack Obama.

Consider the pre-election debates in Kentucky. A reporter asked the Democrat Alison Grimes who she voted for in the 2008 and 2012 elections. She refused to answer—simply refused, not a tough question. Nor a surprising question, especially when everyone pretty much already knew the answer. The reporter surely already knew the answer and was just testing Grimes to see if she would fall for such an obvious trap. She did.

She refused to acknowledge the obvious and did so again a few days later. So even after thinking it over and discussing it with her advisors, Grimes still opted to duck a perfectly reasonable question and make herself look the fool. For Grimes, this suggested a remarkable amateurishness and disdain for Kentucky voters and an even greater fear of Obama's deadly shadow.

To see how easy this was, all Grimes needed to say was "I'm a Democrat. Of course, I voted for Obama. Really, you think I'd vote for McCain or Mitt?" Lemons to lemonade; she could just laugh it off but dared not. In the view of this Kentucky Democrat, at least, Obama was that radioactive.

Throughout the campaign and nationwide, Pres,. Obama was treated by Democrats running for office as a pariah. Nobody wanted him in their state. Well, almost nobody. Lieut. Gov. Anthony Brown stood next to Obama in deep-blue Maryland. Brown was running to succeed the fairly popular Martin O'Malley as governor. Obama was also invited to campaign with Illinois Gov. Pat Quinn on Obama's home turf of Chicago. To be fair, Brown was an uninspiring candidate, and Quinn was something of a soup-to-nuts disaster; but the fact remains Obama campaigned for both, and they both lost on supposedly safe Democratic turf.

So if the story of the 2016 election starts where 2014 left off, then it starts with a deeply wounded Democratic Party and a Republican Party powerfully resurgent if only by default. Worse for the Democrats, they had to find somebody to blame; and the obvious target was their own president, a fact painfully obvious to Obama. A lame duck shunned by his own party, hardly a new story but an important piece of the next campaign's mosaic.

Follow the Money, 2014 Version

Before leaving the story of the 2014 election entirely, a word or two regarding money in politics. The professional handwringing class continually complains about the malevolent role of money in politics, and they have a point. It's hardly a headline to observe through the course of history politicians taking a bribe or two or shading a vote to help a kindly and generous benefactor. However, most politicians at the national level are already rich. They don't need to take bribes; and because their campaigns get enough money from all sides, their decisions are largely inoculated from undue money influence. Democratic Sen. John Breaux of Louisiana once joked, "My vote can't be bought, but it can be rented."[2] He could make that joke because everyone knew that, in fact, his vote couldn't be bought or rented at any price—and he was from Louisiana!

What the handwringers fail to grasp is the general direction of causality. Money flows to those with whom one is generally in agreement, not to influence them to change their minds but to ensure like minds remain in power. Progressive billionaires like George Soros give money to progressives to ensure progressives get into and stay in power. Conservative billionaires like Sheldon Adelson give money to conservatives to ensure conservatives get into and stay in power. Businesses generally give money to politicians of both parties because that's what's expected of them while hoping in the event of need for a fair hearing.

Even so, the professional handwringing class anguishes on over the sums spent on elections. According to OpenSecrets, a website maintained by the Center for Responsive Politics, total spending on congressional races in 2014 reached about $3.8 billion, roughly the same amounts as in 2012 and 2010.[3]

These amounts were broken out as follows:

Inside Money	**Total Spent**	
Candidates – House	$888 million	
Candidates – Senate	$686 million	
RNC & DNC	$291 million	
House and Senate Party Committees	$841 million	
Subtotal Candidate and Party Committees		$2.7 billion
Outside Money		
527 Federal committees	$204 million	
Fully disclosed outside money	$338 million	
Partially disclosed outside money	$ 54 million	
Undisclosed outside money	$172 million	
PAC overhead	$293 million	
Subtotal Outside Money		$769 million
Total spending		$3.8 billion

(Note: Numbers may not add due to rounding.)

Is $3.8 billion a lot, or not, to elect the entire U.S. House of Representatives and a third of the U.S. Senate? How would one know? For comparison, in 2014 Americans spent about $2 billion on toothpaste.

Alternatively, the federal government spent about $3.5 trillion in 2014, raised about $3 trillion in revenue, and through its regulations influenced trillions more in economic activity; so in running for Congress, the contenders raised and spent less than one-half of 1% of the amount of funds spent, raised, or influenced by federal policy.

The takeaway from these figures is not that money was having a vast influence on policy, because if it did, the amounts spent would more closely approximate the amounts influenced. Rather, the data tells us money is a big part of politics but perhaps not a big part of policymaking. Another takeaway might be that the best way to reduce the amount of money in politics would be to reduce the amount of money directed by politicians.

WHAT TO DO ABOUT OBAMA

Every presidential nominee to some extent runs in the shadow of previous presidents from his or her political party and runs against the memory of the most recent president from the opposing party. George W. Bush tried to wear the mantle of Ronald Reagan while running against Bill Clinton's legacy of serial scandals. John McCain could never escape George W.'s negative ratings while Barack Obama won in part by effectively presenting himself as the anti-Bush. So consider the plight of any Democrat running in the 2015–2016.

The country elects someone as president and then probably reelects him (or her, someday). The sitting president obviously did something right. You're running to be the next president from the same political party. You can't escape the sitting president's shadow entirely. You've probably been to White House signing ceremonies, campaigned with the president, had numerous smiley photos taken with the president, and spoken in favor of past actions and policies.

In modern times, only one two-term president had a successor of the same party. Dwight D. Eisenhower's successful presidency was followed by John F. Kennedy. Bill Clinton was followed by George W. Bush, who was followed by Barack Obama. Only Ronald Reagan was able to pass the baton to a sympathetic Vice Pres. George H. W.

Bush. This phenomenon leaves aspiring Democratic White House occupants with a fundamental strategic decision, a decision that could sink their campaigns at the outset if made badly: do I stay loyal to Pres. Obama, or do I throw him under the bus?

Staying loyal means building on a tradition of policies and positions—and mistakes and troubles. This is the default option, but it also makes creating your own distinct brand nearly impossible. In contrast, creating separation can be difficult and awkward, but it creates room to maneuver; and if done in a fashion the current president finds excessive or disrespectful, then even an unpopular president can cause real problems with fundraising, staffing, and public chastisement.

Throughout the 2014 campaign, most Democrats were happy to accept Obama's help with fundraising but otherwise wanted him as far away as possible. Senate Democratic Leader Harry Reid's chief of staff, David Krone, observed, "The president's approval rating is barely 40%. What else more is there to say? . . . He wasn't going to play well in North Carolina or Iowa or New Hampshire. I'm sorry. It doesn't mean that the message was bad, but sometimes the messenger isn't good."[4] Not exactly a warm embrace of his president.

The Timeline

To complete preparations for the story to come, a simple review of the basic timeline is in order. First, one by one the actors approached the two stages: Democrat and Republican. After some preliminary sparring, it's off to Iowa, of all places. This is then followed by New Hampshire; and then the pace accelerates into Super Tuesday when, the theory goes, the two races for the parties' nominations should be decided. This time, it took quite a bit longer. Then it's on to the two conventions for libations, politicking, and party unifying, followed by a few weeks for all to catch their respective breaths. Finally, the gloves came off for the two months of tussle up to election day.

Day 1 – November 5, 2014
Regroup, Recharge, Get Ready

Spring 2015
The Candidates Line Up

August 6, 2015
First Republican Primary Debate

October 13, 2015
First Democratic Primary Debate

February 1, 2016
Iowa Caucus

February 9, 2016
New Hampshire Primary

February 20, 23, 27, 2016
Remainder of Early Primaries:
South Carolina, Nevada

March 1, 2016
Super Tuesday – 12 States

March 15, 2016
Florida, Ohio Primaries

March thru May
Remaining Contests

July 18-21, 2016
Republican National Convention

| **July 25-28, 2016**
| Democratic National Convention
|
Fall 2016 |
General Election Debates |
|
| **November 8, 2016**
| General Election
|
|
|

Wisdom from the National Pastime

Most of the lights were dark on United 1809, nonstop overnight from San Francisco to Dulles, the final flight of the year. The season was over, left in the mess of the fourth game of the National League Division Series, won by the San Francisco Giants. There is no rational way to process such a fate, when the relentlessness of 162 games crashes into a space that, by comparison, feels tightly confined, like crawling from an open pasture into a cramped, airtight box, no room to breathe.

So the plane was mostly silent, mostly dark, completely somber. In the first row one light shone over one open tray table, papers pulled from a folder and spread about. This was the wee hours of October 8, 2014. Yet the papers in front of Mike Rizzo had on them the Nationals' 40-man roster for 2015, what the payroll might be in 2017, depth charts for the future. Not a single item pertained to the bitterness that hovered throughout the cabin.

"This is my therapy," Rizzo said later. On that flight, in Rizzo's calculation, "this year" changed from 2014 to 2015.[5]

The Washington Nationals as constructed by General Manager Mike Rizzo began the 2014 season with expectations of making the World Series. They finished the regular season with a record of 96 wins to 66 losses, champions of the National League East, and owners of the best record in the National League. In early October, they faced off against the San Francisco Giants, winners of the wild-card playoffs against the Pittsburgh Pirates. The Giants won the first two games held in Washington. The Nationals won the third game, played in San Francisco, only eventually to lose the fifth and deciding game by a score of 3 to 2.

What does this have to do with the 2016 election? It would be hard to find a better description of the tension in a presidential campaign, the buildup, the enormous effort and sacrifices rising to a crescendo of climaxes on election night, and, for those immediately involved, the crushing void in the aftermath, far worse for the vanquished than the victor.

In the immediate aftermath of the 2016 election, one imagined Donald Trump battled through exhaustion and elation as he shifted from the manic pace of campaign's end to the manic pace of his new role as president-elect. As is proper, following her post-game interview, Hillary Clinton soon mostly vanished from sight for a period. The media talking heads concluded their joint efforts to establish a narrative for the winner and the loser while quitting their own efforts at competitive perspicacity.

The Congress took a breath, not that it had worked overly hard legislatively the previous year. But some in the House and in the Senate had survived tough reelections, such as Republican Cong. William Hurd of Texas's Twenty-Third Congressional District and Wisconsin Republican Sen. Ron Johnson, while some were giddy at the prospect of being newly elected members going to Washington.

Others, such as New Jersey Republican Cong. Scott Garrett and Illinois Republican Sen. Mark Kirk were not so fortunate, having been booted from Congress by the ever-grumpy electorate. Already shocked and depressed, these now-former Members began the painful process of shutting down their congressional offices in Washington and in their home districts and states.

The wonderful old Bing Crosby/Danny Kaye movie *White Christmas* includes a number by Bing Crosby about unemployed generals after a war. The lead line goes, "What can you do with a general when he stops being a general?" Parades one day, the next day "general who? They're delighted that he came, but they can't recall his name." So it is for Members heading out the door. The phone stops ringing. Staff exit. Pretty soon you lose your office, relegated to a cubicle along with all the other soon-to-be-former Members.

On November 9, 2016, while most of the rest of the country went back to their own lives, going to work, watching soccer games, living, loving, and dying, one particular cadre slept in for a day. Then they went into their offices or perhaps worked from home. And started sifting through poll data, scanning across the races known and expected, all to prepare for the next election in 2018. For a few hours, the political cycle took a break, and then it began to turn again.

But first, the 2016 campaign chronicles . . .

CHAPTER 2
INITIAL RUMBLINGS

Neither party featured a prohibitive favorite going into the 2016 election. The Democrats came closest with presumptive tier-one candidate, former Secretary of State Hillary Clinton. She would surely face challenges from the Left-Wing of the Democratic Party, Massachusetts Sen. Elizabeth Warren appearing the most threatening, while the Republican field led by former Florida Gov. Jeb Bush was wide open. Conventional wisdom predicted Clinton would claim the nomination quickly to face Jeb Bush after a slightly longer primary season.

Initial polls, little more than curiosities, at least provided a test of name recognition. Among Democrats, as of one thousand likely voters released November 25, 2014, showed Clinton with a commanding lead, as expected. She polled at 62% support while Sen. Warren polled at 17%, Vice Pres. Joe Biden polled at 7%, with the Socialist Vermont Sen. Bernie Sanders, former Maryland Gov. Martin O'Malley, and former Virginia Sen. Jim Webb getting a few percentage points each.

The Republicans yielded a cattle call. This poll didn't even include Mitt Romney, though he took top score at 19% in a poll released the next day, followed by Jeb Bush, New Jersey Gov. Chris Christie, and the neurosurgeon and author Ben Carson.[6] All other candidates including billionaire Donald Trump showed in single digits. While the press tried to play up the dynasty story of Clinton versus Bush, Jeb just didn't score high enough to make the story credible, yet.

	Rasmussen	Quinnipiac
Mitt Romney	N/A	19
Jeb Bush	18	11
Rand Paul	13	--
Chris Christie	15	8
Paul Ryan	20	--
Scott Walker	20	--
Ben Carson	--	8

OBAMA SHAPES THE TERRAIN

Following the 2014 election, subsequent events provided clues as to the potential contenders' intentions while shaping the political landscape. Immediately following the elections, Pres. Obama gave the traditional and obligatory post-midterms press conference. Amidst the lukewarm hat tip to the Republicans' strong performance, and how he personally had heard the American people speak, Obama droned on almost more bored with the moment than the American people were to hear him. There was, in fact, little more he could say, and that's about what he said.

Shortly after the midterms, Obama announced a possible executive order to benefit illegal aliens. He had long signaled he would act alone if Congress remained deadlocked on immigration reform; and certainly Republicans building their majority in the House and taking the Senate offered little hope of legislative progress.

In announcing his intentions, however, Obama did far more than act. In colloquial terms, Obama flipped Republicans' "the bird," signaling open warfare on immigration and a perfect willingness to poison the well thoroughly for bipartisan action on anything but the most mundane legislation. In truth, little of substance was expected of the incoming Congress, and less yet Obama would sign into law, but his announcement of a radical executive order on immigration drove minimal expectations to about zero.

With his announcement, Obama also sought to shape the political landscape by gaining the political high ground on immigration for the Democrats. As later events unfolded, however, most notably the ascendant candidacy of Donald Trump and then the rising fear over domestic terrorism, Obama's immigration ploy didn't quite work out as intended.

The second landscape shaping involved a series of related events regarding the future of the Affordable Care Act, also known as Obamacare. Just prior to the election, the Supreme Court announced it would hear a challenge to a central Obamacare component: subsidies for policies purchased through the federal exchange.

While the complex legislation recast much of America's health care markets, Obamacare's structure boiled down to three basic pieces: a mandate on employers to provide health insurance, a mandate on individuals to buy health insurance on their own if they didn't get insurance through their place of work, and a network of subsidies to allow low- and middle-income citizens to afford the insurance they were required to buy along with a tax penalty (the "mandate") if they refused. The states were expected to create the "markets," or exchanges, where all these transactions were to occur; and the federal government would create a national exchange as the default option.

After Obamacare's enactment, as expected and intended, some states built their own exchanges for citizens to buy insurance; but most states just let their citizens buy on the newly created and trouble-plagued federal exchange. As written, however, the legislation restricted Obamacare insurance subsidies to individuals with policies purchased on state exchanges. Whatever the intent, the law of the land was clear; and if the Supreme Court followed the clear letter of the law, then a key component of Obamacare would die and much of the intent of the legislation with it.

Thus the state of play when after the midterms appeared multiple video-recorded revelations of Jonathan Gruber, an academic economist from the Massachusetts Institute of Technology and one of Obamacare's central architects and drafters.[7] Obamacare had already been found to be based on two fundamental falsehoods: First, that it would reduce the budget deficit; second, "if you like your health insurance, you can keep it." Both statements were well understood to be untrue by proponent and opponent alike when the legislation was enacted. Indeed, the claim regarding keeping one's health insurance garnered PolitiFact's 2013 "Lie of the Year." That didn't keep supporters from repeating the falsehoods, of course.[8]

Obamacare suffered a number of other indignities, such as having the Obama administration itself declare one whole section—title VIII, the Community Living Assistance Services and Support Act (CLASS Act) dealing with long-term care financing—to be completely unworkable. Obama also repeatedly, and arguably without legal authority, delayed critical components of the law including, for example, the individual mandate.

But with the videos, we had a key Obamacare designer affirming many other criticisms previously leveled by opponents. As Gruber was shown to be saying, the legislation ultimately depended on the "stupidity" of the American people and by implication the stupidity of many of the Members of Congress duped into voting for it. "Lack of transparency is a huge political advantage and, basically, call it the stupidity of the American voter or whatever."[9]

Gruber also affirmed the legislation was intentionally written to ensure the subsidies went only to purchasers of policies on state exchanges—the very topic the Supreme Court was considering. The tax credit was to induce states to set up their own exchanges and to create enormous political pressure on state politicians who resisted as they were depriving their own residents of this federal largesse.[10]

LOSING LANDRIEU

The post-election "lame duck" congressional session faced a litany of thorny issues, starting with the essential necessity of passing a bill to fund the government for the coming year. Other issues included a bill revising the authorization of the use of military force in Afghanistan and Iraq, the budding scandal over Obamacare and Jonathan Gruber, the ever-festering immigration debate, and the Keystone pipeline.

The Keystone pipeline proved especially fascinating politically because Louisiana Republican Cong. Bill Cassidy faced Democratic Sen. Mary Landrieu in a December runoff election. Landrieu was a strong Keystone supporter as energy production had long played a major role in Louisiana's economy. During her reelection campaign, Landrieu made her ability to help the state's energy sector as chairman of the Senate Energy and Natural Resources Committee a major selling point.

The November election produced a runoff because the Libertarian Rob Maness pulled 13.8% of the vote, giving Landrieu a slight 42.1% to 41% lead in the head-to-head with Cassidy. However, immediately after the vote, Maness threw his support behind Cassidy, who raced to a twenty-one-point lead, meaning Cassidy got all his previous votes, plus the Maness vote. Some of Landrieu's previous supporters changed sides, as well.

Then Senate Democrats threw Landrieu under the bus by refusing a vote on Keystone legislation. Pres. Obama would have vetoed the legislation anyway if it reached his desk, so the only reason to prevent a vote was to sacrifice Landrieu to keep other Democrats from having to cast a tough vote. One should always remember a friend in Washington is someone who will stab you in the chest (not in the back), and a good friend is one who will do so without smiling. Smiles were in abundance among the Democrats who avoided voting on Keystone and in so doing sealed the end of Mary Landrieu's Senate career.

THE FIRES OF DECEMBER

At the end of November, a grand jury in Ferguson, Missouri, announced no charges would be filed against Darren Wilson, a badly trained smallish white Ferguson cop, who shot an unarmed, charging, and menacingly large suspected thief Michael Brown—a black teenage kid. The grand jury's decision triggered a wave of riots in Ferguson and protests across the country leading to the usual media circus surrounding any racial event involving a white cop and a black person.

In response, Pres. Obama put on his sympathetic professorial hat and otherwise did exactly doodly-squat to help the country sort through the issues. In short and as usual, having been elected as the first black president and thus perfectly positioned to help guide the long-delayed and difficult "national discussion on race," Obama retreated to the shadows.

Long before Obama, Bill Clinton while in office was often referred to as the first black president. Clinton, of course, is white; but his sympathy and caring for black issues and the black community were both profound and sincere. Nowhere did his ever-present "I feel your pain" demeanor strike a truer chord. However, Bill's honest empathy apparently did not carry over to Hillary. In a classic case of the dog that didn't bark, Hillary Clinton maintained as low a profile as she could manage as these events unfolded while she redecorated her bunker for the coming campaign. The white community probably didn't notice. The black community probably did but would also probably forget.

A Cajun Exclamation Point and the Senate's Balance of Power

Sunday, December 7, the Washington Redskins under its longtime clown owner Dan Snyder lost its fifth game in a row, at home, to the hapless St. Louis Rams, getting shut out 24 to zip. The only reason the score wasn't worse is the Rams' kicker missed a point after touchdown attempt and two consecutive chip-shot field goals. As yet another disastrous season wound down mercifully to its predestined conclusion, the Redskins were close to the title of worst team in professional football—again.

The day before, the runoff in Louisiana had seen a competent, well-regarded Democratic Sen. Mary Landrieu crushed Redskins style by Cong. Bill Cassidy, 56% to 44%. Even though the national Democratic Party had long since abandoned Landrieu, husbanding its resources and playing down the psychological impact of an expected loss, the enormity of the smackdown was striking. Landrieu's family had very old and deep roots in Louisiana politics. As Cassidy put it, his victory put the "exclamation point" to the Republican landslide, leaving Republicans with a fifty-three-seat majority.

What is one more Senate seat when you have the majority? The obvious answer is you can lose a senator's vote, or two, and still prevail. Sometimes Members are called upon to be good soldiers and vote contrary to their own views or those of their constituents because the party needs the vote. Party leaders generally dislike strong-arming their team this way, but sometimes it just has to be done.

A Member can refuse but often at a price to be paid down the road in terms of committee assignments, amendments blocked, or any of the multitude of other sleights available for a party leader to demonstrate displeasure. Having a few extra votes in his pocket meant Republican Majority Leader Mitch McConnell had more flexibility in determining which votes he absolutely needed to prevail. And prevailing over the minority is one of the majority leader's main jobs.

The less obvious answer as to why the extra seat mattered involved the 2016 election and the ability of Senate Republicans to support a Republican president or to engage effectively with a Democratic president. Going into 2016, Republicans had twenty-three seats up for reelection to nine for the Democrats. The terrain looked promising for Democrats to retake the Senate. Both parties also had a significant number getting on in years. Retirements were an issue, but Republicans had about twice as many.

The picture brightened for Republicans somewhat upon closer inspection. For example, most Republican senators up in 2016 were in relatively safe seats, like Idaho's Mike Crapo; or the seats were held by especially strong campaigners like Ohio's Rob Portman.

Going in, Republicans seemed to have five seats in real peril: Portman, Ron Johnson in Wisconsin, Mark Kirk in Illinois, Pat Toomey in Pennsylvania, and Marco Rubio in Florida. Rubio's name appeared on the list because in Florida a candidate can be on the ballot only once; so if he ran for president as the Republican nominee, he would be unable to run for reelection to the Senate. Each of those states represented a steep climb for Republicans:

- Ohio's Rob Portman was one of the most experienced senators in terms of government service: former House member and consigliere to the House Speaker, former United States Trade Representative, former office and management and budget director. He was also a consummate politician and just a really nice guy who worked hard, but he was running in a very tough state.
- Johnson was miscast as a strong conservative in a deep purple state.
- Kirk, a rare moderate in either party, could survive despite Illinois's Democratic leanings. He was a solid performer and the Illinois Democratic Party could be designated a natural disaster area by the Federal Emergency Management Agency. However, Kirk suffered a stroke in 2012; and while recovered, questions lingered about his energy.
- Toomey seemed too conservative for Pennsylvania, but he was also a solid performer, and Democrats faced big problems finding a suitable candidate other than the highly unpopular Joe Sestak, who'd lost to Toomey in 2010.
- Rubio's departure (for a time) left Florida's outcome completely up in the air. Perhaps a dozen mostly credible candidates were sure to enter the race. The Democrats seemed to have only certifiable wild man, Cong. Alan Grayson, and hyperliberal Cong. Patrick Murphy. The choice of Republican presidential nominee would also influence the outcome of the Senate race as either Jeb Bush or Marco Rubio would likely increase Florida Republican turnout.

Three graybeards were at modest risk: Indiana's Dan Coats, Iowa's Chuck Grassley, and Arizona's John McCain. If any or all chose to run, then they would likely retain their seats, but retirement was an issue, and of these only Indiana leaned firmly Republican. In the end, only Dan Coats retired, putting his seat at risk. All told, with six seats in peril and the ever-present possibility of lightning striking elsewhere, it would be easy to see Republicans losing three seats or more in 2016.

On the Democratic side, absent exceptional events or retirements, only two incumbents seemed at risk. Colorado's Michael Bennet won his seat with only 48% of the vote, and Colorado just elected a Republican senator in Cory Gardner. If Republicans could settle on a good challenger, and that was a big *if*, Bennet's seat could be in play.

In Nevada, Democratic leader Harry Reid barely won reelection in 2010. Reid retired, leaving the seat a toss-up.

If Republicans lost three seats and the Democrats held their two at-risk seats, then the Senate would see a fifty-fifty split. Whichever party then won, the White House in 2016 would control the Senate by the thinnest of margins, the vote of the vice president casting deciding votes. But if Republicans held their losses to two, or even three, while one of the Democrat's seats fell, then a Republican president would have a somewhat more reliable Republican Senate.

As the 1754 edition of Benjamin Franklin's *Poor Richard's Almanac* provides:

> For want of a Nail the Shoe was lost; for want of a Shoe the Horse was lost; and for want of a Horse the Rider was lost, being overtaken and slain by the Enemy, all for want of Care about a Horse-shoe Nail.

Momentous legislation often hangs by a thread in the United States Senate. A single vote, Cassidy's victory in 2014, could prove a very important thread—or a coffin nail as circumstances dictated.

Sine Die

Congress suddenly finished its work on December 16. Relieved shouts of "wheels up" were heard throughout the Capitol, Congress having achieved the bare minimum, which for this Congress might have been considered a passing grade.[11] Most important of all, Congress managed to pass a spending bill labeled a "CRomnibus," combining the two expressions of "Continuing Resolution" and "Omnibus." In short, the CRomnibus funded most of the government's day-to-day operations through the end of the fiscal year, September 30, 2015, at the spending levels set two years earlier in the Ryan-Murray budget agreement.

Not funded through September of 2015 was the Department of Homeland Security (DHS), which instead was funded under continuing resolution (CR) language (meaning all programs are funded without change from the prior year) through March of 2015. DHS was singled out not because it had bad behavior but because it would be the agency most engaged in carrying out the president's hated (by Republicans) immigration executive order. A temporary CR for DHS and full-year omnibus spending for everything else makes a CRomnibus.

The point of the CRomnibus was to give Republicans more time to ponder how to use the denial of agency funding to block the effects of Pres. Obama's executive order. None of this would be particularly relevant to the 2016 election except for the singularly unpopular behavior of one Texas Sen. Ted Cruz. In short, Cruz had once again anointed himself the conservative leader in a spectacularly losing cause, specifically the immediate fight to overturn Pres. Obama's executive order on immigration. While most Republicans seemed in agreement the executive order was ill advised and likely unconstitutional, they also recognized they could do nothing to stop it at this time. Not Cruz, however.

The CRomnibus had passed the House, and Senate Majority Leader Reid prepared to bring it up in the Senate so members could take flight. But no! Sen. Cruz continued his stalling tactics in the hopes of finding some last little lashing he could give the president. (He didn't find one.)

The delay gave Reid the opportunity to complete some additional unfinished business, obtaining votes on presidential nominations that would otherwise expire at the end of the Congress. So Obama got some extra nominations cleared. The CRomnibus passed. Sen. Reid gave his Democratic colleagues a little Christmas present as they left town. And once again, Cruz had achieved exactly doodly-squat aside from alienating all his colleagues including his best Tea Party buddies.

Cruz appeared to be preparing for a presidential candidacy, but he was doing a crackerjack job of marginalizing his support. Too puffed up to read the writing on the wall, even though it was written in very large type, Cruz had again temporarily frittered away his credibility except among the fringiest of the fringe.

The Hillary Factor

As December of 2014 unfolded, two major trends appeared affecting the candidacies of Jeb Bush and Hillary Clinton. First, both Jeb and Hillary came into the nomination process joined by history as each represented an uncomfortable dynastic phenomenon. They also happened to be the two most formidable names in the campaign, at least on paper. Second, they seemed to be going in opposite directions.

Former Secretary of State Hillary Clinton was the presumptive Democratic frontrunner. Her experience and her contacts literally put her in a category by herself. Clinton had worked very hard during the 2014 campaign for Democratic candidates—almost all of whom lost. Had her drawing power outside the Democratic machine evaporated? Time would tell, but in 2014 she certainly played the role of the happy warrior and picked up a lot of political chits in the process.

As a front-and-center candidate, and for all her many strengths, Hillary Clinton began the run for the White House as one of the worst retail politicians on the national scene. Her loyalists loved her, and they were legion. She was reportedly warm and engaging in private, but one can't be "in private" with 360 million people. The simple fact remained she had never really connected with people outside the ranks of the faithful. The 2008 campaign painfully plumbed the depth of this reality when her well-organized, well-funded, well-prepared campaign was crushed by an upstart, no-experience, newly elected, silver-tongued Illinois senator.

Many of her supporters recognized her shortcomings but hoped time and the gravitas and exposure of being Obama's first secretary of state might make her more relaxed so she could better show her human side. Not a chance. Early in 2014 she released her latest "I'm so beautiful I love me" book followed by a massively hyped book tour. This should have been the lowest of the low-hanging fruit, politically speaking. The media and her fans all wanted to bathe Hillary in glorious adulation. The book and the tour were a total flop, a short-lived disaster, and an embarrassment. She still just couldn't do retail.

No one questioned Clinton's intelligence. No one questioned her strong work ethic. No one questioned her toughness or tenacity. But many questioned her judgment, past and present. They questioned her foot-thick armor warding off any sense of shame. They questioned her veracity, or lack thereof. And no one confused her for a strong orator. Pedestrian and shrill was about the best one got when Clinton gave an address.

The other major albatross around Clinton's neck was—no, not Bill—but Obama himself. Try as she might, she could not escape history: Four years she was Obama's secretary of state. Four years in which the seeds of his later foreign policy disasters with Russia, with Iran, with Afghanistan, with Libya, with China, with ISIS all took root. Was she solely or even largely to blame for all these disasters? Of course not, but nor was she an innocent bystander.

Nor could she avoid Obama's poor economic record because time and again her own policies as they dribbled out of the campaign were just variations on Obama's.

Whether she liked it or not, more than any other Democrat save Joe Biden, Clinton was stuck running for Obama's third term. However badly needed, she just couldn't throw Obama under the bus as to do so would infuriate Obama's dwindling but still potent supporters within the Democratic Party and especially within the black community. Obama was very unpopular across the country at the start of the campaign; but within the party—the party from which Clinton was seeking the nomination—he still enjoyed substantial support. Somehow, she had to distance herself enough from Obama to suggest better without alienating his supporters. If anyone could do it, Hillary Clinton could. But how?

THE CLINTON SNOOZE

For all the hoopla and sense of inevitability, through December the Clinton buzz noticeably subsided, proving that in politics as in physics there is no such thing as a perpetual motion machine. Clinton would give a speech and nobody would notice. A recently former secretary of state giving a major foreign policy speech at Georgetown University's School of Foreign Service to empty seats and texting students was not unique.[12]

She gave a speech in New York while accepting an award from the Robert F. Kennedy Center for Justice and Human Rights.[13] She discussed big issues, like the recent Senate Intelligence Committee report on CIA torture practices during the Iraq War. She finally ventured a passing comment on the recent events in Ferguson, Missouri, and a held similar event on Staten Island. Hardly anyone noticed. Not good. On the surface, she seemed to be doing very little to move her campaign forward.

Behind the scenes, however, Clinton prepared to avoid some of the most obvious mistakes of her 2008 campaign, beginning with establishing a disciplined, experienced organization. Some defining characteristics of the Clinton 2008 campaign included chaos, bickering, backstabbing, freelancing, and an amazing inability to make a decision and stick to it. For 2016, the difference started at the top—not the candidate but the chief of staff, John Podesta.

A former White House chief of staff under Bill Clinton, Podesta was brought into the Obama White House as senior advisor, one of those nebulous titles making sense only to insiders and meaning what and only what the president says it means when the president says it. Podesta was brought in to restore order and discipline to dysfunction in Obama's second term. He succeeded.

Podesta was decisive, experienced, utterly loyal, and, perhaps most important, unafraid to tell Hillary where the bear went in the woods. As Dan Balz of the *Washington Post* wrote, "Beyond quiet advice to the candidate . . . because of his long-standing relationship with the Clintons, he can speak authoritatively for the candidate, internally and externally."[14]

Other key additions to the top of the campaign staff ladder included campaign manager Robby Mook, chief strategist Joel Benenson, and media advisor Jim Margolis. Campaigns are inherently fast-paced, barely controlled chaos. Success requires much of the candidate, but it also demands a team approach and discipline under fire from the campaign leadership. If this A-team of American politics failed, the cause of the failure would be traced not to the team but to Hillary Clinton.

WARREN'S CALLING

In contrast to the slow boat on which the Clinton campaign traveled publicly, Sen. Elizabeth Warren's repeated claims she was not running for president increasingly rang hollow. Warren was elected to the United States Senate in 2012. On paper, she appeared to have little to offer when running for the presidency. Before entering the federal policy world, Warren had been a Harvard Law School professor specializing in bankruptcy law. That's right—bankruptcy law. Not a well-traveled path to public fame or high office.

She caught the political bug big time first as chair of the Congressional Oversight Panel charged with monitoring the Troubled Asset Relief Program (TARP) created in response to the 2008–2009 financial crisis. From the panel, she went on to a position as a senior advisor to Pres. Obama. With this curious history as foundation, she then challenged and defeated Republican incumbent Scott Brown to become a United States Senator.

Warren's obvious weakness as a candidate included her lack of basic knowledge of about 99% of the domestic and foreign policy issues a candidate must address and a president must handle. This related to her barely two-year tenure as a senator. Following on the heels of another novice whose presidency suffered early on in many policy respects, the fresh-face factor would seem to pale in comparison with a seasoned hand like Hillary Clinton.

Warren, however, enjoyed strengths Clinton could only dream about. For one thing, Warren's sincerity as a hard-core progressive true believer was absolute. In contrast, Clinton repeatedly wandered left to center and back again over her career as the winds blew, so no one could be sure what she really believed. Warren was an energetic, enthusiastic public speaker imbued with convictions and unchained by too much knowledge. Whatever she said, she left no doubt she believed every word. She voiced perfectly the populist wave building in leftist America. At her best, Clinton could only aspire to a screeching woodenness. Some people can sing. Others can't carry a tune. It's not a character flaw, but it does matter in a chorus.

Warren also had Bidenesque charisma, another noted Clinton shortcoming. Some people had "it," that indefinable personal trait hinted at in the famous Dos Equis beer commercial about the most interesting man in the world. Warren had it. Biden had it. Clinton had very little.

Finally, though, Warren would be dogged by concerns among the party faithful that, while she could inspire and lead the progressives possibly all the way to the nomination, what hope would they have in a general election of winning with a Massachusetts neophyte hyperprogressive? (Similar concerns arose later with Bernie Sanders.) Democrats, far better than Republicans, usually understand politics is about power and winning, not making feel-good philosophical statements hoping to win the next time.

Warren insisted she would stay out of the race, but a powerful vortex of political support was clearly building on the far Left ready to lift her into the campaign as relentlessly as did the tornado lift Dorothy in the Wizard of Oz. And if Dorothy refused, someone else would get drafted, as the progressives were not happy.

Jeb Bush: Mr. Methodical

Whereas Hillary Clinton seemed to be sleepwalking through the early campaign, Jeb Bush gave interviews and got coverage. He increased his buzz factor. Most important, he created an exploratory committee, a legal precursor to a campaign. In the history of American politics, likely no one ever created an exploratory committee without deciding the explorations were favorable for announcing a full-blown campaign.

The former Florida governor almost needed no introduction: son of a president, brother of a president, well-respected within the Republican establishment, and widely distrusted by the party's conservative base despite being a "tax-cutting, fiscally austere, school-choice-promoting, gun-rights protecting, socially conservative, Spanish-speaking two-term governor" in the words of conservative commentator George Will.[15] Then there was the dynasty factor shared with Clinton. Dislike for monarchial succession runs deep in America.

Did Bush have the executive and political experience and the demeanor to be president? Undoubtedly.

But did Jeb Bush have the fire in the belly for the fight? Few knew better what such a campaign would require of him and his family. Running for President of the United States is a brutal, brutish business, an exacting, exhausting undertaking inflicting enormous stress on the candidate but also on the candidate's family. Knowing all this, Jeb had often in years past waved his toe above the water without ever actually dipping.

On the other hand, it was common lore Jeb was the most likely of all the Bush sons to follow in the father's shoes to become president. But in the past, the timing failed. Jeb lost to Lawton Chiles in his pursuit of the Florida governorship in 1994 even as George W. was winning in Texas over the cagey incumbent, Ann Richards, in a brilliant campaign masterminded by Karl Rove. The pain of Jeb's loss reverberated throughout the family. As Papa Bush told a reporter, "The joy is in Texas, but our hearts are in Florida."

Stories are generally best understood when placed in context. For the media's take on Jeb, the very convenient overriding narrative was family—running as another Bush. This narrative worked in part because it was true and in part because it gave the media yet another opportunity to trash George W. Bush. It also provided a sense of drama, of hurdles to be overcome. The media was at least half right. For better or for worse, Jeb had to face facts, which often included the initial reaction "oh no, not another Bush." His only practical response was to declare that he was his own man. He had his own record. And he defined his task as "I have to show what's in my heart," as though he were running for President of the American Red Cross.[16]

On the matter of George W., Jeb Bush's heart was deeply troubled. Bush family loyalty is legendary; and when asked in a *Fox News* interview whether he'd use his brother on the campaign trail, Jeb breezily responded, "Absolutely. I will use my brother, my sister, every relative, every person I can." Good answer, but just the week before in a CBS interview, he fell for the trap, admitting the inherent problems of following in his brother's footsteps and yet distancing himself from his brother "is not something I'm comfortable doing."

Understandable, but he couldn't have it both ways; and his honesty leavened with the pain induced by the question just wouldn't let him hold to the safe line of "I love my brother, and I appreciate his help, but I'm my own man." Strong. Brief. Clear. Honest. But Jeb just couldn't go there. Not yet. Not every time. Because he knew the truth: Jeb Bush had to establish a clear line between himself and W.

Longtime Republican operative Al Cardenas presented the Bush machine's answer well, arguing as the campaign wore on and voters especially in early caucus and primary states started to focus more, "then it will become more about Jeb, not Bush."[17] Sensible, and perhaps the campaign would unfold along these lines; but in early summer of 2015, as Jeb's poll numbers continued to slide slowly, Cardenas's comment had the smell of hopeful spin.

Hillary Clinton had much the same trouble because she had to distance herself from Bill Clinton's presidential legacy of serial substantive scandals and whatever trouble he caused in the present, and she also had to create some space between herself and Barack Obama. She too had two distinct legacies, two distinct traps to avoid. Yet Clinton had one advantage. For her, the process of creating a distinct political image was well underway; and whatever distancing she had to do relative to Bill or Barack would cause her not a wink of night's sleep. Her cold, calculating, methodical approach would not be troubled in the least while Jeb wore his angst on his sleeve. Would he ever have a skin thick enough, a determination strong enough, to maintain the discipline necessary to win a presidential campaign? The jury was out, but the signs weren't looking very good.

The media's preferred narrative regarding Jeb's hill to climb was the family legacy, but another loomed more immediately. The Republican Party had moved significantly to the right since W's administration and even further since his father's. Could Jeb convince enough of the base he was conservative enough?

Conservative media asked this question all the time, with a clear sense regarding their current answer. It wasn't good. The mainstream media generally avoided the question because it would force them to try to understand what conservatives were really saying, and the mainstream media just didn't want to go there. The more Left-Wing media relished the question because, ultimately, they were more afraid of a Jeb candidacy and really hoped Republicans would nominate somebody the country couldn't abide. The Left wanted to reinforce the impression conservatives already harbored that Jeb Bush was not sufficiently conservative to win the nomination. Why not a trifecta? First McCain, then Mitt, then . . . Ted Cruz?

Bush and the New Republican Party

After some post-election personal struggles in 1994, Jeb Bush recovered and won the Florida governorship in 1998, but doing so made running for president in 1999 impossibly awkward. Once again, the old saying "but for a nail" rings true. Had Karl Rove gone to work for Jeb instead of W, Jeb might have won in 1994 while George W. recovered to win in 1998 and Jeb would have run for president in 1999.

George H. W. Bush instilled in his sons a tremendous sense of public service. George W. Bush often remarked before his official campaign launched in 1998 he didn't need to be president, and he meant it. This wasn't his lifelong burning desire. He'd enjoyed his time in business as the owner of the Texas Rangers and as Texas Governor. His life would be complete whether he became president or not. He ran for president because he saw he had the best chance of leading the country forward after Bill Clinton's eight scandal-filled years. Jeb likewise had led a productive life; he didn't need to be president. But he did need to serve, and 2016 seemed to offer his last best chance to serve from the big chair in the Oval Office.

First, however, Jeb would have to earn his party's trust and nomination; and to paraphrase an old Buick commercial, this wasn't his father's Republican Party. The Republican Party had always faced substantial tensions among its constituent parts, though traditionally perhaps less so than did Democrats. The great American commentator Will Rogers once observed, "I'm not a member of any organized political party. I'm a Democrat." Some things never change.

The Republican Party has its northeast centrist/liberal elements, once known as the Rockefeller wing—named for former New York Gov. Nelson Rockefeller. The party has its usually quietly suffering Christian/evangelical wing and its salt-of-the-earth small business wing. Republicans have their farmer wing: the redneck agriculture establishment, at least when its welfare payments a.k.a. farm subsidies are not threatened. No radical advocate for urban largesse can best the fury of the nation's redneck welfare queens when ag subsidies are on the chopping block.

The Republican Party also has its hard-core conservative wing, taking form first in the modern era in and following the Goldwater campaign in 1964, up through the Reagan presidency. The hard-core wing most recently found expression with the "Tea Party," less a "party" in the political sense than an enduring protest movement arising from outrage toward all things Washington, beginning with the Wall Street bailouts during the 2007–2009 financial crisis through the enactment of Obamacare.

To its establishment critics, the Tea Party is a collection of ill-informed bumblers who had managed to lose winnable seats in the 2010 and 2012 elections—the names of Sharron Angle and Todd Akin rising to the top of the list of supreme ineptitudes. To its supporters, however, the Tea Party is also the source of numerous victories such as Florida's Marco Rubio and Iowa's Joni Ernst. More importantly, Tea Party supporters are a vibrant source of political energy and focus. Reflecting its defensiveness and to the displeasure of Tea Party supporters, establishment types could never quite bring themselves to acknowledge the Tea Party had done some real good along with the harm.

The behavior of Tea Party activists and congressional members in Washington often didn't help their cause. Time and again, they rallied to the next great battle, whether fighting against raising the debt limit to repealing Obamacare for the 473rd time to holding the line on spending through yet another government shutdown. Time and again, lacking the raw political power to prevail, they got their butts kicked, handing Pres. Obama another victory in the process. To be kind, just say legislative strategy was not their forte.

But they learned, sometimes. In 2012 they fought great pitched primary battles in Mississippi, in North Carolina, and in other states where Senate seats were up for grabs. And they lost every time. In the past, many Tea Party adherents would have supported a third-party candidate (as indeed many still did in Louisiana), thus standing on principle as they failed in practice, handing the seat to their greater opponent, the Democrat. In 2014, Tea Party voters often licked their primary wounds and supported the mainstream Republican who'd won the nomination for a Senate seat and in so doing ensured the resulting Republican landslide.

Some began to recognize the damage their ineptitude had done to their own brand. Much as liberals had done earlier in preferring the label "progressive," some Tea Party activists shifted to different labels. One part rebranded itself "constitutional conservatives" to highlight the many actions Pres. Obama had taken they regarded as unconstitutional. In the House, adherents changed their name from the Tea Party Caucus to the House Freedom Caucus.

Whatever they called themselves, what would they do in 2016? Revert to their previous antics when their champions fell seriatim? Pick up their marbles and go home? Or if a more mainstream Republican like Bush won the nomination, would they rally their support, finally figuring out something Democrats understand instinctively: winning matters? At least in politics, Vince Lombardi was right when he said, "Winning isn't everything, it's the only thing." Simply put, losers don't govern.

George H. W. Bush faced similar issues in 1979 and came up short to Ronald Reagan. Highly agitated following the ineptitudes of the Carter administration and the depredations inflicted on America's military, the conservative wing firmly backed Reagan. When then Vice Pres. George H. W. Bush ran in 1988, he did so promising to carry on the Reagan legacy while the conservative wing retreated to its customary level of modest discontent.

In 2000, George W. Bush enjoyed a détente among many of the competing forces in the Republican Party. Having experienced eight years in the governing wilderness under Bill Clinton, they'd relearned the importance of winning. As a swaggering Texan, the conservatives were assuaged. W's views on social issues were sufficiently sure and understood, leaving the evangelicals satisfied, while most of the major trouble causers in the party played nice as W wrested the White House from the impeached Bill Clinton's heir, Mr. Inconvenient Truth himself, Vice Pres. Al Gore.

The political landscape Jeb Bush faced in 2015 bore a greater resemblance to that of his father in 1979 than that of his brother in 1999. How he would navigate a landscape sown with landmines would be the biggest question. He would certainly have the funding and more than his share of top-flight campaign talent. But it looked like he might need the conservatives to knock one another off as each tried to claim the title of "Mr. Hard-Core." And then, if he won the nomination, could he unite the party again behind the Bush banner? Very probably, the Tea Party wing had matured enough to know that winning beats losing even if the winner isn't your first choice.

First Mover

Did Jeb Bush after so many prior flirtations finally have the fire in the belly to run, knowing all the difficulties and personal pain ahead? Perhaps, perhaps not. But perhaps he could supplement his personal desire for the highest office with something equally as powerful a stimulant—a sense of duty.

George H. W. Bush ran for president in 1980 and again in 1988 for many reasons, but a sense of duty to country was high on the list. Certainly, he had a personal desire to be president. Beneath his gentlemanly demeanor burned a sense of destiny but also an ego as with any politician. The clincher was a sense he owed his best for the country. That's just the Bush way.

George W. Bush ran for president in 2000 for many reasons, including a big dab of family honor restoration after his dad's defeat in 1992 to Bill Clinton; but high among those reasons stood a sense of duty. Apparently, Jeb got the gene too. But why start the campaign so much earlier than everyone else? He was already the Big Kahuna of the Republican cast. The very possibility of his candidacy was putting a hold on the whole field (and on the potential donors and campaign staff who might otherwise fund and work for someone else).

First and foremost, as the leading candidate and now the first near the water, Jeb could begin to shape the contours of the early campaign like no other. In the marketing world, this is called the first mover advantage.

Events would largely shape the issues lineup, but Bush could shape the initial tone and tenor. He could try to establish an early threshold for civility (Trump killed that), for knowledge of issues, and for the thoughtfulness of his positions. He could also begin to address some issues on which his positions were at odds with current conservative orthodoxy, or at least with the views of a substantial block of the more conservative base, issues like Common Core and immigration.

Common Core is a set of standards for K-12 education formulated and agreed to by a collection of governors, state educators, and education "experts." The stated purpose was not to force school systems nationwide to follow a uniform script but to provide guidelines of expectations that could be followed, could be modified, and against which state performance could be judged. So far, so good. Heaven knows the U.S. K-12 education system under the control of the nation's self-appointed experts and the teachers' unions has largely made a hash of educating far too many of America's kids. Reform after reform has done little but spend more money for little to no apparent improvement. Another approach was needed, and so Common Core was created.

The big problem for conservatives arose when the federal government stuck its nose into the Common Core debate. In the United States, K-12 education is primarily a local government function and, to a lesser extent, a state government function. The federal government, however, being the self-appointed fount of knowledge on all matters into which it deigns butt in, also wants a piece of the action.

Jeb Bush had long demonstrated a sincere interest in improving education in America. Common Core seemed a useful vehicle. Jeb insisted, "Standards are different than curriculum"; and so he rejected suggestions Common Core offered another avenue by which Federal authorities would take over state and local education responsibilities and authorities.[18]

As George Will wrote, however, "it is not about the content of the standards, which would be objectionable even if written by Aristotle and refined by Shakespeare. Rather, the point is that, unless stopped now, the federal government will not stop short of finding in Common Core a pretext for becoming a national school board."[19]

Jeb Bush apparently failed to grasp that, again in George Will's words, "standards will shape what is tested, and textbooks will be 'aligned' with the tests." In short, if Bush did not grasp the federal government's penchant for absorbing all governing authority as a galactic black hole swallows all matter, energy, and light, along with all liberty and local authority, if he did not understand Common Core was a state-approved window through which Uncle Sam would surely climb, then "he should not be put in charge of the executive branch."

Bush's support of Common Core reaffirmed to conservatives they were right to worry as Jeb's attempts to "clarify" his position failed utterly. Knowing his problem, by advancing his campaign early, Jeb Bush created an opportunity to shape the Common Core narrative so as to put his role in a better light. Think of it as curb appeal in house buying. No one buys a house because of a painted mailbox, but a weed-infested lawn can drive buyers away. Some might think this cynical, but that's naive. A lot of politics is marketing. Unfortunately for Jeb, he just made a hash of the landscaping.

Viva, Cuba!

Every once in a rare while, Pres. Obama managed to surprise to the good. December 17 provided such an occasion. Obama announced the United States government would lift its embargo of Cuba, first imposed October 19, 1960.

Pres. John F. Kennedy instituted the Cuban embargo to contain and punish its Communist Pres. Fidel Castro while hoping to bring about a pro-democracy counterrevolution. The Cuban embargo arguably managed to add to Cuba's economic troubles, though whether it made much of a difference in the face of Cuba's access to the rest of the global economy or in light of Castro's own disastrous economic policies would be hard to prove. In any event, by 2014 it would be difficult to name a more anachronistic, counterproductive U.S. foreign policy anywhere at any time.

Not to put too fine a point on it, Communism was dead. China still called itself Communist and at one time explained its peculiar variety as representing "Communism with Chinese characteristics," but even that clever marketing ploy wore thin. China was simply authoritarian built around a well-oiled political machine. Likewise, Vietnam still called itself Communist but was racing to implement free market reforms as essential to building strength to stand against rising Chinese regional hegemony.

In concluding 2014, one really had to ask of the embargo, "What's the point?" Apparently, many Americans were asking the same question. Sure, Cuba had a dismal human rights record and regularly supported various regional anti-American malcontents. But Cuba behaved no worse than any number of hemispheric U.S. cash-receiving "allies" in good standing.

Some reactionaries in the United States erupted in feigned outrage to Obama's Cuba opening. Some, like Majority Leader Mitch McConnell, seemed to do so out of habit while following the age-old adage for leaders in political opposition, "If he's fer it, I'm agin it." Others had made so many speeches supporting the embargo they really had little way of accepting Obama's decision while saving face.

And then there was Florida and its large Cuban American population, which made the Cuba announcement potentially relevant to the 2016 election. Jeb Bush came out in opposition to lifting the embargo, but Marco Rubio responded more forcefully. Rubio, the son of Cuban immigrants, still had deep roots in the Florida Cuban American community, especially around Miami. They were loud, active, and highly motivated. And, historically, they were adamantly anti-Castro. Unlike many who rose in opposition, Rubio's stance was at least completely sincere.

Florida isn't just any state. The Bush-Gore election teetered on Florida in 2000. In any national election, Florida can just as easily go Republican as Democrat; and with twenty-nine electoral college votes, it is the third biggest prize after California with fifty-five votes and Texas with thirty-eight.

The knee-jerk reaction among pundits concluded Obama's lifting of the Cuban embargo in 2014 would make a Democrat winning Florida in 2016 that much harder. Not so fast. The embargo was lifted. That debate was over, and the embargo wasn't coming back.

Lifting the embargo also meant eliminating a traditionally defining issue for Florida's electoral politics. How much of an influence would Obama's decision really have two years later, especially as more and more Cuban Americans were finally able to travel to, and invest in, Cuba? Viva, Cuba! Rather than creating a problem for Democrats, Obama may have eliminated a wedge issue traditionally driving the most politically active in the Florida Cuban American community toward Republicans.

CHAPTER 3
NEW YEAR, NEXT CAMPAIGN

The Dallas Cowboys played the Detroit Lions on January 4 for the right to advance to the National Football Conference's championship game. This was a great football game. Hard fought and close throughout, both teams believing to the end they would prevail.

In nearly the last play of the game, Detroit's tight end, Brandon Drew Pettigrew, lined up as a receiver to the left of the formation. Opposite Pettigrew prowled Cowboys' linebacker Anthony Hitchens. Detroit's quarterback, Matthew Stafford, passed to Pettigrew the throw right on target. Defender Hitchens avoided contact and therefore a pass interference call; but he clearly had his back to the play and arms raised, and just as clearly warranted a "face guarding" penalty. A penalty not called, leading not unreasonably to a torrent of blogosphere accusations once again the NFL through its officiating crews had rigged the outcome of a game to benefit the Dallas Cowboys. It wouldn't be the first time or likely the last.

It wasn't the game itself shaping impressions in the coming campaign. Rather, the pertinent moment occurred when the television cameras panned to the owners' box where Cowboys owner Jerry Jones celebrated as his team clinched the victory. And there, on national television, bounced corpulent New Jersey Gov. Chris Christie in a bright red sweater, looking remarkably like a McIntosh Apple, celebrating joyously the Cowboys' good fortune. The TV commentators noted Christie's exuberance, the red sweater, and almost embarrassed, quickly changed subjects.

As reported by the *Washington Post* a few days later, Christie, it turns out, was flown to the game in Jones's private plane.[20] Did Christie do anything wrong? Apparently not, though for a New Jersey Governor and thus supposedly a fan of the hometown New York Giants to be feted by the hated owner of the hated Dallas Cowboys likely wouldn't go down well in a Jersey diner with or without cawfee.[21]

Bottom line—being seen on national television hobnobbing with the high and mighty after being flown in a private plane by an individual with a vested interest in your executive decisions is not exactly the clean-cut image a presidential candidate is looking to convey. Being seen imitating a McIntosh Apple bobbing in a barrel didn't help either.

Chris Christie's Bridge to Purgatory

After Jeb and Mitt, who were so well-known they could be referenced by their first names a la Hillary, a leading group of soon-to-be-candidates stood out as the campaign got underway. Near the top of the list, oddly enough, appeared Chris Christie, with or without his red sweater.

What could be more absurd than a pseudo-conservative New Jersey knuckle rapper believing he could win the Republican nomination? What if he had a tendency to the surly, a reputation for being a bit of a Soprano's bully type? Politics is sometimes the opera of the absurd; and so, oddly enough at campaign's start, Chris Christie appeared a force to be reckoned with.

Americans, especially Republicans, have a long history of appreciating politicians who speak bluntly to power. Alan Simpson—a cranky, curmudgeonly old Wyoming Senator—was widely appreciated for his willingness as chairman of the Senate Committee on Aging to poke his finger into AARP's eye repeatedly. John McCain built a public persona as a straight talker willing to defy convention. Chris Christie fell right into that mode, having bludgeoned New Jersey

Democrats with his blunt direct New Jersey swagger and his own brand of straight talk.

Christie also had some "it" factor, that indefinable charisma to which people magnetically respond. Among the Republican mentionables, Jeb Bush had some "it," as did Scott Walker; Romney had almost none; Rubio had "it" in spades; many others who entered the race were smart and experienced and enthusiastic but were otherwise "it" less.

Christie was far more than a political barroom brawler. He'd done his political homework, beginning with nabbing the chairmanship of the Republican Governor's Association (RGA) in November of 2013. Using this national office as podium, he campaigned vigorously for Republicans in the run-up to the 2014 election, raising $106 million for the RGA.[22] Not coincidentally, in so doing, he padded his fundraising contact lists, his state political contacts lists, and his national profile. Not many in Iowa knew much about him until he helped Joni Ernst win a U.S. Senate seat. After 2014, many Iowa Republicans knew something positive of Chris Christie.

Christie also benefited from being from anywhere but Washington DC. Generically, many independent voters hope for the best but ultimately put little faith in Washington. This is odd since they often vote for people who promise them the moon, and the voters apparently believe in moonbeams until they are struck with the inevitable disappointment. Voters will readily believe government will do well something it hasn't done before even as the mountainous evidence builds government does poorly almost everything it tries.

Whereas Democrats typically believe in the federal government, and therefore more comfortably vote for those who've made a career of government, Republicans tend to be chary of federal government types. So while Democrats will occasionally nominate a governor, and usually win when they do so (Bill Clinton and Jimmy Carter), they are equally comfortable with a vice president (Al Gore) or senator (Hubert Humphrey, Jack Kennedy, John Kerry, and Barack Obama). Republicans tend to favor governors as their standard bearers, and so Christie began the campaign with a decided advantage over some competitors.

Like all candidates, Christie needed to convince the voters he was up to the job, and he could be trusted to tell the truth, at least as truth is redefined in Washington. A key question for Christie remained whether enough voters could come to like a blunt New Jersey Governor and whether he could hold that affection. If he could, and if he could bring New Jersey with him, then Christie could be a formidable opponent in the general election.

In the fall of 2013, Christie looked to be on a roll. He was the new face and a very different face than your typical Republican. Then, on September 9, some of Christie's aides orchestrated one of the biggest traffic tie-ups in American history, and Christie's campaign came to a screeching halt.

The George Washington Bridge, a twenty-nine-lane double-decked toll bridge linking Fort Lee in New Jersey to Manhattan, reportedly wins the prize as the busiest motor vehicle bridge in the world. The three lanes farthest to the right are ordinarily reserved via removable traffic cones for local traffic entering from Fort Lee.

On August 13, Bridget Anne Kelly, Christie's deputy chief of staff, sent an eight-word e-mail to David Wildstein, a senior official at the Port Authority and another Christie operative. The email read, "Time for some traffic problems in Fort Lee." Wildstein responded to Kelly's email: "Got it."[23]

On September 6, Wildstein instructed George Washington Bridge manager Robert Durando not to tell anyone in Fort Lee about the upcoming closure, not even the police. Prior to the morning rush hour on Monday, September 9, 2013, Christie's aides struck, closing two of the three dedicated toll lanes at one of the Fort Lee entrances. Chaos ensued lasting through Thursday. The following investigation strongly suggested classic dirty politics against local officials who didn't play ball with Christie's people.

The mainstream media went bonkers. What good fun! And a chance to take out a possible Republican challenger even before the midterms! For the usual suspects in the media, this story offered a dream come true, missing only a little hanky-panky or payola to add the necessary steamy side for a first-rate scandal.

Did Christie's behavior suggest a culture of political cutthroats and shenanigans? Absolutely! This is New Jersey, after all, not North Dakota.

Scandals come and go, but good politicians abide. Christie took his hits, got knocked down, and got back up again. But could he still run? Christie mostly saved himself with his nearly two-hour January 9, 2014, press conference. In stark contrast to a typical Clinton press conference, Christie didn't just read a statement or take a couple questions. In a refreshingly direct and open manner, he simply outlasted the reporters. Got a question? Let me have it. For two straight hours, Christie alternated between asserting his own innocence and his sorrow, anger, and humiliation at his staff's behavior. He seemed truly downcast, as much by the scandal as by the press corps running out of questions.

Most commentators concluded Christie's press conference went all right, but he should have gotten off the stage much sooner. As so often happens, in their rush to assert their own superior wisdom, the commentators got it wrong. The press conference marathon meant if Christie was found to have even a shadow of guilt in the bridge matter, then he was toast. But if he was clean, and an official panel of New Jersey Democrats issued a report finding Christie innocent, then Christie's ride to the White House appeared slowed but still moving. Of course, the mainstream media essentially ignored the report, but that's another story.[24]

Peyton Manning as Mitt Portent?

Sunday, January 11, Peyton Manning again led the Denver Broncos into the playoffs against his old team, the Indianapolis Colts. This was the fourth game of the weekend. Earlier in the day, the Green Bay Packers defeated the Dallas Cowboys on a peculiar officiating reversal of a brilliant late fourth-quarter catch by wide receiver Dez Bryant (a makeup call for the previous week's pro-Cowboys officiating outrage?). The day before, the Carolina Panthers were simply outmatched by the Seattle Seahawks; and once again, the New England Patriots with fully inflated footballs found a way to win, twice overcoming fourteen-point deficits to squeak past the scrappy Baltimore Ravens.

The Denver game, however, had a decidedly different feel to it. Outside the state of Indiana, Denver was widely expected to win handily because, well, they had Peyton Manning. Manning was universally liked for his humor and humility. His preparation knew no peer. He was simply one of the greatest quarterbacks of all time, ranking with Denver team owner John Elway, Packer great Bret Favre, and the amazing Joe Montana. But as the game played out, Manning looked very mortal, though the TV commentators mentioned his age nary a once. Having built Manning into a Superman in the pre-game commentary, they couldn't bring themselves to admit Superman had forgotten his cape.

Adam Kilgore of the *Washington Post* summed matters neatly in the opening sentence of his Monday story, "At once, Peyton Manning confronted his athletic mortality and beheld a reminder of what he used to be. . . . As the sky above Sports Authority Field darkened Sunday evening, Manning tossed frail passes and watched Andrew Luck make any play the game asked of him, wearing the same Indianapolis Colts blue-and-white he once donned. Luck's laser beams provided a counterbalance to Manning's wan throws, just as Luck's youth emphasized Manning's age."[25]

Two days earlier Mitt Romney let the word go forth. Spurred on by his quiet yet intense personal competition with Jeb Bush, Romney moved quickly, preparing to enter the race. Romney, of course, was no Peyton Manning of American politics; but he was an established player. Even his astute wife, Ann, previously strongly opposed to another run, had flipped. Bush had too many miles on him to play the role of the Colts' brilliant young quarterback, Andrew Luck; but Manning's last performance sure looked a portent for Romney's upcoming campaign.

One would think, after trying hard in 2008 and coming up short to John McCain in seeking the nomination, and trying again and losing decisively to Obama in 2012, Mitt Romney would have two possible responses to suggestions he might run in 2016: No! and Hell no!

In 2012, it could be fairly said, Romney by far presented the most seasoned, most electable option of a large cast of Lilliputians. His only real competition would have come from Mitch Daniels, the Governor of Indiana; but Daniels bowed out early for personal reasons, leaving Romney's Gulliver to defeat the Lilliputians in a war of attrition.

Not so in 2014, with Bush running and building momentum fast. To make it all the odder, Romney the centrist let it be known he intended to run against Bush—from the Right! This after only months before announcing his support for raising the minimum wage, thereby reversing a position he held throughout the 2012 campaign. Oh, Mitt, what do you really believe?

But oh, the temptations! Romney never seemed to have the fire in the belly a la Bill or Hillary Clinton, but he was also a man not used to failure. Losing for Romney almost demanded trying again, especially when the contest was for the biggest prize.

Romney would see the same landscape Bush saw: an apparently good year for Republicans shaping up as Democrats tried to run simultaneously on and from Obama's legacy, no obvious dominating alternative front runners, and a valuable political preexisting condition: national name recognition. Romney's greatest strength would be in comparison to the Obama administration's government-by-grad-student approach. The country might well appreciate having a proven adult in control for a while. After eight years of Obama and friends, a dose of sure and steady might be very appealing.

On the other hand, in the brutal honesty of politics, Romney was a two-time loser. He was also establishment to his core. And he increasingly represented the old guard. If Clinton claimed the Democratic nomination as expected, maybe a battle of old titans would work out. But wouldn't Republicans be stronger offering up a fresh face, someone from the next generation? And if the Democrats cast Clinton aside for a fresh face like Elizabeth Warren, would Republicans really want an old white guy as their champion? Those same considerations dogged Jeb Bush too, of course.

Peggy Noonan probably nailed it when she described Romney's motivation thus:

> If every voter in America were today given a toggle switch and told, "If you tug the toggle to the left, Barack Obama will stay president until January, 2017; if you tug it to the right, Mitt Romney will be come president," about 60% of the American people would tug right.
>
> It must be hard for him to know that, and make him want to give it another try. But it's also true that America would, right now, choose your Uncle Ralph who spends his time knitting over the current incumbent.[26]

If he ran, Romney would surely have his supporters, and the press would love to play up the spectacle of a Jeb versus Mitt slugfest; but having lost to a weak Barack Obama in 2012, and with real competition from the center right, could Romney compete? His previous performances showed him to be likable but stiff, of malleable of views yet stubborn in approach. He enjoyed the enormous advantage of having previously run two major national campaigns. But as Noonan noted, Romney "is politically clunky, always was, always will be." And he was a two-time loser.

THE FIRST MITT WAVES

As the last temptation of Mitt played out, the campaign's vibe changed noticeably, not so much because of Romney per se but perhaps more because it appeared the two heavyweights—Jeb and Mitt—would have to battle it out in the middle of the ring, raising the hopes of the other viable candidates if they moved soon enough while driving out the "mullers"—those wannabes publicly mulling a run. Thus, Paul Ryan quickly announced he was out. Ryan was never a serious contender, but it never hurts to dangle a candidacy. So as Scott Walker's good friend and fellow Wisconsin native, Ryan's timely retreat was expected.

Sen. John Thune of South Dakota, he of the immaculate hair and steely eye, also took this as a convenient opportunity to find an exit. Thune perennially hinted at a presidential run only to return to the background none too soon. Karl Rove, when chief political strategist in the Bush White House, spent hours and hours with Thune cajoling him into risking his safe House seat for a 2004 Senate run against then-Senate Majority Leader Tom Daschle. With Rove's promises of help, Thune accepted the challenge, won, and for no apparent reason every presidential cycle thereafter Thune's name came up as a possible contender. Once again in 2014, he backed away early. Good call.

Then there was Rand Paul responding to Romney's intentions. "I think he's had his chance, and I think it's time for some new blood."[27] No doubt many Americans agreed wholeheartedly with Paul. And by taking this potshot at Romney, Paul managed to hitch a ride on the Romney announcement train—nothing wrong with a little free pub. This was one of the few smart moves in the Paul campaign early on, yet Paul also sounded oddly defensive, as though Mitt plus Jeb somehow posed a materially greater threat to Paul's campaign. Prior to Romney's entrance, Bush and Paul and Christie, and maybe Walker, dominated the discussion. Maybe the dinner table could only seat four, leaving Paul the odd man out in his own mind?

Interestingly, Bush showed himself the sagacious tactician. Not only did he not respond to Romney's rumblings, but he also muted his whole apparatus while the mini-Mitt storm played out. Don't waste bullets. Don't feed the Romney versus Bush meme and thereby give it traction.

A Quiet Little Chat

Oh, to be a fly on the wall. Jeb and Mitt had long before scheduled a meeting in Salt Lake City for late January, original purposes undisclosed. The natural decision in light of their respective campaign trajectories suggested avoiding an awkward photo op, cancelling the meeting citing new scheduling conflicts. Instead, they went forward as scheduled.

Nothing leaked of the meeting's discussion, but one can imagine it boiled down to a showing of cards in a poker game. "I've got three of a kind."

"Well, I've got a jack-high straight," with names of major donors and key staff as the playing cards. Nothing much seemed to change until word leaked David Kochel, a longtime Romney strategic advisor in Iowa, jumped ship to the SS Jeb. This sure smacked of rats leaving the ship; and indeed on Friday, January 30, Romney announced he was pulling the plug on his campaign, with a few nasty parting shots at Bush. Sore loser—we know now who had the jack-high straight.

In any event, with Romney's exit following fast on the heels of his near entry, the process of building campaign organizations while trying to curry positive free publicity picked up pace. Wisconsin Gov. Scott Walker made a good impression at a key Iowa Republican event while former Alaska Gov. Sarah Palin continued her steady slide into political slapstick. Aside from the Romney sideshow, perhaps the most interesting development was the utter absence of Clinton from public view. Stealth is a fine trait in a burglar or jet fighter, not so much a presidential candidate.

To be sure, stories about Clinton's inevitability, or lack thereof, remained plentiful. But the candidate herself was nowhere to be seen. Clinton's self-designated lackeys in her auxiliary cheering squad, also known as the mainstream media, took up the task of rationalizing away her absence. But how long could this go on?

IF IT BLEEDS, IT LEADS

This motto has long guided American journalism. Before one gets too critical, remember journalism is a business. The alternative is for the media to depend for its financial support on and be dominated by government. There are many examples of this latter form today (China, Russia) and throughout history (Nazi Germany, Imperial Japan); and each is a warning. The Founding Fathers recognized the importance of a press free of government direction, and thus the very first amendment to the U.S. Constitution reads:

> Congress shall make no law respecting an establishment of religion, or prohibiting the free exercise thereof; or abridging the freedom of speech, or of the press; or the right of the people peaceably to assemble, and to petition the Government for a redress of grievances.

A free press is also an industry, an industry surviving on subscriptions and advertising, none of which sells without readers. Readers want information, but they also want entertainment. Sensationalism is the height of entertainment as Hollywood knows well, and minimally credible sensationalism is thus the bread and butter of all media, however staid and serious they may appear in print or on screen. Hence, if it bleeds, it leads.

Even better than a story reporting some sensational event is a story that itself draws blood. Hence the market value of investigative journalism. Better yet is a story that draws blood from an ideological or political opponent.

Only one facet remains unilluminated to grasp why most of what is written in places like the *New York Times* and the *Washington Post* appears when and as it does. To remain credible, all mainstream media carefully project a facade of fair-mindedness and impartiality. Whether readers generally fall for the ruse is an open question; but when a journalistic outfit loses even the facade, exposing itself as supporting predominantly the political Right or the Left, that outfit loses audience, or at least used to.

Before they can get to the bleeds-and-leads phase, these ostensibly serious media outlets must first build up their future victims with puff pieces. A nice Style section piece in the *Washington Post* sometimes satisfies a payback for providing critical information in a previous story but just as likely an over-the-top puff piece (and they have to be over the top to be sufficiently sensational) develops the outlet's record of fairness before the investigative reporter can go in for the kill when the time is right. And, of course, there's also the old adage: the bigger they are, the harder they fall. Build 'em up, and the fall becomes that much more entertaining.

Scott Walker learned all this the hard way. On January 18, 2015, the *Washington Post* ran an article under the byline of the eminently fair and credible Dan Balz titled, "Can Scott Walker's Unflashy Style Break Through in the 2016 Presidential Race?"[28] With his strong performance as Wisconsin's Governor, Walker established himself early as one of the blue-chip candidates.

Then, like a political vampire, the *Post* went looking for blood. The hunt started February 11 with a front-page story on the burning question of why Scott Walker left college.[29] Yes, the whole world wanted to know why Scott Walker left college, and ultimately the story didn't tell us why. After a first-page tease, the story continued on page 6 covering three full-page columns and two large pictures—but no answer or even an explanation as to why we should care.

About the same time, another Walker story ran in numerous outlets about how on a trip to London he "punted" on questions posed by the media on various global issues.[30] In other words, Walker as a midwestern governor and possible presidential contender was on a fact-finding tour to become more familiar with international issues. Recognizing he was not an expert, Walker avoided the lazy traps set for him by the gotcha-hungry media.

A secretary of state would answer those questions. A globetrotting senator like South Carolina's Lindsey Graham or Arizona's John McCain would answer questions past suppertime. midwestern governors have no business pretending foreign policy expertise, and Walker knew it. An equally valid story would have run as "Walker easily evades international media traps," but he had his positive piece a month before. The *Post* would draw a lot more blood before this was over.

WALKER'S RUN

Long rumored to have his eye on the White House, Scott Walker, the 2014 newly reelected Wisconsin Governor, was a true policy wonk inspired by the courage of his convictions and energized with a pugilist's love of contest.

While a Washington outsider, Walker was no outsider to government. He won a seat in the state legislature in 1993 at age twenty-five. Nine years later, he won a special election to become the Milwaukee county executive. After twice winning reelection as county executive, Walker set his sights on the big prize in 2006 but dropped out of the governor's race citing a lack of campaign funds. The Republican Mark Green lost the election in 2006, leaving a clear field for Walker to run again in 2010, winning the governorship with 52% of the vote. Walker then defeated a union-driven recall election with 53% of the vote—amazingly improving on his election score. He then won reelection with—you guessed it—52% of the vote.

Walker could run for president as an outsider. He could run as someone with government executive experience. He could run as someone who would stand up to unions. He could easily appeal to the conservative base yet still run as a nice and decent fellow appealing to moderates and independents. There's something uniquely not scary about smiling midwestern governors. His campaign suggested he could take Wisconsin in the general election, a state Republicans usually have little chance at winning. And just to be helpful, Walker published a very readable book in 2014 to explain his views on a number of issues.[31]

On paper, Walker's only obvious obstacle to capturing the nomination, aside from the competition, was his inevitable naivety on the national stage. Running a national campaign is not like running a state campaign. A national campaign rides a massive, complex, dynamic, rapidly growing, rapidly responding beast charging down a narrow path with similarly agitated beasts. Very quickly, the candidate morphs from decision maker to marketed product with others up and down the chain of command making almost all the decisions about marketing strategy. Could Walker handle the transition? Could he function in this new role? If he could avoid any major missteps, he had a shot. If not, maybe he could go back and finish college, and get the *Washington Post* off his back.

CHAPTER 4
THE FINE ART OF WASHINGTON POLITICAL THEATER

The newly minted Republican Congress could do very little to make straight the paths of the eventual Republican presidential nominee. It could, however, demonstrate some minimal ability to govern. Could they rise above rank obstructionism and their own petty differences to assure the American people they could trust Republicans with the reins of power? Recent history freighted with multiple miscues did not encourage.

In practice, this task should not be overly difficult as American voters from frustrating experience had formed very low expectations. The Republicans' goal distilled to its essence was to avoid saying or doing anything stupid. Don't play games with important matters like the nation's credit rating. Get the basics accomplished with a minimum of fuss, items such as passing a budget and spending bills more or less on time and in proper form.

THE DHS DANCE

One legacy task from 2014 required passing legislation providing year-long funding for the Department of Homeland Security, or DHS. DHS funding had been carved out of the broader spending package for the fiscal year passed earlier because this legislative vehicle appeared to offer the best shot at blunting Pres. Obama's executive order on immigration. To avoid yet another legislative train wreck, in other words to clear the minimal bar set for their governing competence, the Republican Congress faced passing a single funding bill and sending it to the president's desk by the end of February. That didn't mean it would be easy.

A great strategic weakness Republicans faced involved not power but perception. For years, beginning with the Newt Gingrich-inspired calamity in the great 1995–1996 budget train wreck, Republicans had taught American voters to blame Republicans whenever a Washington political spat produced a government shutdown.[32]

Bill Clinton had goaded Gingrich into a fight blocking legislation to fund the government and thereby trigger a "shutdown."[33] Clinton favored modest spending growth in the government's day-to-day spending levels. Gingrich and the House Republicans wanted this spending cut enough to balance the budget in seven years. Gingrich was always itching for a chance to "make his bones" as Speaker, and so he naively succumbed to Clinton's prodding—and got his butt kicked politically.

In case the public had forgotten the Gingrich-era lesson to always blame Republicans whenever the government is shut down, the newly installed Republican House of Representatives orchestrated yet another government shutdown in 2011. Different year, same result: Republicans got clobbered and took the blame.

Led by Ted Cruz and Jim DeMint in the Senate and Allen West and Michele Bachmann in the House, congressional Republicans reinforced the message later in the year by threatening not to raise the debt ceiling. The substance of the matter was pretty simple. Congress had passed spending bills resulting in substantial budget deficits. Those budget deficits would necessitate issuing more debt to finance the spending; and at some point, Congress would have to raise the debt ceiling to permit issuing enough debt to finance the spending Congress had already approved.

Needing to raise the debt limit was thus an obvious consequence of Congress' earlier actions. Failure to raise the debt limit also meant the federal government would be in default at least in a technical sense.

Despite their reasonable concerns over Obama's trillion-dollar budget deficits, and despite their intense efforts, Republicans lost the debt ceiling legislative battle too, both substantively and in the eyes of American voters. More precisely, Obama crushed them. The lesson Republicans taught American voters time and again: in case of shutdown or other fiscal crisis, blame Republicans. Past lessons could not be avoided going into 2014's battle over DHS funding.

In January of 2015, the House of Representatives dutifully passed its version of the legislation on a party-line vote including language blocking Pres. Obama's immigration executive order. Surprising no one, Democrats effectively blocked the DHS funding bill in the Senate. Senate Majority Leader Mitch McConnell announced the Senate couldn't move forward and so called on the House to pass another bill, something more appealing to Senate Democrat sensibilities. This, of course, was absurd. House Speaker John Boehner tartly responded, "The House has done its job. I want you to ask the Senate Democrats when they're gonna get off their ass and do something other than vote 'no.'"[34] Of course, the Democrats' answer to Boehner's query was "when you're done acting like fools." Both sides had a point.

The press, dutifully exemplified by a story in the Washington newspaper the *Hill*, presented the moment as demonstrating Republican infighting, especially as between Boehner and McConnell, attempting to establish the case of Republican governing incompetence, "GOP infighting grows over Homeland Security funding."[35]

To be sure, Republicans certainly splintered as to how to respond to the president's immigration executive order in the context of DHS funding, but they generally agreed as to the best policy. Meanwhile, though the press had its own agenda, even some old Washington hands wondered aloud about the apparent head-butting between Boehner and McConnell. Rubbish. This wasn't head-butting; this was fine Washington theater choreographed by masters.

When in session, Boehner and McConnell probably talked as often to each other as they did to their spouses. In a city of amateurs, especially among Republicans, these guys didn't rise to the top donning fools' caps. They were the professionals, and they knew they would rise or fall together—and rising was better. On display played out a carefully planned sequence of steps designed to pass a bill the president would sign.

The House passed its DHS funding bill, but the Senate remained stymied by the Democrats. Asking the House to vote on a second more conciliatory bill essentially asked the House to negotiate with itself. As the saying goes, John Boehner may have been born in the morning, but not yesterday morning.

McConnell couldn't move a bill Republicans liked as he was blocked by Harry Reid and the Democrats, empowered by the Senate's rules.[36] So senators started looking for a way out, and the easiest out was for the House to do all the work. "Won't you please send us a prettier package, all wrapped with a pretty pink bow?" McConnell played his part and turned to Boehner for his prepared and enthusiastic raspberry.

Eventually, the Senate passed a bipartisan bill without any extra restraints on executive branch action—exactly what the Democrats wanted all along. The House objected, so they were forced at the last minute to pass a one-week spending bill. The House, finally realizing it had no effective leverage, allowed Boehner to throw in the towel and passed a "clean" bill for the rest of the fiscal year—passing it mostly with Democrat votes. Boehner and McConnell knew all along this would be the outcome, but both men had to let their guys vent their spleen for a while first.

For some House Republicans, voting against the Republican bill knowing it would pass anyway presented the path of least resistance. For others who didn't get the joke, this provided another example of Boehner's perfidy. These folks simply could not grow up to understand that, in the end, the votes have to be counted. Bluff, bluster, and bombast could not topple a determined opposition holding the high ground. The president and Harry Reid held the high ground, not on the substance of the matter necessarily but in terms of the legislative process. The prospects for demonstrating responsible Republican governorship looked bleak.

The Republican State of Play, End of February

Many elements of the upcoming campaign came into focus as February faded into March. On the Republican side, it appeared increasingly sure Jeb Bush would be a force, largely capturing much of the establishment support. Wisconsin Gov. Scott Walker claimed a slice of the outsider/Reagan conservative market niche. New Jersey Gov. Chris Christie rounded out the trio of most serious contenders at this early stage, but his campaign obviously struggled.

Stories persisted as to how Christie's operation remained something of a two-bit side show, with the undisciplined candidate himself being its worst problem. Christie, the narrative went, lived "in a bubble," not returning phone calls, taking donors for granted, arriving late for meetings. The main source for the narrative seemed to be the *New York Times*.[37] Not exactly a Christie fan club operation, but sufficient third-party commentary remained to suggest some truth to the rumors.

Florida Sen. Marco Rubio topped the next rung. He clearly wanted to run but appeared to waver. Competing with Jeb for the Florida donor base would present a real challenge, and Rubio just couldn't shake the impression he'd given in past performances of being not quite ready for the big game.

Of the other candidates, Kentucky Sen. Rand Paul continued to claim some notice while most others were noticed most for their absence. Yet all sensed the possibilities and the weakness of the Democratic side, as apparently did billionaire New York real estate developer Donald Trump, who somehow convinced himself the need so dire only he could save the nation. Trump's candidacy seemed utterly laughable at the time.

The end of February brought them together at the annual Conservative Political Action Committee (CPAC) shindig in

Washington, a sort of revival meeting for politically active conservatives and a cattle call for the high and rising—like presidential candidates. As a rule, parties get their energy from the wings: the loony Left and the wingnut Right. But candidates tend to win national elections by appealing to the middle. Swing voters are election deciders, and they're generally very uncomfortable with either extremist wing. Thus, the test in most presidential elections is whether winning would be important enough to the extremes for them to accept a candidate who could appeal to the center.

For conservatives propelled by "Tea Party" energies, perhaps the most meaningful item out of the 2015 CPAC convention was the reaction of Matt Schlapp, the jocular new chairman of the American Conservative Union and CPAC host. Evidencing a profound talent for understatement, Schlapp observed, "Conservatives haven't loved John McCain or Mitt Romney. But eight years of Pres. Obama is a real unifier, and they [conservatives] want to win. They want to pick some judges for the Supreme Court. They want to control the regulatory process. The spirit of 2015 is let's find a horse who can win."[38]

CRACKS IN THE CLINTON FOUNDATION

The Democratic side of the aisle at the end of February was, if anything, more interesting for all that was not happening. In short, Hillary Clinton had not been heard from in weeks. Running for president by going into seclusion suggested a novel approach. Rumors swirled about her health, whether she'd had a stroke and more seriously whether she really had the fire in the belly to charge up the hill again.

Meanwhile the Bill, Hillary, and Chelsea Clinton Foundation garnered all the headlines for the tens of millions of dollars collected from foreign governments while Clinton served as secretary of state. The story had "legs" in part because the Hillary haters on the Right and the Left kept it alive but also because the foundation admitted it had with respect to a half-million-dollar grant from the Algerian government violated an ethics-review agreement the foundation had with the State Department.[39]

One could debate the legalities forever; and if any family had shown they could ride out uncomfortable legalities, it was the Clintons. But there was no debating how bad this looked: Clinton took foreign money while Secretary of State. No, she didn't. Her foundation did. But such distinctions are quickly tossed aside. As events would later show, this was only the uppermost ice crystals on the tip of the Clinton foundation scandal iceberg.

The foundation story eventually faded from the front pages but only because it was pushed off in March by a second Clinton scandal, one that would dog her campaign right up until election day. During her stint at the State Department, Secretary of State Clinton used a very sophisticated very personal email system complete with her own dedicated server operating out of her home in Chappaqua, New York. Like nearly every other State Department employee, she had available a government-issued BlackBerry and a government email account. Unlike every other employee who complied with the law, Clinton decided she strode above law and protocol and national security and so used her personal email for government business.

It didn't take long for even neutral observers to put the stories about her foundation's foreign money raising and the private email address together. After all, if the only reason for the private email system was to keep her emails secret, what was she trying to hide? Her self-serving foundation finances, perhaps?

By itself, the email account story stank to high heaven. Once again, the Clintons were writing their own rules. As Eugene Robinson, lifelong hyperliberal of the *Washington Post*, wrote, "The email flap reminds us once again that she considers herself embattled and entitled."[40] The whole affair reeked of shiftiness. The only reason to use a personal email system of dubious security in lieu of her government-issued account was to keep her emails outside the government archival system. Untraced. Perhaps untraceable. Deleted.

On March 10, Clinton held a press conference to clear the air. It failed. She said she would be turning over copies of thirty thousand emails from her time as secretary of state but didn't say when. She also noted in passing, as though a minor point barely worth mentioning, her staff had deleted over thirty thousand emails. Stop the presses.

It was hard not to draw the parallel between Hillary Clinton's email deletions and the Nixon White House tapes and the famous eighteen and a half minutes of supposedly mistakenly erased conversations from June 20, 1972, between Richard M. Nixon and H. R. Haldeman discussing, among other matters according to Haldeman's notes, a break-in at the Watergate Hotel.

Clinton claimed the deleted emails were personal matters, such as emails sent to Bill, recipes, vacation plans, etc.; but it seemed we would never know. They were deleted. As we later learned, deleted is not "wiped" and thus not the same as necessarily lost forever.

The most immediate crack in Hillary Clinton's story, however, curiously came courtesy of Matt McKenna, Bill Clinton's spokesman. According to McKenna, the former president had sent only two emails in his life to that point, both as president.[41] Bill just wasn't an email kind of guy. But Hillary said many of her emails went to Bill. How odd.

The second crack in her story appeared just as quickly. Clinton's central explanation for using her own private email server rested on convenience. "I thought it would be easier to carry just one device for my work and for my personal emails instead of two." Not so fast, Madame Secretary. Many of us manage to carry two devices without much difficulty, certainly without a retinue of handlers. And surely she would know that it's possible to run more than one email account off the same device.

The lie became embarrassingly obvious when video emerged from her own admission only days before. As observed in the *New York Times*, at a technology conference in Silicon Valley Clinton bragged she used multiple devices, including two kinds of iPads, an iPhone, and a BlackBerry. She said then: "I don't throw anything away. I'm like two steps short of a hoarder."[42] Which is it then? One device for convenience or the many devices of a hoarder? Can't be both.

New York Times columnist Frank Brunni referred to Clinton's press conference as a "prickly apologia."[43] The *Washington Post's* Dan Balz aptly boiled her defense down to two words: "Trust me."[44] And that's about all she could ask, because she nuanced her answers so carefully it was classic Clinton. Like the guy caught in bed with another woman who asked his pistol-packing wife, "Who ya gonna believe? Me or your lying eyes?"

The Clintons' story appeared so incredible her defenders pretty much just gave up. Some resorted to Washington's version of the dog ate my homework: "it's all just politics." This was the same line they used during Bill Clinton's impeachment proceedings. It's all about politics and sex when, of course, it was all about the undeniable and arguably impeachment-worthy evidence of Bill lying under oath.

Others apparently hoped Clinton would just blow past this scandal as she had so many before, and so they stopped trying to defend the indefensible. James Carville, one of the Clintons' most intimate of political intimates, catalogued some of Hillary's many past faux pas on *ABC News*, "All right, we've got another investigation, just like we had the Whitewater, just like you go through the Filegate, you go through Travelgate, you go through seven or eight different Congressional committees."[45]

Carville then broke down and in a fit of political delirium told the real story, "I suspect she didn't want [Republican Cong.] Louis Gohmert rifling through her e-mails, which seems to me to be a kind of reasonable position for someone to take."

Time would tell where this would all lead; and as events showed, this email scandal would practice Chinese water torture on the Clinton campaign with a steady drip, drip, drip of bad news, but the immediate effect was to trigger a relapse of Clinton scandal fatigue.

Americans like to believe their presidents, at least going in. After so many past scandals, and so many ongoing scandals, would the American people not already in her camp once again forgive and forget? Would they trust her? Not with respect to her toughness; few really doubted her toughness and tenacity. But would they ever trust her to tell the truth? About anything? Ever?

At the very least, if Clinton planned to launch her campaign publicly in the near future, at the time rumored for April 1, 2015, then these events pushed her timeline back. Indeed, April 1 came and went, and the revelations just kept coming. First, we learned the State Department had released a handful of emails, some originally sent using her iPad. Her iPad? Really? What happened to the one-device convenience story?

Then we learned the server storing the emails originally had been wiped clean—and possibly in late 2014 after the story broke. References to the Nixon episode were all the more poignant when one remembered Clinton got her political start as a congressional staffer investigating Nixon's Watergate break-in.

As Hillary Clinton's troubles mounted, buzz rose steadily regarding possible alternatives. Alternatives like Massachusetts Sen. Elizabeth Warren, who just bided her time, waiting to be drawn into the campaign should the 2015 version of the SS *Titanic*, a.k.a. Hillary Clinton, suddenly sink and create an irresistible vacuum. The same might be said of New York Gov. Andrew Cuomo, whose loyalty to the Clintons kept him on the sidelines but who, if Clinton sank soon enough, could race in to fill the vacuum. Former Maryland Gov. Martin O'Malley evidenced less patience. O'Malley's efforts in Iowa and elsewhere were making regular headlines. Implausible as it seemed, O'Malley's star was rising a little.

O'Malley Calling

Martin O'Malley, most recently Governor of Maryland, seemed an intriguing alternative to Hillary Clinton, having been a state chief executive and outside the Washington mud pits. But his star dimmed a bit as he left office in 2014 after watching his lackluster hand-picked successor Anthony Brown lose to a Republican, hardly a momentum builder for a national campaign. Even so, O'Malley could run as a Washington outsider, which often proved useful, even for Democrats.

O'Malley was smart, articulate, and well acceptable to the progressive wing of the party. He could attack Clinton from the Left, or the Far Left as circumstances dictated, assuming Warren chose not to run and nobody got to the Far Left first. Unfortunately for O'Malley, Vermont Sen. and lifelong Socialist Bernie Sanders did just that, effectively blocking O'Malley completely. However, O'Malley was running a lean campaign. If he could hold on, do well in the debates, and then watch Clinton falter, the party would have to seek out a viable national candidate as Sanders would lead the party to disaster. But if Sanders continued to block O'Malley, then O'Malley literally had nowhere to run.

Alternative options became more relevant when Hillary Clinton's email troubles reared their head big time in July. The *New York Times* reported government investigators found classified information on Clinton's private email account, contradicting yet another of her earlier claims.[46] Worse, the matter was referred to the Justice Department. "This classified information never should have been transmitted via an unclassified personal system," read a statement by Steve A. Linick and I. Charles McCullough III, inspectors general of the State Department and the intelligence community, respectively.

Clinton email stories were no longer a question of Republicans raising muck. This issue now fell to the FBI and the Justice Department. If matters could look worse, they did. The leaked memo starting the latest firestorm was sourced in a *New York Post* article to a "senior government official."[47] The betting pointed to Valerie Jarrett, one of Pres. Obama's closest confidantes and someone reportedly on a deep mutual hate basis with Hillary Clinton.

Trump and Carly

Other contenders prepared as Hillary Clinton's scandals dominated the winter news cycles. For example, Donald Trump established a campaign committee and seemed to be taking himself more seriously than usual, if that were possible. Apparently, Trump's show *The Apprentice* needed a new theme, and so he decided to make himself the apprentice and let the voters be the boss.

Some people just live life large—very large. They have an outsized influence on everything and everyone they touch. Donald Trump was a billionaire businessman. He was a thrice-married father. He was the centerpiece of one of the most popular television shows ever. No one stood larger than Donald Trump on the national stage at the time, not Barack Obama, not Kim Kardashian or Tom Cruise, certainly not any of the others running for President of the United States from either party.

Donald Trump's biographical essentials included a habit of dating and marrying stunningly beautiful often foreign-born women. But beautiful women never captured Donald's core interest, which remained always the next deal. In one television interview, Trump confessed, "I just know it's very hard for them [his ex-wives] to compete because I do love what I do. I really love it."

Trump was born into the art of the real estate deal, his father, Fred, likewise a successful though much smaller-time real estate developer. From a fairly small start with E. Trump & Son, Donald Trump built the Trump Organization, a limited liability corporation with roughly 22,500 employees as of 2015.

Trump loved attention, and he loved giving the impression of being the world's foremost authority on just about everything but especially on what it takes to win in business. So it was entirely natural for him to parlay his entertainment world contacts into an odd television show in which aspiring young business executives proved, or more often failed to prove, their worth to the scowling master. *The Apprentice* went on for fourteen seasons with Trump weeding out the lesser worthies episode after episode with his trademark "You're fired!" According to his Federal Election Commission filing, NBCUniversal paid Trump almost $214 million for his fourteen seasons of work.[48]

Trump's cutthroat business practices included having individual business units that got in trouble declare bankruptcy. A facet of Trump's businesses perhaps alien to many is that the individual pieces are kept legally and financially separate, so that as much as possible each one rises and falls on its own; and if it falls, then the consequences remain isolated from the rest of the empire.

For example, in 1991 the Trump Taj Mahal in Atlantic City, New Jersey, declared bankruptcy, having taken on unserviceable debt. In 1992, Trump Plaza Hotel went bankrupt; then in 2004, Trump Hotels and Resort Casino went through bankruptcy. More recently, in 2009 Trump Entertainment Resorts went under. Real estate investment often relies heavily on debt. In each case, Trump's company had taken on too much debt, taking a risk that didn't pan out. Some risks prove a winner, some don't. The bondholders had been paid handsomely for accepting the risk, so they merited no sympathy for their losses. Bankruptcy was just a way to reset the specific business's finances, everyone including Trump and the lenders taking a haircut for their mistake. "You know, it's like on *The Apprentice*. It's just business. It's nothing personal."[49]

Trump's comments regarding his companies' many bankruptcies entirely reflected his tough business style, as well as big-time deal making, American style. Some of his political opponents tried to make an issue of this practice but to no apparent effect. Americans seemed to understand Trump played tough, and many liked it.

Trump had also written or co-written seventeen books, the titles of ten of which start with the word *Trump*. In the early months of the campaign, Trump constituted a force of nature, mostly because he said what he thought and he'd obviously given many of the issues at least a little thought. He also could afford to let it all hang out, holding nothing back. He was already rich and famous. He had nothing to lose. And the more he spoke his mind, the more adoration washed his way. The incumbent President, Barack Obama, was likewise imbued with an enormous sense of personal superiority, but on this score even Obama couldn't hold a candle to Donald Trump.

Every modern presidential campaign needs a few joke candidates; and Republicans are often pleased to oblige: Michele Bachmann, Rick Perry, and Newt Gingrich in 2012; Sarah Palin in 2008. Mark Everson, former head of the Internal Revenue Service, was one of 2016's curiouser curiosities. Nice man, smart man; but how running the IRS or getting fired as the head of the American Red Cross for noodling your assistant qualifies someone for being the leader of the free world was never clear. Sorry, Mark. Butterflies and delusions of grandeur are free.

Add to Trump and Everson the confidently urbane pediatric surgeon Ben Carson, a fired former Hewlett-Packard CEO in Carly Fiorina, and a couple has-been politicians in former New York Gov. George Pataki and former Virginia Sen. Jim Gilmore; and it became abundantly clear the Republican campaign would not lack for diversity. Fiorina and Carson, however, would prove very serious if passing entrants.

Fiorina was born in Austin, Texas, in 1954 to an abstract painter and a University of Texas Law School professor, her father later going on to become Deputy U.S. Attorney General. While attending Stanford University where she received her bachelor's degree in philosophy and medieval history, Fiorina spent her summers working as a secretary for Kelly Services, a temp agency. From Stanford she followed in her father's footsteps, attending UCLA law school. After one semester, she realized her mistake, eventually returning to school for an MBA from the University of Maryland, after which she went to work for AT&T selling telephone services to the federal government.

Fiorina's career rocketed thereafter as she rose to Group Vice President of the AT&T spinoff Lucent Technologies and being named the Most Powerful Woman in American Business in 1998 by *Fortune* magazine.

In 1999, she rose to CEO of the venerable but troubled Hewlett-Packard Corporation, the first woman to head a Fortune 20 company. As *Fortune* magazine noted, Fiorina's hiring resulted in part from a highly dysfunctional board, a problem dogging Fiorina throughout her time at HP and ultimately leading to her firing.

Fiorina apparently caught the political bug during the ill-fated 2008 presidential campaign of Sen. John McCain during which she was long-listed as a possible vice presidential running mate. Imagine being beaten out by Sarah Palin!

In June of 2008 Fiorina was named to chair the Republican National Committee's "victory" campaign. Fiorina began to fill in some of her policy and politics knowledge deficiencies, first through service on the Defense Advisory Board and then for two years as chairman of the Central Intelligence Agency's External Advisory Board. Having gotten the political bug big time, Fiorina then challenged U.S. Sen. Barbara Boxer in 2010. Fiorina lost 52% to 42%; but for her first time out of the gate against a well-entrenched incumbent, this wasn't a bad showing. Many a seasoned politician had fared worse.

Fiorina continued her drive into national politics, creating her own Political Action Committee and chairing the American Conservative Union (ACU) Foundation, the oldest conservative lobbying organization in the country. In 2012, she co-chaired Mitt Romney's California campaign.

If the campaign followed anything like the normal course, it was hard to see any realistic path forward for Fiorina to gain the nomination; yet if she somehow won the nomination, it was also easy to imagine her doing very well, especially against Clinton; and it was easy to imagine Fiorina being a very successful president. She seemed to get policy. She understood something of global economics and politics, having run the very global Hewlett-Packard. She knew how to manage large enterprises. And as events showed, the campaign followed anything but a normal course, so maybe Fiorina was a viable candidate after all, at least for a while.

LEARN, ADAPT, OVERCOME?

Like professional athletes, a politician's worst mistakes usually happen when the camera's rolling. Making the "Worst Week in Washington" column is not a badge of courage. Caught stupid in flagrante, some politicians just run and hide, waiting for the voters to forget. Some just raise their voice, hoping to drown out the criticism with bluster. Marco Rubio demonstrated a unique capacity to learn and adapt on the fly and while the camera was rolling. Even the best politician makes mistakes. Admitting the mistake quickly and learning from it separates the best from the rest. Rubio showed signs of possibly being one of the former.

For example, at CPAC earlier in the year, when asked about his ill-starred foray into immigration reform, Rubio admitted he had been wrong in his previous approach. The American people demanded the Mexican border be secured before they would entertain other reforms.

Marco Rubio had joined the Gang of Eight in 2013 (anytime senators join a "gang," look out) seeking to hammer out a comprehensive immigration reform compromise so dazzlingly perfect the Congress would pass it in relief. Other Republicans in the gang included Jeff Flake and John McCain, each of Arizona, and Lindsey Graham of South Carolina.[50] Rubio was widely seen as trying to leverage a big immigration deal into a reputation for being a policy player. Bad move.

When the Gang of Eight finally disbanded, exhausted and empty-handed, Rubio's reputation suffered mightily, seen in conservative circles as a phony and a sellout, and as having been schooled by the Democratic head of the cabal, New York's Sen. Chuck Schumer. Rubio's role nearly sank his 2016 campaign before he'd even hired a lawyer.

Rubio's emphatic confession of error at CPAC implicitly acknowledged he'd been in over his head. At risk of appearing to flip-flop, Rubio's change of heart appeared reasoned and sincere. And by acknowledging his error, he also admitted he didn't have all the answers. Many politicians, and the higher the rank the more this is so, quickly come to believe they're the world's foremost authority on whatever subject piques their fancy when all they were relatively expert in was winning the last election—"relatively" because they didn't even have to be expert in that, only better than their opponent.

For those running for national office, and especially for president, foreign policy is a big pain in the tokus. It's devilishly complicated involving history, geography, economics, military affairs, cultural differences, and pure politics. Very few American voters care much about foreign policy, yet a silly misstep can easily trip up a candidate. So except in time of war, it's a lot of work, nearly all pain, no gain.

Marco Rubio had little opportunity in the U.S. Senate to distinguish himself, the immigration oops notwithstanding; but he had taken his role on the Senate Foreign Affairs Committee seriously. In addition to hearings and the like, committee members and senior staff received regular highly classified briefings from administration officials on events around the world. Rubio, it is said, rarely missed a briefing if he was in town. In debates and on the stump, foreign policy is one area where Rubio could demonstrate his preparation for higher office.

Domestic policy was another matter, with so little happening in Congress. So Rubio took the initiative, and another important step in his candidacy. Along with his colleague Mike Lee of Utah, Rubio released a major tax reform proposal.

The proposal was big and bold, with many fine features and a few serious drawbacks. However, for lack of alternatives, this was for now the big dog in the tax reform debate. And Rubio made clear he would be offering newer versions, filing in many of the gaps, as analysis and comments dictated. Whether it helped or hindered his campaign, only time would tell (tax reform is usually something one talks about in a campaign and nothing more for fear of alienating important constituencies); but as the various candidates started to sort themselves out, with Jeb Bush as the establishment's trusted voice, and Scott Walker and Chris Christie as the hard-charging outsiders, Marco Rubio had clearly taken the lead as one of the few big-think candidates now adding domestic policy meat to his foreign policy bones.

CHAPTER 5
THE PARADE STARTS

April 2015 saw the start of a parade of candidacy announcements. First out of the blocks: Ted Cruz. No more "exploratory committees" or "seriously considering" malarkey. Cruz was in.

Officially announcing a candidacy transforms the POTUS wannabe from celebrity/private citizen/elected official to prisoner of campaign finance laws. Suddenly, the candidate's world becomes heavily entangled in legal dos and don'ts. The prevailing interpretation of Cruz's early entry revolved around poor fundraising as a maybe/probably/thinking about it candidate. Ultimately, the announcement gave him a headline but little else.

Few candidates run for president having worked for a previous president who later observed, "I just don't like the guy."[51] Texas Sen. Ted Cruz rubs many people the wrong way, which is not exactly a plus when running for president.

As a rule, Bushes are known for loyalty; and Cruz is a former Bush guy—a somewhat idle legal policy advisor during the 1999–2000 campaign, part of the Florida recount team after the 2000 election, and a member of the Justice Department transition team before the inauguration, followed by six months as an Associate Deputy Attorney General. Cruz wound up at the Federal Trade Commission largely because it was a posting far from the White House.

Ted Cruz presents some other curious personal history. Born in 1970 in Alberta, Canada, of an American mother and a Cuban father. The family moved to Texas in 1974. He attended Princeton as an undergraduate and then Harvard Law, graduating magna cum laude.

Cruz may be irritating, but his raw intelligence is undeniable: primary editor of the *Harvard Law Review*, executive editor of the *Harvard Journal of Law and Public Policy*, later clerking for United States Supreme Court Chief Justice William Rehnquist. In 2003, Cruz was appointed Texas solicitor general, arguing nine cases before the Supreme Court, an impressive total.

Anyone watching Cruz on the Senate floor, in the debates, or on the stump was sure to be impressed by the polish of his presentations. It was not by accident. In 1992, Cruz won the top prize at the U.S. National Debating Championship and at the North American Debating Championship and was named U.S. National Speaker of the Year. In 1995, Cruz came in second in the World Debating Championship.

Besides indisputable intellectual brilliance, Ted Cruz also exemplified the new kind of conservative—a true Tea Party extremist—and proud of it. Texas had long been represented by an energetic, moderately conservative, and very popular Kay Bailey Hutchison. Hutchison's retirement opened the door for an ambitious Cruz to take on the sitting Lieut. Gov. David Dewhurst, a rather self-important character who worked hard at his craft and certainly looked the part. Dewhurst had the cash and the camera; Cruz had the talent and the endorsements. Cruz won the nomination by fourteen points and went on to paste Democrat Paul Sadler. Cruz's rise was aptly called "a true grassroots victory against very long odds."[52]

Winning election in 2012 meant Cruz in 2014 had the same amount of national elective experience as did Barack Obama when he first ran for the presidency. Indeed, Cruz repeatedly demonstrated the abundance of tactical clumsiness expected of a newbie who failed to grasp you have to understand the rules to win the game. Many of the tactical calamities befalling congressional Republicans in this period were due in whole or in part to the hyperconfident, inexperienced Texas Senator.

Making Cruz unique even among the Far Right was not his beliefs or the strength of his convictions. Many on the Far Right were willing to stand up in the face of fierce opposition to defend what they believed was right, much as those on the Far Left such as Bernie Sanders and Elizabeth Warren were willing to do. What made Cruz and Sanders unique was they could clearly state their respective cases in plain, simple language. For all this, what also made Cruz unique was that George W.'s judgment was widely shared. It was just not easy to like the guy.

The mainstream media appreciated Ted Cruz to a point. He could always be counted on for a quip they could mischaracterize or an argument they could slant to make all conservatives look bad. This role was later usurped by Donald Trump, but Cruz still excelled as fodder for media ridicule, especially when it came to his daytime job as United States Senator.

As good as Ted Cruz was for business, the mainstream media truly loathed Cruz personally and politically; and so in subtle ways, they couldn't resist slighting him. For example, most presidential candidates write a "biography" of sorts. A biography provides a good self-introduction to American voters on your own terms, a chance to explain one's views of America and future policy directions, and a chance to apply a little whitewash to past peccadilloes. It's also not a bad way to make a little pocket cash.

Jeb Bush had a uniquely ineffective entry in this respect with his *Immigration Wars: Forging an American Solution*, co-authored with Clint Bolick, a well-known conservative. Bush tried to "clarify" past positions on immigration deeply troubling to many conservative voters. At another time, Bush's play might have worked; but over the following months, the immigration debate became more, not less, rancorous. The book did Bush no favors.

Rand Paul published *Time for Truth*; Marco Rubio released Taking a Stand; Scott Walker wrote *Unintimidated: A Governor's Story and a Nation's Challenge*. Even Carly Fiorina entered two works in the self-explanation category: *Tough Choices: A Memoir*, published after her rushed exit from Hewlett-Packard in February 2005, and *Rising to the Challenge: My Leadership Journey*, published in 2015. Hillary, of course, had produced a steady stream of works, the latest being *Hard Choices*, preceded by *Living History*, and *It Takes a Village: Tenth Anniversary Edition*.

Ted Cruz published *A Time for Truth* through HarperCollins. In its first week, it sold 11,854 copies, more than all but two books on the *New York Times* Best Sellers list.[53] But guess what, the *Times* refused to put Cruz's book on the list. When HarperCollins queried the *Times* regarding the omission, the *Times* loftily replied Cruz's book didn't meet their standards, nose in the air, sniff, sniff, snort; further elaboration not forthcoming.

The spike has a long tradition in the "news" business. It's not always the stories appearing in the paper slanting the news to fit a point of view. Just as often it's the omission. The story not run. The story the editor spikes.[54] The *Times'* bestseller list guardians were just using the spike on Cruz's book. All media slant their reporting. The *New York Times* is just more brazen than most. Why? Because they can be—for now.

First Casualty and Future Phoenix

In early April, a mini-firestorm erupted over a new Indiana law regarding religious freedom (one interpretation) or legalized discrimination (the alternative interpretation). Oddly, the Indiana law largely modeled a 1993 religious freedom law introduced by Sen. and soon-to-be Senate Democratic leader Chuck Schumer (D-NY) and signed into law with much pomp by Pres. Bill Clinton. Many similar laws were in effect in over a score of other states.

Today's protecting religious freedom is tomorrow's discrimination. Despite the impeccable pedigree, the changing times meant the Indiana law sparked a firestorm of national criticism, including from Sen. Chuck Schumer who'd introduced the federal template legislation and from Hillary Clinton whose husband had signed the template into law.

The firestorm consumed the immediate presidential aspirations of Indiana Gov. Mike Pence. To be sure, Pence supported the law and stated publicly he "abhorred discrimination." It didn't matter. The big stink was on. The Pence campaign was dead. Good-bye, Mikey, we hardly knew you. But then, we'd hear from you again and get to know you very well in one of the very strangest twists in a most twisty campaign.

Early April's next development saw team Jeb announce the endorsement of a group based in Arkansas called Right to Rise Policy Solutions. The organization was permitted by law to accept unlimited donations while the donors' identity remained secret. This was now permitted thanks to the Supreme Court's striking down the heart of existing campaign finance laws in favor of the U.S. Constitution, wonder of wonders.

More than the entity itself, the creation of Right to Rise Policy Solutions demonstrated another step in the creation of a whole new dimension in American politics: vast, financially powerful, professionally run organizations outside the traditional party apparatuses. The national Republican Party and the national Democratic Party increasingly appeared vulnerable to a form of political Darwinism as older species were threatened by devastating evolutionary advantages these new species increasingly exploited—in this case, the deadly combination of unlimited donations and unlimited secrecy. Like them or hate them, these new organizations were changing the face, structure, and strategies of national campaigns.

The Parade Continued

Next in the parade marched Kentucky Sen. Rand Paul. Paul was first elected to the U.S. Senate in 2011, giving him a whopping two more years tenure than Cruz or Rubio. Like Carson, Paul was a medical doctor. Like many, he was a Tea Party supporter, having established the Tea Party Caucus in the Senate with South Carolina's Jim DeMint and Utah's Mike Lee.

Yet for all his similarities, Paul carved out a distinct niche in the political landscape. While most conservatives evince certain libertarian tendencies, Paul is most distinctly a libertarian with occasional conservative tendencies. Both conservatives and libertarians are strict constructionists with respect to the Constitution. Both believe in small limited government. But conservatives distinguish themselves from libertarians by endorsing certain areas in which they believe government has a distinctly substantial, intrusive role to play.

Social conservatives, for example, believe government has a role in defining marriage and protecting the unborn; libertarians typically less so. Some conservatives, often operating under the label "neocon," believe government has a vital role in actively engaging with the world to protect national interests. Neocons also typically embrace a strong national defense against foreign aggression. Libertarians are naturally more isolationist and tend to resist any but the minimally required expenditures for national defense. Some conservatives believe in government intervention in the economy, though until recently this was rare and typically limited to local parochial interests such as farm state legislators protecting the billions in welfare payments to their rock-ribbed, pickup-driving, flag-waving farmers/welfare recipients.

Rand Paul was a smart man with a strong pedigree in national politics through his father, Ron Paul, a former Texas Congressman and frequent presidential candidate under the Libertarian banner. But like many of his competitors, Rand Paul was still something of an amateur on the national stage.

In mid-April, two more candidates jumped in—Hillary Clinton and Marco Rubio—the first two of the early top-tier candidates. Both announcements went well, with Marco (forty-three years old) emphasizing the need for a new generation of leadership—a nice double slap at Jeb (sixty-two years old) and Hillary (sixty-seven years old).

Marco Rubio certainly brought real advantages to the table. Youth, of course, which, however, is always a double-edged sword, especially after the previously unproven Obama.

Rubio also had the advantage of being new to the national scene, naturally feeding into the "fresh face" and "change" narratives contrasting with the Clinton and Bush family dynasties—again, a double-edged sword. True, he was new to the scene, but he was still a United States Senator and therefore suspect in the minds of many. On the other hand, the last neophyte to become president, Obama again, was the central target of Rubio's slings and arrows. The last new face sporting a thin résumé didn't turn out so well, so why would a new, new face?

Another Rubio strength, his family story, epitomized the American dream. The son of Cuban immigrants, Rubio was a natural to appeal to the growing Hispanic community. And he was not just a pretty face. Rubio was one of the most articulate, most effective debaters on the national stage.

With a pause in the email scandal, Hillary Clinton launched her campaign with an emphasis on small carefully choreographed gatherings of fawning sycophants in the ultimate retail political state: Iowa. Clinton was running primarily on experience. In this regard, her strengths as a possible future president were perhaps matched in recent memory only by George H. W. Bush when he ran in 1988: secretary of state, United States Senator, eight years First Lady of the United States, former First Lady of Arkansas, former attorney on the congressional committee investigating Nixon's Watergate episode.

Experience? Sure. But noted accomplishments? Not so much:

- A failed health care reform launch (Hillarycare) during her husband's presidency
- Silently suffering the embarrassments associated with a serial and relentless philanderer husband
- A mile-long train of personal scandals.
- An unremarkable stint as U.S. Senator from New York
- A one-time failed presidential aspirant

- Secretary of state under Obama during which time the seeds were sown for the harvest of foreign policy failures that arose during his second term

Hillary Clinton's greatest handicap: she had almost nothing in common with the common man she championed, and she just didn't connect with people. Ever since arriving on the national stage in 1991, she had been described by those who know her best as warm and funny and personable. The loyalty she inspired in her admirers and closest aides strongly suggests the truth of the rumors. Yet somehow, this human, spontaneous Hillary almost never appeared in public. Private Hillary and public Hillary were two different people, which only heightened the public perception of being inauthentic.

Hillary Clinton, the multimillionaire Washington elitist, had little in common with the workaday voters she needed or was on the same page with the Far Left animating forces in the Democratic Party. The energy in the Democratic Party had swung far away from the establishment, beyond progressivism, to an American Socialist, just as the energy in the Republican Party resided in the Tea Party on the Far Right.

So as Clinton launched her campaign, she did so with a checkered checklist:

- Strong campaign team? Check.
- Experience? Unquestionable.
- Able debater? Check.
- Intelligent? Definitely.
- Accomplishments? Nothing notable.
- Establishment support? Pending but likely.
- Aligned with the party activists? Dubious.
- Trustworthy? LOL.
- Likeable? Fuhgetaboutit.

Naturally, every Republican (and some Democrats) running tried to capture the headline with their biting, pithy, memorable responses to Clinton's candidacy. None of it mattered. None of it stuck.

All that mattered to start was whether voters, and particularly Iowans, could get comfortable with Clinton and could trust her or how much they elevated a relative unknown like Sen. Sanders as an alternative—as they did eight years previously with Obama. Softening Hillary's public persona as aloof, condescending, and imperious was campaign job 1. Most important, she had to be "real." Not the public mask of practiced emotions but the private, rumored, warm Hillary, nothing exaggerated or fabricated. After so many years in the public eye, either she had it or she didn't. And knowing all this, she still couldn't help herself, even on exaggerations that could be easily caught.

Leaving Iowa after an April campaign swing, she flew home in coach and carried her own bags as if to say, "See, I'm just like you." Did she really think the nation and, in particular, Iowans were so gullible? On the other hand, what else was she to do?

Well, she could start by answering simple questions directly. Ever on the alert for the potential gotcha question, Clinton struggled to distinguish between a potential hazard and a simple question like "Do you prefer vanilla or chocolate ice cream?"

Case in point: Early in the campaign, Clinton faced strong pressure by the hard left to join in their Social Security reform campaign to increase benefits financed by higher taxes on higher earners. Clinton said repeatedly she wanted to talk about the issues. Well, here was an issue, and she didn't want to talk about it—at all.

A reporter asked her the simple question of whether she was collecting her Social Security checks. She paid in like everyone else. By dint of age, she was eligible. If she believed in the program, then presumably she would file for her benefits. Had she done so? Clinton refused to answer. The sphinx was more forthcoming; and just like the sphinx, Clinton's political Marie Antoinette attitude was not going to win over the masses.

Charles Krauthammer, conservative columnist extraordinaire, certainly bore Hillary Clinton no admiration; and his commentary typically carried a uniquely sharp bite appealing to the armies of Hillary haters. Even so, he fairly captured some of the unique problems she faced. As he put it, "Hillary Clinton's problem is age, not chronological but political. She's been around for so long that who can really believe she suddenly has been seized with a new passion to champion, as she put it in Iowa, 'the truckers that I saw on I-80 as I was driving here'?"[55] Who could really believe it? But to win, she had to make a lot of people, including those I-80 truckers, believe it.

Who really was Jeb Bush? or Marco Rubio? or Bernie Sanders? Few Americans knew to start the campaign. But everyone already had a pretty firm opinion of Hillary Clinton, and that was both strength and weakness. As Krauthammer went on, "Clinton's unchangeability is the source of her uniqueness as a candidate: She's a fixed point. She is who she is. And no one expects—nor would anyone really believe—any claimed character change."

Perhaps not a character change but rather a softening of the edges? A sense of personhood or shared life experience? An obvious starting point for making someone comfortable includes establishing like personal associations. "You're from Colorado? I went to school there." "You're a Baptist? I'm a Methodist." "I see you have a New York Giants cap. My Dad had season tickets." Hillary Clinton wanted to establish a connection with the immigrant Hispanic community. She liked to remind people how her grandparents were immigrants, and so she understood them—except her grandparents weren't immigrants, and she knew it.

Speaking in LeClaire, Iowa, in April, Clinton said, "All my grandparents, you know, came over here and you know my grandfather went to work in a lace mill in Scranton, Pennsylvania, and worked there until he retired at 65. He started there when he was a teenager and just kept going."[56]

While Hillary Clinton's grandfather was an immigrant (from England) as she said, her grandmother was born in Pennsylvania to immigrant parents. It's a small thing, to be sure. But it's one she repeated often over the years, and even her campaign staff admitted the error, but she continued to repeat it. Remember the old saying that if you cannot be trusted in small things, why should you be trusted in big things? These little faux pas just made it harder and harder for undecided voters to believe she could ever be trusted to tell them the truth about anything.

FEELING THE BERN?

In late March the self-proclaimed Socialist Vermont Sen. Bernie Sanders threw his hat into the ring. In America, conservatives in particular have a habit of labeling various Democrats as Socialists, including Pres. Obama, and occasionally with just cause; and those so named resist the label strenuously. Socialism is too close to Communism; and if there's anything around which one once could get near consensus in America, it is that Communism is a lousy economic or political system.

Thus, the Far Left usually preferred the more anodyne term *progressive*. While Sanders was officially an "independent" in the Senate, he caucused with the Democrats and proudly declared himself a Socialist. Bernie Sanders and a few others on the Far Left had given careful thought to the issues, knew what he believed, and was unabashed in advancing his views. No hemming and hawing. No squishy nuances or Clintonian unintelligible mush. If for nothing else, all Americans should respect Bernie Sanders for his honesty and transparency.

Bernie Sanders "indisputably has the most unusual history of anyone in the U.S. Congress."[57] Just ask him. That's how he described himself, and it was a fair assessment. For example, he was an urban democratic Socialist (again, his label) running from a tiny rural state. Born in Brooklyn, New York, he moved to Vermont in 1964 after earning a political science degree from Brooklyn College and a master's degree from the University of Chicago.

No one should ever accuse Bernie Sanders of thinking small. He first ran for Governor of Vermont at the ripe old age of 31. He also ran for the United States Senate—at the same time. He ran unsuccessfully for the Senate again two years later in 1974 and twice more for the governorship in 1976 and 1986.

In 1981, he lowered his sights to become mayor of Burlington, Vermont, winning by ten votes. He was reelected three times. Burlington is a bustling metropolis of about forty thousand souls on the eastern border of New York State, ninety-four miles due south from Montreal, Canada. Despite its slight population, Burlington is the most populous city in Vermont.

In 1990, Sanders ran unsuccessfully for a seat in the U.S. House of Representatives but won the seat two years later. After sixteen years in the House, he ran again for U.S. Senate in 2006 and won and then won reelection six years later with 71% of the vote.

Sanders is an angry old white guy from an itty-bitty rural state. He owns a righteous indignation toward a multitude of perceived social injustices and remains bent on correcting them—immediately. And, yes, he is a proud Socialist. When asked what that means, Sanders responded in an interview:

> Democratic socialism is taking a hard look at what countries like Denmark, Sweden, Norway (and) Finland . . . have done over the years and try to ascertain what they have done that is right, in terms of protecting the needs of millions of working families and the elderly and the children. And I think there's much that we can learn from those countries that have had social democratic governments and labor governments or whatever.[58]

It's important to examine that answer or, more accurately, that non-answer. To describe what he means by Socialist, he points to other countries and what they've done right. And what is it they did right he so admired? Not tellin'. He does mention he wants to address the needs of working families and the elderly and children. Wow, nobody else in American politics is interested in those things, right?

Sanders continued, "And what the American people are saying pretty loudly and clearly is they want an economy that works for ordinary Americans. For working people." Again, this is hardly revolutionary stuff. Ted Cruz would say the same as would Hillary Clinton or Jeb Bush.

As usual, the intentions were largely shared among most candidates. The differences lie in the means toward the ends. Sanders, of course, had strong opinions about the need to break up the big banks and the pharmaceutical companies. He strongly favored highly invasive regulatory powers to protect everything that needs protecting according to Bernie. He had strong opinions about the use of military force (only as an absolute last resort). He wanted to tax the rich to dust and ignore the consequences for the economy. He believed in a cost-effective, well-run government, which to many Americans is an obvious contradiction in terms.

Perhaps the most interesting biographical tidbit regarding Bernie Sanders regards his honeymoon. Nearby Niagara Falls? Nope. The Caribbean for the warmth? Nah.

Bernie Sanders took his new bride to the Soviet Union for his honeymoon, to bask in the wonders of all Joe Stalin and Nikita Khrushchev had wrought for the Russian people.[59] This more than anything may explain what Sanders meant by democratic Socialist. The Soviets too called themselves democratic and Socialist and Communist. The former Communist East German regime included the word *democratic* in its official name. The USSR stood for the "Union of Soviet Socialist Republics." It didn't fool anyone.

Sanders would likely bridle at any suggestion he pined for the good ol' days when world Communism actively sought to enslave the world. But by tossing around a label he refused to define, one must look for clues in his words and actions. No doubt Sanders believed he would do it better than the other guys marching under the red banner, but every future despot basks in that particular fantasy.

Bernie Sanders's prospects of winning the Democratic nomination, not to mention the presidency, seemed approximately nil. But even in the Senate, his presence as a clear voice espousing firm left-wing principles and their application to national issues could not be ignored; and now as a candidate, this was ever more so. Hillary Clinton now had two competing voices on the left: Sanders, who was loud and angry and far, far left; and O'Malley, who was nearly as clear-voiced, not nearly as angry, and was only Far Left and thus presented a significantly more viable general election candidacy if he could grab the nomination.

Curiously, no other viable Democratic senators or governors appeared to be entertaining a run for the White House.[60] The last times viable Democrats shied from the limelight this way were in 2007 when Hillary Clinton looked to have a lock on the Democratic nomination only to see it slip away to Barack Obama and in 1991 when George H. W. Bush had just kicked Saddam Hussein's sorry butt out of Kuwait and looked unbeatable.

In the latter event, some Arkansas scrub of dubious morals, a gift for gab, and nothing to lose became the only contender and won it all. One had to wonder as the campaign unfolded how many Democratic senators and governors would wish they'd had a little more spine in the face of Hillary Clinton's wobbly campaign. Even Gov. Moonbeam (as California's chief executive Jerry Brown was once labeled), then a still vigorous seventy-seven years old, had to look in the mirror every morning and ask himself, "One more time?"

The Graham Cracker

South Carolina Republican Sen. Lindsey Graham of South Carolina inched toward a candidacy. Lindsey Graham was smart, well-spoken, and sharp on television. Though he called himself a conservative, the label might have applied circa 1976 but didn't fit in 2016, except in one respect. Graham was the only unabashed foreign policy hawk running as either Democrat or Republican. Of all the candidates, only Clinton, Biden (if he got in), and Marco Rubio had a better grasp of the threats posed by ISIS, China, and by a resurgent Russia. And of these, only Graham pushed for a forward-leaning, aggressive role for the United States, the exact opposite of the Obama/Clinton/Biden policy doctrine.

Foreign policy aside, Lindsay Graham's political stances pointed to one of the great ironies of politics in America, 2016 style, especially in the U.S. Senate. Senators like John McCain, Lindsey Graham, and Bob Corker, honorable men all, clung desperately to the label "conservative," much as Jeb Bush sought to do in the presidential campaign. The rise of the Tea Party as a defining force in Republican politics made such efforts essential to political survival. Yet one's imagination stretched to snapping to accept McCain, Graham, or the others as conservatives in 2016. However they defined themselves in their own minds, these individuals were no more "conservative" as the times defined the term than Hillary Clinton was "progressive."

In contrast to the non-conservatives trying desperately to wear the coat, Senate Democrats who would qualify as card-carrying Socialists throughout Europe bridle at being called Socialist and grasped desperately instead to the label "progressive." Notable such progressives include Elizabeth Warren but also Tammy Baldwin of Wisconsin and Al Franken of Minnesota. Many more examples populated the House of Representatives, however, including such national entertainers as Maxine Waters of California.

What distinguishes a conservative from a pretender? A liberal from a progressive from a Socialist? Oftentimes, it's a matter of degree but also one of approach. Some years ago, a self-avowed progressive explained the difference between a progressive and a liberal. On the surface the distinction seemed little more than a rebranding because too many Americans had an ill view of "liberals." But the issue ran much deeper than that, he explained. There is a real difference.

A liberal essentially is a defender of the big government status quo—big government, high taxes, single-payor health care, redistributionism and all that—but without changing much and doing so none too quickly. The unions, for example, occupy the very heart of American liberalism. In a sense, a modern liberal is easily confused for a classic conservative preserving the status quo, accepting change slowly.

A progressive, in contrast, looks to change policies with urgency, to try things even if they don't work and when they don't work, abandon them and try something else even if it's something the conservatives are talking about. The end goals are similar; but whereas liberals move slowly, progressives want change now. The liberals' foremost goal is defending the status quo while staying in power. The progressives' foremost goal is to use government aggressively to achieve a more equitable society without worrying overly much about how it was done in the past and without worrying overly about the immediate political consequences in the sure belief they will ultimately be proven right and duly rewarded by the voters.

How does Bernie Sanders's Socialism fit in? Perhaps one can best think of a Socialist in America as a progressive who is willing to use government powers extensively to trample with little remorse individual rights to liberty and property and opportunity to advance toward this more equitable society he or she envisions. Ill consequences are of little consequence to a Socialist when the ends are so identifiably noble.

This view toward unfortunate or unintended consequences may help distinguish progressives from Socialists. A progressive may be more careful regarding consequences. A progressive is perhaps less driven by rank ideology than a Socialist. A progressive's ideology is results. A Socialist's ideology lies elsewhere; and when the results don't follow, the Socialist's answer is generally more of what failed because the ideology cannot be wrong. And therein lies the flower-lined road to tyranny, to systemic and endemic poverty, and to cultural stagnation. A perfect record of ill consequences never dulls a Socialist's enthusiasm because, of course, previous efforts were flawed while theirs will succeed brilliantly. Just ask them.

STRIPPING AWAY THE MASK

Many forces shape national political campaigns. Typically, the campaign and candidate strive mightily to create a specific image and persona appealing to the base and independents. Getting elected is marketing, plain and simple. Then reality hits. Sometimes reality hits in the form of Iowa coffee shops filled with discriminating, knowledgeable voters who strip away the carefully prepared mask.

Sometimes reality strikes in the form of real-world events for which the candidate is unprepared or which simply reveal the candidate's flaws in ways antagonists and voters never could. Stripped of a carefully constructed image, what is left is the real person in all his or her birthday suit glory.

For example, a timeless moment occurred in 1984 when Massachusetts Gov. Michael Dukakis allowed himself to be photographed driving a U.S. Army tank. He couldn't have looked more ridiculous had he been caught wearing a Big Bird costume. But the moment stuck because it revealed Dukakis for what he was: a little man in a big world.

As Governor of Texas, George W. Bush attended an event at a local volunteer fire department. In pursuit of good publicity, a company had offered to supply heart defibrillators to volunteer fire departments across the country on the condition the state's governor agreed to do a small event. The assembled would make a few remarks; the governor would do likewise and then push a red button on a defibrillator attached to a mannequin for dramatic flourish.

George W. showed up at the event. On a gurney lay a mannequin hooked up to a defibrillator. After saying a few words, Bush pushed the little red button—and nothing happened. The battery was dead. Without missing a beat, Bush deadpanned, "He's a goner." Everybody broke up laughing. W was a natural. Candidates didn't always respond as well.

A similar remarkable event occurred in the 1980 campaign in New Hampshire. Former everything-but-president at the time George H.W. Bush was the favorite and campaigning well while the old warhorse, Ronald Reagan, led the pack right behind.

At the big debate, Bush Sr. wanted to go mano a mano with Reagan, excluding all the other candidates. The local newspaper and vocal Bush supporter, the *Nashua Telegraph*, tried to play right along, having attempted to dictate the rules of the debate. Reagan's sense of fairness would have none of it.

Somewhere along the way, the *Nashua Telegraph* moderator Jon Breen forgot the golden rule: he who has the gold makes the rules. Reagan insisted the four other acknowledged candidates who were waiting offstage be allowed to participate. Breen tried to have Reagan's microphone turned off. Bush threatened to walk off the stage. Reagan told Bush to do whatever he wanted and then declared, "I am paying for this microphone, Mr. Breen!"[61]

Bush's pettiness and Reagan's moment of righteous anger revealed a lot about Reagan, about Bush, and incidentally a lot about the supposed political independence of the press even back then.

At the end of the debate, the moderator asked George H. W. Bush whether Reagan was too old to be president, to which Bush properly responded in the negative. The moderator then asked Reagan if he (Reagan) was too old to be president, to which Reagan responded, "I agree with George Bush." Reagan won the debate with determination and humor, and Bush won a learning experience and eight years as vice president before succeeding Reagan for a term.

An event on a whole different scale occurred in 2008. John McCain was running a typical McCain campaign, muddling along having wrested the Republican nomination on the typically inane Republican basis of "it's your turn." The economy seemed sound enough; so with Afghanistan, Iraq, and China bubbling noisily, foreign policy seemed likely to dominate the campaign. McCain was a foreign policy expert whereas Barack Obama as a two-year junior senator was a neophyte.

Then, the global financial crisis hit. Running while representing the party out of power, the moment created a tremendous opening for Obama to attack, linking McCain to Bush as though Bush's policies somehow caused a global financial meltdown. (Note: nothing in U.S. policy at this time could cause a *global* financial meltdown.) McCain had no clue how to respond—and it showed. He suspended his campaign to rush back to Washington to do exactly . . . nothing but sit by idly doing nothing while others acted with urgency.

Along with a handful of major financial firms, thousands of upended homeowners, and millions of workers, the financial crisis and ensuing Global Great Recession sank John McCain's campaign almost overnight. Helloooo, Pres. Obama.

What events would peel back the veneer to reveal the candidates' true mettle in this campaign? In the spring of 2015, not one or two but four events seemed well designed to perform this Toto pulling back the curtain on the Wizard of Oz–style revelation. Unfortunately for Clinton, while some created problems for Republican aspirants, all looked truly menacing to the SS Hillary.

THE CLINTON (CAMPAIGN) FOUNDATION IS CRUMBLING

A major obstacle facing Hillary Clinton's campaign was her honesty, or the widely perceived lack thereof. As Chris Cillizza of the *Washington Post* led off his May 3, 2015, article, "Is Hillary Clinton honest enough to be President?"[62]

Citing a recent poll, Cillizza noted four in ten Democrats and six in ten independents said "'honest' either barely applied to Clinton or didn't apply at all. It is, unfortunately, common for Americans not to trust their president after a few years in office. Disappointments, compromises, missteps, Washington dysfunction, and so forth will taint the image of any officeholder. But Americans also want to like and trust the nominee when they're voting. Clinton had a big-time likability problem for a lot of voters and apparently an even bigger trust problem. The Clinton Foundation fiasco wasn't improving matters.

As with so many Bill and Hill scandals, the Clinton Foundation fiasco's details were nearly endless, but the summary of the matter was that the Clintons established a foundation to do great humanitarian works around the world. To perform these works, the foundation was to receive enormous contributions from all sorts of interesting sources.

So far, so good, more or less, until Hillary Clinton was nominated to become secretary of state. How, then, would it look if the government of Algeria gave a $500,000 gift to the foundation for the noble purpose of helping the people of Haiti following their devastating earthquake yet "at a time when the Algerian government had dramatically ramped up its lobbying activities at State, where it was under pressure for human rights violations," as the *Washington Post*'s Ruth Marcus observed in an editorial titled "Sloppiness and Greed"?[63]

As Marcus tartly put it, "Did Algeria give simply because its government was moved by the plight of the Haitian people? Pardon my cynicism." Third-world country Algeria, simply put, was putting its money, of which it had little to spare, where Hillary Clinton's mouth was.

Knowing these issues would bubble up, Clinton and the State Department produced a wholly imperfect solution: all donations to the foundation would be publicly reported, previous donors could continue to give at the same amounts as before, but new donors or increased donations would have to be approved by the State Department.

Was the Algeria gift submitted for review? No. And it wasn't the only one. The foundation decided to suspend its observance of the solution the minute Hillary left the State Department. Why? Too much transparency can be very inconvenient.

The foundation's shady doings were well-known. The *New York Times* ran a story in August of 2013 about how a former advisor to Bill Clinton at the foundation had left to create his own consultancy—with Bill as a paid advisor.[64] Typical was Bill's comment upon coming back from a $500,000 payday for a one-hour speech in Moscow, Russia, "I gotta pay our bills," as though he was some Arkansas yokel coming off a part-time landscaping gig.[65]

Bill Clinton's comment dredged up reminders of Hillary's 2014 statement that the Clintons left the White House "dead broke." According to PolitiFact, after reviewing the Clintons' financial disclosure forms as they left the White House, Bill's legal bills from his many scandals left the Clintons about $500,000 in the hole, with three teeny-weeny exceptions.[66] The Clintons owned two homes not required on the disclosure forms: a five-bedroom house in Chappaqua, New York, they bought for $1.7 million and a humble seven-bedroom house on Embassy Row in Washington DC they'd bought for $2.85 million. Of course, the Clintons had mortgages on both properties, but they had put $855,000 down on the Washington house, and both had surely appreciated substantially in the interim.

Oh, and the third exception: the willingness of individuals, organizations, and governments worldwide to pay enormous sums for a few minutes of either Bill's or Hill's time.

It's unseemly for the rich to claim poverty. "Let them eat cake," as history claims Marie Antoinette observed shortly before her date with a guillotine, has never been a popular mind-set. It was stunning for someone running for president, or that person's spouse, to have done so. More than the hubris and enduring impression the Clintons think the laws apply only to the little people, these episodes further fueled the sense in Democratic circles that Bill was a loose cannon and Hillary really was politically tone deaf.

Bill Clinton's timing with his flippant remark could hardly have been worse. Only a couple weeks before, the political reporter Peter Schweizer came out with his hard-hitting and well-researched assault on the Clinton family money machine *Clinton Cash: The Untold Story of How and Why Foreign Governments and Businesses Helped Make Bill and Hillary Rich*. The mainstream media tried desperately to play up the narrative Schweitzer was just another crank conservative doing a hatchet job on the Clintons. But Schweizer was well respected, and the *New York Times* had been one of the first to report on the book in a tone clearly suggesting the *Times* at least felt this book was very serious.[67] Toward the end of April, the Far Left columnist Jonathan Chait captured the moment well in a *New York Times* magazine headline, "If This Is the Best Defense of the Clinton Foundation, She's in Trouble."[68]

The next shoe to drop from the Clinton Foundation fiasco centipede was news the Foundation was going to refile five years of federal tax returns.[69] Why? For misreporting millions of dollars in foreign donations, among other failures. One of two conclusions seemed possible. Either the Clinton Foundation was incredibly ineptly run, and its accountants both internally and those it hired to do its tax returns were woefully incompetent, or the foundation had tried to hide its funding sources and got caught. Tax professionals expressed incredulity such a simple mistake could be made time and again. It was simply a matter of checking a box. Either way, this was an ugly black eye and brought another page to the narrative about shady business involving the foundation and foreign governments.

The hits just kept on coming. With this much smoke, there had to be fire somewhere; and the press increasingly smelled an opportunity to engage in its very favorite activity of all: big game hunting. For example, in late April the *New York Times* reported on another fascinating revelation. It turns out a Canadian charity gave more than $33 million to the Clinton Foundation—all neatly hidden by Canada's privacy laws.[70] The Clinton Foundation's official response provided by Maura Pally, acting chief executive, "This is hardly an effort on our part to avoid transparency." Right. Of course not.

With Clinton scandals, one gets the sense a centipede must be involved because there's always another shoe to drop. The next shoe to drop fell later in May when the foundation disclosed it had received not $1 million or $2 million in contributions not previously reported but $24.6 million from speeches Hillary and Bill had given. That's a lot of speeches given for a good cause, so what was the problem? The foundation had recorded the receipts as "revenues" rather than "contributions." Big deal? Not really, except the foundation didn't have to reveal the source of "revenues" with respect to, for example, Hillary and Bill's agreed-upon rules with the State Department. Contributors would have to be revealed.

Like the Canadian charity issue, it sure looked like the Clintons and their foundation were working awfully hard to hide who was paying their bills. Did the Clinton Foundation do anything wrong? Hard to tell. Perhaps they really did just accept the money. Perhaps they really didn't do anything to launder donations through a Canadian charity just to keep the donors anonymous. Perhaps they really didn't know the difference between $24.6 million in revenues and $24.6 million in contributions. But it sure looked bad, and Ms. Pally's response only sharpened the focus on the key issue.

Of course, these could all be innocent mistakes, like a movie showing some poor slouch in a slapstick comedy suffering a series of innocently disastrous mishaps. But then, this was the Clintons, for whom skirting the law was an art form going all the way back to Hillary Clinton's oh-so-convenient high-paying job at the Rose Law Firm in Arkansas, to her sudden brilliance as a novice commodity trader, to her firing White House travel agents, to the Clintons' involvement in the Whitewater real estate development. Ancient history! her defenders would reasonably insist, and they had a point. But even the dots of ancient history sometimes are packed so closely together one has little choice but to connect them to the present.

Another pair of dots packed so close together they almost connected themselves: was there really that much global demand to hear Bill and Hill speak? Was their wisdom really that profound, their remarks that entertaining? Twenty minutes here, thirty minutes there, for so far nearly $50 million and counting. One began to wonder whether something else was going on here. Was there really a quid pro quo behind the carefully constructed veil of secrecy? Did the speeches' sponsors who had paid so handsomely for a few timely words of Bill Clinton's wisdom expect something more substantive from Hillary Clinton's State Department? Would the media bother to ask? It turns out, no, it wouldn't, because even the foundation fiasco was soon crowded out for a season by the email scandal.

HILLARY SPEAKS (VERY) SOFTLY BUT SCORES A BIG PAYDAY

Meanwhile, not all was quiet on the Clinton front. She wasn't saying anything about the decision to invade Iraq, or about Fallujah falling to ISIS, or about the intense legislative battle unfolding in Washington over Trade Promotion Authority with Pres. Obama and the Republican leadership on one side and the bulk of the

Democratic Party on the other, or about her emails, or about the Clinton Foundation, or about much of anything else as weeks passed with nary a public peep from the potential POTUS.

Clinton understood some in the press would hold her accountable. Some took their responsibilities seriously. They wanted access, and they wanted answers. They got nothing, and this was costing her big time. Reporters have a sense of responsibility. They also have a sense of entitlement. And they have editors who demand cutting-edge stories, and the cutting-edge story increasingly became Clinton's serial stiffing of the media. Turning potentially neutral, objective reporters into angry antagonists is an odd way to run a campaign, the edge of which was captured nicely in a quip by Peggy Noonan, "She's running a silent movie of a campaign."[71]

Silent isn't the same as idle. Hillary was still giving paid speeches. According to the *Washington Post*, Bill and Hillary had earned about $25 million in 2014 giving speeches.[72]

A certain bipartisan group in Washington led by the likes of John McCain want desperately to limit the amount of money in American politics. Bill and Hillary could probably barely control their laughter. Just follow the money. Group X wants to give a big check to the Clinton campaign, but the donors want to remain anonymous. Have her give a speech. Pay an exorbitant amount. The money's then the Clintons' who can just give it to their campaign. Of course, not every candidate makes millions of dollars giving speeches. Only the most established—the elites—can do so. The little guy has to raise campaign cash the old-fashioned way. Some things never change. The Clintons skirted the rules professing angelic innocence; the righteous reformers skirted reality demonstrating their innocence of a different sort.

AN IMMIGRATION DETOUR TO THE RESCUE

As the foundation fiasco rolled on, Team Clinton, with the exception of the painfully irrepressible Bill, tried to keep its head down as much as possible, answering questions and responding to attacks only as absolutely necessary. They also knew they needed to do something to shift the focus back onto the campaign's policy themes. Hillary Clinton gave a speech on immigration reform sure to (A) give the press something else to talk about and (B) excite the base—and the base ate it up.

According to Clinton, radical immigration reform was a central plank in her family-oriented economic policy, though actual American citizens might wonder what this has to do with American families. For once in her life, she followed the modern catchphrase of "go big or go home." At a Cinco de Mayo speech in Las Vegas, Clinton went all in on "hispandering," declaring her support for a pathway to citizenship as well as her support for policies going well beyond Obama's constitutionally dubious executive orders, the very same executive orders Obama had declared at least twenty-two times he lacked the constitutional authority to issue.

The conservative media immediately jumped on her claims to going beyond what Obama had already done. Since Obama's actions to date were unconstitutional, they argued, would Hillary Clinton tear up the Constitution even more? More reasonably interpreted, Clinton intended to seek legislation to advance these policies rather than to resort to constitutionally dubious executive orders. But this more reasonable interpretation would blunt the conservatives' preferred attack line, so it was mostly ignored.

Other criticisms noted Clinton's new flip-flops on immigration. Clinton managed to assert her policies as though they were always obvious and always arose from deep long-held convictions. She proved in politics if you can fake sincerity, then you'll go far. In 2004, she said, "I am, you know, adamantly against illegal immigrants," though what she meant is obviously open to interpretation.[73] Should all immigrants be deemed legal, or should they all be deported? She probably meant neither, but what she did mean would remain one of those enduring unanswered questions.

Family-centered economic policy? In 2014, in response to a question about the massive influx of unaccompanied minors across the southern border, Hillary Clinton offered, "They should be sent back as soon as it can be determined who responsible adults in their families are."[74] Sure.

Clinton didn't care what her right-wing tormenters said. From her perspective, the more they whined about her immigration speech, the more they took all her other troubles off the national radar—another little mission-accomplished moment for Team Clinton—and as usual, the conservatives fell for it. Throw them red meat, and conservatives will always skip their vegetables.

A Few More Candidacy Footnotes for the Record

Beyond all the scandals and policy machinations, May also triggered the announcements of a flock of "me too" candidates. On the Democratic side, in addition to the Socialist Bernie Sanders of Vermont, a long-lost Rhode Island flake appeared on the scene.

Lincoln Chaffee hailed from one of the great families in Rhode Island political history, his father John having served honorably in the United States Marine Corps, as Rhode Island Governor, as secretary of the navy, and finally in the U.S. Senate from 1976 to 1999. As then-Pres. Bill Clinton said of Republican John Chaffee, "He embodied the decent center which has carried America from triumph to triumph for over 200 years." His son, Lincoln, inherited his father's passion for politics but apparently little else.

In 1999 Lincoln Chaffee was appointed to finish out his father's term in the Senate, John Chaffee having died suddenly of heart failure. Lincoln Chaffee won the seat outright in 2000 and then lost it to Sheldon Whitehouse in 2006. He then fled the Republican Party to become an independent, announcing his support in 2008 for Barack Obama. Chaffee went on to become a rather unremarkable Rhode Island Governor and then announced he was switching to the Democratic Party in 2012. Probably the only justification for Lincoln Chaffee announcing a candidacy at this point would be summed up in the expression "got nothin' better to do."

Mike Huckabee, Curiosity

The May Republican entries were better but ultimately no more serious. For example, Mike Huckabee announced he was running—again.

Mike Huckabee in many respects was a clone of Ted Cruz: ultraconservative, thoughtful, intelligent, excellent speaker, Southern Baptist. But Huckabee was a successful Governor of Arkansas; Cruz had no executive experience. Huckabee had run for president in the past with a modicum of success having won the Iowa caucuses; Cruz was new to the presidential game. Huckabee was infuriatingly likeable; Cruz?

Huckabee had pastored churches in Pine Bluff and Texarkana. Curiously, though, he earned his baccalaureate in religion from Ouachita Baptist University. He dropped out of seminary after only one year.

Huckabee's unusually fine command of the media did not come by accident. At the age of fourteen, Huckabee worked at the local radio station reading the news and weather. While pastoring, Huckabee established twenty-four-hour radio stations. After his campaign in 2008 came to naught, Huckabee hosted his own named show on Fox News for the next seven years.

In the past, Huckabee enjoyed a great advantage speaking to evangelicals. His great disadvantages this time included that many could speak evangelical almost as well, including Ben Carson and Ted Cruz. Also, all understood Huckabee had a very limited appeal to any voter group outside evangelicals. Even the evangelicals understood winning mattered, and Huckabee had a metaphysically zero chance of winning.

The Difference between Intelligence and Experience

Ben Carson, a black man, was one of three particularly interesting nonpoliticians to get into the race, the others being Donald Trump and Carly Fiorina. For some, their biographies initially overwhelm their candidacy. Ben Carson is one such. A man of humility, integrity, accomplishment, and intelligence, his story is all the more remarkable because, like many in the race not named Bush, Carson rose from humble beginnings. None matched Carson's modest start.

Carson was born in Detroit, Michigan, in 1951. His father married his mother when she was only thirteen and while he had another family. His parents divorced when he was very young, his mother raising Ben and his older brother, Curtis, while working multiple jobs and aided by food stamps and other government assistance.

He graduated from Southwestern High School in Detroit and went on to graduate from Yale and then from the University of Michigan Medical School. Carson eventually accepted a post as director of pediatric neurosurgery at Johns Hopkins Hospital. While at Johns Hopkins, Carson performed a famous operation for the first time separating twins conjoined at the back of the head.

Carson vaulted to national political attention through his 2013 speech to the National Prayer Breakfast. Carson often referred to the importance of his faith during his childhood and beyond. Interestingly, Carson isn't a Methodist or Southern Baptist. He's a member of the Seventh-Day Adventist Church.

Ben Carson embodied one characteristic unique among candidates running for president: beyond his personal character and intelligence, he utterly lacked any of the usual personal requirements of a presidential candidate. Executive experience? None. Legislative experience? None. Foreign policy strengths? None. Domestic policy familiarity? Essentially none. If elected, Carson would have been the most substantively unprepared president in modern memory.

Elections across the Pond an Omen for the United States?

On May 9, the British national election produced a stunning result of tremendous consequence. The UK election featured the incumbent

Conservative Party led by David Cameron and its centuries-long nemesis, the opposition Labour Party led by Ed Miliband.

For the upcoming U. contest, the most interesting aspect of the UK election was probably the failure of British pollsters to grasp the leanings of the electorate, much as U.S. pollsters had done in some Senate races in 2014.

For months prior, pollsters found the two leading British parties as being roughly tied at 34% support. On election night, the Conservatives claimed over half the members of Parliament. A seventeen-point miss off a 34% base is a big miss.

Something obviously foiled UK polling, so much so the authorities launched an inquiry. Were the pollsters biased? Probably not. Simply incompetent? Probably not. But modern polling techniques were failing, likely an issue for the upcoming U.S. campaign.

Frank Luntz, the American pollster, writing in the *Washington Post* the Sunday after the U.K. election made two telling observations.[75] First, he noted the UK electorate was apparently intensely turned off by the campaign process, so much so a large portion of the electorate had become election-eve or even polling-booth deciders. Luntz had observed this pattern in 2014 and expected to see it again in 2016. Translation: when you hear a poll figure with a stated margin of error of, say, 4%, double or triple the margin of error.

Perhaps heightened by the distaste of the election, trust became exceptionally important as voters cast ballots. "In just about every pre-election poll, Conservatives and Labour were locked in a dead heat, yet voters gave Conservative leader David Cameron a large advantage over Ed Miliband, his Labor challenger, on the question of whom they would trust more to run the country."

Liking a candidate is always important, but ultimately voting is largely a matter of trust. Who do you trust to make wise decisions? Who do you trust to look out for your interests as you see them? Who do you trust to tell the truth? Who do you trust with the future of the country? Brits didn't necessarily like Cameron; but for the most part, they trusted him, and they didn't trust the nice but flaky Miliband.

As Luntz went on to observe, "This is a huge lesson, in particular, for Hillary Clinton." In her upcoming congressional hearings on the Benghazi matter, "Any hint of dishonesty or misstep that undermines her credibility could fatally damage her already embattled campaign." The same could be said of her answers, or lack thereof, to questions regarding the Clinton Foundation, the email scandal, or whatever other nastiness popped up in the coming months. The renowned conservative journalist and commentator, William Safire, once called Hillary Clinton a "congenital liar."[76] While nasty even by the standards of the day, the barb stung most because history was on Safire's side. Could Clinton be trusted to give the unvarnished, unparsed truth? If she made it to election day, that could be the decisive question, and it wouldn't necessarily be reflected in the pre-election polls.

UNFORCED ERRORS, BIG TIME

Every candidate running for office knows the inevitability of uncomfortable questions for which they have to be prepared, and the toughness of the questions generally increases exponentially with the importance of the office. Some questions, usually involving social policy, are obvious and universal. Questions like, are you prolife or not? Do you support gay marriage, or not? Do you support the death penalty? Do you support gun ownership rights or gun control? Whatever your position, you have to know it and be able to answer succinctly, repeatedly, and consistently. Those voters for whom these are their key issues truck no waffling or equivocation.

Some questions are specific to the times. In the 2016 campaign, one such dealt with supporting a path to citizenship for illegal aliens or insisting they all be sent home. Another was the increasingly stale question as to whether Obamacare should be repealed.

Then there are the toughest questions of all for which a candidate simply must be fully prepared with a confident, clear, definitive response. These questions are often particular to the candidate, at least insofar as the issues raised. A good answer demonstrates preparation and confidence; danger avoided, next question.

A weak answer or no answer or a constantly changing answer demonstrates the opposite. Hillary Clinton faced a plethora of such issues from her time in the White House as First Lady (standing by the philanderer in chief, for example), her time as secretary of state (Benghazi), the foundation, and her being tagged for better or worse as Obama's potential successor. She preferred these issues to all just slide under the rug, ignored, forgotten. Fat chance. The longer she delayed in addressing them, the longer they would fester.

Jeb Bush had his own tough questions; and for the most part, he handled them well. For example, there was always the dynasty question. His basic answer boiled down to some combination of "aw shucks, it's just me" and "I love my dad and my brother, but I'm my own man." He could probably get away with this as an answer, though many voters would never buy it just as Hillary Clinton couldn't completely avoid the dynasty issues associated with her husband's administration.

The toughest question demanded of Jeb a clear and convincing answer was "Would you have invaded Iraq?" When he finally faced the question publicly, he flubbed it badly; and as often happens, his huge unforced error revealed a lot about the candidate—none of it good.

To review the bidding, after whipping the Taliban in Afghanistan in 2002, George W. Bush set his sights on Saddam Hussein's Iraq. Bush's justification was the U.S. intelligence community had convincing evidence Saddam Hussein was rapidly developing and would soon have the ability to deploy weapons of mass destruction (WMD)—chemical and biological agents. The claim gained legitimacy because Hussein had clearly used these agents against civilians and military personnel in the past, and so very few people in or out of Congress doubted the allegation. Governments around the world concurred with this assessment, as did Sen.s Hillary Clinton and Barack Obama.

Bush's second argument was nearly as clear-cut: Hussein could not be trusted with these weapons. Yes, they were mostly a threat to Iraq's neighbors, including Israel, but the United States was similarly exposed. How about a nice freighter sailing into New York City harbor loaded with some nerve agent?

The nation accepted Bush's judgment, though not without misgivings, because Bush enjoyed the benefit of the doubt after his resounding win in Afghanistan. The question was put to the Congress. Hillary Clinton voted to give Bush the authority to take Hussein out. Obama, despite his agreement regarding the evidence, voted against giving Bush that authority.

It turns out, Hussein was bluffing. Instead of being a "slam dunk" regarding Hussein's WMD program as former Secretary of State Colin Powell embarrassingly assured the United Nations on the eve of the Iraq War, no Iraqi WMD were ever found.

The political Left, whose hatred of W. knew no bounds, quickly took political advantage. After a short honeymoon to avoid appearing to belittle the U.S. military's stunning accomplishment in taking down Saddam Hussein's mighty Revolutionary Guards, the Left pounced. The critical question (to which no substantive public answer was ever provided) was, how did the nation's, and the world's, intelligence services get something so important about which they were so confident so completely wrong? How did Iraq's WMD go from slam dunk to slam the dunce?

Politically active elements on the Left quickly transitioned from the narrative Bush had blundered badly to the narrative Bush had lied about the WMD. The allegation: Bush knew there were no WMD in Iraq but sold the story anyway to justify an invasion. Why would he do that? The explanations got a little hazy.

One explanation went that Bush sought to atone for his dad's failure to finish the job in Operation Desert Storm, the first Iraq War fought in 1991 following Iraq's invasion of Kuwait. As explanations go, this was pretty absurd but sufficient for the W haters.

Ultimately, explanations didn't matter. All that mattered was the new narrative, which was itself false. As Bob Woodward of Watergate fame, who researched extensively the decisions leading up to W's Iraq War in preparing his own book, observed, "there was no lying in this [the case about WMD] that I could find."[77] Incidentally, Woodward's book was found on Bin Laden's shelf in the compound in which he was killed by a U.S. special operations unit.

"You break it, you bought it" is a common rule in retail establishments. George W had broken Iraq; on behalf of the United States, he accepted responsibility for "fixing" it, seeking to rebuild Iraq into a stable, strong, democratically based Arab nation, spending hundreds of billions of dollars in the process and resulting in the injuries to and deaths of thousands of American personnel. The soldiers, sailors, Marines, and airmen performed with courage and conviction. The policymakers failed, or more accurately they proved once again what candidate George W. Bush had repeatedly asserted prior to taking office: the United States cannot successfully engage in "nation building." Then Obama declared Iraq a great success under his own inspired leadership and withdrew U.S. combat troops. Then ISIS started carving up Iraq like a Thanksgiving turkey.

So the obvious question for which Jeb absolutely had to have a hands-down, pat answer also forced him to either ignore history or throw his brother under the bus.

When asked by Fox News reporter Megyn Kelly if, knowing what we know now, he would have invaded Iraq, Jeb said, "I would have."[78] Realizing later he'd screwed up badly, Jeb called in to conservative radio talk show host Sean Hannity's national program and made some lame excuse about not having understood the question initially, adding, "I don't know what that decision would have been; that's a hypothetical."[79]

The next day, he tried again to clean up the mess. "Going back in time and talking about a hypothetical, 'what would have happened, what could have happened,' I think does a disservice to those who served." As compared to what? Those who served and all the family members of the sons and daughters, fathers and mothers, sisters and brothers who'd lost a loved one wanted the truth; and they proved they could handle it.

It was only after the damage was done that Jeb finally stated the obvious, "Knowing what we know now, I would not have engaged, I would not have launched an invasion." Well, no kidding.

This wasn't a hard question. It wasn't a gotcha question. It wasn't a surprise. The correct answer was simple enough. "Knowing what we know now, of course I wouldn't have invaded."

Obvious question, yet Jeb Bush evolved toward an answer over many painful days even as the debacle unfolded. Part of his trouble probably arose because many of his campaign's foreign policy advisors were former George W. administration officials who were themselves party to the decision and the nation-building disaster that ensued.

If the intelligence regarding Hussein's WMD had proven correct, the wisdom of the invasion would remain debatable; but history would almost certainly have sided with George W. Bush. Commanders must act based on the best information available. W's legitimate indictment lay not with the war but with the nobly intended yet foolishly naïve ensuing nation-building policies.

This may smack of Monday morning quarterbacking; but even if it were no more than that, one would hope come Monday morning someone aspiring to be quarterback would avoid the telegraphed blitz up the middle. But it was much more than that. The Iraq War was a pivotal moment in modern American history and a pivotal moment in the course of the George W. Bush presidency. America's warriors fought bravely and fought well, but there was no denying first the war and then what followed proved to be enormous policy mistakes. If we cannot learn from our mistakes, we will continue to make them. If politicians cannot be honest about the lessons learned, however painful they may be, should they be trusted to tell the truth about future decisions and events?

Nor could these questions have come at a more poignant time, for even as these questions raged at home the Iraqi city of Ramadi teetered and Fallujah had just fallen to ISIS forces as the U.S.-trained Iraqi army backed by American airpower fled the battlefield. Fallujah is the capital city of the Sunni-dominated Anbar Province. Its fall marked yet another example of Obama's foreign policy in tatters.

Whatever one's judgment about the Iraq War, its initial justification, or the aftermath, at the end of the day the war was won; and Bush bequeathed a tenuous peace to Barack Obama. For all the cost in blood—nearly 30,000 wounded and 4,500 Americans killed—and for all the financial burden to be borne in debt by current and future generations, Bush left Obama a reasonably stable and hopeful Iraq. Says who? Says Barack Obama. In May of 2011, he addressed the Eighty-Second Airborne Division at Fort Bragg to mark the end of American combat operations in Iraq. As he noted, all the trials overcome, the sacrifice, the courage had led "to this moment of success," calling it an "extraordinary achievement."[80]

Four years later, under Obama's Middle East policy, Iraq was crumbling while ISIS consumed Syria one city at a time. In May of 2015, Obama held a Mideast summit at Camp David, inviting all of America's allies in the Middle East. Many, including the leadership of Saudi Arabia, publicly snubbed Obama, though Saudi leadership did participate in bilateral discussions. Bahrain's King Hamad bin Isa al-Khalifa chose instead to attend a horse show and celebration in Windsor, England, for Queen Elizabeth.[81]

As Charles Krauthammer observed, U.S. Middle East policy scraped "rock bottom."[82] Following the fall of Ramadi, not the U.S. but the Iranian defense minister was first on the scene as the Iraqi government called on Iranian-supported Sunni warriors to assist in taking back the city.[83] The U.S.-backed Iraqi army flees, and Iranian-backed Sunni warriors ride to the rescue; and still, Obama insisted his strategy was working. Under the circumstances, if Jeb Bush couldn't get the "would you have invaded Iraq given what we know today" question right, then maybe he really had no business running for president, after all. And under the circumstances, whatever problems the Iraqi mess created for Republicans was nothing compared with the problems it would create for the former Obama secretary of state who remained fastidiously silent as though hiding in a CIA safe house rather than running for president.

RUBIO'S RUB

The Clintons were not born to America's upper crust; but by working the system, they had amassed a substantial fortune worthy of their own edition of "America's Rich and Famous." The same could not be said of most of their Republican challengers. Sure, Mitt Romney had gotten rich; but as a Republican candidate, he and Donald Trump were the modern anomalies. Most Republican challengers, while not poor, were certainly not rich.

In late May, the *Washington Post* ran a story on how Marco Rubio had been forced to cash out nearly $70,000 in retirement funds.[84] How desperate must his cash flow have been? Because of the tax penalty applicable to early withdrawals, Rubio probably had only a bit more than $40,000 net proceeds. To most Americans, $40,000 on top of a senator's salary of $174,000 and some other outside income of nearly $60,000 would seem like a lot of money. But try keeping two households—one in pricey Washington and another in Florida—and have four kids in private schools; and you see why Congress increasingly is the province of millionaires, as only millionaires can afford to stay in Congress for long.

Of course, the *Post*'s spin on the story was Rubio's "struggles" with money. This, in turn, allowed them a reference to a particularly unhappy episode in Rubio's life: a three-bedroom house in Tallahassee he bought in 2005 when a state legislator. He bought it with another state legislator and apparently paid way too much as he finally unloaded the property in June of 2015 for $117,000, or $18,000 less than they paid for it ten years earlier.[85]

So in an election, who was better positioned to connect with voters worried about their futures, voters whose wages had languished for years or who were out of work or whose college graduate kids were working as coffee baristas as they paid off their student loans? Would Hillary Clinton with her $50 million in speaking fees and multiple palatial homes be convincing, or would Bush with his hefty finances and family history?

Or would the financially struggling Rubio be more convincing after suffering a foreclosure proceeding, who was underwater on the mortgage, and who ultimately sold his little $135,000 Tallahassee condo nightmare at a loss? If America wanted a president who could relate to the little guy, Rubio had a great opportunity to turn lemons into lemonade.

June and Breakfast at Bernie's

Former Maryland Gov. Martin O'Malley and Vermont Sen. Bernie Sanders officially announced their respective campaigns for the Democratic nomination in late May. Who, if anyone, would play Rochester to Clinton's Jack Benny?

O'Malley, the charismatic progressive, perhaps could serve as the fallback to the so-far-jilted Elizabeth Warren fan club. Smart, talented, and telegenic, O'Malley faced four obvious challenges gaining credibility. The obvious problem involved convincing anyone Clinton was not inevitable. If he could last long enough, he'd probably get his shot; but that meant running a disciplined cheap campaign until the cards broke his way.

Second, O'Malley had not left Maryland's governor's mansion on the best of terms. His hand-picked successor got shellacked by Larry Hogan, a Republican long, long, long shot. Not exactly a selling point for the O'Malley campaign.

Next, before he was Governor, O'Malley had been Baltimore's mayor. Shortly before he announced his candidacy, Baltimore suffered widespread rioting so bad Major League Baseball had to postpone one Orioles game and play another to an empty stadium. What triggered the riots? The immediate cause was another case of a young black man dying at the hands of the police. The larger issue was that Baltimore was increasingly a city of two parts—a gleaming, gentrifying harbor area surrounding by an ever-worsening urban blight a la Detroit. Again, not exactly a selling point for the O'Malley juggernaut.

But the fourth issue would be O'Malley's toughest. He ran as the progressive alternative to the establishment's Hillary Clinton. He ran in a party moving further and further to the Left, and Bernie Sanders owned the Far Left as America's foremost Socialist. In theory,

O'Malley might be seen as the reasonable middle between Clinton and Sanders. In practice, he was blocked coming and going.

In Minneapolis, 3,300 people signed up to hear Sanders speak on May 31. The room was packed to overflowing.[86] As the *New York Times* reported, "A mere 240 people live in the rural Northeast Iowa town of Kensett, so when more than 300 people crowded into the community center on Saturday night to hear Sen. Bernie Sanders of Vermont, many driving 50 miles, the cell phones of Democratic leaders statewide began to buzz."[87]

But Bernie had his own problems. First, he really was a Socialist. Even by European standards, he was extreme; and the center of gravity in the United States body politic remained Center or Center Right.

Second, Sanders was loud. He was aggressive. He was cranky and not particularly likeable. It may seem patronizing, but Americans like to like their presidents.

Bottom line: Sanders knew what he believed and he knew it in detail. He knew how to explain it, and he was a strong debater. He might be defeated, and probably would be, but he would not be ignored. O'Malley had nowhere to run.

CHAPTER 6
THE BOYS AND GIRLS OF SUMMER

As of June 1, 2015, Hillary Clinton looked to have the Democratic nomination locked up, though on the surface it was hard to tell she was running at all. Her campaign had again receded to the background. To the extent she was mentioned at all except in reference to her absence it was in the context of the various circling scandals. Collectively, they looked to be taking a toll. For the first time since she left the White House in 2001, her unfavorable rating at 47.8% exceeded her favorable rating at 45.9, and the trend line was ominous.[88] Among Republicans, only Donald Trump could begin to match Clinton's unfavorable rating at 65%, which was not good company to keep.[89]

According to one poll highlighting Clinton's problem, 57% of respondents said Clinton was "not honest and trustworthy." [90] A couple months earlier, the figure was 49%. She was headed in the wrong direction. Abraham Lincoln's famous quote seems apropos, "You can fool some of the people all the time, and all of the people some of the time, but you cannot fool all of the people all of the time."[91]

Lanny Davis, former Clinton aide and perpetual Clinton apologista, found a friendly venue on MSNBC's Ed Schultz show to put a helpful spin on Clinton's trustworthiness issue. Even Davis had to admit, "It's not just the right-wing conspiracy."[92] Did the conservatives still hate Hillary Clinton? You bet. Were they the source of her trustworthy issues? No way. What was the source? Clinton's past, reinforced by her repeated equivocations and half-truths. To quote the great former New York Giants football coach Bill Parcells, "You are what your record says you are."

Trust is tough to earn, easy to lose, and tougher still to regain. Could Hillary Clinton regain enough of the voters' trust during a street fight of a national campaign? Seemed unlikely, but that didn't rule out a victory. It just meant for her to win she would likely have to be seen as the lesser of two evils.

Far behind Clinton's commanding lead at 60% of poll respondents sat Vice Pres. Joe Biden, who wasn't even running, and Bernie Sanders, who was, each at about 10%. Bringing up the rear were former Maryland Gov. Martin O'Malley, former Virginia Sen. Jim Webb, and former Rhode Island Sen. Lincoln Chaffee, all three in the low single digits. If one discounted Bernie Sanders as being too Far Left even for the Democratic Party, an assumption many made in error as it turns out, and if one set aside non-candidate Biden, then Clinton looked to be a sure bet.

Martin O'Malley should have been a stronger contender. While far back in the polls, he had a long history with long shots: thirty years earlier, he worked on Colorado Sen. Gary Hart's presidential campaign. At the time, Hart was generally unknown; but he was charismatic, engaging, smart, attractive, direct, unafraid to take risks, with great hair and a big smile. With memories of Jack Kennedy still very fresh, Hart appeared the second coming of Camelot.

Like O'Malley, Hart also started his campaign in single digits; but Hart walloped Vice Pres. Walter Mondale in Iowa and New Hampshire to become a major contender with O'Malley and a bunch of kids stocking his campaign. Mondale regrouped and went on to win the Democratic nomination, of course, only to lose to Ronald Reagan, but Hart's out-of-left-field insurgency had put a real scare into Mondale and the Democratic establishment and offered O'Malley a template of hope twenty-two years later.

A Republican Complex

Republicans presented a more complicated picture—and a much more interesting picture for its diversity. For example, the Democrats had an old white woman (Clinton), an older white guy (Sanders), a youngish white guy (O'Malley), and two white guys in between. Republicans in contrast were running the only African American (Ben Carson), the only Hispanic American (Marco Rubio), a Canadian Cuban American (Ted Cruz), an Indian American (Bobby Jindahl), a woman (Carly Fiorina), and a celebrity billionaire real estate developer (Donald Trump). Even one of the white men running was married to a Mexican American (Bush).

For all the diversity in its composition, the Republican's early essentials distilled easily. The top three candidates were Bush, Rubio, and Walker. Jeb Bush represented the Republican establishment but was losing altitude as fast as he was raising money. Lacking any buzz, Bush truly was "low energy" as devastatingly described later by Donald Trump. Every story began with his heritage as the son and brother of former presidents. It's tough to identify a separate identity that way.

Marco Rubio and Scott Walker represented different aspects of the rebellious Tea Party wing. Whereas Bush seemed likeable, steady, and boring, Rubio had real "it" factor, as in enjoying the charisma and appeal some politicians have and some just don't, which helped explain Rubio's best-in-class ratio of 53% favorable to 16% unfavorable ratings.[93]

What Rubio lacked was any executive experience whatsoever, not unlike Barack Obama before his rise to the White House. To be clear, executive experience is not an absolute prerequisite as long as the individual knows how to ask questions and can make sound decisions based sometimes on very limited information. The real chief executive in any administration is typically the White House chief of staff (CoS). If the CoS is strong, as was for example Rahm Emanuel at the start of the Obama administration, and if the president completely trusts the CoS, then all can be well.

Rubio and Walker both represented a more conservative option to Bush but less so than the most Far-Right candidates such as Texas Sen. Ted Cruz. Walker embodied Rubio's mirror image. Rubio of Florida was a recent Washington resident. Walker was middle America. Walker had demonstrated chief executive abilities in spades as Governor of Wisconsin. But he was almost naked of experience and exposure to national domestic policy.

One poll released in early June included an interesting and revealing twist.[94] Most respondents to racehorse questions this early in the process express a fairly lukewarm preference. They may prefer Bush, for example, but Walker or Rand Paul might be almost as good. Unless you actually worked for a campaign, chances were you had no real preference almost eighteen months before the election. That observation is less valid with respect to candidates you don't like, and this is where it got interesting.

According to the poll, the American people had a pretty clear opinion of Donald Trump, and it wasn't good: 59% said they would never vote for him, and only 16% said they wanted more information.

Next up on the hold-your-nose list was Chris Christie at 37% saying they would never vote for him, followed by Jeb Bush and Mike Huckabee each at 24%. In each case, the result could be attributed to an obvious factor. For example, Christie's New Jersey bluster, while entertaining, didn't wear well in the rest of the country. Jeb had the Bush name, which guaranteed some support and much irreconcilable opposition. Huckabee as an in-your-face social conservative turned off a lot of people.

Most of the rest of the candidates came in around the midteens while Walker (8%), Carson (12%), and Rubio (12%) fared best. Discounting Carson as a smart man whose shortcomings as a candidate seemed fatal, this poll lent substance to the impression Rubio and Walker should have real staying power as long as they raised decent money.

The Republican race featured three frontrunners followed by a throng hoping the frontrunners would stumble. This vast field created peculiar problems and not just for the candidates. For the candidates, aside from Bush the central issue remained how to stand out in a positive way. The usual tactic involved taking bold positions and offering harsh attacks of Clinton's many weaknesses, of Clinton as Obama's possible successor, or of the other Republicans.

For Fox News and CNN, the hosts of the first two Republican presidential debates scheduled for late summer, how does one hold a debate with so many candidates? The networks opted to limit the debate field to ten candidates chosen by poll results. Reasonable, perhaps, but then the polls for candidates six through fifteen were all very close. The margin of error for these polls really meant there was no statistical difference between their respective support levels. Further, limiting the debates to the top ten by polling would mean the only Republican woman in the race, former HP CEO Carly Fiorina, would not make the cut or, among others, curiosity billionaire real estate developer/entertainer Donald Trump.

THE TEXAS TWO-STEP

On June 5, Texas Gov. Rick Perry threw his big ten-gallon hat into the ring. If nothing else, Perry looked the part, right out of Hollywood central casting: slightly salted dark hair, strong chin, big toothy smile, tall and fit, penetrating eyes behind stylish dark-rimmed glasses. No one in either party could trump Rick Perry for looking presidential, and he loved retail politicking.

Perry had been Texas's top salesman, not for Kenmore dishwashers but for Texas itself. He excelled at regaling California companies with Texas's strengths while reminding them of California's almost endless problems. Running for office is ultimately about marketing; you try to sell the voters on your appeal, your experience, your common sense. Perry's strengths as a candidate ended with central casting and sales.

He should have done better. Former Air Force pilot, fourteen years governor of a large state, substantial executive experience. Texas's economy was booming. And Perry had gained valuable experience having briefly run a presidential campaign in 2012.

In part, Perry's problem arose because the country hadn't quite gotten over the last Texas Governor elected to the White House: George W. Bush. But Perry's real problem was the impression he was, as the old Texas saying goes, all hat and no cattle.

Rick Perry was for a few brief days a formidable candidate in 2012. Compared with the likes of Newt Gingrich, Michele Bachmann, and Herman Cain, Perry looked to be the only serious adult in the room after Mitt Romney. But shortly after launching his 2012 bid, his extremely limited knowledge of federal policy issues sank him. Perry in 2016 couldn't recover from the 2012 edition.

THE NEW YORK TIMES SETS A RUBIO SPEED TRAP

So many interesting candidates meant a gold mine of interesting pasts. Rubio had finally managed to unload his little house of financial horrors in Florida and seemed poised to move forward unobstructed. Then news broke he and his wife had a habit of collecting traffic violations. Or did they?

On June 5, the story broke Rubio and his wife, Jeanette, had a combined seventeen traffic citations in Florida, including speeding, failure to stop at a stop sign, and reckless driving.[95] A total hatchet job instigated by a local Florida Democratic operative, the *New York Times* immediately picked up the story. The *Times* insisted it had coincidentally and simultaneously done its own independent investigation.[96] Sure it did.

It seems safe to say most drivers occasionally exceed the speed limit, and variations on the old California stop are commonplace, but seventeen citations seemed a lot. At the very least, this just didn't look good, which, of course, was the whole point of the story.

Dig a little deeper, and it turns out Marco had four tickets in about seventeen years—comes across a lot different expressed that way, doesn't it? But four tickets in seventeen years doth not a compelling *New York Times* hatchet job make. Nor could the *Times* even get the basic facts straight. The *Times* accused Rubio of driving an SUV; and to the *Times*, this qualified as an accusation because, after all, SUVs are notorious gas guzzlers. Not like the nifty thrifty little subcompact hybrids no doubt all *Times* editors and reporters drive. For the record, Rubio drove a Ford F-150, the most popular vehicle sold in America and thus one facet more common to America's voters than the *Times*' probable vehicular preferences.

Rubio's wife apparently had the lead foot in the family as indicated, for example, by her $185 fine for driving twenty-three miles per hour in a posted fifteen-mile per hour zone. Heavens! It becomes a *New York Times* story only by combining the two Rubios together over a long span of time, as though Hillary Clinton should be lumped in with Bill regarding all his sexual predations over the years. Fortunately for the Democrats, traffic citations were one scandal not likely to befall Hillary as she hadn't driven a car since 1996. Chauffeurs are such lovely protection in a political campaign.

A Shakeup before Kickoff

Every election campaign presents a new adventure. The public sees the adventure play out in TV ads, debates, gaffes, outrages real and feigned, and in talking head commentary. Good candidates thrive on the energy and process. Behind it all is the "campaign," the tens, then hundreds, then thousands of volunteers joining together to put their guy (or gal) on the victory podium. At the core of the campaign is a relatively small band, most of whom have known one another for years and worked together on numerous campaigns. They learn to hate one another—and love one another—because for a few weeks or months, they're family living cheek to jowl.

Whatever the operatives' experiences individually or collectively, each campaign is a custom job; times change, technology changes, candidates change, the cast of campaign staff changes. At some point, if a campaign lasts long enough, the campaign staff realize some folks just don't fit in. Then comes the shakeup.

Apparently, and long before the announcement, Bush and company realized the campaign wasn't gelling. In a surprise and fairly dramatic move, the trusted and seasoned David Kochel was shipped out to run the Right to Rise Super PAC. Kochel had been widely expected to take over as campaign chief, so much so he had moved to Miami. Having been shunted aside, Kochel's role as campaign chief in waiting then went to the relatively unknown thirty-nine-year-old Danny Diaz.[97]

Kochel, a former Mitt man and native of Iowa—funny how that works, isn't it?—was on good terms with another Bush campaign insider, the very seasoned Mike Murphy, and was widely respected for his calm demeanor and deliberative approach. To succeed, political campaigns need firm, sure, rapid decisions. This isn't chess unless you play it the way they do in New York's Central Park with a time clock and a blur of hands moving pieces.

If the campaign needed energy and urgency, it got a real jolt of both in the tandem of Sally Bradshaw unleashed and Danny Diaz elevated. Sally Bradshaw was the calm, no-nonsense Bush loyalist who reportedly orchestrated the switch from Kochel to Diaz.[98] By all reports, Bradshaw, a.k.a. the "Jeb Whisperer," was a real, live version of one of those tough-as-shoe-leather politicos you see on television. A combination Karl Rove strategist and Rahm Emanuel whip-cracker, she'd been with Bush in one role or another since 1993 and served him as chief of staff when Bush was Governor.

The Four Percent Fantasy

In his announcement speech, Bush called for policies to grow the economy 4% a year on average. "So many challenges could be overcome if we just get this economy growing at full strength. There is not a reason in the world why we cannot grow at a rate of 4% a year."[99]

Apparently, despite having superb economic advisors such as Glenn Hubbard, former chairman of the Council of Economic Advisors under George W. and then dean of the Columbia University School of Business, basic policy quality control remained a foreign concept in Bush's campaign. He was partly right, though. Many challenges could be overcome if the economy grew more rapidly. But why stop at 4%? How about 5% or 6 or even 10%? After all, China grew at about 10% a year for many years. Americans are as good as the Chinese, right? Chinese communists outdo American capitalists? Pssshaw.

Not that 4% growth in gross domestic product would be bad. In fact, it would be tremendous.

Not that it never happened before. In fact, it should have occurred in 2010 through perhaps 2012 under Pres. Obama as the economy recovered from the Great Recession of 2008–2009, but of course the economy only puttered along in the mid 2% range until it downshifted further in 2016. But as just about anyone who understands growth theory 101, every economy has a practical limit to its long-run growth rate, a limit that can be raised modestly (Reagan) or lowered (Obama) depending on public policy.

China and India showed how emerging-market countries can grow faster than 4% for many years, or even decades, if they manage their policies correctly. How? Because their workforce is substantially underutilized, undertrained, and often poorly located. Much of China's economic boom resulted from the mass migration of workers from the countryside where they were relatively unproductive subsistence farmers to the cities where they could be given a little training and then employed more productively in modern industry. China was also playing rapid catch-up in terms of infrastructure, the stock of productive plant and equipment, worker training, and technology adoption.

In contrast, the United States is the preeminent developed country. It wasn't playing catch-up. It's the country to which others were playing catch-up. U.S. growth rates were thus limited by other factors, most specifically and simply the growth in the workforce and the growth in worker productivity. Outside of business cycles, everything in an economy and the effects for good or ill of all public policies distill down to these two factors: labor force growth and labor productivity growth.[100]

The average growth rate in GDP from 1947 to 2008 was about 3.5% a year. Notice the obvious: through good times and bad in the postwar period, the economy grew a full 0.5% below the Bush target. Now subtract off the certain drop in the workforce growth rate due to the retirement of the baby boom, and then the average going rate forward falls to 2.9%. Getting from 2.9% to 4% as Bush suggested was on par with Evel Knievel thinking he could jump the entire length of the Grand Canyon with his Harley-Davidson motorcycle.

The Bush campaign's problems with his 4% growth target went way beyond the particulars. The announcement demonstrated to any and all either Bush lacked discipline or refused to listen to his own experts. A great many solid policy people worked for the Bush campaign, but after his Iraq War comments and now this 4% growth promise, it was clear Jeb Bush thought he knew best. A new Bush narrative developed that despite all his strengths and experience, on policy he might just be another Rick Perry.

Filling Out the Dance Card

Hillary Clinton announced her candidacy on Roosevelt Island in New York City on Saturday, June 12. The event was heavily staged as one would expect and then quickly forgotten. No one seemed to know why Roosevelt Island was chosen, except its location greatly facilitated security and stage management. The goal was to avoid glitches and demonstrate competence, and on both counts her campaign succeeded. After a couple days, Clinton and her campaign went back into hiding.

Jeb Bush made his campaign official on June 15. Donald Trump announced the next day. Surprisingly, Bush and Trump shared some common traits suggesting they might both be around for a while. For example, their campaigns would both be well financed. Bush's establishment-based fundraising machine was first rate, while the Donald could tap his own billions. Both had substantial management experience: Jeb as Governor of Florida, the Donald as head of his Trump empire. Both were over sixty years of age. Jeb was a serious candidate; only Donald and company took his candidacy seriously at first, though, of course, that would change.

Trump announced his candidacy at the Trump Tower in Manhattan. Ever making a grand entrance, Trump approached the gathered throng on an escalator—descending, of course, as though from on high.[101] One Ramirez cartoon suggested Trump's real campaign slogan was that he was running to save America from the arrogant clown in the White House. In his rambling forty-five-minute speech, Trump summarized his cache as "the greatest jobs president that God ever created," proving once again he wouldn't be restrained by excessive modesty.[102]

All humor aside—and there was much humor to be had—Trump fundamentally rewrote the script for American presidential campaigns. As Peter Roff of *US News and World Report* wrote, "Trump is talking about things people care about. He's not wasting time spreading a gospel of prosperity and hope sprinkled with government and public policy jargon. He's just doing a bit of plain speaking. People may like what he has to say and they may not: What matters is that they understand him."[103]

Trump was nothing if not audacious, and he wasn't stupid. Trump: agitator extraordinaire, beholden to no one and no thing.

Trump roared over issues the media wouldn't cover, issues politicians preferred to ignore or to pack into convenient boxes to be set aside. Many of the uncomfortable issues Trump raised resonated with voters whose concerns were glossed over by other candidates because the issues were too icky but also issues often caustic to the national debate, especially his blasting of illegal immigrants. This was John McCain's old "Straight Talk Express," yet with the easy smile and reasonable tone replaced by a sneer, and bravado and quirky charm replaced by a verbal cudgel.

To the chagrin and amazement of many, Trump's approach had an immediate impact as he shot up to tie Ben Carson in second place in Iowa behind Scott Walker and second place behind Jeb Bush in a national poll.[104] Anger had a following. How long bombast could sustain a campaign absent any real proposed remedies was unclear; but while his candidacy remained widely mocked, he would be consequential because the Donald had struck a nerve. This marked the first moment of realization Trump's campaign might not be a lark, after all.

Louisiana Gov. Bobby Jindahl added his name to the candidate's list on June 25, a list then standing at thirteen names. Considered sympathetically, one could reasonably have chalked his announcement up to why not? A sitting governor, son of an immigrant, an Indian American, a policy wonk with experience in Congress.

On June 30, New Jersey Gov. Chris Christie made it official. He was in, making his announcement at Livingston High School in Livingston, New Jersey. Why Livingston? "Because everything started for me here."[105] Job one for any candidate new to the national debate is the self-introduction. Who am I? Where did I come from? It always makes sense to begin filling out the portrait with your roots, establishing the narrative before your opponents rip it from you.

Christie had gone from the new darling of the Republican establishment just a year before to an also-ran in near Rick Perry time. The bridge scandal and Bush's enormous presence cast long shadows on Christie's appeal. Even so, he was still the blunt-talking politician who knew how to appeal to voters. Part of his appeal was his WYSIWYG persona—what you see is what you get. But his market niche was dominated by Bush, and his blunt appeal had been blunted or, perhaps more accurately, out-blunted by Donald Trump. This left Christie with little to go on but his own energy and charisma, much like Gov. O'Malley in the Democratic contest.

Walker on the Wild Side

Scott Walker officially became a candidate for president on July 13. "I'm in," he announced in a video prior to a public speech in Waukesha, Wisconsin. Maybe it was because he was now the fifteenth candidate in the field, but the collective reaction to Walker's announcement was a polite "That's nice." As he waited too long, his big announcement was anticlimactic. Not good. Walker was a leading candidate, a governor of an important state, a solid conservative, and seemingly very approachable—just a nice guy, high school graduate, riding his Harley-Davidson Road King motorcycle while running for president.

Probably the loudest reaction to Walker's entrance came from AFL-CIO President Richard Trumka, who called Walker a "national disgrace."[106] Trumka and the unions were still smarting from the first-class butt kicking they'd received from Walker, the very event that launched Walker to national prominence. Why Trumka chose to remind the world of his own recent and very public defeat remained something of a mystery.

Whatever the reason, Walker's entrance made little splash even though, or perhaps because, he was already leading Bush in Iowa 18 to 12% while 80% of Iowa Republican insiders said Walker would win the caucuses if they were held immediately. His message conveyed that he was a proven fighter and winner (crushing the unions, surviving a recall, and winning a second term lent the claim some cred) and that he would not compromise.[107]

Refusing to compromise, Walker had great appeal to the conservative base, which fair or not viewed Republican leadership in Washington as willing to compromise at the drop of a hat. The fact the Republican leadership rarely had sufficient raw political power, i.e., the votes, to prevail without compromising mattered not a mite to the base. They were angry. Very angry. Thanks to Barack Obama and the Supreme Court, the anger that had created the Tea Party in 2010 had not yet dissipated as so many pundits had predicted. On the contrary, the anger grew, getting more demanding with every outrage.

Walker's absolutism was hardly unique. Most, if not all, the other candidates talked about their big plans for the country. However, none were running to become the next Henry VIII of England, virtually all powerful within the island realm. They weren't even running to become the next prime minister of a parliamentary system in which the majority party can do pretty much whatever it wants until the public loses faith.

These Republicans were running for President of the United States, would likely deal with a rambunctious House of Representatives with its own ideas on everything, and a nearly evenly divided Senate with not only its own ideas but its own institutional quirks designed to ensure whichever party is in the minority has a real voice. In short, the only way any of the candidates upon their victory would get anything done is through compromise. Running as a leader who would not compromise for a job that demanded compromise presented certain irreconcilable contradictions. Fortunately for the candidates one and all, no one ever asked them how they would square that circle.

KASICH THE CABOOSE

John Kasich became the caboose on the long Republican candidate train, but being last didn't necessarily make him least. As his local paper, the *Cincinnati Enquirer*, described him:

> Kasich, who officially launched his bid Tuesday, has the resume and attitude to make a real run as something of a wild card, as reported by The Enquirer's resident Kasichologist, Chrissie Thompson. He's a popular governor of a swing state. He's got blue-collar roots, business experience and budget-cutting conservative credibility. His last name isn't Bush. He's ditching the tendency toward abrasiveness but keeping the candor. He's touting his Ohio record of economic growth and his DC experience as a congressman who helped balance the budget.[108]

Kasich spent eighteen years in the House of Representatives, rising to become House Budget Committee chairman, a position from which in 2000 in a moment of delusion he believed he could run for president. He then spent some years as a Fox News political commentator, gaining exceptional training as a modern communicator on the most important medium. He beat Ted Strickland in 2010 to become governor and crushed his opponent Ed FitzGerald 64% to 33% in winning reelection in 2014. Kasich was smart, energetic, quirky, a policy wonk, short-tempered, and personally engaging in a mildly unnerving sort of way; and he was from Ohio, a key swing state.

Most candidates getting in this late to the contest had essentially no chance. They lacked the fundraising and campaign machinery to make a go of it. As governor of a medium-sized state, Kasich had his own established fundraising operations and campaign machinery, at least enough for a credible beginning. Washington experience, national media experience, executive experience, knowledge about issues the way only these experiences provide, Kasich would prove to be a force in the campaign. Just not perhaps the way he intended.

EMANUEL AME HERE

Wednesday night Bible study, Emanuel African Methodist Episcopal Church, Charleston, South Carolina, one of the South's oldest churches; an overwhelmingly black church. You don't have to be Christian. You don't even have to have a particular religious sensibility to appreciate the sense of family, the joy, the caring, the sense of pure adoration of something wonderful at such a meeting. This is a time for singing favorite songs, for laughing and sharing, for praying.

Wednesday night, June 17, the young and old, male and female, and into their midst came a twenty-one-year-old white man to join the study. The pastor, Clementa Pinckney, invited the young man, Dylann Storm Roof, to sit next to him.[109] There he remained for about an hour, welcomed as a fellow believer, until the study nearly concluded. Then Roof stood up and opened fire. Nine people, including Pastor Pinckney, were dead. Roof was arrested in North Carolina the next day.

Such events are not rare in America or always overtly racist in nature. Sometimes they are religious; witness the Boston Marathon bombing of 2013. Often the event involved young people simply at sea in their personal lives, finding solace in anger, lashing out as in the Columbine, Colorado, High School shooting in 1999. Sometimes it was the radically sick, such as Timothy McVeigh's massive bombing of a federal building in Oklahoma City in 1995 in which 168 people died.

Nor were such events rare in the rest of the world, as much as the press tried to paint the United States as the riotous outlier. In 2012, twenty-three-year-old Mohammed Merah killed three French paratroopers in Toulouse, France, before showing up at a school to shoot three children aged three to eight and a teacher. In 2011, Tristen van der Vlis killed six people and wounded seventeen in the Netherlands before killing himself. And earlier in June of 2015, a gunman killed four people in Hebei, China. Civilization just isn't that civilized.

But the slaughter at Emanuel AME in Charleston was explicitly and unquestionably a racist act. It was shocking, and the nation mourned. For a few days, the nation moved closer to an honest multidimensional debate about race.

It almost seems wrong to relate this event to the political campaign; but just as reporters must report in the midst of war's carnage, the event in Charleston and similar events that followed had ramifications for the campaign and so must be considered.

In such moments, Americans turn to the president for reflection, perspective, and healing. As a black man, Pres. Obama's words and demeanor were especially critical in setting the tone. His initial reaction was on point. He went on radio to advance the discussion, but he did more. He gave it a jolt by intentionally using the ubiquitous but supposedly unspoken n-word: "It's not just about it not being polite to say nigger in public."[110] More than soothing words were needed. To his great credit, Obama tried to make something good out of something terrible. Obama performed at his talented best in giving the eulogy and then largely disappeared once again.

In terms of the campaign, this was one of those unplanned, unexpected major events stripping away the talking points and facades to reveal something real about each candidate. Recall John Hinckley shot Ronald Reagan, his chief press agent, Jim Brady, and two others in March of 1981. When Reagan's wife, Nancy, arrived at George Washington Hospital, Reagan quipped, "Honey, I forgot to duck." As they rolled him into surgery, Reagan turned to the hospital staff to joke, "Please tell me you're all Republicans." These are the moments, far more than any campaign speech, opening a window on a person's true nature.

An old saw runs, "In Hollywood, underneath all that phony tinsel is some real tinsel." Did any of the candidates have more than phony tinsel underneath their carefully crafted images? In the event, most demonstrated low-grade tinsel might indeed be a major component of their characters. Surprisingly, only a non-candidate, South Carolina Gov. Nicky Haley, demonstrated the best in American character.

As the shooting took place in South Carolina, Gov. Haley naturally had a central role helping her own state heal. A long-standing issue for the state and the nation was the tradition of flying the American flag, the state flag, and the Confederate battle flag over the State Capitol in Columbia. A simple symbol of pride and noble traditions for many in the South, for some whites the Confederate flag focused their racial hatreds. For many blacks, it represented a painful present and a sad and hated past.

Gov. Haley grasped the moment to declare, "Today, we are here in a moment of unity in our state, without ill will, to say it's time to move the flag from the Capitol grounds. We are not going to allow this symbol to divide us anymore. The fact that it causes pain to so many is ground enough to move if from the Capitol grounds."[111]

While Gov. Haley set the tone, perhaps Russell Moore, the head of the Southern Baptist Convention's Ethics and Religious Liberty Commission, best captured the moment when he wrote, "White Christians, let's listen to our African American brothers and sisters. Let's care not just about our own history, but also about our shared history with them."[112]

Amen.

Few of the Republicans running for president were as noble or as clear-sighted. South Carolina Sen. Lindsey Graham initially bucked his own governor's laudable direction and instead defended the Confederate flag. But Graham, a politician of many years' service, quickly reversed himself, marking his flip-flop by standing with Haley on the stage almost, but not quite, out of the camera shot.

Sen. Ted Cruz's reaction fell on the other end of the spectrum. Campaigning in Red Oak, Iowa, a couple days after the Charleston event, Cruz cracked, "You know the great thing about the state of Iowa is, I'm pretty sure you all define gun control the same way we do in Texas—hitting what you aim at."[113] At any other time, this would have been standard fare in the ongoing battle over gun control and the Second Amendment. Immediately after the Charleston shootings, however, only a human being imbued with the least ounce of sense necessary for self-awareness could utter such an outrageous remark.

Nor was Cruz finished. With respect to the Confederate flag, Cruz said, "The last thing they need is people from outside of the state coming in and dictating how they should resolve it."[114] As a senator from Texas and a supporter of states' rights, Cruz's position was thoroughly defensible—for Texas, not for South Carolina. But Cruz wasn't just a Texas Senator anymore. He was running for President of the United States, and this was an opportunity and a responsibility to show Americans what and how he thought about issues. Politicians talk a big game on leadership. This was an opportunity to lead. Cruz ducked. Or maybe he did lead and by leading demonstrated the low quality of his vision for America. Neither version reflected well on the candidate.

Sadly, either way, he wasn't alone. There was, in fact, a flock of Republican ducks. Scott Walker was an early duck. Only later, after Haley's announcement, did Walker tweet his support of her decision. Rubio was another early duck, later issuing a statement in support of Haley. Huckabee, a former governor of another Southern state, ducked big time, going on the Sunday morning shows to opine candidates needn't "weigh in on every little issue in all 50 states." You read that right—"every little issue." Nine people murdered.

Rand Paul just issued a statement to say he had no statement, echoing the words of the mid-twentieth-century American philosopher John Cage, "I have nothing to say, and I'm saying it."

Likewise, Chris Christie said nothing whatsoever. Quack, quack, quack.

Of all the other candidates, Jeb Bush was the only one out front quickly. Bush noted, "In Florida, we acted, moving the flag from state grounds to a museum where it belonged."

Carly Fiorina quickly called the flag a "symbol of racial hatred" and called for its removal but then squished by saying it was up to the people of South Carolina to decide. Of course, it was up to the people of South Carolina to decide. But it was up to Carly Fiorina and all the other candidates to express an opinion on what those people should decide. This is part of the role of the President of the United States on deep matters of conscience. Candidates for president need to take these non-canned opportunities to show how they would play that role. Most failed.

Once Haley made her announcement and the political path was clear, the previously reluctant Republican ducks fell all over themselves trying to get back into formation, expressing their personal repulsion at the symbolism of the Confederate flag. Rand Paul, previously square in the "no comment" camp, apparently concluded his navel gazing by calling the flag "a symbol of human bondage and slavery."[115] This, at least, had the benefit of being unscripted as evidenced by the redundancy in the statement.

Their struggle with an appropriate response didn't mean these odd ducks were bad people. However, it did demonstrate their own thinking on certain matters was yet too incoherent to recommend them for the office of the President of the United States.

While most of the attention was on the Republicans, Democrats also had a voice. Hillary Clinton used the Charleston shooting to renew her call for stricter gun control laws, including universal background checks for gun purchasers. The fact the federal government has extensive gun control laws didn't seem to affect her views. Indeed, some weeks later the FBI admitted a mistake in a background check allowed Root to buy the gun: he had a previous drug possession charge.[116] So the best Clinton could do was fall back on the flimsiest of talking points.

The mayor of Charleston Joseph P. Riley Jr. went on television to assert, "It is insane: the number of guns, and the ease of [buying] guns in America."[117]

Mr. Root bought one simple handgun. Under the law, he should have not been able to buy the gun because of a drug possession charge; but otherwise, nothing would have prevented him from buying this one gun. He took one gun to the church. He killed those people with one gun. Neither Clinton nor Mayor Riley nor their friends and allies have any answer for stopping the roots of the world short of repealing the Second Amendment to the Constitution's guarantee of the right to bear arms. As long as that is the case, then for all their frustration, one can only conclude in all frankness that the gun control lobby is just blowing smoke.

On the issue of the Confederate flag, to her credit Hillary Clinton called for the flag to come down from the State Capitol in 2007, creating quite a ruckus at the time; and her views on this hadn't changed. Gov. O'Malley and Sen Sanders likewise called for it to come down.[118]

American Football, Duets, and Lessons about International Trade

Anyone who has ever watched American football will have observed before the snap of the ball the really big guys face each other near the football while the smaller guys are farther away. Why is that? No rule says it has to be so.

Teams line up their players by size and speed to make them as effective as possible. The gazelles are on the outside so they can sprint down the field to catch passes or to defend against the gazellian pass catchers while the mountainous men attempt to gain advantage at the line of scrimmage. They line up the way they do because it works to their best advantage.

The essential principle behind international trade theory is that if everyone and every country does what he or she or it does best, then society will prosper most. This principle was first popularized by the seventeenth-century economist David Ricardo in a theory called "comparative advantage." Even if you play guitar and the piano better than I, you can't perform a duet by yourself. If you play guitar much better and play the piano only a little, then it makes sense for you to pluck strings and for me to tickle the ivories.

An essential reality of economic policy worldwide is governments have a long history of obstructing the movement of goods and services, labor, and capital across national borders; and this generally disadvantages the majority to benefit a small minority. Why do governments enact such policies if the policies are unwise? Sometimes governments make mistakes. Sometimes governments just want to help their friends.

The essential principle of international trade negotiations is to help governments correct those mistakes because it is often best for everyone to move together. There is a sense that if every country has high tariffs, for example, then while it would be beneficial to reduce one's own tariffs unilaterally, it would be better yet negotiating for other countries to reduce their tariffs at the same time.

In the postwar period, the United States had consistently led in advancing global trade negotiations, leading to a consensus on trade principles and numerous agreements involving most trading nations. But the process of negotiating huge comprehensive agreements had broken down for reasons too numerous to mention. In reaction, nations including the United States had negotiated narrower bilateral agreements, multilateral agreements, and regional agreements.

The United States led two such regional negotiations, one with a group of Asia-Pacific nations called the Trans-Pacific Partnership (TPP) and another with the European Union called the Transatlantic Trade and Investment Partnership (TTIP). TPP featured a negotiation dominated by the United States and Japan but involving ten other Pacific nations not including China. If successful, TPP could open up new markets for U.S. companies. It could also create a vital new geopolitical chit for dealing with China. If China wanted the economic and political benefits of the TPP, then China would have to behave as a good global citizen. Otherwise, TPP would become exactly what China feared—another tool for containing China's regionally hegemonic intentions.

TTIP was a different animal. With some exceptions, such as agriculture, few substantial trade barriers existed between the Western powers. This agreement was clearly a "me too" for Europe, which feared the United States would lose interest in its wobbly, irresolute allies across the little pond (the Atlantic Ocean) as it became ever more fixated on the opportunities and threats across the big pond (the Pacific Ocean).

Under the Constitution, the president negotiates such treaties and then submits them for congressional review, debate, and ratification or rejection. This process included the prospect of Congress amending a treaty after the president has supposedly finalized the deal. Obviously, no country would be willing to come to a hard-negotiated deal with the President of the United States only to have the Congress of the United States rewrite the deal unilaterally.

What to do? The long-standing answer was called Trade Promotion Authority (TPA), sometimes called "fast track" authority. Through TPA, Congress tells the president you can negotiate a treaty with country A covering B topics, and this authority lasts for C years. If successful, the president then submits the treaty to Congress for ratification. Congress will then debate it as it chooses and for as long as it chooses, but it cannot amend the treaty in any way, eventually putting the treaty to an up or down vote.

In June of 2015, both trade agreements were advancing, with the Asia-Pacific agreement nearest to conclusion. To finish the job, Pres. Obama pressed Congress to grant TPA. Now the fat was in the fire. Opposition to these trade deals and therefore to TPA was fierce and widespread in Democratic ranks.

To be sure, international competition is fierce and would only get worse, and the future was at least as scary as it was hopeful. But hiding in one's bedroom closet is hardly the answer. For their part, Republicans were leery of giving Pres. Obama this authority because they didn't trust him. Consequently, in the first TPA fight in May the president suffered a severe embarrassment as Republicans joined most Democrats, including House Democratic leader Nancy Pelosi, in opposing TPA.

In the end, thanks to masterful legislative maneuvers by House Speaker John Boehner and Senate Majority Leader Mitch McConnell, TPA was shepherded through the Congress and so the president and his negotiators were given license to proceed.

Among Republicans, only Sen. Ted Cruz's actions were notable in this debate. In April, he and Cong. Paul Ryan penned a *Wall Street Journal* op-ed foursquare behind TPA.[119] Then, the day before the final vote in the Senate, he changed his mind.

And where, in all this, was Hillary Clinton? All the Republican candidates had taken positions for better or for worse. All she could say was "No president would be a tougher negotiator on behalf of American workers, either with our trading partners or Republicans on Capitol Hill, than I would be."[120] How nice.

So where did she stand on Obama's TPA request? Crickets. Sen. Sanders reasonably chirped, "I don't understand how you don't have a position on this issue."[121] Then, finally, she spoke, saying Obama should copy her listening tour technique, in this case listening to Obama's allies in Congress, including Nancy Pelosi. Realizing the unions weren't buying this mush, Hillary Clinton vacated her increasingly uncomfortable seat on the fence and took a position opposing her old boss, opposing TPA.[122]

Hillary Clinton's position was not only late but also conflicted with what she and her husband had said in the past regarding trade negotiations. As President, Bill Clinton championed and signed into law the highly successful North American Free Trade Agreement. As secretary of state, Clinton had pushed her Obama administration colleagues to join the Asia-Pacific trade deal negotiations at the outset, calling it the "gold standard in trade agreements." As NPR noted in her 2014 memoir *Hard Choices*, "Clinton lauded the deal, saying it 'would link markets throughout Asia and the Americas, lowering trade barriers while raising standards on labor, the environment, and intellectual property.'"[123] Hard choices. It's one thing to take a wrong position. It's another to flip-flop, late and weakly, to get to that wrong position.

For Clinton, the damage was done. She had demonstrated a fine facility for evading hard choices as long as possible. She had demonstrated once again a yogic-like facility for positional flexibility. And to the unions on whose support her candidacy depended, even though she eventually ended up in their camp, she had shown she couldn't be trusted, a reality put in stark relief by the strong and early position taken by Bernie Sanders. The Vermont Senator was going to be a real pain in her neck.

SCOTUScare

On June 25, 2015, the United States Supreme Court in the case of *King v. Burwell* sided with the government (Burwell) in sustaining a key provision of the Affordable Care Act, a.k.a. Obamacare. To reach its conclusion, the court engaged in "somersaults of statutory interpretation" resulting in "pure applesauce" in the words of dissenting Justice Antonin Scalia.[124] Chief Justice John Roberts cast the deciding vote and prepared the applesauce personally.

Roberts's role in sustaining Obamacare had precedent. In 2014, Roberts fabricated out of whole cloth an interpretation of an Obamacare provision, recasting an individual mandate as a tax and then declaring Congress has the constitutional authority to levy taxes.[125] Without this magical transformation, Roberts had no avenue for joining with the Court's liberals to sustain the law. Roberts waved his magic want, and Obamacare survived. Ultimately, it was as simple as that.

In 2015, Roberts joined with the liberal wing again, plus the ever-flexible justice Anthony Kennedy, to read into the law something plainly absent, declaring their ability to divine hidden congressional intent in the face of overwhelming credible evidence to the contrary. Said evidence had been provided compliments of Jonathan Gruber, a health economist and key figure in developing Obamacare. Gruber described at length how and why the blank was left in the law. In short, the omission in the text of the statute was no accident, yet Roberts and company ruled the omission entirely accidental and therefore not binding.[126]

Calling this result pure applesauce was much too polite. The Supreme Court had once again usurped Congress as legislative body, which is why Scalia said the act should be renamed SCOTUScare, SCOTUS of course being Washington-speak for Supreme Court of the United States.

Thus, it was all the more fascinating when the Supreme Court the very next day ruled 5 to 4 upholding the requirement under the Fourteenth Amendment that states were required to recognize and issue marriage licenses to same-sex couples. And in writing his dissenting opinion, Justice Roberts opined, "This court is not a legislature."[127] Apparently, the Supreme Court is or is not a legislature in Roberts's view, depending on what? The weather? His digestion?

After years of running its own advertising campaign on behalf of same-sex marriage on its "news" and editorial pages, the *Washington Post* waxed ecstatic at the same-sex marriage ruling. Indeed, while liberals commonly support same-sex marriage, even many conservatives had difficulty justifying as government policy who could or who could not be recognized by government as being married among consenting adults. Individuals may make whatever arguments they may, but using government power to dictate individual relations should require an extraordinarily high bar of justification. None seemed present in this case.

Even so, the *Post*'s use of its pages to champion gay rights at every turn rendered Washington's leading newspaper little more than a propaganda rag. And yet, even so, Justice Kennedy's decision regarding same-sex marriage caused even the *Washington Post* to shake its journalistic head in bewilderment. "Unfortunately, much of Justice Anthony Kennedy's majority opinion is based on dubious and sometimes incoherent logic."[128] Again, this from an ecstatic reader of said opinion.

Or consider the left-leaning the *New Republic*, which ran a piece calling Justice Kennedy's work a "muddled, unconvincing opinion."[129]

In noting that the majority's high ground was the Constitution's equal protection clause, the *New Republic* agreed with Justice Roberts in his dissenting comment, "The majority [did] not seriously engage with this claim. Its discussion is, quite frankly, difficult to follow."

The point is not to criticize either ruling but rather to highlight the pattern of Supreme Court decisions based not on the letter of the law or of the Constitution or even of precedent but solely on the personal views of the Supremes themselves. This practice was not new or showed any sign of abating. It meant the Supreme Court had indeed situationally become a legislative body.

Overstating the magnitude of the Obamacare ruling would be nearly impossible. Obama now knew his signature legislative achievement would survive more or less intact during his term. For the upcoming presidential campaign, the ruling meant Obamacare would remain a major rallying point for Republicans. What they might actually do about Obamacare if they took the White House and held the Congress was another matter as the law would then be seven years old, with millions of individuals and companies having adjusted to it.

TALE OF TWO IMPOSSIBLES

Oddly enough, two candidates who, by universal agreement, had no chance of winning were rising fast, though few wanted to admit it. One poll had Trump pulling only 12%, well back from Bush's 19%; but Trump appeared undeniably on the move despite his bombast and inflammatory remarks, or perhaps because of them.

Trump was many things, including a bona fide modern celebrity. As longtime Republican strategist Charlie Black noted, "A celebrity can get attention and cause trouble by playing on the resentments of a minority of voters."[130] Trump proved the point, and much more, because Trump was appealing to swing-voting women. How? "They don't agree with what he says—but they like the fact that he will say anything and that's he's not handled, not beholden, not packaged.

They hate what politics has become. He is a disruption to that," observed Christine Matthews, a Republican pollster.[131]

Some of Trump's appeal reflected an echo of his many years starring in the most popular TV show in America, *The Apprentice*. Millions of Americans had watched Trump week in, week out. They thought they knew him. They liked his strength. Few others than sitting presidents have ever started a run for the White House so well-known to so many voters.

Much of Trump's appeal derived from his adamant stance on illegal immigration. The debate in Washington remained stymied as both sides believed they got the most political mileage out of their respective bases by holding to their own most extreme positions. Unwilling to wait for Congress, Pres. Obama simply chose to ignore the law and find as many ways of allowing illegals into the country as he could by issuing a series of executive orders late in 2014 protecting up to five million illegal immigrants from deportation. Naturally, Obama waited until after the 2014 midterms to issue the orders—no hint of politics there.

Many Americans were tired of hearing "press 2 for Spanish," were tired of politicians lying to them and doing nothing about illegal immigration, were tired of the squish. Trump gave them the exact opposite of squish. And for the moment, at least, that was enough to gain their support.

The other candidates expected before long "Donald would become a sideshow and a punching bag," in Charlie Black's words.[132] He may be entertaining and refreshing, but he was unserious and angry, and so his ultimate self-implosion seemed assured. The pertinent questions for the campaign were whether the implosion would come before or after the nomination process, or leading up to the general election.

Trump, as it turned out, demonstrated his penchant for what should have been self-destruction sooner than anyone imagined possible. A poll taken July 16–19 showed Trump leading the field with 24% support, nearly twice the level of his closest rival, Scott Walker at 13%.[133] Then, on the nineteenth, Trump seemed to go too far. He questioned whether John McCain was a war hero, saying, "I like people who weren't captured."[134] Really? Let's review the facts:

> McCain had flown A4-E Skyhawks off the aircraft carriers Forrestal and Oriskany on bombing missions across North Vietnam, flying some of the most dangerous missions and earning a Bronze Star among other commendations.[135] He was shot down over North Vietnam, ejecting from his aircraft he suffered three breaks in his right arm, a break in his left arm, and in his right leg at the knee. Captured by a mob, McCain had his shoulder crushed by a rifle butt and was bayonetted in his left foot and abdominal area. He subsequently spent five and a half years in the Hanoi Hilton.

What of the Donald during the Vietnam War? He got four student deferments from the draft and then a medical deferment for a bone spur in his foot.[136] When asked about the bone spur during the campaign, Trump said he couldn't remember which foot had it.[137] Apparently, Trump's bone spur miraculously disappeared, a point the press rarely pressed.

So while John McCain was enjoying the North Vietnam's hospitality in the Hanoi Hilton, the Donald was enjoying the life of the rich preppie at the University of Pennsylvania. If you don't like John McCain, fine. But no one, and certainly no Richie Rich, should ever question John McCain's heroism. With events moving so rapidly, this little episode was just another in a long list of gems soon forgotten.

Trump's nonsensical questioning of John McCain's heroism would in most campaigns presidential or otherwise torpedo a candidacy quickly. In 2016, such absurd, outrageous, or just plain obnoxious statements became commonplace. America had become a coarse, less civil society in which outrageous behavior had become not only acceptable, but lauded.

The Democrats had their own Donald—yes, Vermont Sen. Bernie Sanders. Sanders brought energy. He had ideas. He spoke with clarity and conviction. He spoke from a thoroughly coherent political philosophy. He was interesting to listen to, if sometimes frightening in much the same way Trump could be frightening. He appealed to the leftmost elements of the Democratic Party, especially those frustrated by seven years of disappointment from their erstwhile champion, Barack Obama. Sanders was a revolutionary to Clinton's apparatchik. And he too was rising steadily.

In New Hampshire, Sanders pulled to within eight points of Clinton. This could be dismissed as a location issue. Sanders was from neighboring Vermont, after all. But then, New Hampshire is not Vermont. Vermont celebrates Socialists. New Hampshire sits squarely in the middle of the political road.

Midsummer, Hillary Clinton still maintained a commanding lead in Iowa, 52% to 33%, but her standoffish style just didn't sell well. (She came in third in 2008 behind Obama and John Edwards.) Another poll released mid-July showed Clinton losing to any of the top Republican contenders in Iowa, weighed down by "brutally negative favorability ratings" of 56% unfavorable to 33% favorable.[138]

Clinton's lack of momentum started to unnerve national Democrats. According to the same poll, she was doing just as badly in two key swing states, Colorado and Virginia. Attempting to create some momentum, she gave a big speech in New York on economic policy. The typical reaction? "Meh. What else ya got?"[139] Echoing a theme that would dog her for months, she was long on complex minutia and short on compelling message.

In addition to reminding all concerned Clinton's great gifts lie not in oratory, she suffered from the constraints of a very tight box politically. She couldn't run on a great economy left to her by Obama because the economy just stumbled along. She had to talk about a "fair" economy and middle-class wage stagnation, but how could she do that without indicting Obama's economic policies, the very policies that had left the nation with stagnating wages? And how could she run through the usual litany of economic policy responses, none of which had traction even when Democrats controlled the Congress, without sounding as though she were running as Obama's third term?

Stepping back, the Sanders phenomenon posed an interesting meta-story. Bill Clinton's candidacy and administration created and practiced the modern "third way" middle-of-the-road political approach. Sure, sometimes he veered left, often at Hillary's urging as with the 1993–94 Hillarycare disaster; but then he would veer a bit right as with welfare reform and fiscal prudence. Al Gore ran for president in 2000 under much the same philosophy as did John Kerry in 2004.

Barack Obama broke with the Clinton model, moving the Democratic Party far to the left. He demonstrated the classic approach of the European social democrat. If given a chance, why would the Democratic Party not seek to move still further left with a bona fide Socialist? Sanders said openly and directly what many Democrats believed. For example, in July Sanders explained his economic philosophy simply enough, "Our economic goals have to be redistributing a significant amount of [wealth] back from the top 1%."[140]

As with most Socialists, the fact his economic philosophy inevitably results in widespread poverty rather than prosperity simply did not register. As Larry Summers, former Clinton treasury secretary, observed, the shortcomings of market economies are real, but "it does not follow, however, that governments can bring about economic outcomes they prefer by fiat."[141]

Bernie Sanders promised to take America's leftists to a promised land they had hitherto only dared dream about. This was the essential existential threat to Clinton's campaign. It meant if Sanders won the nomination, then against an even vaguely credible Republican, the Democratic Party would likely go down to a defeat of 1972 McGovern-like proportions, with deep repercussions in down the ticket. However, against a Republican like Trump, perhaps Sanders had a decent chance of success. At the very least, with Trump and

Sanders keeping the show lively, there was little chance of any midsummer doldrums on the campaign trail.

Cash Is King

An old expression rings that cash is king. Cash can't make a king as many aspiring politicians learn the hard way, but a vow of campaign poverty never made a king either. The fundraising totals for the initial six months of 2015 came out in late July, and they included a few surprises.[142]

Jeb Bush came out on top with $103 million raised. Jeb's problem was he had set the bar high, hoping it would scare away the opposition. He failed to scare anyone, but he raised almost twice as much as the next contestant.

Amazingly, Ted Cruz came in second with $52 million, half as much as Bush; but expectations were lower, his campaign operation much smaller, and his expenses commensurately less.

Hillary Clinton came in third with a tidy $46 million, but then her campaign's structure and associated expenses were enormous. She had a lot, and she'd need a lot.

Another surprise was Bernie Sanders, who'd collected $15.2 million. This seemed peanuts next to Clinton's haul, but then his operation was much, much smaller. He might not compete relying on his own extensive organization, but he'd have the cash he needed to compete in Iowa and New Hampshire. Sanders wasn't going away.

The rest of the candidates raised enough to operate and little more, as expected. Probably the biggest surprise: Rand Paul raised only $7 million, a pittance given all the big-moneyed billionaires among libertarian ranks. Even the non-politician Ben Carson did better at $8.5 million.

Hillary Continues to Stumble

Lest anyone think Donald Trump was having all the fun, Hillary Clinton continued her slumping, bumbling campaign, offering up repeated skits worthy of *Saturday Night Live*. As A. B. Stoddard of the *Hill* wrote in a piece titled "Clinton Must Be Joking":

> In just days, Clinton has issued dire warnings about climate change; been caught jumping on and off a private plane; pledged, because of the plane's emissions, to make her campaign carbon neutral (without revealing how); jetted to New York City for a $600 haircut; and refused to reveal her position on the Keystone XL pipeline, which those same voters interested in climate change are asking her about.[143]

Though it already seemed long, the campaign had a long way to go. Clinton was no fool. Her campaign was infused with seasoned, disciplined professionals. But the signs were anything but encouraging for Democrats. And then, Camille Paglia landed her first blow.

Paglia, an academic and widely read social critic, described herself as a "dissident feminist." In a series of *Salon* interviews, the progressive lioness simply unloaded on Clinton:

> Hillary has accomplished nothing substantial in her life. She's been pushed along, coasting on her husband's coattails, and every job she's been given fizzled out into time-serving or overt disaster. Hillary constantly strikes attitudes and claims she's "passionate" about this or that, but there's never any sustained follow-through. She's just a classic, corporate exec or bureaucrat type who would prefer to be at her desk behind closed doors, imposing her power schemes on the proletariat.[144]

This wasn't Donald Trump plastering the Clinton mystique with pigeon droppings. This was a queen of the leftist intelligentsia. And Clinton's chances? "Oh, I don't see Hillary as even getting as far as the debates!" Paglia at least got this wrong.

Clinton's Keystone XL issues provided a substantive example of her many problems. The Keystone XL pipeline would be a 1,179-mile addition to the existing Keystone pipeline network originating in Alberta, Canada, extending across Canada down through the Dakotas and eventually reaching Nederland and Houston, Texas. The Keystone XL component would take a more direct route from Alberta running southeasterly to Steele City, Nebraska.

Some key facts regarding Keystone XL included:

- Rather than a new pipeline structure, it would complement an existing, much larger pipeline.
- Many thousands of miles of such pipelines for oil and natural gas crisscross the United States.
- The Keystone addition would eventually ship crude from Alberta to refineries in the Midwest and the Gulf Coast, replacing crude shipped in from Venezuela and other foreign suppliers.
- Without Keystone XL, Canada would ship the crude to its own Pacific Ocean ports for shipment to world markets.
- Countries all over the world were proposing, building, and expanding such pipelines. This is pretty basic stuff.

In short, there was nothing particularly unusual about the Keystone pipeline extension except it had the ill fortune of getting caught up in political crossfire.

Under the circumstances, opposition to the Keystone XL extension could be chalked up to nothing more than the Far Left's knee-jerk reaction to anything involving crude oil. If the crude would remain in the ground absent the Keystone XL extension, one could at least begin to rationalize the opposition. Without Keystone, the United States would continue to import vast quantities of crude from overseas for U.S. refineries while Canada would transport via first pipeline and then supertanker additional vast quantities to foreign refineries. Keystone would add to an existing pipeline and in the process eliminate both the U.S. inbound and the Canadian outbound oil shipping.

Rational or not, the Left was having none of it. Pres. Obama did what presidents often do under the circumstances: he punted early in his administration to have a study done. The study, done by the State Department of all places, proceeded under the watchful eye of who? Secretary of State Hillary Clinton.

On March 1, 2014, the State Department released its assessment of the Keystone XL pipeline and found "there would be no significant impacts to most resources along the proposed Project route."[145] The Obama administration's reaction? Crickets. Nothing. Nada. Until, in April of 2014, the administration announced the review would be extended indefinitely pending the outcome of a lawsuit set aside on January 9, 2015, by the Nebraska Supreme Court.

The Obama administration had signaled it planned to stall the Keystone XL project until such time as the political environment was safe to kill it. Very brave, Mr. Obama. Finding no legitimate grounds to halt the project, and really no legitimate grounds for delay, yet delay was Obama's order of the day. Which meant Clinton was asked her views. Her response: "If it is undecided when I become president, I will answer your question."[146] Thank you very much, Your Majesty.

And her justification for stonewalling the question? The State Department cleared the project while she was secretary. That's right. Her department released the required environmental impact statement confirming no notable environmental consequences. So as a private citizen, as a candidate for the presidency, she couldn't talk about the report her department released.

How many mistakes can a candidate make and still be a candidate? That appeared to be one question Hillary Clinton was determined to explore all on her own.

Somewhere along the way, even her enemies began to feel sorry for Clinton; so many were writing about her failings as a candidate. In August, Ruth Marcus, liberal journalist and doyenne from the *Washington Post*, added her caustic two cents' worth:

Putting it mildly, the campaign so far has not been kind to Clinton. The issues of her private email server and family foundation finances have been, and deserve to be, a drag on her standing with voters. The latest Quinnipiac poll found 37% of likely voters deeming her "honest and trustworthy," with 57% finding her not. Voters' assessment of Biden was the mirror image, 58% assessing him as honest, 34% disagreeing.

One troubling snapshot from a new Wall St. Journal-NBC poll: More women now view Clinton negatively than positively.[147]

Joe B Stirs

Throughout midsummer of 2015, a serious effort developed to convince Vice Pres. Joe Biden to jump into the race. Biden was conflicted. He knew despite her stumblings the Clinton machine would be formidable. He knew sitting vice presidents ran with all the baggage and little of the glory associated with the president they'd served. And he knew he would be getting in very late.

Biden had long wanted to be president, having run very unsuccessfully for the Democratic nomination in 1988 and 2008. Healthy and vigorous despite his seventy-four years as of 2016, he certainly had no intention of just riding off quietly into the sunset to play golf ad nauseum. And by credible reports, he was more than a little disgusted at the Clintons' money-grubbing mix of political and philanthropic enterprises.[148] According to their own tax returns, the Clintons made $141 million between 2007 and 2014—not bad work if you can get it.[149]

Biden also faced a pressure uniquely personal and powerful: his late son, Beau. Beau Biden was a great son, an army officer, dedicated to his family. He died May 30, 2015, at the Walter Reed National Military Medical Center after battling brain cancer. Beau had wanted

CHAPTER 7
THE BIG CACOPHONY AND BEYOND

The first candidates' debate occurred on August 6, 2015, and what a mess this promised to be.

The Republican debates in 2012 proved a disaster—too many candidates for anyone to stand out and just too many debates. The Republican National Committee (RNC) pared back to ten, still far too many. Debates would follow roughly one a month through December, followed by more debates in early 2016. Neither the RNC nor host Fox News could do anything about the legion of candidates, numbering seventeen.

What was Fox to do with so many candidates? Fox originally announced the top ten candidates by poll ratings would participate. Sounds reasonable enough at first, but which polls? And how fair would it be to a candidate with 2% support to be edged out by a candidate with 2.1% support? And what do you do with those who don't make the cut? And what do you do when the leading candidate, Donald Trump, appeared little more than a firecracker in a henhouse?

The announced solution with respect to the leftovers was to allow them a forum in the afternoon followed by the main event in the evening. Sounds fine superficially, but the margin of error in these polls individually was often three to five percentage points his father to run for president as did Beau's brother, H[...] were powerful inducements Joe Biden could not easily d[...]

For all Clinton's strengths, Biden could tick off certai[...] he would have over her. At the top of the list, Biden was a[...] campaigner. His speaking style was engaging and ente[...] had real charisma. Even Republicans liked him personall[...] disagreeing with him deeply. And Obama would likel[...] first, throw the weight of his team behind Biden. Obama[...] the best way to cement his legacy and defend his acco[...] was to have his vice president as his successor. Just to[...] suspense, Biden let it be known he wouldn't make any an[...] before September.

up or down. The margin of error shrank when combining multiple polls, but a sizable margin remained. Statistically, no meaningful difference existed between Rand Paul averaging 4.7% and Bobby Jindahl averaging 1.7%.

Going into the debates, the most recent polls showed as follows:

Poll Date	Fox News 7/30–8/2	Bloomberg 7/30–8/2	CBS 7/30–8/2	Average 7/30–8/2
1) Trump	26	21	24	23.7
2) Bush	9	8	10	9.0
3) Walker	9	8	10	9.0
4) Huckabee	6	7	8	7.0
5) Carson	7	5	6	6.0
6) Rubio	5	6	6	5.7
7) Cruz	6	4	6	5.3
8) Paul	5	5	4	4.7
9) Christie	3	4	3	3.3
10) Kasich	3	4	1	2.7
11) Perry	1	2	2	1.7
12) Santorum	2	2	1	1.7
13) Jindahl	1	1	2	1.3
14) Fiorina	2	1	<1	1.0
15) Graham	<1	1	<1	0.7
16) Pataki	<1	<1	<1	<0.3
17) Gilmore	<1	<1	<1	<0.3

Trump's position on top and his meteoric rise astounded all, probably even Trump though he wouldn't admit it. As of the end of June, he scored at 4.2%. He'd risen steadily since at the expense of every other notable candidate except Jeb Bush, who at first seemed immune to Trump's effects.

Did Trump tap into the purest forms of frustration and anger of a large segment of the American electorate? Did these people really want him to be the next president? Would millions of Americans vote for Trump for president of the United States in anger or for someone else after cold reflection? Trump was practically devoid of real policies or ideas. He would negotiate a better deal with the Chinese simply because he was a better negotiator, he claimed. No doubt the Chinese found that amusing.

He would build the wall along the southern border and make the Mexican government pay for it. How? He would simply demand it.

No, really. He told Bill O'Reilly during an interview, "Mexico, this is not going to continue. You're going to pay for that wall."[150] And all the world would tremble at his mighty roar.

Aside from Trump's position on top, a few curiosities stood out, beginning with Ben Carson's strong showing, slightly better even than Marco Rubio who was considered one of the eventual top three. Another curiosity was how fast Ohio Gov. John Kasich rose into the top ten while the only woman, Carly Fiorina, remained among the also-rans.

At the bottom of the list sat former New York Gov. George Pataki and former Virginia Gov. Jim Gilmore. Even at the start, both men were long since has-beens. Their involvement demonstrated that long-standing practice of running for president to enhance one's personal brand. Newt Gingrich made this play in 2012 and was stunned when his gambit resulted in his being taken (temporarily) seriously as a candidate. Gingrich would have loved to be president, of course, but what he really hoped for was improved book sales and speaking fees. Pataki and Gilmore followed this same path.

The Democrats had no such issues. Despite three viable candidates (Clinton, Sanders, and O'Malley), a couple outliers (Jim Webb and Lincoln Chafee), and one major entrant lurking in the wings (Biden), they had as yet scheduled no debates. Running scared was no way to run for President of the United States, yet Hillary Clinton apparently could do nothing else, and the Democratic National Committee (DNC) was happy to oblige her.

Clinton had proven a strong debater in 2008. Sanders had the momentum and energy.[151] Clinton had the cash, but she was also spending it rapidly. And in any event, cold cash is cold comfort. A debate would give her a chance to reaffirm her front-runner status or at least hit pause on Sanders' rise, but she dared not, at least not until later in the fall.

On the morning of the Republicans' first debate, the DNC announced a debate schedule.[152] The first Democratic debate was scheduled for October 13 in Las Vegas, with a complete schedule as follows:

October 13	Las Vegas, Nevada
November 14	Des Moines, Iowa
December 19	Manchester, New Hampshire
January 17	Charleston, South Carolina
February	Either Florida or Wisconsin
March	Either Florida or Wisconsin

While late to the party, the Democrats had chosen their sites wisely, all possible swing states depending on the Republicans' eventual nominee.

The Clash in Cleveland

Many Americans associate Cleveland, Ohio, with the old dying rust belt. Older Americans remember a remarkable day in 1969 when the Cuyahoga River, or more accurately the vast quantity of chemicals and refuse floating on the river, caught fire. The Cuyahoga runs through Cleveland just before it empties into Lake Erie.

This memory does no justice to Cleveland today. The Cuyahoga was named an American Heritage River in 1998, and Cleveland has enjoyed something of a renaissance. This renaissance was neither furthered nor hindered by the Republican debate. Surprising to many, a reported twenty-four million Americans watched.

In the afternoon's undercard event, Carly Fiorina clearly won the day, proving herself adept, firm, clear, decisive, and leading many to wish she could stick around for the evening debate. Peggy Noonan of the *Wall Street Journal* called Fiorina "the overwhelming winner."[153]

Mostly the Cleveland debate confirmed preexisting impressions. For example, Donald Trump remained outrageous. Having alleged the Mexican government was intentionally dumping its criminals and other unwanteds on America, moderator Chris Wallace gave Trump an extra thirty seconds to provide any evidence for his claim. Trump provided none, just repeated his claim the U.S. government was stupid, the Mexican government was smart, and these were the facts "whether you liked them or not."[154] This would be Trump's standard operating procedure throughout the campaign.

Jeb Bush proved himself to be the likeable adult in the room. John Kasich demonstrated a refreshing directness. Scott Walker fared reasonably well, no home runs but no strikeouts. Marco Rubio showed again his superior oratorical and communications skills. Remarkably, Ted Cruz said nothing remarkable.

Ben Carson seemed to suggest, since as a noted neurosurgeon he was obviously the smartest person in the room, the choice of nominee should go to the smartest person. His closing statement suggested he was running for surgeon general rather than commander in chief:

> I'm the only one to separate Siamese twins. The only one to operate on babies while they were still in mother's womb, the only one to take out half of a brain, although you would think, if you go to Washington, that someone had beat me to it.[155]

Chris Christie and Rand Paul had the most substantive and sharpest exchange as they debated the very real issues of personal liberty versus national security and the implications for government intelligence programs. Paul delivered a cheap shot when he said Christie was siding with Obama (egads!) and "I remember when you gave him [Obama] a big hug" after Hurricane Sandy hit New Jersey.

Christie then landed the decisive retort, "The hugs that I remember are the hugs I gave to the families after 9/11."

The UK's *Daily Telegraph* provided a useful collection of the night's one-liners.[156] Most knew trying to out one-liner Donald Trump was impossible. Even so, perhaps the top three were:

> "There is no such thing as a politically correct war."
> Ben Carson

> "How is Hillary Clinton going to lecture me about living paycheck to paycheck? I was raised paycheck to paycheck." Marco Rubio

> "Guess what, I just went to a wedding for a friend of mine who happens to be gay." John Kasich (Yes, he really said that.)

Taking a step back, the evening began with all eyes on Trump to see what outrageous thing he would say and how Bush standing next to Trump would react. But as the evening wore on, as one *Hill* staffer wrote, "The strength of the field is overshadowing Trump."[157] It never happened again.

After the Gab

The top story line for Republicans following the Cleveland debate was what to do about Donald Trump. He demonstrated at most a passing association with the Republican Party when during the debate he refused to say he'd support the party's nominee, fueling rumors he might run a third-party candidacy just for grins. This tension gained added intensity by his running battle with Cleveland moderator and Fox News anchor Megyn Kelly. Trump, of course, complained the questions directed his way were unduly mean and unfair. As was so often the case, Trump was alone in this assessment.

The spat with Kelly was particularly fascinating. Hillary Clinton rose to Kelly's defense, as did Carly Fiorina. While this may look like the rise of the political sisterhood in defense of one of their own, it was also appropriate as Trump's comments were inherently low and demeaning toward women.

Trump didn't like the pushback one bit, tweeting, "I just realized that if you listen to Carly Fiorina for more than ten minutes straight, you develop a massive headache."[158] For Trump, whose forays into logic left the rest of the country with a headache, this was understandable.

Michael Gerson captured a classic Trumpism in a *Washington Post* op-ed, "if you actually listen to him and try to follow his reasoning, the result is the intellectual version of a hangover."[159] Gerson went on to deconstruct a classic Trumpism regarding politicians and money: "Every politician is bought by billionaires. Only billionaires can fund their own campaigns to avoid being bought. Therefore, only billionaires can save us from billionaires."

Not all the stories were about the Donald. Carly Fiorina continued to receive wide praise for her performance and a nice spike in fundraising. Others fared not so well. Rick Perry's fundraising collapsed. Not that he'd done particularly well previously, having raised only about $1 million during the year.[160] But with little cash coming, he told his staff he couldn't pay them and they were free to talk to other campaigns if they wanted.[161] Let the weeding of the weak begin.

AND THE WINNER IS?

The Donald proclaimed himself the Cleveland debate's winner. Most campaigns argued their candidate did well. But what did the American people think? Rasmussen released the first follow-on national poll, for the most part confirming the consensus view most of the candidates didn't hurt or help themselves much.[162] But there were exceptions.

Carly Fiorina benefited most according to the Rasmussen poll, jumping eight percentage points and landing in the middle of the upper tier. Marco Rubio also got a nice bounce, clearly shifting him from second to first tier.

Going south was Donald Trump, who lost almost seven percentage points. At seventeen points, he showed the same level of support in Iowa and New Hampshire as he did nationally.[163] Many mused optimistically perhaps Trump's rise had peaked as the Rasmussen headline suggested. Mike Huckabee appeared the other notable loser as his support fell by half, reinforcing the impression that in this field he really didn't impress.

Poll Date		Average 7/30–8/2	Rasmussen 8/9–8/10	Major Changes
1)	Trump	23.7	17	- 6.7
2)	Bush	9.0	10	
3)	Walker	9.0	9	
4)	Huckabee	7.0	3	- 4.0
5)	Carson	6.0	8	
6)	Rubio	5.7	10	+ 4.3
7)	Cruz	5.3	7	
8)	Paul	4.7	4	
9)	Christie	3.3	4	
10)	Kasich	2.7	4	
11)	Perry	1.7	1	
12)	Santorum	1.7	1	
13)	Jindahl	1.3	1	
14)	Fiorina	1.0	9	+ 8.0
15)	Graham	0.7	1	
16)	Pataki	<0.3	<1	
17)	Gilmore	<0.3	<1	

Anyone hoping to see in the Rasmussen poll the early signs of the widely anticipated Trump fade was quickly disappointed. A couple days later, another poll showed him back with 25% support. The Trump phenomenon continued and reports suggested he was now preparing to run a real national campaign, including developing at least the skeletons of specific policy positions beyond building a wall on the Mexican border and throwing the illegals or, as the more politically correct preferred, "the undocumented," out of the country.

BERNIE CONTINUES HIS ASCENT

Paralleling Donald Trump, Vermont Sen. Bernie Sanders's surprising political rise came right out of the deep blue. Surprising to the masses. Surprising to Hillary Clinton. "Feel the Bern" became a new and popular chant as twenty-eight thousand came out to hear him in Portland, Oregon, and nearly as many in Los Angeles. And he was picking up endorsements—most important, union endorsements.

National Nurses United representing 185,000 nurses endorsed the Bern, saying, "He's real. He's authentic." No jab at Clinton there, huh? Even the popular black rapper Lil B The BasedGod (whatever that means) withdrew his endorsement of Clinton to back Sanders: "Right now it's all about Bernie. . . . he's the real he loves us."[164]

Clinton got some union love too, but it was a troubled relationship. The American Federation of Teachers (AFT) with 1.5 million members endorsed her on July 11, only to have its President, Randi Weingarten, suffer a hailstorm of abuse from her own membership. While the AFT claimed it had polled its members, the claim surprised the membership. All signs pointed to Weingarten and the AFT national leadership deciding the endorsement on their own, the views of the membership be damned. As one teacher blogger put it succinctly, when it came to Weingarten and the endorsement, "no freaking way!!!!"[165] This seemed one endorsement subtracting more than it added.

For all the feeling for the Bern, no matter how Far Left (or Right) one is, there's always somebody even further. So it was in Far-Left Seattle, Washington. As a crowd of thousands waited to hear Sanders talk, a Black Lives Matter campaign leader, Marissa Johnson, jumped on stage to declare, "We're shutting this event down—now."[166] On what basis would she do this? The threat of violence, of course. Linking Bernie Sanders with white oppression demonstrated just how ideologically at sea the Black Lives Matter movement had become.

A LITTLE HIGHER ED INITIATIVE

A besieged candidate scrambles to divert attention to something more interesting. Attacking one's opponent directly is usually effective if the attack is credible. Hillary Clinton couldn't attack Sanders from the left because that way led to la-la land. Attacking him from the right as an out-of-touch Socialist, while accurate, would drive the activist progressives and all their money even faster into Sanders's camp.

A reasonable assessment concluded the Bernie wave would crest before he created too many problems. He didn't have the organization for a long fight. He didn't have the money. He didn't have the portfolio of policy proposals. Then again, Clinton concluded much the same eight years earlier against Obama when despite all the foregoing he still proved the unstoppable force. But what was she to do?

Attacking Bernie might work later, but for now that was a losing play. An alternative approach relied on keeping a relatively low profile, giving speeches, raising money, building the organization for the later battles, all in the expectation the current troubles with emails would somehow blow over; but the email issue just wasn't going away.

A third strategy was to go on the offensive, claiming the email business was all a political attack. This wasn't going to fly. Her voice was barely heard in that space; and her counters seemed tired, pro forma, and shopworn. Republicans were anti-woman, she would claim, echoing a popular line from previous Democratic campaigns. But about half of all Republicans were women, so Clinton was claiming Republican women were anti-women? Almost as absurd as claiming Republican men were anti-women as though they hated their mothers, wives, sisters, and daughters. How Democrats got away with this nonsense for so long is a wonder.

Republicans were trying to deprive citizens of their right to vote, she would claim when Republicans demanded people had to show government-issued identification before voting in a federal election. If voting is so important, and the franchise so fundamental (it is, in both cases), then why would anyone resist simple efforts to prevent voter fraud unless, of course, one systematically benefited from voter fraud?

You need a government-issued ID to get on an airplane, rent a car, write a check, or just about any other mundane activity. Very few Americans would object to such a simple requirement. Defending voter fraud also debases the franchise of those who vote legally. What is your vote really worth if it can be offset by an illegal voter or a phantom voter or a dead voter? Once again, to score a point, Clinton found herself on intellectually very thin ice.

Republicans just wanted to help the rich, she would argue, when, in fact, most Republican voters were not rich; and the rich were at least as likely to be progressives as they were Tea Party members. All Republicans had to do was point out they didn't care about the rich, they cared about those who were trying to become richer, but of course this was a message they never delivered effectively either, allowing Democrats to return to this theme again and again.

Finally, a candidate can try to overwhelm the bad news with a steady stream of substantive proposals serving to paint the larger portrait. In effect, soldier on. Clinton had no other choice.

So while trying to find her voice, Clinton rolled out a set of policy proposals touching on key issues. She'd already advanced one soak-the-rich tax proposal and affirmed her stance for raising the minimum wage. Now it was time for higher ed to get its due, and get its due it would in spades if she had her way, a new $35 billion program layered onto all the other often ineffective and wasteful federal programs.

Drip, Drip, Drip in Hillary's Kitchen

When sending an email, some devices make a "swoosh" sound. When receiving an email, some devices make a "ding" sound. For Hillary Clinton, emails meant a kitchen faucet's steady drip, drip, drip of bad news.

First came revelations Clinton had violated State Department policy by using a private email server. Her justifications rang hollow; and many, such as her claim of wanting to use just one device, were easily proven flimsy fabrications. *Drip.*

On July 27, news broke the inspectors general for the State Department and the intelligence community had referred the Clinton email case to the Justice Department to open a criminal investigation. In a sample of forty emails randomly reviewed, four contained classified information, suggesting the number of classified emails sent or received totaled in the thousands. Justice Department criminal referrals don't spruce up an aspiring politician's résumé. *Drip. Drip.*

Initially, the key point was whether this was a criminal investigation. Running for President of the United States while under criminal investigation for violating the law regarding the handling of classified information would be a circle hard even for Hillary Clinton to square. The Clinton camp insisted the case was not "criminal," but sources reported in the *Washington Post* insisted otherwise. *Drip. Drip. Drip.*

As the *New York Times* detailed the matter:

> The email controversy breaks into three clear phases: Mrs. Clinton's initial choices about how to set up her email; her decision to destroy messages she judged to be personal; and the discovery of classified information in an account where it is not allowed by law.[167]

Then came the news of another forced release of emails totaling 2,206 pages, or about 12% of the 55,000 emails extant. (Remember, Clinton had deleted over 30,000 emails before the inquiry.) *Drip.*

On August 12 came news Clinton was turning over her private email server and a related thumb-drive containing work-related emails to the Justice Department.[168] *Drip. Drip.*

The same day came revelations some of the emails found on the server were labeled "top secret."[169] How top secret were they? Some included the classification "TOPSECRET//SI//TK//NOFORN," which translates as follows:

> Top Secret – a broad classification with many levels and specificities
>
> SI – stands for "special intelligence," meaning communications via cell phone and the like typically captured by the National Security Agency requiring special handling and protection
>
> TK – stands for Talent Keyhole, indicating the information was captured via satellite
>
> NOFORN – means information can only be shared with Americans, not foreigners.[170]

As many intelligence community types observed, had they allowed such raw lapses in intelligence security, they would most assuredly have been fired, fined, and jailed. Matthew Aid, a writer on intelligence matters at the National Security Agency, spent a year in jail for far less.

This drip, drip, drip continued. The count of emails containing classified materials grew to one hundred and then over three hundred. Clinton would say she never sent an email with classified materials; but even if true, what was her staff doing sending her these emails? Many, it was later learned, contained information cut from a clearly identified classified email and pasted into regular email. This was a criminal act. Clinton knew it, yet why did she not tell them to stop? Were they above the law, too? *Drip. Drip. Drip.*

The next drip was more of a splat, like a wet washcloth hitting the kitchen floor. Understandably, Clinton got a little cranky about the whole email thing. How was she to have meaningful meetings with fawning Iowa and New Hampshire voters if the press kept hounding her about the blasted emails? It turns out the computer server that housed her private email system had been wiped clean. *Drip.*

In New Hampshire, a reporter asked if she'd personally wiped the server clean. "What, like with a cloth or something?"[171] Not a bad response. Deflect the issue with snark and humor, but she couldn't leave it there. "Well, no, I don't know how it works digitally at all."

Come again? Hillary Clinton, America's queen of micromanagement, Secretary "sweat the details," didn't understand how her email server worked "at all"? Clinton Family Operating Manual: belittle, dismiss, counterattack, and, when all else fails, pretend ignorance or deny plain facts; and when that fails, fall back on "mistakes were made." Anyone watching knew the signs . . . a trapped animal who knew the trap was closing in on her like an FBI dragnet, Eliot Ness and all.

What was she to do? The issue steadily gained a life of its own, threatening to consume her campaign. In late August, she finally "took responsibility for that decision" to use one email server.[172] Well, no kidding. Who else would be to blame, the butler? Classic Clinton—admit what everyone already knows and only what you must and do so only after inflicting the most possible damage on yourself, exhausting every alternative.

Hillary as a child: The dog ate my homework.

Teacher: You don't have a dog.

Hillary: No, it was the cat.

Teacher: You don't have a cat or any other pets.

Hillary: There was no homework assignment.

Teacher: Yes, there was, and everyone else did it.

Hillary: I'm not in your class.

Teacher: Yes, you are. You've been here since September, and it's now February.

Hillary: I'm not enrolled in your school.

Teacher: Yes, you're in sixth grade and have been here since kindergarten.

And on and on it went. Even so, she'd finally accepted "responsibility," finally reaching the final stage of "mistakes were made." She'd turned over the emails, turned over the server. She'd turn over Bill, maybe even Chelsea, if it would help. Would this never go away?

No, not until something else came along, some new shiny object to distract the media's attention. Every batch of emails would have something for the media to chew on. Even without a criminal indictment, even if it were all just a stupid mistake, as long as she remained a top national figure, the faucet would leak. The drip, drip, drip of the email scandal would never end until it was replaced by something juicier, just as the foundation scandal was driven to the back pages by the email scandal.

THE HIGH PRICE OF LOYALTY

Whatever effect the email water torture had on Clinton, it really got to her supporters. Ruth Marcus of the *Washington Post*, a lifetime card-carrying member in the Hillary Clinton fan club, finally snapped with a piece titled "Stop Digging That Hole."[173] Marcus pleaded, "Cut out the Snapchat jokes about your spiffy new account in which '[t]hose messages disappear all by themselves.'"

Marcus observed the many bad mistakes already made could not be undone, like the private email server, deleting some thirty thousand emails, not turning the server over to the Justice Department immediately, and on and on. But Clinton couldn't help herself. She just kept digging the hole deeper. "You ought to stop—now!—with the unconvincing claim that you did nothing different from your predecessors as secretary of state."

You mean, all those predecessors going back to Benjamin Franklin? Apparently not, since she had only two predecessors in the email era. Condoleezza Rice rarely used email and Colin Powell even less. Whatever she did the same as her predecessors, it had nothing to do with email.

So how about a more reasonable comparison? Did any other Obama administration cabinet secretaries use a private email server? So far, as Marcus noted, none had come forth; and none would because, of course, Clinton played by her own rules.

Marcus concluded, pleading for all she was worth, "Stop making light. Stop litigating. Stop the high-handed dismissing. Stop the prickliness with the media; we're not going away. Stop the non-apology apologies. [You didn't do anything wrong, but you wouldn't do it again]."

Probably leading Marcus to her obvious desperation was knowing Clinton would do none of the above. She couldn't. It just wasn't in Hillary's DNA.

An old story goes a scorpion and a fox were each out wandering in the woods. It started to rain hard. A small river rose up blocking their path home. The fox could swim the river with some effort. The scorpion couldn't, and he was getting desperate. At last the scorpion pleaded, "Let me ride on your back across the river so I can get home."

The fox replied, "What? You'll sting me and we'll both die."

The scorpion answered, "I won't sting you. I want to live too. I just want to go home."

Reluctantly, the fox let the scorpion climb on his back, and off they went into the river. All went well at first, but then halfway across the scorpion reached out and stung the fox on the neck.

"Why?" the fox whispered with his dying breath.

"I'm sorry, I'm a scorpion. It's just what I do," the scorpion replied.

Litigating, dismissing, and belittling were the only responses Clinton knew just as insulting people was Trump's pat reaction when backed into a corner. Stop digging? Hillary couldn't.

Even if nothing came of it, at the very least these matters remained an unwelcome distraction. Worse, the stories all suggested Clinton had done something very wrong, and possibly illegal, something that might have imperiled national security. Americans got the joke. An August poll showed only 2% of respondents believed Clinton told the truth about her email mess.

Simply too much smoke not to have a fire smoldering somewhere, and blaming the whole matter as a concoction of the "vast right-wing conspiracy" didn't fly with anyone. The issue involved her former employees at the State Department. It involved the Obama administration's Justice Department. It was reported in the pages of web and paper of even very sympathetic media outlets. Even for the likes of the *New York Times*, blood in the water trumps ideological loyalties. Even among her supporters, the calls for her to pull out of the race were getting louder.[174] Fat chance that.

Trump Gets Positional

In the movies, when an Egyptian pharaoh speaks a decree, the court recorder intones, "So let it be written. So let it be done." That, apparently, was Trump's model for policy development. I want to do this... I want to do that... No, your idea is stupid. I want to do the opposite.

And how would he do it? By being "smart," or "tough," often followed by his signature "Trust me." That it was all a delusion seemed never to occur to him or, more importantly, to his supporters.

On the basis of his own intellect leavened by what he picked up by watching television, Trump evolved his policy positions in public and on the fly. David A. Fahrenthold documented this evolutionary process beautifully in late August of 2015 with respect to Trump's recent positions on dealing with ISIS, immigration, and tax reform, part of which is copied verbatim.[175] Trump's recent policy evolution on immigration:

Version #1: Figure it out later.

> "The first thing we have to do is strengthen our borders. And after that, we're going to have plenty of time to talk about it." (July 23, 2015)

Version #2: Figure it out now: Deport "the bad ones"; work out something so the good ones can stay.

> "If somebody's been outstanding, we try and work something out." (July 24, 2015)

Version #3: Deport the bad ones; maybe let *some* of the good ones stay.

> "We're going to do what's right. Some are going to have to go. And some, we're just going to see what happens." (July 26, 2015)

Version #4: Deport everybody.

"But the good ones—of which there are many—I want to expedite it so they can come back in legally." (July 27, 2015)

Version #5: Maybe we don't deport everybody.

Dana Bash, CNN: "What about the 'Dreamers?' What about people who came here when they were children, they didn't know what they were doing, they came with their parents who brought them here illegally? . . . Should they have to leave too?

Trump: "They're with their parents? It depends." (July 29, 2015)

Version #6: Deport everybody, the sequel.

Chuck Todd, NBC: [talking about the "Dreamers"] "You're going to kick them out?"

Trump: "They have to go." (Sunday, on "Meet the Press.")

After a while, one sensed Trump believed national policy was something best divined on a late-night talk show couch. So let it be spoken, so let it be written, so let it be done—works great in Hollywood and apparently in Trump world.

Trump was convinced he alone had the courage to raise the issues. Consider illegal immigration. "This was not a subject on anybody's mind until I brought it up in my announcement," he declared August 6 during the Republican Debate. Right. Nobody talked before about the wall or the eleven million or so in the country illegally or sanctuary cities or any of it—once again, a legend in his own mind.

Yet even as Trump kept the media entertained and the opposition astounded, his crowds grew, and his evolving policy statements struck a nerve with many angry voters while creating real problems for his opponents. After declaring the United States would build a southern wall and get Mexico to pay for it, after declaring that all, then some, then all the illegals in the country would be shipped out, Trump declared that the children born in the United States to parents in the country illegally would not be accorded U.S. citizenship.

Trump's standard MO apparently involved finding the next biggest, nastiest can of worms and cracking it open with a rock. Declaring he would force every person in the country illegally to leave was so impractical as to be absurd. But the issue of birthright citizenship was another matter entirely.[176] It was a hard issue, and a legitimate one, at least in principle.

The child is obviously not at fault if born in the country to parents in the country illegally. On the other hand, granting of citizenship ought to be up to the discretion of the citizenry. Discussing who should be allowed to become a citizen is a perfectly fair and proper debate; but as Charles Krauthammer observed, birthright citizenship is a symptom, not a cause. "If you control the border, the number of birthright babies fades to insignificance."[177]

In practice, whether the federal government could legally deny citizenship to these children was an issue to be settled by the courts. The Fourteenth Amendment to the Constitution said, "All persons born or naturalized in the United States, and subject to the jurisdiction thereof, are citizens of the United States." America's trained some pretty clever lawyers, but it's not clear how a president or Congress could deny birthright citizenship given the plain reading of the amendment. On the other hand, the Supreme Court in its Obamacare rulings had already managed no less a feat of textual discombobulation.

Nor did Trump care. Executive order, legislation, or constitutional amendment, his policy preference was all that mattered. For campaign purposes, the issue involved less these human or legal issues but rather the perception of being hard on illegal immigrants. An angry backlash blossomed against Pres. Obama's executive orders, of course, but also against the refusal of the federal government to enforce existing laws with respect to border security and deportation.

Birthright citizenship then gave rise to a derivative issue—"anchor babies." A child born in the United States to illegal immigrants gains citizenship and thereby becomes an "anchor" for justifying allowing the parents to remain. Again, this is a derivative problem. Control the border, and the anchor baby issue too fades to insignificance.

Jeb Bush got caught in this particular mud pit, using the term *anchor baby* and then insisting it's not offensive.[178] Memo to all politicians: If someone sincerely finds a term offensive, then it is offensive to that person. You don't get to decide for them. Of course, in a land where nearly every term is deemed offensive by someone, the language of political discourse quickly becomes so much pablum, but that's the participation trophy politically correct world we live in. The left was quick to pounce, revealing a feisty Bush rarely seen—bad timing.

In the ancient Japanese martial art of aikido, the goal is to use the opponent's force to his disadvantage. One instructor of the Okinawan system uechi-ryu, John Carria, used the expression "the fight is in the feet." Not that one kicks a lot, but rather good footwork puts one in position to sidestep and deflect incoming force. Sidestep a punch rather than deflect it. Deflect a punch rather than block it. Less is more, and then be in position to respond on your own terms.

Unfortunately for Jeb Bush, he liked blocking punches with his chin. When asked about the anchor baby issue on a visit to the Texas border, he doubled down on dumb. The politically smart response to his giving offense involved a certain amount of prostration followed by an apology if he offended anyone. Infuriating, because the political correctness Nazis were on the loose again deciding what others could say, or perhaps a better historical analogy would be the Jesuits during the Holy Spanish Inquisition. Private citizens are usually allowed to push back; presidential candidates who hope to appeal to the immigrant vote must prostrate themselves.

Did Jeb Bush do the infuriating but politically smart thing? No, he just got publicly infuriated: "We need to take a step back and chill a little bit as it relates to the political correctness."[179] Absolutely right, but the NHHC (National Hysterical Hispanic Caucus) is not interested in chilling. They're interested in leverage and political power.

But worse, he then extended his error to cover Asian immigrants. "What I was talking about was the specific case of fraud being committed where there is organized efforts – and frankly it's more related to Asian people—coming into our country, having children in that organized effort." Way to pare down Asian American support, Jeb. Care to try for the Irish next?

What about mass deportation? The American Action Forum estimated it would take twenty years and $500 billion. And remember the Donald's latest plan—kick them all out and let the good ones come back. As Krauthammer observed, not only was this morally obscene, but it was "crackpot." "Wouldn't you save a lot just on Mayflower moving costs if you chose the 'good ones' first?"[180]

Taking a step back, an arms race was developing to harness this backlash as various groups; and now Donald Trump tested how far one could go in demonizing illegal aliens. This was getting ugly and a little scary. The only certainty was that this was not going to end well for anyone.

The flip side of the issue was how much or little other candidates were willing to stand with Trump or stand up to Trump. Republicans had been coveting acceptance in the Hispanic community for years, apparently with little success. Trump threatened whatever progress had been made, but in standing up to Trump, a candidate in theory could prove his or her own reasonableness while affirming to Hispanics and moderates that Republicans were not their enemy.

Some Republican candidates jumped aboard the Trump anti-illegals train. Ted Cruz quickly jumped onboard as did Rick Santorum and Bobby Jindahl. Chris Christie waffled, saying the issue should be studied. Sometimes a waffle is just the right meal. Sometimes a little study before adopting a firm position is the smart move, contrary to what so many politicians practice. John Kasich called the issue a "stumbling block" but otherwise stepped around it.

Jeb Bush tried a cleverer finesse. First, he supported birthright citizenship because it was in the Constitution. Fine, but what did he really think? Is the policy right? Bush argued, if it were possible, then the Constitution should be amended to strike the birthright citizenship language in the Fourteenth Amendment. Then he tried striking a firmer tone by claiming we should focus more on those who "abuse the system" and proceeded to mumble off into the distance. For now, nobody was listening.

At first, Marco Rubio's performance suggested maybe he wasn't quite ready for prime time, after all. When pressed by reporters, Rubio fell back on the lamest of defenses, "The majority of it is not a workable plan that could ever pass Congress."[181] At this stage of the campaign, voters want to know what you think, not whether you think a plan could pass some future Congress. The vast majority of a president's proposals, let alone a candidate's, never even get a congressional hearing, let alone passage. This was classic Washington double-talk.

Part of what made Rubio such an intriguing candidate was his anti-Hillariness—that is, his ability to adjust and learn on the fly. It helps when you have a strong and clear internal compass. He quickly regained his footing. Of all the major candidates, Rubio alone forcefully stood up to Trump to declare his support for birthright citizenship and the Fourteenth Amendment as written.[182]

Scott Walker's response on balance showed how candidates avoid traps effectively, if not gracefully. Like Cruz, Walker quickly jumped on the anti-birthright citizenship bandwagon but then had second thoughts. Early on August 17, he was at it again, saying his views were "very similar" to Trump's, whatever that meant.[183]

Later in the day, Walker seemed to be getting fuzzier while emphasizing how enforcing other laws would resolve the issue, following Krauthammer's lead. But then Walker pointed out "even Harry Reid (Senate Democratic Majority Leader) said that it's not right for a country to Americanize birthright for people who have not—for families who have not come in legally." Sounded like Walker was opposed but, again, no direct answer.

By the end of the week, he'd announced, "I'm not taking a position on it one way or the other."[184] This was an odd conclusion since in a short period he had already taken a variety of divergent positions.

After stumbling around, Walker finally managed to avoid the trap the press desperately wanted to spring. Was his position of not taking a position particularly satisfying? No. Not to the "evict 'em all crowd" or to those supporting birthright citizenship. But it was enough. Enough, as the soldier says, to live to fight another day.

Joe's Getting Warmer

What do you do when you've always wanted to be President of the United States? You made it as far as number 2. The leading candidate of your party, an old friend, is flailing badly and looks like she might implode or be indicted any day. The second-leading candidate, another old friend, would if he won the nomination probably have the most disastrous national election since George McGovern lost forty-eight states to Ronald Reagan in 1984. What do you do? If you're Joe Biden, you agonize. In public.

And you meet with fellow travelers, like Elizabeth Warren. You meet with establishment Democratic leaders and donors. And if you're Vice Pres. Joe Biden, you inch ever closer to running.

Heading into the 2015 Labor Day weekend, Biden seemed more and more likely to take the plunge. On the one hand, why not? He'd implicitly have the president and much of Obama's political machine in support. For example, reports indicated Anita Dunn, former Obama White House communications director, and Bob Bauer, former White House Counsel, had recently met with Biden.[185] Consider the Biden checklist:

- Obama insiders' support? Check.
- Senior Obama communications experts? Check.
- Big-time Obama lawyer? Check.

- Ability to raise funds? Check.
- Nationally known? Check.
- Belief in yourself? Oh yeah.

It was all adding up. After all, who better to burnish and protect Obama's legacy than Obama's right-hand man (left-hand man?), and Obama had given his blessing.[186] Biden knew the issues better than any other candidate in either party. He was energetic, enthusiastic, popular, highly likeable even by his political opponents, quick on his feet, and a good speaker—in other words, everything Hillary Clinton wasn't.

More than the Hillary haters in the Democratic Party or the mainstream media or Biden's personal fantasies drove the push for Joe to get in. He was also seeing some interesting data. One poll showed 83% of Democrats viewed Biden favorably compared with 76% for Clinton and just 54% for Sanders.[187] Biden did better in head-to-head matchups with possible Republican opponents according to the poll. Tim Malloy, assistant director of the Quinnipiac University Poll, summed up the results nicely:

> Note to Joe: They like you. They really like you. Or at least they like you more than the others.

Fine, but what about the money people? Could Biden finance a campaign at this late date? One indicator he could was that only 52 of the 770 people who collected checks for Obama in 2012 had either done so for Clinton or held a fundraiser for her. These were the so-called bundlers who raise really big bucks by tapping really large personal networks of other very rich people. Apparently, while a few had signed up to be "Hillblazers," most of the Democrat Party's big donors remained unconvinced. FBI investigations will do that.

Not that Clinton was doing badly moneywise. She raised a record $47 million in the first quarter and had established a phalanx of super-PACs.[188] But, obviously, there was a lot of money still sitting on the sidelines waiting for . . . Joe? You can almost imagine Biden asking himself that question while staring in the mirror every morning as he shaved.

But the downsides were very real, starting with the late start. It would be tough to put together a national campaign at this late date unless Clinton imploded and her operation shifted to Biden. If she stayed in, as seemed likely, the war between Clinton and Biden would be a political bloodbath. For all Hillary Clinton's flaws as a candidate, shying from a fight was not one of them.

While many professed their undying devotion, Biden also knew his enemies would be formidable if he got in. What now appeared a clear path would become a mighty ordeal.

And among those enemies would be many of the same progressives now flocking to Sanders because to the far, far left, Obama's Far Left administration seemed too centrist. To take the Far Left's temperature, Biden met with Warren.[189] First on the agenda was surely to confirm Warren hadn't changed her own mind about running. Second, could Biden count on Warren to rally her progressive supporters. If she was encouraging, it would be a big blue chip in Biden's stack.

As the nation retreated into its Labor Day activities, a deep unease bubbled below the surface. The American people suffered an abiding, growing anxiousness. The issue was much broader than the country's direction. Something was very wrong, but no one could quite put a finger on the deepest causes. Nor was this a new phenomenon, merely a growing one.

A few weeks prior, James Harrison, linebacker, Pittsburgh Steelers, gained widespread attention and favor. Harrison had a reputation as a fierce competitor who delivered crushing and often injury-inflicting hits on the gridiron. He had two young sons who played organized sports; and as is common for teams with young children, at the end of the season, the boys had been presented with "participation trophies." Harrison was not amused.

More precisely, he was incensed. "I came home to find out that my boys received two trophies for nothing, participation trophies! While I am very proud of my boys for everything they do and will encourage them till the day I die, these trophies will be given back until they EARN a real trophy. I'm sorry I'm not sorry for believing that everything in life should be earned and I'm not about to raise two boys to be men by making them believe that they are entitled to something just because they tried their best ... cause sometimes your best is not enough, and that should drive you to want to do better. . . not cry and whine until somebody gives you something to shut up and keep you happy."[190]

A great many Americans heard Harrison and responded in chorus, "Hell yes!" America had become a participation trophy society, and it was galling. This was not all that was wrong, of course, but it was a sign. America was looking for a leader who understood greatness arose from accomplishments, not just from participation (Hillary) or doing your best (Jeb). This was perhaps an important clue explaining the rise and persistence of Donald Trump.

Another example of the participation trophy philosophy appeared out of the 2007–2009 financial crisis. For the United States, the initial spark of the global financial crisis wasn't in finance but in housing. The collapse in housing prices revealed enormous business mistakes and systemic flaws in America's financial system. A good analogy is the difference between a detonator and a stick of dynamite. A detonator (housing) will hurt you; a stick of TNT (financial mismanagement) will kill you.

A great many Americans happily bid up housing prices, bought second homes, and bought homes they couldn't afford assuming subsequent price increases would make up the difference. When the housing bubble popped, these amateur investors found themselves like the coyote chasing the roadrunner that had missed the bend in the curve and found itself plummeting to the chasm below. Puff.

Larry Lindsey, former chairman of the President's Council of Economic Advisers, had a wonderfully simple expression: We have a profit, *and loss*, economy. When people make bad investments, they lose money. The prospect of losses helps govern investment decisions, channeling them hopefully toward better outcomes, while the reality of losses chastens misguided investors. But the system can work only if politicians will let the losers lose.

The Great Global Financial Crisis of 2007–2008 could just as well have been called the great bailout derby. First, the great investment house Bear Stearns was bailed out, sort of. When Bear's investments went south, erasing its operating capital, Bear's investors were wiped out and the company destroyed; but many of its bondholders were protected.

Later, when Lehman Brothers suffered a similar fate, employees, investors, and bondholders were crushed as attempts to orchestrate another bailout failed and the firm evaporated; but a few days later, the vast global financial conglomerate AIG and its bondholders were preserved, though again the equity holders took it on the chin. The federal government's own massive housing-oriented hedge funds, Fannie Mae and Freddie Mac, were crushed. Next came GM's current and former union employees who'd been promised through their unions pension and health care benefits the company never could finance fully.

If you bought a home you couldn't afford, Washington was there to bail you out. If you saved your money and invested in company stocks, then when the stock market crashed, the system functioned normally—you lost. Worse, who paid the tab for the housing, bond, and union bailouts? Everyone not getting a bailout. In Trump and Sanders, the voters finally had champions as angry as they were.

No Tea, No Party

As the financial crisis gained momentum and bailouts and rumors of bailouts spread, many voices railed against the bailouts' massive wealth transfer and violation of basic rules, but no voice raised higher at the time than that of Rick Santelli, financial reporter for CNBC. During Santelli's aired primal scream early in the financial crisis, he remarked almost offhand that maybe what the nation needed was another Boston Tea Party to start a counterrevolution. Sometimes history provides a clear starting point. This was the spark of life for the Tea Party movement.

Tea Party outrage started with the bailouts but quickly extended to many of the actions government took to sustain the economy while preserving the financial system. The anger was undeniably justified, but just as undeniable was how poorly the anger was directed. The Tea Party's anger was directly primarily at those who were trying to limit the damage. This was akin to attacking firemen for the fire. You may not like the mud they track in, but you should be thankful they put out the fire.

Better targets for the Tea Party's ire would have been the scores or perhaps hundreds or thousands of executives at financial firms worldwide who had knowingly bent and in some cases broken fundamental rules of finance, and of the law, in the pursuit of a quick buck times a few billion. Of course, most of these people never spent a day in jail or even lost a dollar of salary in the days, months, and years to follow. Unfortunately, government prosecutors were far more interested in multibillion-dollar fines and settlements ultimately paid by subsequent company shareholders than they were of prosecuting the offending high and mighty. Therein lies a cause worthy of a primal scream.

Other preferable targets for Tea Party fury would have included the politicians who preserved a status quo of regulations and laws utterly incapable of ensuring the security of the global financial system. Those would have included members of both political parties who had worked tirelessly to protect the federal government's housing sector protectors and financial basket cases, Fannie Mae and Freddie Mac.

All of which is to help explain the genesis of the Tea Party movement. More than anything, the Tea Party movement started as a reaction to the vast expansion of federal government powers and authority during and following the financial crisis. Even as the crisis began to fade slowly from memory, Barack Obama's repeated expansions in government power fed the Tea Party fire.

The Tea Party became a major force within the conservative movement first and the Republican Party second. It toppled sitting Republican congressmen and senators and elected many of its own to the Congress, including Rand Paul, Marco Rubio, and Ted Cruz. In 2016, the Tea Party and its counterparts on the Left were hardly the last word in political agitation. Bernie Sanders and especially Donald Trump managed to tap into an even deeper broader vein of dissatisfaction with American leadership and direction. As loud as the Tea Party became, it was eclipsed by Donald and Bernie.

CHAPTER 8

GEARING UP: LABOR DAY TO DECEMBER

Labor Day 2015 provided a natural break for separating political seasons, a moment to take stock, consider what was working and, more often, what was not, and prepare for the big push into the early contest states.

The state of play was a far cry from what most had expected at summer's start. As expected, Bernie Sanders seemed to have peaked, at least temporarily, at a high level of support. Hillary Clinton's campaign still lacked a rhythm while suffering a slow leak of public support. And the Joe Biden buzz continued to build as though Democrats nationally were in a desperate "any credible candidate but Hillary" mode.

On the Republican side, the faux-Republican Donald Trump continued to make the most waves; but like Sanders, he too seemed to have peaked. Ben Carson continued his ascent into second place. Jeb Bush continued to lead among the rest but just barely and seemingly only by habit. Scott Walker suffered the most from Trump's surge and thus appeared in real trouble. The remaining gaggle including Marco Rubio and Ted Cruz seemed just muddling along largely unnoticed.

The post–Labor Day national polls according to the RealClearPolitics average memorialized the race. For the Democrats:

Clinton	47.8
Sanders	23.0
Biden	18.0
O'Malley	2.0
Webb	1.6
Chaffee	0.6

These figures had been largely stable for a month, excepting Biden's rise seemingly cutting mostly into Sanders's totals. In early summer, these national figures were largely mirrored in Iowa, but by mid-September Sanders had raced past Clinton to take a 43% to 33% lead according to one poll.[191] In New Hampshire, Sanders maintained a steady lead with 41% to Clinton's 32%, with Biden at 16%.[192] New Hampshire seemed an outlier as this was a neighboring state to Sanders's Vermont; but Clinton's plummeting in Iowa was ominous, especially after all the time she spent there. In South Carolina and Florida, two other early contest states, she maintained support of 50% or better, but would that support hold if she really lost the first two states? Probably not.

For Republicans, the RealClearPolitics average of the two polls taken just prior to Labor Day showed Trump in the lead:

Trump	29.5
Carson	16.5
Bush	8.5
Walker	8.0
Cruz	7.0
Rubio	6.0
Fiorina	6.0
Huckabee	4.5
Christie	2.0

Paul	1.5
Perry	1.0
Santorum	1.0
Jindahl	0
Graham	0

These national polls were reflected in Iowa and New Hampshire, with a couple notable exceptions. In Iowa, Bush at 6% was in the middle of the pack far behind Carson and Trump. And as September progressed, Walker slipped steadily into the second tier. In a series of polls from August 23 to September 8, Walker's numbers fell from 8 ultimately down to 3%. Walker, the born Iowan and governor of a neighboring state, was vanishing into Perry-Paulville.

The polls' other notable item was the steady, strong performance of Ohio Gov. John Kasich. He had taken over second place in New Hampshire with 12%. Coming in late, Kasich made a wise strategic decision to emphasize New Hampshire over the labor-intensive and candidate-swamped Iowa. The decision seemed to be paying off.

Trump's persistence triggered some real soul searching in Republican hearts and minds. For most Republicans, Trump securing the nomination remained a ludicrous, terrible prospect. But perhaps the situation was not yet quite so dire. Trump was pulling about 30% support, which also meant 70% were not with him. As other candidates faded, where would their support go? Some would go to Trump, but who would be the political magnet drawing most of these now-free supporters? If Carson faded, for example, would supporters of the calm, cerebral, articulate neurosurgeon flock to the bombast in chief? That didn't seem likely. As Labor Day receded, a two- or at most three-man race (sorry, Carly) seemed increasingly likely as Trump's remaining antagonists captured most of the support released by all the other former candidates—thus, the conventional wisdom, at least.

But the poll probably mattering most at this juncture highlighted Hillary Clinton's unfavorability. According to the *Huffington Post*,

Clinton remained stuck at about 52% of respondents viewing her unfavorably since the beginning of summer, with around 7% undecided.[193] As she was about the best-known politician in America after Barack Obama, if push came to shove, most of those undecideds would surely decide against her if given an appealing alternative. It's tough to get elected when at the start of the campaign well over half of all voters already don't like you. No wonder Democrats were praying Joe Biden would get in the race.

JIM GILMORE'S STEALTH CAMPAIGN

Usually, when one runs for President of the United States or for any other elective office, one's campaign actually involves campaigning. Politics may be a rapidly evolving industry, but former Gov. Jim Gilmore was running a most unusual non-campaign.

Gilmore became Governor of Virginia in 1998 on a typical Republican platform spiced with a very popular proposal to eliminate the hated property tax on cars. The tax itself was substantial, varying by county; but being paid once a year in a lump sum really made the tax unpopular. For a $20,000 car in Alexandria, Virginia, outside DC, that's a nearly $1,000 all-at-once tax hit Gilmore reduced to $400.

Gilmore was a nice, decent, mild-mannered conservative who might have won reelection but for Virginia's limiting governors to a single term. So after leaving the governor's mansion, Gilmore knocked around Virginia and national politics until he later ran woefully for a U.S. Senate seat in 2008 against Mark Warner, garnering just 34% of the vote. Thereafter, he tried to remain active in Washington conservative circles but went mostly unnoticed. Thus, it was a surprise when he announced his campaign for president on July 30. In the intervening months, nothing happened. Not a single campaign event. "No handshakes in Iowa. No rallies in New Hampshire. Nothing."[194] The *Washington Post* went on to label him "the hermit candidate" and then went back to ignoring him until Gilmore presented reason to do otherwise. He never did.

Hillary's Filet of Flounder

At this stage of the campaign, Hillary Clinton's problems could be paraphrased in the great 1970s era Eric Clapton song "Born Under a Bad Sign": if it wasn't for bad press, I'd have no press at all. For Clinton, if it wasn't bad press from her email scandal and occasional references to her foundation scandal, she might not get any press at all. The bigger problem was not the scandals themselves as the Clintons were masters of managing scandals largely by surviving, letting time pass, letting Americans and the press get distracted by the next big thing, or just getting bored. The biggest problem was the distraction created by having to manage the scandals, keeping her from really finding her campaign footing. As she acknowledged some months later, "I am not a natural politician, in case you haven't noticed, like my husband or President Obama."[195] Hillary Clinton had to work at her profession, and she worked hard at it, but these scandal distractions kept her from the work she needed to be doing.

With her campaign clearly floundering, Clinton launched a very public reboot beginning with a series of televised interviews what could be called the "I'm almost sorry" tour—sorry in the sense of her bad decisions early on to establish a private email server. This was a modified form of the ageless "mistakes were made" mantra when politicians make mistakes they don't want to admit.

To add to her miseries, Hillary Clinton's accomplishment problem reared its head again. While her tenacity or her impressive résumé was never in question, her list of accomplishments appeared to show not a single entry. Campaign spokesman Brian Fallon responded, "From the Senate to the State Department, Hillary Clinton has a record of results on behalf of children and families, and in her advocacy of America's interests abroad."[196] Specifics offered? None. Marrying Bill Clinton and then not shooting him for his serial philandering didn't count. Surely, when advertising a record of results, one could at least point to one result. It's not like there would be a strategic advantage in playing hide the ball.

Clinton liked to boast she'd flown a million miles as the nation's chief diplomat. Forgive the pun, but as Carly Fiorina noted, that doesn't fly: "Flying is an activity. It's not an accomplishment." Time and again, early on Fiorina showed the most finely tuned political ear, timing, and wit of any candidate on the national stage—except for Trump.

Hillary faced an even bigger problem than an excess of inappropriate emails and a dearth of accomplishments: Obama remained highly unpopular, with an early September poll of 1,500 likely voters indicating 53% disapproval, a figure that hadn't budged since the start of the year.[197] With these numbers, running as Obama's successor seemed out of the question; yet the alternative was to run as an Obama alternative, which necessarily meant criticizing Obama's decisions. For example, in an interview with ABC's David Muir, Clinton said, "I'm going to fight for all the people like my mother who need someone in their corner."[198] Then added, "And they need a leader who cares about them again."

Again? So Obama doesn't care about "them." How was the view from under the bus, Mr. President?

Graham's Crackers II

To say South Carolina Sen. Lindsey Graham's campaign lacked traction is to observe water is wet. And this held even in his home state—an early contest state. According to a PPP survey of South Carolina Republicans, 78% said he should end his campaign while only 36% of Republican voters approved of his job performance as senator.[199] One imagines his approval rating among South Carolina Democrats substantially lower; but fortunately for Graham, he wasn't up for reelection again until 2020.

Even so, Graham showed no signs of abandoning the race. He just kept smiling, preaching a hard line on foreign policy and austerity at home, and maintaining a steady drumbeat of attacks on Donald Trump. Why should he abandon the race? He was never really in it to win it. Like so many who'd gone before, Graham was running because doing so gave him a much bigger megaphone than he had as senator. And Graham very much liked telling people what they should do and why he was right.

This wasn't a leadership thing. Graham loved the personal attention. As long as you don't take yourself too seriously and don't go into debt, running for President of the United States qualifies as fun for a politician, especially one with a typical senator's ego. Quit the race? You can't be serious. Not until it got embarrassing, and that wouldn't be for a long time.

Tax Reform, Anyone?

Republicans are expected to campaign on tax reform, however suicidal this may be, while Democrats are expected to campaign on spending promises, however expensive these may be. Midway through George W. Bush's first term his economic team from Treasury, the Office of Management and Budget, the Council of Economic Advisers, and the National Economic Council (NEC) generally agreed on the need for tax reform and what a better system would look like. The federal tax system was complex, messy, expensive, and bad for growth.

Senior staff met, papers prepared, all seemed progressing well until the reelection team geared up and the tax reform team was told to shut up. Tax reform was just too dangerous, too tangential.

That's where matters stood until two nights before George W. was to receive the party's 2004 nomination at its August New York City convention. Suddenly, the campaign's poo-bahs realized the president's campaign portfolio had a gaping hole. An emergency call went out to Keith Hennessey, then deputy director at the NEC, to draft a suitable, safe, placeholder paragraph on tax reform to be buried deep in Bush's acceptance speech. A few hours later, the lovely vague paragraph written and accepted, tax reform appeared back on the agenda though on the furthest burner at the back of the stove.[200]

Those running for president in 2015 felt they needed to be quite a bit bolder than was W in 2004. But comprehensive tax reform faced a very complex Gordian knot. The good news was the fairly broad agreement, even including many Democrats up to and including former President Bill Clinton: The U.S. corporate income tax rate had to come down significantly. At 35% federal plus about 5% average state, U.S. corporations faced by far the highest statutory income tax rate in the industrialized world. The high rate sapped U.S. companies' competitiveness and contributed substantially to driving business elsewhere.

So far, so good, but federal budget deficits hovered near a half trillion dollars and the Congressional Budget Office projected trillion-dollar deficits in just a few years under Pres. Obama's policies. Significant rate reductions and other pro-growth reforms would reduce federal tax receipts enormously. Nor could one just wipe out so-called tax loopholes to solve the problem. Eliminating every true loophole would offset the costs of maybe three percentage points of rate reduction.

Into this nasty little political bog his brother and father had worked hard to avoid rode Jeb Bush, flag held high. Bush's plan, released September 8, was not the first of the candidates' plans; but it was the most detailed, most thoughtful save Rubio's plan introduced previously.[201] Bush's plan was also more coherent than most.

The plan's primary purpose was to reignite economic growth after eight years of Obama's slow-boat economics. The Tax Foundation estimated the Bush plan would increase total output and income by about ten percentage points over the long run.[202] Even accepting this figure and accounting for the offsetting revenues from higher economic growth, the Bush plan still reduced federal receipts by $1.2 trillion over ten years.

Economic and budget issues aside, Jeb Bush's plan faced an immediate public relations problem: it was comprehensive. As president, he could start a real tax reform debate with this plan. However, in being comprehensive it was then impossible to summarize neatly. Only tax geeks can read and grasp the import of such a litany of provisions and the tradeoffs involved. A campaign needs a thematic tax reform outline for public consumption based on a comprehensive plan kept locked in a safe.

Some other candidates' plans were circulating at this point. Gov. Huckabee had advanced a fanciful plan based on the national retail sales tax. Gov. Kasich had implemented some tax reforms in Ohio; but when it came to running for president, his campaign was uniquely silent.

Marco Rubio's tax plan had been through a number of iterations over the years as he and his staff worked at perfecting it. While opening himself to criticism that his views on tax reform were raw, in fact, Rubio's approach evidenced a refreshing maturity. All blustery speeches aside, very few members of Congress know much about the federal tax system—certainly not freshman senators.

Ted Cruz also had a fairly comprehensive tax reform plan in many ways paralleling Rubio's. Cruz had lower tax rates than Rubio but otherwise had many of the same bells and whistles. One major difference structurally between Cruz's plan and Rubio's was that Cruz repealed the payroll tax. Why would he do that?

In repealing the payroll tax and producing a single unified individual tax, the Cruz proposal was cutting edge, following in the trend of the new flat tax introduced some years earlier.[203] Cruz correctly referred to his tax on business as a "business transfer tax" or BTT. While Rubio didn't call his business tax a BTT, that, in fact, is what it was. A BTT is of a class of tax systems falling under the broader label of a value-added tax, or VAT. Therein lay troubles of an utterly artificial sort.

Cruz was attacked for his VAT because all conservatives hate VATs. The nub of conservatives' ire is the possibility of an additional super sales tax on top of the existing tax system. Ironically, nearly all conservatives, including those attacking Cruz, favored a flat tax, which is just another form of VAT. As a perfect little window on Washington insanity, a conservative candidate (Cruz) was attacked by conservatives as apostate for offering a VAT while his attackers favored their own VATs but refused to acknowledge their preferred tax system was, indeed, a VAT. It's something in the water.

Democrats Do Taxes

Republican tax reform plans focused squarely on raising economic growth and cutting taxes in general disregard to the system's progressivity. For the two leading Democrats, tax plans were squarely focused on raising taxes, most especially on upper-income Americans, disguising their motives behind a ritualistic sacrifice at the "tax fairness" altar and in complete disregard to the harm their preferred tax hikes would do to the economy.

One could fairly argue how much Republican plans would help the economy and how much Democratic plans would hurt, but the essential direction in each case was clear. Apparently, Bernie Sanders and Hillary Clinton had concluded the proper response to the weak economy and how it was failing America's middle class was to weaken the economy further hoping the middle class wouldn't mind as long as the tax burdens of the rich went up.

Sanders's tax plan was especially focused on redistributionism. He raised the top income tax rate to 52%, substantially raised the tax rates on dividend income and capital gains for households with income over $250,000, and imposed an "income-based health care premium" calculated to be the equivalent of an additional 2.2% income tax surcharge on all taxpayers.[204] To complete the picture, Sanders further raised taxes on upper-middle class Americans by imposing the full 12.6% Social Security payroll tax on earnings over $250,000.

To demonstrate his deep concern for middle-class families, Sanders raised their taxes too. He proposed a new 6.2% payroll tax on wages and salaries. The tax would be collected from employers, of course, so employees wouldn't see it, though they would see their wages drop by the amount of the new tax. Further, he also levied an additional 0.4% payroll tax on workers, half collected directly from employees and the other half again disguised by having it collected through the employer. Bernie Sanders, friend of the American worker! Rot.

And for businesses? What did he propose to improve the competitiveness of American businesses? He proposed tax hikes on energy producers and higher taxes on American firms competing abroad, ensuring that before long all American multinational companies would become foreign multinational companies. Just to complete the economic destruction, Sanders also proposed a financial transactions tax.

Sanders called himself a Socialist. Socialist economies have a very long history of poor economic performance. One look at his tax plan explained why. The Tax Foundation estimated the plan would shrink the long-run size of the U.S. economy by about 10%.[205]

Clinton's tax plan wasn't nearly as dramatic and only a tenth as harmful as Sanders's plan, but it would still cause the economy to be 1% smaller in the long run, according to the Tax Foundation.[206] Astoundingly, though they both talked at length as to how the economy was performing so poorly and how the middle class wasn't benefiting, utterly missing from either Sanders's or Clinton's tax plans was a single provision to strengthen the economy so the middle class might hope for better jobs, more jobs, and higher wages.

FALL PRUNING

Texas Gov. Rick Perry, he of the steely gaze and stark black-rimmed glasses, was the first to exit officially, "suspending" his campaign Friday, September 11. Perry could never distinguish himself from the other candidates, and so he made the smartest decision of his campaign—to end it.

Perry's timing was interesting beyond the fact he chose the fourteenth anniversary of the September 11 attacks. The second Republican debate would take place the following week, which meant a lot of hard work in preparation. Why go through all that for nothing? For candidates like Lindsey Graham, Mike Huckabee, and Rick Santorum, each was running for the microphone, not the office; so irrelevance to the contest was, in a word, irrelevant.

Others, like Bobby Jindahl and Rand Paul, had neither the microphone nor a chance. As they prepared for the upcoming debate, they had to be mulling the same questions Perry had asked and wondering how long they wanted to keep this up.

Trump, meanwhile, continued to dominate the national debate with his insults and quips. The quips kept him in the news, earning him free media at every turn; and by staying in the news, he dominated the field. Trump was no dummy, and some of his barbs really hit home. Trump's campaign ran an Instagram video online, mocking Jeb Bush as the low-energy candidate who may need more sleep.[207] Ever helpful, Trump offered Bush some hints on getting more sleep. The barb hit home because, taking a step back, it seemed Bush would be much more at home in a university president's post in some Florida backwater than at the White House. Cerebral, thoughtful, professorial, nice—all well-regarded Bush strengths, but they left Bush boring and, frankly, low energy.

Everyone not named Donald Trump wondered, when would he finally implode? This couldn't continue through to the convention, could it? One theory describing Trump's demise centered on the simple question: how many of those responding to telephone polls saying they favored Trump would, with curtains drawn and hand on the lever, actually vote for Trump? Protests were more than fine, but at some point we have to elect a real president, right? Thus pled the establishment.

The more common theory assumed eventually Trump would say something so caustic, so nasty, so absurd as to turn voters off. For example, in early September a *Rolling Stone* article had Trump disparaging Carly Fiorina's appearance: "Look at that face. Would anyone vote for that? Can you imagine that, the face of our next president?"[208]

Fiorina brushed Trump's comments off gracefully like so much lint on an old dress while Bobby Jindahl managed his only notable moment on the campaign: "I think it's pretty outrageous for him to be attacking anyone's appearance when he looks like he's got a squirrel sitting on his head."[209] Direct hit, Governor. Well played.

Trump tried to backtrack, saying his comments about Fiorina were "as an entertainer."[210] Americans, however, weren't looking for an entertainer. They had plenty of entertainers. The nation needed leadership.

OH CRAP!

Thus, the sentiment heard clearly on both sides of the Atlantic after the English voted on Saturday, September 12. In the United Kingdom, the opposition Labour Party elected Jeremy Corbyn, populist Socialist extraordinaire, as its leader with nearly 60% of the vote, handily defeating four more-centrist candidates.

In recent years the Labour Party had steadily retreated from a Tony Blair, Bill Clinton–style third-way approach toward a muddled progressivism most recently espoused by the vanquished milquetoast Ed Miliband. In defeat, Labour to Socialism. Corbyn favored vastly higher taxes and spending, and he advocated renationalizing key industries, taking the Labour Party back to its heydays of the 1950s and 1960s, a period of unmitigated economic catastrophe for the United Kingdom. Apparently, England's progressives have short memories.

Corbyn might well have relabeled the Labour Party as the English Socialist Workers Party. Surely saner elements in the Labour Party would soon seek out alternatives; and unlike in the United States, other parties can survive in the English system like the more centrist liberal Democrats.

The overarching message of Corbyn's ascension, and one ringing across Europe and the United States, was that anti-establishmentarianism was back with a vengeance. Convinced Bernie Sanders has no chance? When his political kissin' cousin just took over the opposition party across the pond?

Corbyn's rise also played in concert with the anti-establishment movement in the Republican Party. Where once Ted Cruz and Rand Paul were previously the rabid anti-establishment voices within the party, they'd been drowned out by non-politician Donald Trump. In fact, Cruz found himself so marginalized he chose to piggyback on and kiss up to Trump at a Washington rally against the multilateral agreement on Iran's nuclear program. Cruz was so desperate for attention he was caught practically fawning over Trump like many of the thousands of adoring fans spread out on the Capitol lawn.

An "oh crap" of a different sort was heard in the Clinton campaign and throughout the Democratic Party establishment. All those thirty thousand or so "personal" emails she had earlier indicated were deleted? Yes and no. They were deleted but not necessarily lost. Deleting an email is like eliminating a phone number from the phonebook. It doesn't mean the house in which the phone is placed has been wiped out.

In 2013, Hillary Clinton's private email server was replaced with another through a Colorado company, Platte River Networks. That's when the "personal" emails were deleted according to the campaign. However, Platte River had turned the old server over to the FBI and now issued a statement, "Platte River has no knowledge of the server being wiped."[211] That meant some or all of them were recoverable.

Of course, if all those "personal" emails were truly personal, such as family notes to Chelsea and Bill and the like, as Hillary insisted, then Clinton's campaign would be delighted. Except no one really believed all these messages were "personal." Many? Sure. Most? Maybe. All? Nah.

Remember, she said many were to Bill Clinton, yet Bill's spokesman said at the time he'd only sent two emails in his life. There were so many potential smoking guns in those thirty thousand previously hidden emails. How long could the Democratic Party stand by?

Just how anxious had the party become? Ruth Marcus wrote a piece the same day the recoverable email story came out. Message: let's move past those blasted emails.[212] Her message was not directed to the American voters or even Democratic voters. Hers was a plea to her fellow liberal journalists to lay off Clinton. Bury the story, please?

Backstage Talent

Political campaigns are serious business, but they are also part entertainment. As Donald Trump admitted when explaining some of his more outrageous comments, "Many of those comments are made as an entertainer as I made 'The Apprentice' and it was one of the top shows on television."[213] In both politics and entertainment, however good the on-camera talent, good staff matters. Competition among the campaigns for proven talent is as fierce as the competition for air time or votes. So when Lanhee Chen signed up for the Rubio campaign instead of Bush's in September of 2015, the political world took notice.

Chen previously served as former national policy director for the Romney 2012 campaign. After Romney's defeat, Chen did what all good senior Republican staff do when they can: he retreated to the Hoover Institute at Stanford University in California. Hoover is about the only conservative organization that understands the importance of sustaining high-level operatives between campaigns. The Left is exemplary in this regard, ensuring its people are handsomely supported in their careers even after their government or campaign service. On the Right, those who've dirtied themselves in campaigns, or "eek" government, are generally treated as unclean in the Old Testament sense.

Chen joining Rubio's campaign presented a huge coup, not just because the campaign gained Chen's talents (while denying those same talents to the other campaigns) but because Chen's choice also made a very public statement: this is the guy I think would make the best president. Endorsements are always important, but endorsements by respected insiders and involving a paycheck speak loudest. Most Americans wouldn't see the import of Chen's decision, but political operatives across the country understood what just happened.

Nor was Chen joining a bare cupboard. Rubio had quietly assembled a small but impressive cadre of policy advisors. Rubio had earlier grabbed John Slemrod as policy director, formerly an economic advisor for Sen. John Cornyn in his Senate leadership office, and Rubio's political office was chock-full of A-team conservative campaign and policy veterans such as Cesar Conda, formerly on Vice Pres. Cheney's staff, and Brian Reardon, formerly a White House aide at the National Economic Council.

REPUBLICANS RUMBLE IN REAGANLAND

Republicans held their second debate September 16 in the Ronald Reagan Library in California, moderated and televised by CNN.[214] The polls had steadied with Trump capturing about 30%, Carson in second with 20%, followed by the rest at or under 6%. Democrats were still waiting for their first debate to the intense annoyance of a great many Democrats in addition to Bernie's camp.

The marathon debate lasted three full hours. Lest anyone thought the American people didn't care this far out: 22.9 million viewers tuned in to the top-tier debate, making this the largest audience for any CNN program to date.[215] CNN's Jake Tapper did a fine job moderating, keeping the topics moving, giving participants adequate opportunities for give and take, thrust and parry. To the original ten from the first debate was added the steadily ascending and impressing Carly Fiorina.

In the first debate, no one quite knew what to expect of Donald Trump or whether to take him seriously. In the second debate, everyone stood ready to take Trump down, though usually Trump gave as good as he got, highlighting one of the second debate's fundamental dynamics: when the participants threw elbows, Trump usually won. When the discussion turned to real issues and policies, Trump disappeared as he had little to say. He tried early on to engage on foreign policy; but his comments proved so vague, so amateurish, even he realized he looked foolish against the firm particulars offered by Rubio, Bush, and even Fiorina.

Before turning to the first-tier debate, Sen. Lindsey Graham participating in the undercard debate deserved a tip of the hat. In reference to suggestions of deporting eleven million illegals then in the United States, Graham responded, "We're not going to deport 11 million people here illegally, but we'll start with felons, and off they go. And, as to the rest, you can stay, but you got to learn our language. I don't speak it very well, well, look how far I've come?"[216] Graham has a very strong South Carolina accent incomprehensible to many northerners. Well played, Senator.

Some participants in the first-tier debate, like Mike Huckabee and Rand Paul, needed lightning in a bottle. They didn't get it. Their campaigns started with little and were going nowhere fast. The exit beckoned.

Others, like Scott Walker, who had started with such promise, were watching their campaigns slowly deflate like an old bicycle tire. He needed to impress. He failed, though he fared better than in the first debate.

Ted Cruz was direct and forceful but reinforced the impression of something very unappealing about him as a candidate. He reinforced the frequent observation he remained both brilliant in the abstract and clueless about reality. Many conservatives wanted to defund Planned Parenthood following the release of some horrendous videotapes. Cruz insisted Republicans stand up to Pres. Obama and defund Planned Parenthood in the next spending bill even in the face of Obama's veto threat. If it takes shutting the government down to defund Planned Parenthood, so be it, Cruz argued.

A great many Republicans remained sympathetic to Cruz's call. The problem? Republicans had seen this movie too many times before. However fierce their anger, Republicans couldn't win this fight. They didn't have the legislative muscle, plain and simple. So Cruz was advocating once again congressional Republicans dance the self-destruction mambo:

> Step 1: House Republicans pass a spending bill defunding Planned Parenthood, knowing the bill couldn't pass in the Senate.
>
> Step 2: The federal government would shut down for a few days.

Step 3: The president would stand firm, backed by congressional Democrats and most of the mainstream media.

Step 4: Voters would blame Republicans because that's what Republicans have been spending two decades training the public to do.

Step 5: Enough Republicans would eventually get the joke and pass a bill the president could sign.

Step 6: Republicans would have shown, despite earlier hopeful signs to the contrary, they'd learned nothing from past defeats and they were not mature enough to be trusted with the White House. Republican nominees would all see their chances reduced accordingly.

Ben Carson's appearance perplexed, starting with his energy and his clothes. Carson talked at half speed compared with anyone else, and his demeanor suggested so little energy it was a race to see who would fall asleep faster: Carson or the moderator. In contrast, Carson's clothes—a wide pinstriped medium gray suit—looked just terrible, giving Carson almost a sickly appearance. Television is, after all, a visual medium. Carson then underscored his amateur status by completely blowing a question about raising the federal minimum wage.

Chris Christie needed to impress. He did. He had Trump's directness with none of Trump's bile. And with Christie, it's much less "me" and "I" and much more "you" and "Americans." If voters picked up on the difference and believed his directness would translate into action, then Christie might have done enough to restart a viable campaign.

Rubio performed well, demonstrating a strong knowledge of foreign policy but otherwise somewhat stiffly stuck to his standard lines. More than his performance, reactions afterward revealed a curious split. Many observers recognized in Rubio real political talent and expected him to go far. Others simply said, "I hate him." Very curious, but for some inexplicable reason, Rubio really turned some people off. Men, women, young, old, more conservative or less, some reacted quite negatively to Rubio on a personal level.

Carly Fiorina was simply fabulous. Strong, direct, without being rude or obnoxious. She earned widespread praise for making Trump look the total jackass to the point even Trump noticed. And no one demonstrated a better command of issues on the stage than did this non-politician.

Jeb Bush's performance improved over the first debate, but someone apparently didn't get him the memo that rote recitation of past accomplishments is *boring*. However, he did score a body blow to Trump early on from which Trump never quite recovered. Trump had just finished observing how he was his own man and how all these others had taken money from special interests. Bush retorted that when he was Florida Governor, Trump had supported Bush because Trump had wanted to build a casino in Florida. Bush told him no at the time. Trump clearly had no recollection of the event and insisted it never happened, all while knowing Bush was right or he wouldn't have raised the subject. Jeb Bush won that round decisively.

At debate's center by dint of his polls stood Donald Trump. As Peggy Noonan observed in perhaps the most useful observation:

> The gift of Trump is that just by showing up he makes people watch the Republican debates. The force of his presence makes it all bigger, more exciting, as if something important is happening. That elevates the field. The other candidates are noticed too, and get a chance to make an impression. It's enlarging.[217]

Simple fact: without Trump, considerably fewer than 22.9 million pairs of eyeballs would have watched the debate.

The second debate offered hope for some candidates, momentum for others, and above all a chance to puncture Trump's balloon, exposing him as a charlatan; but defeating him would not be easy. Palpable was the angst of a vast throng of the American people, and the throng represented a significant swath of the ideological spectrum. Trump was direct and confident, in stark contrast to the relatively squishy nuances born of a deeper understanding demonstrated by everyone else on stage. After almost seven years of Barack Obama, many Americans were desperate for what Trump was selling. They wouldn't give up on Trump easily.

The first poll out after the second debate captured the voters' shifting moods. Carly Fiorina clearly won as she jumped from 4% to 15% and to second place among the aspirants after Donald Trump.[218]

Besides displaying poise and smarts, Fiorina also delivered one of the few haymakers to land squarely on the Donald's jaw. When asked about Trump's disparaging remarks about Fiorina's looks, Fiorina coldly responded, looking straight into the camera, "I think women all over America heard very well what Trump said."[219] Knees buckling, Trump flailed. "I think she's got a beautiful face," as he sprawled over the mat.

Building on her triumph a couple days later, Fiorina went on *The Tonight Show Starring Jimmy Fallon*, a common vehicle for candidates trying to show their human side. Fiorina scored another win as she flawlessly sang a comical ditty she had written about her dog Snicker.[220] Fallon cracked up completely; and Fiorina just smiled, carrying it off like the next Bette Midler. Human indeed! Fiorina was managing something few candidates even tried—to be genuinely liked and likeable.

Aside from Fiorina, Bush and Rubio each garnered slightly higher numbers in the poll while Fiorina's support seemed to come largely at Carson's expense. The others continued to tread water, which apparently wasn't good enough for Scott Walker, as out of funds he bailed on the campaign on September 22.

In the classic 1988 Kevin Costner/Susan Sarandon movie *Bull Durham*, Costner plays Crash Davis, an aging Minor League catcher traded to the Durham Bulls to mature the raw young phenom pitcher, "Nuke" LaLoosh. Earlier in his career, Crash spent "twenty-one glorious days" in the majors and never returned. A great Minor League ballplayer who just didn't have the stuff for the majors. That, as it turned out, also described Scott Walker.

Walker was also the second "first tier" candidate to flame out early. Recall Christie had been a first-tier candidate at the start of the year only to see bridgegate knock him to the back of the pack. Overly simplified, the race now appeared to be between the two outsiders, Trump and Fiorina, and the two establishment candidates, Bush and Rubio, with a string of wannabes hoping for lightning while hoping not to be the next knocked out.

What really sank the Walker effort? On paper he looked formidable: midwest governor of a swing state, able to appeal to evangelicals and the Tea Party, etc. Some pointed to his early strategy of focusing on fundraising rather than Iowa coffee shops. Others noted his continued naïveté regarding federal policy. Being a policy wonk, he thought he knew it all already. All these propositions rang true, but perhaps Walker was just a really good Minor League ballplayer and leave it at that.

Sometimes it takes time for memorable moments to rise to the surface of America's consciousness. Jeb Bush's defense of his brother was one such. During the debate, Trump went after George W. Bush as a way of undermining Jeb substantively and trying to get under Jeb's skin. He succeeded in the latter; and in one of those unscripted moments, Bush struck back and hit home, "He kept us safe."[221] The audience erupted in applause.

Scripted cuteness or cleverness almost always falls flat. These are politicians, not comics or entertainers—excepting Trump, of course. Spontaneity can be scary because a quip can also do great harm. This one unscripted Bush moment re-energized his campaign, but it also drew into contrast most of the rest of his performance throughout the campaign. When asked a question or given a moment to make a comment, one could almost see behind his eyes as he mentally sought out the page from a briefing book containing the scripted response.

Then he would mentally read the scripted response, sounding wooden and unreal.

CLINTON'S PIPELINE

Throughout the campaign, Hillary Clinton had ducked the question as to her views of the Keystone XL pipeline. The pipeline, a relatively minor proposed addition to an existing vast network of petroleum and gas pipelines crisscrossing the country, demonstrated perfectly why America's economy struggles under the mountainous burden of federal regulations and permitting requirements. However obvious the benefits, America's enviro-progressive movement had made their stand at stopping the pipeline just as they had blocked drilling in Alaska's remote ANWR region a decade before. Neither the proponents nor the enviro-progressive opponents were happy at Clinton's enduring equivocation.

Finally, on September 22, Hillary Clinton climbed off the fence to announce her opposition to the Keystone pipeline, advancing as her argument the perfect non sequitur, "I think it imperative that we look at the Keystone pipeline as what I believe it is—a distraction from important work we have to do on climate change."

So let's see if we have this right: the pipeline is a distraction because it increases the efficiency of moving crude oil and ultimately would reduce pollution through the gained efficiency. Remember: pipeline or no, the United States would use the same amount of oil, refine the same amount of oil, and consume the same amount of oil. The pipeline would reduce costs in part by reducing the amount of crude in supertankers plying the globe's oceans. Rational observers could only laugh at Clinton's contortions or weep this woman might someday be president.[222]

Clinton's evolution on the issue was classic, well, Hillary Clinton. On October 20, 2010, while still secretary of state, she said,

> So, as I say, we've not yet signed off on it. But we are inclined to do so and we are for several reasons . . .

we're either going to be dependent on dirty oil from the Gulf or dirty oil from Canada.[223]

Very true, and the Canadian oil is going to be shipped, if not to the United States via the Keystone pipeline, then all the way across the Pacific to Asia. Then, four years later almost to the day, she said,

> I don't want to inject myself into what is a continuing process or to in any way undermine my successor. . . . I mean, this is one pipeline, there are dozens of pipelines that cross our borders every, bringing energy every day.

True again. There were dozens of pipelines in operation across the country and many more being built worldwide outside the United States. So if there are many older pipelines, what's the problem with this new environmentally state-of-the-art pipeline?

In July of 2015, Clinton found a new reason to stay mum:

> No other presidential candidate was secretary of state when this process started, and I put together a very thorough deliberative evidence-based process to evaluate the environmental impact and other considerations of Keystone [. . .] So I will refrain from commenting because I had a leading role in getting that process started and I think we have to let it run its course.

So to review the history of Hillary Clinton's positions:

1. The United States will import oil from somebody, might as well be Canada.
2. Canada is going to pump, transport, and sell the oil anyway, so it might as well be to the United States, which is far more environmentally safe than shipping it across an ocean.

3. We already have lots of pipelines with Canada, so what's one more?
4. I can't comment because I had a role in the process.
5. Oh, scratch that. I can comment after all because I'm sinking in the polls.

Almost the same day, Clinton gave us another example of her veracity challenge, this time with respect to her private email server. According to Clinton, "When we were asked to help the State Department make sure they had everything from other Secretaries of State, not just me, I'm the one who said, 'Okay, great, I will go through them again.' And we provided all of them."[224]

Classic Clinton: Not a flat-out lie (except perhaps the "OK, great" part; "crap," "damn," or something similar was more likely) but a very selective and artfully spun reading of the truth. Clinton wanted to create the impression this was the State Department's first contact on the subject; but according to the department, they had contacted her three months prior in the summer of 2014. And her "oh great" request was prompted by the department's shocked discovery she'd kept a private email server. When given an opportunity by the *Des Moines Register* to clear up the confusion, all she could say was "'I can't answer."[225] Sometimes even the master Clinton spinmeisters just run out of yarn.

But the story got even better as yet another reverberating "oh crap" was heard in Clintonville. On September 23, the FBI reported it had recovered the thirty thousand or so deleted emails from Clinton's private server.[226] They had been deleted, not "wiped," after all. If the emails proved entirely innocent as she insisted, then her reputation for veracity would gain a boost; but if any real smoking guns were found among the formerly lost emails, the Clinton campaign would be burnt toast, and Clinton could be looking at a criminal indictment. The initial betting didn't look good for the Clintons; and within the campaign itself, a new and deep worry had to waft over the faithful.

CHAPTER 9
FALL MANEUVERS

Some realities in Washington never change, like bad traffic and bad manners. An end-of-year "budget crisis" ranks right up there, along with the high probability Republicans will turn a manufactured political crisis into legislative defeat. As 2015's fiscal year end approached, all signs suggested yet another Republican self-inflicted wound. Remember, they had only two jobs in this Congress: contain Pres. Obama in his waning years and demonstrate minimal governing competency. The Obama administration had remained remarkably inactive in those areas involving the Congress, so containing the administration proved easy enough, but demonstrating governing competency presented an insuperable challenge.

The Republicans appeared to start the year off strong, passing a budget resolution more or less sticking to the 2011 Budget Control Act spending caps while giving defense spending a little extra boost. But they passed it with only Republican votes—no Democratic buy-in. Therein lay the seeds of their utterly predictable future troubles.

Budget passed, over the course of the year, the House then passed appropriations bills for the various areas of government. The Senate remained deadlocked. Nearing the end of September, Republicans faced the moment of truth, a moment given a new charge with the infamous Planned Parenthood videos.

To review the bidding, Republicans controlled the House, which meant when united they could pass whatever they wanted out of the House. Republicans also had the majority in the Senate, which gave them an advantage in setting the agenda and timing; but Senate rules still meant the Democrats could prevent most legislation from moving. Pres. Obama just sat back with his veto pen poised to reinforce the Senate Democrats should they waver.

The Republicans wanted to set spending according to the budget they'd rammed through earlier in the year while also "defunding" Planned Parenthood. The president threatened to veto any bill that did not include a significant increase in non-defense discretionary spending or any bill reducing Planned Parenthood funding.[227] Add to this an upcoming vote on raising the debt ceiling plus some secondary issues regarding the highway bill, reauthorizing the Federal Aviation Administration, and some other nits and gnats, and the essential ingredients for gridlock and crisis once again fell into place.

The script appeared in the can: the House would pass a bill, Senate Republicans would try to pass a similar bill but would be stymied by the "just say no" Senate Democrats, and the president's veto pen loomed over the whole enchilada. The president and Senate Democrats would be mostly responsible for the government shutdown, but would the American people see it that way? Would Republican voices be heard over the president's? Would the American people believe them after they had for so many years in so many ways trained voters to understand government shutdowns were always the Republicans' fault? No way.

The Far Right in the House, now operating under the flag of the Freedom Caucus, threatened to block any bill not defunding Planned Parenthood or increasing non-defense discretionary spending. If they held to that position with enough votes, then to move forward with a bill the president could eventually sign, Speaker Boehner would have to rely on Democratic votes, which meant, in turn, giving the Democrats more of what they wanted, namely, more non-defense spending. This is the enduring "genius" of conservative Republican legislative strategists: even knowing the outcome, they would choose a course guaranteed to give the other side what it wanted. Pyrrhic victories are for losers.

BOEHNER BOWS OUT

Every human being has an endurance limit. After four and a half years, Speaker John Boehner had reached his. On Friday, September 25, Boehner shocked the political world by announcing he would step down as Speaker of the House at the end of October, driven from office not by the Democrats or by lurking usurper but by the bloodlust of the extreme Right in the House itself and by their external allies such as Jim DeMint and Michael Needham at Heritage Action and fellow travelers at the Club for Growth. Their lust was not for power or policy but for Boehner's scalp. They finally got it.

For years Boehner labored to do his job while many House Republicans wanted nothing more than to fail to do theirs. To be sure, they could match in furor any small-town Texas high school football team over the political contest du jour. Every time they would rush onto the field, launching yet another crusade, only to flounder impotently until Boehner rode to their rescue, saving them from further embarrassment by legislating, which typically at that point meant negotiating from a badly weakened position with the Democrats and the president. And every time, Boehner's reward for bailing them out and doing his job was to be flailed mercilessly by the failed crusaders.

Evidencing the curious throes in which the House found itself, the most immediate consequence of Boehner's impeding departure included a broad agreement to pass a bill to fund the government into December, thus avoiding an immediate government shutdown.

A second consequence involved the selection of Boehner's successor as House Speaker. Paul Ryan, House Ways and Means Committee chairman, offered the most capable option; but Ryan was too smart to be lured easily into the awaiting witch's cauldron. As important, Ryan had to fight for his congressional district every two years. As Speaker, Ryan would instantly become the Democrats' target #1, not a good place to be for a House Speaker as Washington State's Tom Foley learned in 1995.

After Ryan, conservative House Republicans offered not a single promising alternative to the affable, telegenic, hardworking, yet untested Majority Leader Kevin McCarthy of California. Others who might be considered, such as Ohio's Jim Jordan, were too smart to fall for the gag. They knew if they won the Speakership or any of the lower leadership positions, then eventually they would be declared heretics by the Freedom Caucus inquisition. So lacking alternatives, the Freedom Caucus labored to convince themselves McCarthy was an improvement over Boehner by referring to him as "inclusive" and "fair" as if these words failed to describe Boehner.[228]

It took only days for McCarthy to get into trouble. As McCarthy sought to sound tough, he bragged about the ongoing investigation into the murder of four Americans at the U.S. compound in Benghazi, Libya, September 11, 2012. Typical of Washington, the investigation was always part substance, part politics, especially the effort to rip apart Hillary Clinton's ridiculous cover story.

The standard Washington script has Democrats in this case complaining about the political witch hunt while Republicans insisted on the issue's import and the investigation's integrity. But McCarthy couldn't keep his role straight. "Everybody thought Hillary Clinton was unbeatable, right?" McCarthy said on Fox News. "But we put together a Benghazi special committee, a select committee. What are her numbers today? Her numbers are dropping. Why? Because she's untrustable. But no one would have known any of that had happened had we not fought."[229] By tying the Clinton campaign and personal poll numbers to the House special investigating committee, McCarthy had blown his guys' cover.

Boehner's exit bode ill for Republicans generally. Recall their one real job having consolidated their hold on the House and gaining control of the Senate in the midterm elections was demonstrating a minimal governing competency. They had avoided a government shutdown, for the moment; but they had publicly deposed and somewhat humiliated their own leader. No way this impressed average American voters.

Krauthammer's Take

While congressional Republicans wallowed in their own political muck, and while Donald Trump continued his ongoing circus of a campaign, the Democrats were arguably in worse shape. As Krauthammer described it:

- They (the Democrats) are running a campaign decrying wage stagnation, income inequality and widespread economic malaise—as if they've not been in office for the past seven years.
- Their leading presidential candidate is twenty-seven points underwater on the question of honesty and is under FBI investigation for possible mishandling of classified information.
- Her chief challenger is a seventy-four-year-old Socialist with a near-spotless record of invisibility in twenty-five years in Congress. The other three candidates can hardly be found at all. The only plausible alternative challenger, Joe Biden, had run and failed twice and, before tragedy struck (to which he has responded, one must say, with admirable restraint and courage), was for years a running national joke for his endless gaucheries and verbal pratfalls.[230]

To this list must be added the following realities. First, Pres. Obama's job approval rating had remained five points underwater for nine months straight. The American people, it appeared, had rendered judgment on the orator from Illinois.

Second, though the economy continued to chug along, it was a very slow chug with no sign of accelerating. Polls continued to show a majority believed the nation was still in recession.[231] According to the economists' definition, the recession ended in June of 2009, over six years prior; but voters aren't interested in economists' definitions. When voters say they think the economy is in recession, they mean the economy isn't doing well enough to do them much good and they're worried about their own futures. When voters believe the economy is doing poorly, it's a bad omen for the party in power.

With apparently everything going wrong in the American political system, it was easy to forget what still worked well. For the most part, state and local political systems continued to function as well as democracy generally permits. To be sure, unfortunate outliers such as Illinois persisted; but for the most part, the nation's governors continued to do their jobs fairly well as did the state legislatures and the mayors and the town councils. The political virus of perfect myopia and dysfunctionality so badly infecting American politics at the national level had mostly not overly troubled the more bedrock institutions of state and local government. Reasonable grounds for hope remained.

Trump's Tax Tanks

Since the last debate, Donald Trump's support had dropped by almost a third, though he still led the pack. To sustain his campaign with more than bluster, Trump seemingly needed to get into the nitty-gritty of real proposals. He started with tax reform, a good move as Jeb Bush had recently released his fairly detailed plan, adding to Marco Rubio's and Ted Cruz's plans in the debate. Could Trump put forward a serious plan or just cobble together a list of talking points?

Answer: talking points. Trump's plan was built around massive reductions in individual and corporate income tax rates. The top individual rate would come down from 39.6% to 25% while the corporate tax rate would come down from 35% to 15%—so far so good for a pro-growth plan but expensive in terms of foregone revenue. Another immediate issue was small businesses typically pay tax at the individual level, and so Trump's plan meant an increase in the tax advantages for corporations from 4.6 percentage points to 10. Not good.

Above all rendering the Trump plan little more than a series of amateur talking points was the budget hole he would create. According to the Tax Foundation, on a static basis, the Trump plan would reduce federal revenues by nearly $12 trillion over ten years or by nearly 30% from the Congressional Budget Office's projected $41.6 trillion.[232] Even accounting for the resulting additional economic growth, the Tax Foundation estimated the total increase in the budget deficit at nearly $10 trillion. This simply wasn't a serious proposal.

How Long Can This Last?

The Bush and Clinton campaigns began the race for their parties' respective nominations as strong presumptive favorites. By October of 2015, an impartial observer might reasonably ask, given their poor performances, how long can this last for either of them?

By conventional wisdom, Bush along with Rubio and maybe Fiorina seemed the likely remnant after Trump and Carson inevitably flamed out. Neither Cruz nor any of the other Republicans were making a noticeable impression. So far, however, Trump was holding a steady 22% in the polls and Carson 17%. Bush remained stuck in single digits. He had the organization and the money but very little else, certainly no momentum or sense of appealing to the times. In short, the candidate had the organization, but the organization lacked a viable candidate.

In contrast, Clinton remained at the top of her polls, but her campaign floundered. After Kevin McCarthy's comments about the Benghazi hearing, Clinton went on the attack but came out shrill and angry. She may have felt better going on the attack, but she looked bad doing so and certainly did nothing to dissuade her detractors.

A group of polls released October 5 illuminated further.[233] In head-to-head polls, each of Trump, Bush, and Fiorina beat Clinton by seven, ten, and fourteen points, respectively. Conversely, in a head-to-head, Sanders beat Trump by five points.

Early head-to-head polls offered little more than midseason sports stats fodder, but one couldn't help but be impressed by Clinton's consistently poor showing. How long can this last? How long before Vice Pres. Joe Biden could no longer resist the pull? Without Biden, Sanders might yet prove the Democrats' best shot, if only because Clinton looked to be a dead candidate walking. But she kept walking and eventually learned to run again, however awkwardly.

THE MARKET'S VIEW

Economists' misplaced confidence notwithstanding, markets are not especially good forecasters of the future. However, they are excellent gauges of what some market participants think about the future. Thanks to the Internet, it's possible to bet on political outcomes. This makes for an interesting additional bit of information. For example, according to PredictWise, Jeb Bush had a slight lead in the market odds, followed by Rubio and Trump.[234]

	PredictWise Odds (percent)
Bush	31
Rubio	28
Trump	13
Carson	7
Fiorina	7
Christie	5
Cruz	4
Huckabee	2
Kasich	2
Paul	1
Others	0

On the Democratic side, market participants betting their own money had Clinton a lot stronger than the polls suggested, with a 69% probability of taking the nomination, followed by Biden at 18%

and Sanders at 11%.[235] Overall, the markets were laying about three-to-two odds Democrats would hold the White House.

What Does Hillary Really Believe?

Throughout her public life, Hillary Clinton exhibited a high degree of flexibility in her policy positions, to put it kindly. No one could ever really be sure what she believed other than that she should be president. Case in point: the Trans-Pacific Partnership, or TPP.

For reasons unexplained yet highly laudable, Pres. Obama had long supported the negotiation of this twelve-nation trade agreement. Perhaps these negotiations reflected his strong and oft-expressed belief in multilateralism. Perhaps he understood the TPP was as much a statement of geopolitical strategy, especially as it related to future dealings with China. In any event, on this topic Obama clearly bucked the overwhelming majority of his party.

On October 5, Pres. Obama and the other parties to the negotiations announced they'd reached a deal. Now it was up to the respective governments to ratify the deal. By and large, Republicans were mostly muted in their reactions, traditionally supporting free trade in theory, including the TPP, but not wanting to give Obama any credit. Once again, Republicans were showing the shallowness of their views and their strategy. What better way for Republicans to drive the wedge deeper between Obama and his electoral coalition than to credit him for a free trade deal! They didn't see it.

From a U.S. trade perspective, TPP was perhaps a bit less than advertised. Indeed, a few months after the deal was struck, Obama's own International Trade Commission released a report confirming the agreement would provide only modest benefits to the U.S. economy.[236] The United States already had free trade agreements with six of the other eleven TPP signatories, covering nearly 40% of American exports. TPP was more about strengthening the economies and solidifying the political relationships of the other TPP members. The new trade bloc would, it was believed, then become a magnet for other countries to join, building an ever-stronger free trade area.

Bernie Sanders immediately denounced the TPP, as expected, but what would Clinton do? As she often noted, she'd helped to launch the TPP negotiations as secretary of state and had spoken out in favor of it at least forty-five times.[237] What would she do now? She came out in opposition to the trade deal. In a sense, she had no choice as the unions were nearly united in apoplexy. On the other hand, if she could flip-flop on this, why should her allies ever trust her not to turn on them if she became president? As David Axelrod, Barack Obama's chief campaign honcho in 2008 and in 2012, noted:

> I think this is kind of a classic political decision—you can flip flop if you flop over to the popular side of an issue. That's the calculation she made. The great risk, though, is that her great liability in this race has been the sense that she is inauthentic—and that of course is one of Bernie Sanders' strengths— and so, this lurch on this issue opens her up to another charge of inauthenticity.[238]

THE FIRST DEMOCRATIC DEBATE

The Democratic candidates held their first debate October 13 in Las Vegas, Nevada, hosted by CNN's Anderson Cooper. Cooper did a superb job. CNN? Not so much, as evidenced by their lame inclusion on the stage of a lectern for non-candidate Joe Biden, as though Biden were ducking the debate. Biden was not and never became a candidate for president in 2016. Tacky, CNN, tacky.

Going into the debate, polling showed Hillary Clinton's support steady in the mid forties, Bernie Sanders in the mid twenties, and non-candidate Joe Biden at about 20%, with Martin O'Malley, Jim Webb, and Lincoln Chafee immeasurably above zero. Unlike the Republican debates, viewership ratings for the Democratic debate were low, as the Clinton campaign intended. Saturday, chosen by the Democratic National Committee at the Clinton campaign's insistence, is a low night for television viewership. To worsen the comparison, the Democrats didn't have a nationally recognized entertainer (Trump), and the debate was up against the LA Dodgers versus the New York Mets in a National League division series game.

Different candidates excel in different venues. John McCain, for example, was master of the town hall setting. Barack Obama was master of the big stage microphone. Hillary Clinton fared passably in a town hall setting, especially before a friendly audience, and poorly on the big stage but excelled in a debate where her discipline, preparation, cool demeanor, and extensive experience gave her a huge advantage.

On this night, she took full advantage of her strengths while blunting Sanders's appeal by highlighting many of the areas where they agreed. For example, Anderson Cooper catalogued a long list of issues on which Clinton had clearly flip-flopped, including same-sex marriage, immigration, the Trans-Pacific Partnership, and many more, concluding with the question whether Clinton would say anything to get elected. Without missing a beat, she said,

> Well, actually, I've been very consistent. Over the course of my entire life I've fought for the same values and principles, but, like most human beings—including those of us who run for office—I do absorb new information. I do look at what's happening in the world.[239]

Notice the genius of this response. First, refute the uncomfortable allegation using positive language. Second, establish a basis to support the refutation. Third, establish a commonality with the audience. Fourth, lay the groundwork for being pragmatic and fact-based.

As usual, Webb and Chafee were simply nonentities in the debate while O'Malley failed to make an impression one way or the other. More than anything, the time these three spent talking provided Sanders and Clinton the opportunity to regroup, catch their respective breaths, and review their talking points mentally.

Sanders provided the most memorable line in the debate, and a huge tactical advantage to Clinton, when he opined,

> Let me say—let me say something that may not be great politics. But I think the secretary is right, and that is that the American people are sick and tired of hearing about your damn e-mails.

To which, beaming, Clinton concurred. Sanders was at least partly right. Both Clinton's supporters and the nonaligned were sick and tired of Clinton scandals. They wanted to hear how these candidates would get the country on the right track again, i.e., not the track Obama had the nation on. Sensible, but tactically this was Sanders's first really big fatal mistake of the campaign.

The one point of consensus among the Democratic contestants was that Pres. Obama's economic policies were failing the middle class. As O'Malley expressed it,

> What I'm talking about is this, our middle class is shrinking. Our poor families are becoming poorer, and 70% of us are earning the same, or less than we were 12 years ago. We need new leadership, and we need action. The sort of action that will actually make wages go up again for all American families.

These Democrats were not running against a Republican president. They were running against the most left-wing president in American history, a president from their own party; and their policy prescriptions were for more of the same that produced this abysmal outcome they collectively bemoaned, all as though Obama hadn't been president the past seven years.

Judged as an academic debate, Clinton clearly won, consistently scoring points, deflecting problems, and putting Sanders on the defensive. Sanders also did well from an academic debate perspective, showing himself to be informed, articulate, direct, and passionate.

However, this wasn't an academic debate. What ultimately mattered was how voters felt the next day and a month later. According to a panel of Democrats assembled by pollster Frank Luntz, about half of whom were self-proclaimed Clinton supporters at the outset, old Bernie won the debate hands down.[240] They loved his passion, his sincerity, his boldness; but they doubted he could win. Clinton might not be loved by all, but her cool and competence were reaffirmed.

The takeaways from the Democrats' first debate were fairly clear:

1) Clinton still got game.
2) Sanders was almost ready for prime time.
3) The rest are and would likely remain temporary cannon fodder.
4) Biden's time was up.

The last takeaway only became obvious in the immediate aftermath. Given Clinton's solid performance and her broad adherence to the Obama line even while attacking Obama's results, Biden's path was restricted to being an emergency substitute in case of a Clinton indictment.

Also, it was fair to ask, if he thought he really should be the next President of the United States, then why was it taking so long for Biden to decide to run? It suggested for all his obvious pluck, Biden had a tough time with tough decisions. As former Obama political advisor David Axelrod summed it up, in this debate "maybe the biggest loser was the man who wasn't there."[241]

Following the debate, the press continued to play up the story Biden might get in the race or that Clinton had plateaued at a mere 20% landslide margin over Sanders—anything to keep the competitive race narrative going because, otherwise, there was no news at all. No news = no newspaper readers.

Alternatively, if the press admitted the Democratic race effectively over, then the only news to be reported about the Democratic campaign would require digging into one of Clinton's scandals, which would be politically highly inconvenient. But absent some shocking development, at this point Clinton seemed to have the nomination in the bag. The press believed it. Biden must have believed it. Sanders suspected it. Clinton prayed it. In any other year, it may even have been true; but this was the 2016 campaign.

As Halloween approached, the race for the White House ended for some and became a nightmare for others. On the Democratic side, Jim Webb and Lincoln Chafee took their leave, each having made almost no impression whatsoever. Then Joe Biden, after weeks of buildup and speculation, made it official: he wasn't running. Martin O'Malley, while still in, had made no more impression than Webb or Chafee. Biden became the unofficial "break glass in case of emergency" candidate. If Clinton stumbled badly in the debates, if she were indicted, or if some new scandal broke out, then the party needed a realistic plan B. *B* stood for Biden.

On the Republican side, Trump continued to dominate as pundits and party establishment types increasingly pondered, and shuddered, at the prospect Trump could go all the way.

Carson was clearly gaining momentum at Trump's expense. Fiorina, having gotten a nice bump in the polls following the debate, slid back to the pack, lacking anything bringing her attention. The pack, including Ted Cruz, showed no sign of going anywhere either up or out. Jeb Bush announced he was cutting his spending rate dramatically, widely interpreted as a retrenchment in the face of the Trump and Carson phenomena but also inevitably seen as possibly the initial steps of a campaign death spiral.

These developments all served to leave Marco Rubio as the only rising candidate seemingly able to pick up the pieces if and when Trump and Carson faltered. Unlike Bush, who'd built a mighty and expensive-to-maintain national campaign organization, Rubio had kept his operation lean and mean. Could Rubio ramp up fast enough if his campaign caught fire? Could he count on the Republican Party apparatus or the many outside groups building their own state-based organizations?

Speaking of Ryan and Benghazi

Congress took its Columbus Day recess just in time. The House Freedom Caucus, having deposed Speaker John Boehner, finished their little victory laps only to wake up realizing they had no viable alternatives. The obvious alternative after Majority Leader Kevin McCarthy blew up his own candidacy was Ways and Means Committee Chairman Paul Ryan. Trouble was, he didn't want the job, at least not yet, in part because he had long wanted to chair Ways and Means and had just taken the gavel, and in part because he knew the Freedom Caucus would continue to be a huge rebellious, undisciplined pain in the neck. So with matters thoroughly up in the air, Ryan flew home to Wisconsin for the recess.

In the end, Ryan claimed enough support from the wingnuts on the right and accepted the post. Only ten Republicans failed to support Ryan when they called the roll, those ten now self-identifying as being the most-out-to-lunch bunch of the Freedom Caucus.

Some disgruntled Freedom Caucus types publicly groused as to how Ryan was dictating terms. Indeed, he was. The out-to-lunch bunch had themselves put Ryan in position to dictate terms. The Freedom Caucus was united with the rest of the Republicans in needing Paul Ryan to limit their further embarrassment. He didn't need them. But again, many of them were just too out-to-lunch to get the joke.

Meanwhile, the House Select Committee on Benghazi held its long-anticipated hearing featuring Hillary Clinton's testimony. The bottom line from the hearing—no new smoking guns, no noteworthy revelations. Eleven hours of testimony and cross-examination leaving Clinton in full command of the moment. Republicans, increasingly frustrated at being unable to land even a glancing blow, shrank in comparison, appearing ever more petty—almost like watching the Wicked Witch of the West in the *Wizard of Oz* melt away after Dorothy hit her with a bucket of water, only this time it wasn't the wicked witch (Hillary) who melted but all the little Dorothies. The

Republicans had Clinton exactly where they wanted her, and she beat them soundly at their own game.

Republicans hammered away at the many requests by Ambassador Christopher Stevens for more security at the Benghazi compound while time and again Clinton repeated that such requests were reviewed and decisions made by the State Department's security personnel and did not come to her attention. As secretary of state responsible for the Benghazi mission, Clinton did eventually accept responsibility for the shortcomings of her Department, though she reasonably argued she obviously didn't review every decision.

Ultimately animating the Republicans under Chairman Trey Gowdy (R-SC) was how the State Department and the White House had grossly misled the nation regarding the 2012 attack at the Benghazi compound. First, the administration said the attack was triggered by an inflammatory anti-Muslim video, that the attack was spontaneous and brief and therefore not a planned terrorist attack, and that a rescue mission was therefore impossible. Additional information confirmed the Administration's claims were pure cover-up: The attack was well organized and instigated by local terrorist cells, it lasted for more than seven hours, and the attack had nothing to do with the video.

Badly weakening her defense that she was unaware of Ambassador Stevens's requests for better security, Hillary Clinton had led the campaign within the administration to topple Libya's longtime crackpot ruler, Muammar el-Qaddafi. Maureen Dowd captured the essence of the substance of the matter:

> Since she [Hillary] was, as her aide Jake Sullivan put it, "the public face of the U.S. effort in Libya," one of the Furies, along with Samantha Power and Susan Rice, who had pushed for a military intervention on humanitarian grounds, Hillary needed to stay on top of it.
>
> She had to be tenacious in figuring out when Libya had deteriorated into such a cauldron of jihadis that

our ambassador should either be pulled out or backed up. In June 2012, the British closed their consulate in Benghazi after their ambassador's convoy was hit by a grenade. A memo she received that August described the security situation in Libya as "a mess."

When you are the Valkyrie who engineers the intervention, you can't then say it is beneath you to pay attention to the ludicrously negligent security for your handpicked choice for ambassador in a lawless country full of assassinations and jihadist training camps.

According to Republicans on the committee, there were 600 requests from J. Christopher Stevens's team to upgrade security in Benghazi in 2012 and 20 attacks on the mission compound in the months before the Sept. 11 siege..[242]

Only lifelong Clinton devotees could fail to see she had utterly failed Ambassador Stevens and the American people. Likewise, only committed Hillary haters could fail to see the committee had been badly outmatched in their contest with Clinton, even though they held every advantage. Clinton had once again received a nice little boost, compliments of her Republican antagonists. One hopes she sent them a nice "thank you" card.

CNBC's Debacle: The Third Republican Debate

CNBC hosted the third Republican debate, this time at the University of Colorado at Boulder, October 28, 2015. Boulder is beautiful but a curious choice as it is one of the most radically progressive cities in the country.

Each candidate's storyline had evolved some since the last debate; but of greatest interest by far were the changes at the top as Jeb Bush continued his descent while Ben Carson had taken the lead over Donald Trump, 26% to 22%, the first time the front-runners had swapped places.²⁴³ This also reaffirmed Carson's building strength in Iowa, where he maintained a solid ten-point lead over Trump. Carson trailed Trump by only one point in Pennsylvania and led in Texas and Oklahoma. Trump still crushed Carson in New Hampshire, but Carson's viability was increasing.

So far for Republicans, 2015 was proving to be the year of the outsider. Only Bush clearly represented the establishment while Cruz, Carson, and Trump made the best case for "outsider" label. Cruz appealed to the modern hard-right outsider. His appeal was strongly ideological.

Trump defied labels. He was no conservative as in recent years he'd been on just about every side of every issue. Curiously, his appeal was in part that he spoke his mind bluntly, yet any voter paying attention would see his mind changed with great frequency. Voters complained politicians told them only what they wanted to hear. They lambasted Hillary Clinton for her serial flip-flopping. Yet here they were raising up the worst case of positional flexibility in memory.

Two differences between Clinton and Trump stood out—one was more or less reliably center left, the other all over the map—and whereas Clinton couldn't sell anything but her supposed inevitability, Trump could sell his supporters anything.

So Carson and Trump both appealed as "outsiders," but Trump appealed without ideology and evinced a "blue collar" appeal whereas Carson was firmly traditional conservative, but gently so, and evinced more of a "white collar" appeal.

Four words summarized Carson's appeal: outsider, humble, intelligent, and nice. Bush and Rubio stumbled on "outsider" whereas Trump failed the humility and nice tests. As Henry Olsen opined in the *National Review*:

> Dr. Ben Carson is doing something no one has done in decades, combine a values-laden conservative message with a soft-spoken, humble persona. Others who have

sought Reagan's mantle have emulated elements of the Gipper's approach, but none have spoken the language of freedom and the morality of the Bible with such eloquence and calm until now.[244]

Olsen went on to a polling data-intensive analysis of Carson's appeal, concluding, "Carson is as close to unifying all wings of conservatism as anyone since George W. in 2000." If by some miracle Carson gained the nomination, he could surely present an awesome challenge to any Democrat. His civility would go far assuaging moderates about his conservatism; and as a black American running for president, he would disrupt the Democratic Party's traditional race-baiting tactics. Just imagine if America elected not one but two black presidents consecutively!

The third Republican debate suffered from two huge disadvantages. The most obvious, known going in, was the debate competed for viewers with game two of the World Series between the Kansas City Royals and the New York Mets (Royals won, 7–1). That meant many viewers flipped back to the debate during the game's commercial breaks. CNBC notched an average of only 14 million viewers compared with the 24 million who watched the first debate or the second debate with 23.1 million viewers.[245]

The second disadvantage was the host. CNBC proved a business news channel flailing badly at politics, apparently trying to turn the event into a circus to bring down the Republicans even as they tried to prop up ratings. The three CNBC moderators—Carl Quintanilla, Becky Quick, and John Harwood—amateurishly played modern media gotcha with the candidates and were repeatedly booed by the audience in consequence. The bar was set low indeed when Quintanilla opened with the general question, "What's your biggest weakness?"[246] Really? That's your opening line?

Fiorina nailed the best answer when she said she'd been told in the last debate she didn't smile enough. She then gave a big smile and said, "Fixed it." Brought the house down. Marvelous.

Looking every bit the serious journalist, Quintanilla later asked Jeb Bush about regulating online fantasy sports gambling. Bush dutifully answered, apparently unable to recognize this was probably number 1,342 on the nation's list of important issues. Chris Christie brought them back to reality, "Carl, are we really talking about getting government involved in fantasy football? We have . . . wait a second, we have $19 trillion in debt. We have people out of work. We have ISIS and al-Qaeda attacking us. And we're talking about fantasy football?"[247]

In terms of political reporting, Harwood was by reputation the most serious of the three moderators; yet his first question to Donald Trump was "Let's be honest, is this [Trump's] a comic book version of a presidential campaign?" One issue was quickly settled: CNBC was a comic book version of a political news network as CNBC became the story.

Becky Quick at least tried to stay on her own turf. After a lengthy buildup to make sure the knife sunk deep, Quick asked Carly Fiorina once again about her getting fired at Hewlett-Packard. Fiorina played Quick like a fine violin. Fiorina noted that she had been brought in to fix a dying company. It required tough decisions, many not very popular; but she saved the company. She was later fired by the board because, guess what, politics plays a big role in business. Her biggest detractor at the time, Tom Perkins, admitted he was wrong and Carly was right.[248]

Quick surely seems a nice person and a decent business reporter, but she was way out of her league. Having tried to set Fiorina up for the kill, Quick was ready to pounce. "Mrs. Fiorina, it's interesting that you bring up Mr. Perkins, because he said a lot of very questionable things. Last year, in an interview, he said that he thinks wealthy people should get more votes than poor people. I think his quote was that, 'if you pay zero dollars in taxes, you should get zero votes. If you pay a million dollars, you should get a million votes.' Is this the type of person you want defending you?"

You could almost read Quick's mind at that point: "Gotcha, right? Admit it, Carly, I got you. Admit it."

Fiorina's response? She smiled and quickly retorted, "Well, this is one of the reasons why Tom Perkins and I had disagreements in the boardroom, Becky." That's what it looks like when you wear the big-girl pants, Becky. Better stick to your periodic trek to Omaha to kneel at Warren Buffett's feet.

The biggest winner out of the debate may have been Marco Rubio, who had a handful of strong exchanges. His most memorable line in response to a question from Quintanilla was "You know, the Democrats have the ultimate Super PAC: it's called the mainstream media." Truth hurts sometimes. Quintanilla staggered.

Quintanilla tried his best to land a punch in return, asking Rubio why he doesn't just slow down and finish his work in the Senate. Rubio responded, "That's an interesting question. That's what the Republican establishment says, too."

Dazed, Quintanilla fell back into the ropes but tried to recover by pointing out how a Florida newspaper, the *Sun-Sentinel*, objected to Rubio's missed Senate votes while on the campaign trail and so called for Rubio to resign. Again, Rubio easily deflected the blow and counterpunched effectively, observing the *Sun-Sentinel* never had a problem when former Florida Sen. Bob Graham missed votes by the score while running for president and didn't have a problem endorsing then-senator John Kerry while he was missing votes in droves while running for president, ditto on then-Sen. Barack Obama.

Quintanilla, eyes glazed over, hit the mat hard as the referee began a ten count and as his CNBC bosses scrambled for a white towel or at least a commercial break.

Rubio saved his best punch of the night for his old mentor, Jeb Bush. Thinking he saw an opening, Bush tried to cover for Quintanilla, saying Rubio signed up for a six-year term and he should "be showing up to work." Rubio easily slipped the slow, looping punch and again countered with a right to Bush's jaw:

> Over the last few weeks, I've listened to Jeb as he walked around the country and said that you're modeling your campaign after John McCain, that

> you're going to launch a furious comeback the way he did, by fighting hard in New Hampshire and places like that, carrying your own bag at the airport. You know how many votes John McCain missed when he was carrying out that furious comeback that you're now modeling after?
>
> I don't remember you ever complaining about John McCain's vote record.

Bush's response distilled to its essence, hammana hammana hammana, as he joined Quintanilla on the mat, little imaginary birdies circling their respective heads as though in a *Looney Tunes* cartoon.

Cruz also performed well in the CNBC debate, showing poise and command. He made only a few impressions, but he landed solid punches not on the Democrats or his opposition onstage but on the moderators. Attacking media bias is standard fare in Republican circles, largely because it's such a target-rich environment; but CNBC had provided real-time examples. Cruz brought the dispute to a sharp point, "The questions that have been asked so far in this debate illustrate why the American people don't trust the media. This is not a cage match."

The *Washington Post*'s political reporter, Dan Balz, crediting Cruz for a good night, observed, "Cruz also drew a contrast with the recent Democratic debate, saying those candidates had drawn only fawning questions. Nobody watching at home believed that any of the moderators had any intention of voting in a Republican primary," he said. One doesn't have to like Ted Cruz to admit when he's right.[249]

Perhaps Peggy Noonan summed the matter best, "There's nothing wrong with mischief from debate moderators, but this was dumb mischief, plonkingly obvious in its ideological hostility." Her advice to future moderators: "Don't be a high-handed snot."[250]

What of the poll leaders, Trump and Carson? Each stayed true to character: Trump, insulting and angry; Carson, calm and Yoda-like and otherwise unremarkable. The other candidates made some noise too but nothing anyone outside their immediate families was likely to remember.

Jeb Can Fix It

Following the third debate, it appeared little had changed other than CNBC's reputation. Reince Priebus, the Republican Party chairman (you can't make this stuff up—"Reince Priebus," really?), sent a letter to Andy Lack (again, you can't make this up—"Lack"?), head of NBC, the parent company of CNBC, cancelling NBC's future participation in GOP debates. Priebus also fired an RNC staffer Sean Spicer as sacrificial goat. Sorry, Sean.

One change gradually emerged, however: Jeb Bush's campaign was on life support. He tried to play the tough guy with Rubio and failed. To his credit, Bush just doesn't do nasty well, which is a problem in a nasty campaign. His candidacy in steady decline, he came up with a new slogan: Jeb Can Fix It.[251] Of course, the *it* is supposed to be all things Washington, but the *it* Bush needed to fix was his own campaign performance. Doubts about fixing his campaign were exceeded only by doubts he could fix Washington.

Doubts about Jeb Bush, and creeping doubts about Donald Trump, achieved numerical precision with the first post-debate poll showing Carson with a six-point lead, 29 to 23, over Trump nationally, with Rubio and Cruz at 11% and Bush at 8%.[252] Despite a decent performance, Fiorina had fallen back to the pack at 3%. Her fleeting moment of fame had passed.

These polls implied Trump had peaked. Like a stand-up comic with one schtick, the audience had heard all the jokes and only the hard-core still laughed. Carson was rising, but his appeal likely also faced a ceiling constructed out of his strong support from evangelicals and his natural inability to reflect and channel the outrage angry voters demanded. The stage was set for a back-in-the-pack candidate to surge in time for Iowa and New Hampshire. But then Trump surprised again. More than recovered, he roared back into the lead.

Early Winds of Change?

Every November in America, somebody is voting somewhere. A big race in November of 2015 was the Kentucky gubernatorial race where a Tea Party outsider crushed the Democratic establishment candidate 53 to 44. Republican Matt Bevin had tried to boot Senate Majority Leader Mitch McConnell the year before and was schooled by the master. Apparently, he learned his lessons well because Bevin whipped the Democrat, Attorney General Jack Conway.

Kentucky would have its first Republican governor in decades, but perhaps the bigger story was the one the media tried desperately to ignore: Republicans also won the lieutenant governor's race. Why was this such a big deal? Because the Republican winner was Jenean Hampton, a black woman. Imagine that—Republicans nominating and then winning with a black woman—in the South no less. This after Mia Love, another black woman, won a congressional seat in deeply conservative Utah the year before. Conservatives electing black women was yet another story the mainstream media tried desperately to ignore in a classic whistling past the graveyard moment.

The immediate narrative from the Kentucky race bolstered the "year of the outsider" meme. Bevin was certainly an outsider. Bevin was such an outsider he wasn't even much of a Kentuckian. He grew up in New Hampshire, went to college at Washington and Lee in Virginia, and moved to Kentucky in 1999. Prior to challenging McConnell in 2014, Bevin had never been in politics.

Outsiders were the new "in," and even the Democratic Party recognized it was in trouble. Kentucky's former Gov. Steve Beshear had aggressively implemented Obamacare, and Democrats in the state regarded it as a big success. Bevin made opposition to Obamacare a centerpiece of his campaign and was duly rewarded with victory. As Elias Isquith put it in the Far Left *Salon*:

> Democrats hoped voters would reward the party for successfully implementing such a major policy. But from today's vantage, it's painfully obvious that they

didn't. And that's not just a problem in the Bluegrass State—it's a problem for all Democrats. Because one of the foundational assumptions behind Kynect, the ACA, and much of the entire Democratic Party agenda is that good policy makes for good politics. In Kentucky, at least, it didn't.[253]

Campaigns as Debating Societies

The fourth Republican debate, moderated by Fox Business News, went off without a hitch on November 10 in Milwaukee. The debate remained substantive and focused on the candidates rather than the moderators, as with CNBC. Overall, the candidates continued in form. For example, it became apparent Donald Trump didn't like Carly Fiorina. At one point, after interrupting other candidates repeatedly, Trump groused, "Why does she keep interrupting people?"

Carson dismantled the recent false attacks on his biography. Delivered in a cool, calm voice, Carson nailed it but was otherwise almost invisible.

Bush did a fair job of damage control. Well enough to continue—no fumbles, nothing notable—and so on balance, he cleared a low bar. Rubio continued strong and confident while Kasich finally let out his inner cranky, the moralizing cranky Kasich those who've watched him for years knew was just bottled up waiting to come out.

Less the debate, what happened after became interesting. At this point, Trump's popularity could be summed up in three words: build the wall. Finish the wall dividing Mexico from the United States. Increasingly, this idea crystallized the complaints of a wide swath of Americans, Democrats, and Republicans alike. The elites don't like it, and Hispanics see this as a personal insult; but after years of double talk and broken promises, the price of resolving the immigration debate started with building the wall.

Even as his campaign chugged along, and maybe even gained some momentum, at this point Trump appeared to have concluded it was time to blow it up. Trump began to question Carson's fundamental honesty, referring to a "pathological disease."²⁵⁴ One can question Ben Carson's aptitude and his training to be president or his positions or many other things, but questioning Carson's veracity made even Trump supporters scratch their heads. What was he doing?

One theory explaining Trump's campaign is he got in on a lark, was shocked by his own success, decided to enjoy the ride, and now had a problem. He never expected to be president, the theory went. He didn't really want to be president; but once you're riding the bucking bull, it's hard to get off without catching a horn. The campaign was supposed to be fun and to help build Trump's personal brand; but his brand was based on Trump the winner, meaning he couldn't allow a loss. As soon as it became clear he couldn't win the nomination, he had to get out of the race, right? But how?

ISIS ATTACKS, THE CAMPAIGN PIVOTS

On November 12, Pres. Obama gave an interview in which he stated that "ISIS had been contained," the statement offered to suggest his policies were working.²⁵⁵

On November 13, Islamic terrorists representing ISIS launched a series of coordinated attacks in Paris, France, killing 129 people and injuring another 433. ISIS made Obama look the fool but even so miscalculated the French reaction.

This attack differed materially from the *Charlie Hebdo* shooting earlier in the year. According to the prevailing narrative, an insulting cartoon could be blamed for the *Hebdo* incident, much as an inflammatory video was conveniently blamed for the Benghazi attacks. Further, the *Hebdo* narrative went, the attacks were in France but not against France. That's what the international elites told themselves, anyway. The November attack was different. They were undeniably and indisputably an act of war by Muslim extremists against France itself.

The French people are not easily roused, but once attacked they are fierce and relentless. France's Socialist and usually milquetoast Pres. François Hollande immediately called the attacks what they were: an act of war. Soon, French warplanes were bombing ISIS targets in Syria. French police began to hunt the terrorists at home, of which they acknowledged there were likely hundreds. Americans instantly embraced the French with whom relations were not always so smooth. Pres. Obama offered his somber condolences and then insisted his policies were working as intended. 'Nough said.

Democrats held their second debate the next day, Saturday, November 14. Once again, held on a Saturday night to minimize viewership. Only an average of 8.5 million viewers watched, far fewer than watched the fourth Republican debate. Most striking of all, not once did any of the candidates on the stage refer to radical Muslims or Muslim terrorists. Political correctness is a real killer.

Otherwise, little came out of the second Democratic debate. Sanders was firmly Socialist, Clinton was firmly Clinton, and O'Malley was well-spoken and otherwise seemingly onstage just to give Clinton a hard time. Even so, the debate served to open a new theme on the Democratic side, a theme Ruth Marcus observed a few days later:

> Saturday's debate revealed this essential truth. The ideological gulf between Sanders and Clinton is as wide between two front-runners as in any Democratic campaign in decades. Sanders doesn't want to talk about her damn e-mails. He wants to talk about her damn worldview.[256]

Though Democrats fielded a smaller assortment, they were nevertheless a diverse lot. Whereas Clinton was a pragmatic bureaucrat politician, Sanders despite being a United States Senator was neither typical politician nor bureaucrat. As Marcus observed, "Sanders is an unabashed revolutionary." If Americans really wanted the second coming of Leon Trotsky, well, he was available.

A Sort of Cajun Bites the Dust

Louisiana Gov. Bobby Jindahl became the next Republican to drop out, announcing on November 17, citing fundraising difficulties and low poll numbers. In many election cycles, Jindahl might have made a formidable candidate—smart, articulate, experienced—but in this cycle he couldn't get noticed if he stood onstage naked. Unlike many of those who remained, at least he had the sense to get off the stage.

Unrelated but of passing interest, shortly thereafter Republican Louisiana Sen. John Vitter lost his bid to become the next governor, losing to Democrat and Louisiana House Minority Leader John Bel Edwards. Vitter had gone from prohibitive favorite to cast-off in just a few short months. In all likelihood, Vitter's vanquishing resulted more from some unfortunate past peccadillos than any statewide turn from Republican dominance.

Even so, Edwards's win raised a question. After Hurricane Katrina hit Louisiana a decade before, thousands of reliably Democrat-voting New Orleans voters fled, never to return. Without the New Orleans base of poor African American voters, the standing assumption was Louisiana would henceforth join the rest of the deep south as reliably Republican. Was Vitter a one-off? Or had something else changed to put the state in play in 2016?

Paris Echoes

In America, the consequences of the Paris attacks continued to reverberate for weeks. Pres. Obama put himself on the wrong side of public opinion, not to mention of many of his congressional allies, by insisting the United States could take in many thousands of Syrian refugees without worry that a fair number of ISIS and al-Qaeda terrorist operatives were amongst the new arrivals. As usual, Obama tried to claim the higher ground while belittling the opposition. It didn't work.

The Paris attacks reverberated through the campaign, as well. Donald Trump found new ways to probe the extremes of American political tolerance, first suggesting the creation of a database for suspicious Muslims already in the country and then repeating a claim he'd made in years past that he'd personally witnessed Muslims in Jersey City, New Jersey, celebrate by the thousands the attacks on 9/11. (It should be noted no evidence was ever uncovered to support this claim.)

Even Hillary Clinton found she had to muscle up her foreign policy statements to avoid sounding Obama like. Now on the defensive, Obama began to assert all the decisive events that needed to occur, like cutting off ISIS financing, destroying its leadership, and so on, as though he'd just awoken from a three-year slumber. The tougher Obama sounded, despite years of minimalist light-touch policies, the more he sounded like Clinton, while she was desperate to sound tougher than Obama, moving her ever closer to the Republicans. Life was never easy on the Hillary Clinton bandwagon.

Taking Stock at Thanksgiving

The Thanksgiving holiday marked a natural end to this stage of the campaign. For the month between Thanksgiving and Christmas, campaigns typically struggle for attention as the nation focuses on turkey, shopping, and the buildup toward the holidays. College football season was coming to a head leading to the various Bowl games; and the NFL was building toward the playoffs.

Thanksgiving therefore provided a good opportunity to take stock. Trump continued to lead the Republican parade with 32%.[257] Trump had shown signs of trailing off until the Paris attacks, but then his strong inflammatory rhetoric juxtaposed to Obama's limp condescension caught hold, and Trump regained his mojo.

Ironically, ISIS may have saved Trump's campaign, whose recovery of momentum came mostly at Carson's expense. At nearly 22%, Carson remained in second place; but he was down from nearly 25% a couple weeks prior. While Carson's approach to the terrorists was stronger than Obama's, Carson's tone was far too meek to allow him to match Trump's ferocity.

The rest of the slate continued much as it had for weeks. However, when asked who they liked as a second choice, relatively few respondents chose either Trump or Carson as their second favorite. Here, Rubio came in first with Cruz also picking up some support.

	First Choice	Second Choice
Trump	32%	13%
Carson	22%	16%
Rubio	11%	17%
Cruz	8%	12%
Bush	6%	9%
Fiorina	4%	3%
Huckabee	3%	6%
Kasich	3%	2%
Paul	3%	5%
Christie	2%	7%
Graham	1%	<0.5%
Santorum	1%	1%
Pataki	<0.5%	<0.5%
Other/No Opinion	5%	7%

The poll also confirmed the inescapable reality the Bush campaign simply wasn't catching fire. Bush just couldn't compete against the language, tone, and firmness of Rubio and Cruz vying to become the leading Trump alternative. He might make a solid executive; but in 2015, Bush failed as a national candidate. Bush, like many of the trailers, hoped for lightning to strike in Iowa or New Hampshire. The state polling, however, was anything but promising.

The RealClearPolitics (RCP) average of Iowa polls closely proxied the national figures except Ted Cruz did somewhat better in Iowa than nationally, likely reflecting the powerful influence of the evangelicals who had abandoned Mike Huckabee. In New Hampshire as in Iowa, Trump still held the lead; but in New Hampshire, Carson was in fourth behind Rubio and Cruz. In all cases, Bush was among the also-rans.

	Iowa	**New Hampshire**
Trump	25.7%	26.6%
Carson	21.0%	9.8%
Rubio	11.3%	12.0%
Cruz	15.3%	10.0%
Bush	5.0%	7.6%
Fiorina	4.3%	4.2%
Huckabee	3.0%	1.0%
Kasich	1.7%	7.2%
Paul	2.0%	4.4%
Christie	2.7%	5.8%
Graham	0.7%	0.8%
Santorum	1.3%	0.6%
Pataki	0.0%	0.2%

The state of the Democratic nomination was strikingly different. Clinton held a commanding lead over Sanders in the national polls, about 56% to 32%, with O'Malley hanging on in low single digits, figures that were closely matched in Iowa. Only in New Hampshire was Sanders showing any real sign of viability, trailing Clinton about 46% to 38% according to RCP. Absent an FBI indictment or some similar catastrophe, the Democrats seemed sure to be fronted by Hillary Clinton, like it or not. But the race was still young, and much would change.

CHAPTER 10
THE IOWA RUN-UP

Candidates talk a lot. They give speeches, visit with voters, take interviews ad nauseam, every opportunity a chance to say something amiss, knowing that anything they say can and will be used against them by the media and their opponents. Campaign staff are typically on full alert to "clarify" the little mistakes while praying major no-nos go unnoticed. Not Donald Trump.

Trump made so many easily disproven assertions his opponents, and the media largely gave up pointing them out. Amazingly, Trump's supporters didn't care. Just as Hillary Clinton's supporters apparently didn't care whether she told them the truth, Trump's supporters only seemed to care that he was as angry as they were.

Even so, some of Trump's more interesting "misstatements" early in the campaign bear noting if only for their comical factor. The *National Journal* provided a useful listing:

- Trump claimed his Boeing 757 was "bigger than Air Force One, which is a step down from this in every way." Except, of course, *Air Force One* is a 747, which is fifty feet longer and has a maximum takeoff weight three times greater.
- Trump claimed, "Our president wants to take in 250,000 [refugees] from Syria," except the actual figure was 10,000.

- Trump suggested China would ultimately be the largest beneficiary of the Trans-Pacific Partnership (TPP). Trouble was, China wasn't a party to the TPP. China reasonably saw the TPP as an effort by its neighbors to fence China in.
- During the October 2015 debate in Boulder, Trump was asked why he referred to Sen. Rubio as Facebook co-founder Mark Zuckerberg's "personal senator" to which Trump insisted, "I never said that. I never said that." Except the observation and the language tying Rubio and Zuckerberg together came from Trump's own website.[258]

The operating theory, and the prayer on his opponents' lips, remained that Trump had gotten into the race on a lark, for a little fun and to build his brand, which meant Trump needed a convenient exit without looking like a loser. His excuse for quitting the race had to be built on some slight or unfairness he could then cite ever more. Yet as Thanksgiving came and went, his opponents failed to land a glove and circumstances provided no convenient excuse. On the contrary, Trump's campaign morphed from lark to the real deal. Likely to his own amazement, voters continued to take him seriously—and he loved it. Exit strategy? Fuhgedaboutit.

An Angry Nation

America was mostly at peace in the sense the U.S. military was not engaged in full-scale war a la Afghanistan or Iraq. The U.S. economy was doing reasonably well in that businesses were creating jobs. Yet the country was unsettled, and it was deeply angry.

Blacks were angry at whites for abuses, real and perceived, from the police and more broadly from (white) society at large. They had substantial cause to be angry given events such as occurred in Chicago where a young black man high on PCP and sporting a short knife was shot by a poorly trained white police officer sixteen times—fifteen times after the man was on the ground—or in Baltimore where six black and white cops threw a black man into a van without a seatbelt so he subsequently suffered a fatal injury. And these were just the stories that got headlines.

Whites were angry at blacks who blamed whites who, for the most part, had no more prejudice than any other race yet were subject to ceaseless insults by blacks whose urban culture prized violence and promiscuity and eschewed personal responsibility. Police shootings gave rise to the Black Lives Matter movement, which became incensed when anyone mentioned all lives mattered, thus reinforcing the sense that racism flowed effortlessly in both directions. The Black Lives Matter movement and the entire national black leadership establishment refused even to acknowledge blacks were murdering blacks by the dozen across the country every month.

American workers were angry at seeing their wages languish for years on end and their kids having few opportunities when they graduated from high school or from college with enormous debts. American businesses were angry at the government for steadily improving its expertise in obstructing simple commerce in ever more inane and irritating ways.

Americans collectively were angry at the rest of the world for always blaming America for the world's ills and then turning to America for help every time there was a problem too great for their feeble resources or resolve. Many were angry at Pres. Obama for making abject apologies to foreign tin pots a central pillar of his foreign policy.

Progressives were angry Barack Obama had done in their eyes next to nothing to advance the progressive agenda despite his victories on Obamacare, gay marriage, an epic flood of regulations, and a more progressive tax system. And they remained highly discontented the big Wall Street banks had faced only modest punishment for the major mistakes leading to the 2008–2009 financial crisis and none of the top financial leaders had gone to jail.

Conservatives and libertarians were angry at the rapid growth in government intrusiveness; in short, they were angry at all Obama had accomplished. Conservatives were also growing in fury at the inability of their own leadership to rack up any positive accomplishments of their own, ignoring that political accomplishments required political power, which still resided substantially with the president.

In summary, Americans were angry because they were unsettled, often scared, at a nation they saw adrift at home and abroad, culturally and economically. Their anger had little to do with ideology. At his weakest, Bill Clinton presented a stronger national leader than Barack Obama was for most his presidency. The nation, indeed the world, sensed Obama's fundamental weaknesses as a leader. The bolder of the nation's enemies around the world took full advantage, leaders like Russia's Pres. Putin and China's Chairman Xi. That's how it goes in the real world.

Donald Trump's persistent strength, and to a lesser extent that of Ted Cruz, and Bernie Sanders could be seen largely as response to this anger and worry. Trump and Sanders embodied and channeled the anger unfiltered. Cruz appealed more to the inherently conservative while channeling anger like Trump.

Nothing highlighted the nation's ill ease more than the president's limp, misguided response to the mass shootings in San Bernardino, California, in early December of 2015. Mass shootings were becoming commonplace, most often by angry individuals acting alone with no more agenda than to lash out. Shootings like the October 2015 Umpqua Community College episode in Roseburg, Oregon, where a mentally unstable mixed-race American fatally shot nine people and wounded nine others before committing suicide. Then there was the mass shooting by another half-deranged hillbilly at a Planned Parenthood clinic in Colorado Springs, Colorado, November 27. These were all terrible events but hardly unusual. There has always been violence in the United States and around the world, even in oh-so-civilized Western Europe, to say nothing of Latin and South America and Africa.

The San Bernardino shooting was different. An American citizen, Syed Farook, born in Chicago, moved to California. He went and found a wife, Tashfeen Malik, in Pakistan. He brought her back to the United States, had a baby girl, and became a terrorist, possibly under Malik's influence. Apparently acting as "lone wolves" in the name of but not directed by ISIS, they planned a devastating attack, including pipe bombs and a remote-controlled bomb. This was no spontaneous burst of anger. This was a premeditated terrorist attack.

On December 2, the couple dropped off their baby girl with her grandmother and went on a rampage, killing fourteen people, wounding twenty-one. Nor was this intended as a suicide attack. The killers wore masks. They hoped to kill and run, probably to kill again; and they nearly got away with it. Four hours after the attack, police caught up with their SUV and killed them both in a modern-day version of the bloody end of Bonnie and Clyde.

Three weeks earlier in Paris, terrorists struck in a coordinated attack, killing 128 people. France's bland, traditionally Pacifist, Socialist Pres. François Hollande immediately observed that France was at war with ISIS. And he acted, decisively, at home and abroad. Très bien, monsieur.

Pres. Obama's response to San Bernardino? After calling for prayers for the victims and their families, the president gave a determined Oval Office address, calling for gun control. The nation yawned. Terrorists strike at home, and the president's response is to disarm Americans. ISIS probably couldn't believe its good luck.

Farook and Malik used common handguns and common low-caliber rifles, all bought perfectly legally. Aside from depriving all Americans of their Second Amendment rights, exactly what gun control did the president have in mind that would have stopped San Bernardino? He didn't say. Nor could he, because every American understood the president was just blowing smoke. Unspecified, irrelevant "gun control" was his "go to," his comfort zone anytime real decisions were needed potentially at odds with his curious worldview.

At the same time, the Middle East refugee problem rapidly grew. Western leaders, most especially Germany's chancellor Angela Merkel, gave a ray of hope to these mostly desperate people just trying to survive and protect their families. Refugees by the tens of thousands set out in pursuit of this faint and flickering ray of hope from homes they deemed utterly hopeless.

Seeking to play his part, Pres. Obama insisted the United States take in a large number of these refugees. A fine humanitarian gesture, but for the United States and Germany and the rest, exactly how would one screen these individuals to make sure ISIS or al-Qaeda–influenced terrorists were not among them? Importing a small army of ISIS terrorists is a strange way to fight ISIS.

The vast majority of these poor souls were utterly unknown to the United States government and little known officially in their own war-ravaged countries, some of which like Syria were enemies of the United States and thus unlikely to share what little information they had. Even many senior Democrats in Congress worried. How could one make sure today's hopeful, thankful refugee from Syria wouldn't later become a terrorist as some radical cleric fanned the flames of religious fervor or personal discontent? Remember, Syed Farook was born and raised in Chicago.

One of the simplest rules of war asserts it is better to fight the war in the opposition's backyard than your own. The American people understood Pres. Obama's humanitarian gesture risked American lives at home by allowing future terrorists to enter the country with a gold-embossed invitation.

So many reasons for Americans to be angry, bringing the discussion back to the topic at hand. This anger would play out in the coming campaign, providing a potent political energy to Republicans able to focus the anger on the president and his party and a huge challenge to the Socialist and especially the former Obama secretary of state who hoped to follow in Obama's footsteps without becoming trapped by Obama's legacy.

INTO THE NEXT DEBATES

In early December, the Republican establishment made it official: they were scared. Not scared of the Democrats who looked primed for defeat but scared of Donald Trump and, to a lesser extent, Ted Cruz. Nor was it just a matter of losing the presidential election but more the enormous damage either man at the top of the ticket could do to downstream voting—Senate, House, and state races. Republicans were establishing themselves as the nation's dominant political party, but it seemed Trump or Cruz could do as much damage as did Richard Nixon fifty years prior.

The establishment let it be known they were reviewing the processes of a "contested convention." If they couldn't beat Trump and Cruz head-on, they would beat them at the Republican convention in Cleveland with political shenanigans. In the eyes of most lifelong Republicans, a contested convention meant limiting the damage in November. A contested convention also likely meant the eventual nominee was toast.

Surprisingly, at first Trump took this talk about a contested convention in good stride. His confidence in his own superiority was such he presumed he would come into the convention with so many delegates the party wouldn't dare deny him, which, of course, turned out to be true.

In truth, Trump was doing very well. In national polls, his scores had jumped from about 25% prior to Thanksgiving to 38%.[259] Trump milked the anti-Muslim/anti-terrorist sentiment for all it was worth, often mixing in tellingly biting statements about Obama's ineptitude along with his usual bluster about all the "smart" and "strong" and "hyuge" things Trump would do.[260]

Trump repeatedly pushed the envelope of what might be acceptable. Millions of American voters just lapped it up. Compared with the namby-pamby Republicans running on nuance and reasonableness (Jeb Bush), Trump captured the anger building up in large swathes of the country.

Even as Trump rose, Ben Carson's support largely collapsed (down from 25% to about 12%), with his support largely flowing to Trump, Cruz, or, to a lesser extent, Marco Rubio. Then there was Jeb Bush, whose support had dipped from the low 6% range to about 3% despite spending nearly $50 million in 2015.[261] Perhaps never before has so much been spent on a political campaign for so little accomplished. Bush still had an enormous war chest. It didn't matter. He had only one useful task left in this campaign, and that was to dedicate all his resources to take out Donald Trump and, if necessary, Ted Cruz. Bush failed at that too.

Iowa polls painted a somewhat different picture than the national polls. In Iowa, Carson's collapse perfectly mirrored the rapid rise of Cruz's support, so Cruz either topped or tied Trump in Iowa in the low thirties or high twenties, with Rubio coming in a distant third with around 14%. The New Hampshire polls more closely mirrored the national polls, with Trump in a commanding lead at 27%, followed by a three-way tie of Rubio, Christie, and Cruz at around 11%.

The December 15 debate in Las Vegas centered on foreign policy and national security. It was a heated affair. Trump said he wanted to "carpet bomb" ISIS, though he obviously had no idea what "carpet bomb" meant or care.[262] In no previous debate was Trump's shallow understanding of issues and facts more apparent. He suffered repeated exposure most especially by Bush, so much so Trump became flustered and pissed. Utterly lacking in substantive responses, Trump fell back on his usual insults and dismissals, to which Bush responded with the most notable line of the night, "You can't insult your way to the presidency." Or maybe he could.

The third debate also produced a pitched battle between Cruz and Rubio on immigration. As a member of the original 2013 immigration reform gang, Rubio had badly miscalculated and later admitted same at the annual American Conservative Union shindig. But with building anti-immigration sentiment further inflamed by Trump, the dial had moved much more toward Cruz's extreme position, leaving Rubio deeply vulnerable regarding past decisions and any residual ambiguities.

Both men threw punches, and both men took hits; but on balance, Cruz definitely came out the winner as his absolute anti-amnesty positions were more in line with the times. Both benefited, in one respect, however: for a few days Cruz and Rubio were the story, not Trump.

The Speaker Speaks

While the debate captured the headlines, House Speaker Paul Ryan's announcement that night probably meant more to the upcoming election: Congress had a budget deal covering spending for 2016, a tax bill addressing a long list of relatively minor issues and addressing a variety of other issues most notably including lifting the ban on U.S. petroleum exports.[263] This meant Congress would have relatively little to do in 2016, suggesting there should be relatively few opportunities for congressional action, read: Republican miscalculations to affect the upcoming presidential campaign.

Ryan and Senate Majority Leader Mitch McConnell knew this budget would require Democrat votes to pass the House and Senate; and of course, the president would have to sign it. All of which meant a multitude of compromises all around, all of which meant nobody was going to be very happy with the final product. Important legislation often requires legislators to use two hands while voting: one hand raised in support, the other hand holding their noses. This was no exception.

The budget legislation also meant, not coincidentally, congressmen and those senators up for reelection could mostly concentrate on their reelection campaigns without being unduly interrupted by the various duties normally associated with legislating and overseeing the federal government.

The Democrats Debate Again. Anyone Notice?

Democrats held their third debate on Saturday, December 20, in Manchester, New Hampshire. One could scarcely choose a better time to minimize the audience size, which was again obviously the intent of the Clinton campaign and its Democratic Party establishment protectors. In this, at least, they succeeded as only about a third as many viewers watched the Democrat's New Hampshire debate as watched the Republican debate.

Stoked by a combination of real events (San Bernardino, the Syrian civil war, etc.) and Trump's rhetoric, the imperative of defeating ISIS had unexpectedly taken center stage in the national debate. In every notable aspect but one, Pres. Obama's strategy seemed to be failing miserably. With Russia fully engaged in Syria against ISIS, Putin simultaneously directed his forces to punish ISIS and the U.S.'s minimally supported rebel alliance against Syria's President, Bashar al-Assad. Putin also muscled the United States out of its leadership role in the region as the United States once again focused on ineffectual training of various splinter combatants while providing material support that often ended up in the hands of the enemy.

Closer to home, Obama's intentions of welcoming tens of thousands of Muslim refugees, but only after they had been "carefully screened," crashed against the facts regarding the two terrorists in San Bernardino. The evidence showed both Malik and Farook had been radicalized long before the attacks; that their inclinations were open for all to see in their online communications and in their U.S. Muslim community; and that the wife, Malik, had come to the United States on a "fiancé" visa and had passed through the various U.S. security checks unnoticed.

No screening system could ensure these terrorists were kept out, if only because the terrorists worked hard to remain unnoticed and documentation was inherently sketchy from that part of the world. No one could guarantee Muslims coming into the country would subsequently not be radicalized through online contacts, in their U.S. communities, or perhaps as a result of simple disillusionment with their personal circumstances.

What aspect of Obama's strategy was succeeding? Minimizing the use of U.S. ground forces to buttress local forces in the various hotspots. After long wars in Afghanistan and Iraq, America's appetite for renewed ground combat was nearly nil.

Taking Stock for Christmas

Heading into Christmas, as Iowa and New Hampshire drew nigh, polls in these states easily eclipsed national polls in importance.

	Iowa[264]	New Hampshire[265]
Trump	31	32
Cruz	40	14
Rubio	12	13
Carson	6	5
Christie	1	11
Bush	2	6
The rest	<2	<5

Riding support from evangelicals, support steadily abandoning Ben Carson, Ted Cruz momentarily took the lead in Iowa. Cruz's success surprised all the more because he alone among the major contenders of either party had been brave enough to oppose the federal government's subsidies for ethanol production, essentially the corn lobby's own special welfare program. Cruz had also taken a commanding hold of the most hard-right elements of the Tea Party movement in Iowa. In contrast, while Donald Trump trailed a bit in Iowa, he continued to dominate in New Hampshire.

Marco Rubio managed a respectable third in both Iowa and New Hampshire polling, meaning he would remain a fully viable candidate. Rubio had been a Tea Party favorite until his 2013 immigration reform boo-boo, but he was less radical right than Cruz. Rubio was also the leading candidate appealing to both the conservative base and the Republican establishment.

Even so, Rubio just wasn't catching fire. Sure, Jeb Bush was still in the race, as were a handful of also-rans; yet only Rubio offered a viable, clear alternative for a broadly acceptable nominee. Yet Rubio's performance clearly lagged, his weak performance demanding an explanation. On December 21, the *Washington Post* provided, Rubio was less than fully engaged.

The *WaPo* narrative: Rubio wanted to be president but seemed unwilling to do the day-to-day campaign grind necessary to win it. It wasn't just the *WaPo* making this claim. Typical of the quoted remarks in the story was this from Al Phillips, a Rubio backer in South Carolina, "Rubio has not put in the face time that he really needs to have, I don't think."[266]

The alternative less dramatic explanation was Rubio was stalking the field, the way a racehorse hangs back through the first turn and down the backstretch. Rubio spent enough time and energy in Iowa and New Hampshire to remain top tier; but with so many candidates and so many wildcards, the race was sure to prove a marathon, not a sprint. Rubio could husband his resources, wait for the also-rans to drop out, pick up their support, and then battle it out down the road. A good theory, if he could pull it off.

In contrast, of the also-rans Chris Christie was almost invisible in Iowa but could score well enough in New Hampshire to remain viable. After that, Christie's campaign was built on a single premise: to win, one had to survive.

Jeb Bush, on the other hand, could see the end of the line if he bothered to look. America showed that for all the whining about money in politics, even the vastest sums are no substitute for a viable candidate.

On the Democratic side, while Martin O'Malley was barely a footnote, Bernie Sanders was quickly making life miserable for Hillary Clinton. The coronation had been put on hold again. Sanders surged and could take both early states, forcing Clinton to rely on money and campaign organization to win an unexpected war of attrition. The parallels to 2008 and her contest with another radical leftist, Barack Obama, were striking.

	Iowa[267]	New Hampshire[268]
Clinton	50	42
Sanders	45	56
O'Malley	4	4

Rubio Tacks to Attack

Immigration remained a sore point between Rubio and Cruz for days after the debate. Rubio knew he had a problem due to his role in the 2013 immigration reform; and thus far, no explanation had defused the problem. Cruz knew he had the advantage, and he never let up. Rubio's response was to go on the attack and in so doing made a grave tactical error.

Cruz led the opposition during the 2013 Senate immigration reform debate. During the debate, Cruz offered the pivotal amendment to remove language from the underlying bill allowing illegal immigrants a path to citizenship but allowing them legal status. Cruz knew his amendment was a poison pill for the bill, which would fail if his amendment passed. He also knew substantial support existed for allowing illegals to remain in the country without citizenship; mass deportations were inconceivable for most people not named Trump.

During the 2013 debate, Cruz suggested he wanted the bill to pass if only his amendment passed. Reasonable people could doubt his sincerity, but he insisted. Cruz made an "all in" bet his amendment would kill the bill; but to be credible, he needed to assure his colleagues he was not against the bill, just this one aspect. On budgetary matters, Cruz's history of tactical decisions was abysmal; but on this occasion, his approach, given his objective, was brilliant. He succeeded: the amendment passed; the bill died.

Two years later during the Republicans' 2015 Las Vegas debate and in the days following, Rubio sought to neutralize Cruz's advantage on immigration by quoting Cruz's own words from the 2013 debate. For example, during the 2013 debate, Cruz had said, "So I would encourage everyone on this committee to roll up our sleeves and fix the problem in a humane way . . . allowing as this bill does a legal status for those who are here illegally."[269]

Was Cruz playing a game in 2013, or did he really support a path to legalization for illegal immigrants? This was a "he said/she said" moment between Rubio and Cruz, with Rubio quoting Cruz's words during the debate and Cruz insisting he had only been trying to defeat the bill.

Alabama Sen. Jeff Sessions, perhaps the Senate Republicans' staunchest anti-amnesty warrior, set the record straight. After recounting the enormous political forces pushing the immigration bill forward, Sessions said, "It was that close to being passed . . . and I think I can say this with integrity. Without the vigorous opposition of Ted Cruz, this bill would have passed."[270]

Rubio accused Cruz of being soft on illegal aliens when Rubio himself had been at the center of the bill's original drafting and voted to support the bill while Cruz had led the opposition. True, Rubio later recanted, but even so his attacks on Cruz's role during the immigration debate reeked of smear politics and hypocrisy. Rubio had intentionally and knowingly mischaracterized Cruz's role. Rubio looked like just another phony Washington politician, and it cost him dearly with conservatives. "Here's the difference between Rubio and Cruz. One of them was in the gang of eight. One of them wasn't. Got it?"[271]

Rubio had drawn attention to his most exposed flank while drawing attention to his opposition's strength. Not smart. He continued this theme by repeatedly arguing Cruz had voted to cut defense spending, the issue involving another one of those moments in the U.S. Senate where votes are easily misconstrued. Attacking Cruz as weak on immigration or defense spending didn't fly. It made Rubio look small.

The National Picture

At this time, Iowa and New Hampshire polls were most significant because they showed how voters were reacting in states getting the most attention from the candidates, yet national polls reflected the broader campaign narrative. A national poll released December 22 showed Cruz with 24%, catching up to Trump at 28%, while Rubio and Carson occupied the second tier at 12% and 10%, respectively.[272] On the Democratic side, Clinton led Sanders two to one, with O'Malley continuing as a footnote.

Trump and Clinton had a lot in common. For example, 58% of those polled said they thought Trump was "not honest and trustworthy" whereas 59% said the same of Clinton. Similarly, 61% said Trump "did not share their values" whereas 55% said the same of Clinton.

Among Republicans, Trump led with 28% as the candidate self-identified Republicans would definitely not support, Bush came in second on this list at 24%, while the rest varied between 5 and 14%. Curiously, while almost three Democratic voters in five found Clinton not honest and trustworthy, only 8% said they would definitely not vote for her.

Among Republicans, Cruz had the highest net favorability rating in December at 61%, with Rubio close behind at 56%. Trump had a net rating about half these figures at 33% while Bush had the worst net rating at minus 15%. Among Democrats, Clinton and Sanders both did better than all the Republicans at 69% and 61%, respectively.

A very different picture emerged among all voters. Considering Republicans, Democrats, and independent registered voters, Rubio and Sanders led with net positive ratings of 9% each. Cruz came in third at 2%. And what of Clinton and Trump? Minus 8% and minus 26%, respectively. Bush led with a minus 28%. Time to go now, Jeb.

Bye-Bye, Lindsey, We Hardly Knew You

On December 21, enigmatic South Carolina Sen. Lindsey Graham gave up the campaign ghost. Graham, a thoroughly decent if peculiar fellow, still believed he was right but acknowledged his message of intensive global interventionism clashed with the times. Americans were tired of playing global cop. Jihadist terrorism was a global problem. It afflicted Russia and China internally. It poisoned the Middle East. It threatened wide swathes of the Pacific basin and Europe as much as it did the United States. The era wherein the world could rely on the United States to lead in every crisis and to shoulder the greatest burden, if not over, was at least suspended.

Why end the campaign now? Graham's campaign was doing no worse or better than it had for months. His ratings were no worse than those of a handful of other candidates. Candidates end their campaigns in defeat at the polls or beforehand for lack of funds or out of sheer boredom. In Graham's case, the answer seemed to be the latter. Amazingly enough, Lindsey Graham seemed to tire, if only momentarily, of telling other people what he thought.

Obama the Almost Invisible

With only an occasional exception, Pres. Obama stayed largely invisible through much of this part of the campaign. Of course, Republicans hammered him and his policies while Democrats danced around both, but the president himself remained largely a nonfactor. Heading into Christmas, a couple events merit mention regarding his diminished influence.

At the urging of the United States, the United Nations Security Council on December 18 passed a resolution demanding "all parties immediately cease any attacks against civilians and civilian objects." As a member of the Security Council, Russia voted in favor of the resolution. Forty-eight hours later, Russia carried out six or more airstrikes against civilian targets in northern Syria, with forty-three confirmed dead.[273] Russian Pres. Putin made very clear what he thought of the United Nations.

To be sure, U.N. Security Resolutions are commonly not worth the hot air with which they are debated. Yet Putin's blow was extraordinary, even by U.N. standards, and by Russia's standards for dismissiveness toward Pres. Obama who had worked to secure the resolution.

On a related front, Obama considered his negotiation ending the Iran sanctions one of his legacy accomplishments. So how was it going? In October, in a blatant violation of the agreement, Iran test-fired a medium-range missile capable of carrying a nuclear warhead.[274] When the Obama administration failed to respond, the Iranians ran a second test in November—again, no response. The State Department's front man on these matters, Steve Mull, testified, "We are now actively considering the appropriate consequences to that launch in October."[275] The Iranians surely were quaking in their boots.

As per tradition, Pres. Obama gave a set of interviews toward year-end seeking to shape the narrative as to how he and the nation fared. The facts being no longer deniable, Obama in a radio interview observed, "Blue-collar men have had a lot of trouble in this new economy," and then he flew off to his winter vacation in Hawaii.[276] The president's economic policies had largely failed America's middle class, and even he couldn't deny it.

THE WAPO STOOPS TO A NEW LOW

The *Washington Post* is the leading political newspaper in the country. Call it home-court advantage. It has also been known in some circles as the Washington Pest or the Washington Worst. Its support for Democrats and liberal causes is as reliable as the sunrise, only endorsing Republicans for office when there seemed no practical alternative. The *WaPo* also carries some conservative columnists like George Will and Charles Krauthammer, thus taking at least an occasional stab at neutrality. Sometimes, though, the *Post* just can't contain its biases.

The *WaPo* couldn't stand Donald Trump, but it also couldn't take him seriously. To the *Post*, it was simply inconceivable Republicans would nominate Trump in the same way it was inconceivable for a person to jump into the air and fly to the moon.

Ted Cruz was another matter. The *Post* would be perfectly happy with Cruz as the Republican nominee if only because the *Post*'s leadership would be reasonably certain he would lose to any reasonable Democrat, even Hillary Clinton. Reasonably certain is not absolutely certain, which made the *Post* more than a little nervous, which allowed an outrageous cartoon showing Cruz dressed up as Santa Claus with an organ grinder and his two daughters depicted as monkeys on a leash also dressed in Christmas garb.

The reaction to the *Post*'s despicable cartoon was instantaneous and fierce. The paper quickly pulled the cartoon. With an apology? No. Did anyone get fired? No. Was the paper sorry? What do you think?

BILL IS FAIR GAME

Despite her service as secretary of state under Obama and previously as New York Senator, the biggest item on Hillary Clinton's résumé remained being the wife of former Pres. Bill Clinton. In part because he had been careful to limit his public exposure, Bill Clinton had remained arguably the nation's top politician even after almost sixteen years out of office. Many argued if he ran for a third term in 2016, then he would likely win. Too many voters knew nothing of Bill Clinton's many scandals, and his media spin machine had worked too well for too long for the scandals to matter much.

Bill Clinton hovered in the background of the campaign, the ever-ready secret weapon to be used when and as needed. Only Hillary Clinton could effectively blunt Bill's effectiveness, and only Trump could call her on it. She did. He did. Even the fawning press had to admit it.

The great comedian Don Rickles specialized in the targeted insult. He would insult a person's looks, clothes, heritage, height, weight, or age. He would insult their intelligence by calling the target a "hockey puck," giving special inflection to the *p* in *puck* to make the point. He got away with it as comedy because he insulted everyone and meant not a word of it. His schtick was the cranky white guy with the crisp New York accent, and it was so obviously a schtick no one got angry. At the end, all he had to do was give that big bald head smile from ear to ear; and everyone knew it was all in good, clear fun.

Donald Trump, in a sense, was 2016's version of Don Rickles. He insulted anyone and everyone, from the outrageous mocking of a *New York Times* reporter with a disability to Hillary Clinton. In contrast to Rickles, however, Trump usually meant it; and so, as the *Washington Post*'s Ruth Marcus noted, Trump was "every 'ist' in the book."[277]

Trump's sexist comments toward Clinton, including a reference to her getting "schlonged" and to her "disgusting" bathroom break during the recent Democratic debate, were no worse than so much else he said. But then Clinton tried to play the sexist card on Trump and the victim card for herself. As she told the *Des Moines Register*, "It's not the first time he's demonstrated a penchant for sexism."[278]

To which Trump roared back in one of his signature tweets, "Hillary Clinton has announced she is letting her husband out to campaign, but HE'S DEMONSTRATED A PENCHANT FOR SEXISM, so inappropriate."

He followed quickly with another tweet, "If Hillary thinks she can unleash her husband with his terrible record of women abuse while playing the women's card on me, she's wrong."

As Marcus observed, "'Sexism' isn't the precise word for [Bill Clinton's] predatory behavior toward women or his inexcusable relationship with a 22-year-old intern. Yet in the larger scheme of things, Bill Clinton's conduct toward women is far worse than any of the offensive things that Trump has said. . . . Clinton has preyed on [women], and in a workplace setting where he was by far the superior."

In one of the great inexplicable paradoxes of American politics, Bill Clinton was simultaneously a sordid sexual miscreant and yet even among women voters still a tremendous asset to the Clinton campaign. But publicly, any political environment involving sexism or women's issues destroyed his political value. At such times, he needed to stay out of the discussion. Hillary should have known this instinctively. She didn't, proving once again for all her strengths she was a poor politician. All it took was one person to make the point emphatically. Trump obliged, with delight.

Who Were These Trumpees?

At 2015's exhausted conclusion, the biggest political question in the land remained: who were these people supporting Donald Trump? Contrary to the prevailing narrative, they weren't predominantly Tea Party voters. An analysis by Civis Analytics suggested Trump supporters overwhelmingly lived in the eastern third of the country from Louisiana to Massachusetts, and far more were registered Democrats than registered Republicans.[279]

Trump did best in states like Louisiana and North Carolina and New York and worst in states like Minnesota, Colorado, and Washington. In the early voting states, Trump showed poorly in Iowa, well in New Hampshire, and fairly well in South Carolina.

Trump overall scored 33%, fairly uniform across the age of the respondent. He did somewhat better among men than women (36% to 33%). Despite his harsh views on immigration, 24% of Hispanic voters preferred Trump. The group with which he scored best? Registered Democrats—43%, compared with just 29% of registered Republicans.

The Civis Analytics data refuted the common narrative of three parallel contests—one a contest between Cruz and Trump for the Tea Party vote, a second among the more establishment-accepted candidates like Christie and Bush, and then a third between the winners of the first two. Rather, the contest was among the Tea

Party champion, Ted Cruz; the boisterous voice of disaffected but less ideological voters, Donald Trump; and everyone else collectively.

Happy New Year (?)

The new year started under subdued tones. The year 2015 had seen too many scandals, too many outrages, too many episodes of mass violence, and all with too little to cheer about to compensate. The U.S. economy had continued its slow and steady growth, the manufacturing sector in a mild recession, and 2016 seemed less of the same. The stock market ended the year much where it started, all of which left Americans uneasy about the future.

All of which showed up clearly as deep concern in two national indicators. Pres. Obama's job approval rating had fallen to about 44%. When asked whether the country was on the right track or the wrong track, about 25% said right track to about 65% wrong track. Bottom line, the terrain of the national mood suggested a fairly hostile environment for Democrats.

The Republican polls showed Donald Trump still leading, with Ted Cruz making a move, Marco Rubio hanging in, Jeb Bush barely hanging on, the rest waiting to exit. Bush's desperation became public as he redeployed his Miami-based staff mostly to New Hampshire while cancelling reserved ad buys in Iowa and South Carolina. New Hampshire was to be his breakout moment or his Alamo. It wasn't hard to predict which.

PS: Former New York Gov. George Pataki officially suspended his campaign on December 29, 2015, continuing the process of thinning the herd. Enough said.

CHAPTER 11
GIVE IOWA A CHANCE

Maria Jahn. For those who play political trivia, that's half the answer to the question, "How did Iowa come to kick off the voting in the presidential nomination process?"

Jahn had been a recorder for Plymouth County in northwest Iowa for thirty-eight years when she retired in 1975. Local Democratic leaders threw a party to celebrate her many years of public service. They needed a speaker and invited everyone they could think of. All said no, except an obscure former Georgia Governor.

Just how obscure was Jimmy Carter? When he appeared on the game show *What's My Line?* he stumped the panel, which failed to recognize him or discover he was a former governor. As George Will wrote, "When George Gallup drew up a list of 38 potential Democratic presidential candidates in 1975, Carter's name was not on the list."[280]

Eleven months later, Carter finished second behind "uncommitted" in the heretofore unremarkable Iowa caucuses and carried his runner-up status all the way to the White House. So the whole trivial pursuit answer is, "Maria Jahn and the peanut farmer."

A Nation Uneasy

As the college football season roared toward its big finale, the 2016 New Year's national championship game between Alabama and Clemson, the political season prepared for pre-season to give way to the Iowa caucuses. The rest of the country seemed otherwise preoccupied.

China's stock market suffered another collapse, quickly spreading to financial markets worldwide. What did it all mean for Americans? Nobody was really sure. Nor were they sure of the implications of the Federal Reserve's decision earlier in the month to raise a key interest rate.

Adding personal to economic insecurity, Islamic terrorists continued their lone-wolf attacks. A man claiming Syrian nationality passed himself off as an asylum seeker living in a German refugee camp, traveled to Paris, and attacked a police station with a butcher knife and wearing a fake explosives vest. Paris police shot him.[281]

A few days earlier in Cologne, Germany, more than one hundred German women and girls came forward describing horrific sexual assaults New Year's Eve near the city's main train station at the hands of men apparently from North Africa.[282] German police were, apparently, otherwise occupied.

In Philadelphia, Edward Archer charged a police cruiser firing a semi-automatic pistol, hitting officer Jesse Hartnett three times in the arm. Officer Hartnett got out of his car, chased Archer down the street, and eventually shot him in the butt. (Bravo! Hartnett.)

Archer was found a few moments later by other police officers, still holding the pistol with which he tried to "assassinate" Officer Hartnett.[283] Archer immediately announced his support for ISIS. Meanwhile, Pres. Obama insisted his policy of mass immigration by Middle East asylum seekers would go forward.

All in all, the country was very uneasy. The economy had slowed markedly in the fourth quarter. While few thought a recession imminent, few expected an acceleration from 2015's tepid performance. All of which explained the persistent polls indicating about one in four Americans thought the country was going in the right direction and Obama's approval ratings persistently running around negative seven points.

Democrats were running in a very difficult environment. Pres. Obama was one of theirs. His policies weren't working. Yet they were proposing more of the same: more taxes, more spending, more regulation. But what else could they do? They were Democrats running further and further to the Left.

Nor could they take advantage of Obama's few legislative successes. Obamacare infused itself into the nation's health care system, yet Obamacare remained broadly unpopular. Its promises of reducing the ranks of the uninsured proved inflated. Its promises to restrain rising health care costs proved a joke.

Obama's administration had begun deporting mostly Hispanic families who'd recently come into the country illegally, gaining no cred from the anti-immigration hawks while stoking opposition in the community. And his one true victory in 2015, negotiating the Trans-Pacific Partnership, had inflamed opposition from the labor unions. Democrats were running away from Obama's policies and their consequences.

In contrast, the only trouble Republicans seemed to face involved figuring out which candidate could best take advantage of the veritable garden of plentiful attack lines to be used against Obama and whichever Democrat survived the primaries. But then the Republicans ran into formidable troubles of their own, starting with Donald Trump.

THE POLLS TO START THE YEAR

The end was coming quickly for former Maryland Gov. O'Malley, as for many of the Republicans who had campaigned for months to no avail. But for the front-runners, it was pucker time—time to scurry, react quickly, seize every opponent's every misstep, time to make an impression on voters, most of whom were only beginning to pay attention.

To start the year, Bernie Sanders threatened to upend Hillary Clinton's 2016 campaign just as had Barack Obama in 2008. Sanders was close enough in Iowa to believe an upset a possibility, and he led in New Hampshire. Spin this as they would, the Clinton campaign couldn't deny Sanders would carry a lot of momentum into the ensuing contests in Nevada and South Carolina. The presumption of inevitability was Clinton's strongest campaign asset. Take it away, and she might be in big trouble. If Republicans were afraid of what Trump or Cruz would do to their party, Democrats were equally nervous about what the Bern would do to theirs. But where Republicans aired their fears, party Democrats mostly hid in the dark, hoping somebody would shine a light and all their fears would come to naught.

Among the Republicans, though Donald Trump led nationally, Ted Cruz showed very well in Iowa and threatened an upset in New Hampshire. Marco Rubio, a more distant third, led the rest and appeared to be gaining strength; but the other wannabes were denying Rubio the majority of the "none of the above" vote and thus depriving him of the momentum he would need in the coming marathon.

The first two national polls to start the year hinted at an ongoing story: the questionable value of polls. Both polls had Sanders at 39% and O'Malley at about 2%. But one poll had Clinton's support at 54% while the other had Clinton at 43%—an eleven-point difference.

	National[284]	Iowa[285]	New Hampshire[286]
Clinton	48.5	48	43.3
Sanders	39.0	45	48.0
O'Malley	2.5	3	2.3

Voter intensity would be the big question for both Republicans and Democrats. It was easy to express a preference over the phone, but who would actually come out to vote? For Democrats, the likelihood of a sympathetic individual voting generally rises with union involvement and with the extent of the voter's enthusiasm. In Iowa, Clinton had the stronger institutional union support while Sanders had the clear edge in enthusiasm. On balance, Sanders would seem to have the edge, meaning polling results based on the wrong assumptions about voter mix would understate his actual vote total.

For Republicans, specific issues often drive voter intensity, which is why "evangelicals" are so powerful in Iowa, often handing the state to a candidate unlikely to win beyond Iowa. Trump's voters, on the other hand, were not your typical Republican voters. It was safe to bet Cruz's voters would come out in large numbers in Iowa, but would Trump's come out in numbers consistent with his polling strength? Many hoped not.

	National	**Iowa**	**New Hampshire**[287]
Trump	34.5	23.5	31.0
Cruz	19.0	27.5	10.5
Rubio	11.0	14.0	13.3
Carson	9.0	10.0	4.0
Bush	4.0	5.5	10.0
Christie	3.0	3.5	9.8
All others combined	8.0	11.0	23.0

HILLARY IN IOWA

Iowa just was never going to be a verdant field for Hillary Clinton to harvest votes. In public she was naturally standoffish, stiff, visibly calculating, almost robotic in her artificiality. When she spoke in public, she was pedestrian; and when she raised her voice to make a point, she came off shrill. As the campaign wore on, some of her outer shell thinned and she became more of a regular mensch; but early in Iowa, her poor retail qualities stood out painfully.

The rest of the country may resent Iowans' odd advantage as the first contest in the presidential marathon, but Americans can at least take comfort knowing Iowans take their responsibility seriously. As a candidate, they want to hear you, talk to you, and to do so repeatedly. This is small-scale retail campaigning at its best; and for Clinton, at its worst.

Clinton played best on the big stage, where the format and lighting and hoopla allow her to make a grand entrance, where teleprompters can carefully guide every carefully rehearsed utterance, where carefully selected supporters provide enthusiastic applause.

In 2008, Clinton came in third in Iowa after Illinois Sen. Barack Obama and former North Carolina Sen. John Edwards. Clinton had started as the prohibitive favorite with more money to spend than she knew how. As Clinton's 2008 Iowa campaign faltered under Obama's assault of positivism and personality, she famously (and reasonably) responded, "We all want change. Some people believe you bring it about by hoping for it. I believe you bring about change by working really, really hard for it."[288] And work hard she did as she did in every task she undertook. Whatever criticisms they want to throw at her, the Hillary haters can never fairly accuse her of sloth. But as a campaigner in 2008, she was simply outclassed; and so eight years later, she tried again.

Part of trying again was avoiding her previous unforced errors. Her 2008 "Hill-a-copter," a Bell 222 chartered so she could descend on county after county as if from heaven, was replaced in 2016 by a silly Scooby mobile. The likelihood of her again buying snow shovels to hand out to her supporters so they could get to the caucuses was probably pretty low. The snow shovels, a last-minute purchase in the campaign, shouted to Iowans, "I don't understand you, I'm not one of you." Memo to all candidates: Iowans know about snow and already have snow shovels. Don't insult their intelligence.

The snow-shovel episode and many of the other last-minute bizarre purchases of the Clinton 2008 campaign offered a substantive warning to any and all campaigns planning on a big bank account to get them through. Beyond a certain point, more money is irrelevant, and especially so toward the end of a campaign. A campaign can only effectively buy so many radio and TV ads, stuff the mailbox so many times, and irritate voters with so many robocalls. In economics, it's called the law of diminishing marginal returns. At some point, an additional TV ad gets you nothing. Beyond that, you're just irritating voters; and marginal supporters change their minds.

This is especially so toward the end of a campaign. As Karen Hicks, a senior advisor to Clinton's 2008 campaign, put it, "The reality is, the closer you get to an election day, the harder it is to spend money in a smart way."[289] To avoid wasting money or, worse, looking ridiculous, "you probably should stop spending." But they won't even if the impression given is of a snow job. In a candidate's eyes, and especially in the eyes of their professional campaign staff, losing a campaign with money in the bank is a cardinal sin.

Early on, most Republican candidates seemed to have a reticence about campaigning full-bore in Iowa. Strategically, this may have been wise. In Iowa, organization is king. This is retail politics at its most retaily. Also, Iowa was practically Scott Walker's home turf. Or, more accurately, it was once his home turf, which was nearly as good. Walker had lived in tiny Plainfield, Iowa, population 450, for seven years as a boy. Plainfield is in the upper northwest corner of Iowa, town motto "The heart of a rural community."

"It might sound trivial, but in Iowa politics, feeling comfortable with a candidate is paramount."[290] Walker "talks like we do," noted (former Iowa Republican Party Chairman) Matt Strawn. "He drinks the same beers we do. The most important thing to be successful in caucuses is, you need to be accessible and authentic. The last few caucus winners have been people Iowans found relatable." Many Republicans, and even some of the Democrats running, could do well on this list: comfortable, accessible, authentic, relatable. Clinton? Not so much.

Iowa First—Why?

Iowa had long strenuously defended its role as lead off. On its face, Iowa's position seems absurd—a small mostly rural almost entirely white state with a history of long-seated, highly capable legislators of wildly diverse perspectives. Ideologically, one could hardly find an odder pair than Sen.s Tom Harkin, ultra-progressive, and Chuck Grassley, moderate conservative; yet the two men served together for years.

To their credit, Iowans understood the importance of this contest for their state's economy, not just for the money spent during the campaign but for the powerful effect Iowa's role had on certain federal policies critical to Iowa, support for ethanol being just the most obvious example.

Iowa came first, but many followed. The complete list of states and their respective 2016 caucus and primary dates were as follows:

	Republican	**Democrat**
Alabama	March 1	March 1
Alaska	March 1	March 26
Arizona	March 22	March 22
Arkansas	March 1	March 1
California	June 7	June 7
Colorado	March 1	March 1
Connecticut	April 26	April 26
Delaware	April 26	April 26
DC	June 14	June 14
Florida	March 15	March 15
Georgia	March 1	March 1
Hawaii	March 8	March 8
Idaho	March 8	March 8
Illinois	March 15	March 15
Indiana	May 3	May 3
Iowa	February 1	February 1
Kansas	March 5	March 5
Kentucky	May 17	May 17
Louisiana	March 5	March 5
Maine	March 5	March 6
Maryland	April 26	April 26
Massachusetts	March 1	March 1
Michigan	March 8	March 8
Minnesota	March 1	March 1

Mississippi	March 8	March 8
Missouri	March 15	March 15
Montana	June 7	June 7
Nebraska	May 10	May 10
Nevada	February 20	February 20
New Hampshire	February 9	February 9
New Jersey	June 7	June 7
New Mexico	June 7	June 7
New York	April 19	April 19
North Carolina	March 15	March 15
North Dakota	June 7	June 7
Ohio	March 15	March 15
Oklahoma	March 1	March 1
Oregon	May 17	May 17
Pennsylvania	April 26	April 26
Rhode Island	April 26	April 26
South Carolina	February 20	February 20
South Dakota	June 7	June 7
Tennessee	March 1	March 1
Texas	March 1	March 1
Utah	March 22	March 22
Vermont	March 1	March 1
Virginia	March 1	March 1
Washington	April 5	March 26
West Virginia	May 10	May 10
Wisconsin	April 5	April 5
Wyoming	March 12	April 9

A Question of Balance

Who should have a voice in choosing a political party's nominee? The obvious answer would seem to be the party's established and recognized members. Imagine the mischief if Democrats were allowed to vote in Republican primaries, and vice versa. Oddly enough, in many states, that is permitted.

Take the question a step further by considering the following. If in the general election a state—Massachusetts, for example—was sure to go to the Democratic nominee, then should its votes count as much in the Republican nomination process as the votes from a state like Utah, which is equally certain to go for the Republican nominee? Should Massachusetts Republicans have a say in the nomination at all?

Or consider the reverse. Should Democrats in Utah have their voices count as much in choosing the Democratic Party's nominee as the voices in Massachusetts? Of course, the moral high ground is firmly occupied by those insisting all votes be counted and all votes weighted the same. But there is a practical side to the question, as well. The point of the exercise is to nominate a candidate who represents the party and can win. This isn't an academic pursuit, a poser for casual rumination. National politics is not a hobby.

Take the question a step further. Since states sure to go for one party or the other are not really contested by definition, and since elections are decided by swing states, shouldn't the Republican voters in swing states count the most in picking a Republican nominee, and shouldn't the Democratic voters in swing states count the most in picking a Democratic nominee? Is the foremost goal to reinforce the party's self-understanding or to win an election? Perhaps there is no right answer to these questions, but the possible answers go far in explaining the behavior of party leaders, and of voters, in the course of the contest.

In light of the timing of the caucuses and primaries, did these questions matter in practice? Iowa, the first state to vote, had gone for the Democratic nominee in five of the last six general elections prior to 2016. New Hampshire, the second state to vote, had gone for the Democratic nominee in, you guessed it, five of the last six elections.

Next up, South Carolina was reliably Republican; but then came Nevada, which had gone for the Democrats in four of the past six elections. After Nevada came twelve-state Super Tuesday, March 1, featuring an even balance of states, some of which were perfectly reliably Democratic supporting, some equally reliably Republican supporting, some trending Republican and some trending Democrat, and some just going back and forth.

Returning to Iowa, one may reasonably wonder if contributing to the Republican's modern habit of choosing poor flag bearers was that states that rarely vote Republican in the general election have an outsized influence on the nomination process by virtue of their front-end status. This, however, became a question more relevant for the future than to the present, because as the nomination process dragged on, memories and the influences of early states like Iowa and New Hampshire quickly faded.

Iowa in Portrait, Politically

As a political phenomenon, Iowa has its full complement of peculiarities. The map of electoral results from 2012 reveals one such. Most states closely follow a pattern whereby urban centers and rich suburbs vote Democratic, rural areas vote Republican, and the battle is joined over the swing non-rich suburbs. For example, in Maryland, Baltimore County and the rich DC suburb of Montgomery County and the largely African American DC suburb of Prince George's County are solidly Democrat while the rest of the state is solidly Republican. In Colorado, the Denver-Boulder axis appears an island of Democratic strength surrounded by an ocean of Republican conservatives. In part, Iowa follows this pattern as well, but Iowa also demonstrates an odd east/west split.

Iowa usually votes Democrat in presidential contests, but not always, and often by only slim margins. In 2012, Obama won with just 52.1%. Iowa's population projected at just over three million in 2016, a relatively small state by population, split almost exactly even between men and women. By race the population broke down as:

White	91%
Hispanic	4%
Black	2%
All other	3%

Iowa has ninety-nine counties. Polk, in the center of the state and dominated by the capital of Des Moines, is the largest by far with a population approaching a half million. The second-largest county is Linn on the eastern side, population just over two hundred thousand and the home of Cedar Rapids. The smallest county, Adams, boasted a population just under four thousand. Combined, Polk and Linn provided almost a third of the state's total voting population. The third-largest county by vote is Scott on the eastern edge of Iowa. Voting in Scott is roughly equal parts Republican and Democrat. In contrast, Johnson County in eastern Iowa and home to Iowa City is Iowa's fourth-largest by vote tallies yet typically provides Democrats a huge margin.

Not surprisingly, agriculture and related activities dominate the Iowa economy, though manufacturing plays a surprisingly large role according to the National Association of Manufacturers (NAM). NAM found that manufacturing accounted for 17.1% of state domestic product compared with Illinois, which one might think of as being relatively industrial, coming in at 14.1%, or Missouri with 13.1%.[291]

WHEN FRONT-RUNNERS GET NERVOUS

Toward mid-January the races tightened rapidly. The front-runners got nervous. Nervous front-runners heretofore smiling and friendly go on the attack.

Donald Trump was ill accustomed to losing. He was losing Iowa to Ted Cruz. New Hampshire was iffy. The Donald was not happy. But finding a way to knock Cruz off stride proved surprisingly difficult. On many of the hottest-button issues, like immigration, Cruz and Trump were in lock step. A few months before, they stood together on the steps of the U.S. Capitol like long-lost brothers.

Other issues, such as Cruz's opposition to ethanol subsidies or his strong faith, were regarded in conservative circles as strengths, not targets of Trumpian opportunity. Trump resorted to the "birther" maneuver. "Whether you like it or not, Ted has to figure it out. . . . you can't have the person who gets the nomination be sued."[292] Trump pointed to Cruz's father's Cuban heritage and emphasized Cruz was born in Canada. Most experts agreed Cruz met the Constitution's requirement to be a "natural-born citizen." But "most experts agreed" was not a definitive answer. Nor could there be one unless a court actually ruled. So for a time, the birther maneuver remained Trump's useful parry, one which he used repeatedly until he found one better, the "lyin' Ted" play.

Hillary Clinton likewise struggled mightily with her opposition. Bernie Sanders was closing fast in Iowa and stood to win New Hampshire decisively. Clinton responded by attacking Sanders on his position on guns. (Bernie would have preferred to repeal the Second Amendment altogether but couldn't advocate that position and win in mostly rural Vermont.) But in general, establishment Clinton attacking Socialist Sanders on being insufficiently progressive was always a stretch. Clinton had her own problems demonstrating, despite what she'd said all her life to the contrary, she was just as progressive as Sanders. Sanders appeared the candidate rank-and-file Democrats wanted; Clinton appeared the candidate they'd accept as the price of winning.

Obama's Last SOTU

On January 12, Pres. Obama gave his final State of the Union (SOTU) address, which could easily have been titled "It's not as bad as some people think." Not exactly an uplifting message.

The president started strong, observing he'd keep his remarks short because he knew many of the senators needed to get back to Iowa to campaign. Obama always did know how to deliver a punch line.

Defensive substance aside, the speech was well written; and Obama delivered it masterfully. Generally avoiding the typical laundry list of problems and proposals, he washed over broad themes, including a strong view along the lines of "people, we're better than this." Still, his off-note cheerleading was perhaps the most memorable aspect.

The president assured us we have the best-trained, most capable military in the world. He omitted that China was catching up quickly while the U.S. military's capabilities were eroding due to persistent overuse and underfunding.

He assured us the rest of the world calls the United States first whenever there's a problem in the world and then went on to describe all the ways in which the United States would not and should not get involved.

The president talked about the longest run of job creation in American history while ignoring that nearly 10% of Americans were either unemployed or underemployed and the steam seemed to be going out of the economy even from its tepid growth of recent years.

He talked about cutting the budget deficit by nearly three-fourths while ignoring it remained nearly a half trillion dollars, that the decline was only because he'd run such enormous budget deficits earlier in his term, and that the deficit was projected to rise back above a trillion dollars annually in just a few years under his policies.

Nikki Haley, the South Carolina Gov. born of Indian parentage, gave the Republican response though it was sometimes hard to watch because her teeth were impossibly white. White teeth aside, Haley cast a bright spotlight on two very different visions of America on display in the Republican Party: on the one side stood those believing in a positive, inclusive America; on the other stood those voicing intense anger and calling it policy.

Those in the latter camp responded quickly—and vehemently. Ann Coulter roared Trump should deport Haley for her views.

Quickly realizing she had gone too far even for the country's many rising radicals, Coulter quickly backtracked, "I was just kidding."[293] Right.

CHELSEA ON THE ATTACK

The Clinton campaign grew more desperate by the day. Bernie Sanders's fundraising ballooned, and his campaign's cost structure remained much smaller than Clinton's. Fund-raising isn't just about spending. It's also an indicator of interest by the party faithful, in many cases a much better indicator than poll results. Sanders was ascendant.

Hillary Clinton knew she couldn't let this continue. The campaign had a long way to go, but still it could be decided in the next few weeks if she didn't slow Sanders's momentum. The solution? Unleash Chelsea Clinton, especially to reach the younger voters flocking to Sanders's radicalism. Heretofore, Chelsea's main job had been to paint her mom as warm and friendly. Tough job, but she did it well.

On January 13 in New Hampshire, warm and friendly Chelsea morphed into attack-dog Chelsea. She ripped Sanders over his proposals on health care and college affordability, stunning Democratic observers. Since when had Chelsea become a policy expert on anything? Where'd she get her chops? The weakness was so obvious. Sanders deflected Chelsea's attack like a kindly old grandfather, "As much as I admire Chelsea, she didn't read the plan." She probably did read Sanders's plan. She just didn't understand it.

The Clinton people had rolled out Bill and found he'd lost the magic edge but retained the downsides Trump so easily highlighted. Hillary had now rolled out Chelsea, and her clumsy effort just made Sanders look good and the Clinton campaign look desperate. Realizing its mistake, the Clinton campaign quickly pivoted, "Her comments were spontaneous"—that is, not planned. Maybe. Wanna buy a bridge?

As if Hillary didn't have enough trouble with Bill, the Bern, her email scandal, her foundation scandal, etc., Hollywood chose this moment to pile on with *13 Hours: The Secret Soldiers of Benghazi*, a thriller of a true story about the six men who went to the U.S. Consulate in Benghazi like Davy Crockett leading his Tennesseans to the Alamo. This, of course, inflamed the debate once again about the Obama administration response to the murder of Americans in the consulate and Clinton's hotly disputed role in issuing a "stand down" order.

JANUARY 14 REPUBLICAN DEBATE—GLOVES OFF

The last debate prior to the Iowa caucuses proved exceedingly entertaining. It largely featured Trump, Cruz, Rubio, and Christie, though Bush, Carson, and Kasich were also in attendance. The top tier was getting very good at this. Trump proved the master entertainer while Cruz proved the best pure debater. Christie showed himself a likeable regular guy while Rubio showed command of the issues and an exceptional capacity to speak rapidly as though auditioning for party auctioneer.

They also agreed on issue 1: Hillary Clinton could never be allowed to succeed Barack Obama. The possibility Sanders might beat Clinton never seemed to cross their minds.

Leading up to the debate, Trump had continued his Cruz "birther" attacks. Maria Bartiromo, one of the Fox Business News' front-line moderators, threw Cruz a softball about whether he was a natural-born American for purposes of constitutional muster. Cruz crushed it. He even pointed out correctly that a few months earlier Trump himself had said it was a nonissue. Trump sputtered lamely.

Developing his own lines of attack, Cruz had gotten into the habit of saying Trump had "New York values." Bartiromo asked, "What are those? I'm a New Yorker, and I don't know." Without missing a beat, Cruz replied that maybe she didn't, but most people across the country did.

When asked to respond, Trump talked about how New Yorkers had come together after the attacks on 9/11 and how he had watched them unite to rebuild a city, as though the citizens of any other major city would not have done the same. Even so, on debating points, Trump did well. On showing a human side to his usual loud, blustering, unpleasant character, again, Trump did well.

However, New Yorkers were none too pleased with Cruz, which in the moment concerned him not at all. Cruz had made his point to the voters in New Hampshire, and especially to those in Iowa, in South Carolina, and throughout the upcoming primary states across the South later on. However, this would come back to bite Cruz when New York voted months later.

Cruz was also asked about a couple loans he'd taken out when first running for the U.S. Senate, loans he had disclosed on his ethics reports and everywhere else but apparently had not disclosed on his FEC filing. This then formed the basis of a *New York Times* hit piece on Cruz and the basis of a buzz campaign by the Cruz haters: won't this mean he will have to halt his campaign? Wish, wish, hope, hope. Balderdash. Cruz patiently pointed out this was just another *Times* hit piece (red meat to conservative voters), and the loans had been disclosed repeatedly elsewhere. If the FEC forms were inaccurate, they'd be refiled. End of story. And that pretty much was the end of the story.

Campaign Strategery[294]

Coming out of the January 14 debate, the campaign had become a three-man race of Trump, Cruz, and Rubio, with Christie trying desperately to hold on and the rest trying desperately to be noticed. So what was the path to nomination victory?

Trump's path to victory depended on getting all his angry supporters to vote. He would have a tough time winning Iowa; but if he won New Hampshire decisively, then South Carolina could be the deciding factor. Best two out of three. His strong suit was the intense coverage his campaign received by the national media soaking up his entertainment value while waiting for his next outrageous statement. Even so, if he came in second in both Iowa and New Hampshire, then the "winner" would be a "loser" and his campaign could collapse quickly.

Cruz had more staying power. He had a strong nationwide campaign organization and solid fundraising. He could win Iowa thanks to more disciplined turnout and a better ground game. That same ground game would likely then get him second place in New Hampshire, if not a victory. Even a strong second in South Carolina would leave Cruz well placed going into Super Tuesday, March 1, where he could conceivably lock up the nomination.

Rubio also had a credible though more complicated path to victory, starting with at least a second-place finish in New Hampshire. Rubio recognized early on he'd have a tough time breaking through in Iowa against Cruz's evangelicals and Trump's angry mob. His goal was just to be respectable in Iowa and then make a mark in New Hampshire. By that point, the theory went, the rest would quit the race—Bush, Carson, Kasich, etc.—and they would certainly all throw their support to Rubio as the respectable alternative to Trump the outsider/entertainer and Cruz the right-wing bomb thrower.

Respectable in Iowa; second in New Hampshire; and Rubio could become the magnet for support making him the top dog out of South Carolina. While Rubio's path to victory was more complicated, it seemed entirely plausible.

In contrast to Rubio, Christie had one shot. First, it would help if Trump or Cruz knocked the other off. But then Christie had to take at least second in New Hampshire to be credible. In that case, all that might have gone right for Rubio now stood to go right for Christie.

While more focused, the Democratic side remained just as interesting. Sanders gained in strength. Clinton gained in desperation. Sanders had the energy. Clinton had the party establishment, the superdelegates, and the inevitability mantra.

Sanders retained one lingering and heretofore fatal handicap: the widespread belief among all but his most naive supporters that, whether he was right or wrong, he couldn't win. The impression the Bern couldn't win in the general election was slowly but definitely changing. True, Sanders had little chance in the general if Republicans nominated a Bush or Rubio or Christie. But what if Trump won the nomination? What if Cruz won? If Republicans went loony, or as Far Right as Democrats went Far Left, then Sanders had a decent shot in the general. Obama won, didn't he? In a race between two utterly unelectable candidates, one of them had to win.

The Republican race actually started to have a positive feedback effect for Sanders. If Hillary wasn't inevitable, and if Bernie wasn't a sure loser in the general, then why support the less appealing candidate? Why not support the real Socialist rather than the pseudo-wannabe Socialist?

THE PALIN DRONE

Fame, for some, is an addiction. Once touched, they cannot help but seek it out even long after the spotlight has moved on. In 2008, Sarah Palin, the former Alaskan Governor, became addicted. Sen. John McCain chose Palin as his running mate.

Palin was funny and attractive, a quick wit blessed with a confidence far exceeding her abilities and equally blessed with blindness to her own shortcomings. Having been ripped from obscurity, Palin popped up from time to time to make a rousing empty speech to conservatives who liked their red meat served rough and raw.

Palin's announcement January 19 she was backing Donald Trump came as a complete shock. Palin was a Tea Party darling. Ted Cruz was Tea Party through and through. They were cut from the same cloth. Trump was a category all to his own with only occasional accidental overlapping with Tea Party ideology. Palin's backing Trump made no sense, on the surface.

No sure explanation appears. Backing Cruz would garner her at most a couple paragraphs in the morning newspaper precisely because it would be expected. Backing Trump gave Palin front-page coverage on the evening news. Would Trump accept Palin as his vice presidential running mate? the media buzzed. Suddenly, if temporarily, Palin again basked in the spotlight.

Palin helped get Cruz elected to the U.S. Senate. They knew each other well, and therein may lie another explanation for Palin's decision. Cruz was 100% Tea Party, but perhaps even to Palin he was in some way just too scary to contemplate becoming commander in chief. Or maybe it really was just that, having come to know Cruz, Palin shared the George W. Bush's judgment regarding Cruz: maybe she just didn't like him.

Would Palin's endorsement, announced in Ames, Iowa, even matter? It could, in Iowa because she still had strong connections to the Iowa evangelical community, the community Cruz relied on for a desperately needed win. Outside of and beyond Iowa, Palin's endorsement probably meant little.

Shortly thereafter, Iowa's longtime Republican Gov. Terry Branstad said, "I don't think Ted Cruz is the right one to be supporting in the caucuses."[295] Why? Because Cruz opposed the renewable fuels standard. When he spoke on behalf of Iowans, Branstad's position made perfect sense because those were *his* corn-raising welfare recipients.

With the Palin announcement, the Branstad critique, and then a poll showing Trump over Cruz in Iowa 37 to 26, Trump tried to close the deal. He unloaded the works with a strong ABC News television interview and his first real attack ad directed at Cruz. On ABC News, he said:

> Look, the truth is, he's a nasty guy. He was so nice to me. I mean, I knew it. I was watching. I kept saying, "Come on Ted. Let's go, okay." But he's a nasty guy. Nobody likes him. Nobody in Congress likes him. Nobody likes him anywhere once they get to know him. He's a very – he's got an edge that's not good. You can't make deals with people like that and it's not a good thing. It's not a good thing for the country. Very nasty guy.[296]

Making these comments so effective was the widespread impression it was all true. Cruz had no endorsements yet from his Senate colleagues, and fellow Tea Party traveler Sarah Palin had turned her back on him. He must be a nasty guy, right?

As if things weren't going badly enough for the Texas Senator, his Princeton freshman college roommate Craig Mazen popped up to fill in some details on Cruz's past calling him, among other things, "creepy."[297]

Trump's persistence in the campaign forced others to reexamine their views. The Republican establishment, for example, did what all long-surviving political animals do: they sought for a way to live with a non-Republican topping the Republican ticket.

Bob Dole, the former Senate majority leader and 1996 Republican presidential nominee, couldn't quite bring himself to say something nice about Trump; but he could accomplish nearly as much by dumping on Cruz, which he did in spades, opining as how "nobody in Congress" liked Cruz, which wasn't exactly a black mark in the eyes of many conservatives. But then Dole observed, "We're going to have wholesale losses in Congress and state offices and governors and legislatures."[298] He also threw Trump a bone. With Trump, "we'd do better."[299] This was certainly on the minds of many Republicans at all levels of government.

The Republican establishment wasn't alone in getting queasy. Clinton's campaign made the strategic decision to lose Iowa with dignity, meaning they would try to limit their losses. The same poll showing Trump with a solid lead over Cruz showed Sanders with a similar lead over Clinton, 51 to 43. And unlike Cruz, who could at least hope a higher percentage of his seasoned folks came out to caucus than Trump's newbies, Clinton entertained no such hopes for her disciplined supporters compared with Sanders's energized hordes.

The Clinton campaign also knew New Hampshire was long gone. Of course, they still had enormous institutional advantages in superdelegates, but first Clinton needed a firewall to stop Sanders's march to the nomination. The next firewalls would likely be Nevada and South Carolina. Clinton's machine was well entrenched having had years to prepare; Sanders ran an entirely fly-by-night affair in comparison. But as the Clinton machine girded for Iowa and New Hampshire results, the next contests seemed a long way off.

SUPERDELEGATES AND CLINTON'S INSTITUTIONAL ADVANTAGE

For all the hard work trying to win caucuses and primaries to build delegate count, a great many Democratic delegates were chosen not by voters but by elements of the national Democratic machine. For example, the rules recognize four different kinds of delegates:

1. District-level delegates
2. At-large delegates
3. Pledged party leaders and elected officials (PLEOs)
4. Unpledged PLEOs, a.k.a. "superdelegates," which are composed of
    a. DNC members;
    b. Current and former Democratic presidents and vice presidents;
    c. Current Democratic Senators and Representatives;
    d. Current Democratic Governors; and
    e. Former Democratic Speakers of the House, House Minority Leaders, Senate Majority Leaders, Senate Minority Leaders, and DNC chairs[300]

For delegates under categories one through three, collectively known as pledged delegates, the selection process was determined by state party rules. For the first vote at convention, pledged delegates were required to vote for the candidate to whom they pledged. Superdelegates, on the other hand, were independent agents, the number of which at any time was a matter of circumstance. (If a Democratic congressman retired early, for example, he or she would no longer be a superdelegate and the count would drop by one.) The 2016 convention would have about 720 superdelegates, amounting to about a third of the total.

Clinton counted on the superdelegates for a huge edge. She was establishment. They were establishment. She had helped many of them in past campaigns. They hoped to remain in office. Just as Cruz and Trump threatened mass losses for Republicans in down-ballot voting, Sanders might inflict the same on Democrats. On the other hand, superdelegates could just as easily feel the need to ride a popular wave should one develop. Just like the wave seeming to build behind Sander's candidacy.

The Republican process was no less complicated. For starters, the totals varied from the Democrats' rules. A Republican needed 1,237 delegates to capture the nomination. Each state chose ten delegates plus three delegates for each congressional district. In addition, states received bonus delegates if they had a Republican governor, or if one of the state's legislative chambers was under a Republican majority, or if the state's congressional delegation had a Republican majority. All these are pledged delegates. Each state was also awarded three unpledged delegates.

Beyond Top Secret

The Clinton email scandal rarely garnered undivided attention but only because so many scandals competed for attention. Even so, a January 20 announcement brought the whole affair back into focus: the private computer server on which Clinton had run her email system while secretary of state had contained emails classified "Top Secret/SAP."[301]

Clinton had insisted no highly classified information ever went through her server. Not true, according to the letter sent to lawmakers by I. Charles McCullough III, inspector general to the intelligence agencies. The letter indicated the server had stored information far above "Top Secret" into levels of classification labeled "SAP," or "special access programs." This meant only someone with a specially designated classification was permitted to see the information. This was way above "Top Secret." Calls for Hillary Clinton to face a federal indictment grew steadily.

On top of the inspector general's revelation, the State Department asked federal Judge Rudolph Contreras for a one-month delay in the release of the last batch of Clinton emails.[302] The justification? A historic snowstorm dropping two feet of snow in the District beginning Friday, January 22, through the evening of January 23.

The storm disrupted everything in the city from a Washington Wizards basketball game to the work of the Clinton email team. Ryan James, the lawyer who started the whole ball rolling with his Freedom of Information Act request, observed in response to the State Department request, "It's baffling why State needs a month to make up for only three days of snow-related office closures." Indeed.

It sure looked as though state intended to abet the big delay. Why a month? Would it have anything to do with timing the release to occur after the Iowa caucuses and the New Hampshire primary?

Cats and Dogs

In the week before the Iowa caucuses, former New York mayor Michael Bloomberg announced he was seriously considering running as an independent if Sanders became the Democratic nominee while either Trump or Cruz became the Republican nominee. Why he thought the country would clamor for another brassy billionaire New Yorker remained a mystery to all, or how he would have a snowball's chance, or how he wouldn't take more votes from the Democrats than Republicans, thereby effectively ensuring a Republican victory whomever the Republican nominee turned out to be.[303]

At about the same time, the National Republican Party made it official: it was pulling out of the NBC debate scheduled for mid-February. Immediately after the previous disastrous CNBC debate, the Republicans fulsomely expressed their displeasure. Apparently, NBC hadn't done enough to assure the GOP there would be no repeat, so the GOP dumped NBC for CNN.

Trump then threatened to boycott the upcoming debate scheduled for the Thursday after the Iowa caucuses and moderated by Fox News due to his ongoing fight with Megyn Kelly, one of Fox's stars. Trump believed Kelly had treated him unfairly, so he tried to have Kelly booted from the debate.

Fox responded by issuing a childish press statement, saying, "We have learned from a secret back channel that the Ayatollah and Putin both intend to treat Donald Trump unfairly when they meet with him if he ever becomes president—a nefarious source tells us that Trump has his own secret plan to replace the Cabinet with his Twitter followers to see if he should even go to those meetings."[304]

Threatening to boycott the debate meant Trump remained in the news, depriving Cruz of a chance to regain the initiative. And if he boycotted the debate as threatened, he would again be the topic of debate. Trump to date had played many roles effectively. No reason to believe he couldn't play the victim, as well.

Trump was also faring well in the endorsement department. After the surprise Sarah Palin endorsement came a couple more surprises. Though Cruz publicly lived his faith and had done so for years (and was counting on a strong evangelical vote in Iowa to put him over the top), Jerry Falwell Jr. endorsed Trump. Falwell, the son of the noted Reagan-era conservative leader Jerry Falwell Sr. and president of the increasingly influential Liberty University in Virginia, said Trump was "a man who I believe can lead our country to greatness again."[305]

Almost as shocking, John Wayne's daughter, Aissa, came out of seclusion to endorse Donald Trump.[306] John Wayne may be associated with boring old Westerns to the minds of younger voters; but to millions of conservative baby boomers, the Duke still represented all that was good about America. And where did the endorsement take place? At a ceremony held at the John Wayne Birthplace Museum in, you guessed it, Winterset, Iowa. Palin, Falwell, and John Wayne's daughter all in one week—not a bad week for Donald Trump.

PREGAME GAB

Polls came fast and furious in the days leading up to the Iowa caucuses. On the Democratic side, it looked a toss-up between Clinton and Sanders. If you believed the polls, Trump seemed to be solidifying his support. The line about Cruz being a "nasty guy," the Cruz birther constitutional question, the Falwell endorsement, and Trump's star power seemed to be taking a collective toll on the Cruz machine. None of the other Republican candidates appeared to be catching on.

An interesting item appeared at this time in a national poll of Republican registered voters. Typical of many other polls, Trump led with 37%, Cruz with 21%, Rubio with 11%, and everyone else below 10%. So if the rest of the wannabes dropped out and endorsed Rubio, then in a two-man race Rubio would go head-to-head with Trump on level ground. Conventional wisdom suggested much of the country would breathe a sigh of relief and likely bolt to Rubio if only out of fear of either Democrat or of Trump.

The more interesting question in the poll plumbed whether the candidate was "unacceptable." Forty-five percent of respondents still said Bush was "unacceptable," a worse showing than any other candidate. In the unacceptable category for registered Republicans:

Candidate	Judged Unacceptable
Bush	45%
Christie	38%
Trump	32%
Carson	30%
Cruz	26%
Rubio	22%

This poll had to discourage Bush and Christie. Neither had done anything particularly wrong, yet not only could they not break through into positives, but their negatives still topped the list. On the flip side, Rubio had to be smiling because even if he scored only 11% positive, he had the lowest percentage of voters deeming him unacceptable. The post–New Hampshire magnet strategy seemed a long shot but quite viable.

CHAPTER 12
VOTERS VOTE, FINALLY

Republicans held their last pre-Iowa debate and their first Trumpless debate on January 28. The Donald was having one of his Trumpertantrums due to his spat with Fox News. Viewership remained high at about 12.5 million, about half the viewers of the first debate (24 million), but higher than the previous debate's 11 million. Trump pointed to the drop from the first debate as evidence he remained the main attraction while everyone else including Fox News pointed to the rise in viewership from the previous debate.[307] Spin, spin, spin.

Trump wasn't completely missing from the national stage as he held a competing event carried in part by CNN and MSNBC with about 2.7 million viewers.[308] Trump's event, a fundraiser for veterans, certainly sounded noble until one realized Trump could donate more out of one day's petty cash earnings than his event could raise. No one seemed to make that connection, however.

On substance, Ted Cruz had some of the debate's highlights and lowlights. To start the show, Cruz observed, "Let me say I'm a maniac and everyone on this stage is stupid, fat, and ugly. And Ben [Carson], you're a terrible surgeon. Now that we've gotten the Donald Trump portion out of the way."[309] It was obviously planned, but it worked, and it made Trump look silly for his absence.

Rather than ask questions, the moderators frequently posed questions in the form of "candidate X said this, what do you say?" This approach was more interesting than asking simple questions as it forced the candidates to debate one another as per the title of the event: a debate. But the questions were petty, pitting candidates against one another even when they were largely in agreement. Cruz, in particular, felt with some justification he was picked on excessively: "I would note that the last four questions have been Rand [Paul], please attack Ted [Cruz], Jeb [Bush], please attack Ted," Cruz said to the Fox News moderator, "If you guys ask one more mean question, I may have to leave the stage," trying to defuse the situation with a little levity. Cruz had a valid point, but his attempt at levity failed.

His reference to leaving the stage was, of course, another dig at Donald Trump, but it didn't help. What the transcript failed to show was how the audience booed Cruz for whining. They booed again when Cruz tried repeatedly to interject himself in others' discussions with the moderators. The moderators let him butt in a couple times and then put a stop to it, but he kept trying and got booed in response. Cruz did himself no favors in this debate.

Marco Rubio probably fared best among the other candidates, striking strong national security positions. Jeb Bush seemed to be saying, "Come on, guys, be nice" while John Kasich tried for the fiscal discipline vote. Chris Christie and the rest tried to be noticed and failed.

Pocketbook Issues

Going into the Iowa caucuses, the federal government announced the economy had slowed from a weak 2% growth rate in the third quarter to an initial reading of less than 1% in the fourth. The stock market was in full swoon; and while employment crept steadily upward, wages remained stagnant. Oddly, Republicans while campaigning said little about the economy's poor performance under Pres. Obama or how the announced policies of Hillary Clinton or Bernie Sanders would make matters worse.

Only Clinton and Sanders were really running on the economy, lamenting its poor performance while trying to avoid blaming the obvious culprit in the White House. And while they had much to say about "fairness" and "income inequality," their proposals for stiffer regulations and higher taxes could have but one consequence if enacted: further economic stagnation. Apparently for Hill and Bern, fairness dictated an equal lack of income growth for all.

Sanders hammered away at Clinton for being beholden to Wall Street interests (she had been a New York Senator) while Clinton and the Democratic establishment hammered away at Sanders for his fantasy-based reforms. Clinton remained in her tight little box: attacking Sanders from the Left was impossible while attacking him for being an out-of-touch Socialist merely inflamed the vast majority of Democratic primary voters and caucus goers who wanted to believe in Sanders's happy land.

Too Top Secret to Release

On Friday, January 29, the State Department indicated twenty-two of the emails found on Hillary Clinton's private email server were too sensitive for public release. Not only were they classified far above Top Secret, but they related to issues still too current to risk disclosure. Some of the emails included "operational intelligence," and their presence on an unsecured server "jeopardized sources, methods, and lives."[310]

Curiously, many of these emails included information in the body of the text cut out of another email in which the high-end security clearance was prominently displayed. Why do that? So highly classified material could be sent to a nonsecure email address. That, boys and girls, was a felony.

The Clinton campaign's best response was to complain about Washington's penchant for over-classification. The claim had merit but was also irrelevant. If the emails were marked classified, then the rules pertaining to classified materials applied. Hillary Clinton and some on her staff had on multiple occasions knowingly and intentionally violated the law regarding the handling of classified material. She was now at legitimate risk of being indicted, or so it seemed.

Republicans naturally jumped all over the latest revelations. Nor was this just "playing politics." The latest disclosures were very troubling.

Even Sanders found himself with a gift he couldn't refuse. Recall, Sanders had in their first debate dismissed the email scandal as a sideshow not worth mention. With these latest revelations, his own candidacy gaining traction, and the Iowa caucuses in sight, Sanders acknowledged, "That is, I think, a very serious issue. There is a legal process taking place, I do not want to politicize that issue."[311] Sanders exercised admirable restraint, but the email scandal was now part of the Democratic contest.

A Five-Candidate Race

As the Monday of the Iowa caucuses dawned, for all intents and purposes, the two parties' races had come down to five relevant candidates. On the Democratic side, Clinton had the machine, Sanders the energy, O'Malley had the opportunity to make someone's day.

Support Levels in Percent

	Des Moines Register/ Bloomberg[312] (likely caucus goers)	RCP average of previous 5 polls
Clinton	45	51.6
Sanders	42	37.2
O'Malley	3	2.2

The internals of the Iowa polls indicated Clinton captured 65% of the likely caucus goers aged 65 and up but did poorly among young voters. Sanders, the oldest candidate in either race, captured 63% of those thirty-five and under. As expected, Clinton had a ten-point lead with women while Sanders had a five-point lead with men.

The polls consistently showed O'Malley with only a few percentage points of support, yet he could still prove decisive because the Democratic rules stipulated a candidate must receive at least 15% support to be recognized. If in a caucus session O'Malley's hardy few fell below 15%, which seemed likely to happen everywhere, then they would be given the opportunity to move to their second choice. Would O'Malley signal a preference? If not, would they opt on their own for Clinton, Sanders, or abstain?

The Republican race represented two races in one. One race matched Trump and Cruz for mantle of the representative outsider/bomb thrower. At one time, Carson looked to be in this race, but his support flagged. About a third of self-identified evangelicals indicated support for Cruz. Bottom line: it appeared if Cruz failed to impress in Iowa, his candidacy would likely be mortally wounded. For Trump on the other hand, a strong second might be a blow to his ego as second place was still first loser. Trump hated losers, but his campaign would continue strong into New Hampshire even with a second-place showing.

Support Levels in Percent

	Des Moines Register/ Bloomberg[313] (likely caucus goers)	**RCP average of previous 5 polls**
Trump	28	28.6
Cruz	23	23.9
Rubio	15	16.9
Carson	10	7.7
Paul	5	4.1
Christie	3	2.4
Bush	2	4.1

The other race within a race was for the non-Trump/Cruz prize, and in this race Rubio's polls suggested a clear lead and strong momentum. Unlike the Democrats, however, Republicans had no minimum threshold for support, so none of the low-digit losing candidates were likely to pull an O'Malley and throw their support to Rubio on Monday night.

Looking at the internals of the Republican poll, amazingly Trump the billionaire did best at 39% support among those who believed the system was rigged against all but the very rich. Trump also closed the deal with his supporters as 71% of his supporters said their minds were made up. The comparable figure for Cruz was 61%. One sign of Rubio's strength is that Rubio was most often a likely caucus goer's second choice while 70% viewed Rubio favorably.

It's worth reviewing how traditional labels had become inadequate in the Republican race. Trump was running as the anti-Democrat or at best as the convenient Republican. He ran almost without any firm ideology or worldview other than the simple principles that he was smart and everyone else was a moron, and his few enunciated policies bore little relation to traditional Republican views.

Cruz likewise defied description. While his roots were in the Tea Party, the same could be said of Rubio and Paul. Otherwise, no known label fit. For his part, dedicated libertarian Paul could at least claim to be running as a "Liberty movement" guy while Bush represented the classic establishment, and Christie represented the non-Washington establishment.

For his part, Rubio was often and errantly grouped among the establishment candidates. He was a junior senator with a strong Tea Party history. He was continuously attacked by Bush the true establishment candidate for his non-establishment positions. What made the establishment label stick to Rubio was, again, his disastrous flirtation with immigration reform.

Democrats had a much easier time of it. Sanders was a democratic Socialist. Most Democratic voters had a pretty good idea what that meant. O'Malley was a progressive, again, a comfortable term for Democrats; and Clinton was Clinton, a candidate of infinitely flexible ideology trying under the circumstances to sound the sensible Socialist, taking positions, which should they become inconvenient she would surely abandon.

Iowa Votes, at Last

On February 1, the cacophony from the politicians, pundits, and cranks was for a few short blessed hours drowned out by the voices of actual Iowa voters—a lot of Iowa voters. This was followed by some quick analysis, and then Iowa was forgotten as quickly as a New Year's Eve party favor.

Republicans and Democrats turned out in huge numbers to have their say. Iowa Republicans gave a shout-out to Ted Cruz, whose meticulous planning, enormous ground game, and maybe some dirty tricks at Ben Carson's expense gave him a 27.7% victory. As expected, Cruz's strength came from the evangelical vote from whom he received 34%. They gave him a win he had to have, but the source of his winning also cast a shadow as the evangelical vote in New Hampshire was much, much smaller. Where could Cruz go for votes in the Granite State?

Iowans told Donald Trump just as loudly, "Close, but no cigar." Trump hadn't fared poorly, coming in second with 24.3%; but by Trump's own lights, if you ain't winnin', you're losin'. Trump had built his whole persona on the premise he was a winner. On this night, Trump was first loser.

Arguably the biggest winner in Iowa was not Cruz but Marco Rubio. Rubio's numbers had risen prior to the caucuses, leading pundits to predict he'd get at most 15%. Rubio nearly clipped Trump at 23.1%. He did well among evangelicals (21%) and especially well among those who prized winning the general election. Rubio was now firmly in the top tier of three, with the rest all gasping for air.

The rational thing for most of the rest to do was to get out. They had poor prospects in New Hampshire and a second decisive, poor performance meant the end of the road beckoned. Former Arkansas Gov. Mike Huckabee showed the best sense by announcing he was getting out "for health reasons," observing the voters were "sick of him." Head held high, going out with humor. Very classy, Guvna. Next.

Others who should have been right on Huckabee's heels included Carly Fiorina, Rick Santorum, Rand Paul, Jim Gilmore, and especially Jeb Bush. It was clear to everyone but the candidates themselves and their highly paid consultants that none of these had any future in the race. Their continued campaigns only served to slow Rubio's climb as the alternative to Trump and Cruz. Carson would likewise have been smart to get out because, though he'd captured 9.3% and was well received by voters generally, his campaign too was going nowhere.

Oddly enough, John Kasich could make a case for continuing despite getting only 1.9%. Kasich entered the contest late, campaigned little in Iowa, and had put almost all his effort into New Hampshire. Despite his paltry 1.8% in Iowa, Christie could make a similar case. They both faced very long odds, but their continued campaigns could be excused under the circumstances.

Surprisingly, the close Republican contest was initially overshadowed by the shenanigans underway on the Democratic side. For starters, the race became a dead heat between Bernie Sanders and Hillary Clinton. At least six precincts produced a perfect tie and were decided by coin toss. Every time the coin was tossed, Clinton won—six times out of six.[314] The odds of that happening? One in 64. Keep in mind, Clinton's ground team dominated among Democratic operatives in Iowa—the very same operatives who were flipping the coins. Ever see a two-headed coin? Both sides bore a striking likeness to Hillary Clinton.

Final count: Clinton had 49.9% of the vote to Sanders with 49.6%. It appeared Clinton won. On the one hand, a win is a win. On the other hand, Sanders had nearly defeated Clinton with relatively little organization and now headed toward his home territory.

Long before the bulk of the results had come in, Martin O'Malley suspended his campaign. Zero point six percent just wasn't enough. In many ways, O'Malley looked an ideal candidate: a progressive's progressive and not from Washington DC. Executive experience as

Maryland Governor. Telegenic and well spoken, O'Malley might have defeated Clinton if he'd ever gotten a hearing, but he was thoroughly blocked by Sanders. Bad luck, Governor. Next.

A massive snowstorm struck the Hawkeye State as the Iowa caucuses concluded. Those who hadn't prepared were stuck. The rest bugged out for New Hampshire, all except Carson who first flew home for a change of clothes.

New Hampshire Awaits

Iowa and New Hampshire shared few traits. Iowa had few Boston émigrés while New Hampshire had few corn farmers. But the citizens of both states take their responsibility in the presidential nomination process seriously. They know and respect their traditional outsized influence on the selection of commander in chief. Citizens of other states may resent the arrangement but at least can take comfort the folks in Iowa and New Hampshire are on the job.

In terms of essential demographics, Iowa's population at about 3.1 million was almost two and a half times that of New Hampshire. The populations sixty-five or over in both states stood at about 16%. Both states were overwhelmingly white at about 92%. Both states had relatively high percentages of their populations having earned at least a high school diploma, and both had relatively high percentages with at least a bachelor's degree.

However, the defining characteristic of New Hampshire voters may be their stubborn independence. Independents make up about 40% of the New Hampshire vote and New Hampshire held open primaries, so anyone could vote in either party's contest. Often more than ideological purity, New Hampshire voters look for quality of character, simple decency and honesty, and some evidence the candidate can really get the job done.

In January, one poll found 44% of New Hampshire undecided voters were likely to vote in the Republican primary, 35% in the Democratic, and 21% were unsure which way they'd go.[315] By February, those numbers could easily move in any direction.

The last three New Hampshire polls of likely voters taken prior to the Iowa caucuses provided a measure of the effects of the Iowa voting. These polls, taken between January 26 and January 31, revealed the following averages among Republicans:[316]

	Percent
Trump	32.7
Cruz	12.3
Rubio	9.7
Kasich	8.7
Bush	8.3
Christie	6.7
Fiorina	3.7
Carson	3.0
Paul	3.7
Huckabee	0.7
Santorum	0.3
Undecided	10.2

These results superficially reassured Trump but really represented a threat to his campaign. Following his second-place Iowa finish, Trump ran the risk of seeing 32.7% become a high-water mark, meaning the narrative thereafter would be of steady slide. This would buttress the broader narrative of a campaign on the road to implosion, a narrative frequently reinforced by Trump's perplexing outbursts and erratic behavior, and a narrative easily becoming a self-fulfilling prophecy.

On the Democratic side, these same polls showed Sanders with a commanding lead at 58.7%, Clinton at 33.7%, and the departed O'Malley at 1.7%, leaving just 5.9% undecided. In theory, Sanders faced a similar high-water-mark problem as did Trump, except Sanders came out of Iowa with tremendous momentum. Also, Clinton's poll numbers had fallen steadily from polls taken January 23 to 26.

At Liberty to Exit

Throughout the campaign, Rand Paul had held the liberty movement flag highest, representing those Americans whose foremost concern is the sovereignty of the individual in the face of government coercion. Many call themselves "libertarians." While often confused with Republicans, libertarians are a sometimes distant cousin.

For example, libertarians typically have no qualms about gay marriage because in their view the state has no legitimate interest in sticking its nose into the personal affairs of sovereign citizens. Conservatives tend to favor traditional marriage.

Libertarians can be highly equivocal on the issue of abortion depending on whether they believe the fetus is a person. They can appear conflicted on matters of race or sexual discrimination because these issues arise between individuals and thus are not government's proper concern, though they strenuously oppose any form of discrimination on government's part.

Libertarians and conservatives a strong preference for smaller less active government. As this is such a major area of policy debate, libertarians and conservatives sometimes appear indistinguishable. On the other hand, libertarians tend to favor a minimal military capability whereas conservatives tend to favor "peace through strength"; and libertarians consistently avoid foreign entanglements whenever possible, whereas some conservatives, and most conservatives some of the time, lean forward aggressively in foreign affairs.

Most conservatives seek some harmony with the liberty movement. For example, Cruz specifically and the Tea Party movement more generally try to appeal to liberty movement supporters on the basis of much smaller government but then diverge quickly on national security and social issues.

Early on, Rand Paul had been feted by the mainstream media as a leading candidate. He was articulate. He had a sense of humor. His views seemed quite new, which is a useful attribute to a "news" media. But as most expected, Paul had little more success than did his father, the über-libertarian, former Texas Cong. Ron Paul. So on February 3, Rand Paul decided to save his political career, abandoning the presidential quest to defend his U.S. Senate seat in the November election. At his leaving, Paul abstained from endorsing another candidate. Interesting man. Next.

The following day, former Sen. Rick Santorum joined the exit parade. Despite his win in the Iowa caucuses in 2012, Santorum's exit garnered about as much interest as did his 2016 campaign. He endorsed Rubio. Nice man. Next.

Knowing When to Stop Punching

Either nobody wrote the memo telling Jeb Bush it was time to get out (unlikely), or he ignored it (likely). Expecting a more or less typical election, Bush, like Clinton, ran on experience and accomplishments. But these qualities had little currency against a rising anti-establishment fervor. How does one gain experience, accomplish great things in government, but by appearing at least a bit establishment? To his credit, Bush knew he had nothing else to run on; so he stayed with it, unlike Clinton, who though (Democratic) establishment to the core tried desperately to portray herself as the über-progressive, revolutionary outsider. They both failed, but at least Bush was honest about it.

Despite the obvious writing on the wall and an honorable exit beckoning, Bush ramped up his attacks on Rubio into the New Hampshire primary. Would Bush really prefer Trump or Cruz? Hard to believe, but his attacks were making it more likely one of the two would get the nomination.

How toasted was Bush's campaign? He had to plead with the audience to clap. As reported by the *New York Times*,

> Speaking at an event at the Hanover Inn near the Vermont border during his final stop of the day, Mr. Bush finished a fiery riff about protecting the country as commander in chief—"I won't be out there

blowharding, talking a big game without backing it up," he said – and was met with silence.

"Please clap," he said, sounding defeated.

At the end of a long and drawn-out fight, a boxer becomes so tired and disoriented he keeps throwing punches long after the bell has rung. Somebody in Bush's entourage needed to play the corner man and walk Jeb back to his stool in the corner—and throw in the towel. Nobody did.

BEN'S NOT-SO-EXCELLENT TED ADVENTURE

Trump's initial reaction to his Iowa defeat was his version of the stiff upper lip. But the defeat mightily rankled. How long could he contain his fury? About two days.

By the Wednesday after the caucuses, Trump had a full head of steam on the claim Cruz had cheated.[317] In fairness, Trump had a point, and he wasn't the only one with a reason to be angry.

Just minutes before the Iowa caucuses were to begin, CNN reported Carson was going home, noting the move was highly "unusual."[318] Apparently most people didn't catch the report, but Cruz's people saw it. Carson later clarified he went home for a change of clothes and to rest, but at the time the explanation was a blank waiting to be filled in.

Cruz's people were all too happy to fill in the blank. They spread the story Carson was ending his campaign, so Carson's supporters should support Cruz. In fact, as the caucus results showed, Carson had significantly underperformed relative to expectations while Cruz overperformed by like amount, suggesting the Carson to Cruz support migration may have been substantial.

As dirty tricks go, this was fairly mild stuff. No doubt much worse occurred episodically in both Republican and Democratic caucuses across the state. For example, some enterprising opponent distributed flyers advertising $25 an hour for people willing to come to Bush's last Iowa event before the caucuses.[319] The implication was the Bush camp already knew they had little support and were desperate to avoid a televised embarrassment. Retail politics is not for the timid.

The Cruz team's dirty trick infuriated Carson, who apparently thought everyone should play by the Marquess of Queensberry rules, but it was enough to give Trump cover explaining his loss to Cruz. "Cheater, cheater, cheater," Trump bleated like a kid who'd lost a game of marbles. He threatened lawsuits. He suggested a re-vote (as though that was even possible). He looked the sore loser; but he had an excuse for his loss, which was all that mattered. That, and he had a new attack line on Cruz "the cheater."

Taking the Cruz-Carson issue to a much higher level of dirty pool was the Cruz campaign's embellishment. Carson said he was leaving Iowa before the caucuses started. The press carried the story and noted it was odd. Cruz headquarters got the word out to their Iowa field army. So far, so good. But then they added the rumor "a major announcement was expected next week." This could only reinforce the impression Carson was getting out, but it was pure fabrication by the Cruz campaign.

A Nasty Tiff in New Hampshire

At first, as Sanders joined the race for the Democratic nomination, Clinton treated him as a useful, convivial warm-up act—a foil to help her sharpen her campaign skills. As Sanders got traction, Clinton initially hid her irritation. Nearly defeating her in Iowa rattled Clinton and her entire machine. Irritation in the open, the gloves came off at the next debate on February 4 in New Hampshire hosted by MSNBC and moderated by resident socialist Rachel Maddow. Both sides punched for blood.

Clinton's core substantive argument was she was just as "progressive" as Sanders but more practical. Sanders was all pie in the sky.

Sanders argued Clinton was a faux progressive, entirely beholden to her big money Wall Street buddies and only hid behind the excuse of practicality. They were both right.

Nasty campaigns are dominated by nasty comments. Clinton tired of the "insinuation" she was tainted by the millions of dollars she and Bill had received over the years from the reviled Wall Street cabals. Anderson Cooper of CNN asked Clinton about the $625,000 (or $675,000—the figures varied from story to story) she'd received for giving three speeches to Goldman Sachs. The average American family would take about ten years to earn that kind of money. She made it in three speeches. Her reaction? She shrugged her shoulders and replied, "That's what they offered."[320] What else could she say?

Sanders's best line of the night was his shout to "Break them up," referring to the mega banks. Clinton countered that her proposed regulatory enhancements would be more effective reining in Wall Street, but her words fell on deaf ears. She might have gotten a better response had she not already gotten rich off Wall Street's beneficence. Her credibility on this was basically squat.

Clinton tried to change the subject, suggesting Sanders's attitude toward her was "sexist," to which Bernie said, "Whoa, whoa, whoa . . . wow."[321] None but the most Hillary sycophantic feminist could fail to be astounded at this accusation. Clinton looked desperate and mean and tired.

As a footnote to the debate, lest anyone think MSNBC isn't fully in the tank for the Democrats, the moderator, Rachel Maddow, hugged both candidates after the debate.[322] Just a love fest all around. Imagine Maddow hugging Ted Cruz! Some wag suggested "MSNBC" really stood for "More Socialist than NBC" just as "CNN" again stood for the "Clinton News Network." (It stings most when there's an element of truth.) It remained unclear what phrase "Fox" stood.

WHO ARE YOUR FRIENDS?

In national politics, a *friend* will stab you in the chest. A *good friend* will look you in the eye without smiling when (s)he does it. Even so, friends and endorsements matter. Who were the candidate's friends? Who endorsed whom? This issue took on new meaning because a big knock on Cruz was he didn't have any friends among his U.S. Senate colleagues.

The friend issue was also important because many Democrat women served as U.S. Senators, and all but one had endorsed Clinton. No sexism there, of course. If a man won't support Hillary because she's a woman, that's sexism; but if a woman supports Hillary because she's a woman, that's not sexism. Never expect politics to be rational.

The one outlying senator, the great Clinton resister among the female senators, was Elizabeth Warren. Warren was no hypocrite. Like Sanders, Warren was a true believer; and she just couldn't accept a phony progressive. And maybe she still had an inkling of running herself if Clinton flamed out and Biden stayed out.

Contrary to popular assertions, Cruz had friends, such as Tony Perkins, the well-respected leader of the Christian values movement. Perkins endorsed Cruz, saying, "Leadership isn't about making deals, leadership is about standing on principle."[323] A reasonable portrayal of Cruz demonstrating why Cruz could make a great statue but a disastrous president.

Leadership involves principles, to be sure, and a leader whose principles are uncertain or overly malleable won't lead for long. But voters elect the President of the United States to run one of the three constitutionally established branches of government. The voters don't elect a dictator or a monarch or an emperor. All meaningful legislation is ultimately the product of compromise among competing visions. Competing visions among Republicans, among Democrats, and between them. If you cannot cut a deal, then you cannot legislate. Unable to legislate, would a Pres. Cruz follow Obama's model and govern by executive order, contrary to every principle Cruz enunciated regarding constitutional government?

Former candidate and former Texas Gov. Rick Perry also endorsed Cruz. South Carolina Cong. Jeff Duncan endorsed Cruz just before the New Hampshire primary, a particularly important voice as Duncan was a Tea Party favorite, and the South Carolina primary followed close on New Hampshire's heels. The only senator to speak up for Cruz was Utah's Mike Lee: "I am his [Cruz's] friend."[324] But Lee didn't endorse Cruz, just "liked" him as though he were on Facebook. As of the New Hampshire primary, Cruz was still seeking his first endorsement from his Senate colleagues.

In contrast, Rubio racked up a tidy list of endorsements including many Tea Party favorites, like South Carolina Sen. Tim Scott, who called Rubio "the real deal."[325] Rubio also received the endorsement of another conservative, Pennsylvania's Sen. Pat Toomey, who just happened to be running for reelection in a tight race.

THE REPUBLICANS' NEW HAMPSHIRE DEBATE

One could be forgiven for concluding the Saturday Republican debate in New Hampshire just prior to voting was more of the same. Trump was obnoxious. Cruz effused eloquence. Kasich remained the happy warrior. Christie, pugnacious; Rubio, intense; Bush, smiling and newly bespectacled; Carson, present and accounted for; Fiorina omitted.

The New Hampshire debate felt different. True, Trump was especially hard on Bush and continued to demonstrate intelligence, strength of views, and the fact he was a rather unpleasant fellow. So much so, the audience repeatedly and roundly booed him—and Trump lapped it up.

Chris Christie seemed to have one goal only—to take out Rubio. Later events showed he largely succeeded. They were essentially competing for the same voters; but as Christie's boat had long since sailed, it seemed by implication his main goal was ensuring Trump got the nomination. Christie called Rubio the "boy in the bubble," emphasizing his lack of accomplishments and experience in contrast to Christie's executive experience as New Jersey Governor. "Each morning when they wake up, a U.S. Senator thinks about what speech I can give or what bill I can drop. Every morning when I wake up I think about what kind of problem I need to solve for the people who actually elected me."[326] He had a point, which is why governors often make better presidents.

Christie hammered Rubio for "cutting and running" when the ill-advised comprehensive immigration package collapsed. So depending on the source, Rubio was attacked for participating in the immigration gang, for supporting the bill, and for cutting and running on the bill. Talk about "can't win for losing."

While Rubio tried to counter, on immigration he remained largely defenseless. Rubio had learned the American people wouldn't tolerate any kind of immigration reform until the border was secured. They'd been conned too often in the past with promises of border security to buy that pig in a poke again. Rubio acknowledged this reality emphatically and repeatedly. He'd learned his lesson during the immigration debate, the biggest issue on which he'd worked, which reinforced the narrative he had too much to learn yet to be president.

Disciplined candidates "stay on message," but it's possible to take it too far. Perhaps as a result of Christie's effective pummeling, Rubio took it too far, earning himself the unfortunate sobriquet of "robo candidate." After many of the questions posed, Rubio offered a glancing response and then quickly circled back to one of his pat talking points. For a candidate who had fared well extemporizing, he suddenly looked—afraid—as though having caught some momentum he was afraid of losing it.

Cruz began the campaign as the best debater and perhaps second only to Rubio as an orator. In the New Hampshire debate, Cruz's debate skills proved extraordinary. He was clear and direct (Hillary, take note). He was impassioned without losing his cool. In response to a question about the growing opioid epidemic, Cruz recited the touching story of his half-sister's addiction that led to her death. For one night, Cruz seemed a mensch.

Hosted by ABC News, for the most part the debate was a well-run affair. Anchor David Muir seemed to understand the purpose of the moderator is to let the candidates be the show. George Stephanopoulos, the Democratic Party's renowned media undercover agent, pretended neutrality as occasional inquisitor while conservative journalist Mary Katharine Ham and WMUR political director Josh McElveen joined in with specific substantive questions. All in all, a balanced affair but for one participant: ABC's Martha Raddatz, who despite one assumes her best efforts utterly failed to keep under wraps her intense dislike for the Republicans on stage. Her questions were fair and well delivered but her repulsion palpable.

Going Ballistic

Just hours before the New Hampshire debate came news North Korea had successfully tested a ballistic missile capable of reaching North America. The North Koreans were also developing a nuclear weapon they hoped to mount on such a missile. The missile launch instantly became fodder for the debate. The sensible question to ask would be how the United State should respond. The question posed by Martha Raddatz as she sought to bait the Republican candidates into a foolish statement was whether the United States should have acted preemptively to take out the North Korean missile.

Some suggested it was a possibility and quickly reaffirmed their absolute intention of protecting the homeland. Some let their testosterone get the better of them and said they would absolutely have taken out the North Korean missile preemptively. Cruz gave the smartest answer, indicating he would have to know the specific intelligence the U.S. government had about the missile and surrounding circumstances before he could answer whether he would have acted preemptively.

A preemptive attack against a North Korean weapons site would have been an act of war, possibly triggering a major international incident, possibly even involving the Chinese. Goaded by the moderator, and loaded with adrenaline and testosterone, most of the candidates onstage fell for the trap of preening their militaristic manhood. (As so often during the debate, Carson wasn't even asked his opinion.) The exception, the candidate who didn't fall for the trap: Ted Cruz. Maybe for the first time in the campaign, Cruz was one of the least scary candidates. Point: Cruz.

Hillary's Speeches and Other Handicaps

Clinton's money-grubbing Goldman Sachs speeches continued to haunt. They kept in the news the story about making enormous sums from Wall Street big shots, thus steadily feeding the Sanders attack machine. They reminded voters she and Bill had parlayed their political connections into becoming one of the richest couples in America. They kept her in defense/response mode. The speeches story elevated the risk of yet another scandal/crisis in the making. The issue: the transcripts.

At Clinton's insistence, her Goldman Sachs speeches had been transcribed; but she didn't want the transcripts released. Having transcripts produced was curious. Keeping them under wraps screamed once again Clinton was trying to hide something. Why refuse to release them if there's nothing to hide? This in turn led to the reasonable conclusion: if she's hiding something, then it must be bad. So Clinton said something bad. What did she say? And the issue then snowballed into yet another self-inflicted wound.

This and many other issues hounded Clinton in New Hampshire. Sanders had clear home-field advantage, but Clinton refused to give New Hampshire up without a fight. Maybe she would lose; but if she closed the gap noticeably, she would blunt the narrative of Sander's momentum. Clinton went all out in New Hampshire. She had fifty staffers in place for months.[327] She had eleven field offices and eight "get out the vote centers," all in a state of only 1.3 million people.

She attempted a clumsy rendition of "we gals gotta stick together," which apparently turned off most young female voters. She brought in former Secretary of State Madeleine Albright, who insisted, "There's a special place in Hell for women who don't help each other."[328] One wonders the reaction if some male Democratic luminary had said, "Vote for Bernie because for God's sakes you don't want a woman in the White House." Hypocrisy is now so commonplace it's only recognized as a matter of convenience.

Hillary unleashed Bill, who looked frail and low energy yet still managed a blistering attack on Sanders—accusing him of sexism, of all things, from a world-famous sexual predator. She unleashed Chelsea, who was still treated by the media like a kid though now a grown woman. She ran ads everywhere she could.

If she succeeded, she'd slow the Sanders surge. But if she failed to close the gap, the narrative would run to the contrary. Clinton took a big risk. She was right to do so, because if she couldn't slow Sanders when the expectations game played in her favor, then Sanders's momentum could sweep her campaign away like so much fairy dust.

Secretary Mush

Clinton came into the 2016 campaign with a record of being about the worst retail politician on the national stage. Would she learn to do better or continue to screech and nuance her way through to the end? For certain, she didn't improve quickly. The New Hampshire debate moderator asked both candidates what would be job one if they were elected. Sanders: unrigging the system. Vague but short, to the point. "So long as big-money interests control the Congress, it is going to be very hard to do what has to be done for working families." Agree with him or not, there was no doubting where the Bern stood, though it was fair to wonder how he would do it.

And Clinton? "I'm for a lot of things. If I'm so fortunate to get the nomination, I will begin to work immediately on putting together an agenda, beginning to talk to with members of Congress and others about how we can push forward." Mush and blather.

She would develop an agenda *after* she gets the nomination? Aren't you supposed to figure that out before you seek the nomination? At least with respect to your top priorities? Isn't that what all those position papers on your website are all about, not to mention the Democratic platform? And then her answer was all about process. "Develop an agenda." "Begin to talk with members of Congress and others." She wasn't enunciating presidential leadership. This was a candidacy for starting an encounter group.

New Hampshire Finally Has a Voice

Primaries and caucuses exhibit very different dynamics. In the Iowa caucuses, participants arrived by 7:00 p.m. to register and then spent a couple hours debating, haggling, arguing, and finally standing for one candidate or the other. It's time-consuming, social, and, for some, intimidating. In a primary, you show up and vote and go about your business—no muss, no fuss.

As New Hampshire voting got underway, all the candidates told a good story. Sanders felt the Bern. Hillary kept grippin' and grinnin' while acknowledging a shake-up of her campaign might be in order. The Republican narrative prior to the debate suggested Rubio practically had the nomination locked up, and then Rubio ran into the Christie buzz saw. Bush's supporters insisted he was finally on his game; and to be sure, Bush had upped his game, though almost surely in the too-little-too-late category. Bush, Christie, and Kasich the happy warrior all battled for what seemed at best fourth place. The exit called for all three like a ghostly siren.

The New Hampshire polls as voting began had settled into a clear pattern. Among Republicans, only Kasich (upward) and Cruz (downward) showed any apparent movement suggesting how independents might break.

RCP Averages

	New Hampshire	National
Trump	31.2	29.5
Rubio	14.0	17.8
Kasich	13.5	4.0
Cruz	11.8	21.0
Bush	11.5	4.3
Christie	5.8	2.5
Fiorina	4.8	2.5
Carson	2.8	7.8
Undecided	4.6	10.6

The polls of the Democratic contenders suggested Clinton hadn't moved the dial despite enormous efforts. The national narrative of

Clinton under siege from Sanders the ascender seemed accurate and prophetic. One curiosity out of the respective national polls was that, by percentages, about twice as many Democrats were undecided despite having a two-person field as Republicans with a large field.

RCP Average

	New Hampshire	National
Sanders	54.5	41.2
Clinton	41.2	36.0
Undecided	4.3	22.8

Clinton needed a decent showing. She needed to close the gap. She failed. Sanders took 60% in a landslide. He did it his way, preaching inspiration, with quiet intensity and credibility. He won the women's vote, the young vote, and seven out of ten independents voting Democratic.

Clinton lost nearly every demographic except voters over sixty-five and voters with over $200,000 annual income. She lost the women's vote by a ten-point margin. She had treated the women's vote as though it were 1966, not 2016. Of course, women had many legitimate issues; and most of the time Clinton's campaign was all about real, pragmatic solutions to real problems; but with women, she'd resorted to rank sexism and New Hampshire's Democratic-voting women didn't like it.

According to exit polls, 34% of Democratic voters rated "honest and trustworthy" as a candidate's most important characteristic; 91% of these voters went to Sanders, suggesting the Clinton scandals did matter to these Democratic voters, after all.

Clinton lost all but three towns reporting results. She won Bedford fair and square. She won Millsfield, which recorded three votes of which she got two. And she won in Waterville by one vote. She lost every other town in the state.

A year before, Clinton's position in New Hampshire appeared unassailable. Sure, the crazy old Socialist from the neighboring state was running, but who really cared? After Iowa, her support was down to around 40%. After enormous effort, her polls going into the primary remained around 40%. When the voting was over, she had fallen to 38%. Fortunately for her, New Hampshire, like Iowa, is not a winner-take-all state, so she still picked up nine delegates to Sander's 13; but Bernie now had the momentum and Hillary had a big problem—or several.

Peter Roff of *US News and World Report* perhaps best summarized Clinton's defeat thusly, "She not only lost to Bernie Sanders, she lost to New York developer Donald Trump, who polled more votes in a field of eight candidates than she did losing in a field of two."[329]

Neither Hillary nor Bill nor the campaign could mask its utter shock and horror at how badly Clinton had performed. Even Clinton sycophants like "journalist" Andrea Mitchell commented as to how Bill was "freaking out" and couldn't hide the shock on his face.[330]

After New Hampshire, Clinton proved once again she was one tough broad, the Rocky Balboa of American politics; and she had grounds for hope. For example, Clinton had built a huge organization in South Carolina and Nevada, the next two states, the latter especially buttressed by the manpower of her union support. Sanders had much less organization, but he would also have an organization spontaneously materialize as the large nebulous progressive movement mobilized.

Race was also in Clinton's favor. Iowa and New Hampshire were "lily white" whereas South Carolina and Nevada had much higher percentages of African American and Hispanic voters. While the demographic differences were indisputable, the consequence was less obvious at the time. Implicit in the narrative was Clinton's long history of broad support from minorities.

Taking a step back, this narrative seemed thinner than a Clinton excuse. An old white woman from New York reeking of establishment connections would necessarily appeal better to minorities animated by Black Lives Matter-style ideology than a fire-breathing anti-establishment old white guy from Vermont? Maybe.

The African American community still seethed from the episodes in Ferguson, in Baltimore, and most notably in Charleston, South Carolina. Sanders led the coalition of the irate. Why would African Americans, or Hispanics for that matter, not be more receptive to his fiery anti-establishment message than to Clinton's more sedate message? Clinton's supporters spinning this story of her support among minorities seemed to be whistling in the dark. As it turns out, the African American community may not have been in love with Hillary, but they did know her. They didn't know Bernie; and as he learned, it takes more to earn the support of the African American community than a sit-down and coffee.

Too Little Winnowing

In the end, the New Hampshire primary meant less for Republicans than many hoped. Trump expected to win. He did, with 35% of the vote, and he got around 35% of every slice of the demographic pie—by age, by income, by sex, by political orientation.[331] The one outlier: 24% said "telling it like it is" was a candidate's most important characteristic. Trump took 65% of those voters.

Cruz expected to do poorly given the small evangelical representation. He did, earning only 12%. Fiorina, Carson, and Gilmore (yes, he was still officially running) were expected to be barely noticed. They were gathering only 4%, 2%, and 127 votes, respectively. (The New Hampshire ballot was very complicated. Gilmore's name appeared first, and so most of his votes probably came from undecided or confused voters who just checked the first box.)

More than the others, Kasich and Christie had made maximum efforts in New Hampshire. They needed to demonstrate viability as candidates. Kasich did well enough. Christie cratered.

Christie had worked hard. New Hampshire should have been fertile ground for him. He only managed 8%. He flew back to New

Jersey to look in the mirror in search of a reason to continue. He didn't find one; and so he got out, another of the early front-runners barely making it out of the starting gate. Christie's campaign epilogue, his high point, had been his Rubio mugging in the New Hampshire debate, thereby wiping out the one guy who could take out Trump and Cruz. Whoever won the nomination should send Christie flowers on his birthday every year. Next.

Even more so than Christie, Kasich had basically run for President of New Hampshire. New Hampshire rewarded him with a solid second-place finish at 16%.

Trump and Kasich: the celebrity took first place, upending much long-standing conventional wisdom. The old-style grip and grinner took second, suggesting conventional wisdom was at least partly valid.

For Trump, the fight ramped up quickly because his campaign style didn't require the typical accoutrements of a national campaign—scores of handlers, schedulers, front men, fundraisers, communications experts, IT help, etc. They had Trump. For Kasich, having thrown all he had into New Hampshire, he had little organization or opportunity to capitalize on his performance going into South Carolina. Kasich seemed destined to be a one-hit also-ran wonder.

Bush needed a better showing. He got it, barely, maybe. He and Rubio both came in with 11%, though Bush edged Rubio by about five hundred votes. Bush had the money and the machine to continue, but did he have a reason other than hubris? A fourth-place finish in a state where he should have done well was not a glowing endorsement of his prospects.

Rubio came out of Iowa seemingly with the nomination practically in the palm of his hand. He'd wipe out the non-Cruz/non-Trump alternatives in New Hampshire and roar into South Carolina. Then the Christie debate mugging stalled Rubio's parade. The most talented, most charismatic natural politician among the Republicans, thanks to Christie's attacks, Rubio had been labeled the "robo candidate."[332] The last national candidate to be called a robo candidate was former Vice Pres. Al Gore, making the comparison laughable.

While Rubio clearly lost momentum, all was not yet lost. He knew he needed to improve. Rubio admitted mistakes. He learned. He adapted. He had about two weeks to fix it.

Thus far, Trump had received 24% in Iowa and 35% in New Hampshire. Cruz had received a dirty-tricks-inflated 28% in Iowa and 12% in New Hampshire. Taking a step back, this meant half the voters liked either Trump or Cruz, and half preferred someone else. The key for traditional Republicans going forward was to identify this "someone else" and quickly; and if they did, then their chances looked good because 50% going to one person beats 50% split between two.

New Hampshire voters had decided. In a loud nearly unanimous voice, they had told the Republican and Democratic establishments, "Go away!" The anger in the country wasn't dissipating. It was coalescing, focusing, gaining coherence as voters considered the state of the nation and where we seemed to be heading culturally, socially, racially, economically, and politically. Candidates who in more normal times would have run strong instead ran into a wall of dissatisfaction. Candidates who in more normal times would have been laughed off the national stage instead took the ring.

This was the reality going next into South Carolina and Nevada to winnow the field further before the supposedly great and merciless crucible of Super Tuesday. Anger would have its say. The nation, and the world, would soon learn how long and loud it would speak.

CHAPTER 13
OF PALMETTOS AND DICE: SOUTH CAROLINA AND NEVADA

As expected, the day after the New Hampshire primary, Chris Christie and Carly Fiorina gave up the chase. Fiorina had made a good if modest impression following the early debates but became screechy and irrelevant thereafter. Nice lady. Impressive. Next.

Christie just never gained traction despite offering a compelling story and performance. Interesting, likeable candidate who later proved the primary voters' judgment sound. Next.

After his big New Hampshire win, Bernie Sanders enjoyed a deluge of campaign contributions, raising $6.2 million in just twenty-four hours.[333] Just as helpful, most of his contributions were of the $10, $20, and $50 variety (his average donation was $37 in this period) whereas Clinton tended more toward max-out donors at $2,700. This meant Sanders could approach his donors again time and again for a fill-up whereas Clinton had to seek out new max-donors in a possibly down market.

As if the nomination process weren't confusing enough, after New Hampshire the Republicans and Democrats went their separate ways. Republicans went first to South Carolina and then Nevada a week later while Democrats voted in the reverse order.

NEW HAMPSHIRE AFTERMATH

"When the exact same problems crop up in separate campaigns, with different staff, at what point do the principals say, 'Hey, maybe it's US?'" tweeted Obama's 2008 campaign mastermind David Axelrod.[334]

Axelrod was no Hillary hater; but like much of the Democratic establishment, he was getting frustrated. Somewhere, buried deep in Clinton's campaign slept a compelling message waiting to awaken, but no one had yet discovered it. Clinton's campaign spun her message as "comprehensive." By one count a couple months later, her campaign platform had twice as many words as Shakespeare's *Hamlet* and was growing like kudzu.[335] To her credit, Clinton could probably discuss every proposal at length, but most were minor refinements on current law. One perspective on her platform was she was seeking to improve what government was already doing. Another perspective recalled the old saw, "If you can't dazzle 'em with brilliance, baffle 'em with BS."

To her credit, Clinton sought to let voters know exactly what she intended. She demonstrated she was fully prepared for the job. Jeb Bush tried much the same. The result in both cases was to offer a comprehensive program for governing appearing to most observers as unfocused white noise. Sanders was only hit and miss with respect to topics but remained sharply focused in comparison, allowing him to speak with clarity and force.

Even before Clinton's New Hampshire debacle, rumors swirled of a campaign shake-up. The problems went beyond muddled message. Her campaign organization sprawled uncoordinated, suffering from "fuzzy lines of authority." Near the epicenter of the problem was Clinton's decision not to appoint a master chief strategist. "There's nobody sitting in the middle of this empowered to create a message and implement it."[336]

The chief target of dissatisfaction appeared to be top pollster and strategist Joel Benenson. But absent a campaign top dog, Benenson had a nearly impossible job. Another problem was and would always be Bill Clinton champing at the bit to play a bigger role. And Hillary would always be Hillary, talking to scores of old friends outside the campaign offering advice and counsel. Clinton turned to campaign manager Robby Mook to bring order to chaos; and over time, he fairly well succeeded. Meanwhile, where was campaign chairman and operative extraordinaire, John Podesta?

DOWN AND DIRTY IN THE DEEP SOUTH

Many localities lay claim to high expertise in low politics. East St. Louis, for example, regularly reports high rates of dead people voting. Oddly enough, South Carolina, famous for genteel Southern charm, is also home to a colorful history of political skullduggery. The ground game fight in both parties was about to plunge deep into the mud.

How bad could it get? The local newspaper launched a website, the *Charleston Post* and *Courier*'s Whisper Campaign, to track reported campaign attempts to start rumors about one another.[337]

One key to an effective dirty tricks campaign is experienced volunteers. On had to know how to strike and not get caught. Clinton fielded a cadre of South Carolinians. This, her desperation, and her willingness to do anything suggested Clinton was about to unleash on Sanders. Ted Cruz too was well positioned to launch an all-out dirty tricks assault, especially on Donald Trump who had very little ground organization with which to fight back.

Claims of dirty tricks in South Carolina ran rampant. The vast majority became apparent only to the campaigns on the receiving end, like reports Cruz supporters ran robocalls in Spanish to Marco Rubio's non-Spanish speaking supporters. Why? Because many South Carolina voters, constantly reminded of Rubio's role in the Senate immigration reform gang, were irate over unchecked Hispanic immigration.

Then there was the obviously Photoshopped picture of Rubio smiling and reaching his hand out to shake Pres. Obama's hand. The Cruz campaign didn't deny this one. Cruz's national campaign spokesman, Rick Tyler, responded, "If Rubio has a better picture of him shaking hands with Barack Obama, I'm happy to swap it out."[338]

Cruz's reputation was so bad he asked for and got an off-the-record meeting with Ben Carson.[339] The purpose? For Cruz to clear the air with Carson about the Cruz campaign's dirty tricks, especially in Iowa. Carson was having none of it.

Why would Cruz care about Carson's hurt feelings and not those of any of the other Cruz tactics victims? Maybe because Cruz expected Carson to quit soon and wanted Carson's endorsement? Would gentlemen Ben rebuff crude Cruz's attempted rapprochement? Forgive and forget? Turn the other cheek? Remember Trump's charge regarding "nasty Ted"?

Carson endorsement? Fat chance, it would appear.

How bad did it get? The day before the Nevada Republican caucuses, Cruz fired his national campaign spokesman, Rick Tyler of Rubio Photoshop fame. As it happened, Rubio ran into Cruz's father and a staffer at a Hampton Inn in South Carolina. The staffer reportedly was reading the Bible. According to a blog post, Rubio reportedly told the staffer the Bible "did not have many answers in it."

Intentionally or not, the blog misstated Rubio's comments to the staffer, yet Tyler quickly posted it to Facebook. Tyler later deleted the post and apologized, but Cruz fired him anyway citing "a grave error in judgment."[340]

To be sure, Cruz's campaign had no monopoly on dirty tricks. With today's technology, any miscreant supporter can put up a Facebook entry or a blog post with a distorted picture or misleading story. Many did, but the loudest complaints were directed toward Cruz's operation and claims Cruz himself was unaware of the many alleged misdeeds wore thin quickly.

Palmetto Polls to Start

Two South Carolina polls taken between January 15 and January 23 showed Trump and Clinton with strong early leads, and they showed little movement immediately after New Hampshire. They also showed Bush had a pulse coming out of New Hampshire, if just barely. And

Kasich, despite his second-place finish in New Hampshire, had a long way to go to find relevance.

	Pre–New Hampshire	Immediate Post[341]
Trump	38.0	38
Cruz	20.5	22
Rubio	13.5	14
Bush	8.5	10
Carson	8.5	6
Kasich	1.5	4
Other/undecided	9.5	6

In contrast, comparing the pre– and post–New Hampshire polls of South Carolina's Democratic voters showed substantial movement in Sander's direction.

	Pre–New Hampshire	Immediate Post
Clinton	62.0	48
Sanders	32.5	47
Other/undecided	5.5	5

BLOOMBERG'S NEWS

Somebody suggested Michael Bloomberg run for president. The thrice-elected mayor of New York City and founder and owner of Bloomberg LP, a global financial and data company, was worth about $41 billion at the time. He loved the spotlight and hated both parties' national campaigns. Bloomberg asked in response, "Why not?"

Bloomberg had yet to enter the race but obviously contemplated it seriously, and indeed, why not? He could fund the campaign himself, more so even than Trump. He already had an organization in place, with the necessary media contacts through his business and political contacts from being the former New York City Mayor.

He would probably have to run as an independent, at least initially. Of course, running as in independent meant Bloomberg had no shot at winning. The system was indeed rigged in many respects to channel the nation's political energies through the two established political parties. So why bother? To make a point. To outline a different vision for the country to rebuild on after the destruction of the current campaign. To enjoy the spotlight at its hottest for a few months.

However, if he ran and stayed in through election day, then he would almost certainly deliver the presidency to the Republicans on a silver platter. Even Rick Perry could win under those circumstances. What point would he really make then?

Bloomberg, a classic New York liberal, sells fine in New York City, would do reasonably well in much of New York State and the northeast in places like New Jersey and Connecticut, but would bomb dismally in most of the rest of the country. The best Democrats could hope for if Bloomberg stayed in to the end was that he wouldn't split the Democratic vote so badly in these deep blue states as to deliver a Delaware to the Republicans.

Then again, maybe if he did well enough, and if Clinton floundered, and if party leaders feared political hari-kari with Sanders, then just maybe the party would turn to Bloomberg to run as a Democrat.

The 2016 election was already one for the record books, but the prospect of Bloomberg entering the race as an independent, absurd under normal circumstances, seemed almost destined. Imagine a general election featuring Sanders, a Socialist transplant New York Jew from Vermont, against a multibillionaire New York Jew media magnate, against a billionaire New York real estate developer/TV personality.

As they say, you can't make this stuff up. Yet such were the possibilities as the race sped away on. Stranger things have happened but perhaps not on this planet, not in the past one thousand years. Shortly after popping up for some national love, Bloomberg again disappeared from the stage. Itch apparently scratched. Next?

Hillary's Up, Down, and Sideways

The pace quickened markedly after New Hampshire. Clinton enjoyed a clear win picking up the Congressional Black Caucus (CBC) endorsement. Surprise, surprise—the black establishment rallied around the Democratic establishment candidate. Increasingly, the Clinton campaign narrative referenced her strength of support among minorities.

Clinton's moment winning the CBC endorsement was quickly crushed when word leaked the State Department's office of inspector general (IG) had opened an investigation regarding the Bill, Hillary, and Chelsea Clinton foundation during her secretary of state tenure. Word also leaked the IG had subpoenaed foundation records relating to Clinton's close aide, Huma Abedin, the foundation itself, Clinton's personal office, and "a private consulting firm with ties to the Clintons."[342]

Recall the essentials of the narrative: Wealthy foreign actors gave vast sums to the foundation, sometimes as payment for a speech, sometimes for some other favor. Lo and behold, Secretary of State Hillary Clinton did something nice for them: give a speech, place a call, nudge a policy, whatever. In the political lexicon, this is called payola. The only differences from typical payola are the payments often went to the Clintons indirectly; the payments weren't in cold, hard cash, and the amounts involved had lots more zeros.

Those were words Hillary Clinton didn't want to see in the same sentence: inspector general, subpoena, Clinton. Under a Democratic administration in which she had previously served, the Clintons were under at least three separate investigations; and she hadn't even secured the nomination yet:

1. The State Department IG's inquiry regarding Clinton and the foundation
2. The State Department's ongoing investigation into the private email server
3. The FBI investigation into the Clinton email server[343]

On top of these bubbled the various Freedom of Information Act exercises proceeding under a federal judge's watchful and impatient eyes.

Regarding the State Department's investigation into the private email server, U.S. District Court Judge Rudolph Contreras had run out of patience. He issued an order requiring all remaining still-undisclosed Clinton emails be released in rapid-fire batches, with all to be released by February 29.[344]

Naturally the State Department missed the judge's previous deadline badly. He dinged the department accordingly. Would state make the new deadline? Was state incompetent or abetting a cover-up for a politically convenient period? Fair questions.

Not a matter of speculation, this story would stay in the news, threatening at any moment to blow up in Clinton's face, at least up to the SEC primary. Ouch.

In the midst of these developments came another Sanders-Clinton debate hosted by PBS and simulcast on CNN. This one got testy, though at least it didn't feature another hug by the moderator. The nation was furious at the state of the country in so many ways, yet Clinton had fully embraced the "Obama's third term" mantra, for in truth she had no choice.[345] This allowed Sanders to add Obama to his targets of gripe. And gripe he did.

The debate was largely scored a draw, following past themes: aspirational "you can have it all" versus "dream, but be practical." Sanders unquestionably got in the best lines. After Clinton chastised Sanders for criticizing Obama, he responded, "One of us ran against Pres. Obama. I was not that candidate."[346] He struck again when Clinton tried putting Sanders in his place with her imperious former secretary of state voice. After referring to her repeatedly as "Madam Secretary," he put a spotlight on her arrogance by scolding, "You are not in the White House yet."

Debate as Debacle

Republicans held their last debate prior to the South Carolina caucuses on Saturday, February 13. For the first time, all six of the remaining candidates were onstage together. It wasn't much of a debate. Debacle described it better as even the happy warrior John Kasich couldn't help but descend into the mud pits for a round or two with Jeb Bush.

If the purpose of debates involved helping voters decide who best reflected their values, had best thought through the nation's problems and had sensible answers, or seemed most suitable to the office of the presidency, then the debate was a total flop. If the purpose was to make as many voters as possible conclude, "a pox on all their houses," then it was a rousing success.

Donald Trump proved, once again, he lived in an alternative reality defended with volleys of insults. He still insisted he would make the Mexican government pay for a wall along the nation's southern border. He still insisted were it not for his candidacy, immigration wouldn't even be discussed. Somehow the huge immigration battles in Washington in recent years escaped his notice, especially the one about which Ted Cruz and Chris Christie had hammered Marco Rubio in the New Hampshire debate with Trump standing right there.

Trump still insisted he would bring back American jobs from China, from Mexico, from Japan. He made a great many such claims; and when pressed as to how he would perform these miracles, the answer always revolved around "being smart" and "hiring smart people." Details not forthcoming.

Then Trump said something awesomely absurd. Trump blamed George W. Bush for allowing the attacks on September 11, as though Bush would somehow know about and be able to stop threats about which his own national security apparatus had been completely ignorant. This was the same national security apparatus that later misled Bush into the Iraq War. But Trump went further. He said, "I will tell you. They lied. They [the Bush Administration] said there were weapons of mass destruction [in Iraq] and there were none. And they knew there were none."[347]

Just to review the known facts, Saddam Hussein had toiled to create the impression he had a stockpile of weapons of mass destruction. His claims were credible because he'd used such weapons on his own people, on the Kurds, and in the earlier Iran-Iraq War. Even many in the United States and elsewhere who opposed the Iraq War believed Hussein had these weapons. Even the Pacifist French were convinced. The dispute was not whether Hussein had the weapons he claimed but what to do about them. Bush was misled and so launched the Iraq War on false grounds, but he didn't lie about the WMD. Trump, simply put, was off his rocker.

But this wasn't the worst of the nastiness. Just about everybody on the stage called someone else a liar. Cruz called Trump a phony conservative, which was at least one credible charge among the many thrown about.

No one should be thought to have "won" this "debate." There were no winners, only those who managed to accomplish something positive during the embarrassment. For example, Rubio showed himself to be the strongest candidate on foreign policy. And he thoroughly recovered from any robotic-like mannerisms of the previous debate.

Cruz did a fair job explaining why Trump was no conservative or at best a very recent and convenient convert. It wasn't hard. Trump was in many ways the Hillary Clinton of the Republican field. At one time or another, he'd been on every side of every issue. Now anti-abortion, he had been a lifelong abortion advocate. Now pro-traditional family, he'd been pro-gay marriage. Now in favor of pro-growth tax cuts, he'd previously and repeatedly supported whatever tax hike was then popular among Democrats.

Bush finally showed he had some fight in him. Trump wasn't just an opponent to Bush; he was a living insult, a crass blight whose very presence on the stage Bush increasingly found repugnant. Moreover, the audience seemed to agree; for just as in the previous debate, the audience booed Trump repeatedly and with gusto. Trump, unmoved, seemed energized by the revulsion directed his way, claiming they were all Bush or RNC plants. Unfortunately for Bush, he found his fight too late.

Carson showed he remained a nice man wholly out of his element. Honorable mention should go to John Dickerson of CBS News, who did a most creditable job keeping the proceedings proceeding despite all the mud being slung.

The Longest-Serving Supreme Falls

Just hours prior to the debate, the nation learned of the passing of the longest-serving Supreme Court Justice, Antonin Scalia. Brilliant even by Supreme Court standards, Scalia was unique in many respects. While capable of writing in typical highbrow legalese, he could also express himself in simple, common-man terms to release his outrage at some of the court's more nonsensical rulings. After he was appointed by Ronald Reagan in 1986, the Senate confirmed him unanimously despite his strong conservatism. Scalia's best friend on the court was widely believed to be its most liberal member, Ruth Bader Ginsburg.

Politics being all-consuming, especially in an election year, the immediate question arose whether Obama would, or should, nominate a successor. In a rational world, the answer would obviously be yes. The Supreme Court, representing the pinnacle of the third branch of the federal government, required a full house to do its job properly. However, there were complications. For example, a nomination would take time to clear the Senate, which meant the new justice would be seated long after the court completed much of its work for the year.

The real issue was not timing but politics, and Republicans quickly united behind the position the new justice should be nominated by a new president. All the Republican candidates at the South Carolina "debate" agreed; each wanted to be the president to appoint the next supreme.

Pres. Obama let it be known just as quickly he intended to put forward a nomination. Step one was to try to bully or embarrass Republicans into letting him put another liberal on the court. Obama had nothing to lose by trying.

The president chastised so-called constitutionalists who insisted on reading the text of the Constitution with the meaning, or construction, it bore when it was written. If one wants the Constitution to say something different, Scalia would argue, then you have to amend the Constitution and the document lays out two means to do so. You cannot simply read something into the text that is plainly not there or simply read something out of the text because you do not like it. The Constitution, the foundation of our entire legal structure, ought not shift based solely on personal preferences lest the legal structure be unsound, eventually producing incoherent and conflicting results.

Obama chastised the strict constructionists for ignoring the plain text under which the president is to nominate a candidate for the Supreme Court and the Senate is to give due consideration under "advise and consent." As one who opposed the "constructionist" point of view and who had tried repeatedly to refashion the Constitution according to his own preferences, Obama was exercising his own supreme hypocrisy in trying to argue the Republicans' hypocrisy.

Further, nowhere in the Constitution does it prescribe how or how long the Senate is supposed to take in exercising its "advise and consent" responsibilities. Tradition and precedent are useful reference points, but they are not dispositive.

Congressional Republicans were simply playing hardball. And if they found themselves in some future debate where a lame-duck Republican president was about to nominate a Supreme Court Justice, they would no doubt exercise their God-given right to be total hypocrites, stand on the Constitution, and blame Democrats for obstructionism—just as Democrats did this time.

In 2007, with eighteen months to go in the George W. Bush presidency (roughly twice the time frame at issue in 2016), New York Sen. Chuck Schumer said, "I will recommend to my colleagues that we should not confirm a Supreme Court nominee except in extraordinary circumstances."[348] He went on to add the proviso that, of course, if Bush were to nominate a candidate Schumer liked, that would be OK.

The press covered these developments with a straight face and barely hidden snigger. It was a spectacle. Spectacles sell newspapers. As long as the American people tolerate this nonsense, it will continue.

In reality, any Obama nominee at this point would be lucky to get a hearing in the Senate Judiciary Committee; and if he or she received a hearing, it would be brutal. Then, unless the nominee proved a complete disaster, the committee would hold no vote on the nomination, insisting in a pinch there wasn't enough time to vet the candidate properly. And if by some miracle the nomination were reported out of committee, Senate Republican Leader Mitch McConnell made it immediately and abundantly clear there would be no Senate confirmation vote.

Rather than offer up a sacrificial lamb, the more sensible course was for Obama, Clinton, and Sanders to lambast Republicans for politicizing the process as though it hadn't been thoroughly politicized decades ago (remember Robert Bork and Clarence Thomas?) and then have Clinton and Sanders acknowledge Obama should defer so that they, either Clinton or Sanders, could make the appointment and have it be considered by the next Democrat-controlled (they hoped) U.S. Senate.

Perhaps the most sensible course but not Obama's course. He found someone fully qualified by all initial appearances and someone willing to risk months of torture for little prospect of success. On March 16, Merrick Garland dove into the cauldron. Although he was a respected chief justice of the U.S. Court of Appeals for the District of Columbia, as expected, Garland's nomination went nowhere.

Another Clinton Email Drip, with a Caddell Kicker

The State Department conveniently released another batch of Clinton emails just before the next Republican debate: 551 emails; 1,000 pages; 84 emails retroactively classified of which three were classified "secret." The emails and their contents weren't really news; but the release kept the bigger story in the news, once again reminding the public how Clinton had kept a private server while secretary of state; that she had done it for her own convenience (read: to cover her tracks); that doing so was contrary to the rules applied to everyone else in the State Department, indeed in the federal government anywhere; and that, as a result, a great deal of extremely sensitive information could had been hacked by America's enemies as Guccifer later confirmed.

While some Americans took note of the Clinton email release story, the Democratic establishment took note of comments by Pat Caddell, Jimmy Carter's former pollster, television commentator, and Democratic political advisor. Clinton, Caddell explained, had used her connections at the State Department to enrich her family, her friends, and her foundation. "They all ought to be indicted. This is worse than Watergate."[349]

Caddell continued, "They were selling out the national interests of the United States directly to adversaries and others for money. There is nothing that satisfies them. They are the greediest white trash I have ever seen."

Coming from a Tea Party Republican congressman, comments like these would have led off the evening news and been as quickly dismissed with the typical tut-tutting to the effect conservatives aren't really house-broken. Coming from Pat Caddell, these comments had to send a deep chill down the spines of the Democratic establishment who hoped to install Hillary Clinton to remain in power. Worse, as an AP story released in late August of 2016 confirmed, and then the pre-election WikiLeaks email dumps laid bare, Caddell was 100% correct.³⁵⁰

Trump Fights with the Pope

The last thing one might expect in a political campaign akin to a drunken barroom brawl was to see the pope butt in, scepter and all, yet that's exactly what he did. In a visit to Mexico, the pontiff opined, "A person who thinks only about building walls, wherever they may be, and not building bridges, is not a Christian." Further, "I'd just say this man is not Christian if he said it this way."³⁵¹ Note the words "this man."

A papal spokesman later tried walking back the pontiff's comments as not being directed against Donald Trump or any presidential candidate, which gave new meaning to the term *papal bull*.

The pope then learned an important lesson about playing with the big boys. Trump blasted him:

> If and when the Vatican is attacked by ISIS, which as everyone knows is ISIS's ultimate trophy, I can promise you that the Pope would have only wished and prayed that Donald Trump would have been president because this would not have happened. ISIS would have been eradicated unlike what is happening now with our all talk, no action politicians.
>
> The Mexican government and its leadership has made many disparaging remarks about me to the Pope, because they want to continue to rip off the United States, both on trade and at the border, and they understand I am totally wise to them. The Pope only heard one side of the story—he didn't see the crime, the drug trafficking and the negative economic impact the current policies have on the United States.

> He doesn't see how Mexican leadership is outsmarting Pres. Obama and our leadership in every aspect of negotiation.
>
> For a religious leader to question a person's faith is disgraceful. I am proud to be a Christian and as president I will not allow Christianity to be consistently attacked and weakened, unlike what is happening now, with our current president. No leader, especially a religious leader, should have the right to question another man's religion or faith. They are using the Pope as a pawn and they should be ashamed of themselves for doing so, especially when so many lives are involved and when illegal immigration is so rampant.[352]

Calling the pope out as "disgraceful" was typical Trump and could only work if the pope's behavior had indeed been disgraceful. Once again, Trump scored a direct hit. Later, Trump again surprised by attempting to tone down the dispute, calling the pope "a terrific person" who just didn't understand the extent of the "crime problem" caused by illegal immigration.[353]

Would this little spat hurt Trump's campaign? The pope was popular. Conventional wisdom said Trump should have hurt himself. He didn't. The pope tried his best "holier than thou" routine and got punked because, in fact, he'd crossed a line religious leaders especially dared not cross: questioning a person's faith.

The whole episode added to Trump's tough-guy image, a welcome alternative for many to that of the current president and most politicians. As Jeb Bush noted in a television interview on his own failed campaign months later, "[The Pope] was talking about basically open borders at a time when the whole Trump phenomenon was to build a wall and make Mexico pay for it. [The Pope] literally goes to the wall for a massive mass. I don't think he understood he was intervening in our political affairs."[354]

In taking on a politically inept pontiff, Trump added to his tough-guy persona, which many voters across the political spectrum were rewarding as an alternative to squish and nuance. Also, in South Carolina, where "evangelicals" still occasionally murmured over papist conspiracies, a little righteous papal pushback just might be welcome.

Nikki's Nod

South Carolinians elected Nikki Haley Governor in 2010. The Palmetto State Republican establishment was not happy. They were happy to control the governor's mansion, but they wanted one of their own. Haley was an outsider in a state where good ol' boys were used to runnin' things. Haley had been urged to run by outgoing Governor, now Congressman, Mark Sanford, he of the Argentinian fling. The good ol' boys split into two competing camps; and Haley drove her campaign bus right between them on up the mansion's driveway, winning 51 to 47%.

Haley was reelected in 2014, 55.9 to 41.3%. An articulate woman, Haley was born in South Carolina to parents who'd emigrated from Punjab, India. As evidence of her "rising star" status among Republicans, Haley had given the Republican response to Pres. Obama's final State of the Union Address a month earlier and was on many Republican shortlists as a vice presidential candidate.

Obviously, Haley's endorsement would carry a lot of weight in South Carolina. Endorsing Trump would have been a shock. Endorsing Cruz would have surprised. So that left Rubio, Bush, and Kasich as logical recipients and all three vied hard for her favor. But Bush wasn't catching fire, and Kasich looked increasingly the one-shot wonder. Marco Rubio was the natural beneficiary; and indeed on Wednesday, the seventeenth, Haley endorsed Rubio, adding her voice to that of Tim Scott, South Carolina's African American Tea Party Republican Senator. A Rubio-Haley ticket sure looked formidable.

TRUMP GOES LITE ON POLICY

Donald Trump's campaign was built entirely on his persona. The guy who pushes back. The guy who told it like it was. The New York tough guy in contrast to Pres. Obama's faculty-lounge approach to national leadership. The enthusiastic guy for whom everything good was "hyuge." The mug who described anyone who disagreed with him as "stupid." The sensitive guy who complained adverse events are always because somebody did something "unfair, unfair." His campaign was not built on policy expertise.

Trump's immigration policy? Build a wall and make Mexico pay for it. His economic policy? Make U.S. companies like Ford and GM move their operations back to the United States. How? By making the United States a more attractive place to do business? No, he'd just make them come back, details pending.

Trump's tax plan was by far the most amateur of any candidates', Republican or Democrat. What about health care reform? The only discussion on his website referred to the "drug epidemic," an important topic to be sure, but only an isolated piece of the health care reform debate. When pressed, Trump said he'd get a bunch of experts in the room until they came up with a solution. And who were these experts? Trump wouldn't say, and no one would confess. As Michael Cannon, a respected health policy expert at the CATO Institute, observed, "He seems to be a one-man policy shop."[355]

The problem is not finding substantive solutions. The problem for Social Security reform, as for Medicare reform or tax reform or many of these areas, is finding a political consensus and the political will to guide the experts in choosing among the many possible solutions. The president is supposed to provide that direction so the experts can do their jobs. Trump didn't understand the president had to do more than empanel a bunch of experts. Presidents need to lead.

Flaming Tongues of Fire

The feud between Donald Trump and Ted Cruz ramped up rapidly. Cruz attacked Trump as a know-nothing, lying, phony conservative. Trump attacked Cruz as a pathological liar and "nasty guy." Rubio saw a chance to wound Cruz, so he jumped on the "Cruz is a liar" bandwagon: "He's [Cruz is] lying, and I think that's disturbing."[356]

Trump speaking of Cruz said, "He holds up the Bible nice and high but he lies and I think the evangelicals have figured it out because I'm leading the evangelicals by a lot."[357] The latter statement was undeniably true. The evangelicals were supposed to be the core of Cruz's base, especially in South Carolina; yet Trump had almost twice as much South Carolina evangelical support as Cruz according to the polls.

Trump also threatened to sue Cruz about an ad Cruz ran in South Carolina regarding abortion, and he threatened to sue Cruz about his ability under the Constitution as Canadian born to be president. Cruz replied, "Bring it on, and I'll 'take the deposition myself.'"

Trump's mistake was forgetting Cruz was, for all his oddities, a brilliant lawyer. In a lengthy and detailed press conference, Cruz took Trump apart, "You know I have to say to Mr. Trump, you have been threatening frivolous lawsuits for your entire adult life. Even in the annals of frivolous lawsuits, this takes the cake.... It is a remarkable contention that an ad that plays video of Donald Trump speaking on national television is somehow defamation."[358]

For his part, Jeb Bush and his supporters could only wonder what went wrong: so much money, so much top-flight campaign talent, such a nice guy. Bush was getting really frustrated and couldn't hide it anymore. At a campaign rally in South Carolina, Bush was caught on camera asking, one presumes rhetorically, "I should stop campaigning, maybe?"[359] His solution? He stopped wearing glasses. Bold. And for all the campaigning and effort, the polls weren't moving, at all.

Game Day for the Gamecocks

The week prior to the South Carolina Republican primary provided all the pyrotechnics a political junkie could ask for; but in the end, they changed little. Hundreds of volunteers flown into the state. Campaign coffers drained on TV ads. But when the South Carolina campaign started, Trump was on top at around 30%, Rubio and Cruz were jockeying for second, while Bush, Kasich, and Carson each prayed for a miracle. And that's how the voting played out, except there were no miracles; and the three bringing up the rear actually fared worse than expected.

South Carolina Polls

	Pre-Vote Polls[360]	Voting Results
Trump	31.5	32.5
Rubio	18.8	22.5
Cruz	18.5	22.3
Bush	10.7	7.8
Kasich	9.0	7.6
Carson	8.9	7.2

To his credit, Bush was honest enough to realize the game was up; and so on Saturday night of the vote, he "suspended" his campaign. Feelings were still too raw in Jeb land to take the next sensible step of endorsing Rubio; but it seemed inevitable at the time, if not before the Nevada caucuses on Tuesday then certainly shortly thereafter.

Kasich didn't say much at all about his poor performance, and Carson just seemed to be amazed that in a technical sense at least he was still hanging around. But Carson and Kasich both had scored worse than Bush, and Kasich was a nonentity before and after New Hampshire. It was time for all the pretenders to give up the game.

Ted Cruz liked to proclaim the Republican establishment was deeply frightened by the rising grassroots movement he represented.

He was partly right but less because his conservatism was so edgy or that he would threaten all the cozy relationships between the political class, the media class, and the business class. Sorry, Ted, but presidents just don't have that much power. Or, as many a bureaucrat thought, and some said when their newly arrived political appointee arrived in a new post, "Sir/Madam, we are all WeBes here: We be here when you got here. We be here when you're gone."

No, Cruz scared the political establishment because his judgment had been so poor for so long when leading budget legislative battles. It was time for Bush and Lindsey Graham and Chris Christie to get on the phone with Kasich to tell him, "John, you've run a good campaign. One you can be proud of. But the writing is on the wall: you can't win. But if you stay in much longer, we may not be able to stop Trump or Ted. For the good of the country, we're asking you to consider getting out, like we all did when the cause was lost, and then we're all going to endorse Rubio. Staying in now is about hubris, not service. We need to put the country first."

The sting of Saturday's loss was still too fresh, but perhaps by Monday Bush could make such a call. There wasn't much time, however, as the Republicans caucused in Nevada on Tuesday. Apparently, they never made the call.

Cruz was having a very bad week:

- Coming in third in South Carolina, a state he was expected to trounce in
- Firing his chief spokesperson for validating the claims made against his campaign regarding dirty tricks
- Bush getting out of the race

Yes, Bush's exit was bad news for Cruz because it was great news for Rubio. Suddenly, every name on Bush's massive donor list became a potential Rubio donor. True, some would go to Cruz and some to Trump and maybe one or two to Kasich, but Rubio would get the lion's share. Rubio should soon be rolling in dough. Also, Rubio benefited from a flood of endorsements once Bush was gone.

Suddenly, Rubio was the clear messianic anti-Trump for whom the saner world pined. Whether these shifting fortunes would have time to manifest in Nevada was unclear, but to matter they had to show up in spades on Super Tuesday.

SANDERS'S ROLL OF THE DICE

The Democrats' Nevada caucuses followed immediately after the Republicans' South Carolina primary. Nevada was to be part of Clinton's firewall against an insurgency; and a couple months before Iowa, it sure looked that way. She had the organization, especially the powerful Las Vegas unions. Though he pretended neutrality, in reality she had the shadowy support of the reigning king of Nevada, Senate Minority Leader Harry Reid. Clinton had the money. And she was way ahead in the polls. But after New Hampshire, the ground shifted rapidly.

As a relative latecomer to the campaign, one would imagine Sanders's organization would be spare and Sanders at a substantial disadvantage—not so. As of early February, he had more than eighty staffers on the ground and more offices in the state than Clinton. He had also spent more than $3.5 million on ads in English and Spanish.

Just to protect themselves from too much embarrassment lest Nevada didn't go their way, the Clinton campaign early on tried the "whites only" defense. Clinton spokesman Brian Fallon noted 80% of Nevadans are white.[361] "There's a reason to believe the race will tighten even there."

The polling data and the momentum suggested Clinton had cause for concern. One poll taken in late December showed her leading 50 to 27, with 23% undecided.[362] Another poll taken a few weeks later showed the race tied at 45%.[363] A huge swing, and only 10% of respondents were undecided. Clinton was one of the best-known politicians in America. The remaining 10% knew her well and yet weren't persuaded while Sanders was becoming very persuasive.

Sanders's tactics going all in were undoubtedly correct. He had the momentum. He had Clinton on the ropes. He needed to press the attack. Yet he failed. He came close, but the victory went to Clinton in a squeaker. She could breathe a little easier, if just barely.

	Nevada Polls[364]	Nevada Results
Clinton	48.7	52.7
Sanders	46.3	47.2

One could fairly ask at this point whether Sanders had much of a chance after Nevada. Next up was South Carolina, where Clinton was strong and the black vote substantial; and after that came the SEC states where, again, she had organization and strength. Sanders couldn't build a viable organization in each state, and he couldn't throw an army of volunteers into each state as he did in Nevada. If Clinton strung together a set of strong wins, Sanders likely would never recover. Everything seemed much brighter in Hillary land as long as the money kept coming and the scandals were contained.

Republicans Try Their Luck

The Nevada caucuses on February 23 magnified the prevailing narrative. Trump was winning before, and he won big in Nevada, for the first time getting a higher percentage than his nearest two rivals combined. Rubio continued his run of second-place finishes. Cruz continued his recent run of bad news. Kasich and Carson remained in the race, still for no discernible reason.

The last two polls prior to voting were released Sunday night by Gravis and CNN/ORC and were taken February 14–15 and February 10–15, respectively. These dates are important because it meant the polls didn't reflect any effects from the South Carolina voting or Jeb Bush's exit.

Average of Two Polls

	Pre-Voting	Nevada Results
	(In Percent)	
Trump	42	45.9
Rubio	19	23.9
Cruz	21	21.4
Kasich	7	3.6
Carson	6	4.8
Bush	4	n/a

Without question, Trump won Nevada big. His victory speech was totally Trumperian: "We weren't expected to win too much and now we're winning, winning, winning the country. And soon the country is going to start winning, winning, winning."[365] How the country would start "winning" if Trump were elected remained a campaign secret.

THE TEXAS GANG FIGHT

You've trained for years in the "sweet science," learning the pugilistic arts. You've learned to jab like lightning. You've learned to slide side to side, to slip punches and counter, to bob and weave. You get in the ring for the big fight, lace up your gloves, and looking over see your opponent has a foot-long knife in one hand and a six-foot chain in the other.

This picture describes the previous Republican debates. Donald Trump was always the one with the chain and the knife. In the Texas debate held the Thursday before Super Tuesday, hosted by CNN and moderated by Wolf Blitzer, Ted Cruz and Marco Rubio brought their own chains and knives. Had the debate been rated by the Motion Picture Association of America, it would have received an R rating for verbal violence.

The Texas event wasn't a debate. Politically, it was worse than a debacle as everyone looked really bad. The Texas event was a barrio street fight; and for the most part, it was two on one with two spectators and an occasionally outmatched referee in Blitzer. Cruz and Rubio had obviously concluded if they didn't take Trump out now, then nothing else mattered, their campaigns wouldn't survive the week, while Kasich and Carson were in the ring smiling like this was all afternoon tea.

In the final score, everyone lost. As had become their custom, they repeatedly called one another a liar. They openly mocked one another, interrupted one another, talked over one another louder and louder. Through it all, Blitzer managed as best one could, often teeing up tough questions and pressing for real answers, especially from Trump. At times, all Blitzer could do was allow the fury to spend itself.

Trump still came out the fighter; but for the first time, the blows directed his way landed solid. Trump repeatedly looked outmatched. He was left "sputtering," attempting to parry the attacks with personal jabs that for once left Cruz and Rubio unfazed.[366]

Just hours before the debate, former Mexican Pres. Vincente Fox went right after one of Trump's most popular lines in declaring, "I'm not going to pay for that f——ing wall."[367] Blitzer asked Trump about this directly. "How are you going to make Mexico pay for building the wall?" Answer: "I will, and the wall just got 10 feet taller, believe me."

Fine, but how would he force the Mexican government to pay for the wall? Never an answer, though in later days he referenced the possibility of halting remittances from Mexicans in the United States back to Mexico as possible leverage, a possibility the legality of which was highly dubious.

Blitzer asked about health care reform. Trump's solution was to allow insurers to compete across state lines. Increase competition and prices fall while service improves. All good, but what else? As Dana Bash, another CNN moderator, pressed, "But, just to be specific, what you're saying is getting rid of the barriers between states, that is going to solve the problem." Trump responded, "That is going to solve the problem."³⁶⁸

On health care, Rubio then rode Trump like a carnival mule until finally Bash brought Trump's meltdown to a close with "Is there anything else you would like to add to that [interstate competition]?" Trump's response: no, there's nothing to add.³⁶⁹

Interstate competition is a sound idea included in the plans laid out by all four of the other candidates. But it's only one relatively small piece of health care reform. After repealing Obamacare, another item they all agreed on, what else would you do for health care reform, Mr. Trump? "Nothing."

What about providing low-income people the resources to buy their own insurance? Obamacare had various direct subsidies; most alternative plans had some combination of refundable tax credits and the like. What did Trump's plan have? Crickets.

Trump's tax reform plan would cut taxes by nearly $12 trillion over ten years according to the nonpartisan Tax Foundation, a figure widely cited and broadly accepted.³⁷⁰ The latest Congressional Budget Office projection had the federal debt already rising by $10 trillion from 2016 to 2026 under current policies, with deficits eventually far exceeding $1 trillion annually. Cutting taxes massively under the circumstances was insanity by any lights. Blitzer challenged Trump to say how he would offset those costs.

Trump's only answer was to observe we needed to reinvigorate our economy, which was true, and that his tax plan would do that, which was doubtful. According to the Tax Foundation, the revenue feedback from economic growth due to Trump's plan reduced the tab to just over $10 trillion. This was astounding. It's not easy coming up with a tax plan reducing revenues by nearly $12 trillion over ten years and yet get so little additional growth in response.

Trump's tax plan was symptomatic of all Trump's policies: naive and simplistic. The other candidates also had tax plans with large tax cuts; but as usual, Trump's was far bigger and less effective in every way except further degrading the nation's finances.

Speaking of taxes, one rite of presidential politics is that a candidate releases his or her tax returns. This is an outrageous invasion of personal privacy, but voters like to be sure you are who you say you are, and you've paid all the tax owed under the law. Trump hadn't released his tax returns; so Mitt Romney called him out on it, suggesting maybe Trump had something to hide.[371] Why Romney? Because his own campaign nearly collapsed in 2012 resisting the call to release his returns.

Trump harrumphed. He insulted Romney. He tried to change the subject. During the debate, Blitzer challenged him on releasing his returns. Trump said he'd love to, but he's being audited and can't release the returns until the audit was complete. How convenient. He'd submitted the returns already. He signed the returns. Nothing about an IRS audit precluded him from releasing his returns. Surely he could at least release earlier returns not currently under audit.

All the rest said they'd be releasing their returns immediately. Rubio had the best line: "I'm happy to release my returns. They're pretty simple." One of the few advantages of being of modest means.

Thursday's mud wrestling continued well into Friday. Rubio had obviously decided the best way to beat Trump was to match Trump pettiness for pettiness, insult for insult; so in Texas the two men engaged in a childish tit for tat. Rubio repeatedly made fun of Trump for being a serial tweeter and misspelling his tweets to boot. Rubio called Trump a "con artist" and Trump called Rubio a "choke artist," referring to Rubio's halting performance in the New Hampshire debate.[372]

"It's time to pull the mask off and see what we're dealing with. What we are dealing with, my friends, is a con artist," Rubio challenged.

Trump punched back, "When you're a choke artist [referring to Rubio], you're always a choke artist."

Rubio questioned Trump's business acumen and veracity. He observed that during the debate, "he [Trump] wanted a full-length mirror. Maybe to make sure his pants weren't wet."

Trump fired back calling Rubio a "lightweight" and a "nervous little puppy." All in Cruz's backyard and yet Cruz was nowhere to be seen. Perhaps for the first time in his life, Ted Cruz had nothing to say.

Rubio also came back to hammer Trump repeatedly on some substantive issues, like a $1 million judgment against Trump in a court proceeding in which he was charged with conspiracy to hire illegal aliens to work on Trump Tower and another judgment against him on a money-laundering charge.[373]

Could this get any weirder? The day after the Texas barroom brawl, Chris Christie endorsed not John Kasich, not Rubio, or even Cruz. Christie endorsed Trump, thereby distracting some press attention from Rubio's very effective attacks. One tactic Trump excelled at was timing a surprise or event to take positive attention away from an antagonist. Recall earlier he had delayed his press conference following a campaign victory to push Clinton's press conference much later in the evening.

Trump had just recently gotten his first two congressional endorsements, from Buffalo, New York, Republican Chris Collins and Californian Duncan Hunter. But Christie was the first national-stage Republican to endorse Trump, arguing Trump was "the best person to beat Hillary Clinton in November."[374]

Perhaps Christie meant what he said; but a cynic might wonder whether Christie knew his future in New Jersey was cloudy and a tidy cabinet spot, maybe even the vice presidency, in a Trump administration might do nicely. For a long time, Christie had been seen as the Republican establishment's favored candidate, and here he was endorsing a candidate threatening to destroy the Republican establishment in toto.

Next Up, Dems in South Carolina

The curious structure of the Nevada and South Carolina voting produced something of a ping-pong feel to the race. Attention shifted again to South Carolina. Just in time, Hillary Clinton suffered another bout of the drip, drip, drip email scandal. U.S. District Court Judge Emmet G. Sullivan ordered certain State Department officials and top Clinton aides to be questioned under oath regarding apparent efforts to thwart federal open-records laws.[375]

The judge also ensured this torture would continue well into the campaign. The respective parties had until April 12 to come up with a detailed investigative plan the judge would have to approve, after which the plan would take some months to execute. Judge Sullivan also indicated he might require the State Department and Clinton to turn over all emails relating to Clinton's private account, not just those state and Clinton had previously deemed work related.

This story came on the heels of the widely reported full lemon-puss answer Clinton gave about whether she ever lied. Yes, it got so bad even the mainstream media had to address it, and Clinton flubbed it badly. In a lengthy on-camera interview, well-known Hillary fan Scott Pelley of CBS News asked, "You talk about leveling with the American people. Have you always told the truth?"

Clinton's response, "I've always tried to. Always. Always."[376] Always *tried to* tell the truth. Not a simple "yes, of course." She "tried."

Truth teller or no, Clinton looked to be set for a crushing win in South Carolina. The latest polls released prior to voting had her up over Sanders about 60 to 30%. In the voting she did even better, shellacking Sanders 73% to 26%, picking up thirty-nine delegates to his fourteen.[377] She won every county in the state. She won among Democrats four to one. The only worrying sign was she lost by a small margin among independents.

After Nevada and South Carolina, Sanders appeared to be a one-hit wonder: New Hampshire, with a near miss in Iowa. Sanders had been a strong-momentum candidate until Harry Reid ambushed him in Nevada. Reid would insist he'd not endorsed either candidate to allow a full debate, but in truth he'd fired up his impressive campaign apparatus to ensure Clinton's narrow win. Not that Reid liked Clinton all that much or disliked Sanders, but Harry Reid hated losing. He was retiring, and he didn't want Sanders at the top of the ticket, giving away his seat to the Republicans. And he didn't want Sanders giving away the White House either, which seemed likely if Sanders rather than Clinton won the nomination.

Having lost his momentum in Nevada and a big loss in South Carolina, it appeared the end was coming soon for Sanders, but once again he surprised.

Who's Got the Numbers?

With four contests down and Super Tuesday up next, the respective delegate counts began to matter. Trump and Clinton were winning contests and had what appeared to be sizable leads in delegates. Yet Trump's 81 delegates meant he still needed another 1,156 to win the nomination, and Clinton was in a similar position. On March 1, Super Tuesday, the race for delegates would intensify markedly. Many of these states were winner-take-all.

Delegate Count after South Carolina and Nevada

	Iowa	New Hampshire	Nevada	South Carolina	Total
Trump	7	10	14	50	81
Rubio	7	3	6	0	17
Kasich	1	4	1	0	17
Carson	3	0	1	0	4
Clinton	23	9	20	39	91
Sanders	21	15	15	14	75

The Narrative Process

Media talking heads rely heavily on "the narrative process" to know what to say, what to dispute, and what to argue. The narrative can always change on a dime, and almost always those who espoused the old narrative with utmost confidence will shift to the new narrative effortlessly and without acknowledging the switch. For a long time, the national narrative had Trump as a curiosity, a nuisance, a buffoon, an entertainer, anything but a serious candidate. The media invested so heavily in this narrative they were loath to abandon it and didn't really know how. In the end, they created a new sub-narrative: I was wrong, and I still don't know why.

The new narrative about the Republican contest appeared only moments after the South Carolina primary was called for Trump, who was no deemed "unstoppable," "inevitable." He had a "stranglehold" on the nomination. Only Cruz in Iowa following a disputed result (remember the pre-voting rumors of Carson allegedly quitting the campaign) had beaten Trump; and since Iowa, Trump appeared to be racking up solid victories. But was Trump really unstoppable? After three events in which almost 70% of the voters preferred another candidate, according to the new reigning narrative, Trump had the nomination nearly sewn up.

Recall the narrative after New Hampshire's primary: Hillary Clinton was on the ropes, and Bernie Sanders seemed unstoppable. The media want a narrative, however fleeting, because it's the safe place from which to pontificate; and they prefer near absolutes because those are simpler to explain but still leave some room to speculate. That's all fine as long as one doesn't fall for the show.

The typical counter to the "inevitable Trump" narrative suggested as the field narrowed, most of the votes previously going to Christie, Bush, etc., would go mostly to Rubio. Bush, Christie, Rubio, and Kasich all largely appealed to the same block of voters; and those voters were generally leery of Cruz and disliked Trump. Eventually, the 70% who didn't support Trump would coalesce around the remaining anti-Trump, and Trump would be finally trounced. That was their fervent prayer anyway.

CHAPTER 14
MARCH, THE SUPER MONTH

The campaigns quickly shifted gears with the voting over in Nevada and South Carolina. Much less retail grip and grin, campaigning was more about the celebrity fly in and bye, the big stage event, free media, and paid advertisements.

Among Republicans, Ted Cruz was wounded, Marco Rubio was wobbly, and Donald Trump counted his past victories expecting many more. On the Democratic side, Bernie Sanders appeared to be dead man walking, while Hillary Clinton, despite herself, seemed in position to deliver the coup de grace.

March 1, a.k.a. Super Tuesday, was sometimes also called the SEC Bowl because so many southern states participated, many of them members of the collegiate Southeastern Conference. All told, eleven or twelve or thirteen states were voting depending on how one counted. For many states, no publicly available polls had been released in weeks.

An Odd Calm

With a couple fleeting exceptions, an odd calm descended on the campaign after Clinton stomped Sanders in South Carolina. Reporters reported while candidates made the rounds of the Sunday morning talk shows then flitted about the country. Yet there seemed little suspense, as though the country needed a respite from the ugliness.

Trump continued to pick up endorsements. Particularly surprising, the strongly conservative and normally judicious and gentlemanly Alabama Sen. Jeff Sessions endorsed Trump while Bush and Mitt Romney and an innumerable host of Republican establishment voices remained on the sidelines further reinforcing their utter irrelevance to the nomination and the future of their own party. Some so-called leaders simply didn't know whether to piss or get off the pot. One notable exception was strong conservative and former Oklahoma Sen. Tom Coburn, who came out in support of Rubio, claiming Trump was "perpetrating a fraud."[378]

Many conservatives agreed with Coburn, so it was difficult explaining Sessions's endorsement of Trump. One possibility was Sessions's very strong views about illegal immigration and the need to secure the southern border, but this suggested he could endorse Cruz. Another possibility was Sessions's strong familiarity with Cruz from their time together in the U.S. Senate fighting shoulder to shoulder. Perhaps Sessions agreed with so many others that for all his brilliance and conservatism, Cruz really was unsuited for the White House.

One exception to the calm arose out of the Democratic National Committee leadership. The party's vice chair and rising star congresswoman Tulsi Gabbard of Hawaii resigned in protest over Chair Debbie Wasserman Schultz stacking the deck in Clinton's favor, a theme that would return again in coming months. Gabbard endorsed Sanders immediately after resigning.[379]

Another break in the calm arose when Trump, after repeated questioning on CNN's morning show, refused to disavow the support of former KKK leader David Duke. Trump immediately suffered a storm of abuse from all quarters. Oddly, not until the next day did Trump explain he'd been given a faulty earpiece. He did the CNN interview from a private home in Florida and could "hardly hear" what Jake Tapper in studio was asking.[380] While the delay seemed suspicious, Trump had disavowed Duke's support the previous Friday, giving the whole episode the coloring of another media hit piece.

Even so, the story lived on; but why Trump allowed it to live on remained a mystery. Trump could have killed the story with a quick series of clarifying interviews. But he didn't. The Monday night news programs ran story after story, and many columnists opined at length as to how this proved Trump morally unfit for office. Still, Trump offered no response beyond his faulty earpiece claim while his disavowal of Duke's support even before the earpiece flap never broke through the din.

SUPER TUESDAY BY DESIGN

Super Tuesday featured a mix of caucus and primary voting, some winner-take-all and some proportional distributions of delegates. Most states employed a hybrid system, often shown below as 50–20. This is winner-take-all if the candidate receives more than 50% of the votes. Otherwise, it's proportional except no delegates are awarded to candidates receiving less than 20%. Other states had proportional rules, except no delegates were awarded to candidates below a different threshold, such as Massachusetts with a 5% threshold.

As if this weren't confusing enough, press reports couldn't decide if eleven states were voting or twelve or thirteen. Republicans (thirty-seven delegates) and Democrats (seventy-nine delegates) in Colorado held caucuses on Super Tuesday too, but this was just the first step in a months-long process ultimately awarding delegates, a process that would get a lot more interesting further down the road. Wyoming Republicans also held first-step caucuses on Super Tuesday. Rocky Mountain folk need to reacquaint themselves with the KISS rule: keep it simple, stupid.

Republicans

	Delegates	Type	Special Rule?
Alabama	50	Primary	50–20
Arkansas	40	Primary	50–15
Georgia	76	Primary	50–20
Texas	155	Primary	50–20
Oklahoma	43	Primary	50–15
Tennessee	58	Primary	66–20
Virginia	49	Primary	no
Massachusetts	42	Primary	5% min
Vermont	16	Primary	50–20
Minnesota	38	Caucus	10% min
Alaska	28	Caucus	13% min

Generally, on Super Tuesday Democrats voted in the same states and using the same procedures as did Republicans, except they didn't vote in Wyoming and they did vote in American Samoa. In all states, Democrats awarded pledged delegates using a proportional system, with a 15% minimum to receive delegates.

Democrats

	Delegates	Type
Alabama	60	Primary
Arkansas	37	Primary
Georgia	116	Primary
Tennessee	76	Primary
Virginia	110	Primary
Massachusetts	116	Primary
Vermont	26	Primary
Texas	155	Primary
Oklahoma	42	Primary

Minnesota	93	Caucus
Colorado	66	Caucus
American Samoa	11	Caucus

Super Tuesday Results

For Republicans, Super Tuesday provided Donald Trump a clear victory but not a strong one, certainly not as strong as the initial narrative suggested. Trump won eleven states, taking 226 of 532 delegates, or about 42%. Massachusetts gave Trump his best showing, hardly a hotbed of Republican agitation. His average vote across all states was just under 35%.

Ted Cruz also had a fair night. He won Texas, of course, along with Oklahoma and Alaska. But even in Texas, Cruz received only 44% of the vote.

Even Marco Rubio had a story to tell after Super Tuesday. He finally won a state, Minnesota, and managed three second-place finishes. Hardly a resounding victory, but neither was it a vanquishing loss, especially with Florida anchoring Rubio's calendar two weeks later. Rubio could also claim his "con man" attacks on Trump were working and would turn the tide in his favor. This latter was speculative, but it gained credence as more and more of the nation's leaders political and otherwise rose up to stop Trump at any cost.

One interesting pattern arose in exit polls across the Republican candidates. Republicans most often described Trump as the guy who would "tell it like it is." Cruz appealed to the hard-core conservative who remained immune to Trump's allure. And Rubio appealed most to Republicans who put a premium on winning in November.

Republicans

	Trump		Cruz		Rubio		Kasich		Carson	
	Pct	D	Pct	D	Pct	D	Pct	D	Pct	D
Alabama	43	36	21	13	19	1	4	0	10	0
Arkansas	33	16	31	14	25	9	4	0	6	0
Georgia	39	40	24	18	24	14	6	0	6	0
Texas	27	38	44	99	18	4	4	0	4	0
Oklahoma	28	12	34	14	26	11	4	0	6	0
Tennessee	39	31	25	14	21	9	5	0	8	0
Virginia	35	17	17	8	32	16	9	5	6	3
Massachusetts	49	22	10	4	18	8	18	8	3	0
Vermont	33	6	10	0	19	0	30	6	4	0
Minnesota	21	8	29	13	37	17	6	0	7	0
Alaska	34	11	36	12	15	5	4	0	11	0

Total Delegates
Super Tuesday	237	209	94	19	3
Previous 4 states	82	17	16	6	5
Overall to Date	319	226	110	25	8

Needed to Win: 1,237

THE KASICH/CARSON EFFECT

Obvious to all for weeks, John Kasich and Ben Carson had zero chance scoring on Super Tuesday and zero chance of winning the nomination. Carson had stayed in the race for grins and giggles and little more. Kasich dreamed of using the Ohio primary, March 15, as a springboard.

How much effect did these two hangers-on have? That depends on what would happen to their votes if they got out. As so often in life, one can ask, "What would have happened if?" Some of Kasich's votes in some states were likely independents or Democrats who would not otherwise have voted in a Republican contest. Politically and in temperament, Kasich was least like Trump and most like Rubio; so suppose one allocated Kasich's votes 70% to Rubio, 20% to Cruz, and 10% to Trump.

Likewise, even though Carson later rallied to Trump, his supporters were likely least drawn to Trump but were instead probably slightly more drawn to Cruz than Rubio; so suppose one allocated Carson's votes 40% to Rubio, 50% to Cruz, and 10% to Trump. Under these assumptions, Cruz would have taken Arkansas from Trump while Rubio would have taken Virginia and Vermont from Trump. Overall, in this alternative reality, Trump and Cruz both win four states while Rubio wins three. In short, if Kasich and Carson had quit playing games and their votes split as assumed, then Super Tuesday could have produced a three-way tie.

To almost everyone's relief, the day after Super Tuesday Carson announced he was getting out. In a perfect example of a MOTO (master of the obvious), Carson didn't "see a political path forward."[381] Nice man, very smart, but out of his league. Next.

Democrats on Super Tuesday

Like Trump, Hillary Clinton definitely had the better night on Super Tuesday. She won seven out of eleven contests and took 486 out of 811 delegates (denoted "D" in the table below), or nearly 60%. But she didn't deliver the knockout blow she'd hoped. Of course, Bernie Sanders would win his home state of Vermont; but he also took Oklahoma, Minnesota, and the swing state of Colorado. Further brightening Sanders's day, his campaign announced they raised $42 million in February.[382] He'd outraised Clinton in January $20 million to $15 million. If Sanders had a reason to continue the race, he'd have the finances to do so, and Super Tuesday gave him four big reasons to continue. Clinton might prefer to shift to a general election campaign mode riding a sense of inevitability to end the contest, but that wasn't going to fly.

Democrats

	Clinton		Sanders	
	Pct	D	Pct	D
Alabama	78	44	19	9
Arkansas	66	22	30	10
Georgia	71	72	28	28
Tennessee	66	42	32	22
Virginia	64	61	35	33
Massachusetts	50	46	49	45
Vermont	14	0	86	16
Texas	65	145	33	74
Oklahoma	40	28	59	38
Minnesota	38	29	62	46
Colorado	40	24	59	35

Total Delegates
- Super Tuesday   513   356
- Super Delegates 457   22
- Overall to Date 1,033 408

Needed to Win: 2,382

Another, Ahem, Debate

Thursday, March 3, Republicans gathered for another clash of the serial insulters. Modern American politics reached a new low. As usual, everyone onstage not an Ohio Governor called everyone else a liar. Donald Trump reverted to calling Rubio "Little Marco," to which Rubio eventually responded, "OK, Big Don." It was all amusing in the same way a demolition derby crash might be amusing.

A few days prior to the debate, Rubio made a passing, fairly ridiculous comment about the size of Trump's hands, suggesting they were smallish and suggesting by innuendo other aspects of Trump's physical person that might be below specs. Never one to lose a battle of insults, Trump responded, "Look at those hands, are they small hands?" as he held them up to the audience.[383]

Trump continued, "And, he [Rubio] referred to my hands—if they're small, something else must be small. I guarantee you, there's no problem. I guarantee." Male genitalia had made its first passing reference in presidential politics since "Tricky Dick" Nixon.

Peter Roff, humorously insightful conservative commentator for *US News and World Report*, may have had the best tongue-in-cheek reaction:

> Inside Washington I am considered, by those who know me well, as something of an authority on the "inappropriate." For this reason I feel well-qualified to say to GOP presidential candidate Donald Trump that public references regarding the size of your "manhood" and that of your opponent is always, underline always, inappropriate.
>
> You, Mr. Trump, are running for President of the United States, not President of the second grade class, and it is time you started acting like it.[384]

A Steady Parade of Election Results

The campaigns were in high swing, and election reporters were tiring. The pace didn't let up after Super Tuesday. The next two weeks saw a series of election contests leading up to the next big day on March 15, a second Super Tuesday.

On Saturday, the fifth, Louisiana, Nebraska, and Kansas would vote. Maine Republicans would vote on the fifth while Democrats voted on the sixth. Republicans in Puerto Rico voted on the sixth. The following Tuesday the spotlight shifted to Mississippi and Michigan.

If Trump could be stopped, this would be a good time. Opposition to Donald Trump within the Republican Party was widespread.

It was not just the old guard or the establishment. Many lifelong grassroots Republicans didn't believe Trump's recent conversion to select Republican talking points. Trump was attempting a hostile takeover of a party with which he'd had little past association and the party didn't like it. Marco Rubio insisted, "If we nominate Donald Trump it will be the end of the modern Republican Party."[385]

Trump's opponents had counted on Republican voters coming to their senses. Opponents had counted on the other candidates dropping out until the one remaining would overwhelm Trump's support. It hadn't happened. Establishment Republicans started taking matters into their own hands. Meg Whitman, CEO of Hewlett-Packard, joined up with billionaires Todd Ricketts and Paul Singer to start Our Principles PAC for the express purpose of stopping Trump.[386] They hired Tom Miller, previously communications director for Jeb Bush's campaign, and started running anti-Trump ads immediately. Politically speaking, Trump was a demonstrated force of nature, but nature has many forces. We would now see whether Trump could overcome this new obstacle. No sweat, as it turned out.

Drip, Drip, Drip—Immunity

On March 2 the *Washington Post* reported the FBI has granted Bryan Pagliano immunity from prosecution.[387] Who was Pagliano and why did this matter?

Pagliano worked on Hillary Clinton's 2008 campaign and set up her private email server in 2009. The FBI was pursuing a "criminal investigation into the possible mishandling of classified information." To demand immunity, Pagliano must have felt at risk of prosecution. He'd already invoked his Fifth Amendment right against self-incrimination while testifying before a congressional panel in September. He was a little fish. The FBI gives immunity to the little fish to catch bigger fish.

To underscore the sensitivity of the investigation, Attorney General Loretta Lynch affirmed to a congressional hearing a month earlier the matter was being handled by career independent law enforcement officials, FBI counterintelligence agents, and career independent attorneys with the Justice Department's National Security Division. And to whom would they make a recommendation? To James Comey, FBI Director who reported to whom? To Lynch, of course, an Obama political appointee.

Knowing the White House pressure Lynch would be under to whitewash any Clinton wrongdoing, Comey emphasized he was "very close" to the investigation. If criminal prosecution proved warranted by the evidence as judged by Comey, then Lynch would have a tough time turning a blind eye knowing Comey could go public unless, as some professional conspiratorialists alleged, the fix was already in. The key was Comey.

The Democratic Party was in a pickle. They seemed about to settle on a flag bearer who could, any day before convention or before the election, be indicted by the Obama Justice Department. Or Clinton could win the election only to face indictment shortly thereafter and enter the White House with little political momentum usually found in a president's honeymoon period. She would face ceaseless House Republican investigations, quite possibly a special prosecutor, and possibly impeachment, a dubious honor she would then share with her husband. Or this could all blow over. But what a risk they were running.

And what an irony—the Democrats were about to choose a nominee who might be indicted and have to depart under a plea agreement. The Republicans were about to suffer a hostile takeover of the party by an outside agent who might do anything if elected.

Hopes for a Trump Virus Vaccine

As Donald Trump's victory seemed ever more likely, the number of voices expressing a collective "oh crap" increased exponentially. Two examples from Thursday, March 3, exemplified the panic. On the left, the *Washington Post*'s Ruth Marcus admitted a mistake—in print. In an earlier piece, Marcus had played the "ghastly parlor game of choosing between President Donald Trump and President Ted Cruz." She chose Trump.

But in March she wrote, a "Trump presidency, or so I reassured myself, at least offered the prospect of unprincipled deal making in the service of what is Trump's only guidepost: promoting the greater glory of Trump." Marcus then confessed, "I was wrong."

After citing a long list of particulars wherein Trump had proven on the campaign trail to be far worse than earlier advertised, Marcus observed, "Trump is Nixon with all of the megalomaniacal willingness to abuse power and none of the crafty realpolitik."

Scary Ted Cruz remained a major concern. Yet even to the Left, Trump represented such a grave threat to the nation they could not risk the chance he could win even if they thought his gaining the Republican nomination substantially increased the likelihood Hillary Clinton would win. Some risks one just doesn't run.

On the right, Mitt Romney could contain himself no longer. He launched an "epic take down," a point by point, issue by issue shredding of Trump's candidacy.[388] Romney attacked Trump's honesty, his character, his business acumen, his claims of wealth. Trump responded in kind, of course, tossing back his own litany of insults toward Romney. But at some point, the volume of criticisms leveled at Trump had to take a toll. In America, when the Right and the Left are united in opposition, such a rare consensus is rarely without consequence; incredibly, the consequence was that Trump got stronger.

Just When the Path Seemed Clear

After Super Tuesday, the respective campaign trajectories settled into predictable if uncomfortable realities. Donald Trump might lose a state here or there, but his string of victories made him appear as inevitable as did Hillary Clinton's even stronger string of victories. But then, something odd happened. The voters upended conventional wisdom, again.

On Saturday, May 5:

- Ted Cruz decisively won Kansas and Maine, picking up sixty-nine delegates;

- Trump barely beat out Cruz in Kentucky and Louisiana, picking up fifty-three delegates;
- Marco Rubio came in a distant third in all four states, yet still gained eighteen delegates; and
- John Kasich came in an even more distant fourth, earning ten delegates.

Then on Sunday, May 6, Rubio scored his second overall win, taking Puerto Rico and its twenty-three delegates in a romp. Puerto Rico might seem a distant sideshow politically, but it was important because Florida voted in nine days. Rubio had to win Florida to make an argument for continuing his candidacy. More than a million Puerto Ricans lived and voted in Florida.

Even if Rubio won Florida, the center of gravity of the anti-Trump forces had already moved and likely irretrievably to Cruz. Even those discomforted by Cruz found ways to console themselves with the elixir of not having Trump take over the Republican Party.

To recap: over the two days, Trump had picked up fifty-three delegates, or less than a third of the total at stake. Talk of a contested convention took off—again. Hope Trump might be stopped took off—again.

Among the Democrats, Bernie Sanders did an equally good job of upending conventional wisdom. Inevitable Hillary? Maybe not:

- Sanders easily won Kansas and Nebraska and then won Maine the following day for a total of sixty-six delegates.
- Clinton had to console herself with a solo win in Louisiana and a total delegate gain of sixty-three, nearly matching Sanders.

The convention math: Sanders up by three. The political-appearances math: Sanders won the weekend three to one. The overarching theme for months: it's tough to insist you've won when you keep losing.

Yet Another Flinty Debate

In sports, teams that play one another regularly tend to have the fiercest rivalries: Alabama versus Auburn in college football, the New York Yankees versus the Boston Red Sox in baseball, UNC versus Duke in college basketball. A similar pattern developed with respect to the debates. While the Republican slugfests passing for "debates" got most of the attention in part because they featured Donald Trump the entertainer, Hillary and the Bern spared no sharp elbows in their next debate, held in Flint, Michigan.

The centerpiece was unquestionably the government-made disaster involving Flint's dangerous drinking water. Both Hillary Clinton and Bernie Sanders were in high dudgeon, more than happy to hang this problem around the neck of Republican Gov. Rick Snyder, conveniently absolving both Obama's administration and the Democratic city leadership of Flint altogether. Otherwise, the two combatants agreed on very little.

Sanders bashed Clinton on trade. Clinton countered by noting Sanders voted against the 2009 bailout that saved General Motors (or, more accurately, the UAW's health care fund). Clinton attacked on gun control, a definite point of weakness in much of liberaldom, knowing Sanders coming from rural Vermont had repeatedly been "soft" on gun control. Clinton apparently forgot she was in Michigan, where a high percentage of voters, and especially blue-collar union voters, are lifelong members of the NRA, own many firearms, and like to hunt.

The two candidates agreed on one policy: ending fracking. Fracking is the common term for hydraulic fracturing, the modern technology allowing vastly more efficient production of oil and natural gas in huge areas of the country. Ever since the oil crisis in the mid-1970s, experts confidently predicted the United States would never be close to energy independence. Fracking proved the experts wrong—again.

Fracking allowed the United States to increase its oil and natural gas production so much and so rapidly the nation effectively became energy independent. Indeed, thanks to fracking, the United States in 2016 had the world's largest proven oil reserves, surpassing both Russia and Saudi Arabia.[389]

The fracking revolution and all the investment and jobs it entailed provided much of what little economic growth occurred midway through the Obama presidency. Fracking drove the global price of oil down from over $100 a barrel to as little as $30 a barrel, saving consumers enormous sums and depriving ISIS of the resources needed to wage war.

All this is what Clinton and Sanders pledged to reverse if they were elected president. While the *Washington Post* buried the money line in trying to whitewash Clinton's comments to make Sanders seem the less reasonable, other news organs ran the essential Clinton quote, "I do not think there will be many places in America where fracking will continue."[390] Not quite as definitive as Sanders's "No, I do not support fracking," but the effective difference was nil. For the future of fracking in America, the difference between being regulated to death and summarily shot was a distinction without a difference.

Shortly after the Flint debate, former New York City mayor Michael Bloomberg had an adult moment. Late in 2015 Bloomberg suggested he might run as an independent. Finally, Bloomberg made a decision. He wasn't running. Why? "When I look at the data, it's clear to me that if I entered the race, I could not win."[391] Well, no kidding. That was true when he first suggested he might run.

So what was the real reason? "As the race stands now, with Republicans in charge of both Houses, there is a good chance that my candidacy could lead to the election of Donald Trump or Sen. Ted Cruz. That is not a risk I can take in good conscience."

Tweener Tuesday

The story out of Tweener Tuesday between Super Tuesday and the next really big day had Donald Trump on a roll and Hillary Clinton stumbling badly.[392] Both stories were oversold but only a little. By the topline, Trump won three states, including the big enchilada of

Michigan, as well as Mississippi and Hawaii. Ted Cruz managed a win in Idaho while Marco Rubio faded fast. John Kasich had hoped for and badly needed a decent showing in Michigan to preserve credibility into his home state of Ohio. He didn't get it, coming in third at 24.3%.

	Trump		**Cruz**		**Rubio**		**Kasich**	
	Pct	D	Pct	D	Pct	D	Pct	D
Mississippi	47	24	36	13	5	0	9	0
Michigan	37	25	25	17	9	0	24	17
Idaho	28	12	45	20	16	0	7	0
Hawaii	42	10	33	6	13	0	11	0
March 8 delegates	71		56		0		17	
Total delegates to date	458		359		151		54	

The only states up for Democrats were Mississippi, which Clinton won in a landslide, and Michigan, where Bernie Sanders squeaked a victory 49.9% to 49.2%. Even though this gave Sanders only seven more delegates than Clinton (65 to 58), the win had greater impact because going in Clinton had been leading in the polls 57% to 37%. Getting beat when you anticipated a big win is a big deal.

Clinton barely won in the three counties surrounding Detroit where the unions were strongest, but Sanders swept most of the rest of Michigan.

	Clinton		**Sanders**	
	Pct	D	Pct	D
Mississippi	83	29	17	4
Michigan	48	58	50	65
March 8 delegates	87		69	
Total delegates to date	760		546	

Early Tuesday evening, Trump came out to give some remarks and answer questions, timing it nicely so Clinton's press conference got pushed back to when fewer viewers would watch. More than anything Trump's performance that night harkened back to the good ol' days of Johnny Carson's late-night television monologues. Part stream of consciousness, part showtime, in between laugh lines and assurances that he loved whomever he'd just referenced (Florida, Mississippi, former New York Yankees baseball great Paul O'Neill, who stood front stage in the audience). Trump also got in some carefully planned digs.

He ripped into Cruz as a liar—again—and then ignored him. He tactfully observed Rubio would have to make his own decision about getting out. He announced his relish at focusing on Clinton, who he would beat; no, he would stomp; no, he would obliterate in the general election. He then took special delight in going after Mitt Romney.

In his remarks a few days prior, Romney attacked Trump for a long list of failed businesses including a steak business, a bottled water business, a magazine, and an airline, all called "Trump." So Trump had big steaks on the stage—raw steaks, out of the package—from his ongoing steak business, doing very well, thank you. He had bottles of water from his water business. He had a copy of the latest issue of his magazine. And about the airline? He sold it and made a nice profit by the way. It was all very entertaining if one didn't listen too carefully. Romney again looked outclassed and outgunned.

Trump then went on a long monologue as to why he would win Florida and then Ohio and New York and on and on. And the centerpiece of his explanation in each case was that he'd built some magnificent property or properties there and had many employees there. Never before in American history had a candidate's selling point been his developed real estate portfolio. And, of course, after each state and property noted, Trump would reassure us he "loved" the state and he "loved" the people there.

Back to reality, one interesting subplot out of Tweener Tuesday involved Trump winning less than half the delegates awarded. He won the most individually, but Cruz and Kasich together won more.

Counting Ben Carson's eight delegates, Trump had to date won just over 44% of the awarded delegates. The contested convention dream was alive and well.

Rubio faced a tough choice. On the night he'd recorded two third-place and two fourth-place finishes, averaging about 11% across the four states. The polls had him behind Trump in Florida 40% to 24%. Rubio was facing a rising chorus calling for him to get out so Cruz could take on Trump mano a mano.

Rubio had to know his campaign was finished. He had chosen not to seek reelection to the Senate. His best shot at a political future seemed to involve running for Florida Governor in 2018 at the end of Rick Scott's term. Losing to Trump in Florida would hurt his chances badly. Even so, Rubio rolled the dice one more time, betting big on a home-state win. Bad call.

Hillary, Trade, and Another Kama Sutra

Aside from California, few states are more obviously affected by international trade than Michigan. Yes, it's pretty much all about cars. Americans buy a lot of cars and trucks. Many of those cars and trucks have foreign labels. Many of those cars and trucks with foreign labels are built in the United States while many with domestic labels are built abroad. It's complicated.

Michigan manufacturing is much more than cars and trucks, but that's what the rest of us see. And while we happily buy up those imported cars and trucks and electronics and shirts, international trade also makes us uneasy because some foreign worker and some foreign company is eager to take our jobs.

In the global economy, we have two options. We can hide behind walls and shrivel up and die. Or we can or roll up our sleeves; pass reforms that help U.S. companies and American workers compete, get stronger, faster, smarter; and take the competition head on. There just isn't any option C.

Republicans and Democrats both get tangled in this web of unpatriotic outsourcing. But Hillary Clinton had been at it far longer than most, and so once again she'd managed a full kama sutra of position changes, many of them neatly organized in the International Business Times. For example, in 2004 Clinton took to the Senate floor, "I do not believe it [outsourcing] is a good thing."[393] When the pursuit of expanding international trade resulted in outsourcing, then this was a "strategy for decline. This is a strategy for the destruction of the American job market." The next day she introduced a Senate resolution attacking outsourcing. Pretty clear her position at this point.

In 2012 on a trip to India, Clinton sat squarely on the fence, "Well, it's been going on for many years now, and it's part of our economic relationship with India. And I think that there are advantages with it that have certainly benefited many parts of our country, and there are disadvantages that go to the need to improve the job skills of our own people and create a better economic environment. So it—like anything, it's about pluses and minuses."

In 2016 in Michigan Clinton was again firmly in the quasi-protectionist, head-under-the-blanket camp. An old saw runs that an advantage to always telling the truth is you have less to remember. An analog is the advantage to having core values reflected in your policy positions is you have less to remember and less to explain later. One sure sign Clinton was, if nothing else, extraordinarily capable: she could remember all the opposing positions she'd taken over the years and could usually concoct some plausible explanation to paper over the inconsistencies.

STAYING IN CHARACTER: THE RISE AND FALL OF MARCO RUBIO

Throughout the campaign, Donald Trump said things no other candidate for political office, and certainly not for president, would dare say. He was belittling, caustic, insulting; and voters rewarded him with high poll ratings and strong vote counts. Trump's performance broke every rule in the book short of facing a criminal indictment, yet he succeeded. How?

The immediate answer was that he tapped into voters' anger better than anyone else. And he was so transparent about his approach to leadership and his intentions he captured almost all the support of those prioritizing pure painful honesty—"telling it like it is." But how did he manage to insult his opponents and get away with it? This wasn't presidential behavior, and in the modern era at least Americans had always expected a certain civility in their presidents. How could he behave so unpresidentially and still succeed? By staying in character.

Americans over years of exposure believed they knew exactly who and what Trump was thanks largely to his having had the most popular "reality" show on television for years. He stayed in character, so he could behave in ways no other candidate dared. Marco Rubio proved it.

Early in the campaign, Rubio had been the aspirational next-generation voice of the Republican campaign. He used his personal story effectively to reaffirm his faith in the greatness of America's promise. Over time, voters rewarded him well; and from the New Hampshire primary to Super Tuesday, Rubio's star ascended as lesser candidates faded.

Then, just before the New Hampshire primary, Trump and Chris Christie unloaded on Rubio. Christie called him a robot because Rubio repeatedly fell back on his talking points.[394] Trump mocked him, ridiculed him, called him "Little Marco," leaving Rubio sputtering. It halted Rubio's momentum cold, but he remained a leading candidate.

Rubio thus provided an important if difficult lesson for all political campaigns: the need to adapt to circumstances. Candidates are always told to stay on message because off the straight-and-narrow path hides all manner of missteps and misstatements. Those who cannot manage the discipline typically provide the opposition deadly ammunition.

Rubio was disciplined about staying on message, a trait reinforced by his campaign's tendency to allow exchanges with the media only on specific clearly defined terms. Rubio had his lines down pat. He'd turn to them again and again, and he did this so often he sometimes became robotic. He was capable of spontaneously engaging, better than most; but he stuck to the playbook—even in those moments when the playbook had no answers.

That's when a candidate has to know to throw the playbook away, when to go unscripted, when to adapt to circumstances. When Christie attacked Rubio as robotic after the New Hampshire debate, the blows landed because Rubio had programmed himself to be disciplined and he had no programmed response. Had he relied on his political instincts instead, he could have easily deflected Christie's attack. Instead, he relied on his playbook. It failed him. A candidate has to know when to adapt to overcome.

Rubio changed tactics in the Houston debate on February 25. Trump had been the candidate lobbing mud from the gutter. Rubio decided the only way to beat Trump was to out-Trump Trump. Rubio surprised Trump and made him miserable. But in the process, Rubio self-inflicted a mortal wound. The aspirational candidate showed much less and in so doing debased his greatest asset.

One view at the time was that all the other candidates needed to shift tactics to stop Trump. As described earlier, they'd been coming to a boxing match with gloves neatly tied and facing Trump brandishing a knife and a six-foot chain. Whether Rubio's new tactics made even a dent in Trump's support will never be known. However, Rubio's campaign never recovered.

How could Trump behave as he did while no one else could copy it? Trump was in character. Rubio had stepped out of character. For that one night and the following couple of days, Rubio came across as a fighter but also as a phony, as "inauthentic." Rubio had provided future candidates two important lessons: know when to go off script and adapt to circumstances, and whatever you do, be yourself. The aspirational candidate was gone, replaced for a time by a mudslinger. Rubio stayed in a few more days, but his exit was already written in the script.

Two More Debates—Sigh

Everybody—media, candidates, voters—was dead tired of debates. Yet debate they would, with Democrats meeting Wednesday, March 9. Once again, Hillary Clinton and Bernie Sanders did their best to match Republican nastiness. Little new occurred except they attacked each other as being insufficiently sensitive to illegal immigrants and inadequately hostile to international trade.

Seeing an opportunity, Clinton then went further the next day, announcing an immigration policy far to the Left of Pres. Obama's. In short, nobody in the country would be forced to leave, no way, no how, not ever.

Clinton and Sanders also continued their running battle on who did the most or the least to "save" the American auto industry during the financial crisis. All this was rather humorous since nobody had "saved" the American auto industry. Ford was never in trouble. Fiat had bought Chrysler. Only General Motors was at issue, and the company was never bailed out. Rather, Obama had bailed out GM's unions, which had vastly overpromised pension and health benefits to their members in retirement. That's right: American tax dollars went to bail out high-end union pensions and retiree benefits.

Republicans held their final debate before the big Tuesday showdown, hosted by CNN and moderated by Wolf Blitzer, he of the Yoda-like patience. To everyone's amazement, the candidates behaved themselves, even Trump. They actually debated real policy issues. It was quite refreshing. Quickly apparent in the Coral Gables affair, Trump sought to look more presidential and substantive while Rubio sought to re-establish his persona as a smart, positive next-generation conservative.

Debates can have many layers. On the surface, Trump unquestionably fared well—confident, mostly reasonable, relatively subdued, in full command of his own views. Dig a little deeper, however, and Trump was badly exposed as amateurishly naive. He repeated previous comments he wanted to remain "neutral" with respect to Israel, hoping this would allow him to mediate a lasting peace between Israel and its neighbors, especially the Palestinians. This on the same day he commented and later repeated, "I think Islam hates us."[395]

Dana Bash pressed Trump on how he would fix Social Security. The other Republican candidates all candidly acknowledged reform was essential and inevitable—something Democrats refused to acknowledge—and all put forward solutions with sufficient detail the audience could see the outlines. Trump reverted to cutting "waste, fraud, and abuse" and foreign aid. To be sure, as Rubio acknowledged, one ought to eliminate "waste, fraud, and abuse"; and one ought to scrutinize foreign aid spending, but even complete success in these areas make a dent in Social Security's financial plight.

Trump believed other countries take outrageous advantage of Americans when it comes to international trade. In response, he suggested if these countries didn't behave properly, then he would punish them with a 35% tariff. Ted Cruz dismantled Trump on this point like a prosecuting attorney dismantles a street thug caught on video.[396]

Cruz first acknowledged that, once again, Trump had correctly identified a problem but then proposed an absurd solution. This is pretty simple, really. Imposing a prohibitive tariff on imports hurts the foreign importer a little but mostly hurts U.S. consumers of the imported products because they would then face vastly higher prices. Slamming American consumers and American workers as punishment for alleged foreign misdeeds is absurd. This was not ideological. It was Econ 101.

Religious Curiosities and Minor Contests

Americans were not behaving normally. Nowhere was this more apparent than in the matter of religion. The three Republicans expected to do best with "evangelical" Christians had been Mike Huckabee, based on his biography and past performance; Ben Carson, based on reputation; and Ted Cruz, based on natural affiliation. Huckabee quickly washed out as the evangelicals moved on to "new and improved." Carson washed out as being wholly unsuitable to the anger of the times. Cruz managed substantial evangelical support; but the thrice-married, twice-divorced, coarse-language-speaking Donald Trump did just as well. How strange was that!

Few confident theories explained Trump's appeal to evangelicals. One suggested the term *evangelical* had become so vague as to be meaningless. There were nominal evangelicals who were really just renamed Christian voters. There were "cultural evangelicals" who were active Christians, usually Protestants, driven less by traditional evangelical issues such as faith, marriage, and life than they were responding to a natural affinity for a messianic figure and so were attracted to Trump. And then there were more traditional hard-core evangelicals who were naturally more attracted to Cruz.

This seemed a good start on a theory until one remembered Jerry Falwell Jr., President of Liberty University and presumably a more traditional evangelical, had early on endorsed Trump, and Trump had done very well with traditional evangelicals in South Carolina. Once again, the Trump phenomenon did not lend itself to easy explanations.

Democrats had their own religious conundrum. No Jew had ever come so close to winning the White House, though Connecticut Sen. Joe Lieberman came closest as Al Gore's running mate in 2000. Bernie Sanders was certainly no Orthodox Jew, but he embraced his heritage and the expression of his faith seemed fairly close to that of most American Jews. Yet Hillary Clinton seemed to be getting more than her share of the Jewish vote.

Stranger yet, no American president had done more to put Israel's survival at risk than had Barack Obama, whose legacy Clinton was promising to continue. In supporting her so strongly, it seemed a large segment of American Jews had a very limited real interest in the survival of Israel or their own Jewishness.

In analyzing political trends and voting patterns, the tendency is to seek frameworks within which events can be explained. It's no surprise when blacks vote for a black man and when women favor a female candidate; but when it came to religion, the pattern appeared less clear-cut. Jews weren't necessarily backing a Jew, and traditional evangelicals weren't necessarily backing an evangelical Christian.

In most presidential contests, the big story is about the big states, like Texas on Super Tuesday, and Ohio and Florida and Illinois on Super Tuesday II. In this campaign, with multiple candidates seeking every delegate to be found, even little contests adding a handful of delegates mattered. On Saturday, March 12, Marco Rubio won the contest in the District of Columbia, capturing 37.3% of the vote, just beating John Kasich with 35.5%. Rubio picked up ten delegates; Kasich nine; the rest were blanked.

In Wyoming, Ted Cruz notched a victory with about 66% of the vote and claiming nine delegates while Trump and Rubio picked up one each and one delegate remained uncommitted. The residents of Guam also voted, picking twelve delegates who would be free to support whomever they chose.

American Politics Takes a Decided Turn for the Worse

The Trump and Sanders campaigns were fed by the fire of anger. Not so much their own anger as the latent anger of large swaths of the American people. No obvious single answer explained Americans' anger, but anger was in abundance.

Some were angry about Obama's crappy economy, or rising health care costs, or high taxes for themselves or low taxes for somebody else, or bad traffic, or the way America was repeatedly insulted by petty foreign despots happy to take American cash all the same. They were angry at how Obama had become a serial apologist. They were angry at the prospect of America in decline.

Hispanics in the country legally were angry at being insulted for being Hispanic. Non-Hispanics were angry at illegal immigrants, and sometimes all immigrants, and at having to wait for hours in a hospital emergency room because of a long line of Spanish-speaking people with common ailments and no health insurance. They were angry at hearing "Hit One for English" every time they called a government agency or company telephone number.

Most of the time, Americans suffered their indignities and anger in silence. Lacking a suitable outlet, the vast majority just went about their lives as best they could. Bernie Sanders and Donald Trump had given them a voice and a powerful outlet to express this long-suppressed fury. It was a fire turning ugly. Trump's rallies began to attract protestors along with throngs of supporters. Trump's supporters were in no mood for the protestors' crap.

At a Trump rally in Fayetteville, North Carolina, Rakeem Jones, a defiant young black man in a white T-shirt, stood up and started shouting a protest.[397] Seventy-eight-year-old John Franklin McGraw, a white man with a ponytail and cowboy hat, came up and dropped Jones with one punch. Police immediately arrived to subdue the already-subdued Jones and then later arrested McGraw. The order of those events said a lot. The whole incident was caught on a cell-phone camera and went viral.

By Saturday, Trump was stoking the fires, telling one protestor in St. Louis, "Go home to mommy," as the protestor was led out in handcuffs.[398] Trump insisted he "did not condone" violence, but he didn't mind it either.[399] Trump insisted many of these protestors were organized outsiders, and many were directed to disrupt the Trump rallies by the Sanders campaign, a charge Sanders vehemently denied.[400]

At an Ohio rally, one protestor stealthily approached close enough he could charge the stage where Trump was speaking, only to be tackled by alert Secret Service agents. The threats of violence were so intense Trump canceled a Chicago rally. Black Lives Matter activists wasted no time in claiming a victory.[401] In fact, it was later learned Trump was mostly correct. Many of the protestors were organized not by Sanders but by the Democratic National Committee's (DNC) dirty-tricks squad.

The mainstream media immediately blamed Trump for the mounting unrest. To be sure, Trump wasn't backing down one bit.

But equally clear, Trump was partly right. In New Orleans, more than two dozen Black Lives Matter protestors disrupted a rally.[402]

While Black Lives Matter and the Clinton campaign/DNC nexus were the most visibly organized of the anti-Trump protest movement, many lone wolves would protest in their own way. The more they protested, the more severe Trump supporters responded.

While painting the conflict as a simple matter of black versus white or Hispanic versus bigot provided the easiest press narrative, it also completely missed the point. Yes, race certainly played a role on both sides, but so did ideology as the protestors were often from the radical left. Many had their own reasons for anger and saw in Trump a chance to strike back by striking at Trump.

At some point, it seemed, Trump supporters would invade the Clinton and Sanders rallies. It was reasonable to conjecture that at some point somebody was going to bring a gun. Shots would be fired. Somebody would be shot. There is likely a point of no return in this behavior, where civility and tolerance break down completely, where street battles and anarchy become commonplace. America seemed to be inching—no, racing—toward that point. Fortunately, America gingerly stepped back from the brink, at least for the moment.

John Kasich's Own Little Fantasy

Conservatives are often just too hard on Republican politicians. But then, the politicians often give them cause. A fundamental distinction between liberals and conservatives involves the trade-off between equality and prosperity. Both want prosperity and both worry about "too much" inequality, the difference being in emphasis.

Herewith a river of generalities; they seem fairly accurate: Liberals are communal and protecting while conservatives are more self-reliant and opportunistic. Conservatives support the principle of a social safety net but resent being taken advantage of and insist those using the safety net do so only temporarily. Liberals are willing to "spend" some prosperity (usually somebody else's) to gain greater equality while conservatives tend to believe everybody does better when everybody does better—a rising tide lifts all boats (well, most, anyway).

Conservatives tend to argue the liberals' concern for the poor is too often a false facade. That the liberals' main objective is to amass political power to sustain themselves in power. Of course, many non-political liberals care deeply about their fellow man (and woman), but there is support for the more jaundiced view when applied to political leaders, as why else would liberals so fiercely resist reforming programs serving the poor that serve the poor so poorly?

The mainstream media and liberals broadly like to spin conservatives/Republicans as favoring the rich over the little guy, but this is cartoon thinking. As often as not, the "rich" in America are liberals; and in fact, most conservatives don't give a hoot for the rich. Many years ago, the arch-conservative Republican Dick Armey, House Majority Leader from Texas, was on television with classic über-liberal Jay Rockefeller, vastly wealthy senator from West Virginia. At one point, Rockefeller accused Armey of just wanting to protect his rich friends, to which Armey responded to the effect, "Jay, you're the only rich person I know, and frankly I don't like you all that much."

Conservatives want everyone to have the opportunity to achieve whatever their talents and efforts can provide; and if those talents and efforts make the person rich, then great. If not, well, that's the way the cookie crumbles. However, if a person falls too far, then a decent social safety net must catch them but not one so generous the individual wouldn't rather be on his or her own way. To be sure, these characterizations are all simplifications, but they seem to bear out in practice.

Which brings us back to the issue of conservatives' displeasure with nationally elected Republicans. While to prosper, economies require the rule of law and some regulatory constraints, conservatives believe economies prosper most when incentives are least distorted by public policy, whether tax, regulatory, or otherwise. "Picking winners and losers," for example, is a distinct no-no (unless the winners are corn farmers and dairymen and the like).

Yet increasingly, elected Republicans demonstrate a willingness to inject their own views and opinions into private economic decision making. The issue isn't always just one of hubris. Sometimes policymakers have explicit policy goals beyond simply encouraging good jobs and rising wages. On March 13, in commenting on outsourcing John Kasich opined:

> I think the point on outsourcing, and I have talked to at least one CEO who wanted to move operations out of the U.S.—and I made it clear to him that there's more than just profits. There has to be a value system that underlays our free enterprise system.[403]

Kasich was right about one point: there has to be a value system underpinning our free-enterprise system. There is. It starts with the rule of law. It includes the pursuit of opportunity and self-interest. It leaves to individual discretion support for charitable activities. It includes a robust, comprehensive social safety net but not one that traps those who fall into it.

But Kasich, like many Democrats, had something else in mind. They believe included in the value system is a sense of community and a patriotic duty.

Americans should be patriotic. American businesses should obey the law, compete, treat their workers fairly, respect their customers, do the best they can by their shareholders, and leave the patriotism to living beings. Kasich, apparently, didn't understand the difference or didn't see its importance. A thoughtful conservative would do both.

Super Tuesday II

A powerful sense of finality descended on the Republican campaign going into March 15. Surely some questions would be answered at last. This was do-or-die day for Marco Rubio and John Kasich. In Rubio's case, it looked more die than do as he trailed Trump badly in

Florida polls. For all his insistence to the contrary, this was win-at-home-or-go-home time for the promising Florida Senator.

Though trailing Rubio in every meaningful category, Kasich appeared the stronger force as he stood a good chance of winning Ohio. Ted Cruz didn't seem to be winning anywhere but would pick up delegates in the three non–winner-take-all states. The path seemed reasonably clear to the contested convention apparently needed to stop Donald Trump.

To review the topline, Trump had 460 delegates and needed another 777. He needed to win about 62% of the remaining 1,251 delegates to claim the nomination outright. Thus far, he'd collected about 45% of the delegates awarded. If he won Florida and Ohio and their 99 and 66 delegates, respectively, the math suddenly became a lot easier as he would need to win only 56% of the remaining delegates.

However, if Trump lost either Ohio or Florida, then a contested convention would seem likely. With Florida slipping away from Rubio, Ohio became the focus of the stop-Trump effort. Mitt Romney campaigned for Kasich in Ohio, though whether that helped or hurt on balance was unclear. In a remarkably smart and mature move, Rubio told his Ohio supporters to back Kasich. Kasich didn't return the favor, suggesting anew, despite protests to the contrary, Kasich's campaign was a lot more about Kasich than the country's future.

The run-up to the Democratic contest frankly wasn't nearly as exciting. The final results explained why. In Florida, Hillary Clinton led in the polls by a wide margin. In all the other states, she led by a very small margin.

The wide variety of methods by which states determined their delegate representations on Super Tuesday II was enough to confuse even seasoned professionals. For Republicans:

- In Florida, Ohio, and the Northern Marianas, all delegates were awarded to the statewide winner, whether the top vote getter received 25% or 95%.

- In Illinois, voters select three individuals from each of the eighteen congressional districts. Voters don't choose one of the presidential contenders but rather vote for a neighbor who may or may not declare for a candidate. In addition, fifteen delegates were pledged to the statewide winner.
- In Missouri, five delegates were elected winner-take-all for each of the eight congressional districts and twelve delegates were awarded to the statewide winner.
- In North Carolina, delegates were awarded on a strictly proportional basis.

In all five Super Tuesday II states, Democrats allocated pledged delegates proportionally subject to a 15% threshold.

Indisputably, Clinton won big on Super Tuesday II. She won Missouri and Illinois in squeakers, but she won all five contests. She picked up 396 of the 688 delegates available. It seemed she had finally snuffed out the Bern. Surely, he would abandon the race now and throw his support to Clinton. Not.

	Clinton		**Sanders**	
	Pct	D	Pct	D
Florida	65	141	33	73
Ohio	57	81	43	62
Illinois	51	79	49	77
North Carolina	55	59	41	45
Missouri	49.6	36	49.4	35
March 15 delegates	396	292		

The Republican side was nearly as decisive. Trump crushed Rubio in Florida, who then dropped out before the sun set in California. He gave a great speech and then exited stage right. Next.

As expected, Trump had a very good night but not good enough to put his competition away. He won four out of five states, including two of the winner-take-alls (Florida and Illinois), but Kasich took Ohio.

Kasich spun his lone victory not as a home-state win but rather the first big step on the road to the White House. One had the sense he really believed it, which probably reinforced one big knock against Kasich as a candidate—his capacity for self-delusion. After Super Tuesday II, he had a couple dozen fewer delegates than Rubio, who'd just exited. Political observer Stuart Rothenberg characterized Kasich's belief he could still win "bizarre."[404]

Though he won no states, Cruz probably had the second-best night among Republicans because he picked up delegates where he could and because Rubio, his main opponent, was gone. Indeed, one of Rubio's top aides reportedly tweeted shortly after Rubio's speech that Rubio's supporters should now all rally to Cruz's flag.

	Trump		Cruz		Rubio		Kasich	
	Pct	D	Pct	D	Pct	D	Pct	D
Florida	46	99	17	0	27	0	7	0
Ohio	38	0	13	0	3	0	47	66
Illinois	39	54	30	9	9	0	20	6
North Carolina	40	29	37	27	8	6	13	9
Missouri	40.9	37	40.7	15	6	0	10	0
No. Marianas	73	9	24	0	1	0	2	0
March 15 delegates		228		31		6		81
Total delegates to date		693		424		166		144

Looking at states as opposed to delegates, a clear pattern emerged among Republican voters. Thus far, voting occurred primarily in eastern and especially southeastern states. If one drew a line from Virginia westward to Oklahoma, then every state on or below the line had voted as had the uppermost northeast and some western states. But New York and the surrounding states had yet to be heard from, as well as the far west.

Among those that had voted, Trump, the New York State real estate developer, was the clear winner of the "bubba vote." The South and the Great Smoky Mountain states were Trump country. How strange was that?

Move farther west into cowboy country and Cruz dominated. Many more such cowboy states were yet to vote, so Cruz saw a fertile field for harvesting delegates. On the other hand, Trump could look at the New York vicinity as his own backyard and could expect to do well. The Pacific West seemed open for bidding.

After Super Tuesday II, a full month would pass before another decisive day of voting. March 22, Utah and Arizona and American Samoa would vote, followed by a string of three singletons (North Dakota, Wisconsin, and New York). Then would come April 26, when the candidates and the nation could hope the immediate future would be settled at last. Not quite.

Another Stage, Another Grind

By all appearances, Hillary Clinton had effectively won the Democratic nomination and needed nothing more than to run out the clock on the Sanders campaign. Sanders and Democratic voters would soon remind how appearances can deceive. For their part, Republicans settled into a five-week slog until the late April voting.

Pres. Obama, seeing a window to act between events, nominated Merrick B. Garland, Chief Justice at the District of Columbia Court of Appeals, to be the 113th Supreme Court Justice. The president, many of his congressional allies, and the media immediately labeled Garland a centrist no reasonable person would oppose. When one sits on the Far, Far Left (or Right), one's conceptions of "centrist" can be a bit peculiar. Garland wasn't an extremist, but he was very much in the mold of a typical liberal justice.

As evidence of Garland's position on the ideological spectrum, the Far Left had to strain mightily to hold its tongue at the lost opportunity to put another of "theirs" on the court to join the president's other Far-Left appointments in Sonia Sotomayor and Elena Kagan. Bottom line: a standard liberal white male, really?

Conservatives immediately opposed Garland, with Senate Majority Leader Mitch McConnell affirming his previously stated position Garland's nomination would never see the light of this Senate's floor.

In other developments, Florida Gov. Rick Scott, who had quietly not endorsed anyone in the recent contest including his home-state senator (nice, gGovernor), endorsed Donald Trump.

The RNC had scheduled another debate for Monday, March 21, in Utah. First Trump, then Kasich, and finally Cruz pulled out. As Trump observed, "I think we've had enough debates. How many times can you answer the same question?"[405] Point, Trump.

Back in Washington, House Republicans sought to craft and pass a budget resolution. It wasn't going well. The House Freedom Caucus still fumed at the year-end budget deal Speaker Ryan had struck with Pres. Obama hiking discretionary spending.

Considered from their perspective, one can understand the Freedom Caucus's frustration at the higher spending, and a great many other things. But the essential political realities remained: the Senate would not reduce spending and the president would with gusto veto any bill reducing spending. But by withholding support, the Freedom Caucus made it nearly impossible for Speaker Ryan to move a budget without Democratic support, an option he was loathe to entertain. On the other side of the Capitol, it appeared Senate Republicans would not even try to pass a budget. For years, Republicans had severely criticized Democrats for failing to pass a budget—payback, boys.

Ryan—No!

Speculation swirled about a contested Republican convention leading to much study of the standing rules regarding delegates and setting convention rules. Trump, fully aware of the speculation and that it was largely directed at stopping his candidacy, not so subtly suggested his supporters would "riot" if the party pulled any shenanigans.[406]

Two fundamental facts could not be avoided. First, whatever happened at the convention, many Republican voters would be displeased. Filling a big happy tent just wasn't in the cards. Every convention left some malcontents, but their ranks would be swollen out of Cleveland.

Second, whatever happened at the convention, the Republican candidate would emerge wounded. The election would seem to be Clinton's to lose. She wasn't a very good candidate, so she might manage to lose the election all on her own, but it seemed likely Clinton would have to blow it for a Republican to win.

And so, speculation continued. What if Trump could be stopped? What then? The party didn't like Cruz much, and Cruz would have won fewer delegates than Trump. If you're going to deny Trump, why not deny Cruz too? But who then? Turn to Romney, the stiff two-time loser? Or turn to someone generally and widely admired within the party excepting the malcontents in the House Freedom Caucus, a next-generation candidate, someone like House Speaker Paul Ryan?

As the speculation continued, Ryan felt compelled to respond. So on March 16: "I've been really clear about this. If you want to be president, you should run for president. We should select our nominee from among the people who are running for president. Clear and simple. So, no, I am not going to be the president."[407]

Ryan's statement sounded definitive enough. But one word kept popping into his statement: the word *should*. Very little about the 2016 campaign in either party had been constrained by "should." In fact, by normal lights, Ryan should not even be Speaker of the House. Ryan had been tapped when the Freedom Caucus toppled his predecessor, John Boehner, without any clue as to who'd be the successor. Ryan accepted the job because his party needed him and the country needed him—a lot like the disaster scenario apparently shaping up for the Republican convention. Preferences and protests aside, Ryan had already set the mold of being swept by history to where he didn't want to go.

An Army of One

Political campaigns rely on staffs who carry out instructions down the chain of command and percolate ideas and observations up the chain. Donald Trump had other ideas. Used to being his own brand, following his own advice, Trump had little use for experts in various policy areas, whether health care, technology, or tax.

For example, Trump had long been pressed to name the key members of his foreign policy team. Who did he talk to for advice and counsel? Finally, he admitted, "I'm speaking to myself, number one, because I have a very good brain and I've said a lot of things. . . . My primary consultant is myself, and I have a very good instinct for these things."[408]

Whoa, even for Trump, this was breathtaking. Some days later, in a *Washington Post* editorial board interview, Trump finally rattled off a few names, such as Walid Phares, a former Romney advisor then at the National Defense University; energy consultant George Papadopoulos; and a couple more.[409] Even within foreign policy circles, these were not exactly household names. Trump—truly an Army of One.

The exhausting month of March finally came to an end, leaving an eerie five-week hiatus when little appeared likely to happen, for which almost everyone involved seemed grateful. March had been kind to Hillary Clinton, but without clearing Bernie Sanders from the field, while leaving Republicans in a fine state of disarray; but for the moment, a breather.

Arizona, Utah, Idaho, American Samoa

Each state a battleground: On March 22, three states and a territory voted. The results: another inconclusive split decision. For Republicans, Donald Trump won Arizona's winner-take-all contest with 47%, picking up fifty-eight delegates, while Ted Cruz and John Kasich drew 25% and 10%, respectively. The import of these numbers: (1) Trump still had yet to cross the 50% threshold in any state; and

(2) even if Kasich had gotten out of the race and all of his votes had gone to Cruz, then Cruz would still have lost.

In contrast, Cruz romped in Utah with 69%, picking up all forty delegates. In American Samoa, Trump took all nine of its delegates, so on the day Trump claimed sixty-seven delegates to Cruz's forty. These results reinforced Cruz's strategy of not trying to overtake Trump but just to be in position to outmaneuver him at the convention.

Among Democrats, another split decision. Hillary Clinton took Arizona (58 to 40%) while Sanders took Utah (80 to 20%) and Idaho (78 to 21%). Apparently, Clinton wasn't getting a lot of love in the Rocky Mountains. Overall, Sanders won the day in a squeaker: 57 delegates gained to Clinton's 51. Sanders now lagged Clinton in pledged delegates 1,170 to 870. Gaining a net six at a time wasn't going to close that gap.

One final feature worth noting about the March 22 voting: in Arizona, voter turnout was enormous. Not only were Americans angry, but they were waiting in hours-long lines for the chance to register their anger.

Cruzian Realities

All along, the narrative ran that if the rest of the candidates would get out of the way, then the remaining option (in this case, Ted Cruz) could finally take on and defeat Donald Trump mano a mano. One indisputable fact at this point gave Cruz's narrative credibility: Trump had yet to break 50% in any state.

The trouble for Cruz was he drew his support entirely from the agitated hard-core conservative base—the constitutionalist/fiscal policy wing, the "I'm-more-scared-of-Trump" wing, and the evangelical wing which he split with Trump. These voters made up between 40% and perhaps as much as 50% of the Republican Party. Two other wings of the party making up the balance were the moderates and, for lack of a better word, the establishment types.

Historically, moderates found themselves in the party either by dint of tradition or because they were driven there by a Democratic

Party too Far Left to accept. Long ago, that is, before Ronald Reagan, moderates often ran the show in the party. By 2016, they lacked the energy and the numbers to run much of anything. Most often, their influence on the party is imperceptible. What's worse for them, they are strongest in states that typically vote Democratic in presidential elections—like New York and California. It's hard to influence a political party when you have little chance of adding to the elected representation.

The establishment types in the party more often than not agree with the hard-core conservatives on policy. Higher minimum wage? No way. Balance the budget? Absolutely. Strong national defense? Of course. Rule of law? Without a doubt.

While policy disagreements occasionally arise between the establishment types and the hard-core right, the real bone of contention is over tone and method. Whereas the hard-core, especially the modern Tea Party movement, thinks nothing of shutting the government down in a losing legislative battle, establishment types prefer negotiations and progress. Consequently, the Tea Party/hard-core wing sees the establishment types as "sell-outs" and "squishes" while the establishment types see the hard-core wing as fanatical serial losers.

Moderates and establishment-type Republicans generally abhorred Trump. Cruz's problem was they abhorred him nearly as much. Cruz essentially understood this as his main sales pitch, especially after Rubio's exit, became that he, Ted Cruz, was the only Republican who could stop Donald Trump.

Think about that for a moment. Cruz had the hard-core supporters. To win, he needed the moderates and the establishment types. He didn't even try to win them over on the merits. "I'm the only one who can stop Donald Trump."[410] Cruz was telling them: "Look, I *am* the lesser of two evils." He convinced Jeb Bush, who despite their profound differences in style, endorsed Cruz on March 23.[411] Who says they don't know marketing in Texas?

Cuba and Brussels

In mid-March, Pres. Obama took the next step in normalizing relations with Cuba, becoming the first American president to visit since Calvin Coolidge. Obama proclaimed, "It is time now to leave the past behind us."[412]

As is common for U.S. presidents, Obama took the opportunity to speak down to his Cuban hosts about human rights. Cuban Pres. Raúl Castro was not amused. Obama expected his host to sit obediently while Obama lectured on the need to improve human rights in Cuba. Castro was having none of it, pointing out that education and health care are free in Cuba. Political freedoms are fewer, but some economic freedoms are more abundant.

A few days later, Fidel Castro could contain his indignation no longer. In a missive titled "Brother Obama," ol' Fidel showed he still had some fight left in him.[413] "Leave the past behind" as Obama suggested? Not with distant memories of the Bay of Pigs and more recent memories of an economic embargo still fresh in the old dictator's mind. Waiting for American generosity? No. "We don't need the empire to give us anything." Fortunately for President Obama, he had gotten used to being slapped around by petty blowhards.

While Obama was enjoying his Cuba visit, ISIS terrorists struck in Brussels, with bombings at the Brussels airport and main train station killing 31, wounding 270. The Belgian police had a couple days before captured a leading ISIS operative, Salah Abdeslam. Thinking the terrorist cell had been or was about to be compromised, the remaining members attacked rather than wait to be arrested.

Countries throughout Europe had permitted entire neighborhoods to be taken over by Muslim immigrants who then presented ISIS large numbers of potential converts to radical Islam. Rather than assimilating into the local culture, often these neighborhoods became hotbeds of anti-West fervor and places the police dared not go except heavily armed. National authorities did little more than tut-tut at expensive meetings with expensive dinners, drinking expensive cognac.

This was far from a new experience for Europe. After World War II, Germany needed more workers to help rebuild a nation. Tens of thousands of mostly Turkish men responded. The plan was these guest workers would come for a few years and then go home. They came and mostly stayed. They brought their wives to Germany and had families. And for the most part, they didn't assimilate into German culture in part because it was so foreign to Turkish culture and in part because the German government permitted it. Fortunately, Turks in Germany were little inclined to radical Islam.

After the Belgium attacks, the German newspaper *Die Zeit* observed, "Wir sind im Krieg," translated: We are at war.[414] French prime minister Manuel Valls reiterated Pres. Hollande's earlier comments, "Yes, we are at war."[415] Newly installed Canadian prime minister Justin Trudeau trotted out his Pacifist flag, observing his country was not at war with ISIS, but then, his country hadn't been attacked—yet.[416] How convenient.

And what of Pres. Obama? At his initial Havana press conference, Obama began his remarks referring to the Brussels attacks, observing, "We will do whatever is necessary to support our friend and ally, Brussels, in bringing to justice those who were responsible."[417]

Question: Was the Brussels attack an act of war or a criminal act? To be sure, it could be both, but if both, which would be the more essential? Most of Europe understood the Western world was at war with ISIS. Not that it wanted to be. Not that it knew what to do in response. But ISIS had declared war with every means at its disposal. This had to be faced honestly. The Europeans faced facts and did little. For the U.S. government and the Canadian, the attacks were seen as a cowardly act, a heinous act, but ultimately just a no-drama-Obama criminal act. Herein lay a fundamental feature of the Obama doctrine in foreign policy—terrorism is first and foremost a criminal act.

When the United States launches air strikes against ISIS positions in Syria or Libya or Iraq, those are acts of war. When ISIS blows up a train station in Brussels, that is a criminal act, according to Pres.

Obama. Americans increasingly found Obama's thinking on these matters simply incoherent.

On the other hand, compared to Ted's and Donald's responses to the Brussels attacks, Barack Obama looked positively logical. Ted Cruz announced, "We need to empower our law enforcement to patrol and secure Muslim neighborhoods before they become radicalized."[418] And once they are radicalized, senator? What then? Burn 'em out?

Not wanting to appear the weaker reactionary, Donald Trump said the recently captured Salah Abdeslam should be tortured: "He'll be talking a lot faster with torture."[419] Trump also called for special police patrols in Muslim neighborhoods in the United States.

Hillary Clinton just kept quiet, hoping nobody would remember she was Obama's former secretary of state.

Gathering Forces in Self-Defense

Republicans of all stripes increasingly resigned themselves to two realities: Donald Trump was likely to be the nominee and would suffer a stunning loss. The only chance of preventing the former was supporting Ted Cruz.

To most non–Tea Party Republicans, Cruz remained an awful option. Few had forgotten how many pointless legislative disasters Cruz had orchestrated for congressional Republicans. Trump's sobriquet of "Lyin' Ted" wasn't helpful; but for many in the Republican Party, Cruz remained far less scary than Trump. Stephen Rodriguez, a former Bush administration official, expressed it well, "I don't know what's worse—having Trump say all those ridiculous things and being totally clueless, or having him say those all those things and actually mean it?"[420] If Cruz failed and Trump won the nomination, many lifelong hard-core conservative Republicans seriously contemplated supporting Hillary Clinton.

If Trump clinched the nomination, some might support Clinton; but what about the rest of the Republican ticket? Trump was no Republican; and so, the thinking went, the party would just have to isolate him as it would a cancerous growth. The election defeat would sever the appendage, but how to keep the rest of the body whole?

The obvious answer was to focus on the downstream races and protect as many as possible against the pending Trumpocolypse. By late March, such efforts were widely underway, uniting Republicans from the Koch brothers to Crossroads GPS.[421] Each in their own way began to develop plans to protect the most important or most threatened Republican incumbents.

Trump Sinks to a New Low

One pastime for American political observers in 2016 was guessing how low Donald Trump could sink. He'd long ago insulted Carly Fiorina for her looks and John McCain for having the bad form of getting shot down over North Vietnam and spending years in the Hanoi Hilton. He'd butted heads with the Pope. He regularly called Cruz "Lyin' Ted." He'd encouraged his supporters to beat the crap out of unruly rally protestors, offering to pay their legal bills. He'd advocated torture for prisoners. He'd referenced the size of his male organ. Could he sink any lower?

One lesson from the campaign was never underestimate Trump. He'd already confounded the political experts in surviving the early days of the campaign by breaking every rule short of not committing a felony on camera. Toward late March, Trump proved he had not yet plumbed the depths to which he would sink: he compared his wife Melania's looks with those of Cruz's Heidi. Heidi Cruz was a smart, lovely life partner to the Texas Senator. Melania, a regal former model, was Trump's third wife and twenty-six years his junior.

First, Trump threatened to "spill the beans on your wife."[422] Cruz responded in the rather quaint, old-fashioned way by calling Trump a "coward." He later elaborated, calling Trump a "sniveling coward," telling Trump to "leave Heidi the Hell alone."[423] Cowards are often sniveling, of course, but one struggled to imagine Donald Trump ever actually sniveling.

Cruz then climbed out of the gutter for a moment to make the reasonable observation, "Real men don't try to bully women. That's not an action of strength. That's an action of weakness." One sure way to get Trump agitated was to question his manhood, and this time he had to know Cruz had hit the bull's-eye. Grrrrr. Point, Cruz.

Enquiring Minds and the Lawyer's Offer

On March 23, the *National Enquirer* ran the story alleging Ted Cruz had a history of extramarital affairs with five secret mistresses.[424] Ted was not amused. Nor did anyone really take the story seriously. This was, after all, the *National Enquirer*, a comic strip involving real people. Whether his reaction was sincere or manufactured, Cruz immediately accused Trump of planting the story.

The natural reaction would be to brush off *National Enquirer* nonsense. Reacting by blaming Trump only kept the story alive a few hours longer. We will likely never know the truth, of course.

The most likely scenario is the *National Enquirer* just made it all up. But somehow, it wasn't hard to believe Trump planted the story, as unlikely as it would seem under normal circumstances. Consider, for example, a front-page story that ran a couple days later in the *Washington Post*.[425] According to the *Post*, during Trump's famous battle with a little old lady in Atlantic City whose home was disrupting Trump's development plans, Trump made an offer to hire the old lady's attorney, Glenn Zeitz, to represent Trump in a far more lucrative matter. Zeitz declined, citing the obvious potential "tangled web of conflicts" such an arrangement would produce. Zeitz found the offer "bizarre." It was bizarre, but that's just the kind of guy Trump was. And why it wasn't hard to believe he'd planted the *National Enquirer* story, just as Cruz claimed.

Hillary Cruisin', Bernie Bruisin'

While the Republican front-runners were field-testing various new forms of mud to throw at one another, the Democrats actually engaged in selecting a nominee. On Saturday, Democrats voted in Alaska, Hawaii, and Washington State, thus concluding March's festivities.

Bernie Sanders kicked butt, and Hillary Clinton didn't seem to care. She had simply ignored the three contests. Hawaii, Alaska, and Washington State all went overwhelmingly for Sanders.[426] Alaska went for Sanders 440 to 99. Yes, just over 500 Alaskans voted. On balance, he picked up fifty-five delegates to Clinton's twenty, for a net gain of thirty-five. This wasn't a big shift, but Sanders was setting a pattern of winning and Clinton was setting a pattern of losing. Winning beats losing.

	Clinton		Sanders	
	Pct	D	Pct	D
Washington	27	27	74	74
Alaska	18	3	82	13
Hawaii	30	8	70	17
March 26 delegates		38		104

Donald Trump took a week off from campaigning because, well, he was Trump. He did that sort of thing. The next contests were a few days away and this was another campaign rule he could break.

Sanders was gaining momentum, so why was Clinton coasting? In a word, superdelegates. The Democratic Party's human infrastructure had long before lined up behind Hillary, to the tune of 469 committed superdelegates to Sanders's 29 as of late March. Clinton assumed first that the supers once bought would stay bought and that therefore she was assured of the nomination no matter what Sanders did. This was a dangerous assumption. If Bernie went on a tear of winning states and closing the gap, would the supers remain loyal to Hillary even as the party was voting time and again for Sanders? This seemed a foolish risk to run.

CHAPTER 15
WISCONSIN CHEESE TO ACELA PRIMARY

March produced epic clashes revealing clear winners. Clashes? Yes. Clear winners? No. Neither political party knew who would bear their flag in the coming election. Hillary Clinton looked to be in the driver's seat; but a string of losses to an aging Socialist, her own unpopularity, and her dogged scandals dimmed her prospects. Her candidacy would be in peril but for her indomitable spirit buttressed by hundreds of superdelegates and her campaign's fundraising prowess.

Compared with the Republicans, the Democrats looked in fine shape. The candidate still out front was a non-Republican: Donald Trump. His main antagonist, Ted Cruz, boasted friends, little experience, and a history of disdain for the majority of his own party. Neither appeared to have a sure path to a first-ballot win. The coming Cleveland convention promised disaster with serious downstream consequences. The Republicans' hold on the U.S. Senate was expected to be shaky, with 24 seats to defend compared with the Democrats' 10, but now control of the House also seemed in jeopardy.

Is You Is or Is You Ain't a Republican?

One touchstone of party politics demands all contestants within the party support the party's nominee. Usually not an issue because the contestants understood the importance of party loyalty and usually disagree more with the other party's nominee. As usual, 2016 did not unfold the usual campaign. Early in 2015 Donald Trump waffled on whether he would support the Republican nominee if he didn't win, which was understandable since he had no real allegiance to the party. Eventually, if only to discard the distraction and knowing he could change his mind later, Trump relented and committed.

Tellingly, as the race narrowed to a mostly Trump versus Cruz affair, Cruz allowed in a CNN interview he would support the nominee no matter what but only because he had previously said he would. By March, the fight between Trump and Cruz had sunk so low, so dirty, so personal both candidates were hounded by the press with the question: after all the terrible things you've said about him, would you really support the other guy? While Cruz kept to his word, Trump threatened to renege on the loyalty pledge he had previously signed. Does he hold to the pledge? "No, I don't."[427] No one could ever accuse Trump of being ethically inflexible.

In addition to his flexibility, Trump also gained enormous advantages in offering up outrages with such rapidity as to prevent anyone from really digging into any single episode. At a March 8 press conference in Jupiter, Florida, former Breitbart reporter Michelle Fields got a little too close and a little too pushy for Trump campaign manager Corey Lewandowski's comfort. Fields alleged Lewandowski grabbed her arm roughly and pulled her back. Lewandowski denied the allegation. Trump backed his campaign manager.

There the matter sat until, as they used to say in the sports world, "roll the tape."[428] Jupiter Police got hold of the video from the ballroom. The video backed Fields's version. Lewandowski was charged with battery. He continued to maintain his innocence. Trump sided with his campaign manager. Millions viewed the video online rendering their own judgment.

The issue would have passed with hardly any notice had Lewandowski or Trump any sense: apology offered, apology accepted, move on. With all the brutality in the campaign, and in America, a mildly rough exchange between a pushy reporter and a campaign operative becomes a sensation? Yes, because Trump and his crew were not the apologizing sort. This created a free-fire zone for a press corps the members of which wanted nothing more than to be the one who took Trump down in a journalistic version of big game hunting.[429] Meanwhile, Trump must have laughed at how he'd distracted his adversaries again.

Wisconsin Cheese

Republicans had two upcoming contests: North Dakota on Friday, April 1, and Wisconsin on Tuesday, April 5. Respects to North Dakota, but Wisconsin offered the more interesting race. To begin, in the general election North Dakota was almost certain to go to the Republican, whereas Wisconsin leaned Democrat but could be contested.

Second, the candidate apparently waiting off-stage for some contested convention magic was none other than House Speaker Paul Ryan—of Wisconsin. Ryan had recently given a high-profile speech decrying the nastiness of the Republican race while donning the mantle of the sensible adult in the room.

Third, Scott Walker, former top-tier presidential candidate, endorsed Cruz on March 29, declaring Cruz "is the best positioned by far" to beat Clinton.[430] Walker's stock in Wisconsin had fallen as he neglected state affairs during his brief presidential campaign, but he was still popular and he was still the governor. The RealClearPolitics average of polls prior to Walker's endorsement had Trump at 33.0%, Cruz at 32.3%, and Kasich, as usual, trailing at 23.0%.

Sanders Goes Super

Bernie Sanders knew it would be almost impossible to have more pledged delegates than Hillary Clinton by the convention. He trailed 1,243 to 975. Sanders also knew he had all the momentum, and the campaign was swinging after Wisconsin to the northeast, where he could do very well.

Against these positives stood a deficit of 440 superdelegates. These were the Democratic Party pooh-bahs who had more or less pledged to support Clinton. But they might change their minds, right? And so, Sanders set out to help them. In a conference call with reporters, Sanders laid out his strategy based largely on momentum (his), a lack of electability (hers), and the supers' freedom to change their minds.[431]

Campaigns are full of irony and hypocrisy, most of which goes unnoticed and unremarked. However, a tweet out of the Clinton campaign following Sanders's reporters' conference call bears noting. Clinton's argument ran: even if Sanders won more delegates, he couldn't win because of her stockpiled nonelected superdelegates. The tweet? "Summary of Sanders spin: Voters only count for real or mean anything when they vote for Sanders."

Ah, Hillary? The voters didn't vote for the supers on whom you're counting to seal the deal. The headline on the *New York Daily News*' March 30 edition perhaps had the best response describing Clinton's hold on the supers: CROCK THE VOTE.

Drip, Drip, Drip ... Discovery

Hillary Clinton had bigger problems than Bernie Sanders' flirtations with her superdelegates. Yes, that old email thing again. How serious was the FBI investigation? The agency had not one or two ready-to-retire backbenchers but dozens of agents working the case.[432]

Then, on Tuesday, March 29, Federal Judge Royce Lamberth, watching over a related but separate matter and citing evidence of "government wrongdoing and bad faith," allowed Judicial Watch to pursue legal discovery regarding the email account as part of its Freedom of Information Act requests.[433] Judicial Watch would now be allowed to depose under oath various Clintonistas associated with the scandal, likely including Clinton herself, all of which would then be part of the public record.

The Clinton people would be very busy and not just on campaign matters. In addition to the pending Judicial Watch depositions, the FBI contacted the attorneys for a number of Clinton's top aides to schedule interviews.[434] Anyone who has watched a good crime drama knows the story: start at the bottom and work your way up. Reporting suggested these interviews meant the investigation's preliminary background work neared completion.

This had to dog Clinton. Even if she was totally innocent of anything other than a few bad decisions come back to haunt, the Judicial Watch case guaranteed the story would be reported on again and again. And the FBI seemed to be spending too much time and effort in a high-profile case to come up empty-handed. Somebody's scalp seemed sure to be going up on a wall somewhere. Everybody in Clinton land believed it. No one volunteered to be sacrificed just yet.

The FBI was also in a tough spot and would ultimately rely on the personal credibility of Director Jim Comey to see them through. If Comey shielded Clinton, or if upon seeing all the evidence the generally supine and hyper-political Justice Department didn't indict Clinton, then even neutral observers would suspect a cover-up and the FBI would share in the suspicion. On the other hand, indicting Clinton would be very delicate for a former secretary of state and former New York Senator. Indicting Clinton, leading candidate of the president's own party to cement his legacy, would be historic. Would an indicted Clinton would fight—her instinctive reaction—or fold?[435]

The Abortion Issue

Few issues produce a more virulent personal reaction in America than abortion. Few issues have ended amateur politicians' careers faster. For most, the political guidelines are clear:

1. Spend some time to understand thoroughly what you believe.
2. Be able to explain your views clearly and succinctly in common terms typical of that position.
3. Never vary; never dwell on the topic; move on as quickly as possible.

These simple rules follow because most Americans don't want to talk about abortion. It is an ugly issue. Large numbers of highly animated citizens are on one side or the other, with a large bloc in between. As a politician or a candidate, not having an opinion is not an option. If you're clear and unwavering, one side will support you and the other oppose; and if you don't dwell on it, then the large bloc of voters in the middle will appreciate talking about other issues. But if you waver or waffle in any way, chances are you're going to lose because your opponents will oppose you and those who may agree with you won't trust you.

For most of his life, Donald Trump had supported a woman's right to abortion on demand. To run as a Republican, Trump switched sides, he said. Because they're a trusting sort, many abortion opponents accepted his conversion. Then, toward the end of April, Trump's amateurishness and arrogance snagged him in a bramble of his own making.

It started during a conversation with MSNBC's Chris Matthews. Trump argued if abortion were made illegal, then there should be "some kind of punishment" for having an abortion.[436]

In a coldly analytical way, Trump's position made sense. Usually, when someone breaks the law—and remember, the predicate was if abortion were illegal—an appropriate punishment follows. But for those opposing abortion, an essential element involved remembering the emotional and sometimes physical distress of the woman. While abortion proponents sought to cast opponents as being anti-woman, the charge was obviously absurd given the millions of American women who opposed abortion; but it often gained currency through thoughtless comments such as Trump made regarding "punishment."

Trump is not heartless, one presumes, but he clearly hadn't thought this through. Within hours he flip-flopped, saying the doctor should be punished but that "the woman is a victim in this case, as is the life in her womb."[437] Ooops.

His intentions were obvious in trying to show understanding and compassion, but calling women who have abortions "victims" is both absurd and insulting. Women who have abortions know full well the decision they are making, and its import from their own personal perspective. They cannot be both self-empowered and "victims" at the same time.

Matters worsened a couple days later. When pressed by *Face the Nation* moderator John Dickerson, "But you don't disagree with that position, that it's [abortion's] murder?" Trump responded, "No, I don't disagree with it."[438]

An ugly issue; if one believes the unborn is a human being—a child—then abortion is murder. There's no escaping it. Just as there's no escaping the fact that a pregnant woman gives up a great deal of the control over her own body during a pregnancy. Demanding a woman carry an unwanted fetus to term is exceptional, unconscionable. But if the unborn is a child, the alternative seems even more so. On the other hand, if one is certain the fetus is not a human being until born, not a child in any relevant sense, then there is no reason to oppose abortion.

Abortion tripped Trump up, as it had many an amateur before him; but it also tripped up the most experienced candidate in the race. Also on *Meet the Press*, Hillary Clinton said, "The unborn person doesn't have constitutional rights. . . . Now that doesn't mean that we don't do everything we possibly can in the vast majority of instances to, you know, help a mother who is carrying a child and wants to make sure the child will be healthy, to have appropriate medical support."[439] Ooops.

"Unborn person," "a mother who is carrying a child"—this is game-changing terminology and Planned Parenthood pounced quickly, saying Clinton's comment "further stigmatizes abortion." Clinton was saying that abortion kills a "person" and not just any person but a "child." If she really believed this, and unlike Trump, Clinton had most assuredly given the matter a great deal of thought, then her view was that abortion might be restricted in certain instances but otherwise the entire matter should be a woman's choice even if that choice meant she was killing a child. That was her position according to her own words. Not surprisingly, neither the Washington Post nor the New York Times bothered to report on Clinton's Meet the Press comments or the ensuing dustup.

Trump's NATO Air Strike

In the 2016 campaign, Donald Trump was many things: insulting, nasty, inconsistent, entertaining. He was also a raw agitator, asking questions the American people wanted asked or would want asked if they thought about them. Americans also wanted the questions answered honestly even when national politicians preferred to remain silent; example: Trump's questioning of America's membership in NATO.

NATO, the North Atlantic Treaty Organization, was the umbrella defense alliance of the United States and Europe after WWII to present a united front against the Soviet Union's expansionist plans. NATO helped integrate military plans and capabilities among its members, who agreed upon joining to defend as one any member attacked by a nonmember. By any measure, NATO was the most effective defense alliance in history against a mighty and determined adversary. After the collapse of the Soviet Union, NATO's justification likewise collapsed. But NATO remained.

NATO remained even as the United States bore most of the cost and while the military capabilities of most European participants withered to naught. Once again, Europe was free-riding on the American taxpayer, and nobody wanted to ask why. Trump not only asked but concluded there was no justification, calling the body "obsolete."[440]

Fundamentally, Trump made a strong case. In the first two decades following the Soviet Union's collapse, a badly weakened Russia was disinclined to foment trouble while Middle East problems essentially fell outside the alliance's remit. Even Pres. Putin's rebuilding of Russia's military, his military agitations in Georgia, the annexation of Crimea, his hostile ministrations in the Ukrainian civil war and in Syria all failed to justify NATO's continued existence under its original charter.

Europe, of course, benefited greatly from a military alliance as long as the alliance had both teeth and credibility as Putin made no bones about wanting to reconstitute Greater Russia and its strategic orbit of neighboring countries, many of which were more inclined to turn to the West. But Europe's military had very few teeth capable of chewing, let alone biting; and its political leadership mustered zero credibility in suggesting it might use what little capability it had in thwarting Putin's ambitions. Without the United States backing NATO, Europe's military was a small paper tiger. Europe's interests were clear, but why should the U.S. taxpayer pay for defending Europe when Europe's taxpayers refused to do so? This was essentially the question Trump asked—and answered.

Then Trump's position evolved. The focus shifted to the undeniable fact the United States was paying disproportionately for NATO.[441] In Trump's view, the Europeans needed to pony up—big time. "Either they pay up including for past deficiencies or they have to get out. And if it breaks up NATO, it breaks up NATO." But why pay at all for something that is obsolete? If it's not obsolete, then demanding that all the members pay their fair share is obvious. If it is obsolete, distributing the burden fairly doesn't change its obsolescence or justify U.S. involvement. Once again, Trump had asked a good question but hadn't thought through his answer.

Naturally, the establishment quickly rose to NATO's defense. Pres. Obama had a showy meeting with NATO's head. Hillary Clinton donned her former secretary of state hat to defend NATO.

Many Republicans did, as well. Of course, they'd sat by for years and accepted the status quo, so either they became the "me too" chorus to Trump while explaining away their previous complacency, or they played the reactionary while defending their past and now uncomfortable acquiescence to the status quo. To the extent the American people knew what NATO was, however, Trump scored the political points.

Only Bernie Sanders, the Left's temporary agitator in chief, went a different direction, suggesting, "We need a new NATO" including Russia to defeat ISIS.[442] Let's review the bidding: NATO exists first and foremost as a bulwark against Russia. Russia gets mad anytime one of its non-NATO-neighboring countries hints at joining NATO. Russia, of course, still had its own regional military alliance. And Russia was in a contest with Europe for control of Eastern Europe. So Sanders's solution was to bring Russia into the organization it had opposed to one degree or another for about seventy years. As the Beatles once sang, "Strawberry fields forever."

Trump's Independent Streak

Donald Trump suffered from a fairness complex. Time and again he fixated on whether he was treated "fairly." In early April, Trump again raised the possibility if he weren't treated fairly by the Republican Party, then maybe he'd run as an independent. This joke was getting stale, so RNC head Reince Priebus responded, "Those kinds of comments, I think, have consequence."[443]

Having sent a shot across the bow, Priebus cleverly steered the audience's eyes away from his real target. He talked about whether Republican voters could support a candidate during the Republican primaries who maybe would run from the party later on. Fair point, but those weren't the consequences Priebus had in mind.

When Trump signed the "loyalty pledge," he signed an agreement whereby the RNC would provide the Trump campaign with certain voter information and other logistical support. The same support went to all the candidates, contingent upon signing the agreement.

If Trump went back on the agreement having received the support, then he would be reneging on a contract, likely resulting in legal action by the RNC against Trump and his campaign. Those were the consequences to which Priebus alluded. Trump understood. His talk of an independent campaign quickly subsided.

Feinstein Trips on Accomplishments

With all the rancor and tension of a national political campaign, one ought not ignore the funny moments. To her chagrin, California's Sen. Dianne Feinstein, a longtime Hillary Clinton supporter, provided one such moment.

Sen. Feinstein was well respected in the U.S. Senate by colleagues from both parties for her diligence, hard work, and steady hand. She first came to the Senate in 1992, having previously spent ten years as San Francisco's mayor. Feinstein evidenced the consummate professional for so long her flubbing of a question in early April came as a surprise for Feinstein and an embarrassment for Clinton.

On March 30, Feinstein was visiting with the *San Francisco Chronicle*'s editorial board, something she had done scores of times over the years. Asking a fairly simple question, the *Chronicle*'s editors probably had no idea they had guided Feinstein over a trap, "As someone who worked with Hillary Clinton for over a decade in the Senate, what in your view is her signature accomplishment as a senator?"[444]

Ummm . . . ummmmm.

No, that wasn't Feinstein's meditative mantra. It was the good senator struggling for an answer. Finally, she turned to Google for an answer and found none. Feinstein later admitted, "I didn't come prepared for this."

Feinstein's reputation meant she needn't worry her little faux pas would affect her standing. But the Clinton campaign had to worry Feinstein had inadvertently blown the cover off a troubling feature of Clinton's past: her lack of accomplishments. Her résumé of positions held was long and distinguished. Her list of notable accomplishments to date had nary an entry other than logging frequent flyer miles as secretary of state and not bashing Bill with an ashtray for chasing after other women. A paucity of accomplishments was not a selling point for someone trying to distinguish herself from the Socialist competition on the basis that she could get things done in Washington.

Accomplishments a Nuisance, the FBI a Threat

Hillary Clinton should be so lucky as to only have accomplishment issues, but she also had FBI issues. The FBI was lining up senior Clinton aides for interviews and then would turn to Hillary. As H. A. Goodman wrote in the leftist *Salon* magazine:

> The FBI's upcoming interview of Hillary Clinton will be a turning point in the race for Democratic nominee, especially since Clinton won't be able to speak to James Comey and his FBI agents in the same manner her campaign has communicated with the public. Unlike loyal Hillary supporters who view the marathon Benghazi hearings to be a badge of courage and countless prior scandals to be examples of exoneration, the FBI didn't spend one year (investigating this email controversy) to give Clinton or her top aides parking tickets. They mean business, and lying to an FBI agent is a felony, so Hillary Clinton and her aides will be forced to tell the truth. The doublespeak involving convenience and retroactive classification won't matter to seasoned FBI agents whose reputations are on the line; the entire country feels there's a double-standard regarding this email controversy.[445]

No evasions, no time limits, no doublespeak, one reasonably presumed Clinton would have to tell the truth, the whole truth, and nothing but the truth (wouldn't that be novel?); or she would be in deep kimchi. And with twenty-two top-secret emails on her email server by the latest count, claiming ignorance wasn't going to fly.

Goodman rattled off a top ten list of questions the FBI would surely pose (and remember, this is from a leftist publication. Imagine what else the FBI might ask):

1. What was the political utility in owning a private server and never using a State.gov email address?
2. Were all 31,830 deleted private emails about yoga?
3. Why didn't you know that intelligence could be retroactively classified?
4. Why did you use a Blackberry [sic] that wasn't approved by the NSA?
5. What did you say to Bryan Pagliano [Clinton's IT specialist who set up the private server]?
6. Why were 22 Top Secret emails on a private server?
7. Was any information about the Clinton Foundation mingled with State Department documents?
8. Did President Obama or his staff express any reservations about your private server?
9. Did Bill Clinton send or receive any emails on your private network?
10. How was your private server guarded against hacking attempts?

This was for starters. Each and every question could trigger a series of follow-ups. This might take more than a day. Better clear the schedule for a while. (Little did anyone suspect the FBI interview to be little more than afternoon tea.)

Fiscal Fantasies of a Trumpian Dimension

When Barack Obama took office, publicly held federal debt stood at $6.8 trillion. By the time he left, projections were for $14 trillion, or roughly double. The Congressional Budget Office projected the debt to climb another $10 trillion over the following decade under the policies then in place and assuming no wars or recessions. Then the crushing burden of the nation's inadequately funded entitlement programs would really hit.

Over these years, federal tax receipts would rise from just above 18% of GDP, roughly the post–World War II norm, to over 19%. With such plentiful revenues, why was the enormous debt? In one simple and irrefutable word: spending. Under Pres. Obama, federal spending soared, and then remained far above normal, until it was projected to soar even further.

Heretofore, the various candidates' contributions to the debate over fiscal policy involved making the debt picture markedly worse. Hillary Clinton and Bernie Sanders battled to see who could offer up the most debt-busting spending increases while Donald Trump offered the same effect through a massive tax cut. While Clinton and Sanders were rarely criticized for their spending, Trump was blasted for the size of his tax cut. Trump's response was to dismiss the critics and claim his plan would create so much growth the deficit would actually fall.

It apparently occurred to Trump his theory was a little thin, so he simply claimed he would eliminate the debt in eight years. This was the kind of silly statement that might be tolerated with a polite snicker if made by an incoming freshman Member of Congress. As is his wont, Trump had once again raised the bar on absurdity.

The only way to reduce the debt is to run a budget surplus—spend less than you take in. Set aside Trump's tax cut for a moment. The CBO projected an average deficit of about $860 billion annually from 2017 to 2026.[446] To eliminate $14 trillion in debt over eight years meant running an average surplus of $1.75 trillion over these years. Doing so would require a net change in the deficit of over $2.5 trillion *a year.* Federal spending was projected to average about $4.9 trillion, so Trump was claiming he could cut spending roughly in half, or roughly by the total of all spending on Social Security, Medicare, and Medicaid. He might as well have said he would build a wall the length of the Mexican border and make Mexico pay for it.

This man wanted to be President of the United States. Many voters seemed to want him to be President of the United States. Amazing.

BADGER VOTES

The Colorado Republicans' convoluted process begun March 1 finally managed to allocate six of its thirty-seven delegates, all of whom went to Ted Cruz. Cruz also outmaneuvered Trump in Louisiana, thus matching Donald Trump's haul of eighteen delegates even though Trump received almost eleven thousand more votes. Cruz also claimed all ten Republican delegates from North Dakota on April 1. Cruz was on a nice roll going into Wisconsin, April 4.

The Badger State appeared unfriendly territory for Trump, especially after the terrible two weeks he'd just had. It wasn't really Cruz territory either, but conservative and Republican forces finally united behind Cruz if only to stop Trump. Wisconsin also has a very active cadre of local conservative radio hosts, most or all of whom spent a good ten days battering Trump mercilessly.

In the end, the combined firepower proved sufficient: Cruz won with 48.2% to Trump's 35.1% and Kasich's 14.1%. Most immediately, this meant Cruz picked up another thirty-six delegates to Trump's six. Kasich, who took exactly zero delegates out of a state he should have done well in, continued his campaign for reasons still no one could explain.

More broadly, Wisconsin and the other events noted brought Cruz to 517 delegates, still behind Trump's 743; but he was closing steadily. At least as important, after Wisconsin, the odds of a contested Republican convention rose dramatically.

On the Democratic side, Bernie Sanders scored yet another victory in Wisconsin, receiving 56.6% to Hillary Clinton's 43.1%, and taking forty-seven delegates to her thirty-six. This gave Clinton 1,279 pledged delegates to Sanders's 1,058. Sanders wasn't closing the gap quickly, but he was closing it. More importantly, he had strung together six wins since March 22 to Clinton's one win. Sanders had the momentum and it showed in solid fundraising.

ON TO THE EMPIRE STATE

New York offered the next big voting event on the calendar, April 19, though the Democrats would make a quick pit stop first in Wyoming April 9. Curiously, three of the four top contenders called the Empire State home. Hillary Clinton lived there and had twice been elected senator from New York. Bernie Sanders was born in Brooklyn and lived in neighboring Vermont. Donald Trump hailed from the Big Apple, and his business had a huge footprint in the city.

Only Ted Cruz lacked an obvious New York attachment, which meant anything less than a clear victory for Trump would be a clear embarrassment. Kasich was expected to win Ohio. Rubio was expected to win Florida (and dropped out when he failed). Cruz was expected to win Texas. Trump was expected to win New York.

New York Republicans had a common and complex system of allocating their ninety-eight delegates, ninety-five of whom would be bound by the voting and three of whom were the state's allocated RNC members. Of the ninety-five bound delegates, eighty-one would be allocated three per congressional district while fourteen would be awarded by statewide voting.

Unlike many states, New York had a closed primary, meaning only Republicans could vote in the Republican race. A candidate had to win more than 20% of the vote to receive any of the fourteen statewide delegates. If a candidate won more than 50% of the statewide vote, he took all the delegates. (Trump consistently polled at about 54%.) The eighty-one delegates awarded by congressional districts were similarly allocated, so in most cases the district winner would receive two delegates and the runner-up would receive one.

While Trump faced substantial pressure, Clinton's back was to the wall and she was fighting mad. Two things Clinton knew how to do were to fight and to go for what she perceived to be the jugular. The New York primary was open only to the party faithful, so Clinton questioned whether Sanders was really a Democrat. He was running as a Democrat, sure, but he had insisted he was an independent in the U.S. Senate. "I think he himself doesn't consider himself to be a

Democrat," she offered helpfully.[447] She elaborated the next day, "He's a relatively new Democrat, and in fact I'm not even sure he is one." It was a fair point, just as questioning whether Trump was a Republican was a fair question.

Clinton also questioned whether Sanders was fully prepared to be president: "I think he hadn't done his homework and he'd been talking for more than a year about doing things that he obviously hadn't really studied or understood."[448]

Sanders proved equally pugnacious. While not his nature to throw the first punch at a fellow leftist, he showed no reluctance to counterpunch. "My response is if you want to question my qualifications, then maybe the American people might wonder about your qualifications Madame Secretary," he said.[449]

Sanders added, "When you voted for the war in Iraq, the most disastrous foreign policy blunder in the history of America, you might want to question your qualifications. When you voted for trade agreements that cost millions of Americans decent paying jobs, and the American people might want to wonder about your qualifications. When you're spending an enormous amount of time raising money for your Super PAC from some of the wealthiest people in this country, and from some of the most outrageous special interests. . . . Are you qualified to be President of the United States when you're raising millions of dollars from Wall Street whose greed and recklessness helped destroy our economy?"

This little exchange reminded Clinton of a nasty reality. If she wanted to engage in a slug fest, then she'd have to stand toe-to-toe with Sanders in the middle of the ring. It wasn't clear who would be standing at the bell. She had to find a better way if she wanted to survive Sanders' challenges.

A Cycle Without Pause

National campaigns typically follow certain cycles: announcements, debates, Iowa, New Hampshire, Super Tuesday; then a pause as the presumptive nominees prepare for the conventions; a pause for the

Summer Olympics; then a mad dash after Labor Day to election day—thus, the normal cycle but not this cycle. The traditional spring pause never came. This was going to be a very long year.

On Saturday, April 9, Bernie Sanders added to his string of consecutive victories, winning Wyoming 56 to 43%.[450] Symbolic of his tough week, however, Sanders and Clinton split the Wyoming delegate take seven each. In part, Sanders's troubles began with his success. Even after his good start, the media hadn't given his candidacy much of a chance and so had given his statements and positions relatively little scrutiny. His continued success brought more scrutiny. He didn't handle it well. The heightened scrutiny perhaps began with his suggestion Clinton wasn't "qualified" to be president. This got the mainstream media's attention because by and large they believed Clinton was eminently qualified and that she should and would be the next president.

The scrutiny took on a sharper edge with Sanders's incessant attacks on Wall Street, especially his demands the big banks be broken up. This attack was not only sincere and broadly popular but also tactical because Clinton was well-known to have close ties to the Wall Street big-money boys. But exactly how would Sanders break up the big banks? And which ones?

For a very long time, Sanders offered no answer. Then, finally, he referred to a flimsy piece of legislation he'd introduced previously and to some powers granted federal regulators under the post-financial crisis regulatory reform. Sanders's position with respect to the big banks was crystal clear. His explanation of how he would break up the big banks was, in contrast, almost Trumperian in its opacity.

Sanders's explanation of his big bank proposal fit a pattern, so much so the *Washington Post* ran a telling editorial page cartoon showing Sanders next to a large blackboard titled "Sanders Platform."

Under the title were lines numbered one through ten as follows:

1. don't know
2. it's complicated
3. got me there
4. I'll look into it
5. haven't decided
6. to be determined
7. details, details
8. that's a puzzler
9. haven't thought it thru
10. will get back to you

In the cartoon, Sanders stood next to a donkey speaking the words, "That's not what I meant about filling in the blanks."[451]

CRUZ THE DELEGATE MASTER

Bernie Sanders wasn't the only candidate having a tough time. Ted Cruz was schooling Donald Trump in the fine art of backroom politics. Trump was a master of hardball business tactics, but either Cruz or someone high on his staff was a master at hardball nomination politics.

First, Cruz managed to squeeze a few more delegates out of Louisiana right out from under Trump's nose. Next, he began a meticulous process of working delegates already pledged to Trump. In some circumstances, some might be convinced to vote for Cruz at the convention, some on the first ballot, many more on the second or third. Next Cruz claimed the last thirteen of Colorado's thirty-four delegates, giving him a clean sweep.[452]

Trump's Colorado debacle showcased Cruz's mastery of the process and Trump's amateur status. Colorado was one of six states and territories employing a convention rather than a primary or a caucus to decide on delegates. Cruz put staff in Colorado a year before. They knew the rules and were well prepared. Trump's team were few, recently recruited, and outclassed.

For example, the morning of the convention the Trump team distributed white flyers with Trump's delegates' names on the ballot. Some of the names were misspelled, and many had the wrong ballot number. As Colorado's freshman Sen. Cory Gardner explained in a tweet, ".@tedcruz showed up to the @cologop convention @realDonaldTrump only sent a surrogate." Cruz swept. Elections are won by those who show up.[453]

The story ran deeper. According to Alan Cobb, a Trump campaign senior advisor in Colorado, "our slate was correct at the time of print."[454] Probably true, but then what happened? Just maybe the State Republican Party had renumbered? Why would they do that? Hint: Cruz had his people on the ground in the state for a year, and the party bosses didn't like Trump. Not very smart for a man running as the smartest man on earth. Trump's response was utterly predictable. He called the situation "totally unfair."[455]

To be sure, Colorado Republicans had instituted some of the nation's most convoluted rules for picking delegates. But the rules were known. Cruz used them well. Trump didn't. Back on March 15, Trump won Florida's Republican primary with less than 46% of the vote; yet he won all the delegates. Those were Florida's rules. They don't sound very fair, winning less than half the vote yet getting all the delegates. But they were the rules, and no one whined when Trump got all the delegates. No one complained, "It's not fair."

Republicans weren't the only ones with Colorado issues. The Colorado Democratic Party admitted it misreported March 1 caucus results from ten precincts.[456] Correction made; Sanders picked up another Colorado delegate. Mistakes happen, but then something curious happened. The Colorado Democratic Party quickly told the Clinton campaign of its lost delegate. They didn't tell the public or the Sanders campaign. Hmmmm.

Trump's experience in Colorado was largely repeated in Nebraska, though with less fanfare. In the first week of April, Nebraska Republicans held their local county conventions. Trump's supporters were scarcer than an Oklahoma Sooner fan at a Cornhusker tailgate party. "I didn't see any Trump supporters," observed John Orr, chairman of the Washington County Republican Party.[457] Which meant when Nebraska held its primary May 10 in a winner-take-all battle for thirty-six delegates, Trump looked to strike out. An old expression, the rule of six *P*s, reads "previous planning prevents piss-poor performance." Unlike Cruz, Trump was severely lacking in previous planning.

Time and again, Cruz mastered Trump. Missouri Republicans voted March 15. Trump won thirty-seven delegates; Cruz, fifteen. But who were these delegates? Three of them were RNC members, but the rest still had yet to be chosen. Republicans caucused on April 9 to decide. Typical is what happened in Wild Horse Township in the county of St. Louis.[458] Former Missouri House Speaker and Ted Cruz supporter Tim Jones offered a slate of delegates, all perfectly within the rules. Trump's people offered their own. Jones won, all within the rules. All the delegates on Jones's ballot were Cruz supporters, meaning they would vote for Trump on the first ballot if that's how their congressional district went; but after the first ballot, they were free agents—free, that is, to vote for Cruz or anyone but Trump.

Trump had apparently come to understand he needed some more seasoned campaign hands. To this point, the campaign had been a small tightly knit affair with Trump being his own top advisor and Corey Lewandowski operating as chief lieutenant. Trump brought in some help, starting with longtime senior Republican operative Paul Manafort, hired to manage Trump's convention-related activities.

Manafort apparently fit right in. Just days after his hiring, Manafort was on *Meet the Press* complaining about Cruz's "Gestapo" tactics at conventions.[459] Trump serially complained about "unfair" behavior. Manafort complained about "Gestapo" tactics. Gentlemen, if you don't want to play hardball, stay off the field. Whining is unbecoming.

Trump followed Manafort's hiring with Rick Wiley, Gov. Scott Walker's former campaign manager, a highly experienced political operative.[460] Shortly thereafter, the campaign's national field director,

Stuart Jolly, submitted his resignation. Under the new organizational chart, Jolly was to report to Wiley, not Lewandowski. As one campaign insider put it, "Stuart will not work with Rick Wiley. It just wasn't going to happen."[461]

Only those on the inside truly knew the dynamics between Manafort and Lewandowski; but from the outside, it certainly appeared Manafort intended to build a professional parallel organization to supersede and quickly devour Pac-Man style the existing Lewandowski operation. If so, and if Trump already had the nomination sown up, then the Manafort maneuver might be just the ticket. In the middle of a political death match, the Darwinian conflict would lead to dysfunction and paralysis at the worst possible time. The old saying holds true: it's tough to change racehorses in the middle of a race.

Trump, like Sanders, also still couldn't explain his policy proposals so anyone not at a bar pounding his fourth or fifth Bud Light might understand. Take immigration and the Mexican wall. Trump had long said there had to be a wall all along the U.S.-Mexico border. Regarded as excessive in previous years, the idea of such a wall had become mainstream. As Marco Rubio repeatedly observed, the American people aren't going to trust Washington with immigration reform until the wall is built.

All true, but Trump said he would force Mexico to pay the $8 billion to $10 billion cost. How would he force Mexico to pay? In the past, he simply reiterated, Mexico would be forced to pay for the wall. "Trust me."

Finally, Trump elaborated. Mexicans in the United States remit billions back home to Mexico every year. Trump's solution to force Mexico to comply with his wall-building demands was to block all remittances.[462] Mexico's economy relied to a significant extent on this external income flow. Block the flow, and Mexico would have to comply. Or so Trump insisted.

That Trump would lack any legal authority to block the remittances didn't trouble him. That the Mexican senders would easily evade whatever measures he took to block remittances didn't trouble Trump. That Mexico, a neighbor and sometimes ally, might respond in alternative ways than Trump anticipated, like arresting Americans in Mexico or blocking all repatriations of profits earned by Americans in Mexico or any of a dozen other unpleasantries, didn't trouble Trump.

Cruz and "New York" Values

In the campaign's early days of Iowa and South Carolina, Ted Cruz had derided "New York" values. Chickens, meet roost. New York, the next really big enchilada on the primary calendar, showed Donald Trump polling way out in front at around 56%. John Kasich polled at around 22% with Cruz at around 15%.

Trump, of course, was from New York and so expected to do well; but New York State, while deep blue overall, is diverse culturally. Away from the Big Apple, much of the state is a chilly version of Arkansas. Cruz and Kasich combined stood a good chance of keeping Trump below the 50% threshold, so the game was on.

Naturally, New York City denizens cared little for Cruz's disparaging remarks about "New York values"; but Cruz also knew there was no way to sugarcoat his comments. He didn't need to. "Everyone in New York and outside of New York knew exactly what I meant by that. And it is the liberal values of Democratic politicians who have been hammering the people of New York for decades."[463]

John Edwards, the now-disgraced former Democratic Senator from North Carolina and former presidential candidate, once distilled the national debate down to the phrase "two Americas."[464] One America, according to Edwards, was prosperous and hopeful. The other America struggled mightily and seemed destined to continue to do so. He had a point, which is why the theme resonated and later merged into the budding debate over income inequality.

An alternative, equally valid two Americas perspective is to observe there is the America of liberal values and big government, an American where "it takes a village" in Hillary Clinton's famous words or the "nanny state" according to former Vice Pres. Dick Cheney. This

America is typically found in the big cities, especially in the northeast and among the "beautiful people" inhabiting coastal California from the Oregon border to the City of Angels.

Then there is the America of individualism and in-your-face patriotism, where individual liberty and self-reliance are paramount, where pickup trucks outnumber hybrid sports cars, and where distrust of government is pervasive and palpable. It's not that any or all these characteristics are not found in both Americas, but the preponderances and emphases are very different between the two.

Ted Cruz had put a label on one America, the America of "New York City values." Cruz might stumble in New York by labeling liberal values as "New York values," but conservatives across the country knew what he meant. And they approved. New Yorkers also knew what Cruz meant and probably broadly agreed. They just didn't like the term used as disparagement.

WHAT IS PAUL RYAN UP TO?

In early April, as Republicans sped toward a contested convention, hope sprang up like spring daisies—hope, in the form of one Paul Ryan, Speaker, United States House of Representatives. Ryan insisted he wasn't running, even after giving a high-profile speech in March, even after he cut a video looking suspiciously like a campaign ad.

To be sure, the chances of Ryan parachuting into a contested convention maelstrom and coming out a viable candidate lay between slim and none much as the idea of Joe Biden parachuting into a similarly chaotic contested Democratic convention seemed preposterous. But . . . but . . . what scenario for the Republicans didn't seem preposterous at this point?

Donald Trump's candidacy was preposterous, yet he was leading. Ted Cruz could claim credit for momentarily denying Trump his victory, but Cruz would have even fewer delegates. Slowing Trump would gain Cruz little support from the party regulars he'd attacked so intensely for so long.

So what about John Kasich? Really? The guy who had only won his own state?

Ryan's candidacy seemed unlikely but not much more so than any other scenario. Ryan could unite the party, at least long enough to mount a campaign. The key for Ryan was simple—deny, deny, deny—and just do your job, staying in the public eye just enough. He did all this—and did it well.

On April 12, Ryan tried the Shermanesque approach, "Let me be clear. I do not want, nor will I accept, the nomination for our party."[465] Ryan's problem, of course, was this was about what he insisted when his colleagues first turned to him to succeed John Boehner as Speaker. Further, this was exactly what he needed to say if he meant it or if he didn't. In all likelihood, the first part was true. He didn't want the nomination, which would probably lead to a catastrophic political defeat, though one no worse than seemed likely under any alternative scenario for Republicans.

But what about the second part: would not accept? If the party convention lay in ruins, a perfectly reasonable expectation, and rallied more or less united in calling to Ryan, would he really not answer the call? One didn't have to observe Paul Ryan of Wisconsin for long to conclude he would, reluctantly, do his duty once again.

BLACK LIVES MATTER, MEET BILL. BILL, MEET BLACK POLITICS

Bill Clinton enjoyed boundless political talent. He had rare charisma. He had an appetite and a temper. The former got him into trouble throughout his career; the latter got him into trouble in Philadelphia.

On April 7 at a Hillary Clinton rally, Black Lives Matter protestors traded barbs with Bill for fifteen minutes, yelling repeatedly, "Black youth are not super predators," recalling a term Hillary had used with respect to the 1994 crime bill signed into law by Pres. Bill Clinton.[466]

In 1994, America had a major problem with rising violent crime, so Congress responded with a crime bill. Who supported the bill? In addition to Bill and Hillary Clinton, there was Bernie Sanders, for example.[467]

In a 1996 speech defending her support for the crime bill, Hillary Clinton had said, "They are often the kinds of kids that are called 'super predators.' No conscience, no empathy; we can talk about why they ended up that way, but first we have to bring them to heel."[468] Black Lives Matter protestors didn't like the "super predator" label, perhaps because it shined a spotlight on the escalating violence in neighborhoods across the country from Baltimore to Chicago to San Francisco.

Even as the mini-dustup over Bill's comments continued, John Rufus Evans III was stabbed inside the Washington Metro Orange Line station at Deanwood.[469] Evans had moved to Richmond with his mother to escape DC's violence but returned to deal with some personal obligations. Back in DC, Evans ran into an old enemy, Jovante Hall. Hall attacked, stabbing Evans in the neck. Hall was arrested a couple days later. Evans died, a young man with a future no more. No one from Black Lives Matter showed up for the funeral.

Nor did they show up in New Orleans to mark the murder of former Saints football star Will Smith. About the same time Evans was being murdered in DC, Smith, thirty-four years old, former NFL first-round draft pick, was shot eight times in the back, his wife twice in the legs, in a road rage incident. As respected national sports commentator Kevin Blackistone observed, what distinguished Smith from the year's thirty previous New Orleans murders was Smith's fame. Other than his fame, "Smith was like almost all the other homicide victims in New Orleans—young, male, and black."[470]

As is typical of such articles, Blackistone made no mention of the fact that in Smith's case, as in almost all the other thirty murders in New Orleans, mostly of young black males, the murderer was also a young black male. Instead, Blackistone went down the more common more politically correct road of blaming the ubiquity of guns.

To be sure, Smith was shot repeatedly. Evans was stabbed in the neck. What did they have in common? They were young black males. What else did they have in common? So were the murderers.

This makes the death of Evans and Smith no less tragic, no less depressing, no less outrageous, no less frustrating. It does suggest that the search for scapegoats is never going to lead to change, never going to manifest the deep reality that, indeed, black lives do matter!

In Philadelphia, Bill tried to defend Hill, "I don't know how you would characterize the gang leaders who got 13-year-old kids hopped up on crack, and sent them out in the streets to murder other African American children. Maybe you thought they were good citizens—she didn't."

The protestors kept at it, trying to get under Bill's skin. He played the good host—at first. "Here's the thing. I like protesters, but the ones that won't let you answer are afraid of the truth. That's a simple rule."

But Bill has his limits. Eventually, it was temper one, limits zero. He exploded, "You are defending the people who killed the lives you say matter."

Bill Clinton had a valid point but not a politically correct one. In a society where victimhood is a political tool, one is not allowed to question the victimhood creed. And so, for his outburst of sanity, Bill was again in hot water. As the *Washington Post*'s Dan Balz observed, "[Bill] Clinton is caught in a time warp, having to grapple with how much the era in which he served, the events that occurred then and the actions he took as president have been reinterpreted and, by many in his own party, rejected."[471]

How sensitive were racial sensitivities? Even hyper-liberals could run afoul of the racial sensitivity political correctness police. At an Inner Circle dinner in New York City, Mayor Bill de Blasio signed off on and performed in a satirical skit poking fun at . . . himself. During the skit, to explain why he'd endorsed Clinton so late in the campaign, de Blasio said he was "running on CP time."[472] The expression "CP time" may not be familiar; but it rankles some with cause because in an earlier era it stood for "colored-people time," alluding to the old Southern belief blacks, usually lacking watches, were commonly late to meet for appointments, to show up to work, to show up at church, etc.

The expression today sounds anachronistic and alien, but de Blasio knew what it meant, and so did Clinton, who in the skit responded "cautious-politician time." Most in the audience got the joke and chuckled. Some didn't chuckle.

If the participants had been Ted Cruz and some Republican mayor, then this little episode would likely have set off riots and received daily front-page coverage in all the major media outlets. No one said politics is fair. But the press did cover the reaction to the skit if only in its own astonishment that anyone could infer racist overtones in a rarely used racial expression by a hyper-liberal New York City mayor while endorsing a hyper-liberal presidential candidate from New York.

Of course, Clinton quickly threw de Blasio under the bus, emphasizing it was his skit, as though she hadn't read the text beforehand (she had, of course), as though she didn't know what "CP time" meant (she did, of course), as though she bore no responsibility. De Blasio went under the bus, but really, that's what campaign buses are for, isn't it?

Sanders's First Endorsement

Much had been made of Ted Cruz's lack of endorsements by national Republican figures. This played well into the narrative his colleagues didn't like Cruz. Likewise, Donald Trump had few Republican endorsements, but this didn't appear noteworthy since, after all, Trump wasn't really a Republican, and all but a handful of political neophytes understood that.

Even while chortling over Cruz, the press remained studiously mum regarding Bernie Sanders's lack of endorsements. Not even his home state colleague, forty-one-year Senate veteran Patrick Leahy, had endorsed Sanders. Why the fuss over Cruz's lack of endorsements and the silence about Sanders's lack of endorsements? Was it because of media bias, as most Republicans would conclude? Or because, as some in the media were beginning to realize, Sanders's campaign had heretofore not been considered credible, and so Sanders himself had mostly gotten a media pass?

Whatever the reason, the ice finally broke on April 12 as Oregon Sen. Jeff Merkley became the first Senate Democrat to endorse Sanders. In a *New York Times* op-ed, Merkley explained his thinking.[473] Clinton, according to Merkley, would be a "strong and capable president." But the country needed someone more radically aggressive, someone "boldly and fiercely addressing the biggest challenges facing our country." In short, Hillary was OK, but Bernie was rad. Merkley went with rad.

Merkley had, in fact, captured the essence of the Democratic choice from an ideological vantage: Clinton, the practical, practiced, pragmatic establishmentarian versus Sanders, the hair-on-fire radical who didn't much care if his proposals made sense as long as his complaints were delivered with sincerity and passion.

Brooklyn's Electric Kool-Aid Acid Test

While the Republican debate stage remained cluttered, each episode outdid the prior in pure vitriol. Republicans, Democrats, the media, the nation all agreed the Republicans looked terrible. On April 14 in Brooklyn, Hillary Clinton and Bernie Sanders proved they were no slouches at throwing mud. The cuddly old codger proved the sarcastic, snarky old man while the tough old broad proved she could still wield a rhetorical rolling pin with the best of them.

The two didn't so much interrupt one another as simply yell over each other from start to finish. Finally, an exasperated Wolf Blitzer, one of CNN's moderators, interjected in a momentary pause in the bedlam, "If you're both screaming at each other, the viewers won't be able to hear either of you."[474]

Led by fellow CNN moderator Dana Bash, Clinton and Sanders discussed their shared policy of breaking up banks deemed "too big to fail." Clinton trotted out her nifty standard riff that "no bank is too big to fail, no executive too big to jail." She then sought to reaffirm her bona fides, arguing, "I stood up against the behavior of the banks when I was senator. I called them out on their mortgage behavior."

In rapid response, Sanders tittered, "Secretary Clinton called them out. Oh my goodness, they must have been really crushed by this. And was that before or after you received huge sums of money by giving speaking engagements? So they must have been very, very upset by what you did."

Clinton continued her defense but, in the judges' opinion, point Sanders. And that was the point of the exercise—to score points. No one was convinced, except that maybe both candidates were simply too unpleasant to be president—just like the Republicans. If you were a progressive and anger your fuel, then Bernie was still your man; and unfortunately for Hillary, those attributes described many Democratic primary voters.

By the Numbers

April 15 found millions of Americans crunching the numbers in their tax returns and so provided as good an excuse as any to review the numbers on the economy and the political scene.

The unemployment rate remained a fairly low 5%, though millions of Americans who wanted to work full-time were working part-time, and real wage growth remained anemic. More broadly, the economy had slowed markedly and forecasts for 2016 and 2017 were on a steady downward trajectory. For example, when Blue Chip first released a forecast for 2016 in January of 2015, the "consensus" was for healthy 2.9% growth. By April, the consensus forecast had fallen to 2.0%, suggesting the downward trend would continue, which it did.

Still, no recession loomed, and the U.S. economy for all its weaknesses still looked one of the better old nags at the international glue factory. Japan flirted with recession and deflation. Much of South America wrestled with rapid contraction and high inflation. Europe stumbled with a panoply of vexing problems. China kept its economy moving with the economic equivalent of a double latte and a Red Bull.

The federal budget deficit in Pres. Obama's last year looked to be about a half trillion dollars despite record tax receipts, with deficits projected to rise back well above a trillion dollars annually even without a recession.

On the campaign front, candidates from both parties managed one remarkable accomplishment: by looking so bad, they had made Obama look good in comparison. Ever since mid-2013, Obama had suffered a net favorability deficit—his unfavorables exceeded his favorables—with a peak deficit of 16.1% in December of 2013. Two years later, Obama's favorability deficit remained 7.9%. As of March 13, 2016, Obama had turned the corner with a positive rating of 0.4, and he rose from there.

Hillary Clinton had amassed 1,289 pledged delegates to Bernie Sanders's 1,038, but she held a 469 to 31 lead in superdelegates. She had also received 9.4 million popular votes to Sanders's 6.9 million for a roughly 2.4 million vote advantage. On the other hand, Sanders had won seven of the last eight contests and had essentially tied Clinton in the national polls, but of more immediate consequence, in the New York State polls. Given Sanders's advantage in voter intensity, Clinton looked to be at serious risk of losing her home state, likely inflicting a near-mortal wound.

Donald Trump had won 755 delegates; Ted Cruz, 545; and John Kasich, 143. Cruz had won three of the last four contests and had repeatedly outplayed Trump in the delegate-picking game. On the other hand, Trump seemed likely to win New York big, regaining badly momentum. Further, the voting a week later in Connecticut, Delaware, Rhode Island, Pennsylvania, and Maryland—the Acela primary—all looked ripe for Trump victories. And yet, even with strong performances, his chances of taking the nomination on the convention's first ballot seemed so-so.

In the abstract, Republicans continued to debate the best way to minimize their losses and leave the party in the best place to recover in 2018 and 2020. Perhaps just let Trump win the nomination and lose the general election massively. How bad did it look? A March 2016 poll showed Trump losing to Clinton in Utah—yes, Utah—and losing to Sanders by even more.[475] And Trump's favorability deficit remained around minus thirty-five for months.

Option two: Perhaps turn to Cruz, someone regarded by many as far too ideological to represent the party. Lose in the general but do so respectably. After all, his favorability deficit was a comparably rosy minus 21. Or turn to Kasich, whose main claim to fame was he didn't quit the race, but he would represent the party faithfully and lose in the general after a fair try. Kasich was then breaking even on favorability but had only a month earlier been around plus 20.

But then, Republicans could look at the Democrats and imagine that anyone could beat either Clinton or Sanders. True, Barack Obama had largely proven to be the demi-Socialist his antagonists claimed, but he didn't admit it. Sanders shouted his Socialism from the rooftops. Surely, American wasn't ready to embrace a cranky old socialist, was it? Or Clinton, a candidate who though competent was trusted by few and who boasted a mountain of smelly baggage.

RNC to Trump: Quit Your Kvetching

Over the course of the campaign, Donald Trump had added new elements to his ritual riffs. First it was the wall with Mexico, how American had negotiated stupid trade deals, and how he would "carpet bomb" ISIS. Then he added the positive spice: everything he did would be great and "hyuge." Then there was the "little Marco" and "lyin' Ted" mantras.

Especially after Colorado, Trump added the riff the game was "rigged." It was, of course, to an extent. No group sits back without reacting to a hostile takeover attempt. But mostly, it wasn't that the election was rigged so much as Trump didn't play it well. The big-persona game he played brilliantly. It was the Republican contestant game he played poorly.

Trump tweeted that RNC chairman Reince Priebus "should be ashamed of himself because he knows what's going on." Priebus tweeted back, "Nomination process known for a year + beyond. It's the responsibility of the campaign to understand it. Complaints now? Give us all a break."[476]

Trump ran an op-ed in the *Wall Street Journal*, claiming, "The system is being rigged by party operatives with 'double-agent' delegates who reject the decisions of voters."[477] He hammered the RNC at every opportunity. Finally, the party had enough of Trump's kvetching. Remember, the guy had recently said he might go back on his commitment to support the nominee if it were somebody else. So Sean Spicer, RNC communications director, wrote, "Each process is easy to understand for those willing to learn it." And "it ultimately falls on the campaigns to be up to speed on these delegate rules."

TED GIVES DONALD MORE GROUNDS FOR WHINING

Somebody in the Cruz campaign knew his or her business. In state after state, most prominently in Colorado, team Cruz carefully exploited every opportunity under the rules. Donald Trump had learned late, probably too late, campaigns were about more than debates and speeches, insults, and slams. Campaigns were also about preparation and knowing the rules. Sometimes it was just a matter of showing up.

Wyoming voters had cast their ballots in county conventions on March 12; Wyoming's statewide delegates were chosen a month later. In the county conventions, Ted Cruz had taken nine of the twelve delegates available, Trump and Marco Rubio had each won one, and one remained uncommitted.

Cruz addressed the Wyoming delegation in April while Trump skipped it, complaining, "I don't want to waste millions of dollars going out to Wyoming many months before to wine and dine and to essentially pay off these people, because a lot of it's a payoff, you understand that?"[478] Tough to win when you don't show up. Result: Cruz swept, capturing all fourteen available delegates.

Cruz's preparations extended deeper yet. Anticipating a contested convention where no one took the nomination on the first ballot, Cruz's operation began preparing for the second ballot and the third. In conventions in Virginia, Georgia, and South Carolina, Cruz went to work ensuring Cruz-friendly delegates were chosen. These delegates would likely back Trump or whomever they were bound to on the first ballot at the national convention as per the rules, but then they would bolt to Cruz on the second ballot.

In South Carolina's first district, won narrowly by Trump in February's primary, Cruz supporters won all three delegate slots. Likewise, Georgia's eleventh district, which had gone for Trump with 35% of the vote, meaning he would get two votes on the first ballot, Rubio getting the third of three. But Georgia chairman Scott Johnson and former Cong. Bob Barr—both Cruz supporters—won the delegate slots and would abandon Trump after the first ballot. No other conclusions could be drawn. Trump was probably screwed at a contested convention, and Cruz's operation was truly impressive.

JUST HOW IN THE TANK WAS THE WAPO?

The *Washington Post* made no secret it (a) disdained Trump, (b) intensely disliked Cruz, (c) could have lived with Bush or Rubio, (d) feared Sanders, and (e) only in comparison vastly favored Clinton. As of April, the paper hadn't yet officially endorsed Hillary Clinton as appearances had to be preserved for a season, but its coverage laid bare its biases. How in the tank was the WaPo for Hillary?

On Sunday, April 17, the *Post* ran an op-ed by Kareem Abdul-Jabbar endorsing Hillary Clinton—smack in the middle of the page, extra bordering for effect.[479] Abdul-Jabbar was one of the all-time greats in National Basketball Association history, a fairly ancient history by modern standards. He was also a thoughtful man. He was also a black man. He was also a Muslim. But why anyone should particularly care who a great former basketball player endorsed remained a superficial curiosity. The answer, of course, was the *Post* was seeking to bolster Clinton's support within the black community. Not so much to ensure her victory in the coming New York State contest but nationwide for the general election. No doubt the *Post* would be running additional Clinton endorsements as the need arose.

New York Votes

The Empire State delivered big for Hillary Clinton and Donald Trump, as expected. Trump took 60.4% of the vote; John Kasich, 25.1%; Ted Cruz, a paltry 14.5%. Apparently, whatever New York values, it wasn't Ted Cruz. With this vote, Trump picked up eighty-nine delegates; Kasich, four; Cruz, zip.

The New York outcome for Kasich meant little. He was irrelevant before. He was irrelevant after. He only remained in the race hoping for a special miracle in a contested convention. Cruz, on the other hand, saw a good portion of his campaign's justification evaporate. In the general election, New York would go for any Democrat over any Republican, but still, 14.5% was embarrassing.

Clinton did almost as well as Trump, winning 57.9% to Sanders's 42.1%. However, her delegate haul wasn't nearly as robust as Trump's. She took 139 delegates to Sanders's 106, padding her lead but not by much.

Sanders should have done better in New York, perhaps not winning but coming closer. The problem was less Sanders or his campaign. The problem was New York knows how to control (Sanders and Trump would say "rig") the process, a lesson other states and even the national parties might want to consider in light of the 2016 campaign.

A debate in all such primaries is whether to allow "outsiders" to vote. Should Democrats or independents be allowed to vote in a Republican primary? Should Republicans or independents be allowed to vote in a Democratic caucus? These are reasonable questions.

If you want your nominee to have broad appeal, perhaps you should let more people vote for him or her. On the other hand, political parties have adherents and supporters, associated because to one extent or another, they embrace certain principles and represent particular points of view. Shouldn't the party's nominee represent those points as espoused by party members? Many states went for the inclusion route. New York's party leadership insisted this is our club and we decide who's running it.

For example, a prospective New York voter had to register by March 23. If registered to vote but with a different party, then you had to switch parties by the previous October. These rules effectively blocked meddlesome crossover voting and blocked those who generally didn't vote or decide to vote late. They kept much of Trump's family from voting because, oops, they'd voted Democrat in the previous election. While there were likely few New York Republicans wanting to vote for Sanders, his support among young voters and the commonly disaffected was exceptionally high, and very few of these would have registered in time.

Clinton did well enough in New York to reclaim some momentum but certainly not well enough to drive Sanders out, though much of the media tried to suggest as much. Would Sanders just please pack up and go away? Not if his fundraising provided any clue. Two days after the New York primary reports circulated Sanders through his vast army of small donors had raised more money than Clinton for the third month in a row: $42 million from more than nine hundred thousand donors.[480] Sanders also knew states voting a week later, like Maryland, Rhode Island, and Connecticut, generally didn't have these institutional firewalls against possible Sanders voters. Finally, Sanders always knew, as did every Democrat, that on any given day the FBI could bring its case against Clinton to the Justice Department recommending an indictment.

Even as New Yorkers cast their votes promising Clinton and Trump big wins, the candidates first suffered a bit of bad news. One poll came out showing that whatever New Yorkers thought of them, the rest of the country liked none of the candidates all that well, but Clinton and Trump least of all.[481] Almost a third of the country liked Clinton. The problem? Fifty-six percent had an unfavorable opinion, for a net favorability deficit of 24%. And perhaps as big a problem: Sanders had a net favorability rating of 9%.

The good news for Clinton? The country liked Donald Trump even less. Trump had a net favorability deficit of 41%. Ted Cruz didn't do much better at minus 23%. In Cruz's favor, however, he was relatively unknown nationally, so he had a chance to move his numbers up—or down.

Next Up

Collectively, the next contests were even more momentous than New York. Dubbed the "Acela primary" as the Amtrak Acela train ran through Maryland, Delaware, Connecticut, and Rhode Island missing only Pennsylvania, these states seemed to bode well for Donald Trump and Bernie Sanders. Trump's northeast roots demonstrated in his resounding New York win should play well in all five states while Sanders's left-wing ideology should do likewise, especially as Clinton wouldn't be protected by New York–style restrictive voter registration requirements.

With so many contests in a short period, organizational strength would be key. Voters would be blasted with every political tool available. To assess how the campaigns performed, the table below shows the most recent polls up to the New York primary. (Rhode Island and Delaware were rarely polled publicly.)

Typical Post–New York Poll Results

	Trump	Cruz	Kasich	Clinton	Sanders
Maryland[482]	41	25	26	58	33
Pennsylvania[483]	40	26	24	53	37
Delaware[484]	55	15	18	45	38
Connecticut[485]	48	19	28	51	42
Rhode Island[486]	61	13	23	45	49

The big story after New York revolved around internal Republican Party machinations at the party's spring meeting in Hollywood, Florida. The existing rules, largely based on the rules controlling the House Republican Conference, precluded anyone but Trump and Ted Cruz from gaining the nomination. Some attendees wanted to switch to Robert's Rules of Order to facilitate a "white knight" candidate such as Paul Ryan. In the end, the party chairman insisted the rules would stand as any change would be interpreted as an attempt to thwart Trump's rise. If Trump failed to claim the nomination, the failure had to be Trump's and his alone. At least, that was the hope RNC chairman Priebus held to closely.

As the campaign progressed, the profusion of polls increased. National polls, statewide polls, statewide head-to-head polls, favorability polls—you name it. Any university political science department with a scintilla of initiative tried to squeeze the funding to do a poll for its fifteen minutes of fame. Through it all, one poll included some particularly interesting information. It showed 56% of Trump's and Clinton's "supporters" said their support was more a statement of opposition to the other candidate than support for their own.[487] Fewer than 40% of Trump supporters actually supported Trump, and fewer than 40% of Clinton's supporters actually supported Clinton.

After New York, it became clear Trump would arrive at the Republican Convention with the most delegates but perhaps not with a majority. Some argued he should receive the nomination, anyway. Others argued the process should be followed. If he failed to get the nomination on the first ballot, then what happens next happens. As Cruz had been doing a masterful job of ensuring his delegate count would rise substantially after the first ballot at Trump's expense, what would happen next is Trump would storm out angry, creating at best a destructive spectacle.

Over the April 23–24 weekend, a number of states picked delegates from earlier voting. Again, Cruz completely outmaneuvered Trump. Cruz took nineteen of the twenty Maine delegates available.[488] He picked up nine delegates in three Minnesota congressional districts originally won by Marco Rubio. Cruz picked up thirty-six of the thirty-seven available Utah delegates, missing only Utah Attorney General Sean Reyes who refused to reveal whom he supported.

To increase his chances of gaining the nomination on the first ballot, Trump needed to capture as many of the few "unbound" delegates as possible. Unbound Republican delegates were similar to the Democrats' superdelegates in that they could vote for whomever they wanted on the first ballot. But unlike superdelegates, who were almost exclusively bigwigs in the Democratic Party, unbound Republican delegates were simply those chosen in the course of the campaign from states like Kentucky, Pennsylvania, and Delaware where the delegates were not required to state a preference before the primary.

For example, on March 5 Trump narrowly beat Cruz in the Kentucky primary, but on April 23 at the Kentucky Republican Party conclave, party leaders presented and the convention adopted a slate of twenty-five delegates picked for their work in the state party.[489] While they would almost surely vote according to the rules on the first ballot in Cleveland, these delegates were not chosen according to their stated preferences, so no one could say how they would vote in a second ballot.

Delaware wasn't quite as big a prize as Pennsylvania, with only sixteen delegates; and Trump was expected to do well in the popular voting, perhaps taking them all. But Trump also wanted to ensure his supporters were the chosen delegates, so Trump sent a former Ben Carson aide, Joe Uddo, to twist some arms.[490] Bad idea because Uddo apparently took the expression "twisting arms" almost literally. "One of our delegates is just a little old lady," complained one source who remained anonymous.

Uddo's hardball tactics didn't sit well with the Delaware Republican Party. They didn't appreciate suggestions of being sued because, guess what, Trump thought the Delaware rules in place since 1996 were "unfair." Trump could be pretty sure most of his first ballot delegates from Delaware would follow the results of the election, but many would switch on the second ballot if there was one. Call it the "Uddo effect."

This matter of unbound delegates made Pennsylvania's vote an especially bright red-letter day on this season's primary calendar. Pennsylvania would choose seventy-one delegates, seventeen allocated to the statewide winner and three delegates each per congressional district. Making Pennsylvania unique, the fifty-four congressional district delegates ran as individuals, not necessarily as representing or favoring a particular candidate. Most important of all, these delegates were unbound according to state party rules.

A Flaky Alliance

When John Kasich held the gavel of the House Budget Committee in the 1990s, he was known as an energetic, inquisitive team player. Nice guy, sincere, he was also considered something of a flake. Apparently, that last attribute remained true as of 2016.

Kasich was running campaign TV ads in Washington DC presumably to convince the establishment his campaign had a heartbeat. In one ad, he repeated his claim to having led the fight that led to budget surpluses in the late 1990s. To be sure, as House Budget Committee chairman, Kasich was involved; but he took his marching orders from Speaker Newt Gingrich; and in any event, the surpluses surprised everybody, and resulted far less from Republican-related spending restraint than from an unexpected and temporary burst of tax revenue driven by the dot-com bubble. The 2016 TV ad also had Kasich saying he had sat on the House Armed Service Committee for sixteen years, as though sitting was a major accomplishment, even for a congressman.

For Cruz and Kasich, the facts were simple: stop Trump or go home. After the Acela primary came most notably Indiana, a winner-take-all state, and its fifty-seven delegates, followed by hotly contested New Mexico and Oregon with a combined fifty-two delegates. On Sunday, April 24, Cruz and Kasich struck something of a deal: Kasich would leave Indiana to Cruz, and Cruz would agree not to campaign in New Mexico and Oregon. Denying Trump a win in Indiana was essential, while denying him either New Mexico or Oregon would practically guarantee a contested convention. As Kasich's chief strategist John Weaver confirmed, Kasich's campaign would "focus our time and resources on New Mexico and Oregon, both areas that are structurally similar to the northeast where Gov. Kasich has done well."[491]

The plan seemed reasonable in the abstract. Even though Indiana neighbored on Ohio where Kasich should have done well, Cruz was polling at about 33% to Kasich's 19% (Trump polled at about 40%), so Cruz had the best chance of beating Trump in Indiana. No publicly released polls for either New Mexico or Oregon were available at the time, but Weaver's argument seemed a plausible justification.

In practice, the pact survived a few hours before John Kasich showed he hadn't changed. When asked about the pact in a Philadelphia diner, Kasich said, "I've never told them [his Indiana supporters] not to vote for me. They ought to vote for me."[492] A bevy of psychologists might with enough time settle on the proper diagnosis describing John Kasich's particular quirks, but for present purposes, "he's still a flake" works fine.

Northeasterners Take the Acela Primary

As expected, Donald Trump and Hillary Clinton did very well in the April 26 Acela primary. Trump won all five states outright, his lowest percentage occurring in Maryland at 54% and his best showing in Rhode Island with nearly 64%. The day after, Trump could claim 105 more delegates. John Kasich and Ted Cruz? Five and one delegates each, respectively. Nice job, boys.

The outstanding question mark remained Pennsylvania's fifty-four uncommitted delegates. As results were finalized, Trump was declared the winner in all eighteen congressional districts, meaning he collected at least forty-two delegates; so even if Cruz picked up all the uncommitted delegates, his tally for the state would be a paltry twelve. Pennsylvania had been very kind to Trump.

In total, and not counting Pennsylvania's congressional district delegates, Trump had at least 992 delegates, or nearly 53% of those awarded. He needed another 245 out of the remaining 556 to claim the nomination outright. If he stayed on pace, then he'd just barely make it. That was the good news, plus the fact New Jersey with 51 delegates held its primary June 7 and was surely Trump country.

The bad news: the next two states, Indiana and Nebraska, with ninety-three delegates between them, should be Cruz country and were winner-take-all. Worse, four of the last five states were also winner-take-all, and these included South Dakota and Montana with another fifty-six delegates. So even if Trump won New Jersey, if he lost all four of the upcoming Midwest and western primaries, the climb would quickly get a lot steeper. Trump's victory at this stage was in no way assured.

On paper, Hillary Clinton did nearly as well as Trump, taking all but tiny Rhode Island in the Acela primary, and picking up a net of sixty-five delegates over Sanders (194 to 129). In fact, while Trump picked up more states, Clinton had the better night.

As Wednesday morning dawned, the Sanders campaign had to look hard in the mirror to wonder why they continued. Sure, the campaign had plenty of money but no obvious purpose, harkening back to the position in which Jeb Bush found himself just before his exit. Absent some major new development, Clinton looked set to become the Democratic nominee. Sanders could do little more than drive up her unfavorable ratings with ongoing attacks, hardly a productive vocation. In fact, Sanders did still have one good reason to stay in: the possibility of Clinton's FBI indictment.

Some might think it cynical to suggest Sanders's campaign had morphed from head-to-head contest to indictment gambit, but this isn't tiddlywinks. And if the FBI believed an indictment warranted, whether or not the Obama Justice Department carried through or went all political and shielded Clinton, the Democratic Party would be desperate for a new champion. Thus, Sanders's campaign's new justification: meet Bernie Sanders, prospective savior.

CHAPTER 16
THE FINAL ROUNDS OF TWO EPIC FIGHTS

After following similar tracks since before the Iowa caucuses, the campaigns within the two parties left the Acela primary heading in different directions. Hillary Clinton appeared to have sown up the Democratic nomination, barring any untoward FBI indictment bombshells as Bernie Sanders pondered his exit strategy.

In contrast, Republicans faced a series of pitched battles in which Donald Trump faced the possibility of a string of painful losses culminating in a convention battle of two well-armed and highly motivated guerrilla armies. Trump had the momentum. Ted Cruz needed a bold stroke to set the battle. The moment had some eerie historical parallels, as recorded by Lee Edwards:

> The magic number needed to capture the Republican presidential nomination in 1976 was 1,130 delegates, and Ronald Reagan was oh so close as the national convention prepared to convene.
>
> After losing six straight primaries to President Gerald Ford early in the year, Reagan had come roaring back, attacking Ford for his weak foreign policy and deficit spending and winning the crucial North Carolina

primary with help from Sen. Jesse Helms. Reagan achieved a political resurrection and posed the most serious challenge to an incumbent Republican president since 1912 when Theodore Roosevelt had taken on William Howard Taft.

After Reagan won the Texas, Indiana, Georgia and Alabama primaries, a nonplussed GOP establishment that favored Ford struggled to understand the former California governor's appeal. Conservative author Richard Whalen made it easy for them: Reagan was doing well because he was "unsullied by Watergate, untainted by Vietnam, and uncorrupted by a Washington system that isn't working."

However, after failing to carry Ohio although easily winning his home state of California, Reagan realized that the political momentum was shifting back to Ford. Something dramatic had to be done. Breaking a long-held precedent, he announced his running mate before the convention: Sen. Richard Schweiker of Pennsylvania, a moderate conservative with a high rating from the AFL-CIO. Schweiker assured Reagan and his aides that he could pry loose delegates from Pennsylvania and other Northern states.

It was a bold gambit, but it failed.[493]

It Ain't Over Till the Skinny Lady Sings

History suggests that Reagan's 1976 VP tactic may have been sound, but the execution was flawed. Choosing the ideologically suspect Richard Schweiker muddied Reagan's message and proved to be without compensations as not only did Schweiker fail to turn any of

Pennsylvania's delegates, but in reaction to picking Schweiker, the entire Mississippi delegation also shifted decisively in Ford's favor.

Ted Cruz faced a similar situation, but he avoided Reagan's error. In picking Carly Fiorina, Cruz picked as his running mate someone who could complement him without shading his ideological message. Earlier in the campaign, Fiorina had proven an adept debater, an energetic campaigner, and a dynamic speaker. Perhaps most important of all—no, not her gender—Fiorina was very likable.

The media narrative on Cruz's move immediately jumped to a "hail Mary" theme. After all, Cruz had just gotten clobbered in five states. Desperate times demanded desperate measures. This narrative had the strengths of simplicity, familiarity, and drama. The only problem was that as usual, the media got it wrong.

Cruz wasn't desperate. He had just fought five battles on grounds favorable to his opponent and was now moving to contests where the ground appeared favorable to his campaign. Cruz had every reason to be optimistic. He had a good Veep candidate, he had grabbed the attention from Trump, and he had recaptured the initiative heading into these favorable contests.

The good times didn't last. Cruz stumbled badly into the Hoosier State. For starters, Trump consistently held a 40 to 33% lead in the polls, with Kasich once again bringing up the caboose at 20%. Unless Kasich's voters found it within themselves to support the disliked Cruz to stop the hated Trump, Cruz's campaign could effectively end in Indiana.

Cruz then suffered some self-inflicted wounds, one previously inflicted that just then manifested. Former House Speaker John Boehner unloaded on Cruz, calling him, among other things, "Lucifer in the flesh" during a talk at Stanford University. "I have Democrat friends and Republican friends. I get along with almost everyone, but I have never worked with a more miserable son of a bitch in my life."[494]

Cruz had risen in stature among the hard-core Right in part by losing fights in the fiscal battles with Pres. Obama. Rather than admit his own mistakes, each time Cruz scapegoated "sellouts," specifically naming John Boehner. In no small measure, Cruz had made his political bones at Boehner's expense. Boehner had his moment to deliver a little sweet revenge.

Boehner's remarks, exceedingly biting though they were, would have passed with fleeting notice, but for one thing—when an event or a statement fits into a preexisting narrative, it strikes deeper and lasts longer. Cruz had few friends. Trump had repeatedly called Cruz "a nasty guy," among other things. Boehner's blow fit right into the prevailing narrative.

Then Cruz messed up big-time. While campaigning at the very same iconic Indiana basketball court in which one of his favorite movies, *Hoosiers*, was filmed, Cruz observed, "The amazing thing is, that basketball ring in Indiana, it's the same height as it is in New York City and every other place in this country."[495] You could almost imagine his nearest staffers cringingly whispering, "Senator, it's not a ring. It's called a 'hoop.'" In any other state, this would be an "oops." In Indiana, it was the desecration of a sacred talisman.

What better time for Bobby Knight representing the unofficial religion of Indiana (basketball) to come out and forcefully endorse Trump. Knight won 902 NCAA Division I basketball games, mostly at Indiana University, from 1971 to 2000. Aside from his victories, Knight was perhaps most famous for choking a player and throwing a folding chair across the basketball court during a game to demonstrate his extreme displeasure with the quality of the game's officiating. Hoosiers are classic midwesterners—polite, respectful, civil, yet they love Bobby Knight, who was none of these things.

Knight was fulsome in his Trumperian praise: "There's never been a more honest politician than Donald Trump," Knight said. "After you've seen and listened to him, I think you'll be in a hurry to get out there and vote for him. I want you to know you have this great opportunity to push him over the top as soon as you can and putting him in the best position that this country has been in getting going where we all want to be."[496] After all this, especially Knight's endorsement, Cruz looked to have about as much chance beating

Trump in Indiana as Ivy Tech Community College had in playing Indiana University.

TRUMP GOES ALL FOREIGN

Donald Trump started the pivot to the general election with a major foreign policy speech laying out his vision—the Trump Doctrine.[497] Imagine an aging swashbuckling pirate donning a coat, top hat, and tails. Trump didn't look comfortable, and it wasn't just the teleprompter he criticized Obama so often for employing. Trump described his doctrine unabashedly: "America First will be the major and overriding theme of my administration."[498]

The intelligentsia universally decried Trump's speech. First, it was Trump, so it had to be bad. Second, they knew it would appeal to Americans after years of being treated for decades like patsies by every foreign tinpot with a grudge and particularly so under Pres. Obama. Third, it was scary language because it harkened back to the America First Committee movement prior to World War II, those folks who had sought to keep the United States out of the war at all costs, the folks who were fairly well shut up on December 7, 1941.

Was Trump unaware of the linguistic parallels? As Bret Stephens described it in the *Wall Street Journal*, "Either Mr. Trump stumbled upon his worldview through a dense fog of historical ignorance. Or he is seriously attempting to resurrect the most disastrous and discredited strain of American foreign policy for a new generation of American ignoramuses."[499] The third possibility, and almost surely the correct answer, was Trump didn't know about and didn't give a hoot about historical parallels and knew that neither did many American voters.

Trump's message was ultimately quite simple. Under his administration, the United States would be a patsy no more. America's allies would have to appreciate America's help and would have to make substantial contributions themselves to their own security. America would rebuild its military and restrain its foreign engagements except to the purpose of destroying ISIS. America would seek common ground with Russia and China, but would no longer kowtow to them overtly or through silence, or to Iran, or to North Korea.

In rawest form, Trump's foreign policy vision bore a striking resemblance to something Clinton or Cruz or Obama might say. The difference is Trump, as usual, didn't bother with the "but fors" and "yes buts," the subtleties, and nuanced language. He gave it to America straight and in direct language so everyone understood his meaning.

Germany's Foreign Minister, Frank-Walter Steinmeier, opined none too pleased: "I can only hope that the election campaign in the USA does not lack the perception of reality," adding this was why 'America first' is actually no answer to that [the changes in the global security infrastructure]."[500] America First did not mean isolationism or unilateralism. It meant simply that America had to look out for itself first, just as the Germans were doing in the eurozone crisis they'd helped create. Every other country in the world looks out for its own interests first, as their citizens would rightly demand, yet for Trump to speak the words apparently threatened to topple the whole world political order. If so, then maybe Trump had a point.

The Award for the Second-Limpest Endorsement Goes to . . . Mike Pence, Governor of Indiana

As attention shifted to the coming Indiana primary, Indiana Gov. Mike Pence responded to demands that he name his preference as between the three Republican candidates. Once considered a leading contender for the nomination, Pence's prospects were clipped by a nasty in-state dustup.

Pence went to a local radio station to give an interview in which he rambled on and on as to how he'd met with all three candidates and liked all three candidates and could vote for all three candidates. Nice, nice, nice . . . get to the point, Governor. Finally, he did get to the point, not exactly endorsing Ted Cruz, but acknowledging he would be voting for Ted Cruz. Rarely has anyone given a less rousing endorsement.

Even less enthusiastic than Pence's limp endorsement was silence from Indiana's senior and soon-to-be-retired Senator, Dan Coats. Coats had enjoyed a long and distinguished career as a congressman, then a senator, then as U.S. Ambassador to Germany, and then back in the United States Senate. When it was time to move on, Coats sensibly obliged. Coats had earlier endorsed Rubio for president, but Rubio was out of the race. Who would Coats endorse now that it mattered? Crickets.

Even after Pence (sort of) endorsed Cruz, Coats just couldn't bring himself to follow suit. Coats had nothing to lose. He was retiring. A smart, kind, classy, midwesterner type, the kind of senator respected by all his peers, Coats surely abhorred Trump's behavior; but even so, he just couldn't bring himself to endorse Cruz despite all that was at stake. Coats had served with Cruz, had watched him up close. And just couldn't do it.

Further Delegate Machinations

At the end of April, Virginia Republicans met in Harrisonburg, home of James Madison University, to pick the thirteen statewide delegates going to the national convention. Donald Trump had won the state, sort of, on March 1, taking 35% of the vote. Trump received the most votes, but one in three is hardly a landslide. In late April, Virginia reminded once again the difference between winning a state and picking the delegates. Once again, the Cruz machine completely outplayed the Trumpists, electing ten Cruz supporters to Trump's three.

How hardball did the Cruz people play? Remember Jim Gilmore, former Virginia Governor, former head of the Republican National Committee, former (and technically still) presidential contender with a total of 145 national delegates? The Cruz people blocked Gilmore from gaining a delegate seat. Gilmore observed that Cruz "is trying to take a state where the people went and voted in an open primary for

Donald Trump and convert that into a Ted Cruz state. It was a very ruthless display. They were decapitating any potential for alternative leadership on the delegation."[501]

Ted Cruz did even better in Arizona. Trump won the winner-take-all state by twenty points over Cruz, but even as Virginians were sorting through delegates, the Arizona Republican leadership tweaked the online voting system to disadvantage Trump delegates, even outfoxing Gov. Jan Brewer, a Trump supporter, who exclaimed, "The people of Arizona got cheated, I got cheated, and the Trump delegates got cheated."[502]

Arizona GOP Chairman Robert Graham called such charges "laughable." For now, Trump could only whine "unfair," and it probably was unfair; but Cruz was winning the game at the party level because, after all, Trump was a convenient Republican. Cruz was certainly laughing. Despite losing the state badly, he picked up about forty-six "Trojan Horse" delegates out of fifty-eight.

These maneuvers and those that came before brought into the discussion the role of a little-known group called the RNC's Committee on Credentials. The task of the 112-member Committee is to ensure that all the delegates arriving to vote at the convention are certified to do so. Certification involved such matters as whether the individual is a registered voter or a citizen of the state he or she is representing and also includes whether proper procedures were followed in the selecting of delegates. The Trump campaign hired a top-notch attorney, William McGinley, to look into these and related matters.[503]

"If there is an allegation that proper procedures were not carried out, then it is possible to undertake a procedure that is elaborate but outlined in the party rules a multi-step procedure whereby you can challenge the credentials of people who are claiming to be delegates," observed longtime Virginia Republican and RNC member, Morton Blackwell.[504] In 2012, Ron Paul lost his Maine delegates as the result of a credentials challenge after Paul's supporters pretended to be Romney supporters during the delegate selection process.

Naturally, given the Credential Committee's potential importance, the campaigns battled to ensure their representatives won Committee seats. Once again, the party leadership fairly effectively blocked Trump supporters. In New Hampshire, the state party blocked Trump representatives from gaining any seats on the coveted Rules or Credential Committees.[505] Sometimes, winning big battles is about winning the little ones.

Could Trump present Credentials Committee challenges as effectively as had Romney? Possibly, but with one big difference. In 2012, the party lined up behind Romney, so weeding out nuisance Ron Paul supporters was an easy call. In 2016, would the Credentials Committee party regulars who opposed Trump be as vigilant in weeding out Cruz delegates? Doubtful.

According to prevailing wisdom, these maneuvers mattered only if Trump failed to secure the convention nomination on the first ballot. However, Kimberley Strassel of the *Wall Street Journal* introduced another interesting wrinkle.[506] As Strassel noted, a growing faction of first-ballot Trump voters questioned whether they could vote otherwise. According to Curly Haugland, unbound North Dakota delegate and longtime member of the party's Rules Committee, only in the contested 1976 convention were delegates bound by national party rules. The pertinent rule was rescinded in 1980.[507]

If so, then the convention lacked specific rules about binding delegates and might or might not be inclined to police whether delegates adhered to their state's party rules. Thus the rub—lacking a national convention rule, only the states' rules applied, and no one at the moment of voting could police the delegates to ensure they abided by their state's rules.

If, for example, the delegates from Virginia whom Trump had won by popular vote but Cruz had installed during the party convention decided to foreswear Trump and vote for Cruz on the first ballot, or even abstain, who could stop them? This suggested Trump might have in practice far fewer delegates at the convention than his front-page numbers indicated. If delegates who were supposed to vote for Trump on the first ballot voted for someone else, or abstained, depriving

Trump of a victory he would otherwise claim, then there would be bedlam and lawsuits aplenty. In short, the Republican Party would have a total disaster on its hands, but then, as May 2016 dawned, that seemed likely in any case.

Getting Hairy at the Trump Rallies

Earlier episodes of violence at Trump rallies subsided, allowing some hope the punches thrown henceforth would be rhetorical in nature. Then Trump campaigned in California. California's leftist fascists, it turns out, take their protests seriously.

In late April in Burlingame, California, a suburb of San Francisco, matters escalated.[508] Anti-Trump protestors locked arms to block traffic near a Grand Hyatt scheduled to host a Trump rally, only to discover the police had already cordoned off the area. They threw eggs at the police and at Trump supporters. They burned the American flag while hoisting the Mexican flag, a nice touch if the goal was to incite a racial riot while maximizing anti-immigration sentiment. They broke through police barriers seeking to storm the hotel, but the police stopped them. They attacked Trump supporters, smashed police car windows, and generally behaved as the criminals Trump claimed many of them to be.

Donald Trump ditched his motorcade, approaching the hotel on foot with his security detail and entering the hotel through the back entrance. "That was not the easiest entrance I ever made," Trump commented. He added, "Oh boy, it felt like I was crossing the border, actually. I was crossing the border, but I got here."[509] At least we know Trump had a sense of humor.

"This Is Nuts"

Just as Hoosiers were about to go to the polls, Donald Trump revisited the loony bin. In a call-in interview with *Fox News*, Trump ranted, "His father was with Lee Harvey Oswald prior to Oswald's being—you know, shot. I mean, the whole thing is ridiculous. What is this, right prior to his being shot, and nobody even brings it up. They don't even talk about that. That was reported, and nobody talks about it. I mean, what was he doing—what was he doing with Lee Harvey Oswald shortly before the death? Before the shooting? It's horrible."[510] The "he" to whom Trump referred was Ted Cruz's father.

The only halfway sane element in the whole rant was that there was a report that Cruz's father was with Lee Harvey Oswald at one point. The report ran in the *National Enquirer*, a newspaper famous for running stories about alien abductions, Hitler living in Argentina, and magic potions capable of triggering vast psychic powers. This, apparently, is where Trump got his news. After reviewing the claim, PolitiFact gave Trump's claim its highest award for political nonsense—"pants on fire."[511]

Almost as surprising, Trump's claim left Ted Cruz almost speechless. At a news conference in Evansville, Indiana, Cruz finally reacted. "Now, let's be clear, this is nuts. This is not a reasonable position. This is just kooky."[512] Cruz knew of kooky. He went on to call Trump a "pathological liar," among other things.[513]

Any other candidate for office in America making an accusation as absurd as Donald Trump's claim about Ted Cruz's father would have been laughed off the stage, instantly unelectable for county deputy dog catcher. For Trump, this was fine. It was almost expected. The more outrageous his statements, the more his candidacy thrived, so much so that he crushed Cruz in Indiana's primary.

SAY GOOD NIGHT, TED

For Ted Cruz, Indiana was all or nothing. After losing the five Northeast primaries badly, he needed a strong win in Indiana to maintain momentum and allow his careful planning for a contested Cleveland convention to succeed. He failed. Trump won 53.3%. Cruz took 36.6%.

Cruz threw in the towel early in the evening, announcing he was suspending his campaign. "Together we left it all on the field in Indiana. We gave it everything we've got, but the voters chose another path and so with a heavy heart, but with boundless optimism for the long-term future of our nation we are suspending our campaign."[514] He never mentioned Trump. Next.

Cruz was gone, and with him incidentally was, once again, Carly Fiorina. So too was further talk of a contested convention.

Also done was John Kasich. Not that anyone cared, but Kasich took a whopping 7.6% in Indiana. He got out the next day. Not that anyone cared. Irrelevant man, leaving Trump the last one standing. Next up, Clinton or Sanders?

The end of the Cruz campaign also affirmed one of the major thesis of the 2016 campaign, a thesis likely holding in every presidential campaign, perhaps in every campaign. The thesis is that no campaign, no matter how well funded, no matter how well organized, can materially outperform the candidate. The candidate sets the campaign's ceiling. Jeb Bush had a professional campaign, national name recognition, and plenty of cash, but went nowhere because Bush was a terrible candidate for 2016. Jeb Bush himself established the low ceiling for his candidacy.

Scott Walker had done the same months before. Popular governor, strong fund-raising, but ultimately Scott Walker proved to be a AAA ballplayer faking it in the bigs.

And now, Ted Cruz, brilliant lawyer, superb debater, strong fund-raising, clear antiestablishment candidate, had fallen short. Why? Ted Cruz. Most voters found, perhaps to their own astonishment if they'd known, that they were in strong agreement with George W. Bush. Recall Bush's comment about Cruz: "I just don't like the guy."

In contrast, Trump's campaign was Trump, and his performance rose above those of all the others. It rose above his minimal campaign organization. It rose above his own fumbles with facts. It rose above his many gaffes and outrageous statements. It rose above his unpresidential demeanor. Trump had written his own playbook, followed it paragraph by paragraph, and came out on top in the first game of his two-game match.

Game two against Hillary Clinton in the general election had slightly different rules:

- This was no longer an intraparty affair.
- While the mainstream media cared little as to who took the ring in the Republican competition, they cared a great deal about who won the general election, and they wouldn't want Trump.
- During the primary, every state mattered in proportion to its delegate count. As a practical matter, for both Clinton and Trump in the general, some states could be won with little effort, some were lost at the outset, and then there were the battleground states.

Would Trump's playbook still work in game two? Could he revise or add to it to be successful?

As Republicans turned to the general election, everyone tried to play nice. Even Trump found something nice to say about Cruz: "Ted Cruz—I don't know if he likes me or he doesn't like me—but he is one hell of a competitor."[515]

Reince Priebus, Chairman of the Republican National Committee, did his best to put lipstick on this pig when he commented, "It's time to unite. It's time to come together, and I said—you may recall—months ago, I thought that we would have more clarity in our party before the Democrats do." Notice the clever transition: We're bad, but the Democrats are in worse shape.[516] A debatable proposition, but at least it was something hopeful to say.

The reality was much darker. Trump had claimed the path to the Republican nomination, but he was no Republican, certainly not in the eyes of the vast bulk of rank-and-file Republican voters. Trump might yet convince them otherwise. Or he might barely win their support if only to keep Hillary Clinton from the White House. Or the rank and file might just sit this one out, concluding with respect to Trump: Not my circus. Not my monkeys.[517]

Indiana's Bernin'

While Donald Trump was knocking Ted Cruz out of the race, Bernie Sanders was giving Hillary Clinton the fits. Sanders gained a solid win in Indiana, 52.7 to 47.3. Sanders's victory covered almost the entire state. Clinton won only the upper northwestmost county outside Chicago, plus a strip of counties along the southern border with Kentucky.

Sanders needed a win to sustain his campaign. He got it. What he didn't get was a lot of delegates. He won 44, but Clinton won 38. Clinton at 1,683 delegates to Sanders's 1,362 underscored Sanders's math problem. To close a 321-delegate deficit, not counting the supers, going forward, he needed to win just slightly more than two delegates out of every three. Netting six delegates a state wasn't going to win any prizes or the nomination.

In one important sense, it didn't matter. Sanders's main path to the nomination ran not through primaries and caucuses, but through Clinton's indictment lottery. Would he yet have the winning ticket? And if the indictment came, would the Democratic Party really sit by and let an avowed socialist become cannon fodder for Trump's legions? Or would the party grab a hammer and break the Joe Biden emergency glass case?

In many respects, Indiana was a fairly normal state. It tended to elect Republicans, but recently elected a Democrat to the Senate. It had a mix of agriculture and industry. It had some big cities in Indianapolis and Fort Wayne and a fair amount of demographic diversity. The Indiana primary therefore provided a useful event to review some exit poll basics. The following are examples:

- Women outnumbered men by three to two, so why didn't Hillary win? Half of all women voters went for the Bern.
- Sanders won the youngest voters by three to one and the next youngest by two to one. In short, the oldest candidate won the youngest voters.

- White voters outnumbered nonwhite three to one. Sanders won the white vote almost three to one. Clinton won the nonwhite vote almost two to one.
- Clinton had a small edge with voters having a high school diploma or less while Sanders had the edge with those having some college. Otherwise, education level had little effect on preferences.
- Clinton had a small edge with voters earning $30,000 a year or less. Sanders had an edge with everyone else, the edge increasing with income.
- Clinton had a slight edge among self-identified Democrats, whereas Sanders had a three-to-one advantage among self-identified independents.
- Sanders had a slight edge among both union and nonunion households.[518]

The summary from the exit polls was Clinton did best with lower-income and nonwhite voters, had a problem with young people and independents, and her support from unions remained tepid.

Exit polls also offered some interesting tidbits relevant to Donald Trump's future:

- Forty-seven percent of Republican voters were women and 47% of those supported Trump, the rest split between Cruz, Kasich, and "no answer." For all the media's bleating as to how Trump had a huge problem with women, it didn't seem so in Indiana.
- Trump did well with young voters but especially well with voters over forty-five years old.
- Seventy-three percent of Republican voters self-identified as Republicans while 23% self-identified as independents. Trump took about 54% of each.
- Five percent of Republican voters self-identified as Democrats and voted Republican primarily to support Trump.
- Trump took half the self-identified evangelical vote.

Trump's performance among women and Democratic crossover voters was especially interesting. If Trump could appeal enough to Democratic voters to get them to cross over, this could have a telling effect in states like Ohio, Michigan, and Pennsylvania. If Trump could redesign the traditional electoral college map, it might well start with these Democratic crossovers. In the event, it did.

Why Trump?

Donald Trump morphed from laughable novelty, the outsider with zero prospects, to presumptive nominee despite breaking all the rules. Those who in May dismissed his chances were in all likelihood still whistling in the dark, just as they had since Trump first announced. The doubters could still be proven right, but probably not for any of the reasons they offered at this point. The impossible candidate had made sensibly analyzing the coming election nearly impossible.

Trump through his candidacy essentially laid the American voters on a psychologist's couch, plumbing the depth and breadth of their dissatisfaction with Washington, with politics, with the direction of the country, with whatever other topic Trump raised. Voters knew they were unhappy, but because they didn't dwell on it often, focusing instead on families and careers and hobbies, their unhappiness remained mostly buried below the surface of their respective consciences. They carried on, occasionally grumbling, because there seemed no alternative. Trump was drawing their unhappiness to the surface like a poultice drawing toxins to the skin. Trump was offering them an alternative. The more he offered, the more they wanted it, never asking or even seemingly caring whether he could deliver any of what he promised.

What would happen if Trump's expressions of anger outran the voters' actual anger? Or what would happen to Trump's appeal if the voters' anger, finally vented, left the SS Trump without an ocean on which to sail? In short, could Trump keep it up to November? And if anger was the primary currency of his campaign and he actually won, on what basis could he govern? After Indiana, these were questions rarely asked in public.

Drip, Drip, Drip in May

Hillary Clinton insisted her email server was absolutely safe and secure. To be fair, how would she know? She's the one who, when asked whether she'd wiped the server clean, responded, "Like with a cloth or something?" Let's be fair. How many of us not in the IT business and over the age of thirty really understand how these things work? After all, she had to rely on the experts who worked for her. When government agencies and major corporations are regularly hacked, which of us can ever say their systems were safe? Months later, former Secretary of State Colin Powell's private emails were hacked and leaked, as were Clinton campaign Chairman John Podesta's.

When told of Clinton's claim regarding the security of her email server, Guccifer just laughed. Guccifer, real name Marcel Lehel Lazar, the famous Romanian hacker whose actions helped expose the Clinton server in the first place in March of 2013, told *Fox News*, "For me, it was easy . . . easy for me, easy for everybody."[519] Not only did Guccifer claim he'd easily hacked the Clinton server, in the course of his wanderings around Sidney Blumenthal's email and the Clinton email server, Guccifer also found he had many fellow visitors. "As far as I remember, yes, there were up to, like, 10 IPs from other parts of the world." Later, reports largely confirmed this statement.

Lest anyone forget, the slow march of justice likewise signaled in early May that Clinton still had some serious legal problems to overcome. On May 3, Judge Emmet Sullivan (a Bill Clinton appointee) of the U.S. District Court for the District of Columbia set forth the rules governing how at least six Clinton aides and associates would be deposed in the review of the use of her private email server, with an expectation of completing the depositions before the Democratic convention.[520]

Sullivan observed, "Based on information learned during discovery, the deposition of Mrs. Clinton may be necessary. If plaintiff believes Mrs. Clinton's testimony is required, it will request permission from the Court at the appropriate time." The plaintiff in the case was Judicial Watch which had triggered this particular investigation with a Freedom of Information Act (FOIA) request the State Department had wrongly but effectively stonewalled. One could safely predict Judicial Watch would indeed require Mrs. Clinton's testimony as part of the FOIA request.

Named as subject to deposition were Clinton's close personal aide, Huma Abedin, former Chief of Staff Cheryl Mills, Undersecretary for Management Patrick Kennedy, former Executive Secretary Stephen Mull, and Bryan Pagliano, the IT official reportedly responsible for setting up and maintaining the server.

Judge Sullivan's case was entirely separate from the FBI and State Department investigations under way involving the email server and the possible misuse of highly secret government documents. To be clear, Judge Sullivan presided over a FOIA request-based lawsuit, not a criminal investigation, but what the investigation uncovered would be made public, promising juicy nuggets to be used by her enemies and fodder for the government investigations.

To be sure, Hillary Clinton was a very sharp cookie and arguably the most nuanced twister of simple truths in American politics, but one would expect her deposition if done with the FBI's usual thoroughness would be no cakewalk. For those who care to remember, Bill Clinton's impeachment in the U.S. House of Representatives arose because he lied about his involvement with Monica Lewinski during a court-ordered deposition. That Bill lied under oath is not in dispute. Whether this transgression merited impeachment remains debatable. Surely Hillary had not forgotten what happened to Bill when he got caught lying under oath.

These looming depositions also cast an inescapable pall over the Democratic Party. The three investigations continued apace, each repeatedly dredging up reminders of Clinton's blatant and lazy falsehoods regarding her email server and often inconveniently reminding the nation of how the Clintons had used their charitable foundation to launder funds for their own benefit. How much baggage could the Clinton campaign carry and still move forward, especially into the face of Hurricane Donald? A fair question, and many in the party had to be asking it.

The State Department then added to the dripping faucet by responding to a FOIA request from the Republican National Committee. State claimed it could not find any text messages sent to or from the former secretary of state.[521] Further, it could not find any emails sent to or from Bryan Pagliano who had already cited his Fifth Amendment rights when called before the House Select Committee on Benghazi.

Though few in the press covered it, there was a big smoldering pile of stink underneath this story somewhere. Secretary Clinton, she of the one BlackBerry for convenience, oops, no multiple electronic devices, hadn't received any emails from her State Department or White House colleagues, ever? An IT expert had forsworn email while on duty? This was simply absurd.

One possibility was either the State Department didn't do a thorough search. Or perhaps State searched thoroughly and was just lying. Both possibilities seemed unlikely.

The other seemingly more likely possibility was that IT expert Pagliano had indeed "wiped" clean any electronic records of his and Secretary Clinton's activities while at the State Department. While Clinton might wipe her home email server with a cloth, if anyone knew how to cover his trail electronically speaking, it might be Pagliano. No wonder he pled the Fifth. This fellow was going to jail if he wasn't very careful.

Unity? Bah, Humbug

Donald Trump and the Republican Party had a huge task ahead—burying the hatchet. The standard refrain was "unify the party." Good luck with that. Trump expected everyone just to fall in line, and if some didn't, well, he said he didn't care.

Conversely, much of the party had little interest in Trump. New Hampshire Sen. Kelly Ayotte released a statement through her

Communications Director, Liz Johnson, saying, "As she's said from the beginning, Kelly plans to support the nominee. As a candidate herself, she hasn't and isn't planning to endorse anyone this cycle."[522] Ayotte was locked in a tight reelection battle with the popular Democratic Governor, Maggie Hassan. Under the circumstances, if she could stand the Republican nominee, then of course she'd endorse him. Rough translation of Ayotte's position: I won't play in his sandbox, but he'd better stay out of mine.

Ayotte wasn't alone. The parade of nonendorsements came fast, highlighted by House Republican Speaker Paul Ryan. When asked by *CNN*'s Jake Tapper if he would endorse Trump, Ryan responded, "I'm just not ready to do that at this point. I'm not there right now." Ryan continued, "What a lot of Republicans want to see is that we have a standard bearer who bears our standard."[523]

At this point, most national Republicans seemed more than willing to be conned into pretending Donald Trump was one of theirs. They would play their part in a charade if Trump would play his part just a little, but Trump could only play Trump. For example, Senate Republican Majority Leader Mitch McConnell, echoing Sen. Ayotte's line, expressed tepid support for Trump in a statement released May 5: "I have committed to supporting the nominee chosen by Republican voters, and Donald Trump, the presumptive nominee, is now on the verge of clinching that nomination."[524]

Ryan was like the guy in a bad marriage who refused to be the one to say "it's over." He would let Trump pull the plug, and Trump at first seemed happy to oblige. Speaking at a boisterous rally in West Virginia, Trump responded, "I am not ready to support Speaker Ryan's agenda."

On the evening of March 5, Nebraska Sen. Sasse led a conference call among Republican senators as to what they should do. An early Trump antagonist, Sasse suggested that Republicans rally behind their own flag bearer, though declined to run himself.[525] Absurd, but also wonderfully symmetrical in its own Alice in Wonderland way: An apolitical Independent had taken over the national Republican Party, so why not have a nationally recognized Republican run as an Independent? He or she would lose, of course, and badly, but at least real Republicans would have someone they could vote for in November.

Trump's Veepstakes Anew

Media political coverage is one part fact, one part fantasy, and four parts speculation. Donald Trump having been raised to the status of presumptive nominee, speculation turned to his veepstakes. Few seemed interested. While the media mentioned John Kasich and Marco Rubio and New Mexico Gov. Susana Martinez, none were interested.

Chris Christie as an early Trump endorser made the media's list, though one presumes Trump would be smarter than that. At this point, Christie brought nothing to the table.

Sarah Palin was asked if she would consider the job but declined, noting she would bring a lot of baggage to the campaign. "I wouldn't want to be a burden on the ticket and I recognize that in many, many eyes, I would be that burden."[526] So instead, she threatened to support a campaign in Wisconsin to defeat Paul Ryan, the House Republican Speaker.[527]

Newt Gingrich insisted that Republicans, and most especially Paul Ryan, should rally to Trump, instantly putting his name at the top of the veepstakes list.[528]

Another odd name that floated at this time was that of Michael Steele, former and utterly failed head of the Republican National Committee. Steele had buried the RNC in debt to no apparent purpose, only to be tossed out on his keister when the party awoke and turned to Reince Priebus to pick up the pieces. Steele, however, was African American, rhetorically gifted, and available.

The Ever-Varying Candidate

Donald Trump had been accused of many things. An excessive fealty to consistency was not one of them. As Zach Carter of the *Huffington*

Post wittily expressed it, "Analyzing Donald Trump policy proposals is a fool's errand. I am a fool: Behold my errand."[529]

Throughout the campaign, Trump had bragged he was self-funding his campaign (mostly). Voters needn't worry about his being unduly swayed by campaign contributions from corporations and the "rich." As the presumptive nominee, however, Trump was more than happy for all the financial support he could muster. He hired former Goldman Sachs executive Steve Mnuchin to be his chief fund-raiser and to build a national fund-raising machine capable of tapping into traditional Republican donors as well as nontraditional sources. Flip-flopping on fund-raising was just the start of the unveiling of the new Donald.

Trump had previously opposed raising the minimum wage. Now he supported it, remarking, "I mean, you have to have something that you can live on."[530] So Donald Trump, billionaire businessman, running as a Republican, thought it perfectly fine to make mostly small businesses responsible for the national social policy of income support for low-income individuals and families.

Trump had previously backed an enormous tax cut heavily skewed to tax relief for upper-income taxpayers; now, not so much. "I am not necessarily a huge fan of that. I am so much more into the middle class, who have just been absolutely forgotten in our country."[531] Suggesting the middle class had been "forgotten" seemed rather preposterous since every candidate for office anywhere talked about the middle class, but Trump's broader point was certainly valid—middle-class incomes had barely budged in years under Barack Obama. Trump promised to change all that without telling anyone how, as opposed to Hillary Clinton and Bernie Sanders who made the same charges and whose solutions largely involved doubling down on the Obama policies that had led to middle-class income stagnation.

Something of a cottage industry developed highlighting all Trump said and later reversed or that was demonstrably false. While examples of Trump-catching became too numerous to track, the *Washington Post*'s designated fact-checker, Glenn Kessler, included some of Trump's best doozies to date in early May.[532] One example involved Trump's repeated assertion he was against the 2003 Iraq War. Problem: Numerous news organizations had extensive publicly available evidence that Trump supported the war. Yet in interview after interview, on this as in so many examples, the media failed to press Trump on his inconsistencies.

Finally, Bret Baier of *Fox News* pressed him on the Iraq War inconsistency. Trump's response: "I said very weakly, well, blah, blah, blah, yes, I guess." Of course, Trump went back to claiming he opposed the war all along.

Trump's problems with consistency were so legion none gained sufficient prominence to allow the point to really sink into the American psyche. These inconsistencies were like Clinton scandals— Hillary's now and Bill's when he was in office—neither the media nor the public could keep track of them all long enough to really matter. In Trump's case, for most of his supporters, perhaps it wouldn't have mattered in any event, just as Clinton's scandals and her well-documented difficulties with truth telling didn't matter to her supporters. Perhaps Trump's supporters really didn't care what he said as long as he was angry and confident and promised to make America great again.

Multiplying flip-flops paled in comparison to Trump's net incredible revelation—it was just fine if the United States were to default on its debt. "I would borrow, knowing that if the economy crashed, you could make a deal," Trump told CNBC.[533] The deal would then go like this: I took your money and promised to give it back with interest. Just kidding.

This is how Trump ran his businesses and why sometimes his businesses ended up in bankruptcy court. That's business. The lender took a risk and was compensated accordingly. The lender lost.

That's not how governments operate, not if they want to borrow at the best rates in the world. Trump had said, in the famous words of Roseanne Roseannadanna of classic Saturday Night Live fame, "Never mind."

GOP's Existential Angst

Torn by so many forces, lifelong Republicans didn't know what to do. A few actually supported Donald Trump. Some felt honor-bound to the Republican Party, no matter what. Some were so fixated on having a "Republican" in the White House, nothing else mattered. Some were so afraid of Hillary Clinton, or just loathed her to such an extent, they would support anyone to defeat her, recalling the famous Winston Churchill quip, "If Hitler invaded Hell I would make at least a favorable reference to the devil in the House of Commons."

This was a contest of principles. The principle of "winning at all cost" versus the principle of defeating Hillary Clinton at all cost versus one's core principles. Increasingly among Republicans, the latter principle won out. Many conservatives were conservatives first and Republicans second. Most of the time, the differences didn't matter. In recent years, the differences mattered more with the rise of the Tea Party. In 2016, the difference mattered much more because few Republicans and very few conservatives saw in the presumptive Republican nominee anything they recognized as Republican or conservative.

This distinction was most obvious in the veepstakes, but it extended far and wide. Just how far it extended, and how rapidly, became apparent in an article describing how Trump would have a very tough time staffing his administration with people who had a clue what to do. Jim Capretta was a highly experienced former Office of Management and Budget official and one of the nation's foremost experts on health care reform. Capretta insisted, "I would never serve in a Trump Administration. The person at the top is unfit for the presidency."[534]

Capretta was not alone. Keith Hennessey, former head of the President's National Economic Council under George W. Bush and an extremely capable political operator then living large at the Hoover Institute in California, commented on his willingness to serve a Trump Administration: "This is not a tough call. Trump is an ignorant, unprincipled, amoral policy lightweight." Tell us how you really feel, Keith.

Why would the most competent people stay away? As Matt McDonald, another former senior official, put it, "I don't agree with half his ideas, and the other half I don't really believe what he said." Even so, many might agree to serve if called because that's what public servants do, especially when the president asks for help.

Many people want to work in the senior levels of government. They want to do so for the best of reasons—to serve the country, or for the experience, or to support the president, or just for the fun of it, or to get that bullet point on a résumé. It takes about four thousand senior-level people to fill out the president's executive branch team. These people are called on to function in environments wholly unlike anything found elsewhere in business or society. It takes several months before a new senior government executive has a handle on the job and a year before they are proficient—assuming they really were qualified substantively, organizationally, personally, and politically.

This is why for an administration to function, the vast majority of the most senior people must have previous government management or policy experience. Rookies make messes the professionals have to clean up. As one former Bush administration official put it, "Trump will be able to fill these jobs because there is a whole class of people who want these titles so badly it doesn't matter who is president. But these are B- or C-level people."

Trump wasn't helping matters. His waffling on core policy positions led Republicans and especially conservatives to doubt him. Ben Carson, he of zero federal government experience yet oddly enough led Trump's veep search committee, said Trump might appoint a Democrat as his running mate, though Trump later contradicted Carson.[535] Trump suggested he didn't really need to unify the party. "Does it have to be unified? I'm very different than everybody else, perhaps, that's ever run for office. I actually don't think so."[536]

In truth, Trump had run an exceptionally unique campaign to win the nomination, and he'd succeeded, besting some very good opponents. If past success provided any basis for confidence, then he had good reason to believe he could run a general election campaign his way.

Maybe Trump didn't need to unify the party to win. Maybe he didn't need the corps of reliable Republican volunteers in every state, every district, every precinct in the country to identify voters and make sure Trump's voters voted. Maybe he didn't need the base of Republican donors to fund his campaign. Maybe.

THE DEMOCRATS WERE STILL BATTLING

With so much attention devoted to the uneasy dance between Donald Trump and the Republican Party, the race for the Democratic nomination was easy to miss. The nation was about to be reminded. Almost completely unnoticed, Clinton had won the Guam primary, collecting four delegates to Sanders's three, but on May 10, West Virginia would have its say.

In a March townhall meeting in Ohio, as she spun up on environmental policy, Hillary Clinton let her guard down and revealed a basic truth about her policy intentions. She promised "to put a lot of coal miners and coal companies out of business."[537] Perhaps inspired by Bernie Sanders's direct speech, she of the infinite nuance finally said what she really meant in simple terms.

The coal miners of West Virginia heard her loud and clear and remembered in May. Of course, when she campaigned in West Virginia, she tried to change her tune, insisting she'd "misspoke."[538] The ruling queen of the global climate change political class "misspoke" when she said she was going to destroy the coal industry? She must really think coal miners are stupid. At least have the integrity to say what you believe and stand by it as Cruz stood by his comments about "New York values." Not Hillary Clinton.

West Virginia thanked Clinton for her kind thoughts with a crushing defeat. Sanders won 51% to 36%, picking up 18 delegates to Clinton's 11. This was yet another 2016 election irony as Bernie Sanders believed in man's role in global climate change every bit as much as Hillary Clinton, and certainly his intentions were as dark toward the coal industry as Clinton's. The only difference was Sanders had not been caught saying so publicly.

Sanders netted only seven delegates out of West Virginia, but he was winning states. A week later, Oregon and Kentucky with a combined 116 delegates would have their respective say. Oregon was a deep blue state which should prove fertile ground for Sanders, especially after demonstrating anew his viability with the West Virginia win.

Kentucky appeared to pose an even greater problem for Clinton. While the state had shifted solid red, it still had a very strong and vibrant Democratic Party built in part on union strength. Which unions? In particular, the United Mine Workers—coal. Kentucky produced the third-most coal of any state. Kentucky also was smack-dab in the middle of fracking country—another industry Clinton frowned upon.

Trump won West Virginia with 77% and Nebraska with 61% of the vote, about as expected as no other Republican was running. One might be forgiven thinking nothing much had happened by looking at the *Washington Post*'s front page the next day. No story about Sanders whipping Clinton in West Virginia. No story about Trump's two victories. Instead, the *WaPo* ran a story rehashing ancient history about how Trump had been something of a playboy in his youth.[539] It seemed a bit early for the *WaPo* to turn itself completely over to the Clinton media machine.

WHY CAN'T WE BE FRIENDS?

Donald Trump and the Republican Party establishment agreed 100% on one, and arguably only one, point—defeating Hillary Clinton. The Republican Party membership in Congress and around the country certainly was not in lockstep on any or even most issues. Contrary to the impression fomented in the media, intellectually, Republicans did represent a "big-tent" party. Substantial disagreements continued on immigration, free trade, nationalism versus globalism versus isolationism, abortion, gay rights, and a long list of subjects. But overall, there were some defining elements running through their ranks, giving coherence to what might be termed the modern Republican policy view—smaller government, lower taxes, less onerous regulations, respect for the Constitution, respect for states' rights, a strong national defense. And of course, there always remained the unifying political view they sometimes remembered—winning beats losing.

This unifying political view provided a foundation for the meeting between Trump, Reince Priebus, and Paul Ryan at Republican National Committee headquarters in Washington DC on May 12. Trump had very strong if typically skeletal policy views. Paul Ryan had spent a lifetime developing his understanding of policy. They disagreed on much, which wasn't going to change, but could they learn to work together to defeat Clinton? That was the overarching question as the three men met.

Ryan brought the matter to a very practical level—I don't know you, Donald Trump. I want to support you. Let's get to know one another, find areas of agreement, and see if we can unify the party. "While we were honest about our few differences, we recognize that there are also many important areas of common ground," Trump and Ryan said in a joint statement. "We will be having additional discussions, but remain confident there's a great opportunity to unify our party and win this fall, and we are totally committed to working together to achieve that goal."[540]

In his press conference after the meeting, Ryan masterfully refused to be maneuvered or badgered into endorsing Trump, or not endorsing him, or explaining why he would or would not endorse Trump. Ryan created a backdrop that inherently gave both men time to find a functional relationship they could live with. "This is our first meeting, I was very encouraged with this meeting, but this is a process. It takes some time, you don't put it together in 45 minutes."[541]

Trump, being neither rebuffed, rebuked, nor insulted, indicated he was fine with the outcome. "Great day in D.C. with @SpeakerRyan and Republican leadership. Things working out really well!"[542]

Going in, a strong undercurrent in Republican circles suggested this meeting provided Ryan a way to check the box. Ryan's exceptional handling of the situation created at least the possibility the two sides could work together to win in November. Many Republicans would never support Trump no matter what, but Ryan created at least the opportunity for Trump to shrink the ranks of the #NeverTrump supporters.

Trump's Bummer Taxes

So far, Donald Trump had broken nearly every rule in the playbook, from rhetorically head butting the Pope to refusing to build a national campaign organization. If nontraditional or just plain crazy was working for you, why change?

Now that Trump was the presumptive Republican, calls renewed for him to release his tax returns. When this first came up, Trump refused to release his tax returns under the bogus defense he was being audited. That dog wouldn't hunt, but there were so many other issues floating around, his opponents didn't bother to follow up.

The press took another run at the tax return issue. ABC's George Stephanopoulos broached the question. Trump's response: "It's none of your business."[543]

Aghast, Stephanopoulos fell back on the liberal's favorite line of "rights." The voters, insisted Stephanopoulos, "have a right" to see his returns.

Ah, George, where is this "right" written down? It's not in the Constitution, or the Bible, or any official document. It's not even written in law (not that such a law would pass constitutional muster). It's not a natural law, nor a physical law, nor any other kind of law.

Voters have no "right" to a candidate's tax returns. Trump said as much: "I don't think they do." However, voters have every right to *demand* to see the returns. Having a right to demand to see the returns and having a right to see the returns are two different matters. Candidates have every right to show their tax returns or not as they choose, and then voters have every right to exercise their franchise accordingly. Herein lay yet another breaking of the traditional campaign rules. Would voters let Trump get away with this one too? Time would tell.

Trump's tax troubles didn't end with his returns. In previous days, Trump had wobbled on a few of his earlier positions, such as his opposition turned acquiescence to raising the minimum wage. Then he backed away from some of his tax reform plan because it cut taxes for the wealthy and big corporations too much. Trump told CNBC, "I'm not necessarily a huge fan of that."[544]

Either way, according to interviews the two gave *Politico*, Donald Trump had tasked conservative tinkerers Larry Kudlow and Steve Moore to fix the plan. "What we've been trying to do is help advise him a little bit to try to reduce the cost of the plan" and still encourage economic growth, Moore said in an interview.[545]

Kudlow, one of the nicest people you could meet, a serious, conservative public policy economist, had found a very lucrative niche expertly and entertainingly distilling financial news on cable television. Steve Moore, a frequent sidekick to another famous conservative economist, Art Laffer of Laffer curve fame, had for many years been the chief economic editorialist for the *Wall Street Journal*'s editorial page, but had become something of an anchorless dabbler since leaving the *Journal*. To be sure, both were well-versed in tax policy basics, and both were favorites of Republican leadership in part because their views were trusted rock-solid conservative and they spoke plain English the average congressman could understand. Neither, however, was in any sense a tax expert capable of designing, let alone fixing, a deeply flawed tax reform plan.

Kudlow and Moore got to work, even contacting the Tax Foundation to rescore the plan, the cost of which had been brought down from $10 trillion over ten years to $3.8 trillion. Then for whatever reason, Trump's campaign backed off their backing off their own tax plan. Hope Hicks, Trump's spokesperson, blast emailed, "There are no changes being made to the plan." And as for Kudlow and Moore, "They do not speak for Mr. Trump or the campaign."

To which Moore eloquently responded, "I'm a little bummed out if his spokeswoman says they're not going to make any changes to the plan." Bummer, dude. Later, however, both Kudlow and Moore were brought back fully into the fold.

Predictions vs. Disruptive Forces

I think there is a world market for maybe five computers.
—Tom Watson, President of IBM, 1943

There is no reason anyone would want a computer in their home.
—Ken Olsen, CEO, Digital Equipment Corporation, 1977[546]

Technological advance and its transformative powers have long been known but never before emphasized to such a degree. The automobile replaced the horse. The refrigerator replaced the local iceman. The cell phone replaced the landline. Email replaces snail mail. The PC replaced the typewriter, and the tablet has partly replaced the PC. Investors, technologists, forecasters, and the just plain curious watch for the "next big thing." Typical was a McKinsey Global Institute report released May 2013, "Disruptive technologies: Advances that will transform life, business, and the global economy."[547]

Some advances are flash in the pans, such as the Nintendo Wii and the pet rock (we still prefer cats and dogs), while some endure, evolve, and transform further. Disruptive technologies are truly disruptive and typically make past and contemporaneous forecasts seem foolish. Donald Trump was a massively disruptive technology in the national political sphere, but would he be an enduring one?

Trump had certainly upended the Republican nomination process, utterly dismissed at the outset and for most of the race by professional political operatives and the media alike. The *Washington Post*'s Dana Milbank had written a typically arrogantly confident column assuring his readers Donald Trump had exactly zero chance of getting the Republican nomination or he would "eat his words." He ate his words, literally, and streamed a video to prove it.[548]

Ducks gotta swim, birds gotta fly, forecasters gotta forecast. The *Washington Post*'s Dan Balz ran a Page 2 Sunday article detailing many of the early forecasts for Donald Trump's candidacy in the general election.[549] One "Democratic strategist" of whom Balz thought especially highly speculated on a "not-for-attribution basis" Clinton would probably at least match Obama's performance in 2012 with 332 Electoral College votes.

Balz cited Larry Sabato of the University of Virginia, predicting Clinton "in a romp," taking 347 Electoral College votes. The Cook Political Report showed Clinton with 304 Electoral College votes solid, rising up to as many as 348.

Maybe they would all be proven right. Even some Republicans were hoping Trump would get thoroughly thrashed. Mac Stipanovich, longtime GOP consultant and campaign manager for Jeb Bush's first run as Florida Governor, was quoted as saying, "I hope he gets clubbed like a baby seal."[550] No doubt, Stipanovich was popular with animal rights activists, but his views were widely shared as Republicans thought about the elections after November 2016.

By the normal standards of political prognostication, predicting Trump's defeat while allowing a small possibility of his victory made perfect sense, until one recalled three realities. The first reality was Trump would likely be up against Hillary Clinton, a potentially decent president who was nevertheless a very poor candidate whose deeply negative likeability rating was exceeded only by that of Trump himself.[551]

Second, as a contest between the lesser of two evils, voter turnout might be very low with many voters too disgusted to bother. On the other hand, with so much anger and frustration in so many large pockets of the electorate, the protest vote might be very high. Among these various forces, which voters would actually show up to vote and who would benefit from the anger?

The third reality was Trump as disruptive force. Predicting Trump's effects on voter turnout by state was like predicting the effects of 1960s mainframe computers on how little Johnny does his second-grade homework on a tablet in 2016. Just about every political prognostication at the start of the primary season predicted that Trump would flame out early. Professional political operatives and prognosticators are paid to know stuff, and sometimes they distill the stuff they know into forecasts. A forecast that concludes "I have no idea" doesn't feed the bulldog, but would probably be the only intellectually honest forecast possible.

Drip, Drip, Drip, Mills Takes a Walk

Cheryl Mills was a name Americans were about to hear a lot more. Every longtime politician collects a staff of current and former ultraloyal, highly competent aides. The politician learns to trust this inner circle as the members of the inner circle learn to anticipate the politician's every whim, thought, and concern. Mills, former Chief of Staff to the Secretary of State, was in the innermost inner circle of the Hillary Clinton solar system. She was also at the heart of the FBI's Clinton email investigation.

Complex criminal investigations are systematic affairs, exercises in data gathering, interviews, etc. They typically begin on the ground level and work their way up the chain of command. This investigation was getting close to the first link in the chain. The FBI interview of Mills in mid-May indicated the investigation was nearing the end. Those involved were getting a little tense.

As reported in the *Washington Post*, the U.S. Department of Justice had agreed to some peculiar ground rules for Mills's FBI interview, including areas of inquiry that would be deemed out of bounds.[552] Interviewees do not like it when the FBI goes on a fishing expedition. Oddly enough, one such off-limits area was Mills's role in how the State Department would respond to the FOIA request that triggered the whole episode. As this area appeared at the heart of the investigation, the FBI agreeing to rope it off suggested the FBI was shielding Mills and, by implication, Clinton. If you suspect the evidence is in the refrigerator, agreeing not to search the kitchen can only mean one thing. This was the first real clue the fix was in.

Crossing the Line

People of various political persuasions like to pick on the press, but then the press provides so many opportunities. Case in point, the *Hill* ran a front-page story on May 17 headlined "Hillary's unlikely ally in 2016: The media."[553] "Unlikely" ally? As they say, you can't make this stuff up.

To be sure, the media would run its occasional critical piece when circumstances demanded, such as coverage of any of the ongoing investigations or if Clinton wandered too far from accepted orthodoxy. But come on, an "unlikely" ally? The mainstream media would do anything and everything it could to ensure Clinton was in the White House as long as she remained a credible candidate. The *Washington Post* had already run numerous stories criticizing Bernie Sanders for any number of policy violations.

It got better. In the same issue on page 8, the *Hill* ran a story as to how a Donald Trump hit piece the *New York Times* had run the previous Sunday was based on a series of interviews, and one of the interviewees then claimed the *Times*'s reporters had completely mischaracterized her words.[554] The *Times*, having done what it could to ensure Trump took the nomination, was now dedicated to making sure Clinton trounced him in the general election.

The *Times* piece itself was typical modern hit piece journalism. Titled "Crossing the Line: How Donald Trump Behaved with Women in Private," the piece painted Trump as a sexist and a misogynist.[555] As many people thought Trump a boar, adding sexist and misogynist seemed not much of a stretch. Trouble was, one of the women who was quoted, Rowanne Brewer Lane, spent hours with the *Times* because she wanted to explain "how well Trump treats women."[556]

Lane went on to assert, "They [the NYT] have an agenda to make Trump look unfavorable at this point in the race." Well, no kidding.

As Ben Carson responded to the matter, "It's *The New York Times*. What did you expect?"557

Washington Post media critic Erik Wemple wasn't buying it. "By any standard of decency toward women, the act of ogling a 20-something model is piggish."558 From this, one can safely draw three conclusions:

1. Of course, the *Times* ran a hit piece and of course they mischaracterized Lane's statements.
2. Of course, many people found Donald Trump's past behavior unseemly and "piggish."
3. Erik Wemple was either a world-class hypocrite or a dolt. The *Washington Post* had for years downplayed Bill Clinton's incredible behavior toward women as Governor of Arkansas and then as President of the United States and had given Hillary Clinton a complete pass in her role as Bill's suffering defender.

To reinforce the point, the *Wall Street Journal* reported the Clinton Global Initiative had funneled $2 million to a for-profit firm part owned by friends of the Clintons, and not just any friends.559 Julie Tauber McMahon, a wealthy divorcee, lived a couple of miles from the Clintons and reportedly visited the Clinton home frequently. Her Secret Service moniker was "the energizer."560

Most opposition candidates wouldn't know how to exploit the opportunity Bill Clinton presented. Most opposition candidates were not Donald Trump, who fed off such opportunities as a shark feeds off chum. Even as Bill tried to warn off Republicans from building a smear campaign around the "energizer" revelations, Trump was already landing blows. "You know, it's right next to my golf club. I have a great golf club up there—Trump National Golf Club, literally a few minutes away, and people have been talking about that [Bill's affair with the 'energizer'] for years."561

In another interview, Hillary Clinton had suggested she'd put Bill in charge of "revitalizing" the economy after eight years of lousy performance under Barack Obama. Trump struck again: "Crooked Hillary said her husband is going to be in charge of the economy.... Will he bring the 'energizer' to D.C.?"[562]

The *Washington Post* followed up a few days later with its own hatchet job on Trump, trying a different angle—linking him with mob figures.[563] The story was superficially credible, at least, as one can hardly imagine a major New York real estate developer not crossing paths with organized crime. New York isn't Iowa, after all.

The character in this case was Felix Sater, a Russian-born businessman awaiting sentencing for his role in a "Mafia-orchestrated stock fraud scheme." Sater insisted he had a long-standing relationship with Trump. Trump insisted he wouldn't recognize Sater if he were sitting in the same room. The truth? Nobody knew, but the *Post* achieved its goal of raising the questions. Few subjects did as well selling newspapers as suggestions of Mafia ties.

On the other hand, the mainstream media did all it could to suppress unseemly stories of Bill's exploits. Consider the case of Jeffrey Epstein and the "Lolita express."[564] Epstein was a wealthy New Yorker who spent thirteen months in prison and home detention for solicitation and procurement of minors for prostitution. Epstein has an airplane, a Boeing 727 to be exact. According to the airplane's logs, Bill Clinton took at least twenty-six flights on Epstein's plane, many of them without Secret Service escort. Giving Bill the full benefit of the doubt regarding any personal impropriety, ahem, why would the former president risk traveling repeatedly with a convicted pedophile and pimp and without his Secret Service detail?

More to the point, why would the mainstream media spike a story widely reported elsewhere? *Fox News* broke the original story. It also ran in the *Washington Times*, the *Washington Examiner*, the *Daily Caller*, England's *Daily Mail*, and many, many more. Where did the story not appear? The *New York Times*, the *Washington Post*, or any of the other cable news networks. Curious, that. These are news organizations, right?

Even the mainstream media couldn't avoid covering the next shoe to drop. Trump gave a highly advertised interview with Megyn

Kelly of *Fox News*, his old nemesis, on the inauguration of her new television show. Trump did fine, but Kelly, who is known for her smarts and toughness, basically engaged in a down-filled pillow fight with Trump, missing only the giggles.

Then perhaps just to make sure no one thought he'd lost his tougher side, Trump did another interview with Sean Hannity in which he dropped the political equivalent of a nuclear device. Hannity ran through the usual list of Bill Clinton's alleged victims, Juanita Broaddrick, Paula Jones, Kathleen Willey, "In one case it's about exposure. In another it's about groping and fondling and touching against a woman's will."565

"And rape," Trump quickly interjected.

Trump had thrown down on the Clintons at one of their most vulnerable points. The *New York Times* hack job on Trump had reinvigorated this whole line of discussion. Trump took full advantage. If Hillary Clinton intended to use Bill in the campaign, if she intended to pretend she could invigorate Obama's lackluster economy with Bill's supposedly magic touch, she was going to have to carry all of Bill's baggage too.

KENTUCKY, OREGON, AND BACK TO NEVADA

On May 18, Kentucky and Oregon voters nudged the campaigns toward a conclusion. In Kentucky, Hillary Clinton nipped Bernie Sanders by a nose (about 1,900 votes out of 423,000 cast), giving both candidates 27 delegates. Sanders needed a strong victory in Kentucky. He didn't get it.

Sanders got his victory in Oregon, winning about 55% to 44%, but getting only 4 more delegates than Clinton. This was the story of the campaign at this point—Sanders winning more than he lost, but making imperceptible progress, closing the pledged delegate gap that stood at 279 with only 781 remaining to win. Sanders needed to win about 68% of the remaining delegates to come even with Clinton, not counting the superdelegates.

Apparently, Sanders was willing to fight for the nomination in more ways than one and the Clinton's people gave them cause. Nevada Democratics met to pick delegates to send to the national convention. Clinton's people appeared to rig the game.[566] As recounted by Gayle Brandeis, a Sanders supporter at the convention, picking up shortly after the convention opened,

> at 9:30, a full half hour before registration closed, (party Chair) Lange read the results of ballots that had been passed out to early arriving conventioneers regarding temporary rules for the convention, rules which would discount the results of the county convention (the second tier of the caucus process, where Bernie had won more delegates), rules which would require that all votes at the convention be decided by voice alone, and which ruled that the decision of the chairperson would be final. These temporary rules had passed by flying colors, which did not sit well with the Bernie delegates, many of whom had not been given ballots. Suddenly half the people of the room were on their feet, shouting "No!!!!"[567]

Sanders's supporters demanded a recount. Lange called for a voice vote as to whether the results should stand. Clinton supporters yelled "aye," and then Sanders's supporters responded. Brandeis continued, "When it was time for the 'Nay' vote, the response was so loud, I felt it shake my every cell, felt it alter my heartbeat. The room was explosive with 'Nay's, roaring with it, and yet Lange decided in favor of the 'Aye's, which only set off more yelling."

Lange had railroaded the convention. In response, Sanders's supporters threatened her life. She documented the threats by posting online some of the emails she received.[568] Not to depose her, but to kill her and her family.

Sanders supporters shouted down California visiting Sen. Barbara Boxer, a Clinton supporter. They started throwing punches and then throwing chairs. A medic was called to the front of the auditorium to help one laid-out Clinton supporter. The State Police came in and cleared the room. Once the delegates were chosen, Sanders had exactly the number he was supposed to get from the previous election.

When asked about his supporters' violent behavior, Sanders just walked away.[569] Finally, his campaign issued a statement saying it did not "condone" violence and then went on to attack the Democratic Party, which was quick to respond in kind.[570] Democratic National Committee (DNC) Chairwoman Debbie Wasserman Schultz, herself a hard-core Clinton supporter, went on *CNN* to call Sanders's response "unacceptable."[571] One can only imagine Sanders's colorful private reaction. Somehow, nobody seemed to have noticed that trying to bully Sanders would only make him fight more fiercely. The Bern was burning at high intensity. Any chance of his standing down soon to help Clinton evaporated in Nevada's heat.

Sanders's ripping of Wasserman Schultz apparently kicked over a bigger anthill than at first appeared. Stories persisted that she might be fired as head of the DNC—stories with named quotes.[572] A lot of Debbie dissatisfaction had been bubbling out of sight, dissatisfaction Sanders had brought to the surface. One sure sign she was in trouble was the absence of senior Democrats running to her defense. New York's Sen. Chuck Schumer, expected to become the Democrats' Senate leader in the next Congress and one almost always ready to defend the Democratic establishment with a quotable quote, took a pass. As did Patty Murray, (D-OR), the highest-ranking woman in the Senate. Harry Reid begged off too: "That's not up to me."[573]

Democrats had tried for months to argue that they and their party were in much better shape than the Trump-bedeviled Republicans. It wasn't true at this point. The Democrats still suffered an increasingly nasty primary campaign. Republicans suffered Trump, but at least they made some effort to come together. Now a whisper campaign was blossoming to take out Wasserman Schultz.

It wasn't all coming up roses for Clinton either. Judicial Watch, the conservative watchdog group whose FOIA request had led to the discovery of her little email server shenanigans, announced that six current or former State Department staffers, including Clinton aides Cheryl Mills and Huma Abedin, had been served subpoenas setting the deposition dates. Drip, drip, drip.

The next day came yet another story noting how depositions in one case had been taken while the Judge in a second case was preparing to decide on a schedule for a second round of depositions. Drip, drip, drip.

To reiterate, none of this meant or confirmed that Clinton had done a single thing wrong. Stupid and misguided, even she would admit and had. But so far, not wrong in any legal or national-security-endangering sense. The steady drip, drip, drip of stories about ongoing investigations did, however, strongly *imply* wrongdoing, steadily reminding voters how the Clintons lived by their own rules and how scandal followed them the way a cloud of dust follows Pigpen of Peanuts cartoon fame.

About this time, some unkind soul put together a thirteen-minute YouTube video summarizing some of Hillary Clinton's more famous or more incontrovertible difficulties telling the truth.[574] One highlight of the video was Clinton talking about how she landed in Bosnia under sniper fire and had to run across the tarmac to safety, followed by a clip of Clinton actually landing in Bosnia on that occasion with Chelsea in tow, smiling, shaking hands with a little girl, and waving to the various dignitaries and American soldiers waiting to receive her and then strolling to waiting cars.

Clinton tried to explain away the contradiction by saying she had been tired when she made the remarks about snipers and running. The trouble was she had told the story many times, many of them shown on the video.

Trump Goes into the Bridge-Building Business Big-Time

The election calculus for conservatives was fairly simple. If Republicans held the House, then against a Clinton Administration, they would likely stand firm most of the time, thus preventing anything too egregious from passing in domestic policy. That left two areas of concern: judicial nominations, especially the Supreme Court, and foreign policy. Donald Trump's foreign policy, like his domestic policies to date, presented a witches' brew of bluster and naïveté, well-seasoned with fantasy. What would happen with judicial nominations under a Trump Administration was unknown. So bottom line: having a solid defense on domestic policy and no particular reason to trust Trump on judicial matters or foreign policy, Republicans and especially conservatives at this point had no particular reason to support Trump over Clinton.

Trump couldn't do much very quickly about his policy peculiarities, but he could move smartly regarding judicial appointments. This was a bridge he could build quickly. He did, releasing a list of eleven judges he would consider nominating to the Supreme Court, all of whom quickly found favor with conservatives who followed such matters.[575] With Justice Scalia's untimely death, and with three sitting Justices aged seventy-eight or older, Trump's list probably did more to draw conservatives in than even he imagined.

Trump also moved quickly on another front—fund-raising. Trump needed to raise a lot of money. The Republican National Committee needed to raise a lot of money. Thus, the RNC had to coordinate with its nominee. Here was an obvious opportunity to learn to live together, so on May 17, the two sides announced a joint fund-raising agreement allowing individuals to give up to $449,400 to two joint fund-raising committees versus the $2,700 limit on individual donations to the Trump campaign.[576] Trump Victory would raise money for the Trump campaign, the RNC, and eleven state party committees. Trump's Make America Great Again would direct all its funds either to the RNC or to the Trump campaign.

These moves complemented the more or less campaign-independent Super PACs already up and running to raise millions for the Trump campaign. For example, Great America PAC, with the understood tacit support of Trump campaign guru Corey Lewandowski, was very active, while the Committee to Restore

America's Sovereignty, believed to be supported by Paul Manafort, Trump's other senior campaign aide, had just launched.[577]

Absent any overarching leadership, the various groups and big-donor players quickly engaged in a classic ego-driven pissing match over who was authentic and who was a "sham PAC," as Republican Roger Stone labeled Great America. This left many big-dollar donors in a quandary, not wanting to throw their money down a rat hole. For example, Sheldon Adelson, a Las Vegas casino magnate, told Donald Trump he could donate as much as $100 million, but he was sitting on the sidelines for the moment as he was unsure how to give the money.[578]

Lest one suffer the misimpression Hillary Clinton was at risk of being outgunned, she raised over $213 million through April and had multiple massive PACs raising enormous sums. While fund-raising for downstream races followed its own pace and timing and amounts, for the two presidential campaigns, the biggest problem could well turn out to be finding campaign advisers shameless enough to submit bills large enough to soak up all the money. A shortage of cash was not going to influence this presidential election, it seemed.

National Polls

A trio of polls in mid-April had Clinton leading by 11 points, by 7, and tied, respectively. Broadly speaking, these polls reflected the state of play since the start of the year, with (a) Clinton leading by about 10 points and (b) the various polls producing wildly different results.

By mid-May, the tide had turned, at least for the moment. Two polls of likely voters showing Trump ahead by about 4 points with about 10% undecided. These were the first polls taken after the two combatants had begun training their fire on each other. Trump was clearly winning the early rounds. Once again, America's intelligentsia appeared to have underestimated Trump's popular appeal.

One interesting side note to these poll results: In national polling, Trump was beating Clinton while Clinton maintained a steady 7-point edge over Sanders, yet Sanders maintained a steady

11-point edge over Trump. To review: Trump beats Clinton; Clinton beats Sanders; Sanders beats Trump. Obviously, there was something seriously wrong somewhere. Either the polling was way off or the American people were a thoroughly confused lot—or both.

Clinton should have been on top of the world at this point, having pretty much secured the nomination. She wasn't. That pesky socialist wouldn't go away, had won two of the last three contests, and nearly won the third. Sure, the nomination looked secure, but you don't look like a winner when you're mostly losing.

Nor was Bernie Sanders going away. Three weeks would pass before the voting would come to a final glorious conclusion on June 7 with South Dakota, North Dakota, New Mexico, New Jersey, Montana, and the big enchilada, California—a grand total of 694 delegates. The Virgin Islands and Puerto Rico would vote just before, and the District of Columbia on June 14, but June 7 should decide the match. In the meantime, Sanders could continue to bedevil Clinton.

In political terms, the election was still far in the future, but Democratic donors and activists surveying the landscape had to be nervous. Nervous donors and activists are much more time-consuming than fat and happy donors and activists. No, Hillary Clinton was far from on top of the world in mid-May 2016.

A *WaPo* Day in the Life of Hillary

The *Washington Post*'s Sunday, May 22, edition presented an interesting overall impression of Hillary Clinton's campaign and the media's response. Page 2 featured a "fact-checker" analysis by Glenn Kessler of a National Republican Senatorial Committee (NRSC) radio spot.[579] According to the spot, Hillary Clinton "defended an accused rapist, then laughed about his lenient sentence." As Kessler recounted, the case arose in 1975 when Clinton was a twenty-seven-year-old attorney practicing in Arkansas.

The Judge in the case of a forty-one-year-old factory worker accused of raping a twelve-year-old girl "asked" Clinton to serve as the accused's court-appointed attorney. These are not the kinds of requests an ambitious young attorney can turn down and hope to have a legal career in the area, so despite her revulsion over the case, Clinton took it on and threw herself into her new responsibility. In the end, the prosecution reduced the charge and the defendant pled guilty.

In the mid-1980s, Arkansas reporter Roy Reed recorded an interview with Clinton including a discussion of the case. On the recording, Clinton is heard giggling repeatedly about certain aspects of the case and the outcome. As Kessler notes in defending Clinton, "This is a complex situation that has been reduced to a misleading sound bite." Kessler continued, "The laughter is open to interpretation, certainly some might find it disturbingly lighthearted." He then goes on to give the NRSC three Pinocchios.

The trouble with fact checkers sometimes is they are so deep into the details and analysis they can't see the forest for the trees. Even the harshest Hillary hater, taking a step back, would have to doubt seriously if a young woman forced to accept a case she resisted would take the rape of a twelve-year-old girl lightly, so lightly in fact that she would later cackle at it callously. Or would a wife, someday soon a mother, do so? Or did Clinton laugh because recalling the episode was so distasteful her laughter was purely a form of psychological self-defense? Clinton had no shortage of faults, but could she really be that much of a monster? No. Period.

For his part, Kessler was so desperate to exonerate Clinton he sullied what little remained of his own reputation. This was not a case of an allegation in the face of opposing facts. Even Kessler acknowledged that the situation was "complex." The fact is the only honest appraisal from the "fact checker" is he could not judge the facts one way or the other. The only honest appraisal from the facts would be, "I can't tell." The situation didn't call for a fact check; it called for judgment.

Judgment: Is Hillary Clinton such a monster the NRSC claim was reasonable? No. Four Pinocchios, not three.

In the same issue, the *Post*'s Ruth Marcus referenced a piece she'd written earlier about referring to one of the presidential candidates as a "stonewaller, shape-shifter, and liar."[580] Some of her readers assumed she was writing about Clinton. No, "my target was Donald Trump." The rest of her column was her attempt to explain why she wasn't a Clintonista and why it was fair to call Trump these names and not Clinton.

In an example of monumental understatement, with regard to stonewalling, Marcus wrote, "It is fair to say that Clinton has a penchant for secrecy." She then proceeded to explain that, yes, Clinton is a shape-shifter, but all politicians do it, and she minimized doubts regarding Clinton's veracity by narrowing the issue to the Benghazi attacks and Clinton's dubious self-defense. Marcus then concluded in explaining how Trump is so much worse than Clinton, "she plays within the goal posts of ordinary political behavior." That is probably true, if one's definition of "ordinary political behavior" included Tammany Hall and Richard Nixon. All ideology aside, Marcus was better than this.

Clinton also figured prominently in two other *WaPo* stories that day. One noted how the race was on to see whether Clinton or Trump would have the worse favorability ratings.[581] As of mid-May, the race was dead even: Both carried a 57% unfavorable rating, but Clinton nipped Trump with a 46 to 45 "strongly unfavorable" rating, while Donald had a 40% favorability rating to Hillary's 41%. Could the country have settled on two less-popular options? Not easily.

Clinton was winning in one respect, however. Always ready to complain about the role of money in politics, she would know because she'd raised nearly $300 million (and spent much of it) to Trump's relatively paltry $59 million.[582] However, as noted, Trump hadn't until recently bothered much with fund-raising. Now he was engaging in more traditional means such as Super PACs and his arrangements with the RNC.

Drip, Drip, Drip, Brick Wall

On May 24, the State Department's Office of Inspector General (OIG) released its report on the former secretary of state's performance.[583]

It wasn't damning, but it did suggest a few days in heated purgatory. Bottom line: Hillary Clinton had thumbed her nose at Department policy with respect to compliance with the Federal Records Act.

> Secretary Clinton should have preserved any Federal records she created and received on her personal account by printing and filing those records with the related files in the Office of the Secretary. At a minimum, Secretary Clinton should have surrendered all emails dealing with Department business before leaving government service and, because she did not do so, she did not comply with the Department's policies that were implemented in accordance with the Federal Records Act.

In all, the OIG's office interviewed five current or former Secretaries of State. Secretary Clinton was the only one to refuse an interview request. Her former Chief of Staff, Cheryl Mills, as well as top deputies Jake Sullivan and Huma Abedin likewise stonewalled the OIG.

The report concluded the following:

- Hillary Clinton had systematically and intentionally violated core procedures and protocols established by her own department.
- Her staff had worked hard to ensure she could play by her own rules.
- She had repeatedly insisted her exceptional email system was authorized, but produced no evidence to corroborate that claim, and the IG's investigation found none.
- The substance of the Federal Records Act was not followed.
- Clinton and her staff had erected a protective wall of silence rather than the transparency and cooperation she'd promised.
- To this point, nothing pointed to Clinton having done anything illegal in these particular matters.

What so infuriated friend and foe alike was Hillary Clinton's self-destructive penchant for secrecy reinforced by that of her associates. "OIG sent 26 questionnaires to Secretary Clinton's staff and received 5 responses."

"In addition to Secretary Clinton, eight former Department employees [most of them Clinton aides] declined OIG requests for interviews." *CNN*'s Wolf Blitzer reasonably asked Clinton spokesman Brian Fallon, "If she didn't do anything wrong and she had nothing to hide, why didn't she cooperate with the Inspector General?" It was a fair question. It was never answered.

Part of the Clintons' political genius appeared in the art of the subtle, unnoticed deflection. This genius was on full display as the story behind the OIG report unfolded. First, we learned the State Department had gone to extraordinary lengths to accommodate the new secretary's peculiar computer needs, going so far as to offer her a "stand-alone" computer giving her Internet access without entering a password or going through the Department's network.

Lewis A. Lukens, then executive director of Clinton's secretariat, was told that the offer of a stand-alone computer was turned down because Clinton was "not adept or used to checking her emails on a desktop." Oh OK. Move on, nothing to see here. And most readers probably did just keep reading.

No, wait a minute. Rewind that one—Clinton couldn't use an extraordinary stand-alone computer not even requiring a password because she wasn't used to checking email on a computer? The very elderly seniors who grew up with single-speaker radios can figure out email without an IT department showing them how. The typical five-year-old can figure it out. Hillary Clinton couldn't figure it out—this woman reportedly of exceptional intelligence who was seeking the highest office in the land?

An absurd comment made so casually and matter-of-factly, accepted so easily. Yet obviously absurd, and equally obviously, further evidence Clinton made Herculean efforts to hide her activities. She had erected a stone wall hidden behind a smokescreen and a guard of loyal aides. What was she doing that was so dangerous to her career and reputation? We may never know. The rest of us can only shake our collective heads at the Clintons' audacity, but then, why not? The Clintons always got away with it. The press bought the deflection and moved on.

Elites in America, from Wall Street to Main Street to Washington DC, Republicans and Democrats alike, live to write detailed rules to dictate the lives and decisions of the unwashed masses (hint: that would be you and me), while ignoring those rules themselves when and as they choose. Unlike Bill Clinton, who is less the elitist than an impish cad who learned from a charmed life he can get away with almost anything, Hillary Clinton embodied the consummate elitist. Early in her career, her elitist attitude flowed from her unwavering belief she was the political equivalent of the Caped Crusader and her intended goodness washed away her ethical and legal lapses.

Now, Hillary Clinton's elitism flowed from her résumé, her wealth, and the establishment support she received in exchange for her defense of their own elitist status. Her supporters among the unwashed masses apparently didn't care she was running as the antiestablishment elitist, as oxymoronic as that obviously is, just as they apparently didn't care she would tell the truth only when it was convenient. Grouse as one might, that's their privilege.

Trump Gains a New Antagonist—Pocahontas

Hillary Clinton needed all the help she could get. Sen. Elizabeth Warren, silver-tongued darling of the Bernie Sanders wing, was happy to oblige. While Warren hadn't endorsed Clinton, she saw an opportunity to take on Donald Trump. She took it. Normally restricting herself to 140-character sniping, Warren gave a speech dedicated to rallying opposition to Trump. "He inherited a fortune from his father, and kept it going by scamming people, declaring bankruptcy, and skipping out on what he owed."[584] Warren started her career as a bankruptcy law attorney, so these issues were familiar ground.

Having won the nomination, Warren said Trump was then "kissing the fannies of poor, misunderstood Wall Street bankers." Warren called Trump a "small, insecure money grubber who doesn't care who gets hurt, so long as he makes some money off it."

Warren, a smart and determined lady, was out of her league, and every counterpunch Trump landed hit Clinton by implication. Trump called Warren a "hypocrite," noting that in the 1990s, she'd "rapidly bought and sold homes herself, loaned money at high interest rates to relatives and purchased foreclosed properties at bargain prices." And again, "Goofy Elizabeth Warren, sometimes known as Pocahontas, bought foreclosed housing and made a quick killing. Total hypocrite!"

None of this would endanger Warren in Massachusetts, but she was spending her credibility rapidly in a battle she couldn't win. With luck, her Senate colleagues wouldn't call her "Pocahontas" to her face, despite her having claimed Native American heritage only to admit later it was little more than unsubstantiated family lore. One thing was for sure: Warren provided Trump amusement and fodder, just the way he liked it.

Trump's Take on the Press

"Dishonest," "not good people," "the most dishonest people I have ever met" were some of the kinder things Donald Trump had to say about the press in a scorched-earth press conference to announce the recipients of the funds raised at his veterans' event four months earlier.[585]

The press smelled blood mode, wondering what had happened to all the money raised, a total of $5.6 million, to be exact. The press's fixation was rather peculiar. The veterans' event was pure theater from Trump's perspective. He put in $1 million personally or about 1% of what he earned on petty cash in a year (rough estimate). Did the press think billionaire Donald had run off with the money? Or that he was simply unable to manage collecting and paying out the funds?

Chris Cillizza of the *Washington Post* did an admirable job attempting to defend the press, noting that it was a journalist's job "to find out who he gave to and how much."[586] The vital importance of a free press to a free society is its mandate to hold the powerful accountable. To be clear, there are a great many fine journalists in America who more or less manage to keep their personal views contained while covering their stories. Then, like all professions, there are the schmucks who make the rest look bad.

The trouble was the press pointed to its journalistic mandate the way teachers' unions use kids as shields while they explain away the education system's shortcomings and demanding for their members more money and better benefits. The press doesn't demand better pay in this instance. They demand the right to shape the information we receive. In this case. they demanded the right to go into attack mode to destroy someone they abhorred, to see if a pack of little hunters could take down big game. It sells newspapers.

The veterans' benefit result was a press-concocted phony story. Trump was not pleased. "I'm the only one in the world who can raise $6 million for the veterans, have uniform applause by the veterans' groups, and end up being criticized by the press." Trump then proceeded to read, one by one, the names of the recipients of the funds and the amounts received, a process that took over five minutes.

Bottom line: It wasn't hard for Trump to make a convincing case members of the press were more or less everything he accused them of being. He also showed most of them had glass jaws and withered when faced down.

The Era of Non-Ringing Endorsements

"Ah, crap, I guess so" about captures the tone of endorsements slowly accreting to the respective candidates. In an open letter to California Democrats and independents, the Golden State's Governor, Jerry Brown, wrote, "I have decided to cast my vote for Hillary Clinton because I believe this is the only path forward to win the presidency and stop the dangerous candidacy of Donald Trump."[587]

The next paragraph praised Bernie Sanders effusively. Then Brown acknowledged Clinton was OK, concluding by raising alarms over Donald Trump. Hardly a ringing endorsement, but with the California primary only a week away and the race a dead heat, Clinton needed all the help she could get. She was on track to claim the nomination easily by delegate count, but she needed victories to avoid arriving at the Democratic convention a badly wounded duck. She needed to finish Bernie off once and for all.

Most of Trump's endorsements carried a similar "hold your nose" aspect. Marco Rubio was asked by a Miami radio station if he'd endorse Donald Trump. "I've always said I'm going to support the Republican nominee . . . and that's especially true now that it's apparent that Hillary Clinton is going to be the [Democratic] nominee."[588] Notice the pattern: I'm endorsing X, not because I think they'd be a good president, but because Y is too awful to contemplate.

House Speaker Paul Ryan completed the set with his endorsement of Trump on June 2. Ryan's endorsement in tone and method could have won an award for polish: He published an open letter in his hometown newspaper, the *Jaynesville Gazette*, Jaynesville, Wisconsin.[589] Ryan admitted he was a policy wonk and he came to Washington to pursue policies that solve problems. Many politicians say as much, but none match Ryan for putting actions to words.

Ryan needed someone in the White House to partner with Congress. "One person who we know won't support it [the House plan] is Hillary Clinton." No doubt about that. So Ryan spent several hours talking through the House plans with Trump and concluded, in the end, this is a person he could work with. "Through these conversations, I feel confident he would help us turn the ideas in this agenda into laws to help improve people's lives. That's why I'll be voting for him this fall."

But Ryan also made clear, "There's no secret he [Trump] and I have our differences." Again, an endorsement, but hardly a ringing endorsement.

Three's a Crowd

While the Republican and Democratic Parties have dominated American politics for decades, every election cycle brings out a raft of "third-party" candidates. In modern history, with its very tight elections, third-party candidates have occasionally influenced the outcome. Not that they had a chance themselves, but they could take enough votes to decide the outcome between the mainstream candidates.

In 1992, the peculiar diminutive billionaire Ross Perot took 19% of the vote, mostly from George H. W. Bush, possibly pushing Bill Clinton across the finish line. Likewise, Ralph Nader's Green Party candidacy in 2000 may have stripped enough votes from Al Gore to give the win to George W. Bush. Nader took 97,488 votes in Florida, which Bush won by 538. Almost all of these votes would have otherwise gone to Gore.

In 2016, Republicans continued to talk about running a third-party candidate such as Mitt Romney just to give the anti-Trump crowd somebody to support.[590] The problem was that only a few of the anti-Trump voters would vote for Hillary Clinton. Many would just stay home, but most in the absence of a third-party option might hold their noses and vote for Trump out of fear of Clinton. So a Republican third-party candidate in a tight election might just take enough votes on net to swing a key state to Clinton.

Another perennial option was the Libertarian Party. Americans were exceptionally fed up with government (hence the two flavors of "burn the house down" in Sanders and Trump). Maybe this would be the year the Libertarians finally broke through to relevance. The Libertarians met at the end of May in Orlando, Florida (no references here to Disneyland, Goofy, or Mickey Mouse, please), to nominate former Republican and New Mexico Gov. Gary Johnson and former Republican and Massachusetts Gov. William Weld as their ticket.

It was fair to suggest before they made a claim to credibility that the Libertarians should win one Senate seat, or one House seat, or one governorship, or one mayoral election; to date, zip. In the

2012 election, Johnson managed about 1% nationally. In 2016, some national polls showed around 10% when matched up against Clinton and Trump.[591] In combination with the Greens, the Never Trumpers, and the socialists, the libertarians might toss a state or two to one of the top candidates, but which states, and would it matter to the final outcome?

HILLARY TAKES HER BEST SHOT

"Bizarre rants, personal feuds, and outright lies"—can you tell which candidate said this of the other? Probably not, which is why this line of attack probably would not play well.

Hillary Clinton knew her best shot at defeating Donald Trump lay in attacking his person. Sixteen Republican candidates had tried that approach and failed. Many television pundits and similar gasbags tried, and with each one, Trump only seemed to get stronger.

At the very least, Clinton needed to get in the ring with him, exchange some big-boy blows, and show she could land a punch as well as take one. So on June 2, she gave a major speech, billed as a foreign policy speech, but it was nothing of the sort. This was a major Donald Trump takedown.

The Clinton News Network, a.k.a. *CNN*, titled its lead story, "Hillary Clinton's evisceration of Donald Trump."[592] Much of the mainstream media accepted the narrative Clinton had begun the dismantling of the Trump mystique. Some, like foreign policy expert K. T. McFarland, didn't buy it.[593] One of Clinton's better lines was "He [Trump] says he has foreign policy experience because he ran the Miss Universe pageant in Russia." In contrast, Clinton touted all her foreign policy experience dealing with real issues, like Russia, Libya, Iraq, Afghanistan, and Syria.

Oh, maybe she shouldn't have mentioned those. None were working out so well, as McFarland noted. "They [Obama and Clinton] lost three wars: Afghanistan, Iraq, Libya. Four if you count Syria."

Clinton talked about Trump "bragging" and "tweeting" his way through policy. Indeed, even as she spoke, Trump was tweeting away,

"Bad performance by Crooked Hillary Clinton. Reading poorly from the teleprompter. She doesn't even look presidential."

But it was Clinton's reference to Trump lying that probably rang the most off-key. Here was a person once called a "congenital liar," who provided regular confirmations of her own struggles with veracity, calling someone else a liar? This was a subject Hillary Clinton should have just left on the cutting-room floor.

Violence Comes to Cali

It fascinates how those who criticize others for being intolerant are typically among the least tolerant.

Donald Trump held a campaign rally in San Jose on June 2. As his supporters streamed out of the arena, they were met by a hailstorm of eggs and abuse, punches and shoving. The Trump supporters, of course, were mostly white. The anti-Trump forces were entirely Hispanic. Neither side was innocent, but the anti-Trump forces were the clear instigators. The anti-Trumpers were ready for a fight. They wanted one. They got one.

Politics isn't an afternoon tea party. Sometimes it gets rough, but partly what keeps the violence in check is the adult calming reactions of civic and political leaders. Trump was no angel, having earlier promised to pay the legal bills of anyone who punched a protestor, but consider too the reaction of San Jose Mayor Sam Liccardo: "At some point, Donald Trump needs to take responsibility for the irresponsible behavior of his campaign."[594]

Let's see. One side has a political rally. They are then caught in a planned ambush by opponents, and the mayor defends the ambushers (as does the mainstream media). In fact, the ambushers were kind enough to supply the video proving who were the aggressors.

A Climactic Finale

With the voting on June 7, the races for the respective parties' nominations came to a close. For the first time in a long time, voters in California, Montana, New Jersey, New Mexico, and South Dakota finally had some influence on the outcome, if only a little. Donald Trump swept all five states.

The Democratic results were almost as anticlimactic. Sanders hoped for one last miracle, especially in California. He didn't get it, though he did manage a respectable pair of wins in Montana and North Dakota, coming very close as well in New Mexico and South Dakota. The big states in terms of delegates on this day were New Jersey and California. Clinton won both with 63% and 56%, respectively. The District of Columbia voted a week later, giving Clinton one last victory.

The nominees now set, barring Clinton's indictment or Trump's random implosion. Sanders and Clinton began a curious dance of rapprochement while Trump tried to figure out how to act more presidential, or even if he wanted to bother. On the Democratic side, especially, the center of attention quickly shifted to speculation about Clinton's running mate, with the early preference going to Sen. Warren to ensure sufficient rabid progressivism on the ticket. Curiously, far less speculation arose as to who would be Trump's running mate, or even who would want to be, other than Chris Christie, of course.

CHAPTER 17
THE STORM BEFORE THE STORM

Without exception, political candidates in free societies feel they are treated unfairly by the press. Without exception, they're generally right.

Often, the press is just sloppy, either because the reporter is writing under a deadline or because he or she really doesn't know the subject and is just winging it, hoping the reader knows even less. Sloppy reporting is easily confused for malicious reporting and thus seems unfair to the victim. And yes, sometimes, the press is just unfair, twisting quotes out of context, ignoring basic facts, and cherry-picking others to fit the intended narrative. To paraphrase Winston Churchill with respect to democracy, a free press is a terrible way to communicate information publicly, except by comparison to all others.

Donald Trump had much earlier in the campaign established a mantra of being treated unfairly by whomever he regarded as impolitely critical. When it came to the press, he didn't just complain; he took away their credentials. In a Facebook post, Trump announced he was taking away the *Washington Post*'s press credentials due to the paper's "incredibly inaccurate coverage."[595]

The *WaPo* wasn't the first to suffer this indignity, *BuzzFeed*, *Politico*, the *Daily Beast*, and the *Huffington Post* having previously been ostracized, but the *WaPo* was by far the most meaningful recipient of Trump's displeasure. More than personal pique, however, Trump's cavalier attitude toward "the fourth estate" also highlighted how individual elements in the media, and to an extent the mainstream media in toto, had become increasingly dispensable to the political process. What did it mean to Trump to toss out the *WaPo* when there were so many ways to get the message out to huge audiences? This, in fact, was the secondary message of the Trump decision. He didn't announce the action in a press release. He announced it in a Facebook post.

OH, ORLANDO

In the early morning hours of Sunday, June 12, a man having pledged allegiance to ISIS opened fire inside a crowded gay bar in Orlando, Florida, killing forty-nine people and injuring fifty-three.[596] Omar Mateen (the gunman, a twenty-nine-year-old security guard) was then killed by police.

Mateen's parents had immigrated from Afghanistan, and he was born in New York. The early narrative suggested Mateen was homophobic, but information quickly surfaced, indicating he'd frequented the club in the past, suggesting a more complicated storyline. His ex-wife said he was gay.

Another interesting bit of information: the FBI and the Department of Homeland Security had kept an eye on Mr. Mateen for some time, including bringing him in for "interviews." In a mostly free society, neither the FBI nor the DHS could do anything more until Mateen did something, and then it was too late.

The Orlando shooting quickly became fodder for the campaign, with Donald Trump immediately staking out the most inflammatory position while Pres. Obama staked out the most passive. Hillary Clinton found herself having to use what was for her very uncomfortable terminology in referring to "radical Islam."

Conservatives didn't quite know what to say in response to the Orlando shooting. Some sided with Trump, but his rhetoric was too extreme, too vitriolic for most. Many liberals, rather than deal with the issue of domestic acts of religious terrorism, quickly pivoted to their political happy place of "gun control."

The Orlando shooting raised at least two sets of legitimate questions. One set of questions revolved around who in America should be allowed to buy or own guns, and which guns they should be allowed to buy. A second set of questions revolved around domestic Islamic terrorism. Republicans were willing to tinker around the edges of increasing background checks for gun purchases, but nothing more. Trump wanted to meet with the National Rifle Association to see what they would accept. Mostly, the Republicans were focused on Islamic terrorism.

The Democrats saw another opportunity to move down the road toward abolishing the Second Amendment altogether, and the president absolutely refused to utter the words "Islamic terrorism," once again preferring to treat these episodes as one-off criminal acts. Democrats also saw another opportunity to champion LGBT rights, seeing the Orlando shootings as an anti-gay "hate crime," neatly ignoring that the shooter was himself bisexual.

Twenty-four hours after the Orlando shooting, a French police captain and his partner were stabbed to death at their home in a small town northwest of Paris.[597] The attacker, Larossi Abballa, had earlier pledged his loyalty to ISIS chief Abu Bakr al-Baghdadi. Abballa was killed by police in the couple's home.

In a barrel of one hundred apples, one can usually spot the bad apple pretty quickly. It's harder with people. How was Western society to distinguish between the ninety-nine Muslims living peacefully in their midst and the one bad apple who may or may not be sufficiently radicalized to resort to domestic terrorism?

Muslims had every reason to resent being shunned, insulted, and discriminated against. But then, non-Muslims had every reason to be uneasy. If the ninety-nine didn't find a way to work with the society in which they chose to live, then there would be no satisfactory solution.

The Obama Administration's intense desire to avoid references to Islamic terrorism reached absurd heights with the release of the transcripts of the back and forth between the police and the shooter in the latter stages of the attack. The first version of the transcripts released by Attorney General Loretta Lynch's Justice Department had a great many sections redacted, though any thoughtful reader could easily fill in the blanks. Somebody in the administration quickly recognized how utterly stupid the Department looked, so they released a less redacted version a few hours later.[598] The DOJ still looked ridiculous.

Drip, Drip, Drip Plus $18 Million

Less riveting to the reader but more relevant to the campaign, U.S. District Judge Emmet G. Sullivan ordered Bryan Pagliano to set a date before the end of June to give a videotaped deposition in the matter of the Clinton email server.[599] Recall, Pagliano had earlier invoked his rights under the Fifth Amendment of the Constitution against self-incrimination before a congressional investigation.

Particularly interesting, Pagliano's attorneys said Pagliano was given limited immunity by Federal prosecutors in an ongoing FBI criminal investigation into the mishandling of classified information. Key words: criminal investigation.

The same day, we learned the Clinton Foundation received $18 million in contributions from foreign governments while Hillary Clinton was secretary of state.[600] How did we learn? Clinton Foundation officials released the information through a New York State charity board filing. No information provided as to which governments had demonstrated their generosity. This was the third "official" revised version of the Foundation's financial statements. For all Clinton's troubles with her email scandal, the bigger smoking gun politically appeared to be the Foundation scandal.

Hillary Clinton liked to say she would be the most transparent presidential candidate in history. Jay Leno, guest hosting the June 15 *Jimmy Kimmel Live!* show, asked the audience, "OK, so how many of you can see right through Hillary?" All hands went up.

Vlad Hacks the DNC

In a curious twist, the Russian government penetrated the computer networks of the Democratic National Committee (DNC), gaining access to, among other information, the DNC's complete dossier of opposition research on Donald Trump, including all related email.[601] The hackers enjoyed access to some elements of the DNC system for over a year.

This case of classic industrial espionage applied to politics likely occurred frequently as apparently many of the candidates' computer networks had been compromised. The Russians, of course, insisted the government had nothing to do with any of it and then asked if anyone was interested in buying a bridge.

Russian Pres. Putin rose to become a lieutenant colonel in the KGB before becoming a modern czar. His wasn't an idle curiosity. He was looking for information he could use against a future adversary, whether Trump or Clinton. What made this especially interesting is the Russians had not merely penetrated the DNC system. They lingered, knowing the longer they lingered, the more likely they would be caught—and they didn't care.

It turns out the Russians had also hacked the Clinton Foundation servers.[602] Maybe now the public would see all the Clinton emails, including those 33,000 supposedly private emails Clinton's people had tried to delete. Curiously, the Clinton Foundation said it was unaware of the security breach. Among the information hacked by a group calling itself Guccifer 2.0 was a list of donors who had made large contributions to the Clinton Foundation.

This was all highly relevant to the various investigations under way regarding national security and the Clinton email server. The known facts were that Clinton's private emails contained an enormous trove of information classified at the highest levels of Top Secret, and the Russians had been able to walk through the Clinton email server like a Sunday stroll in the park.

Distinguishing Heart, Mind, and Muscle

As Republicans struggled to come to grips with the Trump phenomenon, increasingly the media described what occurred as Donald Trump executing a hostile takeover of the Republican Party. A piece in *The New Yorker* used this language as early as January.[603] This characterization wasn't quite right. To be sure, Trump had in a most hostile manner wrenched the presidential nomination from the party, but he hadn't taken over the party itself. He may have become its mouth, but he wasn't its mind, or heart, or muscle.

Trump himself began to realize this reality. He further realized he would never gain acceptance during the campaign among much of the party's heart, mind, and muscle—the governors, mayors, local legislators, donors, and even Washington representatives and all their supporters who really *are* the Republican Party. The Donald wasn't happy. At a mid-June rally in Atlanta, Trump said, "This is tough to do it alone. But you know what I think I'm going to be forced to. I think I'm going to be forced to."[604]

He was also peeved about attacks from Republican Party leaders on his comments about the judge in the ongoing trial against Trump University, and especially their criticisms of his comments after the Orlando shooting. He told them collectively, "Be quiet. Just please be quiet. Don't talk. Just please be quiet."[605]

Trump was risking a three-front war. One front was against Hillary Clinton on his left. A second front was against the media in his front. These were inevitable, but the third front, a rear-guard action against the party itself, could very well be the one to defeat him.

There was no shotgun available to force this marriage. The bride would insist on a certain degree of civility and adult behavior on the part of the notorious bad boy, or she wasn't saying the words at the altar. Yet most days, the bad boy showed up on his motorcycle stinking of beer. One at a time at first and then more and more, Republican leaders publicly walked away. Larry Hogan, Maryland's surprising and surprisingly popular Republican governor, was typical. After ducking the question for weeks, when asked if he would vote for Trump, Hogan replied, "No, I don't plan to. I guess when I get behind the curtain I'll have to figure it out. Maybe write someone in. I'm not sure."[606]

There were a couple of ways this could go. Somebody could find a shotgun to force the marriage, or the bad boy would tone it down, or Trump would run as the Republican nominee while the vast corpus of the party scorned him, focusing entirely on their own concerns. The third option seemed the more likely.

Trump knew something was going very wrong among the campaign staff, so he delivered his famous verdict to a loyal supporter. He told Corey Lewandowski on June 20, "You're fired." Lewandowski had been with Trump from the very beginning. It seemed he wasn't going to make it to the end.

Lewandowski was a force of nature, and sometimes that force bore an uncomfortable likeness to an F5 tornado. But there was no denying his loyalty or his central role in assisting the oddest candidate in modern U.S. presidential history to the very steps of the nomination. However, as they say in baseball when releasing a player who no longer fits the plans, "the organization has decided to make a change."

In part, something had to be done to as Trump had suffered a string of bad weeks. The problem wasn't necessarily Lewandowski, though his warfare with Paul Manafort didn't help. When a ball club is underperforming, you can't fire all the players. So you fire the manager. The problem was Trump as team owner, not Lewandowski as manager, but Trump couldn't fire Trump, so he fired the manager instead.

To his credit, Lewandowski went on *CNN* to praise Trump effusively and thank him for the opportunity. Lewandowski may be the SOB many suggested, but on this occasion, he was a stand-up guy, and he was rewarded for his loyalty in a subsequent campaign shake-up.

Firing Lewandowski would not slow the rapidly building revolt in the Republican Party. The anti-Trump forces knew changing the convention rules to release all delegates to vote their consciences on the first ballot was a long shot, but they were going to give it their best shot. They really had no idea what they would do if and when Trump had been turned back. It didn't matter. They simply figured anyone would be better than Trump.

The Republican revolt was manifesting as well in an entirely different venue—money. According to published reports, Clinton's campaign had $42 million in the bank as of May 31.[607] Her Super PAC, Priorities USA, had another $52 million. The Donald? $1.3 million.

To be sure, Clinton's campaign went through cash for staffing and overhead at a prodigious rate while Trump kept his operation lean—no need for an army of policy advisers, for example, when you have essentially no policies. Trump's problem was the Republican Party's major donors weren't particularly interested in helping out. As a multibillionaire, if need be, Trump could fund his own presidential campaign. "I spent $55 million of my own money to win the primaries, 55, that's a lot of money, by even any standard." But Trump continued, "It would be nice to have some help."

If party donors turned their backs on Trump, then he would turn his back on the party's fund-raising for downstream races. Typically, the party relies on its nominee to act as a cash magnet to help nationwide. If Trump wouldn't help, then the party would have to switch business models quickly. The donors were still there and a passel of Super PACs could do the fund-raising, but would it work as well, and would Republicans suffer downstream for want of cash? This was another sign the Republicans were coming to a fork in the road.

First Rumble

Donald Trump suffered a string of bad weeks entirely due to his own self-inflicted wounds. If Paul Manafort could instill in the Donald a little presidential self-restraint, plenty of time remained to right the ship, but these bad weeks showed in the polls, where Hillary Clinton was maintaining a steady 5-point lead nationally.

Despite her fund-raising advantages, Clinton knew she was in a weak position, and she knew Trump was momentarily weaker. It was time to attack. First, she gave a lengthy "foreign policy" speech, little of which touched on her own foreign policy views as each and every one would be a variation on Obama's policies, which aside from the recent gains by the Iraqi Army had produced nothing but failure after failure. Her speech instead was an all-guns broadside on Trump's foreign policy. Both candidates enjoyed a target-rich environment when it came to foreign policy.

A few days later, she gave a speech on economic policy including hardly a word about her own policies and instead featured another all-guns broadside on Trump's economic policies. She blasted his views on debt and the enormity of his tax cuts, and on and on. First problem, Clinton was attacking a businessman for his approach to economics when said businessman had made billions of dollars. She gave speeches to Wall Street for hundreds of thousands. On paper, at least, he had more credibility on economic policy than she did.

Second problem, the disappointing economic performance over the previous seven years under Obama were the best one could hope for from Clinton as she largely followed Obama except where she would make matters worse. Even as she was speaking, Trump was tweeting responses to soften the blows. Clinton knew Trump would counterattack, but perhaps she wasn't quite prepared for the ferocity of the counter, blasting her tenure as secretary of state and how she used it as her own private hedge fund. He referred to Clinton as a "world-class liar" who "may be the most corrupt person ever to seek the presidency."[608]

For all the charges and countercharges, Trump had the advantage because the American people largely already believed Clinton had great facility with falsehoods, and her "pay-to-play" scheme through the Clinton Foundation gave substance to Trump's claims about corruption. Clinton, it seemed likely, would lose this battle badly;

but once again, she faced the same fundamental issue she'd faced so often in the campaign—what else was she to do?

Clinton did make one particularly valid point. She and her campaign had fairly specific goals for the economy and had also developed detailed plans for how she thought she could achieve those goals. Trump had vaporous goals and essentially no plans. She acknowledged the economy was underperforming in general and for the middle class especially, but asserted she could fix it following much the same policies producing the failings. That her plans were merely updates of Obama's policies and would categorically fail didn't detract from Clinton's basic point that Trump had little idea what he would do.

In 1976, Pres. Gerald Ford was running for reelection against former Georgia Gov. Jimmy Carter. A cartoon ran showing a young man staring up into a summer sky at a big billowy cloud in the shape of a person's face. It was Jimmy Carter's face with his famous enormous warm smile. The young man asked the cloud, "What will you do for the country?"

> The cloud responded, "I will heal the land."
>
> The young man asked, "What will you do for my family?"
>
> Jimmy Carter the cloud responded, "I will heal your family and you will prosper."
>
> The young man pleaded, "But how, when national politics is so evil?"
>
> The cloud responded, "Because I am good, and I mean you well."
>
> The young man was then seen running toward the cloud crying, "I believe, I believe."

Jimmy Carter ran as the good and decent man from outside Washington who could heal the land after the Vietnam/Nixon/Watergate debacles. Trump was vastly more accomplished than the former peanut farmer, yet he still appeared the 2016 version of Jimmy Carter—vacuous, overpromising, utterly unprepared. Like Carter, Trump spoke to the most basic psychic needs of a large portion of the country in the moment. The voters went with the happy place dream of Jimmy Carter as against the bland Nixon-pardon-tarnished but competent Gerald Ford in 1976. Forty years later, would they again eschew the bland, tarnished, but competent for the flashy and emotionally satisfying?

What a Week!

The penultimate week of June presented an amazing array of events. To start, on June 22, Bernie Sanders made it almost official—he wasn't going to win, but he wasn't dropping out entirely, not even "suspending his campaign." He was still a candidate, just not running anymore. He was angling for leverage at the convention, knowing his leverage was shrinking daily. Further, his candidacy was still very much alive in the one respect where it was always strongest—the Clinton indictment sweepstakes. It was a bit like Powerball—spend a couple of bucks and have a long-shot chance to get rich.

With Bernie as appetizer, next came the main course for the week: The decision by UK voters to leave the European Union (EU), a.k.a. "Brexit." Aside from an immediate and quickly reversed stock market crash, Brexit's immediate effects were to drive the UK's Prime Minister, David Cameron, to resign. Cameron had bet his future on "remain" and lost. Unfortunately for the United Kingdom, no one appeared ready to step into Cameron's shoes.

Brexit also meant Pres. Obama once again had to scrape egg off his face. Obama had publicly pushed hard for the United Kingdom to remain in the EU, a public position many on both sides of the pond found utterly inappropriate. Obama went so far as to warn that if the United Kingdom left, then negotiations on a trade deal or other matters between the United States and the United Kingdom would go to the back of the line.

A more ham-handed approach would be hard to script. After the vote, Obama quickly backtracked, referring again to the "special relationship" between the two countries. Hillary Clinton also shared in the egg-scaping exercise, though she'd had the sense to express herself in more muted tones.

Donald Trump had been in Scotland opening two new golf courses (odd way to run a presidential campaign). Trump offered a surprisingly sensible reaction:

> The people of the United Kingdom have exercised the sacred right of all free peoples. They have declared their independence from the European Union and have voted to reassert control over their own politics, borders and economy.[609]

At about the same time, the Supreme Court slapped down the Obama Administration with respect to its unconstitutional approach to immigration reform, letting stand a lower court ruling putting a stop to the centerpiece of Obama's immigration policy. This didn't mean the immigration issue had advanced toward a solution—far from it. The pressure on Congress to act, pressure it would continue to ignore, grew substantially. The ruling did suggest the Constitution still had some life in it.

The same week, Marco Rubio made it official—he would run for reelection to the U.S. Senate, after all. Even before his presidential run, Rubio had made clear his dislike for the Senate and insisted he would not change his mind about leaving. He changed his mind. Reason? Partly to ensure the seat remained Republican. His chances of reelection were very high, while if he left, then the chances of Republicans holding the seat were fifty-fifty.

Another reason to run again—so he could run again. Rubio was still young and full of promise. Running for governor, or running for president again in 2020, would be a lot easier from the Senate than from the sidelines.

Cleaning Up After Your Own Parade

In the course of his slash-and-burn primary campaign, Donald Trump made more than a few over-the-top comments, so he decided to take a rhetorical tour of clarification, attempting to take a little of the sting out of his previous remarks. After a parade has passed by, along with the confetti and similar detritus, the horses and elephants and other animals leave behind their own little presents. Somebody has to come along and clean it up. Trump tried to clean up from his own parade.

First stop in the cleanup parade: international trade. Trump had denounced just about every trade deal the United States had inked in the modern era. Was he anti–free trade, or did he just think government after government, Republican and Democrat alike, had negotiated bad deals? After his speech on June 28 in Pennsylvania, the only reasonable answer was—both.

Trump blamed free trade for leaving "millions of our workers with nothing but poverty and heartache."[610] He called the recently negotiated but as yet unratified Trans-Pacific Partnership "a rape of our country," pretty strong language for a trade deal that didn't do much economically.[611] He vowed to pull the United States out of the North American Free Trade Agreement with Canada and Mexico if the other countries refused to renegotiate it.

Trump painted himself as a neoisolationist nationalist and painted Clinton as part of a "leadership class that worships globalism."[612] Trump's accusation about Clinton was largely true, which is why it hit so hard, though as the campaign wore on, she insisted she had resigned her membership in Globalists United.

To be sure, like every piece of major legislation, a trade deal is a collection of compromises. There's always much to criticize. International trade always demands workers, companies, and industries to adjust, sometimes in ways they really don't like. The whole point of negotiating a free trade deal is to help the countries involved to prosper by giving consumers greater access to more goods and services at lower prices while improving fundamental economic efficiencies. The downside, almost always: in the pursuit of those greater efficiencies, some domestic workers and companies suffer.

Freer trade can easily be attacked with simplistic one-liners, and when many were hurting, many were willing to be beguiled by those one-liners. Competition means some win a lot, some win some, and some lose. Often, those least able to bear the losses are the losers, like low-skilled workers in older companies and industries.

The alternative to vibrant competition is stagnation and decline for all. The history on isolationism is extensive and consistent—it is a sure prescription for national decline. Nearly a century before, the United States had inflicted enormous pain on itself when it enacted the Smoot-Hawley tariffs, which, combined with the Federal Reserve's abysmal monetary policy, produced the Great Depression.

One moves either forward or backward. There's no standing still. Moving forward is hard work and always carries risk while moving backward requires little effort and always involves decay and failure. Were past trade deals the best the United States could do? Almost certainly not, but in most cases, a long expanse separates less than best from harmful. When it came to trade policy, Trump didn't clean up after the parade; he fed the elephants plenty and then told them to keep marching through the city.

ISIS Losing Ground, Winning the War

On June 28, the Select Committee on Benghazi released its final report.[613] The basic conclusions:

1. The State Department's bureaucratic morass had resulted in its ignoring Ambassador Stevens's repeated requests for increased security at the United States compound in Benghazi.
2. U.S. military forces were prepared to respond to the attack, but no specific order was given.
3. When National Security Council Director Susan Rice went on television Sunday morning to blame the episode on an inflammatory video, her comments "were met by shock and disbelief by State Department employees in Washington."

Bottom line: While Secretary of State Clinton bore the ultimate responsibility, the Committee's report failed to lay a glove on her while exposing Susan Rice as a political hack who defended the Administration with a politically convenient fiction.

The next day, ISIS struck again, this time at the Istanbul airport in Turkey, leading to the deaths of at least 43 people, with another 239 or so wounded. The attack, carried out by Russian, Uzbek, and Kyrgyz nationals, was believed to have been planned by ISIS leadership in Raqqa, Syria.[614] To one made a reference to an inflammatory video.

In response, Pres. Obama insisted ISIS was losing: "Beyond killing innocents, they are continuing to lose ground, unable to govern those areas they have taken over."[615] All three elements of that sentence were accurate, yet the statement was still false. ISIS *had* perfected the tactic of killing innocents. In some areas, like Iraq, ISIS was losing ground, though it was gaining ground in Syria and in Libya. ISIS had shown little capacity to govern, certainly not without income from terrorism, extortion, and blackmail, not to mention oil receipts when oil prices were high.

Yet to suggest ISIS was losing the war at this time was a stretch. ISIS's political tentacles continued to spread throughout North Africa.

Their ability to strike throughout the world was undiminished. Their ability to force their enemies (us) to respond and react was, if anything, expanding while their enemies' ability to strike at ISIS strategically was sorely limited.

ISIS operatives struck again two days later in Bangladesh. Gunmen stormed a restaurant in a posh neighborhood of Dhaka, killing 28 people. Shortly thereafter, ISIS agents exploded a truck bomb in Baghdad in a busy shopping district, killing at least 215 people.

True, its actions did not a caliphate make, but just as war is politics by other means, effective widespread terrorism is war by other means. As James Robbins wrote in *USA Today*, if these actions "are a sign ISIL is losing, I'd hate to see what winning looks like."[616]

Syria was a real pain in Barack Obama's neck. ISIS was using it as a base for launching attacks elsewhere. So Obama went hat in hand to Russian Pres. Putin to propose, and got, a new deal on Syria.[617] Under the deal, the United States would provide Russia with intelligence on al-Qaeda targets inside Russia. In exchange, Russia would agree to stop picking on America's few remaining rebel allies in Syria seeking to topple Syria's Pres. Assad. Note the previous deal Obama arranged with Putin also asked the Russians to stop picking on America's allies, a commitment Putin broke within hours.

Drip, Oh Huma!

On Monday, June 25, another 165 pages of Hillary Clinton's emails from her State Department tenure came out under court order, including nearly three dozen she'd earlier said were deleted.[618] In March of 2009, Clinton wrote to her aide, Huma Abedin, "I just realized I have no idea how my papers are treated at State. Who manages both my official and personal files? . . . I think we need to get on this ASAP to be sure we know and design the system we want."

Later in June, Abedin was deposed as part of the ongoing Freedom of Information Act investigation. In her sworn testimony, Abedin confirmed Clinton maintained her own email server account to maintain her personal privacy, which was certainly understandable.

What was not understandable, or legal, was for Clinton to keep her official email traffic secret from her own Department.

Toward week's end came news the Justice Department had asked U.S. District Court Judge Rudolph Contreras for a twenty-seven-month extension to comply with the request for emails from former State Department employees Huma Abedin, Cheryl Mills, Melanne Verveer, and Michael Fuchs.[619] Apparently, State had found some inconvenient truths in all those emails. The Obama Justice Department was more than happy to help protect the former secretary of state until long after the election.

Drip, Drip, Phoenix

It's happened to everybody. It's easy to understand. No big deal. You're sitting on the tarmac in your own little airplane at the Phoenix, Arizona, airport. An old friend just happens to be in Arizona, just happens to be in Phoenix, just happens to be at the airport. So your old friend who just happens to be in the neighborhood pops up to your plane for a quiet, friendly visit to talk about the grandkids. Sure.

That, at least, was Attorney General Loretta Lynch's story when she explained her little one-on-one with former Pres. Bill Clinton. Yes, that former president whose Foundation was currently under investigation by the FBI. Yes, that former president whose wife was running for President of the United States and whose decision to use her own email server while secretary of state was under investigation by the FBI. Yes, that FBI which was almost at that very moment "interviewing" Hillary Clinton for three and a half hours. Yes, that FBI, the chief investigative arm of the Justice Department. Sure.

Lynch and Clinton originally tried to keep the meeting under wraps. They failed, and the firestorm in the press was instantaneous. The firestorm within the FBI was even hotter. The immediate narrative was that Bill messed up again, and Lynch, in obliging him, did too.

The FBI was supposed to make a recommendation regarding indictments to the Justice Department. Senior Justice officials would review the recommendation then pass it along to the Attorney General for a final decision. After Lynch's meeting with Clinton, her position became wholly compromised. She spent the next day trying to contain the damage. She failed.

"I certainly wouldn't do it again because I think it has cast this shadow over what it should not, over what it will not touch. It's important to make clear that the meeting with Pres. Clinton does not have a bearing on how this matter will be reviewed and resolved."[620] Apparently, Loretta Lynch thinks the American people are just plain dumb.

Lynch spent the next two days explaining the extent to which she would or would not simply accept the FBI's recommendation.

Maybe the initial narrative was correct. Lynch and Clinton had just done something stupid. After all, Lynch was only the Attorney General of the United States, the chief law enforcement official in the country; and Bill Clinton had only suffered the most extensive experience with independent counsels, scandals, and investigations of anyone alive up to and including impeachment. Sure, they just messed up. And I have a bridge to sell you.

"Bill Clinton has made a mess. It was either out of foolish indifference or plain foolishness," piped Dan Balz in the Sunday *Washington Post*, page 2.[621] On page 19, Ruth Marcus roared, "Attorney General Loretta Lynch's tarmac conversation with Bill Clinton wasn't just stupid, although it certainly was that. It was a colossal misjudgment on both sides, most especially hers."[622]

Right. Just a big boo-boo. We all make mistakes, right?

Another possibility was that the FBI was nearing the end of its investigation into the email server and was interviewing Hillary, that Lynch knew where the investigation was going, and that Lynch was the most politically corrupt Attorney General in memory. Lynch had sent word to Bill they needed to meet, and so they did away from prying eyes, on the tarmac, in Phoenix. Marcus's article titled in the printed version, "When the system seems rigged," may have been closest to the truth.

Drip, Drip, Drip ... Walk

The hubbub over the Bill and Loretta tarmac chat quickly faded with the shocking news the FBI would not indict Hillary Clinton. FBI Director James Comey, apparently cut from the same political cloth as Attorney General Loretta Lynch, did his best to scold Clinton in lieu of indictments. As detailed by *CNN*, Comey's seven most damning criticisms of Clinton were as follows:

1. "Although we did not find clear evidence that Secretary Clinton or her colleagues intended to violate laws governing the handling of classified information, there is evidence that they were extremely careless in their handling of very sensitive, highly classified information."
2. "There is evidence to support a conclusion that any reasonable person in Secretary Clinton's position, or in the position of those with whom she was corresponding about those matters, should have known that an unclassified system was no place for that conversation."
3. "None of these emails should have been on any kind of unclassified system, but their presence is especially concerning because all of these emails were housed on unclassified personal servers not even supported by full-time security staff, like those found at agencies and departments of the U.S. Government—or even with a commercial email service like Gmail."
4. "Only a very small number of the emails containing classified information bore markings indicating the presence of classified information. But even if information is not marked 'classified' in an email, participants who know or should know that the subject matter is classified are still obligated to protect it."
5. "While not the focus of our investigation, we also developed evidence that the security culture of the State Department in general, and with respect to use of unclassified email

systems in particular, was generally lacking in the kind of care for classified information that is found elsewhere in the government."[623]

6. "We do assess that hostile actors gained access to the private commercial email accounts of people with whom Secretary Clinton was in regular contact from her personal account. We also assess that Secretary Clinton's use of a personal email domain was both known by a large number of people and readily apparent."

7. "She also used her personal email extensively while outside the United States, including sending and receiving work-related emails in the territory of sophisticated adversaries. Given that combination of factors, we assess it is possible that hostile actors gained access to Secretary Clinton's personal email account."

After all that, Comey decided charges weren't "appropriate." Comey explained, "Our investigation looked at whether there is evidence classified information was improperly stored or transmitted on that personal system, in violation of a Federal statute making it a felony to mishandle classified information either intentionally or in a grossly negligent way, or a second statute making it a misdemeanor to knowingly remove classified information from appropriate systems or storage facilities."[624]

As Michael Mukasey, a former U.S. Attorney General, observed in a *Wall Street Journal* op-ed the next day, "The felony statute requires no such evidence, and no such intent."[625] Nothing in the law refers to whether one *intended* to break the law or whether one *intended* to jeopardize the security of the nation or whether one *intended* to buy a double latte. The law centers on what you did. Through her actions, Hillary Clinton "improperly stored" and "transmitted" classified information on her personal system, and her actions were "extremely careless." Yet she walked because Director Comey ignored the law so she could.

On the other hand, if one wanted to play the "intent" game, consider that Clinton certainly intended to set up her own email server; she intended to violate Department rules regarding email communications on a nongovernmental account; she intended to send and receive classified emails. "She meant to do what she did. And she did it. Intentionally."[626]

Others didn't have the benefit of being the Democratic candidate for the presidency. As Judge Napolitano observed, two years prior, the Justice Department had prosecuted a young sailor for sending a selfie to his girlfriend. The problem? The selfie showed a submarine sonar screen in the background. The Justice Department had prosecuted a Marine Lieutenant in Afghanistan who inadvertently used his Gmail account instead of his secure government account to alert his superiors of al-Qaeda operatives nearby.[627] Yet somehow, Clinton walked because Comey could find a difference between "extreme carelessness" in his words and "gross negligence" in the words of the statute, and he could magically read an "intention" facet into the statute where none existed.

In short, Hillary Clinton had been a naughty girl, but she would skate because that's what usually happens with elites in America. It's just the way it is. The fix was in. Any doubt was erased shortly after Comey's announcement when the FBI admitted Clinton had not been under oath when deposed the previous Saturday. The FBI further acknowledged, by the by, there would be no transcripts of the interview because none had been made. Whitewash is such a lovely color. Apparently they bought it in bulk in FBI Director Comey's office.

Naturally, Clinton quickly went into "move on, nothing to see here" mode, and after the obligatory twenty-four-hour pause, the media largely accommodated her. Donald Trump didn't get the memo. He pounded "corrupt Hillary" over and over and to great effect because he wasn't making it up. He was just repeating what the vast majority of Americans already knew.

Speculation continued as to why Comey gave Clinton a pass. He had a reputation as a solid nonpolitical professional. The evidence as he himself had laid it out was so damning, Comey concocted his own reinterpretation of the law to find an escape chute for Clinton.

Comey's torture would continue a little while longer as he was called to Capitol Hill to explain himself. Time and again, Comey would confirm the known facts and insist they didn't support an indictment.

What we would not learn, and may never learn, is why Comey ducked. The simplest explanation, and Occam's Razor points in this direction, is that Comey was simply a political hack doing what hacks are called to do. He used his office to execute an unassailable coverup.

Charles Krauthammer offered a more generous interpretation. Hillary Clinton was the presumptive nominee of the Democratic Party and favored to win in November—unless she were indicted, in which case her campaign would evaporate in hours. Did the FBI Director really want to be the one to pull the plug on the presumptive nominee/likely next president's campaign, thereby dramatically changing the course of American political history so dramatically? If Clinton imploded and Trump won, and Trump did something crazy, would some of the blame fall on Comey and the FBI because he did his job? "Comey didn't want to be the man remembered as the man who irreversibly altered the course of American history."[628]

Never in modern times has an FBI Director faced such a momentous decision. Under Krauthammer's interpretation, Comey had a choice—fidelity to the judicial system and to the job he had sworn to do faithfully or duck an epic decision. He chose to duck. One can understand if he couldn't bring himself to do his job faithfully given those choices, but then the honorable thing would have been simply to resign. Comey chose to stay. He chose to duck. The race continued.

Another curiosity one can chalk up to serendipity, or luck good or bad, is how Pres. Obama and Hillary Clinton had arranged for the president to make his campaign debut with Clinton on Tuesday, July 5, the very day the FBI released its report.

The Media Meets Its Match

The mainstream media's reaction to Donald Trump ranged from fear to abject hatred, so they took every opportunity to twist Trump's words into pretzels to make him look bad. Not that Trump didn't provide good raw material, but how the media used it was often just plain wrong.

The heart of the media's mistake was they were up against someone who could more than fight back. He could take their pretzel and beat them with it. Truth be told, it was often fun to watch.

Part of Trump's advantage was he was very entertaining and he could go on at great length beating on them mercilessly, without notes, without a teleprompter, just his own Trumpian stream of consciousness. Ultimately, the media care most about ratings, and a Trump monologue meant ratings. So they covered many of these monologues at great length without commercial interruption. Trump could then dissect at length and in detail every blatant media misstatement and mischaracterization.

On July 5 in Raleigh, North Carolina, Trump gave such a monologue. One topic was fighting terrorism. He wandered into talking about Saddam Hussein, the former and now quite dead Iraqi President. Over and over, Trump called Hussein a "bad guy." There really wasn't much question Trump thought Hussein a bad guy, but then Trump added that Hussein was good at one thing—fighting terrorists in his own country.

"He was a bad guy—really bad guy. But you know what? He did well? He killed terrorists. He did that so good. They didn't read them rights. They didn't talk. They were terrorists. Over."[629]

Did the mainstream media go with the narrative that Trump thought Hussein was a "bad guy," or that he "once again expressed a preference for keeping dictators in power in the Middle East"?[630] The *Washington Post* picked up the thread the next day, referring to Trump's "regular praise for authoritarian governments and dictators."[631] Some in the media know no shame.

Trump didn't say anything suggesting a preference for dictators. In the course of repeatedly calling Saddam Hussein a "bad guy," he had just revisited Pres. Obama's down pillow fight against terrorists and made the simple point that a better tool was a baseball bat.

Trump would take the time, time and again, to dissect the press's unfair coverage, exposing them in detail in simple terms so everyone could see the truth. The American people's sense of the media's trustworthiness ranked right down there with their opinion of Hillary Clinton's veracity, so Trump's critique fell on fertile soil even among listeners who didn't like him.

In Ohio, Trump gave another lengthy monologue in which he dissected another case of stupid media bias. Trump's son, Eric, had overseen the work leading to the reopening of Trump International Golf Course in Aberdeen, Scotland, named by *Golfweek* as the best modern course in Britain and Ireland. The reopening had been long scheduled, and unfortunately the date coincided with Brexit—the UK referendum on escaping the European Union.

The initial press story was Trump in going to Scotland demonstrated his lack of seriousness in running for president. After all, who (besides Trump) runs for president by going on a vacation overseas? Trump explained he went to Scotland for a two-day trip to support his son.

During a press conference, in light of the dramatic fall in the British Pound following the Brexit vote, a reporter asked what the Pound's decline would do for Trump's golf course, to which Trump responded that if it made it cheaper for foreigners to come, it would be good for business. "Look, if the pound goes down, they're going to do more business."[632] A pretty obvious answer the press then twisted into Trump praising the Pound's decline.

The examples go on and on. Trump's campaign included a tweet with a six-pointed star. The press tried to paint that as anti-Semitic, neatly ignoring the many close Trump family members who were Jewish.

Most Americans already knew the press is often biased, lazy, unfair, and inaccurate. Many in the press are none of those things, and for these few we should be thankful, but Americans are not always so discriminating. Trump taught the American people a simple lesson: When the press attack me, don't believe them. See how many times they've attacked me and every time it was unfair and inaccurate? So don't believe them. It largely worked.

A Bad Night in Baton Rouge, in Minneapolis, in Dallas, in Chicago

A homeless man outside a convenience store in a sketchy neighborhood of Baton Rouge, Louisiana, approached a large black man asking for money.[633] The potential donor, Alton Sterling, showed the homeless man a gun and told him to get away. The homeless man called the cops. The cops showed up. Sterling died, much of which was captured on two separate police videos.

Thirty-seven-year-old Sterling was no angel. He'd fathered five children with multiple women and had never been married.[634] He'd been in and out of jail his whole life. He had a forty-six-page arrest history, absolutely none of which was relevant to the moment. Sterling was a citizen minding his own business when the police showed up.

Sterling was also a big man in a rough neighborhood. The two responding cops were big men, and they had reason to believe Sterling had a gun. The situation was dicey from the start. After some words, the cops rushed Sterling and wrestled him to the ground. One cop pulled his weapon, pointing it at Sterling's chest. The struggling continued. The cop's weapon went off at least six times. Sterling died. Sterling was black. The cops were white. It was all caught on tape. Again. Again. Again.

At about the same time in St. Anthony, just a few miles northwest of Minneapolis, Minnesota, a white police officer stopped a car with a broken taillight. The driver, Philando Castile, was black. When the officer approached the car, Castile properly alerted the officer to the fact he had a permit for a concealed weapon. When Castile reached inside his pocket to retrieve his wallet with driver's license and proof of insurance anticipating the officer's usual and proper demand, the officer shot Castile in the chest, the entire episode recorded by

Diamond Reynolds sitting in the right-hand seat, her four-year old daughter sitting in the backseat.[635]

Hours later in Dallas, a lone gunman executed a carefully planned ambush of Dallas police on duty to preserve the peace at a Black Lives Matter protest. The gunman used a rifle and handguns, had taken up an elevated sniping position, and opened fire, killing four officers immediately. Another later died at the hospital. Eleven more were wounded, some critically. Two civilian bystanders were also wounded, one of them a protestor. The gunman, Micah Johnson, was a former U.S. Army soldier sent home early from Afghanistan and discharged.[636] After an extensive negotiation, Johnson was killed by an explosive device. The dead cops were all white. Johnson was black. The press at first worked very hard not to mention these last two facts.

The nation seemed on the verge of an epidemic of violence not seen in decades. In Roswell, Georgia, a gunman in a passing vehicle shot at a police officer on patrol.[637] The cop, Officer Brian McKenzie, was uninjured. He was white. The shooter? Guess.

In Bristol, Tennessee, Lakeem Keon Scott, thirty-seven years old, started shooting indiscriminately at passing cars on a highway from a room in a Days Inn. One woman died, three were injured, including a police officer. You can guess the races of the individuals involved. Scott said he was angry at the police shootings, which certainly explains why he shot at a desk clerk at the Days Inn.[638]

A few days later, Pres. Obama flew to Dallas with Michelle to give what seemed like his 1,000[th] memorial speech. It clearly seemed that way to Obama too. He was flanked by George W. and Laura Bush. Obama gave a brilliant speech that captured well the sense of frustration and deep, deep down-in-the-marrow sadness the nation felt at these senseless killings, of the police officers, of the Charleston churchgoers, of Alton Sterling, and on and on.

This speech was almost as much about Obama's self-reflections and his recognizing his own inadequacies in helping the nation to a postracial future as it was about the events that had brought the attendees to Dallas. But Obama's address fit the moment perfectly.

The nation was hurting, and if Obama could channel the hurt through his own, well, that was more than OK.

By the third week of June in Chicago, 307 murders had been committed since New Year's. The police solved about one in five.[639] By summer, shootings were occurring at the rate of ten a day in the Windy City as the murder rate increased at double-digit rates for the third year in a row.[640]

The point of this little snapshot is simply that violence in America was rising rapidly and no one on the campaign trail wanted to talk about it. The bright light of hope in 2009 when Barack Obama took the oath of office had gone completely dark. Hatred, racism in all directions, and violence were winning. While hardly the most important aspect, this part of the nation's story also influenced the campaigns in a deep, uncomfortable way.

As violence escalated, naturally some political candidates would tap into the growing popular unease picking up the ancient and effective mantle of being the "law and order candidate." Clinton obviously couldn't, so naturally Donald Trump did. Calling Clinton the "secretary of the status quo," Trump declared, "We must maintain law and order at the highest level or we will cease to have a country."[641]

The 2016 campaign had seen more than its share of buffeting real world events, but most such didn't affect voters directly and so had at most a passing political consequence. Violence in our communities was of a whole different sort. People were afraid in their homes, on the streets, at events, and if Trump could channel this fear into a political force as he had done with anger over immigration policy, then Trump could become unstoppable. Not that he had any solutions, for as usual he had nary a one, but the first step to solving a problem is identifying the problem. So far, Trump was the only one identifying the problem and finding a proven political theme to address it.

Smarter Democrats immediately recognized the threat. Vice Pres. Joe Biden went on ABC News to talk up the Clinton candidacy for the watching party faithful and was asked about Trump's law and order candidate claim. Biden just flashed a grin and laughed.[642] There really wasn't anything he could say, so he tried to deflect the issue by mocking the concept. The fact was, however, on this issue, Trump held all the aces if he knew how to play them.

Drip, Drip, Drip, DOJ Referral

Hillary Clinton was under oath when she testified before Chairman Trey Gowdy's Benghazi investigation committee. She swore to tell the truth. She testified she never sent nor received on her personal email account material marked classified. She testified she had sent all her work-related emails to the State Department. When FBI Director Comey laid out his bill of particulars before ignoring them all, two of those particulars directly contradicted Clinton's sworn testimony. Ooops.

The purpose of having a witness swear to tell the truth is then if they lie during testimony they can go to jail for perjury. Clinton swore to tell the truth. Either she lied or she had quite a remarkable failure of memory for such a brilliant detail-oriented professional politician. The testimony was all on camera. The truth was in the FBI report. House Government Reform and Oversight Chairman Jason Chaffetz (R-UT) and House Judiciary Chairman Bob Goodlatte (R-VA) referred the matter to the U.S. Attorney for the District of Columbia. "The Department [of Justice] should investigate and determine whether to prosecute Secretary Clinton for violating statutes that prohibit perjury and false statements to Congress," the committee chairmen wrote.[643]

The Obama Administration's DOJ investigate Clinton after they'd done such a thorough job of protecting her? Fat chance. The elites, having reaffirmed their own special rules, weren't about to backtrack now.

The drip, drip, drip continued on other fronts, keeping Clinton in the news but always in a bad light. Attorney General Loretta Lynch testified on Capitol Hill for over four hours, presenting a most effective stonewall. Meanwhile, the Judicial Watch civil lawsuit remained very much in the news. The Clinton camp, having now ducked an indictment, went on the offensive, arguing in a legal filing on July 12 with U.S. District Court Judge Emmet Sullivan that every question Clinton might be asked was already answered and on the record.[644] Sullivan set a date for a hearing on the motion for July 18, assuring yet another opportunity for the public to be reminded of Clinton's many scandals.

VEEPING

The selection of the nominees settled, and Clinton's most immediate legal issues momentarily becalmed, the press quickly turned to the next major sporting event—choosing Veeps, vice presidential running mates. These sorts of political parlor games are great sport because them media can speculate ad nauseum without knowing a thing, and it's all good fun in the same way listening to sports radio prior to the NFL draft is good fun. For the most part, reporters haven't a clue what the deciders are thinking, but are rewarded with airtime for having firmly held opinions backed by vapor-thin arguments.

For both Trump and Clinton, the press went through a sort of Veep flavor-of-the-month fetish. At first, the list of names bandied about was very long, but then the Veepstakes settled on a few front-runners. New Jersey Gov. Chris Christie initially went to the front of the pack in the media narrative. Christie had endorsed Trump early on and had been a reliable sidekick. The downside to Christie was he had run for president and bombed, which was hardly a selling point, especially for the self-designated winner of all things, Donald Trump.

Bored with Christie, the media moved on to the ever-telegenic former Republican Speaker, Newt Gingrich. Gingrich had much going in his favor, including a firm understanding of Washington's political mechanics and an ability to speak flawlessly on just about any issue. He wouldn't do much for Trump, but he likely wouldn't hurt him. Trump's people probably started talking to those who'd worked with Gingrich for years. Even many of Gingrich's biggest fans understood this was a man who should never be one heartbeat away from the Oval Office. Next.

The next flavor of the month was Indiana Gov. Mike Pence. This was also ironic because Pence by 2014 had geared up to run for president himself but had been waylaid by a silly in-state hubbub. He was arguably the first (almost) candidate knocked out of the race, but since he'd not run, he didn't suffer the same problem as Christie of having run and failed. Pence was a nice, genial, solid option.

The Democratic side was much quieter. Virginia's Sen. Tim Kaine garnered much attention, and indeed he would make a solid choice for the general election. Aside from a reputation as having something of a thin skin, Kaine's problems were that Clinton was already doing well in Virginia and Kaine, as something of a moderate, would further inflame Bernie Sander's highly agitated army.

When the press tired of Kaine, they moved on to a possible Warren flirtation, then to Housing and Urban Development Secretary Julian Castro. Possibly because Clinton wasn't as entertaining as Trump, and partly because the Republican convention came first, the press seemed much more interested in Trump's pick at this point.

A Supreme Puts More Than a Toe over the Line

Donald Trump's candidacy, his person, and his statements drove many an establishment Republican crazy, but his effects on establishment Democrats were worse. Even believing Clinton would crush Trump in November, Supreme Court Justice Ruth Bader Ginsburg just couldn't contain her revulsion. A Supreme living in her cozy bubble can only take so much.

In an interview with the Associated Press, Ginsburg commented on the possibility of a Trump presidency: "I don't want to think about that possibility, but if it should be, then everything is up for grabs."[645]

Two days later, she gave an interview to the *New York Times* in which she said, "I can't imagine what the country would be—with Donald Trump as president." She added what her late husband might have said: "I guess it's time we move to New Zealand."

In case we didn't get the message, the next day she was at it again, calling Trump a "faker," adding, "He says whatever comes into his head at the moment. He really has an ego."

Trump responded by calling Ginsburg's comments "highly inappropriate." It really was rather humorous hearing a Supreme talk about somebody else's ego.

Every American has a right to speak his or her mind, but sometimes when one takes a job, part of the deal is that this right becomes circumscribed, out of either legal necessity or simple decorum. That Ginsburg detested Trump was no surprise. That she spoke out against him from her perch as a Supreme Court Justice was not only a surprise, it was indeed highly inappropriate.

Ginsburg's behavior was so over-the-line the *New York Times* felt compelled to suffer the double indignity of agreeing with Trump while chastising one of its own. A *Times* editorial led off with "Ruth Bader Ginsburg needs to drop the political punditry and the name calling." The Times concluded it was "baffling that Justice Ginsburg would choose to descend to his [Trump's] level and call her own commitment to impartiality into question. Washington is more than partisan enough without the spectacle of a Supreme Court Justice throwing herself into the mosh pit." Indeed.

The Midsummer Polls

Rasmussen released a poll of 1,000 likely voters taken July 5 showing Trump in the lead by 2 percentage points. Reuters/Ipsos released a poll of 1,345 registered voters taken July 2 through 6 and reported Clinton as having an 11-point lead. A 13-point swing between the two polls could only mean one thing—one or both of the polls was essentially crap.

No obvious solution existed to fix this problem beforehand. Even when polls are taken the day before voting occurs, one cannot be sure a poll result that differs substantially from the election result was bad, nor can one conclude that a poll result nailing an election result. Hint: respondents change their minds, and sometimes lie.

Remember the surprise Bernie Sanders laid on Hillary Clinton when he took Michigan.

The fallback solution in recent years had been to use the RealClearPolitics average of recent polls in hope the resulting larger total pool size would mitigate errors in individual polls. Maybe, but if all the pollsters were subject to the same limitations, or making the same errors, or being systematically misled by the respondents, then the RCP average was really no better than any of the individual polls.

What matters in an election is who comes out on top, which means the absolute levels matter. However, in the course of the campaign, what matters most sometimes is movement—who's rising and who's falling. Whatever errors are built into a given poll, or in all of them, those errors are likely constant over time, and so even though they may not give a reliable sense of the current standings, they probably do give a reliable sense of the direction of movement. They were moving profoundly against Clinton.

One poll had Clinton up by 5 points over Trump for weeks leading up to another taken June 20 and 21. A poll taken June 28 and 29 had Trump up by 4 points; a week later, he was up by 2. A week later, Trump led by 7 points.

Various state polls at this time likewise showed surprising Trump strength, but there seemed no obvious pattern. The polls shown below were primarily pre-Clinton nonindictment.

	Trump	Clinton	Poll
Florida	42	39	Quinnipiac
Virginia	37	44	Fox News
Pennsylvania	43	41	Quinnipiac
Ohio	41	41	Quinnipiac
Iowa	39	42	NBC/WSJ/Marist
Wisconsin	41	45	Marquette
Colorado	41	43	Gravis
Michigan	41	48	Gravis

Bottom line: Going into the Republican convention, Trump was doing surprisingly well. Justice Ginsburg's comments and the further erosion of Clinton's trustworthy factor following her near indictment all gave Trump some wind at his back. One other item in Trump's favor—Clinton had been spending tens of millions on television ads. Some were designed to make her look good while others were pure attack ads on Trump. Trump had spent hardly anything on advertising since wrapping up the nomination. Yet he essentially tied Clinton if the polls were to be believed. Clinton couldn't be feeling very good at this point.

CHAPTER 18
CONVENTIONAL WISDOM

Various Republican National Committee committees completed their preliminary work as Republicans began final preparations for their Cleveland convention. The Rules Committee reaffirmed the convention's rules but also crushed the last gasps of the "Never Trump" movement. The Platform Committee finished work on the party platform to the extent it mattered to Trump.

Thursday before the convention, word leaked Trump picked the genial Indiana Gov. Mike Pence to be his running mate. Talk about the odd couple! Pence had gone from being on no one's list to topper in a matter of days. Very few in the media who'd played the parlor game of Guess the Veep even had Pence on their radar until the very end, once again affirming these media exercises are for entertainment value only.

Pence excited no one, but he was rock solid and Trump didn't need a coagitator. He needed someone who understood the challenge and could be relied upon through thick and thin. His pick also helped calm the establishment types.

A suitable few moments after the Pence pick, the media shifted to speculating on Hillary Clinton's Veep pick, and in the meantime they could cover the Republican convention, which seemed likely to have all manner of entertainment value.

Trump was forced to delay the announcement of his Pence pick as a Tunisian immigrant named Mohamed Lahouaiej-Bouhlel had zigzagged his truck at high speed through the Promenade des Anglais in Nice, France, during a Bastille Day celebration.[646] At some point, he stopped the truck, jumped out, and started shooting, methodically killing more people for a final tally of 85. The French police shot him dead. The victims included two Americans, Sean Copeland of Lakeway, Texas, and his eleven-year-old son, Brodie.[647]

As French police continued their investigations, they learned Lahouaiej-Bouhlel had planned his attack for months and that some number of acquaintances either knew of his plans and said nothing or were active accomplices. ISIS supporters the world over celebrated.[648] Pres. Obama still insisted ISIS was losing.

How do you protect a major American city during a political convention? Cleveland would be on lockdown, but nobody attending the convention could feel completely safe from terrorists either domestic or imported.

One additional outcome out of the Nice attack worth noting—it showed Trump was right in skipping former House Speaker Newt Gingrich as Veep nominee. Immediately after the attack, Gingrich said, "Let me be as blunt as I can be. Western civilization is at war. We should frankly test every person here who is of a Muslim background, and if they believe in Sharia, they should be deported."[649]

American citizens of a certain belief should be deported. That's what he said, this former Speaker of "the People's House."

Many American citizens are Muslims. Likely some of these American citizens believe in Sharia law, the legal framework regulating public and private life in a strictly Muslim state. Gingrich was right that Western civilization was at war with a barbaric enemy and severe measures were needed, but Gingrich apparently had forgotten an old saying his parents had surely taught him: "You don't throw the baby out with the bathwater." Instead, Gingrich had resurrected the old saw from the Vietnam War, "You have to destroy a village to save the village."

The mainstream media immediately went into high apoplexy over Gingrich's comments. But before the media went too far in ostracizing Newt Gingrich, they might have recalled another old saying about he who lives in glass houses shouldn't throw stones. For years, the liberal elite at America's colleges and universities have pilloried conservative authors and pundits when they dared speak on campus.

Likewise, individuals who fell under the label of "climate change denier" had long suffered attacks and insults, but recently, Attorneys General from individual states had sought avenues by which they could prosecute climate change deniers, having banded together to form "AGs United for Clean Power."[650] Even the U.S. Attorney General Loretta Lynch acknowledged, "This matter has been discussed. We have received information about it and have referred it to the FBI."[651]

Whatever one's views about climate change, these actions by state and Federal law enforcement leaders attempting to stifle opinions contrary to their own should be universally condemned. They weren't. Soft fascism is alive and well in America and may be politely sipping a Chardonnay at a cocktail party near you.

THE TWO SHADES OF BIAS

In America, finding a member of the fourth estate not completely political would be harder than finding a needle in a haystack in a field of haystacks. This is perfectly understandable. Reporters and editors have personal opinions just like anybody else. Some schools of journalism may still teach the need for objective reporting, but if so, then these lessons are quickly overwhelmed with messages on social justice and the like, all teaching the importance of reporters using the medium to better society as they see it. *Fox News* recognized the absurdity, and so one of its catchphrases offered always with a straight face was "we report, you decide."

Translation: We report what we want you to know, and you decide you agree with us. Isn't that nice? At least Fox was somewhat honest about it.

Respects to the *New York Times*, the *Wall Street Journal*, and other wannabes, the *Washington Post* is the most important news organ in the country when it comes to political reporting because it is, as noted earlier, the hometown newspaper of American politics. The *Post* is as partisan as they come, but usually tries to be subtle about its bias until it fesses up and endorses a clean slate of Democrat candidates. That's fine. They're not fooling anybody.

That the *Post* would support Hillary Clinton to the hilt had been obvious since the start. Not that it wouldn't critique her when she varied from the *Post*'s preferred line, and not that it wouldn't report on developments in any one of her various scandals or court proceedings—they still need to sell newspapers, after all. Remember: if it bleeds, it leads. There's no such thing as too much sensationalism when presented tastefully.

Going into the Republican convention, the *Post*'s focus was all on Donald Trump. Center of the front page of the Sunday edition, July 17, appeared a typical picture of a mildly scowling Donald. To the left of the picture was a story about Mike Pence's troubles as Governor of Indiana. Page 4 offered two stories, one with a headline as to how Pence would have trouble with women's voters, the other a story as to how Trump, in introducing Pence, spent the whole time talking about himself.

The *Post* then carved out space on the middle of the op-ed page for a Jeb Bush piece on how Trump wasn't the future of America or the Republican Party. (Note to Jeb, you lost, son. Lost badly. Have the good sense to leave quietly, please.)

Entirely appropriately, the *Post* dedicated an entire insert to the Trump convention, but mostly about Trump, with nary a flattering story in the lot. Somehow, the *Post* didn't find a way to sneak in a snarky story on Trump in the Metro section, or Sports, but it did shoehorn a piece in the Business Section, front page, on "Trump's most enduring—and unbefitting—trait." Just to ensure the reader detested and feared Trump more than ISIS itself, the front page of the Outlook Section featured a side-profile picture of Trump's head. Trump's brain matter in the picture was illustrated by the image of a nuclear explosion mushroom cloud, obviously echoing Lyndon Johnson's famous TV ad against Barry Goldwater showing a nuclear mushroom cloud. The title of the piece? "Anger Management."

The *Post* would campaign for Clinton mostly subtly. Its attacks on Trump would be nonstop and about as subtle as, well, a nuclear explosion mushroom cloud.

A World in Tumult

Periodically, the whole world seems to spiral out of control. Thankfully, it doesn't happen too often, and the world has in the past always eventually been restored to a degree of normalcy. Perhaps the American people sensed the danger in much the same way deer sense a storm coming. Perhaps this more than anything explained the emergence of a candidate effusing bravado defying all the usual rules of politics because the world seemed to be spiraling again.

Following Ferguson, and Baltimore, and Charleston, and Orlando, and Baton Rouge came Baton Rouge again as an honorably discharged former U.S. Marine Corps Sergeant used the military skills honed in Iraq to plan and execute an ambush of Baton Rouge police, killing three, wounding four. The shooter, Gavin Long of Kansas City, Missouri, had come to Baton Rouge to celebrate his twenty-ninth birthday. He was black. Two of the dead cops, Matthew Gerald and Brad Garafola, were white; the third, Montrell Jackson, was black.

Domestic terrorism now had two distinct flavors: One involved radicalized Muslims associating themselves formally or informally with ISIS and targeting anyone not of their radical orientation. The other involved radicalized racists, both white and black, the latter now targeting the police. Underlying it all lay a peculiar acceptance of violence, but where had this acceptance come from, and what could be done about it? Pres. Obama gave another speech and ordered that once again the flags over the White House be flown at half-mast, a position that had become fairly common.

Events were spiraling just as badly internationally. The European Union tottered after the Brexit vote while pressures from Middle East immigration simply overwhelmed Europe's limp institutions. Radical Islamic terrorism erupted repeatedly, most recently in the Nice attack and increasingly in Germany. Europe also faced a Russian President, Vladimir Putin, who credibly threatened to resort to the kinds of military adventurism the likes of which Europe hadn't seen since the last World War.

As usual, the Middle East was in turmoil, though the sources of agitation changed over time. Significantly adding to the tensions, elements of the Turkish military attempted an old-style coup July 15. Though the coup was snuffed out, Pres. Erdogan went on a rampage of snuffing out his political opposition in government, in the military, in the media, and in the broader society. Turkish society and its own self-image had been rocked badly. As a member of NATO bordering on Russia, Turkey's troubles rebounded on the EU's defensive posture in a most unpleasant fashion.

In Asia, China's farcical "nine-dashed line" map, which China had used to seek to legitimize its claim almost to the entirety of the South China Sea, had properly been rejected by an international court in The Hague. The ruling was no surprise, but it was a source of embarrassment to China and its President, Xi Jinping. China's ongoing efforts to control the South China Sea would continue apace, neither sped up nor slowed as a result of The Hague decision, but China now had nothing but brute force, belligerence, and intimidation as its weapons. No one doubted it would use them as and where needed.

I Like, You Like

The candidacies of Donald Trump and Hillary Clinton were simply bizarre. Trump held the record as the most disliked national presidential candidate since such records were kept, but Clinton was catching up fast. Among registered voters, 57% had an unfavorable view of Clinton and 47% had a "strongly unfavorable" view of her.[652] This was ugly.

Of those polled who said they would likely vote for Clinton, 54% said they would do so to oppose Trump. Of those polled who said they would likely vote for Trump, 57% said they would do so to oppose Clinton. Hard to find better evidence that this would truly be a "lesser of two evils" election.

With two such extraordinary candidates, it was hard to know how voters would compare them. Would the old metrics be in any way relevant? There was no way to know until the voters decided.

One has to use the tools available. At the start of July, one poll examined voters' perceptions of the two candidates on specific issues. By an 8-point margin, voters thought Trump would do a better job with the economy than would Clinton.

Taxes are always a big issue for voters, but the importance soars when taxes seem the most painful—that is, when they're perceived as unusually high or when incomes are stagnant. Overall, the Federal tax burden at about 18% of GDP was normal for modern times, while State and local taxes crept up steadily. However, by 2016, incomes of middle-class families had remained fairly stagnant under Pres. Obama's policies, so taxes were another big concern. Trump led Clinton on tax policy by 7 points.

With so much domestic and international terrorism, Americans were naturally uneasy. Trucks ply streets across the country. After the attack in Nice, which truck was the next used in an attack? Crazies were shooting people, even ambushing police. Trump had donned the "law and order" mantle, and voters mostly approved, giving him a 6-point advantage over Clinton on fighting terrorism.

Clinton had some relative strengths, too, in voters' eyes. While she essentially tied Trump on dealing with immigration, she whopped him on foreign policy (18-point advantage) and race relations (30-point advantage). Who looked stronger on net? The candidate with the advantages on the economy and terrorism, or the candidate with advantages in foreign policy and race relations? Not a tough call, which reinforced the impression Trump was in a relatively strong position.

Unity

National political conventions have certain well-defined purposes, above all to create an event major enough to get voters excited about the candidate and to force party factions to set aside past grievances to unify to beat the other party's nominee. Neither party seemed likely to achieve this latter purpose in toto. Many senior Republicans were proving highly adept at finding excuses not to go to Cleveland.

Ohio Gov. John Kasich, still waging a quiet political guerrilla war with Trump, was nowhere to be found. Speaking at a breakfast, Trump's campaign manager, Paul Manafort, called Kasich "petulant" and said he was "embarrassing his party in Ohio."[653] The convention was being held in Cleveland, Ohio, after all.

Ohio Sen. Rob Portman was locked in a tough reelection campaign with former Ohio Gov. Ted Strickland. Yet unlike Kasich, Portman endorsed Trump. The press tried to drag Portman into the Manafort versus Kasich spat. Portman refused to fall for it. He would come to the convention. He would play the good soldier since he bore much of the credit or blame for convincing the party to hold its convention in Cleveland. And then he would go back to campaigning his own way. "I told them I was doing my own thing, you know."[654] Indeed we do.

Picking Mike Pence as his running mate definitely helped Trump convince many conservatives to support the ticket. Pence had thought through all the major issues carefully from a conservative perspective. If Trump would listen to him, and it was a big "if," then Pence could help guide The Donald on a wide variety of matters, conservatives told themselves, if not always confidently.

The second essential purpose of a convention is to sell the nominees to the voters. This required a spectacle grand enough the American people would want to watch, especially the acceptance speeches of the Veep candidate and the nominee. Very few people outside of Indiana knew Mike Pence. If circumstances dictated, could he be president? Americans wanted to know.

A third purpose is to have a big party. Yes, copious amounts of alcohol would flow. Many fine dinners would be had—however, not as many as usual. With so many elected Republicans staying away, and with Trump as the nominee, many of the law firms, corporations, and associations that would normally host such affairs just wouldn't bother in Cleveland.

Unlike the Republicans, the Democrats would have few problems with top elected officials missing their convention. The vast majority would rally to Clinton's flag. Even so, many of the law firms, corporations, and associations that skipped the Republican convention would skip the Democratic convention too. Many wanted to go to the Democratic convention, but one standing rule hadn't been rewritten yet—go to both or go to neither.

Republican Convention, First Night

The Never Trump movement fired its last blanks on the convention's first night. They attempted to force a roll call vote on the convention rules, hoping to allow pledged delegates to vote their consciences (i.e., not for Trump) on the first ballot regardless of the delegate's home state party rules. A roll call would go name by name through all 2,462 delegates present. The Never Trumpers believed they had the signatures to force a roll call vote, but they didn't have the gavel. He who has the gavel enforces and sometimes makes the rules. The presiding officer, Rep. Steve Womack of Arkansas, had the gavel. He declared the rules approved and tried to move on.

The hall erupted at this travesty, as indeed the Never Trumpers had followed the rules and were due a vote. Womack left the stage for a moment, came back, and called for a voice vote. Voices were raised both "yeah" and "nay" in what appeared to many to be roughly equal volumes. Womack declared "in the opinion of the chair the ayes have it," and the rules were adopted. The Never Trumpers never had a chance.

Spectacle is essential to a successful convention. To start the evening's entertainment, Donald Trump strode onstage and firmly announced the introduction of the "next First Lady of the United States," his wife, Melania. The statuesque former model then graced the stage to Queen's "We Are the Champions" in a beautiful off-white gown, addressing the audience in soft, calm tones in her East European accent.[655] Showbiz.

Melania Trump spoke, with no one much noticing what she said. Nobody remembers what's said at these events, so no slight to Melania. Just about every poignant phrase and every deep thought lurking in the consciousness of Man had been long since uttered many times.

Unfortunately for the campaign, one aspect of her talk stood out. She copied two extended elements directly from a 2008 Michelle Obama speech.[656]

The plagiarism became a major brouhaha, but was just a simple mistake. The story emerged that Melania had read some text she liked over the phone to the speechwriter, Meredith McIver, to give McIver a sense of direction. McIver dutifully jotted down the words and included them in the speech, not knowing Melania had read directly from a Michelle Obama speech. McIver offered to resign, but Donald learned the facts and so refused the resignation.

The Trump campaign's initial response to the plagiarism gaffe was just plain boneheaded. Campaigns make mistakes. Candidates make mistakes. When you're caught, admit it, promise to figure out what happened, and move on. When the plagiarism in Melania's speech was noted, did the campaign admit its mistake and promise to look into it? If they had, the issue would have quickly faded. Instead, the "scandal" lingered, initially casting something of a shadow on the convention. Instead of keeping the convention focused center stage, the campaign denied the plagiarism charge, even sending campaign chairman Paul Manafort out to do interviews in which he blamed the Clinton campaign for the whole dustup.[657]

Next up was Sen. Jeff Sessions of Alabama, who despite his strong southern accent gave a rousing speech even Bostonians could understand. Then came former New York City Mayor, Rudy Giuliani, who provided his usual rousing full-frontal assault on Pres. Obama's national security policies.

Just to remind everyone how Hillary Clinton had failed the people under her charge in Benghazi, the next to speak was Pat Smith, the mother of Benghazi victim Sean Smith. One conventioneer toward the front held up a large sign saying "Hillary for Prison." Smith, weeping at the loss of her son, pointed to the sign, declaring, "That's right. She deserves to be in prison." This was not George H. W. Bush's "kinder, gentler" Republican Party.

Republicans, Days Two and Three

Day 2 centered on the nomination voting itself. Surprise—Donald Trump won. No longer the "presumptive" nominee, he was now the nominee.

Day 2 also featured remarks by many of the Trump kids. Melania had not tried in her remarks to fill in some of the human-side blanks of her life with The Donald. She'd spoken of loftier things. For Trump's kids, the story was a simple one—my Dad is a really great Dad. Donald Trump may be a real SOB to the rest of the world, but if family closeness matters to a voter, then Trump's kids had for a few hours at least suggested Donald can't be all bad.

Day 3 of the Republican convention should have been a relatively routine affair. Mike Pence would give a nice uplifting, aspirational speech accepting the Veep nomination. Other notables would give nice speeches alternatively hammering Obama and Clinton or praising America while calling for party unity. Then everybody would go to their evening soirees and prepare for the big day of Trump's speech.

It should have been relatively routine, but this being 2016, of course it wasn't. Ted Cruz couldn't follow the script. He gave his speech in prime time, but never endorsed the nominee. He congratulated Trump for winning the nomination. He didn't say anything bad about Trump, but Cruz didn't endorse Trump, pointedly urging Republicans to "vote their conscience." As the boos for Cruz reached a crescendo, there he stood in all his arrogance, defiant to the end.[658]

In response, Trump dismissed Cruz as one would a fleck of lint, tweeting, "Wow, Ted Cruz got booed off the stage, didn't honor his pledge! I saw his speech two hours early, but let him speak anyway. No big deal!"[659]

This was a first-term senator who'd accomplished exactly doodley-squat in the Senate and who'd lost the race for the nomination. This was the man who had vowed at the outset he would support the Republican nominee and who when later pressed on the matter acknowledged he'd vowed to support the nominee and so that is what he would do. Yet here he was prime time at the Republican convention, pointedly not endorsing the nominee.

If Cruz couldn't endorse Trump contrary to his repeated previous commitment, then the adult approach would be to just stay away as so many had done. John Kasich had earlier promised to support the nominee, yet Kasich hadn't endorsed Trump and had just stayed away from the convention held in his own state. For all those who'd committed to supporting the party's nominee and who just couldn't bring themselves to endorse Trump, how they reconciled their promises with their actions was up to them—as long as they, like Kasich, stayed away.

But here's the deal: As the nominee, this was Trump's big bash. If you speak at the bash as a former candidate, then you have to endorse the nominee. To do otherwise, to behave as did Ted Cruz, just proved that all those people were right who had concluded as did George W. Bush: "I just don't like the guy." As Peggy Noonan observed, "What a jerk."[660]

As Ted Cruz finished speaking, Heidi Cruz stood in the audience near former Virginia Attorney General Ken Cuccinelli. Cuccinelli so feared for Heidi Cruz's person he had to ward off members of his own delegation to whisk her to safety. "People behind her were getting very ugly and physically approaching her. It was not a pretty situation."[661]

In the end, Mike Pence may have had the toughest job, following on Ted Cruz, the first man or woman to be booed off the stage while speaking at a party convention in modern memory. Pence delivered. He gave a nice speech including at least one memorable line. In referring to Trump, "He is a man known for a large personality, a colorful style, and lots of personality. So I think he was just looking for some balance on the ticket."⁶⁶² Nicely played, Governor.

One other item from Day 3 worth noting: The extent of animus toward Hillary Clinton had reached frightening levels. In addition to chants for Mike Pence and Donald Trump came the refrains repeated louder and louder: "Jail her" and "Send her to prison." The politics of personal destruction, building now for decades, boiled over. Convention attendees didn't simply want to defeat Clinton. They wanted to send her to jail, or truth be told, had she stepped onto the stage in Cleveland, she might have been torn limb from limb.

Republican Convention, Day Four

Topic no. 1 throughout the early hours of Day 4 continued to be Ted Cruz. He was criticized by the Texas Delegation, by former candidates, by former supporters.

Once the evening's entertainment was under way, Trump's stamp on the convention was quickly restored. For example, Silicon Valley billionaire Peter Thiel wowed the crowd in prime time. What's so special about a billionaire praising another billionaire? Thiel was a Silicon Valley darling who'd cofounded PayPal and was the first outside investor in Facebook. That made him high-tech royalty. Far more important, Thiel was openly gay. "I am proud to be gay. I am proud to be Republican."⁶⁶³

This should not have been a big deal, but it was for the Republican Party, and it sent a signal to the LGBT community. Most encouraging of all, Thiel was met not by sniggers and scowls, but by thunderous applause.⁶⁶⁴

Thiel was followed by the marvelously entertaining Tom Barrack, another real estate billionaire out of Los Angeles. Barrack entertained by telling stories and riffing at length about his relationship with Donald Trump, all without notes or a teleprompter.

Ivanka Trump then came on to introduce her dad. Ivanka had become an especially trusted adviser in the course of the campaign. *CNN* called her his "composed, well-spoken daughter—a powerful figure in her own right."⁶⁶⁵ In watching Ivanka and imagining a Trump Administration, one could easily imagine a Nancy Reagan–like force.

While spectacle and warm-ups were useful, only Donald Trump could sell the American people on Donald Trump. He went on for seventy-five minutes trying to do just that. This was no "Morning in America" speech. The bottom line: America was in trouble, and Trump was the only man in the universe who could fix it.

"This is the legacy of Hillary Clinton: death, destruction, terrorism and weakness," Trump boomed.⁶⁶⁶ He claimed the nomination having become the megaphone for the nation's angry and frustrated masses. This he intended to remain: "I am your voice." The specific words in his overly long address didn't matter as much as the tone he set for his campaign going forward. As Peggy Noonan observed, the speech was "not an eloquent speech, not lofty, very plain and blunt . . . with a certain grimness."⁶⁶⁷

As painted by Trump, this campaign would be about the status quo in Clinton offering four more years of Obamian malaise versus taking a risk on an unproven and highly disruptive agent of change in Donald Trump. If Americans wanted to upend the applecart, they knew who to call.

As usual, Trump received a tidy bump in the polls following the Republican convention. Clinton maintained a firm 4-point lead prior to the convention. Following the Cleveland confab, Trump had a 3- to 4-point lead. The media was all agog at how Trump had taken the lead, conveniently if momentarily forgetting Clinton was about to have her coronation at which she would receive a compensatory bounce.

Remember the two goals for the convention—put on a momentum-building spectacle and unite the party. On the first, Trump succeeded marvelously; on the second, not so much. At the convention, the party failed to unite "not because the party had poor leadership or because the nominee didn't know how to do it, though both are true. More killingly, it failed to unite because it didn't *want* to."⁶⁶⁸

Much of the wealthy and well-connected simply stayed away. Many who traveled to Cleveland still didn't know what to make of Trump, but concluded a combination of the Supreme Court, Mike Pence, Trump's inescapable reality, and "what the heck" allowed many establishment elites to conclude they would work toward Trump's victory and hope for the best. For their part, Trump's real supporters had no particular love for the high and mighty wrestling with their consciences. Cleveland, a blue-collar working-class city, had hosted a no-violence blue-collar working-class political convention. It just happened to be the Republican Party's convention.

Running with a Kaine

Apparently aware of leaks within the campaign, Hillary Clinton texted her announcement of Virginia Sen. Tim Kaine to be her running mate late Friday evening. Tim Kaine then texted his delight. If her goal was to minimize immediate attention, then her timing and method were spot-on. However, usually when running for office, the goal is to maximize as much positive "free media" as possible.

Kaine was a former Mayor, former Governor of Virginia, and former head of the Democratic National Committee, so he was well-known in the Democratic Party if not to the rest of the country. The issue for Clinton—Kaine had over the years earned a reputation as something of a moderate. If she intended to tack to the right, then Kaine fit the bill perfectly, but Clinton now had to face the Democratic convention in Philadelphia where a lot of fidgety, angry former Far Left Bernie Sanders voters were waiting in ambush. Picking Tim Kaine looked more like salt than salve in the wound if Clinton had Sanders's voters in mind.

As the country got to know the two Veep nominees, Tim Kaine and Mike Pence, it was likely voters would prefer to jettison Trump and Clinton altogether and pick between Kaine and Pence for president. Both men were qualified, experienced, genial, and, well, presidential.

The timing of the Kaine announcement appeared even more peculiar as the world fixated on the release by WikiLeaks of almost 20,000 emails previously hacked, possibly by the Russian government, from the Democratic National Committee (DNC) email database. WikiLeaks called it "part one of our Hillary leaks series."[669] Many of these emails detailed issues involving major Democratic Party donors and communications between party officials and Clinton allies on how the party could derail Bernie Sanders's campaign.

One email written May 5 to DNC Communications Director Luis Miranda from "marshall@dnc.org" suggested the party could help Clinton by raising questions about Sanders's faith. "It might make no difference, but for KY and WVA can we get someone to ask his belief. Does he believe in a God? He had skated on saying he had a Jewish heritage. I think I read he is an atheist. This could make several points difference with my peeps. My Southern Baptist peeps would draw a big difference between a Jew and an atheist."

The *Washington Post* tried to bury the story on page A8, but Sanders's voters saw it and understood the confirmation of Sanders's oft-repeated claim "the game is rigged." What would Sanders's voters do at the convention with this information? What would they do come November?

Now, the Democrats

The intended Democratic narrative for the weekend between the conventions was to highlight the many dysfunctionalities of the Republican convention and to anticipate the smooth running of the Democratic convention. To be sure, the Republican convention hadn't gone particularly smoothly. The Melania plagiarism episode and the multiple Never Trump agitations at the outset were followed by over-the-top calls to "lock her up," the "her" being Hillary Clinton and the justification being the Comey-whitewashed email scandal. Then came the real jewel of dysfunction—Ted Cruz's failure to endorse Trump when Cruz had center stage.

No, the Republican convention hadn't been a smooth affair, but even as Democratic operatives shifted into full titter, they faced their own problems. Problem one was Tim Kaine. The Far Left believed that Bernie Sanders's performance winning twenty-one states earned them some say in the Veep selection. Hillary Clinton thought otherwise. The Far Left was displeased and immediately began to plot as to how they could use convention rules to block Kaine's nomination. Apparently, the Far Left agitators hadn't learned from the Republican Never Trumpers that he who has the gavel makes the rules. Clinton had the gavel. Kaine's opponents had no chance.

The friendly media, starting with the *Washington Post*, immediately began running stories pointing out all the ways Tim Kaine had always been a strong liberal.[670] If the *Post* had run those stories when Kaine first ran for his U.S. Senate seat, then he would likely have been aghast and might have lost; now, new circumstances, new stories, all good.

On many issues, such as gun control and labor law, Kaine's liberal standing was strong. On other issues, his views were problematic. Kaine supported the Trans-Pacific Partnership, for example. As a strong Catholic, Kaine also opposed abortion. Even so, the AFL-CIO and the leading abortion advocacy group both confirmed they got the joke, immediately endorsing Kaine.[671] Sometimes the discipline within the Democratic Party is impressive.

As the opposition and the media combed through the first batch of DNC emails released by WikiLeaks, each new item threw a gasoline-soaked branch onto a burning bonfire of anger. During the campaign, Sanders complained repeatedly as to how the DNC was helping Clinton. Few doubted him at the time, but concrete proof was lacking. The emails provided damning proof, over and over and over.

The first batch of DNC emails contained a long list of ugly items.[672] Ugly, because they showed a truth about American politics the system's defenders long sought to hide. Items like numerous emails discussing how best to reward major party donors. How about a roundtable dinner discussion with Pres. Obama? Numerous emails complained about Sanders and what DNC operatives could do to torpedo his campaign. Then there were the more run-of-the-mill uglies, from planning dirty tricks to pull on Donald Trump to one about a DNC member killing horses for insurance money.

Debbie Wasserman Schultz served as Chair of the DNC. She was scheduled to Chair the convention, including gaveling it to start and conclude. Few claimed she did a good job, but Pres. Obama as de facto head of the party made no effort to remove her, and Clinton apparently decided (a) at least the DNC was working on her behalf during the primaries and (b) getting rid of Wasserman Schultz would raise a distracting stink Clinton didn't need.[673]

Then the email scandal blew up, and the party needed a sacrificial lamb. Good-bye, Debbie. She decided not to gavel the convention to order on Monday and would resign her position upon the convention's conclusion.

How bad did it get? On the convention's first day, Wasserman Schultz spoke to her own state delegation and was booed off the stage, escorted from the room for her own safety.[674] The Clinton people and the DNC were smart to react quickly in canning Wasserman Schultz, but the response proved inadequate.

The next Sunday, Clinton and Kaine went on CBS's *60 Minutes* for an interview with Scott Pelley. They both did very well, Kaine showing a good sense of humor, Clinton clearly in command from start to finish, though to be sure Pelley's questions all qualified for slow-pitch softball.

The interviews were taped, of course, giving CBS News ample opportunity to edit out any unpleasantries. One segment hitting the cutting-room floor but somehow leaked to the Web included Pelley asking Clinton about the hacked DNC emails.[675] Clinton insisted she "doesn't know anything about these emails," which was as preposterous a statement as she'd ever made. No wonder the American people didn't believe she tells the truth, and no wonder CBS News cut this from the show.

Now that the WikiLeaks outpouring had created a stink, the FBI announced it was investigating the hacking of the DNC email server, but why didn't the FBI investigate the hack when it was first announced? Perhaps hoping it would all go away? The FBI's involvement also played into attempts by the Clinton campaign to confuse the issue by asserting the Russian Government had done the hacking and sent the emails to WikiLeaks. Even if true, the Russians didn't write or send the emails. They just allegedly hacked the DNC system. DNC staff sent and received the emails.

Of course, Wasserman Schultz and her DNC colleagues only did what the president and the party establishment wanted, but somebody had to take the fall, and after all, nobody liked Wasserman Schultz that much, anyway. Donna Brazile, a seasoned and very capable Democratic operative/TV talking head, was tabbed to replace Debbie. While the dustup over the emails was unwelcome, and even more the timing, replacing Wasserman Schultz with Brazile likely was a net plus for the Clinton campaign.

However, the lovely narrative of competent Democrats versus dysfunctional Republicans was now in tatters, with more to come.

MICHELLE O HAS HER SAY

First Lady Michelle Obama highlighted the first night of the Democratic convention. The choice was inspired. Michelle Obama was very well liked by the American people and basically adored by Clinton and Sanders supporters alike. Michelle's words, but even more her presence, acted as a balm to many angry wounds and raw nerves on display on the convention floor. "Don't let anyone tell you this country isn't great, that somehow we need to make it great again. Because this, right now, is the greatest country on earth."[676]

Then she delivered the punch line: "And as my daughters prepare to set out in the world, I want a leader who is worthy of that truth, a leader who is worthy of my girls' promise, and all our kids' promise, a leader who will be guided every day by the love and hope and impossibly big dreams that we all have for our children."

Amen.

Michelle provided the balm, but it didn't last. The wounds were too deep. Bernie Sanders had launched a revolutionary movement even he could no longer control, but he honestly tried, beginning with a rousing speech Monday night following Michelle Obama and continuing all the next day. In response to booing from the California delegation reacting to Sanders's calls for party unity, Sanders responded, "Our job is to do two things—to defeat Donald Trump and to elect Hillary Clinton. It is easy to boo, but it is harder to look your kids in the face if we are living under a Trump presidency."[677]

Many enlistees in Sanders's revolution weren't listening. His supporters staged a sit-in in the media tent. A wave of his revolutionaries attempted to scale an eight-foot wall protecting the convention compound. Many were arrested. An Israeli flag was burned to cheers of "long live the intifada." Through Day 2 of the Democratic convention, the hard-core Sanders revolutionaries weren't giving up, nor did they succeed in either materially disturbing the convention or drawing positive attention to themselves.

Do Democrats Even Know Islamic Terrorism Exists?

On Day 1 of the Democratic convention, sixty-one people spoke. Terrorism, ISIS, al-Qaeda, and the Taliban were mentioned not once.[678]

The day before the convention opened, a twenty-seven-year-old Syrian refugee wearing a suicide vest and proclaiming allegiance to ISIS killed himself and injured twelve others at a music festival in Ansbach, Germany.[679] Over the previous weekend, Islamic terrorists had committed multiple assaults across Germany, including a machete attack by a twenty-one-year-old Syrian refugee on a pregnant woman in Reutlingen.[680] The German government tried but largely failed to tamp down the story that Germany and Angela Merkel had allowed an invasion of terrorists who now threatened every burg and stadt.

The next day, two men went into a Catholic church in Normandy, France, during morning mass.[681] They approached the priest, eighty-four-year-old Jacques Hamel. While one man filmed, the other slit the priest's throat, beheading him. They were shot dead by French police as they emerged from the church shouting "Allahu Ahkbar." Both men had long histories with the French police.

The Democrats desperately wanted to establish a theme of working to make a good nation better to contrast with Donald Trump's "all Hell is breaking loose" narrative. This was a classic juxtaposition: those in power arguing things are good and getting better and those on the outside emphasizing doom and gloom. The Democrats had by far the harder task because the anemic economic recovery had passed many voters by, and race relations were nearing a modern low and threatening to get out of hand entirely. America had already seen its share of Islamic terrorist attacks. Altogether ignoring these many fears and concerns would not serve the Democrats well.

BILL TAKES THE SHOW

Though his first few outings on the campaign stump had featured multiple stumbles, low energy, and misstatements, going into the Philadelphia convention, former Pres. Bill Clinton had clearly gotten his old mojo back. He still connected on a personal level with an audience as well as any politician in America, and he still loved being center stage.

Bill had one problem he couldn't fix, though. The hopeful center-left "third way" Democratic Party he'd created and led as president had been replaced by an angry Far Left Party that hated many of Bill's foremost achievements, like fiscal restraint, financial market reform, and the North American Free Trade Agreement.

On the second night of the convention, none of those disagreements mattered much. As he took the stage, Bill Clinton again in his element, he delivered. A subnarrative of the convention, just as it had been for the Republicans, was to paint the human side of the nominee. Bill tried to splash color and warmth over the well-known cold and calculating Hillary caricature. He mostly succeeded, albeit temporarily.

Bill also sought to emphasize how Hillary Clinton would be "the best darn change-maker" they could ask for, by implication in contrast not just to Trump but also to the mostly status quo–maintaining Barack Obama.⁶⁸² This posed a major problem Bill only partially resolved. Hillary Clinton, Queen of the Democratic establishment and Mother Superior of the Church of Incremental Change, was now to take the gavel of the radical Agent of Change Caucus and worthy successor to the previously designated Agent of Change who in fact in the minds of the audience had changed very little.

Bill Clinton emphasized how Hillary had fought for this or that or the other thing, all of which was surely true. Hillary Clinton was passionate about policy, and some of those things, like support for New York after 9/11 and Obamacare, had come to pass, but she was never the one making it happen.

Many policymakers and politicians fight for their issues. At the end of the day, to be an agent of change, one has to be the one actually changing something. Remember how Sen. Feinstein was tripped up in a friendly interview with the *San Francisco Chronicle* when asked to name some of Clinton's accomplishments—and couldn't, even after searching on Google. Fighting for issues, like racking up frequent flyer miles as secretary of state, are not accomplishments.

TIDBITS OFF THE FLOOR

When the roll was taken and she had officially claimed enough delegates for the nomination, Bernie Sanders went to the floor in a carefully choreographed display to move Hillary Clinton be declared the Democratic nominee for president by acclamation. This was an important symbolic act, signaling to the party the war was over and it was now time to defeat Donald Trump and the only way to do that was to elect Hillary Clinton.

Sanders played his role very well, but this was Sanders's last act as a Democrat. Shortly thereafter, he announced his return to the U.S. Senate as an Independent and officially separate from the Democratic Party and the Senate's Democratic caucus. What Sanders really did was show he was a phony, after all. Not a phony socialist, but a phony Democrat, or at best a Democrat of convenience, just as

Clinton had suggested prior to the New York primary. Sanders had simultaneously told his Democratic supporters to rally to Clinton and that he'd duped them. Of course, he got away with it.

Another side development off the convention floor provided a reminder that even the best at a profession sometimes make stupid mistakes. Many Americans remain enamored of the idea of a citizen legislator. It is a fine ideal in a time when issues are simple and government's tasks few and well-defined. Today, the citizen legislator is an amateur doomed to failure, as many a Tea Party congressman quickly demonstrated.

Politics is a profession. Some take it seriously, and some are very good at it. Every senator, congressman, governor, state legislator, and mayor is prone to the delusion they are good at politics because they got elected. More often, their election only meant they were either luckier or less inept than their opposition.

Some, however, are good at their profession. Virginia Gov. Terry McAuliffe was very good at his profession. McAuliffe was also one of the Clintons' oldest, closest advisers. Despite being what some might call a lifelong political hack, he'd been elected Governor of Virginia in part because he was very good at his business and in part because Republicans had nominated one of the least electable candidates in modern Virginia history.

Yet despite all his experience and talent, McAuliffe made a major booboo during the convention. The issue was the Trans-Pacific Partnership (TPP), an agreement negotiated by the Obama Administration with Pacific Rim nations in part to facilitate international trade and in part as a foundational element in a political alliance to contain China if such were needed down the road. Hillary Clinton had vigorously pushed for the TPP as secretary of state and, indeed, Bill and Hillary had long championed the importance of international trade to economic prosperity and international political relations.

Thanks in large part to the economy's anemic performance and the stagnation felt by large blocs of the American middle class, international trade agreements were intensely unpopular among nearly all Democrats and among many Republicans. So of course, candidate Clinton flip-flopped and came out against the TPP, but many anti-TPP Democrats didn't really believe her. They believed she'd sell them out in a New York minute once she was in the White House.

Enter Terry McAuliffe: "Once the election's over, and we sit down on trade, people understand a couple things we want to fix on it, but going forward, we got to build a global economy."[683] Does that mean she would reverse her position once in office? "Yes. Listen, she was in support of it. There were specific things in it she wanted fixed."

Headline: Clinton confidant confirms Hillary Clinton is lying to you. A firestorm erupted, and within twenty-four hours McAuliffe backtracked, saying the "agreement would only go forward if the changes that she wants are implemented and that everyone is in agreement."[684] This would have helped if McAuliffe, or the campaign, could describe what those changes would be and why they were important. They didn't, or couldn't.

So McAuliffe tried again: "Hillary is against TPP and is always gonna stay against TPP. Let me be crystal clear about that." Almost reminds one of Richard Nixon saying, "I am not a crook."

The point isn't that Clinton would flip-flop on TPP. The point isn't that McAuliffe had screwed up and then flip-flopped himself. Terry McAuliffe was still one of the most professional politicians in America. The point is that even the best sometimes screw up on the big stage.

Day 3 Oratorical Notables

Day 3 featured some of the party's brightest luminaries. Pres. Obama, Veep nominee Tim Kaine, and Vice Pres. Joe Biden all gave solid speeches, the main theme of which distilled down to "We're the good guys, Donald Trump, and the Republicans are the bad guys. Get it?"

As befitting the party in the White House, Obama et al. also tried hard to paint a picture of a thriving, prospering America that nevertheless had some pesky problems to solve. It was a lovely, uplifting portrait, but recent history had shown that a great many voters weren't buying it. Of course, Trump and the Republicans were painting a dark picture only they could change, but even Sanders and Clinton during the campaign had explained the need for their own policies by complaining how America's middle class had been left behind by the Obama recovery. Switching art forms, Obama et al. offered a lovely string quartet playing a Brahms lullaby while much of the country, and especially much of the Party base, was in the mood for some deep, dark, loud heavy metal.

Perhaps the most noteworthy aspect of the headliners was Pres. Obama's amazing self-absorption. This was supposed to be about Hillary Clinton and the handoff, where Obama began the process of, he hoped, handing over the baton of leadership, governing, and the Democratic Party to Clinton. Yet during his speech, Obama referred to himself 117 times, surely a new league record.[685]

The undercard speakers tried to hit the same basic themes, but their purposes differed from the mainliners. For the undercard, convention speeches are auditions. Give a great speech, connect with the audience, and your political career gets a major boost. What most of the speakers in both campaigns failed to grasp is that a great speech doesn't start with the speechwriter. It starts with having something worth saying and then talking to the audience sincerely, humbly, with conviction and passion, as though imparting that something worth saying is the most important thing in the world; Michelle Obama's speech, for example.

Instead of the risky and difficult task of connecting with the audience, convention speeches become a contest to see who can deliver the best one-liner, as though the speakers were really trying out at the local comedy improv. It's not that the speakers had nothing to say, but they had little more than the basic narrative, delivered over and over.

Vice Pres. Joe Biden got in what was probably the best one-liner because it provided the Democrats with their best attack line on Trump. Attacking Trump for being unqualified, or unpleasant, or anything else on their long list, just played Trump's game and would provide little benefit to the Democrats just as it had provided little benefit for the sixteen Republicans Trump had dispatched during the primary season. Biden found what could be the one attack that would matter: "He is trying to tell us he cares about the middle class. Give me a break. This is a bunch of malarkey."

During his convention speech, Donald Trump declared to all the disenfranchised in America, "I am your voice." This was like Bill Clinton speaking to a convent of nuns-in-training proclaiming himself the patron saint of chastity and fidelity. It seemed absurd, and the best response wasn't to argue the facts but to state equally emphatically, "This is a bunch of malarkey." Would she be able to grab that line and run with it? Sadly for Clinton, no.

Hillary's Big Moment

Hillary Clinton strode confidently onto center stage to accept the Democratic Party's nomination. Clinton was famous for hiding her true feelings and carefully choreographing her mannerisms in public. For this one night, she failed. For this one night, she radiated, her joy and delight could not be contained. She was in her moment and played it perfectly. Strictly from a human perspective, it was beautiful to watch.

She delivered her acceptance speech with force and determination, calling on America's better spirits against Trump's drumbeat of fear and doom. She insisted she was the only one who could unify the country to solve America's problems, to make America even greater than it was. Her speech had no surprising dimensions or exceptional phrases because as noted earlier, these had pretty much all been plumbed years before, but she did have a few good lines for which credit is due. For example, in referring to Trump's preferred means of communication, "A man you can bait with a tweet is not a man we can trust with nuclear weapons."[686] Not exactly a logical progression, but clever nonetheless.

It has often been said of Hillary Clinton she was a workhorse, not a show horse, and there's certainly truth in that. So Clinton tried to give this trait a little humor and remind the voters why this was a good thing when she said, "I sweat the details."

For all the clever lines and superb production, the Democratic convention in Philadelphia still concluded with two big conundrums Democrats had yet to resolve. They were smart to focus on all that was good and right in America since, good or bad, they owned it politically, but to millions of Americans and especially to millions of Democratic voters, things weren't all right in America, and a few pretty speeches weren't going to convince them otherwise. Worse, Barack Obama owned these results, and Clinton was inescapably running as more of the same of what had produced these unsatisfactory results.

The second conundrum was perhaps even harder to solve. The American people really did want a leader who could at least credibly attempt to unify the country, bring people together, reduce the partisan tensions, and solve problems. Hillary Clinton insisted she was that person. Upon a moment's reflection, most Americans not already totally sold on Clinton had to think following Joe Biden's exclamation, "This is a bunch of malarkey."

Hillary Clinton, one of the most divisive individuals in modern American politics and continually so over the past quarter century, was now going to be a unifying president? Hillary Clinton, whose veracity was accepted by almost no one? Hillary Clinton, for whom scandal was always close behind? Would she be more divisive than Barack Obama? That was hard to imagine as he had set the bar very high, but Clinton as unifier was as preposterous as Donald Trump winning the Nobel Peace Prize just for succeeding Barack Obama.

Last, it must not go without mention that America had now nominated first a black man and now a woman to lead one of the nation's two leading political parties. The black man had been elected twice to the highest office in the land. Hillary Clinton had a very good chance of winning the upcoming election. If only one thing was going right in America, it was that America was still maturing as a nation. In some respects, at least, artificial barriers of gender, sexual orientation, and racial discrimination were falling not merely in word, but also in deed. This, if nothing else, provided grounds for hope.

CHAPTER 19
THE AUGUST LULL THAT WASN'T

Donald Trump loved the spotlight. He didn't mind sharing the spotlight . . . but keep it short. He was also an agent of chaos and disruption. Combine those two characteristics and you explain Trump's comment on Day 3 of the Democratic convention: "Russia, if you're listening, I hope you can find the 30,000 emails that are missing," referring to the missing emails from Hillary Clinton's private server.[687]

Trump's comment was outrageous and nearly universally condemned. All improprieties aside, and with Trump that was a common caveat, his statement was brilliant, completely off-footing the Clinton campaign, which aside from a bit of humor was of course the whole point.

Trump had drawn attention to a Clinton scandal in which the overwhelming opinion agreed she'd been "recklessly careless" at the very least and really should have been indicted but had gotten a pass from a rigged judicial system compliments of the FBI Director himself. Trump had also deflected the issue of whether Russian Pres. Putin, in hacking the personal email server of Clinton campaign Chairman John Podesta and releasing the emails to WikiLeaks, had sought to help his reported good buddy, Donald Trump.

Then when Trump declared the next day he'd just been sarcastic, he sprang the trap.[688] Of course, Trump had just been sarcastic.

Remember the essential element of politics—staying in character. Did anyone really think he was asking Russia to track down missing emails? If Clinton had played the sarcastic card, then she'd have been accused of flip-flopping, and her defense would have fallen flat because Americans expect her to flip-flop and dissemble. Trump was just being his usual sarcastic, disruptive, smart-ass self and so his "sarcastic" defense made perfect sense. His enemies fell for it, lock, stock, and barrel.

The episode also revealed Mike Pence hadn't quite figured this all out yet, issuing a statement that if Russia or others "are interfering in our elections, I can assure you both parties and the U.S. Government will ensure there are serious consequences."[689] One could almost hear Vlad Putin's guffaw all the way from Moscow. Of more immediate importance, Pence had signed up to ride the elephant in the circus. Where the elephant went, Pence was going to go, whether Mikey liked it or not. That's the deal. You buys yer ticket, you takes yer ride. Better figure it out, Mikey.

THE WRATH OF KHAN

After the conventions, the nation seemed quite ready for a little break from all the politics and nastiness. The dog days of August beckoned, and the Rio Olympics were on tap. A short respite before the Labor Day to Election Day sprint seemed just the ticket. Not.

Actually, Hillary Clinton would have accommodated the request, spending her time more on raising money and campaigning wherever opportunity offered, but Donald Trump just couldn't help himself. So he got into a fight with the parents of a soldier killed in Iraq.

Before recounting the tale, some context—specifically, Trump's military service. Donald Trump grew up in the Vietnam War era and received repeated college deferrals from the draft. He then received a medical deferment because he had bone spurs in his heels, spurs which magically disappeared some years thereafter.

During the Democratic convention, Khizr Khan spoke about his son, U.S. Army Captain Humayun Khan, who died at his base outside Baquba, Iraq, trying to stop a suicide bomber and in so doing protected the lives of his own men.[690] The Khans had immigrated to America from Pakistan in 1980. Captain Khan died a hero in the service of his adopted country, attempting to protect the men in his unit, posthumously earning a Bronze Star and Purple Heart. Mr. Khan was none too pleased with Mr. Trump, and he let him know it. "You have sacrificed nothing and no one." Mr. Khan "electrified" the audience and hit Trump where it hurt.

A normal person would have responded by ignoring Mr. Khan, if possible, or by expressing sorrow and appreciation at Mr. Khan's profound sacrifice, thanking all who served, and politely adding that as a matter of policy, they would simply have to disagree. A normal person would have let the matter pass as quickly as possible. Not Donald Trump.

Instead, Trump got into a prolonged very public pissing match with a man who'd lost his Bronze Star–awarded son. First, Trump observed that Ghazala Khan stood by her husband during his convention speech and said nary a word. Trump suggested, "She had nothing to say. Maybe she wasn't allowed to have anything to say."[691] Mrs. Khan later indicated she was still too overcome at the loss of her son to manage to say anything. No one, not a heartless boar, doubted her.

Mr. Khan went on to question whether Trump had ever read the United States Constitution and insisted Trump had a "dark heart."

Indeed, Mr. Khan went overboard in his attacks, mockingly holding up a copy of the Constitution during his convention speech. While the resulting applause was loud, the stunt was petty and diminished Khan. It didn't matter, though, because he gained instant Teflon through Trump's responses. Trump complained the attacks were "unfair" and full of "inaccuracies." He then went on to equate the sacrifice of a son in military service to his own work. "I think I've made a lot of sacrifices. I work very, very hard . . . I think I've made a lot of sacrifices."[692]

No one questioned Trump worked hard. Certainly, Trump had to "sacrifice" in earning his billions, in much the same way every mother or father who goes to work day in and day out "sacrifices" for their family, though almost always for less of a payday than Trump enjoyed. However, to equate the sacrifices of commerce with those of military service, and most especially with parents losing a child or a child losing a mother or father in military service, was breathtaking. The Khans had "laid so costly a sacrifice on the altar of freedom" as Abraham Lincoln once famously wrote to a Mrs. Bixby of Boston, Massachusetts.[693] Donald Trump had sacrificed a tee time.

Naturally, Hillary Clinton and Tim Kaine and the mainstream media were quick to pounce on Trump's latest outrage. Republican leaders were just as quick to disassociate themselves from his comments, mostly without attacking Trump directly.

Trump just couldn't let it go. On August 2, he went on Bill O'Reilly's *Fox News* show and did little more than complain about *CNN* and to whine as to how he had been "viciously" attacked by Mr. Khan, a phrase he used at least three times. Was he supposed to be attacked and not respond? Trump wondered aloud.

The media then tried to emphasize how evil Trump was by observing that attacks on politicians are par for the course, but attacking an ordinary citizen, and a Gold Star American family at that, was just not at all appropriate. Curiously, Trump and his allies never made the fairly obvious observation that Mr. Khan, by speaking at the Democratic convention, had abandoned the usual protections accorded private citizens outside the ring of politics. Khan was now in the thick of the political conflict and could not expect to be treated as a noncombatant. Bronze Star or no, Mr. Khan was fair game, to a point.

During their convention, Republicans had repeatedly attacked Pres. Obama and Hillary Clinton. Donald Trump attacked both Obama and Clinton again and again. Of course, the Democrats attacked Trump during their convention and thereafter, and if their attacks were vicious, then by this standard, many of the Republican attacks had been vicious. As Mike Huckabee had said a few days prior, "If you can't stand the sight of your own blood, don't run for office."[694]

The episode highlighted a few basic realities of Trump's world. For example, Trump still had a very thin skin. He also was willing to pick a fight with anyone, and he delighted in counterpunching. He had no reliable internal control in this regard, nor any sense of proportion or propriety when responding. All that mattered to Trump was that he won the argument in his own mind.

Surely, this would be the moment for Trump's long-awaited implosion, picking a fight with the parents of a fallen soldier and then letting the fight linger for days; surely, but maybe not. Remember, this was the candidate who earlier picked a very public fight with the Pope. In that instance, however, the Pope had been both in the wrong and on thin ice. He had been in the wrong by questioning Trump's faith, and on thin ice in that he appeared to dismiss many Americans' concerns over out-of-control immigration.

Many Americans seemed uncertain what they thought about Trump's central issue in this little dustup—the intentional and thorough vetting of Muslims coming from countries where terrorism was rampant. Those attending the Democratic convention who cheered Mr. Khan so boisterously were perhaps not quite capturing the mainstream view in America on this point, and this gave Trump some firmer ground on which to battle.

On the other hand, one would expect Trump to be way behind the eight ball in criticizing a man who'd lost his son in military service and in equating the "sacrifices" he'd suffered in his hard work earning billions building golf resorts to the sacrifices of veterans who served and the fallen who came home draped by a flag. It was very hard to see how this could, or should, turn out well for Trump.

Trump's troubles continued for days. One of his strengths was his tendency toward simple, clear declarative sentences. Unfortunately for Trump, they often directly contradicted each other. For example, on multiple occasions, Trump claimed a relationship with Russian Pres. Putin:

- In November of 2013, Trump told MSNBC reporter Thomas Roberts, "I do have a relationship with [Putin]."[695]
- In a May 2014 address to the National Press Club, "I was in Moscow recently and I spoke directly and indirectly with President Putin, who couldn't have been nicer."[696]
- During the Fox Business News debate November 2015, "As far as the Ukraine goes . . . if Putin wants to go in . . . and I got to know him very well because we were both on *60 Minutes*."[697]

But then on Sunday, August 1, he insisted "I have no relationship with Putin" and "I have never spoken to him on the phone."[698]

Trump playing fast and loose with basic facts was hardly news. The mainstream media had created a new cottage industry exposing Trump's nearly daily misstatements and false claims, but this was different. Donald Trump and Hillary Clinton had one thing in common: they were both intensely disliked. Clinton also had a firm reputation as someone who could lie repeatedly, directly looking into the camera and without a whiff of qualm. For example, on July 31 during a *Fox News* interview, Clinton said the FBI Director "said my answers were truthful, and what I've said is consistent with what I've told the American people" regarding her email server and classified information.[699] She said it entirely with a straight face, which must have taken practice.

Attempting to characterize Clinton's statement, the New Jersey *Star-Ledger* opined, "You could call it a blatant lie, which is closer to the truth." In contrast to Clinton, Trump had been attacked for many character flaws including ignoring reality, but flat-out lying Clinton-style had not previously been one of them. Trump was at serious risk of matching Clinton in this respect and possibly crippling his reputation as someone who would "tell it like it is." Fortunately for Trump, this episode too was lost in the broiling river of bizarre events.

Trump took another hit August 2. In a formal press event with the visiting President of Singapore, Lee Hsien Loong, Pres. Obama "launched a blistering attack on Donald Trump, saying he was 'woefully unprepared' to be president."[700] He further called Trump "unfit to be president."[701] Obama posed a series of rhetorical questions scorning Trump's comments about Muslims, questions such as, "Are we going to start treating Muslims differently? Are we going to start subjecting them to special surveillance?"[702] Obama then dropped the hammer: "Do Republican officials actually agree with this?"

Obama could have chosen other venues to charge into the political arena to vent his spleen, but he chose a formal, diplomatic event to announce not only to the American people but also to the world his profound distaste for and disagreement with Donald Trump. Obama had raised his beef with Trump from the political to a moral plane and called on the Community of Man to render judgment as to who was right.

As to the substance of the charges, many would agree Trump was "unfit to be president." Trump could act the calm, sober leader Americans had come to expect, as he demonstrated in his late August meeting and press conference with the Mexican President; but in public at least, Trump was more naturally a carnival barker.

However, for Barack Obama to call Trump "unprepared" was another matter. Recall when Obama ran for the presidency he was a senator with a total of two years' service following a limited career as a local community activist. Many might agree Trump was woefully unprepared, but just about anyone *but* Barack Obama could argue the point.

Just to complete the chaos of the moment, at the same time as he was battling Mr. Khan, the vast biases in the mainstream press, Pres. Obama, and in his spare time the Clinton/Kaine ticket, Trump let it be known he "wasn't there yet" in endorsing either John McCain or Paul Ryan in their respective primary races.[703] This was not a meaningless gesture.

Ryan was in something of a primary battle with businessman Paul Nehlen. Nehlen had no major state endorsements and almost no money, but he had Trump's implicit backing and he had the precedent of a similar unknown in Dave Brat knocking off House Majority Leader Eric Cantor in Virginia four years prior.

John McCain in Arizona was locked in an even tougher battle with state senator and medical doctor Kelli Ward. As of early August, polls showed Ward and McCain tied at 41%.[704] Whereas McCain was an occasional conservative, Ward was more in line with Tea Party activists and expressed great comfort with Donald Trump at the top of the ticket.[705]

Donald Trump did receive one odd bit of good news at about this time. Apparently, French Pres. François Hollande wasn't a fan. Hollande said Trump "makes you want to retch."[706] Once again, it appeared Barack Obama and the French President had a lot in common. This was good news for Trump in two respects. First, Americans don't generally much care what French politicians think, and second, nearly 90% of his own fellow citizens disapproved of Pres. Hollande's performance.[707] Being attacked by a French disaster presiding over a country under repeated attack by mostly homegrown Islamic terrorists couldn't be all bad.

For all its ugliness, the Trump-Khan spat didn't seem to make much difference in the polls Otherwise, both campaign teams seemed to have real challenges in the weeks ahead. For the Clinton team, the nomination

- left Democrats still laboring with the nation's worst top-tier retail politician;
- didn't transform Clinton's screechy, wooden-speaking style;
- didn't change her high unfavorability rating;
- didn't transform her into a person that voters trusted to tell the truth;

- left many of Sanders's revolutionaries fuming and determined to be a pain in the neck;
- didn't resolve Americans' widespread displeasure with the country's direction under Pres. Obama, and she was promising more of the same; and
- didn't eliminate the lingering worries about the next WikiLeaks email dump or the next disturbance from any of the many ongoing investigations involving Hillary and the Clinton Foundation.

In addition, the Clinton team had to deal with the reality that many in the Democratic base responded better to Trump's nebulous nationalistic neoisolationism than they did to Clinton's questionable pseudoprogressivism.

Trump's team had its own problems with which to wrestle. These started with Trump's thin skin. Beyond skin issues, Trump, it appeared

- would have to construct a new political coalition as it appeared much of the conservative base would not vote for him even if it meant voting for a write-in candidate;
- would never have a strong, consistent relationship with down-ballot candidates; and
- could not rely on the RNC the way Clinton could the DNC because so much of the Republican Party establishment was still in some combination of "hold your nose" and "Hell no" mode.

Trump and Clinton both enjoyed important strengths as well. Clinton was disciplined, experienced, and tireless; but her message of a bright and happy future didn't jive with the anger, fear, and frustration felt in much of the nation, including large segments of the Democratic base. Her sales pitch distilled down to, "I'm Hillary, that's Trump, he's terrible, so pick me." In contrast, Trump's whole persona reflected anger and frustration, and an almost militant insistence

America would do better if only because Trump wanted it that way, "trust me."

Catching Up with the Polls

The first two polls following the Democratic convention showed Clinton/Kaine with a 5- to 6-point lead. Clinton had gone into the conventions with a slight lead.

Other polls bear noting at August's start, if only as curiosities. For example, polls taken between July 25 and August 1 regarding Pres. Obama's job approval ranged between -14 to +11. RealClearPolitics averaged the lot and came up with +3.2, but really with such disparate results, one had to wonder whether these polls had any validity.

In contrast, Congress's job approval rating remained fairly steady—in the tank. It ranged from -61 to -74. These polls were peculiar in their own way since Congress was an institution, not an individual, and the polling didn't differentiate between House and Senate or between Republican and Democrat. Americans generally liked their own senators and congressmen as evidenced by high reelection rates, but Americans apparently generally disliked everybody else's senators and congressmen.

Another common poll asked whether the country is heading in the right or wrong direction. These results again had a familiar theme, but a wide range from -37 to -50. It was almost as though the right direction/wrong direction question averaged the approval ratings of the president and the Congress.

Trump's Very Bad Week

When Donald Trump accepted the Republican nomination, he knew he had prevailed in a tough campaign against sixteen opponents, many of them strong candidates in their own right. He also knew he would face a long, hard, ugly one-hundred-day slog against Hillary Clinton, Pres. Obama, the mainstream media, and even some strongly resisting elements in the Republican Party. In the first week of August, Trump faced his toughest opponents—his big mouth and bigger ego.

Faced with his ill-advised comments toward Mr. Khan of Democratic convention fame, Trump apparently recognized he needed to change the topic, so he got into a pissing match with leading national Republicans like Sen. Kelly Ayotte of New Hampshire, Sen. John McCain, and House Speaker Paul Ryan over endorsements. Bad move, as Republicans began to wonder publicly if (a) Trump had set out to blow up his own campaign so they needed to review the party rules about replacing a nominee or (b) Trump would continue his self-destructive ways and they needed to determine how best to put him in political isolation to save as much of the party's candidates in November as possible.

Trump's behavior was not that different from what he'd done since he first launched his campaign, but there was one big difference—he was now the nominee. He might really become President of the United States. Would the voters hold him to a higher standard as nominee than before? Apparently, they would, and this meant big problems for Trump. Without doing anything more than sitting back and watching Trump self-destruct, Clinton jumped out to a 7-point lead nationwide, with some polls giving her a double-digit lead, and some states like Colorado seemed to be slipping away from Trump beyond recovery.

Trump needed to regain the initiative, shifting the national discussion away from Mr. Khan and the endorsement dustup. He started with the obvious step of publicly endorsing everyone he'd previously said he might not, including Paul Ryan and John McCain. This was good news to his supporters and even those Republicans hoping to be able to support Trump. It meant he could at least recognize the most obvious steps.

Then he did it again. Trump thought he was taking a positive step in announcing his cabal of economic advisers, but in fact, the names released were perplexing. The announcement amounted to another self-inflicted wound. What was wrong? His council of economic advisers was dominated by billionaire businessmen who knew almost nothing of economic policy. There was Harold Hamm, the oil industry billionaire, and Steven Mnuchin, a hedge fund CEO, real estate investor Tom Barrack of Republican convention fame, and other major business leaders.[708] Amazingly accomplished people in their own right, if one were setting up a mega–real estate development corporation, these people would make outstanding partners. But as economic advisers of a political campaign for President of the United States, this group didn't add up.

Trump had a couple of credible people in his group, such as David Malpass, a very strong and experienced Wall Street economist and commentator. Malpass was also one of the few with Washington government experience.

Another was Steve Moore, longtime hard-core conservative and economic policy kibitzer. Moore was an excellent writer and an effective guest on television shows, but above all, he had an uncanny ability to convince people who knew little economics that he, in fact, knew a lot.

Trump continued attempting to right the ship with what the campaign billed as a "major speech" on economic policy delivered at the Detroit Economic Club on Monday, August 8. The campaign did all it could to draw attention to the speech, even sending out surrogates like former New York City Mayor Rudy Giuliani to the Sunday talk shows.

So what did Trump say? Not much that was new, and even less that was coherent. The centerpiece was Trump's version of tax reform built around reducing income tax rates substantially and more in line with the sensible starting point released weeks earlier by Ways and Means Committee Chairman Kevin Brady (R-TX) and the House Republicans.

The rest of Trump's economic plan featured more of the isolationist, retrograde trade policies guaranteed to ensure the United States steadily slid into also-ran status in the global economy. Trump insisted he would withdraw from the Trans-Pacific Partnership, which didn't matter much at this point as Clinton also opposed the TPP and it had little chance of making it through the Congress. He also said he'd renegotiate the North American Free Trade Agreement, though to what purpose he never explained. He would label China a currency manipulator (which was true once but hadn't been true for years) and would generally be a lot tougher on our trading partners. There's nothing wrong with negotiating tough trade deals, as long as in the end you get the deal done and increased trade follows.

How Bad Did It Get?

Nothing he did seemed to help. The central problem had become Donald Trump himself. The election had become a referendum about Trump, his person, his character, his qualifications, not about Hillary Clinton as Pres. Obama's successor. Increasingly, traditional Republican Party members decided they just couldn't take it anymore. Maine's Sen. Susan Collins, a respected moderate Republican, penned an op-ed in the *Washington Post* to declare she would not vote for Trump. "My conclusion about Trump's unsuitability for office is based on his disregard for the precept of treating others with respect, an idea that should transcend politics."[709]

That Trump wasn't Collins's cup of tea was hardly surprising. Susan Collins was, in short, everything one would expect from a Maine Senator; and that did not include brash, arrogant, insulting, and disrespectful. Likely Collins would have opposed Trump even if Trump carbon-copied Collins's policy preferences item by item.

Trump might be no better than Clinton on balance in all other respects, but the promise of appointing the right people to the Supreme Court was reason enough to support him, many conservatives consoled. As nonfan George Will wrote mockingly of those who clung to this list, "stickler that he is for consistency and predictability, he [Trump] will stick to this script written by strangers."[710] Sure, he would. (Well, he did.)

With so much going wrong for Trump, the *Washington Post* decided it was safe to give Hillary Clinton a little grief. Clinton was running as Obama's successor. Obama's economy had steadily created jobs for seven years, but even so, it still hadn't returned to full employment, a mark it should have hit around 2011 or so. Clinton bragged she would create lots of new "good-paying jobs," just as she did in economically depressed upstate New York when she was senator. The trouble was, "there is little evidence that her economic development programs had a substantial impact on upstate employment."[711]

The point isn't that Clinton made a promise she had no chance of keeping. Senators generally don't have that kind of power over a state's economy, a fact Clinton knew full well. The *WaPo* story was fair and well-written. The point is the story never would have seen the light of day had Trump been up 7 points rather than down 7.

THE TIGER'S STRIPES

Hillary Clinton stayed in character with iron discipline. Trump likewise stayed in character. If incendiary and outrageous got you the nomination, you stick with it, like suggesting in a *CNN* interview that Pres. Obama was the "founder" of ISIS.[712]

Even sympathetic voices like Hugh Hewitt found this one hard to swallow, so in an interview, Hewitt tried to build Trump a bridge to firmer ground, suggesting Trump meant "he [Obama] created a vacuum, he lost the peace."

"No," Trump objected, "I mean he's the founder of ISIS." Trump elaborated, "The way he [Obama] got out of Iraq that that was the founding of ISIS."

In typical Trumpian fashion, he made the assertion about Obama being the founder of ISIS on August 10 and doubled down on it on the eleventh as his interview with Hewitt made clear. Then when he realized he'd gone too far, he backtracked August 12 with the tweet "Ratings challenged @CNN reports so seriously that I call President Obama (and Clinton) 'the founder' of ISIS, & MVP. THEY DON'T GET SARCASM?" Trump wasn't being sarcastic when he made the initial charge, and he wasn't being sarcastic with Hugh Hewitt. He was just being Trump.

Even before his Obama-as-ISIS-founder comments, large numbers of Republicans were throwing in the towel on Trump. More than seventy senior Republican leaders, including many former senators, congressmen, and RNC operatives, signed a letter to RNC head Reince Priebus urging the RNC to abandon Trump altogether and focus all its resources on House and Senate contests.

> We believe that Donald Trump's divisiveness, recklessness, incompetence, and record-breaking unpopularity risk turning this election into a Democratic landslide, and only the immediate shift of all available RNC resources to vulnerable Senate and House races will prevent the GOP from drowning with a Trump-emblazoned anchor around its neck.[713]

Early in the primary season, the Democratic establishment anguished over Clinton's campaign. It was lackluster. It lacked a theme beyond Clinton's inevitability. It was beset with investigations and scandals. Once she'd dispatched Sanders, gotten a pass from the FBI, taken the nomination, and watched Trump be Trump, the establishment started feeling a lot better about itself—just as the Republican establishment began a new phase of panic.

Hillary's Returns

Earlier in the campaign, Donald Trump was pressed, and refused, to release his tax returns because, he observed, they were under IRS audit. Being under audit meant the final resolution was not yet known and so the returns were subject to change. It also meant the IRS already had the information.

With the caveat Trump and the IRS hadn't settled all their outstanding matters, there really was no reason not to release his most recent returns. Odder still, the IRS wasn't auditing Trump on his returns since time began, only the most recent years. So why couldn't he release the earlier returns not under audit? No answer.

Seeking to pressure Trump, Bill and Hillary Clinton released their 2015 returns, and what a window into their world this provided. In 2014, these renowned champions of the working people made $28 million. In 2015, they made "only" $10.6 million.[714] They also donated $1 million to the Clinton Family Foundation, a different entity from the famous Clinton Foundation. Somehow the press missed the fact the Clinton Family Foundation paid its Vice Chair, who just happened to be Chelsea Clinton, an annual salary of $600,000. In effect, the parents took a charitable donation deduction for paying their own daughter. Cute, but so typically Clinton.

Tim Kaine also released his tax return. The Kaines made $313,441 in 2105, about one-thirtieth what the Clintons had made in their down year.[715]

What Campaigns in Trouble Do

They shake things up.

When the Trump campaign first struggled, Trump brought in a tough, seasoned pro in Paul Manafort. It worked for a while despite tensions with the previous honcho, Corey Lewandowski. When it next struggled, Trump canned Lewandowski, sort of, and put Manafort on top, sort of. All of these were "sort of" changes because even as he signed on with *CNN*, Lewandowski also remained a shadowy Trump campaign adviser who often spoke directly to Trump and reportedly spiced his commentary with unpleasantries directed at Manafort.

The Trump campaign was again struggling badly. Trump was especially angry about talk inside the campaign and out, suggesting what his senior campaign team needed was to stick a bit in Trump's mouth to control him, to force Trump to become a more consistently presidential candidate. They were wrong, and Trump knew it. He had to run as Trump, warts and all. As Trump said, "You know, I am who I am. I don't want to change. I don't want to pivot. You have to be you."[716]

Campaign struggling and the candidate angry, it was time for another shake-up, this time demoting Manafort and bringing in

Breitbart's CEO, Stephen Bannon.[717] Bannon, a former banker, was known for his fierce antiestablishment views and so could fit right in to the Trump mind-set. Bannon also knew modern communications methods and social media. However, Bannon had nearly zero political experience.

Picking Bannon reaffirmed one of Trump's revealed management traits, a trait previously revealed with his announced cadre of economic advisers. Trump wanted people around him who were smart, loyal, and almost perfectly aligned with his own views. So far, so good, but what didn't matter to Trump was whether the individual had any knowledge or experience for the job.

Ah, but with Trump, the rule often permits the exception. Along with Bannon, Trump also brought on Kellyanne Conway. Conway was a bona fide conservative political communications and polling expert with extensive national experience. She also seemed to quickly earn Trump's confidence.

Drip, Drip, Drip—FBI Dump

Hillary Clinton had gone so long without a scandals story ding she may have thought she was in the clear. Not.

On August 16, the FBI did its own data dump, this time releasing to the Congress a "number of documents" relating to the emails, including notes from when the FBI investigators interviewed Clinton not under oath and without producing a transcript.[718]

Much of the material was labeled "Secret." Even diligent, antagonistic, cherry-picking staff would need some time to wade through the new information, but this news had to send a chill down the collective spines of the Clinton campaign. Clinton's antagonists did identify some essentials quickly. "Hillary Clinton is out there saying there's not very much sensitive information in there, that she didn't trade in sensitive classified information. It's so sensitive and so classified that even I as the chairman of the [House] Oversight Committee don't have the high level of clearance to see what's in those materials," Utah's Jason Chaffetz told MSNBC's *Morning Joe*.[719]

Paul Manafort's demotion in favor of the Bannon/Conway tag team arose out of Donald Trump's frustrations that he was being handled. Handled in the sense his team wanted him to play by their rules, not exactly traditional rules of campaigning, but more traditional than Trump preferred. This was like caging a grown lion used to going where and when he pleased. Given a strong cage, you might do it with a lion, but he would never be happy. You couldn't do it with Trump for long. He owned the zoo.

In late August, we had Trump unleashed. This made the Republican establishment even more nervous. It also made Clinton even more nervous because Trump would lay her every falsehood and mistake out in full view in ways most politicians wouldn't dare. Of course, it also gave Clinton grounds for hope because the odds of Trump's own self-destruction rose substantially. For their part, the media were almost delirious with delight. Trump would provide so much raw material for outrage and biting commentary they couldn't believe their good luck.

Trump unleashed also had a surprising effect on Trump. It made him more relaxed and finally able to admit when he made a mistake. He actually apologized. "Sometimes, in the heat of debate, and speaking on a multitude of issues, you don't choose the right words and you say the wrong thing. I have done that, and believe it or not, I regret it. I do regret it particularly when it caused personal pain."[720]

The media were delighted to report on Trump's admission, but they forgot they were helping to portray Trump as something less of a monster than the narrative the media preferred. It also meant reporting the second part of Trump's revelation: "I will never lie to you."

The timing of Trump's statement was interesting because Trump's promise not to lie coincided with incontrovertible proof Barack Obama had just told a doozy. The backstory is that the Iranian government held some Americans hostage. The Obama Administration had tried for months to negotiate the hostages' release. The U.S. Government had long before frozen some $400 million in Iranian funds held in

U.S. banks. The Iranians wanted their money back, and that was the deal. Give us our $400 million, and you can have your citizens back.

When the deal was finally struck, the Iranians got their $400 million, delivered by aircraft in the form of pallets of cold, hard cash, which is much more convenient for paying off terrorists in the field.

On August 3, Pres. Obama insisted, "This wasn't some nefarious deal. We don't pay ransom for hostages."

Much of the world simply replied, "B——t." Sen. John McCain plainly observed, "Whatever the administration may claim, it is clear this payment was a ransom for Americans held hostage in Iran."[721]

Then a few weeks later, State Department spokesman John Kirby demonstrated a breakdown in basic Departmental training. He told the truth. At a press briefing, Kirby was asked, "In basic English, you're saying you wouldn't give them $400 million in cash until the prisoners were released, correct?"[722]

Kirby's response? "That's correct."

Many wondered anew what color the sky was in Barack Obama's world. No doubt he had found some way to torture the facts to convince himself what he had assured the American people about paying ransom was in some way the truth. Does that make what he said a lie? To most people, the answer was probably "yes." To some, the response to Pres. Obama probably remained "B——t!"

MANAFORT TO THE UKRAINE

When Corey Lewandowski "managed" the Trump campaign, Trump was fully antiestablishment and hair on fire. Lewandowski was pushed out to make room for Paul Manafort so the team could grow into the kind of organization necessary to run a more traditional national campaign, to impose some order on the chaos, and to establish some normal ties to the Republican establishment. Manafort also became a regular guest on the national TV news programs, often "clarifying" Trump's remarks and filling in some of the many gaps, a role later assumed by Veep nominee Mike Pence and by former New York City Mayor Rudy Giuliani.

Rule one in Trump world: Only The Donald is allowed to linger center stage. Trump didn't like the constraints Manafort tried to apply. He didn't like Manafort taking the spotlight, and he didn't like it when it turned out long before he joined the campaign that Manafort had done business with some reportedly shady and suspicious Ukrainians.[723]

Hence Manafort steadily lost influence. Then he was demoted in favor of Bannon and Conway. Finally, recognizing he'd lost Trump's ear, Manafort resigned on August 19. No muss. No fuss. Thanks for the giggles. I'm out of here.

The media immediately jumped on the narrative that this represented another round of shake-up and turmoil in the Trump campaign (it was) and demonstrated that Trump knew he was in trouble (it didn't). To be sure, Trump had suffered a couple of bad weeks, allowing Hillary Clinton to establish a modest but persistent lead in the polls, but it was highly unlikely Trump thought his campaign was in trouble. This was just another episode of *The Apprentice* and another Trump associate heard, "You're fired."

For obvious reasons, much of the media and the Democratic establishment hoped desperately this meant Trump was in big trouble. In contrast, the Republican establishment hoped Trump *recognized* he was in big trouble and would then mend his ways. However, without Manafort in the fold, it was hard to see the Bannon/Conway team doing anything other than encouraging Trump to throw more and bigger bombs.

What they all generally failed to grasp was while Trump's campaign team was in turmoil at the top, it didn't matter much. Trump's campaign was about Trump. He would win or he would lose because he was Donald Trump. The campaign had one essential asset. Manafort and company had sought to misuse that asset, to fit a square peg in a round hole. Bannon and Conway and Donald Trump understood they could win only if Trump remained 100% himself every day of the campaign.

Drip, Drip, Drip... Surprise! More Emails

Donald Trump lived the old adage that even bad news is good news if they spell your name right. He wanted the attention. Hillary was glad to let him have it. Clinton wasn't doing anything particularly right, yet she jumped out to a solid lead just by lying low and visiting her many rich friends harvesting campaign contributions. Matters were going so well her name was again linked with the term "inevitable," and stories began to come out as to how she was getting ready for the transition and her new administration.

Why not? Even the steady stream of stories about her email issues and her Foundation payola scheme failed to break through the din of Trump's personal calamitous cacophony. Then she faced another drip, drip, drip from the email scandal when U.S. District Court Judge Emmit G. Sullivan said she had to answer in writing questions submitted by Judicial Watch.[724] She didn't have to appear in person for a sworn deposition, but she had to cooperate, under oath, and her answers would become part of the public record. This also meant another story was coming when she submitted her answers.

The drip continued a couple of days later when the Justice Department revealed it had found 14,900 more emails from Clinton's stint at the State Department, nearly 50% more than originally admitted by Clinton's lawyers.[725] U.S. District Court Judge James E. Boasberg gave Justice until September 22 to come up with a plan for reviewing and releasing these new emails. That hearing, and then the series of releases, again meant the story wasn't going away.

There was yet another drip in the Clinton campaign kitchen when it came out that Clinton's allies tried to use highly esteemed former Army General and former Secretary of State Colin Powell as a human shield.[726] The notes the FBI turned over to Congress regarding its investigation into her private email server indicated that Clinton told the agents Powell suggested the private server. According to Powell, however, the Clinton story was bogus and in fact, "her people have been trying to pin it on me." Query: Do you believe Hillary Clinton and her minions or General Powell?

The *Washington Post* ran a front-page story based on the recently released emails showing how various major donors to the Clinton Foundation and others had called in their chits with Secretary of State Hillary Clinton via her Deputy Chief of Staff, Huma Abedin, asking for all sorts of help.[727] The payola story was alive and well.

The Clinton Foundation itself was also again in the news, which was never a good thing for Hillary. One report said the Foundation hired FireEye, a cyber security firm, after its hack attack.[728] Another story reported the Foundation vowed not to accept donations from corporations or foreign governments if Clinton were elected, as though receiving major donations from *individuals* seeking influence with a Clinton Administration were perfectly fine.[729] None of these stories were particularly damaging in and of themselves, but every story about the emails or about the Clinton Foundation refreshed the impression of scandals and dishonesty surrounding the Clintons.

Questions about the Clinton Foundation's foreign supporters and what they did or did not get from Clinton's State Department continued to swirl. In a television interview, campaign manager Robby Mook was asked why it was OK for the Foundation to accept donations from foreign donors and corporations while Clinton was secretary of state and not OK for it to do so if Clinton became president. Mook's response: Hammana hammana hammana.

Failing any response whatsoever, Mook went on the attack, calling Trump a puppet at the end of Putin's strings, suggesting "real questions are being raised about whether Donald Trump himself is just a puppet for the Kremlin in this race."[730] Those "real questions" were no doubt being raised solely within the confines of Clinton campaign headquarters and perhaps only after some substantial late-night libations. There appeared a lot more to the Clinton Foundation payola scandal than we knew.

We learned more quickly. The Associated Press (AP) sought Secretary of State Clinton's calendar and schedules beginning in 2013.[731] The State Department's stonewalling procedures operating at peak efficiency, three years later, the AP got them. Three years.

At least the AP got a response. Their Freedom of Information Act petition was among almost 240 State received and ignored from 2009 to 2013. State responded to three such petitions within the legally required time frame. No suggestion Clinton was above the law, of course.

When the AP finally got its hands on the information, the resulting story was explosive. According to the AP:

> More than half the people outside the government who met with Hillary Clinton while she was secretary of state gave money—either personally or through companies or groups—to the Clinton Foundation. It's an extraordinary proportion indicating her possible ethics challenges if elected president.
>
> At least 85 of 154 people from private interests who met or had phone conversations scheduled with Clinton while she led the State Department donated to her family charity or pledged commitments to its international programs, according to a review of State Department calendars released so far to The Associated Press. Combined, the 85 donors contributed as much as $156 million. At least 40 donated more than $100,000 each, and 20 gave more than $1 million.[732]

The bottom line to the AP story: The Clintons used their charitable Foundation to run the most high-profile, big-dollar payola scheme in recorded history.

Chris Cillizza of the *Washington Post* reacted, echoing the best feature of ESPN's *Monday Night Football* pre–game show. "COME ON, MAN. It is literally impossible to look at those two paragraphs and not raise your eyebrows. . . . It just plain looks bad. Really bad."[733]

Clinton would insist there was nothing to see here, her defense boiling down to "you can't prove a thing" and "trust me." She was probably right about the first. The Clintons were expert at covering just enough of their trail to avoid an indictment—that is, unless somebody involved messed up and pulled out a blue dress.[734]

Even so, the whole episode was breathtaking. The Clintons knew all along she expected to run for president after Obama's second term. They knew the scrutiny of their affairs personal and financial would be fierce. Yet they couldn't help themselves. One explanation for their behavior was that the Clintons were just stupid. That answer would be ridiculous.

A far more plausible answer was that as much as they loved attention and power, they loved money even more. That was plausible and well supported by the evidence, but inadequate given the facts.

Another answer which may go along with the love of money is they just liked proving how smart they were by bending and breaking rules and getting away with it. They were like kids who got a thrill out of stealing candy from the neighborhood convenience store. They were political escape artist thrill junkies who couldn't resist a chance to get away with something just one more time, especially if it meant they made a buck or two.

The Clintons recognized the AP story as a real threat. First, they attacked the AP story directly, as though the AP was part of the famous "vast, right-wing conspiracy." This was so absurd it merely served to highlight how much a threat the Clintons thought they faced.

Then they unleashed their surrogates to insist this was much ado about nothing. Clinton even called into Anderson Cooper's *CNN* evening show at nearly 10:00 p.m. EST to insist, "Look, Cooper, I know there's a lot of smoke and there is no fire."[735] You could almost hear her then conclude with, "Trust me."

To review the bidding: Hillary Clinton set up a private email server for one purpose and one purpose only, and it wasn't convenience. It was to hide what she was doing.

What did she want to hide? The leading candidate was the nexus between her role as secretary of state and the Clinton Foundation.

Why did she feel she needed to hide it? Was she doing something illegal? Once again, the nation would explore the boundaries between improper and illegal. The issue: "access," for which people paid her Foundation. This from a woman and a political party that complained incessantly about the unseemly role of money in politics because it suggests buying "access."

Every new piece of information exposed a little more of Clinton's big stink. Kimberley Strassel summed it up nicely. Clinton used a private email instead of a State Department email to hide the fact "there was no divide between private and public. Mrs. Clinton's State Department and her family foundation were one seamless entity—employing the same people, comparing schedules, mixing foundation donors with State supplicants."[736] Some pieces were still missing from the puzzle, and it was all so complicated nobody had yet put it together in a succinct, compelling narrative. As long as Clinton could keep the issue a muddled blur, she would muddle through as she always did.

Trump Wobbles on Immigration

Throughout his campaign, Donald Trump could be counted on to be absolutely sure of what he believed—at the moment. The next day? Who knows?

Trump had practically launched his campaign by being tough on immigration. The better he did, the tougher he got. It worked for him. Throw the illegals out. Build a wall. Make Mexico pay for it. It all worked.

Then Trump had second thoughts. Maybe there was a better way. He met with some Hispanic leaders. The campaign announced a major speech on immigration. Then postponed it. "Here's the Republican nominee kinda-sorta, maybe, walking back a central tenet of his campaign—over the course of several days, on national television."[737]

Trump's position evolved from "We're going to follow the law," which according to *Fox News*'s Sean Hannity's interpretation meant illegal aliens were going back from whence they'd come. But a president can propose and Congress can pass new laws. What did Trump think was the right answer? Trump elaborated, "No citizenship." Well, naturally, if you sent them back, they wouldn't be citizens of the United States.

Trump dug his hole even deeper: "They have to pay back taxes . . . there's no amnesty." So they're not going back even though the law requires it, but they have to pay back taxes when they stay. Got it.

Then at the end of an incoherent stream, Trump concluded, "Can they go through a process or do you think they have to get out? Tell me—I mean, I don't know."[738]

At the start of the primary season, Trump staked out the toughest position on immigration. Ted Cruz repeatedly tried and failed to top Trump. Trump was No. 1 when it came to building walls and tossing illegals out of the country, and he flailed poor Jeb Bush and Marco Rubio for their wimpier stances. Yet now here was Trump moving to a position indistinguishable from Jeb Bush's, and maybe even softer.

Many of Trump's supporters were aghast. On his radio program, Rush Limbaugh said, "Let me regain my composure. Who knew that it would be Donald Trump to come out and convert the GOP base to supporting amnesty the same week Ann Coulter's book comes out. Poor Ann. Oh, my God, she's got this book, 'In Trump We Trust,' and in it she says the only thing, the only thing that could cause Trump any trouble whatsoever is if he flip-flops on abortion or on immigration, goes amnesty. It looks like he's getting close to it, and she's just beside herself with this. I mean, what timing."[739]

Ann Coulter had been one of Trump's earliest, fiercest defenders on national television. She had just come out with a book supporting Trump called *In Trump We Trust*, yet here was The Donald flip-flopping on the most core policy of his campaign. If he could go wobbly on this, was there anything on which he wouldn't wobble? Trust Trump? Sure. But to do what, exactly?

What really inspired Trump to waffle on immigration? Reports surfaced suggesting New Jersey Gov. Chris Christie had been working on Trump to develop a more "nuanced" approach, reports then verified by Rudy Giuliani.[740] After a few more days of twisting in the wind, Giuliani and Trump set out to "clarify" Trump's position, returning to something similar to Trump's original stance, and Trump again scheduled a major speech on immigration where the old hard ass was back in charge.

Trump the Surpriser in Chief

Just to cap off a thoroughly confusing foray into an evolving immigration policy, on the evening of August 30, Trump announced in a tweet that he had accepted the invitation of Pres. Enrique Pena Nieto of Mexico to meet, would do so the next day in Mexico City, and would then travel to Arizona to give his much anticipated "major speech" on immigration.

This was a bold move on Nieto's part after all the nasty things Trump had said about the Mexican Government. No doubt Nieto had expected Trump to decline the invitation, but Trump was full of surprises. Now Nieto, who had a basketful of troubles at home, had given Trump a platform from which he could try to assuage American Hispanics with the Mexican President standing nearby.

Hillary Clinton could not have been pleased. Nieto's office quickly "clarified" he had extended invitations to both Trump and Clinton. Trump accepted quickly, leaving Clinton weighing arranging her own little trip to Mexico City without looking too much like a "me too" tourist.

The media reaction to Trump's Mexico jaunt and his ensuing Arizona speech was almost more interesting than the events themselves. The *Washington Post* ran a front-page picture of a scowling Trump walking away from the podium at the conclusion of Trump's press conference with Nieto. The *Wall Street Journal* ran a front-page picture of a smiling Trump reaching out to shake hands with the Mexican President. Those who opposed Trump all declared the event unproductive, counterproductive, or disastrous for Trump's candidacy. Trump's fans all thought the event fabulous.

Steve Hayes, certainly no fan of Trump (or Clinton), concluded that for Trump, "It worked."[741] One sensible attack line the Clinton campaign used repeatedly against Trump insisted Trump was a loose cannon and ill-suited to the global diplomatic stage. Of course, with his many outbursts during domestic events, Trump provided fodder galore for Clinton's critique; but thanks to his performance in Mexico City, Trump "made those concerns look overblown." Trump showed he could play the calm, sober diplomat when necessary.

Charles Krauthammer, another nonfan of either candidate, concluded, "Trump really helped himself."[742] Trump appeared "presidential" and took command of the stage even on Nieto's home turf. It was Nieto's show, but "Trump took charge."

What mattered most for the campaign, however, was how Trump's speech in Arizona ended the momentary flirtation with a "kinder, gentler" pivot on immigration. After all the bluster and histrionics, Trump's policy after his Mexican foray boiled down to three simple principles:

- Absolute border security, beginning with the wall (and less emphasis on who would pay for it).
- Deporting illegal aliens who committed crimes, as per current law.
- As for the rest, that was TBD, which meant they could stay in the country legally for the time being.

For all his wanderings in the immigration policy supermarket, Trump ended up pretty much where everybody else ended up. The only real difference was he expressed himself with anger and a determination easily interpreted as bigotry. He needed the anger because that tapped the energy propelling his supporters, but he couldn't escape the sense of bigotry that proved a major stumbling block for those who might otherwise support him.

INTO THE MUD PITS, DEAR FRIENDS

While Donald Trump hoisted himself on his own immigration reform petard, Hillary Clinton came along to bail him out. She did this by prematurely launching a new and decidedly ugly dimension to the campaign. No one could doubt the campaign would sink ever deeper into the accusational mud pits eventually, but Clinton apparently believed in a First Strike strategy and so began the plunge before Labor Day.

In a major speech in Reno, Nevada, Clinton accused Trump of cavorting with white racists and the Alt-Right movement. She attacked Trump for "taking hate groups mainstream."[743] This was rather comical for a candidate trying desperately to find accommodation with the Black Lives Matter movement.

Trump responded in kind by calling Clinton a "bigot" in a *CNN* interview.[744] Trump then again showed why Clinton had to be very careful in how she got down and dirty with the master. Recall when Clinton called Trump a "sexist" and Trump blew it up by throwing Bill Clinton's past sexual predations in her face. This time, Clinton called Trump a racist, and so Trump merely redefined the charge to his advantage. Trump roared, "She lies and she smears, and she paints decent Americans—you—as racists."[745] First, Trump restated what almost everyone believed about Clinton's trouble with the truth. Then Trump recast Clinton as saying not that Trump is a racist, but that she called "you" a racist. She didn't call anyone but Trump a racist, of course, but now Clinton was in the difficult position of proving the negative—proving she didn't do something.

Drip, Drip, Drip—Not Again!

Hillary Clinton and her allies were just getting over the latest scandal eruption involving the complex Clinton Foundation payola scheme when the darned email scandal erupted again. Clinton couldn't catch a break, but then that's what happens when you behave as the Clintons had done for years.

Recall Clinton's staff had deleted over 30,000 emails from her private email server, which she assured the nation included nothing but minor personal emails with friends and family such as exchanging recipes and yoga schedules. Guess what else was a lie.

The Clinton team didn't just "wipe" the emails "like with a cloth." They didn't just delete files as one would by hitting a Delete key. They really scrubbed the server digitally trying to ensure nobody but nobody could ever figure out what was in those emails. The Clinton team used a special program called "BleachBit," which is an "electronic shredder that permanently scrambles data."[746]

On August 30, the State Department announced the FBI had recovered at least thirty of those intensely scrubbed previously undisclosed "personal" emails.[747] The announcement, made by government lawyers during a U.S. District Court hearing, related to the Judicial Watch lawsuits. The lawyers acknowledged that many of these supposedly "personal" emails dealt with the Benghazi attack in which U.S. Ambassador J. Christopher Stevens, U.S. Foreign Service Officer Sean Smith, and two former U.S. Navy Seals working as private contractors died. Judge Amit Mehta gave the parties until September 6 to recommend how best to proceed. Another "drip" in the email scandal was already scheduled.

Wheezing into Labor Day

No doubt Hillary Clinton was giving important speeches and releasing new policy ideas, but none of it mattered. As the Trump campaign din abated, the din surrounding Clinton's scandals grew. There must have been something positive happening somewhere in the campaigns, but no one noticed.

Traditionally, the period between the conventions and Labor Day offers the campaigns a chance to prepare for the last big push. Donald Trump spent most of the time tending to his own self-inflicted wounds. As noted, Clinton spent much of the time managing her various crises, which truth be told she handled fairly well, in part because there were so many and they went on for so long only the truly dedicated could keep track even with a scorecard. Clinton also kept busy raising money, at which she had proven especially adept.

Typical was a story of a Clinton fund-raiser held on Cape Cod for twenty-eight lucky fawners at a mere $50,000 a pop. According to reports, Clinton was raising money at a $10 million a week clip.[748] This put repeated stories about her failing health to shame. Even traveling with a professional entourage, Clinton's efforts were worthy of a political decathlete.

The essential lines of the campaigns became more coherent through all the noise. Told from Trump's perspective, the race offered, well, Trump, the world's greatest (fill in the blank) in his own mind, against a corrupt, lying establishment, existential threat to the future of the Republic.

Clinton promised a continuation of a poorly performing economy likely to perform a little worse, or the country could take a risk to see what Trump would really do since nobody really knew. On immigration, Clinton would continue some variation of an open-borders policy whereas Trump would at least try within the limitations set by Congress and the law to secure the border.

The one aspect Trump and Clinton had in common was both were intensely disliked. At the end of August, Clinton hit a new high in terms of Americans disliking her, at 56%, though Trump still topped her at 63%. However, among registered voters, Trump was just slightly worse at 60% to Clinton's 59%.[749]

Interestingly, those groups who previously had most liked Clinton now liked her a lot less:

- Among women, her unfavorables had jumped from 46% to 55%;
- Among liberals, her unfavorables had jumped from 24% to 37%; and
- Among Hispanics, her unfavorables had jumped from 29% to 45%.

To be sure, among liberals and Hispanics, at least, she still maintained a positive net favorability rating, but her support was eroding. The question was whether she was just returning to her norm, or was this decline now part of a trend that would continue as the campaigns got uglier?

From Clinton's perspective, the race offered a hardworking, well-prepared progressive versus an utterly unfit sexist braggart who was woefully unprepared for the Office of the President. Clinton offered fairly coherent policy ideas, mostly making incremental changes as opposed to Trump's policy-on-the-fly scary major-changes approach.

A Labor Day Snapshot

Labor Day before an election provides a natural calendar marker for assessing the state of the campaign. Throughout August, Clinton maintained a steady 4- to 5-point edge in the polls, whether or not they included the Libertarian's Gary Johnson and the Green Party's Jill Stein. At the end of August, her lead vanished into the margin of error. For what it's worth, PredictWise, the market-based election forecast engine, indicated Clinton would win with 78% probability.

Pres. Obama's own approval ratings continued to benefit substantially from the comparison to the two candidates vying to be his successor. Obama had done nothing notable, nor was anything going particularly well in the United States at this time as indicated by the persistent -35 rating to the question whether people thought the country was on the right track or the wrong track. Yet thanks to the comparison, Obama's net favorables had averaged a fairly steady plus 6% throughout August.

Many of the U.S. Senate races had come into focus by Labor Day. In Ohio, Sen. Rob Portman had largely put away his opponent, former Gov. Ted Strickland, as the Democratic Senate Campaign Committee "postponed" (really, canceled) its planned September ad buy.[750] Sen. Marco Rubio won his primary race walking away and looked in very good shape to beat his Democratic challenger, Cong. Patrick Murphy. Sen. John McCain easily dispatched Kelli Ward in the Republican primary in Arizona despite a desperate last-minute push by the hard right to help Ward. McCain would have to hustle to beat Cong. Ann Kirkpatrick for his sixth term, but his odds were much better than fifty-fifty.

It wasn't all looking rosy for Republicans, however. Joe Heck was locked in a tight race with Catherine Cortez Masto seeking to claim the Senate seat being vacated by Harry Reid, while Pennsylvania Sen. Pat Toomey was in a small but persistent hole to Katie McGinty. Fortunately for Heck and Toomey, their troubles lay almost entirely with the national environment rather than their own weaknesses or their opponents' strengths.

Democratic Sen. Michael Bennet of Colorado looked to be winning in a romp while Republican Sen.s Ron Johnson of Wisconsin and Mark Kirk of Illinois looked about to be ushered out of office. The odds were close, but on balance, it looked very much like the Democrats might win control of the Senate come 2017, though the House of Representatives seemed to be lost to the Democrats for another cycle.

CHAPTER 20
THE SEPTEMBER OF OUR DISCONTENT

The Labor Day weekend traditionally marked the start of the days of decision. Citizens of a more politically active nature had engaged throughout the primary season. Millions more paid attention albeit fleetingly to the conventions. Many just went about their lives ignoring the political storms until the election demanded a conclusion. That's how the calendar was supposed to play out. As usual, 2016 was different. Donald Trump made it different.

Trump was a one-man sensation, or train wreck, depending on one's point of view. Only those in a coma hadn't seen or heard of Trump at some point, most having done so repeatedly. From bowling alleys to the ladies' Sunday tea, one had to make at least a passing reference to Trump even in polite conversation, much as one would when Neil Armstrong first walked on the moon or when Pres. Kennedy was shot, again, depending on predisposition.

The 2016 campaign differed in another way. Typically, at least one of the two leading candidates is relatively unknown to the general public (Obama in 2008, for example), adding a unique dimension to the general uncertainty. Would the unknown(s) become sufficiently known by Election Day to be trusted by the voters? Would the unknown(s) impress by their "newness," or would they suffer a series of amateurish gaffes (Romney in 2012, for example)?

In 2016, the leading candidates were two of the most famous people in the country. Just about everybody knew something of Trump. Just about everybody had a pretty firm opinion about Hillary Clinton. So absent some monumentally disastrous moment, Election Day polling *probably* wouldn't look much different than the Labor Day polls, polling errors notwithstanding. A relatively small minority of voters would vacillate between candidates, between voting and not, between sticking with the two traditional political parties or voting for a protest third-party candidate. As these vascillating few wavered from Labor Day to Election Day, the polls would follow.

By the Slimmest of Margins

In the 2012 election, Barack Obama received 65,918,507 of the 129,235,558 votes cast, or 51%. That may seem a very small majority, but he beat Mitt Romney by almost 5 million votes, which may seem a decisive victory. In the Electoral College, Obama won 332 to 206, again giving the impression of a pretty strong win.

Dig a little deeper and the picture shifts once more. Fundamentally, Obama won by less than a half-million votes, or by about 0.3% of the total votes cast. So again, the 2012 election looks a squeaker.

Arguing big win or small cannot diminish Barack Obama's accomplishment. Anyone who can convince nearly 66 million Americans to cast their votes favorably deserves all credit due. However, if just a quarter-million indecisive voters in select states had woken up in a Romney state of mind instead, Romney would have won. Close elections in America are decided by incredibly few voters. Chances are, you're not one of them. Sorry.

The issue is not how one can torture numbers to confess to a desired result. The issue is how few voters really decide close national elections, despite all the national hoopla.

How can this be? The explanation begins with recognizing the central role in close elections played by so-called "swing states," by which is typically meant Florida, Iowa, Ohio, New Hampshire, North Carolina, and New Mexico. Depending on the election, in a close election to this list may be added Virginia and Colorado. If states are subtracted from this list or new ones added as in 2016, then it suggests a substantial shift in American voting patterns. As all four past national elections have been close, the choices made by voters in these six to eight mostly small- to medium-population states have been decisive.

In the 2012 election, six of these key swing states went for Barack Obama—all but North Carolina, contributing to his substantial victory as measured by Electoral College margin. The victory in all six states was razor thin. Whether a candidate won 50.1% or 99.1% of the vote in any of the other states was immaterial because when it comes to the Electoral College, it's winner take all.[751]

In 2012, Obama won 332 Electoral College votes, but needed only 270. The good news is he won 62 more than he needed. The bad news: Only Florida, New Hampshire, Ohio, and Virginia needed to go for Romney to retire Obama. By what cumulative total did Obama win those four states? By 429,522 votes.

Of course, if Obama had won a state like North Carolina that he narrowly lost (Romney won North Carolina by two percentage points), then Romney would have needed to switch another Obama swing state; but even then, these are states where the winning margins were very narrow.

No matter how you slice it, close national elections are won and lost not in megastates like California, Texas, or New York despite the enormous numbers of votes cast. What matters is the Electoral College. What matters in most close elections is a handful of swing states. And what really matters is a relative handful of voters in those swing states, voters who often don't decide who to vote for until the weekend before the election, or the night before, or as they close the curtain in the voting booth.

The 2012 election was fairly close, despite Obama's Electoral College margin. What about an election won with a wider popular vote margin, like the 2008 election?

To recap, in 2008, Barack Obama won nearly 53% of 131,473,705 votes cast, establishing a total vote margin over John McCain of more than 9.5 million votes. In the Electoral College, Obama won 365 to 173. By any measure, this seems a substantial margin of victory; yet if McCain could have convinced a select half-million voters of that 9.5 million vote margin to vote for him instead of Obama, John McCain would have become president.

In 2008, Obama won all six swing states—Florida, Iowa, Ohio, New Hampshire, New Mexico, North Carolina—along with both second-tier swing states, Colorado and Virginia. His Electoral College margin: 96 votes. If Florida, Iowa, Ohio, New Hampshire, and North Carolina had gone for McCain, along with the surprising Indiana, McCain would have claimed the necessary Electoral College votes to win.

That still seems like a tall order, so let's check. Obama's margin of victory across those six states? A margin of 990,320. Just half that nearly million vote swing spread over a handful of states would have turned a strong victory for Obama into a squeaker defeat.

Not surprisingly, the previous two very close elections in 2000 and 2004 followed similar patterns. In 2004, Pres. George W. Bush beat Sen. John Kerry with 50.7% of the vote, winning the Electoral College 286 to 251. Kerry needed just three states to flip – Iowa, (which he lost by 0.7% of the votes cast), New Mexico (by 0.8%), and Nevada (by 2.6%). Total cumulative votes needed to wake up feeling Kerry on Election Day for the Massachusetts Senator to move into the White House? A total of 37,547 out of 122,303,590 cast nationwide.

The standard narrative of the 2000 election was alternatively how the Florida Supreme Court tried to ignore the law to give Vice Pres. Al Gore the state of Florida and thus the election, how the U.S. Supreme Court blocked the Florida Court's plans, how Texas Gov. George W. Bush beat Gore by 537 Florida hanging chads thanks to the U.S. Supreme Court's intervention, or how Al Gore lost to Bush despite winning the national popular vote by over half a million votes. The few-voters thesis would seem to be illustrated in bright lights by observing that a mere 537 Floridians ultimately decided the election, but that's too easy. Suppose instead Florida had gone for

Gore. What Gore swing states would Bush have had to turn to have won the election anyway?

Gore won Iowa, Oregon, and Wisconsin with particularly small margins. Had they gone for Bush, Gore could have won Florida walking away and Bush still would have become president. How many additional votes in those three states would Bush have needed in 2000 under these circumstances? A total of 16,617.

This "few-voters decide" thesis ought not be carried beyond reasonable bounds. Obviously, a candidate has to mount a sufficiently credible, effective national campaign to be in a position for these few voters to decide who wins and who loses. But even in elections that appeared to be won handily in terms of overall votes or Electoral College totals, only a modest shifting of votes in a few select states would have pushed the election the other way. How unsettling for the victor! How frustrating for the loser! Just ask Mitt, or McCain, or Kerry, or Gore.

Drip, Drip, Drip—the FBI Reports

Recall the Friday afternoon data dump is every administration's favorite technique for putting out bad news; the Friday afternoon of a three-day Labor Day weekend is even better. This time, the data dump came compliments of the supposedly nonpartisan Federal Bureau of Investigation (FBI), ahem. The data in question involved the FBI's forty-seven-page summary of its investigation into Hillary Clinton's private email server.[752] Given its contents and Director Comey's now apparent objective of protecting Clinton, they were wise to release it on Friday.

As detailed by the *New York Times*, hardly a Clinton antagonist

- Mrs. Clinton regarded emails containing classified discussions about planned drone strikes as "routine";
- she said she either was unaware of or misunderstood some classification procedures; and
- Colin L. Powell, a former secretary of state, had advised her to "be very careful" in how she used email.[753]

Of these points, one can be sure she regarded planned drone strike discussions as "routine," as she treated all such classified information with a remarkably cavalier attitude. Any low-level State Department official who mishandled classified information and then tried the defense they were unaware of classification procedures would have been summarily fired and likely jailed. Remember, Clinton proudly proclaimed that she would "sweat the details." For a former First Lady to suggest she was unaware was preposterous. For Clinton to assert ignorance was just a lie. There just wasn't any reasonable alternative conclusion, but there was more.

Consider the timing of events. News of Clinton's private email server broke in March of 2015. Weeks later, an unnamed computer specialist deleted the archive of Clinton's emails. Coincidence? Sure. Wanna buy a bridge?

Three weeks later, the unnamed specialist realized an archive of emails slated for deletion a year earlier hadn't been wiped. This is when the data eradication program, BleachBit, first came into the picture. As Jason Chaffetz (R-UT), Chairman of the House Government Reform and Oversight Committee, correctly observed, "These were not Hillary Clinton's emails—they were government records," a reality every government bureaucrat understands full well.[754] But Hillary "Sweat the Details" Clinton somehow didn't?

Aside from the emails themselves, the FBI's behavior in this matter under Director Comey's direction was atrocious. Certain agencies of the Federal Government are supposed to be and really must be absolutely nonpartisan to maintain public confidence. The FBI's Friday-before-Labor-Day data dump was a classic partisan move. So much so, Comey felt compelled to issue an internal memo to all FBI employees (which was quickly leaked) insisting the release was not politically motivated, that the FBI would release materials as they are ready, "no matter the day of the week."[755] Right, just as the FBI just happened to interview Hillary Clinton not under oath and without transcription on the Friday before the three-day Fourth of July holiday. Only two possibilities remained regarding James Comey—either he was stupid, or he thought everybody else in the FBI and the vast majority of Americans were stupid. The one thing he knew, however, was he would get away with it.

Drip, Drip, Drip . . . Bill's Excellent $17.6 Million Education Adventure

If all of America's CEOs were as aggressively entrepreneurial as Bill and Hillary Clinton, very few companies outside the United States would stand a chance. The Clintons, it seemed, never missed a trick or a chance to make a buck, as a post–Labor Day story affirmed.

The steady stream of emails recovered from Clinton's private email server had already shown the Clintons were amazingly good at turning Bill Clinton's status as former president and Hillary Clinton's tenure as secretary of state into cold, hard cash. One avenue involved Bill hiring out as a consultant to a company able to leverage exposure and access at the State Department into future business deals. For example, Bill Clinton signed a tidy $17.6 million consulting deal with Laureate International Universities.[756]

Stop and consider that sum for a moment: $17.6 million over five years. Even working tirelessly for five straight years on nothing else, exactly what kind of educational consulting could Bill provide that could be worth that kind of money? Some CEOs of major companies don't make that kind of money.

Answer: access. Access, like attending State Department dinners with the secretary of state and various national and international higher education leaders.

Hillary Clinton's involvement in Bill's excellent education adventure was uncovered in the recovered emails. In one email to Cheryl Mills, Hillary's Chief of Staff at State, Clinton emphasized that one Doug Becker should be invited to a bigwig dinner because Bill liked Becker "a lot." Who was Becker? Laureate's CEO. How much did Bill like Becker? About $17.6 million worth.

This is just how the Clintons did business.⁷⁵⁷ At one point, Clinton's State Department was evaluating options for imposing additional sanctions on Iran. Certain Swedish companies could be especially impacted. These companies opposed additional sanctions. So what did the Swedes do? They convinced Bill and Hill to set up a Swedish fund-raising arm into which the Swedes plunked some $26 million. Bill personally pocketed $750,000 for one speech. The additional sanctions were never imposed. The Swedes no doubt thought this money well spent.

Hillary's Health

Stories involving Hillary Clinton's health hung around like a nagging cough. A nagging cough was one of those stories. At a Labor Day event in Cleveland, Ohio, Clinton coughed through the first four minutes of her talk.⁷⁵⁸ It happened again when Clinton was speaking to a gaggle of reporters on the press plane.⁷⁵⁹ The coughing fits grew so bad even *NBC* and *CNN* were forced to cover them and got blasted by Clinton defenders in turn.

It wasn't just the coughing, which in fairness could be attributed to the fact the woman was campaigning for President of the United States, which involved a lot of talking. Clinton's coughing was a sign she was working herself sick, possibly to exhaustion, not necessarily or even probably a sign of a major health issue. But Clinton had previously acknowledged some health issues. For example, in her FBI interview, Clinton referenced a concussion she'd suffered as a possible explanation for her faulty memory during the interview.⁷⁶⁰ She also acknowledged in the FBI interview at least three episodes with blood clots.

Just as Clinton with the help of her mainstream media allies finished tamping down the health issue, it came roaring back, complete with video. At a Sunday 9/11 memorial ceremony in New York City, Clinton was forced to leave early and was shown on video collapsing as she approached her SUV, losing her shoe, and being half carried by Secret Service agents.⁷⁶¹ The polite term used by a protective media was she "stumbled." Rubbish. She was collapsing when her aides caught her and carried her to her waiting car.

Then the truth came out. The previous Friday, she'd been diagnosed with pneumonia.[762] On Sunday, she got overheated and dehydrated, the story went, even though the temperature was a moderate mideighties with low humidity. Pneumonia, which is an inflammation of one or both lungs, is not typically a big deal if caught early, unless the individual involved is a bit older rather than younger and has a schedule that would exhaust an Olympian and consequently has a weakened immune system. Had Clinton not been caught stumbling on camera, we likely would never have learned about the pneumonia. Now the health questions were back and weren't going away soon.

As usual with a Clintonian episode, the facts (and the falsehoods) just kept trickling out. Clinton called into *CNN* to acknowledge, "I've passed out a few times I don't remember."[763] Oh OK, move on.

This wasn't all the right-wing media in a tizzy. Further feeding the fires of concern, Don Fowler, former head of the Democratic National Committee, observed that Pres. Obama and the party's leaders should come up with an emergency contingency plan. "Now is the time for all good political leaders to come to the aid of their party. I think the plan should be developed by six o'clock this afternoon."[764] Fowler was surely correct, but offering this suggestion publicly surely wasn't appreciated by the Clintons.

The Clinton campaign insisted Hillary's pneumonia wasn't contagious, and as usual, the media just accepted the assertion. Except Clinton was diagnosed with bacterial pneumonia, and those are contagious, a fact many had to find disquieting to learn, like those press and campaign staff cooped up in Clinton's plane when crisscrossing the country. And what of the people she met, some of whom may have had compromised immune systems? What of Chelsea's baby, Aidan? When Clinton collapsed after the memorial, she insisted she be driven not to the hospital where they might have to answer uncomfortable questions. She went to Chelsea's—and Aidan's—apartment with her contagious pneumonia.

Clinton's enduring difficulties with truth telling were on full display for even her protective media to see. All coughing and pneumonia and stumbling aside, by all appearances, Clinton seemed to be in very good health. Many people decades younger than her then sixty-eight years of age would collapse trying to maintain her strenuous schedule, whether fighting pneumonia or not. However, Clinton had trained the country to doubt her veracity whenever she said anything, and that included statements about her health. As Maureen Dowd put it, "It isn't about the health, it's about the stealth."[765]

They're Back!

Congress returned from its August recess with a well-defined "to-do" list and little appetite for doing anything. After months of warning about mosquitos and the Zika virus and the possible health disaster it posed over the summer, a disaster that could only be averted with a hefty slug of additional Federal spending, summer came and went without major Zika incident.

Even so, the House and Senate resumed negotiating a compromise on Zika funding. Any compromise would involve more spending, which meant more deficit spending. The original excuse for not offsetting the Zika funding with other spending cuts was this was an emergency and there was no time to identify $1 billion of less-important spending in the nearly $4,000 billion the government would spend in 2016. From the outset, but especially after months of negotiations, these excuses proved insultingly vacuous. By September, neither the House nor the Senate expressed an interest in offsetting the spending increase, providing yet another perfect example of the legislative behavior generating a half-trillion-dollar annual budget deficit.

A handful of other items on Congress's agenda paled in comparison to the only must-pass item, a spending bill needed by September 30 to avoid a government shutdown. It wouldn't be easy. The essentials of the debate were common and simple enough. Some

Republicans wanted more defense spending, and others wanted to hold the line set by the 2011 Budget Control Act (BCA). Democrats didn't object to the defense spending so much, but they wanted an equal increase in nondefense spending. Republicans had found a budget gimmick to increase defense spending by $18 billion without explicitly breaking the BCA's spending limits. Democrats objected.

There the matter would stand for weeks. The two sides would argue publicly. On occasion, they would appear to negotiate. September 30 would approach and little progress would be made, so Congress would pass a Continuing Resolution (CR), keeping the government funded at the previous year's levels until after the election when they would return to try again in a postelection lame-duck session. This was a lousy way to budget and a lousy way to govern, but the least was the best they could do.

Congressional Democrats came back from the August recess fairly invigorated at their prospects. They believed in Hillary Clinton or perhaps more simply remained incredulous Donald Trump could win, and so they felt pretty good at their chances of retaking the Senate. Over in the House, Democratic Leader Nancy Pelosi tried to match the Senate's optimism, suggesting if Clinton won by a decent amount, say 54–46, then "oh my God. It's all over."[766] At the time, it seemed as if Pelosi was smoking something.

The House Freedom Caucus (HFC, previously known as the Tea Party Caucus) returned to DC ready to play its old tricks. Many were accepting of Donald Trump. Many cheered him. Many HFCers adamantly opposed a short-term CR and threatened to withhold their support for any bill not extending current funding levels well into the next calendar year. They were legitimately concerned (from their perspective) about the kinds of ugly deals a politically untethered lame duck Congress might strike.

Without most of the HFC, Ryan wouldn't have the votes to pass a short-term CR. That meant he would have to rely on Democrats to pass a bill to avoid a shutdown. "How'd that work for John Boehner?" asked Cong. Paul Gosar (R-AZ).[767] Here we had the House Freedom Caucus once again threatening a government shutdown battle, a battle they would surely lose badly, while threatening once again to depose their own House Speaker without, once again, any clue who they might offer as Ryan's successor. Nancy Pelosi probably couldn't believe her good luck: first Trump, then the House Freedom Caucus.

The Ideological-Political Complex

How was it that otherwise intelligent people elected to the House and Senate could make the same mistakes time and again? Even the dumbest puppy eventually learns to scratch at the door. Part of the answer arises from the profound disagreements over policy on display in the parties' campaigns for the presidency to the down-ballot races across the country.

Much of the answer could be found back in Washington. Pres. Dwight D. Eisenhower coined the term "military-industrial complex" to refer to the close and politically powerful post-WWII relationship between industry and the U.S. military. Eisenhower's military-industrial complex was a pittance compared to the ideological-political complex (IPC) taking root in the wings of both parties.

The IPC is in three parts. On the political right we see the Members of Congress, governors, and state and local politicians who consider themselves deeply conservative, often Tea Party members. They have very strong beliefs about politics and culture, just like their counterparts on the IPC left—that is, the progressive/socialist contingent—and they are willing to stand up and fight for those beliefs, just like their counterparts on the left.

The second part of the IPC are all the citizens, but especially those with fat wallets, who use their resources to fund the politicians with whom they agree. Again, in this respect, the IPC on the right is indistinguishable from the IPC on the left.

The third part of the IPC includes some "think tanks" and media personalities who have learned that a fast way to riches is to be as loud and incendiary as possible, to attack their opponents and especially their less-pure fellow travelers as viciously as possible, and to never ever compromise to make progress. For conservatives, these media personalities are found primarily on radio, though a few thrive in television, whereas for liberals and progressives these media personalities dominate television.

The IPC's refusal to compromise is crucial to the operation and to understanding Washington's profound dysfunction. The think tank/personality component of the IPC is ultimately indifferent, and often actively hostile, to enacting policy reforms. Any accomplishment is one less issue about which to rail when raising money from suitably agitated donors. When you win a battle, the associated money stops. Rather than advance an agenda, it is far better to lose a battle on principle and blame sellouts who need to be thrown out, thus requiring more money from Mr. or Ms. Deep Pockets.

All of which explains the House Freedom Caucus (HFC) attitude on the pending 2017 Continuing Resolution. HFC members were told by their so-called outside allies they had to stand firm and follow the hard-right line to remain a right-wing member in good standing. Despite all the past defeats, this time would be different, with Pres. Obama weakened and on his way out. Victory was at hand if they just hung together.

If the HFC forced another government shutdown, then Republicans would once again show their supporters they had spine worthy of the vast monies raised, and would show the American people they lacked the maturity to govern. After a few days, either the HFC would crack or Ryan would pass a bill with the Democrats. Either way, the outside groups would then be given another opportunity to scream against Washington sellouts, and if they took down the pilloried Ryan as well, then they could brag about that too. Once the dust had settled, HFC members would wander around stunned, leaderless, tarred and feathered, wondering about the number of the bus that had just run them over. Meanwhile, the third leg of the IPC would ready another fund-raising appeal.

The Candidates Go Intrepid and Get Defensive

Prior to Election Day, many voters pay most attention to candidates during the debates. The primary debates revealed much about the candidates' respective natures, strengths, and weaknesses. Too often, however, the primary debates devolved into nasty shouting matches featuring competitive insult hurling. On September 7, Hillary Clinton and Donald Trump participated in a different forum, with generally good results. They each spent a half hour being interviewed by Matt Lauer of NBC News and answering questions from the audience aboard the retired aircraft carrier USS *Intrepid*, anchored in New York City harbor.

Billed as the "commander-in-chief" forum, Lauer started off by grilling Clinton about her emails. Clinton squirmed uncomfortably, but managed in her screechy, lawyerly way to grind through her answers well enough, raised eyebrows and feigned innocence aplenty. Lauer also pressed Clinton on her 2003 vote in favor of the Iraq war, a point Bernie Sanders had hammered Clinton with earlier for which she still had no credible response. She just couldn't say, "I was wrong," and leave it at that.

Then came a question from a retired flight officer who observed, correctly, he would have been "prosecuted and imprisoned" if he had handled classified material as Clinton had done and then asked why the military should have any confidence in her leadership after she had "clearly corrupted our national security" with her cavalier attitude toward security in the context of her private email server.[768]

What could she say? "Yes, I get special rules, sorry, that's the way it goes"? Was the woman for whom personal confession was an alien concept now going to admit publicly she'd been wrong? Obviously not, so she insisted she always treated these materials with the seriousness they deserved as she tuned up her best condescending Madame Secretary voice. This was one moment one could really hear the voice of the Red Queen from *Alice in Wonderland*.[769]

Broadly speaking, Clinton came off as Clinton—stiff, informed, patient, utterly competent, occasionally imperious, and unable to give away fresh birthday cakes to a room full of hungry ten-year-olds. Trump, in contrast, arrived with his calm and deliberate suit on, apparently saving his sarcasm and bile for when he faced Clinton directly. Without a doubt, Trump presented far less substance than Clinton, but he also seemed much more "authentic," more at ease with himself, the venue, and the audience. As Neil Newhouse, former pollster for Mitt Romney, described it, unlike Clinton, with Trump, "you never got the sense that Trump was on the defensive."[770]

STRONGER TOGETHER

Irony and absurdity were in abundance in the 2016 campaign, though often the moment passed unnoticed. Case in point: everywhere Hillary Clinton spoke, on her banners and painted across her campaign's airplane, were the words "Stronger Together."

On the one hand, "Stronger Together" was a classic MOTO—Master Of The Obvious. What group isn't stronger together? Who could argue with that?

The obvious implication was Clinton intended to be the new "uniter in chief," bringing us all (or at least most of us) together, and the nation would be stronger as a result. This is where the motto became ironic and absurd.

For a quarter of a century, Clinton had by far been the most divisive character in American politics. In 2016, many Americans had turned away from Barack Obama, finding him weak and ineffective, and while many despised his policies and his arrogance, few really hated Obama personally. Even those who opposed him still generally respected him. Tens of millions of Americans hated Hillary Clinton deeply for her elitism, her arrogance, her lies, her breaking the rules and often the law with impunity time and again.

America would indeed be stronger if we were more together. The person in public life most certain to increase the nation's divisions was Hillary Clinton. On the other hand, Donald Trump probably came in a close second with his own aspirations for first place.

Hillary's Basket of Deplorables

Candidates running hard for public office talk a lot. They give interviews and speeches. They get tired. Sometimes they say something really outrageous. Donald Trump built much of his campaign on making outrageous statements, but whether preplanned or not, they couldn't be chalked up to exhaustion. Trump was often at his most outrageous when he was his most energized.

That's not the norm. The norm for political candidates is they make outrageous comments when they're tired. They screw up. It happens. Early in September, Hillary Clinton offered her best entry for politically dumbest statement of the campaign. Speaking at an LGBT fund-raiser in New York City, Clinton spouted,

> You know, to just be grossly generalistic, you could put half of Trump's supporters into what I call the basket of deplorables. Right? The racist, sexist, homophobic, xenophobic, Islamaphobic—you name it. And unfortunately, there are people like that. And he has lifted them up.[771]

She was tired. She was speaking in front of "family" in a political sense. She let her guard down and said what she really felt. It happens. Even with Hillary Clinton, the truth occasionally manages to sneak out.

Roughly half the country supported Donald Trump. Clinton had just lumped half of Trump's supporters into a basket of sexist, homophobic, xenophobic deplorables. A little quick math revealed she thought that about a quarter of the nation's population were pond scum. "Stronger together"?

Afterward, she admitted she'd made a mistake, but she never repudiated her comment. And so the campaign moved on, the mainstream media content to participate in the moving on as the media largely shared in Clinton's little soul-bearing episode.

A Quick Look at the Polls

The polls had tightened appreciably by mid-September, with Hillary Clinton holding a slight edge nationally, but Donald Trump showing well in key states. For example, in Florida the average of three polls taken September 7 to the twelfth had Trump with a 2-point lead. He had a 2-point lead in Georgia and Arizona. He was up 5 points in Iowa, a state Republicans often struggle to win, and up 9 points in Missouri. The key battleground state of Ohio seemed to lean strongly toward Trump, with three of the four latest polls showing him up 4 or 5 points.

Not all states were leaning Trump. Colorado still sat firmly in Clinton's column with a 5-point lead, but the poll was taken in late August, much earlier than the noted Florida, Georgia, and Arizona polls. In those other states in late August, Clinton had been on top as well. Had Colorado stayed with Clinton, or had Trump turned the Colorado corner as he had in those other states?

Some other battleground states had clearly stuck with Clinton to this point. Michigan favored Clinton by between 5 and 8 points depending on the poll while New Hampshire favored her by 2 points. Virginia, Pennsylvania, and Wisconsin likewise had so far resisted Trump's entreaties.

Even with the Trump resisters, he clearly had the momentum as Clinton had gone through a bad period while Trump had mostly managed not to self-inflict additional harm. The Trump trend became so obvious the mainstream media took notice. Chris Cillizza of the *Washington Post* ran a story for which the headline told you all you needed to know: "Don't look now, but Donald Trump has all the momentum in the 2016 race."[772]

Only part of the Trump momentum could be attributed to Clinton's gaffes. Part of it reflected the ongoing process of Republican voters convincing themselves they could vote for non-Republican Trump. The thought process could be distilled down into a few basic points. First, one of the two of these characters was going to be the next president. All other options were fantasy.

Second, neither candidate was fit to be the next president. The choice was between the serial insulter and the serial liar, between bombast and rank corruption, between a man of unchecked appetites and a lifelong defender of same. Clinton, it could be argued, was temperamentally more suited to the position if one ignored her failings with veracity, her inability to connect with much of the American people, and her many scandals that would continue because that's who the Clintons were, including a husband who was still "dicking bimbos at home," according to Colin Powell's leaked emails.[773] On the other hand, Trump could act presidential when pressed, but then fell back into far more comfortable barroom brawler mode.

On policy, the choice was as simple as it was painful for struggling Republican voters. Clinton presented a policy agenda she believed in and thoroughly understood, an agenda of more Obama. Trump presented a flimsy policy agenda with which he had at best a passing familiarity and interest, but one with which most Republicans agreed in the main.

In short, to struggling mainstream Republicans grown up enough to get past the fantasy, the choice was between the definite awful and the possibly less bad. Possibly less bad was winning Republican hearts and minds, and thus so was Trump.

Trump Struggles Pretending to Be a Republican

In mid-September, Donald Trump reminded Republican voters just how hard this was going to be. Ford Motor Company announced it was shifting all small car production out of the United States, mostly to Mexico. The problem was simple. Manufacturing in the United States is expensive given the relatively high cost of union labor combined with a heavy regulatory burden. High domestic costs were intolerable, especially with respect to small cars, which generally carried exceptionally small profit margins if not outright losses. Ford either stopped making small cars in the United States or stopped making small cars altogether for the U.S. market.

Hillary Clinton kept a low profile as her campaign was still struggling to get out from behind the pneumonia eight ball. Into her silence Trump roared. After a visit to Flint, Michigan, Trump traveled to northern Ohio to observe, "It used to be cars were made in Flint, and you couldn't drink the water in Mexico. Now, you can't drink the water in Flint and cars are made in Mexico."[774] Whatever else you think of Trump, you have to admit that's a great line.

Then Trump turned his ire on Ford. "If you think you're going to make cars and you're ... going to sell them through our borders like we're stupid people ... not going to happen that way." He resurrected his proposal to levy a 35% tax on every car Ford imported into the United States.

From the specific to the general, the 35% import levy proposal wasn't very smart for a man who said he would hire lots of smart people. Who would pay the tax? Ford? Not in a million years. Ford's customers, if Ford had any, would pay the tax.

Would the tax apply only to U.S.-labeled cars coming into the United States? Toyota and Honda and Volkswagen probably loved that idea.

If Trump tried to levy the tax on all car imports, the United States would be slapped with a World Trade Organization filing so fast even Trump's head would spin.

The smart move substantively and politically was to observe the obvious: Ford was leaving because the Federal Government had driven it out. The pressures forcing Ford to scram had grown substantially under Barack Obama, and under a Clinton Administration would only get worse. Instead of attacking Ford, Trump should have turned his anger toward Clinton and Obama to declare he would make the United States such a great place to do business that Ford and every other car company would rush production into, not out of, the United States.

Americans were angry, but they wanted to be hopeful. They weren't angry because they liked being angry. They were angry for cause. They were not doing well, and their hopes for the future were dimming. Trump could embrace the anger. He could channel the anger. He could wield the anger. But in this case, intellectually, he couldn't make the obvious pivot to changing policy to become hopeful. The Republican view is to roll back government policies that weaken the economy, policies like uncompetitively high tax rates and overly aggressive regulations, not hiking tariffs like a third world despot in a temper tantrum. Once again, Trump showed he wasn't really a Republican.

He showed his true colors again in another area: child care. Trump's plan was right out of the Democrats' playbook, which is usually a problem if you're running as a Republican. For example, Trump's plan involved mandating that all employers provide their employees with six weeks of maternity leave.[775] To be clear, extended maternity leave was clearly beneficial to families, and increasingly, employers were revising their practices to allow for longer maternity leaves for mother and father. However, Trump's was precisely the kind of government mandate thinking that distorts labor markets, artificially drives up costs, and drives companies like Ford to vacate the premises.

Nor is extended maternity leave free. One way or another, younger workers were going to pay for this enhanced benefit, either through lower wages or through reductions in other benefits like health insurance.

Trump's folly, and an odd one for someone with a business background, was in thinking that a government-mandated extended-maternity-leave policy was costless to employers or that employers would just suck it up and bear the higher costs. Not in competitive industries, they wouldn't. Even those businesses already offering extended maternity leave did so knowing the employees affected valued this benefit more than some other, so the employer provided more of one and less of the other. But there is and will always be a trade-off.

Trump went further. He proposed expanding the deduction for child care costs, capping the benefit for families earning $500,000 or less. This meant the benefit was unavailable to the truly rich who didn't care anyway and mostly helped the modestly affluent because low-income and many middle-income families pay little or no Federal individual income tax.

Middle-class incomes had stagnated for over a decade, as a Census Bureau report issued at about this time reminded.[776] As of 2015, real (that is, inflation adjusted) median household income had yet to return to the level achieved in 2007. Raising a family was tough. Child care expenses were high and painful to a young family.

All that said, Trump had once again taken a flip approach to a serious issue. High child care costs? We'll help pay for them and pretend the "we" is the "government," when in fact the "we" paying those costs are now everyone else not getting the generous new benefits. Rather than emphasize the true source of the problem— stagnating middle-class family incomes—Trump went all Democrat and copied Clinton. Giving middle-class families a thriving economy where their incomes are rising steadily is a much better solution to painful child care costs. Republicans once again asked themselves— Trump's *our* nominee?

TRUMP AND BIRTHING

Donald Trump loved the spotlight. Hogging the spotlight proved an effective campaign technique. Hillary Clinton had just suffered a bad week of self-inflicted wounds comparable to Trump's usual experience, with her belatedly admitted pneumonia validating the "health question" and her "basket of deplorables" comment sure to haunt her through Election Day. Clinton needed to establish some positive vibes. Trump blocked her by staying in the spotlight. The topic: assertions that Pres. Obama was not even an American.

Trump may not have been a card-carrying member of "birther nation," the common label for those denying Barack Obama had been born in Hawaii as Obama insisted, but Trump was certainly a fellow traveler. Trump refused to reverse his earlier view doubting Obama's American heritage. To be clear, Obama had finally produced his long-form birth certificate in 2011.[777] To this point, the issue had churned ever since it became apparent Obama would be the Democratic nominee in 2008.

One might reasonably wonder why Barack Obama waited until 2011 to release the document unless it was to keep his opponents arguing incessantly about something utterly absurd. If the delay was a campaign tactic, it worked brilliantly. By 2016, Obama's birth certificate was part of the public record, leaving birther nation with nothing left but to ignore the plain fact or to allege the birth certificate was forged.

Trump didn't argue the forgery case, but he was reluctant to acknowledge the validity of the birth certificate and the implication that Obama was, as asserted, born in Hawaii. Finally, Trump acknowledged Obama's legitimate citizenship to the great delight of the mainstream media, which succumbed to the illusion it had forced Trump to do something he didn't want to do.[778] In reality, Trump had played the media like a violin, depriving Clinton of a chance to regain a positive theme while staying in the spotlight on something only Obama, the Democrats, and the mainstream media cared about.

Just to make sure the press understood it had been played, the Trump campaign issued a press release advertising a major news event to be held at the new Trump hotel in Washington, DC. The national press dutifully gathered. Trump took the stage and proceeded to talk about his nice new hotel. Trump had orchestrated a lovely infomercial compliments of the mainstream media. It got better.

Trump turned to a long line of veterans, Medal of Honor winners, and senior military leaders who'd come to voice their support for Trump. *Fox News* and *CNN* rolled the cameras nonstop for twenty minutes as Trump watched these military leaders express their intense support for his candidacy. *CNN*'s Jake Tapper eventually got the joke, and he didn't like it. "It's hard to imagine this is anything other than a political rick roll."[779] Indeed it was, and Jake Tapper and the rest of the mainstream media played their parts well as background actors. Don't mess with the master, grasshopper.[780]

Events, Dear Boy

Harold Macmillan served as Prime Minister from 1957 to 1963 during a particularly turbulent period in the United Kingdom's history. Macmillan can be credited with numerous worthy bon mots apropos the 2016 election. One such described that the life of a typical British foreign secretary was as a person, "forever poised between a cliché and an indiscretion." During the campaign, much the same could be said of either Trump or Clinton.

Macmillan was also credited with a second darkly applicable witticism. When asked what a Prime Minister most feared, he responded, "Events, dear boy, events." Major real-world events can utterly upend a campaign strategy, can distract national attention just when momentum is building, or can target a major weakness with Klieg light intensity. Such an event occurred on September 18.

In the Chelsea neighborhood of Manhattan, New York, an improvised explosive device (IED) went off late Saturday night, injuring twenty-nine people.[781] Another unexploded IED was found four blocks away. An earlier blast went off in a trash can at a train station in Elizabeth, New Jersey. The New Jersey blast occurred as a bomb squad robot attempted to disarm one of five IEDs found in a bag in the trash can. No one was injured in the New Jersey blast.

On Monday, a bar owner in Linden, New Jersey, called police about a man sleeping in his doorway. When Officer Angel Padilla arrived, he recognized the individual as Ahmad Khan Rahami, a twenty-eight-year-old naturalized citizen from Afghanistan on whom the FBI and New Jersey State Police had a few hours earlier issued bulletins as a person of interest in the bombings. Rahami pulled out a gun and shot Padilla in the chest, but was then in turn wounded by another arriving officer and taken into custody.[782] Fortunately, Padilla was wearing a flak vest. He and Rahami survived.

At about the time, twenty-two-year-old Dahir A. Adan, self-described "soldier of ISIS," went on a knife-wielding melee at the Crossroads Mall in St. Cloud, Minnesota. He injured ten people, none fatally.[783] He was then shot by Jason Falconer, an officer with the Avon

Police Department. Nothing immediately linked the St. Cloud knife attack to the New York and New Jersey bomb blasts, but credulity strained attempting to argue these were entirely unrelated, even as authorities tried to paint each as the result of a lone-wolf assailant.

A week prior to these attacks, Pres. Obama had marked the Muslim holiday of Eid al-Adha with a call for tolerance. "And as a nation, we remain committed to welcoming the stranger with empathy and an open heart," after which he observed that the United States had already reached its goal of accepting 10,000 Muslim refugees.[784]

Hillary Clinton was in a tough spot. Obama appeared as indifferent to the concerns of his fellow citizens as he was insistent on America's role in providing a humane haven for as many Muslim refugees as he could get over the border. He still refused to refer to radical Islam or to label as terrorism such acts as occurred in New York, New Jersey, and Minnesota. Clinton was linked at the hip with Obama. It was hard to argue the humanitarian gesture when bombs were going off in downtown New York City and radicalized Muslims suddenly appeared in Minnesota suburban malls brandishing knives.

Clinton called for vigilance, to which most Americans probably responded, "No sh——t." She proclaimed she was "prepared, ready to actually take on those challenges," of internal security against imported and homegrown terrorists. What would she actually do that would help? Crickets.

Clinton attacked Trump for not having a plan: "You don't hear a plan from him [Trump]. He says he has a secret plan. The secret is he has no plan."[785] Yet she couldn't distract from the obvious truth she had no plan either, except to continue to accept tens of thousands of Muslim immigrants from war-ravished lands in the Middle East.

Clinton didn't like Trump's plan, but not liking a plan doesn't mean there wasn't a plan. Trump's plan was to stop importing any more "soldiers of ISIS." While a fairly obvious first step, and one Clinton wouldn't dare espouse, Clinton was right about one thing: short of oppressive, police-state measures, Trump too had no plan to deal with homegrown terrorism.

Neither candidate could propose much to enhance Americans' security against domestic terrorism, any more than could France or Germany. On this issue, the difference between Clinton and Obama on the one hand and Trump on the other wasn't one of plans, but of attitude. Obama's approach was to ignore his fellow citizens' concerns in pursuit of his ideals manifested in humanitarian gestures. Clinton's demeanor and approach delivered in her ever-so-superior tone was to stay calm and do nothing. Trump reacted like a guy who'd been punched in the nose and intended to punch back. Not hard to see which attitude typical Americans found most appealing.

What Clinton and Trump said mattered little at this point. No one doubted Clinton would do much the same as Obama. No one doubted Trump would be little concerned with the niceties and would do everything possible to ferret out domestic terrorists and to stop importing foreign terrorists. These events drew attention to an area where Trump appeared at his strongest, whether he made sense or not, and Clinton appeared at her weakest, whether it fair or not. "Events, dear boy, events."

Hillary Sliding into the Debate

Hillary Clinton's campaign became largely centered on arguing that Donald Trump was "unfit" to be President of the United States. This approach had a certain credibility as the assertion was supported by a Trumpian mountain of evidence, but arguing Trump's unfitness raised its own problems. First, it meant the campaign was about Trump as the unfit agent of chaos, not Clinton as worthy successor to Barack Obama.

Second, even those inclined to acknowledge Trump was unfit to be president could reasonably insist Clinton was equally unfit. True, Clinton was vastly better prepared, but it wasn't about preparation. The issue she raised was fitness, moral and ethical. Clinton threw that card away again and again with her lack of transparency, her defense of Bill Clinton's lifetime of inappropriate behavior toward women, her pay-to-play Clinton Foundation shenanigans, and her lifetime honorary membership in the National Veracity Challenged Club.

Trump had momentum. Clinton had none, and it showed in the polls as Trump slowly but steadily climbed into parity both nationally and across the battleground states. Even many near-battleground states typically tough for Republicans were moving Trump's way. In Iowa, Trump was up 8 points.

In Nevada, Rasmussen had Trump up 3 points.[786] In North Carolina, Trump was averaging plus 2 points, and in Georgia and in Colorado he was averaging up 4 points. Trump was up slightly in Florida and tied Clinton in Maine.

Democrats continued to buck themselves up with talk of an Electoral College lock, but the RealClearPolitics Electoral College map showed Clinton with 200 votes to Trump's 164. An advantage, to be sure, but one quickly disappearing as twelve states since September 1 had moved toward Trump in some way—from leaning Clinton to toss-up or from toss-up to leaning Trump.

Health issues continued to dog Clinton. The standard protocol for recovering from pneumonia is an antibiotic regimen and rest. Neither is negotiable. The pneumonia didn't care she was running for president. Those who try to scrimp on the rest end up taking much longer to recover and meanwhile suffer low energy. Clinton hadn't learned her lesson from nearly passing out at the 9/11 Memorial Service. She still insisted on trying to "power through." Big mistake. All the will in the world cannot indefinitely replace the oxygen necessary to generate energy. Clinton canceled event after event.

She was scheduled to do a little fund-raiser in North Carolina for those willing to pop $100,000 just to meet her.[787] All she had to do was a celebrity flyby and her guests would understand. She canceled, just as she canceled a California event due to flagging health.[788] The pneumonia would pass, eventually, but Clinton's stubbornness was effectively feeding the narrative she had substantial health issues that might properly disqualify her for the presidency.

That wasn't all of Clinton's bad news. With Trump at the top, Democrats had assumed they would build on their strong 2012 showing with Hispanic voters. Obama took 71% of Hispanic votes compared with Romney's 24%, for a 47-point margin. One poll showed Clinton's margin was only 35%. She was winning big with Hispanics, but not as big as Obama had, and in a close election the difference could really matter in pivotal states.[789]

Democrats were also increasingly worried about the black turnout. Clinton would win the black vote by a large margin, but those are percentages. Obama gave the Democrats high watermarks for turnout. How much drop-off would Clinton suffer? At a black-tie Congressional Black Caucus dinner, Obama threw down the challenge, declaring it would be a "personal insult" if blacks didn't come out to vote for Clinton.[790]

Clinton bombarded battleground state airwaves with radio and television ads, hoping to turn the tide. She'd raised a lot of money. That's what it was for. It turns out Trump raised an astonishing amount himself in a very short period and he had spent very little. Clinton had amassed 2.3 million "small dollar donors" over decades of work. These donors give less than $200. Trump signed his first email fund-raising letter June 21. He reported $100 million raised from 2.1 million donors. "I've never seen anything like it," commented a senior operative who'd worked with the program. "He's the Republican Obama in terms of online fund-raising."[791]

TRUMP FLAWS, FOIBLES, AND FUNDAMENTALS

Donald Sr. and Donald Jr. each had issues, but different kinds. Donald Sr. apparently used a quarter-million dollars from his charitable Trump Foundation to settle some lawsuits.[792] If true, this sort of self-dealing involving a nonprofit organization is a definite no-no. The Trump campaign quickly alleged the reporter got the facts wrong, but failed to indicate which of the reported facts were in error.

On the one hand, this little episode was absurd. While the amounts involved were substantial to most individuals and reporters, to a multibillionaire, this was literally chicken feed. It was difficult to imagine why he did it. Whatever the reason, it didn't look good, but it only mattered to Trump's haters and the mainstream media.

On the other hand, any questions about Trump's mishandling relatively minor amounts from his Foundation paled in comparison to Bill and Hillary's payola scheme involving their infamous Clinton Foundation. Hillary Clinton probably cringed every time she heard the word "Foundation," up to and including references to her own cosmetics.

Donald Jr.'s issues were of a different nature, as they struck a twitchy nerve among the nation's intelligentsia. Donald Jr. tweeted a picture of a bowl of Skittles candy with the caption, "If I had a bowl of Skittles and I told you just three would kill you. Would you take a handful? That's our Syrian refugee problem."[793]

The ensuing outrage was as predictable as it was contrived, as Trump's opponents hoped this could be spun to slow Trump's momentum. There were just a couple of problems. First, Trump's opponents were all talking amongst themselves. Trump's supporters and potential supporters weren't listening. Why? Because they got it.

Many Americans were reasonably concerned about Obama's (and by inference, Clinton's) plans to allow tens of thousands of immigrant refugees from throughout the Middle East. Most of these immigrants were desperate and needed help. America is a big country with a big heart.

However, some of these desperate immigrants would be ISIS supporters. Possibly a great many would be. Who could tell? Some would arrive hopeful and then be radicalized like the bom bomber in Chelsea, New York. Clinton and Obama could not and did not argue the contrary. The United States Government had no effective way to screen immigrants adequately either before or after they entered the country.

The inevitable implication was that Clinton and Obama and the rest of the intelligentsia were willing to risk the possibility if not likelihood that some of these desperate Muslim immigrants would kill Americans in their own neighborhoods. Most Americans were less willing to take that chance. Donald Jr. had explained a most inconvenient truth in a most transparent way. Skittles. Beehive duly rattled, the bees came out mad as, well, angry bees.

Once again, the vast majority of Americans were on one side of the issue—their own security—and the elites were on the other side, safely protected (they thought) in their gated communities. If the Trump campaign stayed firm, then the media's own fury would translate into renewed energy for the Trump campaign.

Trump Advantages to Not Being Republican

In one of the most insightful moments of the campaign, *CBS News* explained some of Trump's surprising strength.[794] *CBS* sent a news crew to the working-class neighborhood of Struthers, Ohio, just southeast of Youngstown and a few miles from the Pennsylvania border. The crew picked a typical neighborhood block and knocked on every door on the block.

They found some Clinton supporters, such as Halle Minchin Skook, a special ed teacher at the local middle school. "I don't understand how any educated person who watches all the political things on TV can vote for him [Trump]."

In fact, in this steelworker town full of lifelong, card-carrying Democrats, a lot of people planned to vote for Trump. "They know he's not really a Republican, and that Mitt Romney hates him, so that helps," observed Paul Sracic, a longtime resident and chair of the Department of Politics and International Relations at nearby Youngstown University.

Notice the key phrase there—they know Trump's "not really a Republican," so voting for Trump wouldn't really be like voting for a Republican. It would be more like voting for a strong, traditional Democrat in camo, a point reinforced by the fact a recognized establishment Republican (Romney) hated Trump, and all real Democrats know (or believe) that all real Republicans stick together.

How bad did it get for Democrats in this Ohio union stronghold? During the Ohio Republican primary, Struthers's Democratic mayor had a Trump for President sign on his front lawn.

Why vote for a Republican in camo when you could vote for the Democratic nominee? Jeff Kulow, twenty-five-year member of the Teamsters Union, was a self-described "lifelong union guy, a working guy." For Kulow and guys like him, Obama changed everything. Obama was "against everything I believe in." Clinton had gotten one message through the din: She was running as Obama's third term, carrying on his legacy. For many working-class, lifelong Democrats, that was the kiss of death. Many felt as did Kulow. "I can't see myself ever going back [to voting Democrat]." Trump spoke their language. Clinton and the Democratic establishment had become the enemy.

Not Again!

The location: Tulsa, Oklahoma. The event: Another white police officer shot a black man. It was captured on video from a dash cam and from a police helicopter circling overhead, both videos publicly released immediately.[795]

Officers were called to a two-lane where a white SUV was reported abandoned on the road. When the first police car arrived, a large black man in white T-shirt and shorts stood in the road with the SUV straddling the center line a few feet beyond. Forty-year-old Terence Crutcher turned around and began walking to his car, putting his hand on the top of the car near the driver's side door. A second police car arrived along with the police helicopter. Crutcher was quickly tased and then shot and killed within seconds of the initial contact.

The location: Charlotte, North Carolina. The event: A black police officer shot an armed black man.[796] Keith Lamont Scott was in a vehicle around midday when police arrived to serve an arrest warrant on another man in a nearby apartment complex. Scott got out of his car. He was clearly armed, according to police. He was told to drop his weapon. He refused. At some point, Brentley Vinson, a black police officer, shot Scott four times.[797]

Charlotte's black community erupted for days of rioting in which many were hurt. One person was shot by a protester in a hotel doorway. He died shortly thereafter.

Charlotte suffered a nasty bout of urban rioting and so the National Guard restored order. But according to a Charlotte-Mecklenburg police spokesman speaking with *CNN*'s Erin Burnett, "probably 70% of those [arrested during the protests] had out-of-state IDs."[798] These weren't fed-up local citizens. They were outside agitators flocking to the opportunity to make trouble. Maybe Tulsa was just too far a drive.

No community can tolerate police overstepping the lawful and proper use of force. No community should tolerate police harassment. On the other hand, society had become incredibly violent. Black Lives Matter continued to protest and agitate, but never against rampant black-on-black violence, only when the police were involved. In such an environment of pervasive violence, the police were daily put in highly dangerous situations. Sometimes they overreacted. Sometimes the police made mistakes. Sometimes people died.

In Tulsa, Terence Crutcher was dead for no apparent reason. Later, toxicology reports confirmed Crutcher had the hallucinogen PCP in his system at the time of his death, but this fact appeared to have no bearing because Crutcher had at no point appeared in any way violent.[799] A five-year veteran of the force, Officer Betty Shelby, "overreacted" as the District Attorney observed, plain and simple, and was quickly charged with first-degree manslaughter.[800] The Tulsa community remained calm and let the judicial process work.

In Charlotte, the officer apparently acted entirely appropriately. When faced with an individual carrying a pistol and refusing to obey commands, at some point that individual is going to be shot. The officer was black. The chief of police was black. The dead man was black. The officer followed procedure. The city erupted in riots.

Difficult issues, but what did this have to do with the election? Only this—the depth and breadth of frustration with the course of the country was daunting. In crassest political terms, if this is how the black community feels with a black president, what could possibly motivate them to come out to vote for an oldish white woman who promised at best more of the same? The rest of the country was looking for somebody with the firmness of purpose he or she would restore some semblance of law and order. Did that sound more like Trump or Clinton? Clear advantage: Trump.

FUNDAMENTAL DIFFERENCES: GROWTH VS. REDISTRIBUTIONISM

American voters may not "sweat the details" as Hillary Clinton insisted she did, but they eventually got the big picture pretty well. According to one poll, nearly three out of four Americans believed the economy would continue to perform poorly or even worse for the next decade.[801]

Why the pessimism? Experience is a great teacher. After seven years of the Obama Administration's policies, an anemic economy had downshifted from slow. All the happy talk from the administration's supporters fooled no one. For example, the same poll also showed that over half the respondents believed the very professional Bureau of Labor Statistics (BLS) manipulated the data to produce the reported and historically low 4.9% official unemployment rate.[802] In fact, BLS played it straight, but the low rate certainly didn't reflect the weakness of the labor market as perceived by many.

What about the future? Overall, Americans are by nature an optimistic lot. But again, they get the big picture. Consider the presidential nominees. On the one hand, Donald Trump had what might generously be described as an indifferent familiarity with public policy. For example, on one of the most basic issues of tax policy, it took his campaign days to figure out whether all or only half the country's business income should benefit from a lower tax rate. After much public fumbling, the campaign finally decided, yes, small businesses should also get a tax rate reduction. To their credit, at least Trump discovered the right answer in the end.

Then there was Hillary Clinton. Her husband, the former president, seemed to get it, as during a CNBC interview Bill Clinton advocated a substantial reduction in the corporate income tax rate.[803] Hillary Clinton didn't get the memo about economic growth and tax policy. Instead, she doubled down on her proposed increase in the death tax, proposing to raise the top rate to 65% for especially large estates.[804]

Hillary Clinton's new proposal affirmed her views on economic growth as expressed in her previous tax policy announcements for much higher individual income and capital gains tax rates. In short, Clinton's proposals underscored she really only cared about redistributing income and wealth and didn't care much whether the economy crawled at a snail's pace. She might insist she did care, but her proposals said otherwise. Americans may not sweat the details, but between Trump's policy incoherence and Clinton's coherent antagonism to economic growth, the poll suggests they got the big picture on the economy's future.

HILLARY BETWEEN TWO FERNS

The polls suggested Clinton struggled to appeal to millennials. By late September, her support among millennials appeared to be collapsing.[805] Only a month earlier, she led Trump among millennials by 25 points. By late September, her average advantage had slipped to 3 points. Historically, millennials had a fairly low voter turnout rate, but Clinton needed their support to win. The silver lining came from indications only a portion of Clinton's loss was Trump's gain as many millennials shifted instead to the Libertarian ticket of Johnson/Weld and the Green Party ticket of Jill Stein.

Arresting this slide wouldn't be easy, so Clinton tried something different and, frankly, rather courageous. She went on "Between Two Ferns" with actor/comedian Zach Galifianakis and posted on the web site, *Funny or Die*.[806] The show was a one-man conversation/comedy roast. Clinton seemed at once dubious and yet engaged and wryly funny.[807]

Clinton knew the host would throw decorum to the wind. To set the tone, Zach asked what would happen if Hillary got pregnant. "Are we going to be stuck with Tim Kaine for nine months?"

Galifianakis asked how Obama liked his coffee since she had been his secretary (of state). Then he observed her pantsuits made her look like a "librarian from outer space."[808] This from a guy who looked like he'd just woken from a beer-induced nap and forgot to comb his hair.

At one point Clinton said, "I really regret doing this." One couldn't be entirely sure if she meant it.

In addition to cautious, Clinton also seemed tired, or as Trump might have called it, "low energy." At one point, her answers confirmed something was amiss. Galifianakis asked her what she would do if Trump won. This is one of the oldest tricks in the book, and every decent politician knocks it out of the park. Clinton fell for it.

The correct answer is something along the lines of, "I think I'm going to win because I'm the better candidate, so the question is meaningless." Instead, Clinton answered that if Trump won, then she would work to keep Trump from doing bad things. She posited Trump winning. Trump could win, of course, and insisting the contrary would be silly. But that's not the same as insisting she would win. A rested Hillary Clinton, even a moderately tired Clinton, would never make this mistake.

At the end of the five-minute session, Zach said, "We should stay in touch. What is best way to reach you? Email?" Hillarious! Clinton just stared him down.

Even if you don't like her, give the lady her props. It took guts to go on the show. She handled it well. For five minutes, Hillary Clinton was almost cool.

TED CRUZ RETURNS AND PRESIDENT PSEUDONYM

When last we'd heard from Texas Sen. Ted Cruz, he was being booed off the Republican National Convention stage, having been given a prime speaking slot in Donald Trump's coronation and then failing to endorse Trump. Oddly, Cruz then changed his mind. He endorsed Trump, after all. Had Trump changed? No. Had Hillary Clinton become even less appealing in Cruz's estimation? Unlikely. Why endorse Trump now? Reason No. 1 given was Cruz had promised to support the nominee, and so he would do so. Why reason No. 1 wasn't obvious to Cruz before his convention speech defied explanation.

As Reason No. 2, Cruz offered the same thought process so many Republicans were exploring. Trump is bad. Clinton is worse across the board. Bad is less bad than worse. Again, why this wasn't obvious to Cruz at the Republican convention may not seem obvious.

Friday afternoon—time for another FBI data dump from the thoroughly politicized chief investigative arm of the United States Government. The timing of the data dump reaffirmed the FBI under Director Comey didn't even try to pretend it wasn't an extension of the Clinton campaign anymore. However, the substance of the data dump did reveal the FBI was not yet prepared to go so far as to break the law to help Clinton, which was something.

This 189-page data dump included something new. It showed Pres. Obama had participated in the Clinton email cover-up. Obama used a pseudonym in some of his communications with Clinton run through her private email server while she was secretary of state. As reported by Politico,

> In an April 5, 2016, interview with the FBI, Huma Abedin [chief aide to the secretary of state] was shown an email exchange between Clinton and Obama, but the longtime Clinton aide did not recognize the name of the sender.
>
> "Once informed that the sender's name is believed to be pseudonym used by the president, Abedin exclaimed: 'How is this not classified?'" the report says. "Abedin then expressed her amazement at the president's use of a pseudonym and asked if she could have a copy of the email."[809]

The FBI report didn't indicate what Obama used as his pseudonym, which was apparently known at least to his inner circle. This latest report brought the topic back into the news, reminding voters once again of Clinton's email scandal.

The report also laid bare that Obama didn't tell the truth when he went on *CBS News* in March of 2015 to clarify when he'd first learned of Clinton's private email server. "The same time everybody else learned it through news reports."[810]

Apparently not, as Obama knew of it when he was emailing Clinton, using his pseudonym to her private email account. A government email address is very clearly identified with the trailer ".gov." Clinton's private email server used a different extension. As we later learned, Clinton's people tried to get the administration to "clean up" the president's remarks, but to no avail.[811]

Clinton's Mounting Desperation

Hillary Clinton may have been almost cool sitting between ferns, but her campaign had gone cold on the trail. The race was a dead heat, and both sides suspected Trump had a few percentage points of support not showing in the polls because respondents wouldn't tell pollsters the truth. Nothing Clinton did helped. Her main attack line was that Trump was unfit and unprepared. Most voters likely agreed, but most also believed she wasn't fit for the office either, and while she was highly prepared, the next questions were, "To do what? More of Obama? No thanks."

Hillary tried nibbling at the edges. For weeks, Clinton's mouthpieces complained of unfair coverage, that the mainstream media was treating Clinton more harshly. Anyone not on the campaign could consider the evidence for a moment and only conclude, "You've got to be kidding, right?" The mainstream media continued to cover for Clinton by ignoring as much as they could while hammering Trump on everything they could dream up.

Chutzpah was the only word to describe the Clinton campaign's other complaint. Robby Mook told ABC News, "We haven't seen anything like this. We normally go into a debate with two candidates who have a depth of experience, who have rolled out clear, concrete plans, and who don't lie, frankly, as frequently as Donald Trump does."[812]

No doubt Trump had a serious problem with simple truths. Mook was right in one respect—no politician in modern history had gotten away with anything like Trump's behavior. Campaigns in the past were manically scrupulous trying to keep every statement defensible with citable facts. This was just another area in which Trump was unique. He got away with it because he just dismissed the criticisms.

In most instances, however, Trump's exaggerations and blatant misstatements were venial sins. Like his past claims, he was a big pal of Russian Pres. Putin, only to disavow any such friendship or even suggesting the contrary. Or like his repeated statements he had always been against the Iraq war, statements he continued to make despite video evidence to the contrary, evidence he'd seen and reacted to with essentially, "whatever." To be sure, whether one supported the Iraq war or not was not really tangential, but it was, in the current context, ancient history.

In contrast, Hillary Clinton rarely exaggerated beyond the pale and rarely misspoke. In this, she was a consummate professional politician. Throughout her life in public office, she saved her lies for the really big things and crafted the wording with exquisite care. These traits had most recently been on display involving the Foundation and her private email server. The Clinton campaign needed to avoid certain topics like the plague. No one on the Clinton campaign should have ever used the words "server," or "email," or "Foundation," and most especially "lies." How desperate was the Clinton campaign? They'd lost track of the basics.

The First Debate

The month prior to the first debate was a pundit's feast. Everybody opined on what Trump or Clinton should or shouldn't say. As Macbeth observed at the death of his queen, so too the predebate cacophony. The campaign punditry was "but a walking shadow, a poor player that struts and frets his hour upon the stage, and then is here no more. It is a tale told by an idiot, full of sound and fury, signifying nothing."

Yet the sound and fury went on, hour after hour, for what else were the punditry to do during this pause between the conventions and the first debate? Apparently, many Americans were content to hear, muse, and be entertained by the many poor players on stage. Pollster Frank Luntz offered typical advice when he said Trump needed to go from prosecutorial to presidential. "You do not need to shock with spectacle. You need to surprise with sincerity."[813] Good luck with that.

Trump's great advantage was the bar had been set so low it should have been easy to exceed expectations. Be the Donald Trump who met the Mexican President and then Trump might convince some wavering voters he could be president. As they say in California, "Fake it 'til you make it."

Clinton's task was notably more difficult. If she tried to prod Trump into a mistake, an ill-considered comment or attack, she would have to tread carefully. She had to protect her image of substance and, above all, avoid appearing petty. Going in, it seemed all Clinton could do, all she should do, was to be herself—calm, composed, knowledgeable, and firm . . . and wait for Trump to attack or stumble.

Levity for the moment was provided via the silliness of some last-minute antics. For example, Mark Cuban, the oddball billionaire owner of the NBA's Dallas Mavericks and an inconsequential if vociferous Trump critic, threatened to sit in the front row of the debate. This could have proven interesting as Cuban famously exhibited his own brand of histrionics when his team played.

Trump responded by suggesting maybe he'd have Gennifer Flowers sit in the front row, Flowers having had a long-running affair with Bill Clinton, an affair he denied for years until he finally came clean but only because he was under oath.[814] But then others from Bill Clinton's history wanted a seat, including Paula Jones and Juanita Broaddrick. If all of Bill's accusers came forward, they might need to go to two rows.[815] It seemed unlikely Chappaqua's Julie "the Energizer" Tauber McMahon would be in attendance, however.

Finally, the antics ended; and on Monday, September 26, the two candidates faced off for the first time. In most modern campaign debates, the two candidates clearly shared some degree of mutual respect, mutual distrust, and mutual dislike. Trump clearly had a low opinion of Clinton, but he likely didn't care enough about her one way or another to have a sustained dislike. Clinton, on the other hand, loathed Trump. It showed.

Clinton mounted the stage wearing a neck-to-toe bright red pantsuit, going for the full power look, looking confident and well rested after her pneumonia bout. Trump came out in a dark blue suit with a bright blue tie.

The evening at Long Island's Hofstra University started civil enough. Lester Holt opened with some initial remarks about the ground rules and then proceeded to his first question in which Holt planted his flag clearly in Clinton's camp. Holt observed the economy had created millions of jobs over the previous six years, and the latest Census report showed middle-class incomes rising at the fastest rate in decades.[816] All true, but equally true would have been to observe that even seven years after the recession, millions of Americans remain locked out of the workforce by the anemic economy, and middle-class incomes according to that same Census report were still below the peak during the George W. Bush Administration.

After using his subtle spin to signal his bias, Holt exposed himself in other ways. For example, six times when Trump gave an answer, Holt would follow up to press him on some point. How many times did Holt press Clinton with a follow-up question? Not once.[817] Holt interrupted Clinton seven times in the middle of an answer. He interrupted Trump forty-one times.[818]

For all his obvious bias, Holt otherwise did a fine job. He seemed to understand what so many baseball umpires can't accept—it's not about them. The night was about the candidates and the voters, not the moderator, just as a baseball game is about the players and the fans, not the men in black.

Holt interrupted Trump often, but Trump also had a habit of rambling off subject, much more so than Clinton. Trump also had a tendency to vagueness in response to direct questioning. Clinton was frequently nuanced and shaded but rarely vague with the points she made, so it made sense for Holt to follow up more with Trump to push for detailed responses.

Holt let the candidates debate. He let them mix it up, without letting the discussion get out of hand and without exceptional violations of time allotments. He asked tough questions. It would always be possible to nitpick certain points. On balance, if the subsequent debate's moderators did as well, then the nation would be well served.

The candidates started civil enough, but Clinton had no intention of waiting for Trump to throw the first elbow. She got in first. The debate went back and forth with testiness and substance mixing in with occasional agreement. Unquestionably, Clinton came off as the more polished and poised, the more self-controlled, the better-prepared candidate in terms of facts. She exuded strength, confidence, and determination. She also spoke like a president, using the cadence and terms of her profession.

In contrast, Trump was clearly much less prepared, adding meat to the predebate rumors he had done little prep work. Even when questions were asked he knew would come, his answers were grossly inadequate and appeared to suggest he thought he could just bluster and bluff his way through.

And yet Trump spoke clearly, offering the compelling message America wasn't doing well enough, whether the issue was ISIS or cybersecurity, job growth or poverty in black communities. Trump insisted the country could do much better and that people like Clinton who'd been in charge for decades were responsible for messing it all up. Above all, Trump spoke like a regular person even as Clinton spoke like a professional politician.

Three issues really stumped Trump. The first was his refusal to release his tax returns. Clinton pressed hard. Trump lamely responded he would happily release the returns but his lawyers had told him since he was under audit he should keep them private. To review: The IRS had the returns already. The man was running for president. Tell the lawyers to stuff it.

Then Trump turned the issue to his advantage. He said he'd defy his lawyers and release the returns if Clinton would release the 30,000 emails she'd deleted. The danger in this gambit was Trump had said he could release his returns under at least one condition. Running for president apparently wasn't enough. The condition was Clinton would release her deleted emails.

The second issue to trip Trump and which Clinton pressed to great effect was Trump's only belatedly acknowledging Barack Obama was born in America. In truth, Trump's behavior on this was bizarre and could be perhaps only be chalked up to stubbornness. Having ill-advisedly raised the issue for years, thus stoking the sense he was a closet racist, Trump struggled to admit he had been wrong.

Trump tried to throw up a cloud of dust on the "birther" issue with ramblings about finding birth certificates and repeated references to Clinton confidant Sidney Blumenthal and how Blumenthal had suggested Clinton raise the "birther" issue in 2008 when she was running against Obama. There may have been a thread of substantive argument somewhere in these ramblings, but it would take an expert hours of rabbinic textual parsing to find it.

The third issue to bedevil Trump was the Iraq war. Clinton set up the issue perfectly. Trump continued to insist he had always opposed the Iraq war. The video evidence was plain and public: Trump supported the war at least at one point. Clinton called Trump on it and Trump again insisted he had always opposed the war. The moment passed because there was nothing more to debate. There was a charge, a denial, and the facts.

Yet again, Trump failed to turn the issue to his advantage. As a New York Senator, Clinton had voted to support George W. Bush's Iraq war. Her war vote stirred tremendous anger on the Far Left. Trump allowed himself to get caught debating a falsehood rather than using Clinton's vote for the war as another example of her alleged bad judgment. It was a line he used repeatedly on the campaign stump so it should have come easily, but he missed it.

For all his missed chances, Trump still landed some powerful blows. He painted Clinton as part of the political class that had failed the country in economic policy, social policy, and foreign policy. The blows landed because the assertions were credible, because he seemed sincerely frustrated at what the political class had wrought, and because he spoke his mind in plain language. They also landed cleanly because on this point, many voters, even traditional Democrats, largely agreed with Trump.

As simple proof of the many and manifest failings of America's ruling class, Trump emphasized how the economy was widely believed to be doing poorly. Clinton tried to recover, arguing things weren't really so bad, a particularly unfortunate tack as many voters agreed with Trump.

Clinton argued Trump had no plan to address these ills whereas she had a mountain of detailed plans. Here, Clinton was correct. Trump really had few plans to address the identified problems, whereas Clinton had scores of detailed plans. The problem with her plans, and the point Trump failed to make, was that Clinton's plans were minor variations of more of the same that had left the country in its current condition. She had no plans for restoring prosperity, or restoring America's reputation around the world, or restoring a more civil society.

Trump also trotted out the "law and order" issue. Clinton tried that angle as well, but it just came out as more of the same policies and muddleheaded thinking leading to lawlessness and disorder. Her strongest argument substantively was to refer to criminal justice reform, which to most voters just meant letting criminals out early—not very comforting. Trump didn't have much else to say on the matter, aside from the constitutionally questionable policy of "stop and frisk."[819] As usual, Trump had little substance, but he insisted credibly that he would restore law and order.

Trump's position on law and order received a substantial boost the day after the debate when the FBI reported the murder rate was up more than 10% in 2015 over 2014, and 2016 was likely to see another big jump, especially as Obama's hometown, Chicago, was spiraling out of control.[820]

Clinton's goals in the debate had been simple—get under Trump's thin skin without lowering herself to his level and otherwise present herself as the sane, sensible presidential candidate on the stage. Trump's goals were to present himself as the fed-up outsider who really could be president.

The essence of her candidacy was, "I'm ready, and I'm not crazy like Trump." The essence of Trump's candidacy was, "We can't keep doing this. Maybe you agree with me. Maybe you don't. But wouldn't it be better to take a chance rather than passively accept more of the same?" Both sides conveyed these points effectively.

As one would expect, the media immediately declared Clinton the winner. Very little of the initial commentary and analysis merited attention because it was all so tainted. For example, Howard Fineman of the *Huffington Post* declared, "Trump's Debate Performance Was the Worst Ever."[821] One wondered if Fineman had written the piece before the debate. Contrast Fineman with Charles Hurt's inexplicable hyperventilation in concluding Trump won a "decisive victory" in the debate.[822]

Michael Moore, ultraleftist Hollywood celeb and the one bloviating bombast capable of making Trump seem decently human by comparison, agreed with Hurt, concluding Trump "won" and "we all lost."[823] Moore tweeted throughout the debate, becoming increasingly agitated Clinton refused to go full Trump on Trump, convinced he would win if the Clintonistas didn't wake up.

If one suspended credulity for a moment and just considered the debate and the state of the race in general, one could conclude Hurt and Moore, coming from opposite ends of the political spectrum, were correct. Clinton was formidable in the debate and held a strong position as a candidate, but she was losing ground to Trump and the debate had done nothing to arrest her slide. Trump really could win, it seemed.

Pundits' opinions were worth doodley-squat. Who won, according to the voters? It would take a few days before meaningful poll results appeared. Online polls, which are little more than curiosities if that, were nevertheless all one had in the moment. Amazingly, the online polls showed Trump dominated:

	Trump	Clinton
	(percent)	
Drudge[824]	82	18
ABC News	54	10
Time	54	46
Breitbart	76	24
CNBC	67	33

Drip, Drip, Drip—More Immunity

The FBI conveniently provided another example of its playing politics with the Clinton investigation. Along with news of the email data dump, the realization finally broke through the din: the FBI had granted Cheryl Mills immunity from prosecution in exchange for her cooperation.

The FBI wanted Mills's laptop computer from her time as Clinton's State Department Chief of Staff. The FBI could use a grand jury subpoena to compel Mills to hand over the laptop. Instead, they gave Mills immunity in exchange for the laptop. Why immunity? Mills was worried something on the laptop might put her in legal jeopardy. This was all very strange. As Andrew McCarthy, a former U.S. Attorney, put it, "it's like telling a bank robbery suspect, 'If you turn over that bag, I'll give you immunity as to the contents'—which means if the money you robbed is in there, I can't use it against you."[825]

Though Mills was granted immunity, she was still a witness in the investigation. Yet Mills was still allowed to act as Hillary Clinton's attorney in Clinton's interactions with the FBI regarding the email server. Congressional Republicans, some of whom began their careers in the justice system, thought this all rather odd. They asked Director

Comey to testify and clear up the confusion before Jason Chaffetz's (R-UT) House Judiciary Committee.

For the most part, Comey was his usual calm and deliberate self, but this time the smokescreen proved too thin to hide his own inconvenient truth. Tom Marino (R-PA), a former Justice Department prosecutor, asked the Director why the immunity for Cheryl Mills. Why not just get a subpoena?

Comey's response appeared straightforward. "It's a reasonable question. . . . Any time you are talking about the prospect of subpoenaing a computer from a lawyer—that involves the lawyer's practice of the law—you know you are getting into the big megillah. . . . In general, you can often do things faster with informal agreements."[826]

Reasonable enough, nothing to see here. Move on, please.

No, wait a minute, back that up.

There was that phrase "lawyer's practice of law." The Director was obviously referring to the attorney-client privilege. Something on the computer might, if disclosed, violate the attorney-client privilege. So to get the computer, the FBI had to create a no-danger zone.

Oh right. Can we move on now, PLEASE?

As Peter Falk playing Columbo might have then asked as he donned his old raincoat, "Uh, just one more question. Did this computer involve Cheryl Mills' role as Secretary of State Clinton's Chief of Staff?"

Well yes, it did. This meant Mills wasn't Clinton's lawyer at the time, which meant there was no "megillah" attorney-client privilege issue. Mills had gotten away with this nonsense because she claimed she didn't know anything about the server until after she had become Clinton's attorney, after she had left the State Department. This, then, would reestablish the attorney-client privilege.

Oh OK, nothing to see here. Now can we move on? PLEASE!?

Columbo, crumpled hat in hand: "Oh OK, but, I'm sorry, just one more question. You want us to believe that when everybody surrounding Secretary of State Clinton knew of her private email server, including the president using a pseudonym, that her Chief of Staff didn't? What about this 2010 email here from Cheryl Mills to Justin Cooper [hired by the Clintons to maintain the server], 'hrc email coming back—is server ok?' To which Mr. Cooper replied, 'Ur funny, we are on the same server.'"

The evidence was clear: Mills knew of the server all along. Her assertions to the contrary were false, so the claim of ignorance was false, and there was no basis for asserting an attorney-client privilege. The FBI knew all this. The FBI has more than a few top-notch lawyers, after all. Director Comey knew all this too, yet the FBI gave Mills immunity and gave Clinton a pass. No wonder Comey protested during his hearing, "You can call us wrong, but don't call us weasels. We are not weasels," amazingly reminiscent of Richard Nixon's insistence of "I am not a crook."[827] If not a weasel, perhaps another smaller rodent, then? Perhaps we should let Comey's professional colleagues at the FBI decide on the best choice of varmint.

Obama's Iraq, Hillary's Missed Fact Check

Though he hid it well, Pres. Obama suffered quite an embarrassment when events forced him to reverse course in a mighty way in Iraq. Recall in July Obama announced he was sending 500 more combat troops to Iraq to fight ISIS. At the end of September, he announced he was sending an additional 615 troops. That brought the total to nearly 5,000 plus another 1,500 in country on a "temporary" basis.[828] Recall as well, Iraq was the hot spot over which Obama had previously declared victory when all the troops were first withdrawn. Sending in thousands more combat troops where the flag of victory had already been planted established conclusively the flag had been planted prematurely and the troop withdrawals a bad mistake.

Relevant to the campaign, the issue of troops in Iraq had come up in an interesting way during the first Clinton-Trump debate. Many experts argued it was a mistake for the United States to withdraw all of its combat troops from Iraq when Obama did so at the end of 2011. Others disagreed. Only future developments could show who was right. Pres. Obama insisted the United States was leaving a "sovereign, stable, and self-reliant Iraq."[829] Iraq quickly unraveled as a nation and was nearly overrun by ISIS. The Iraqi government stabilized and then staged something of a comeback largely with Iran's help.

During the debate, Trump argued forcefully it had been a huge mistake to remove all U.S. combat troops from Iraq, as Iraq's subsequent near collapse proved. Clinton responded equally forcefully the United States could not leave U.S. troops in Iraq because there was no Status of Forces Agreement (SOFA) between the United States and Iraq. A SOFA would establish the legal basis for the United States to continue to have troops in Iraq. Clinton was at least partly correct. The Iraqi government had wanted U.S. troops out of the country to reassert its sovereignty and thus refused to negotiate a suitable agreement.

There was, however, one little problem with Clinton's argument. While her statement was superficially correct, Obama had already proven Clinton's statement about the prerequisite of a SOFA to be fundamentally flawed. There was no SOFA at the end of 2011, and there was still no such agreement in 2016, even as U.S. in-country troop strength climbed steadily.

CHAPTER 21
THE LAST MILE

As September gave way to October, the vibe of the campaign shifted markedly. Donald Trump clearly had the momentum prior to the first debate. Hillary Clinton was back on her heels and bleeding support in important demographics as Trump watched Republican voters come home.

While initial online polls showed Trump had won, most initial accounts confirmed by traditional polls suggested Clinton won the first debate on points and Trump had flopped. Most polls, now consistently of "likely voters," showed Clinton maintained a steady 3- to 4-point lead. The persistent outlier among polls was a tracking poll showing Trump leading by 5 points.

Despite his immediate postdebate bravado, Trump clearly agreed he lost the debate. He was embarrassed, and he was pissed. According to reports, well over 80 million Americans had watched, meaning 80 million Americans had watched Trump flounder.

The debate didn't fully explain the campaign's shifting fortunes. The mainstream media concluded its job was no longer to report the news or even to infuse the news with the media's usual biases. The mainstream media concluded its job was to save Western civilization by stopping Trump. This is not to say all of the media were necessarily overly enamored of Clinton, though some clearly were, but she was the alternative to Trump. So be it. Trump had to be stopped. End of subject.

Trump's Bad Week

Donald Trump suffered a prolonged bad spell following the debate. First, he tried to blame his poor debate performance on a bad microphone. This led to hearty sniggers until the debate's sponsor, the Commission on Presidential Debates, announced a few days later, "There were issues regarding Donald Trump's audio that affected the sound level in the debate hall."[830]

This led Trump to observe, "It was bad—I wonder why it was bad. Think of that." The bad microphone probably was an innocent mistake, but given all that was going on, it was not unreasonable to suspect maybe someone on or working for the Commission had pulled a dirty trick. As we learned later, the Clinton campaign had some pretty expert dirty-trick operatives.

The Clinton campaign then dredged up an old story as to how Trump had called the 1996 Miss Universe, Alicia Machado, "Miss Piggy" because, apparently, she gained some weight after winning the award.[831] This, of course, was supposed to provide further evidence Trump held women in low esteem and indicated the extent to which the Clinton campaign would go to dredge up ancient dirt. The media ran wild with the story, including as often as possible a picture of the still beautiful Ms. Machado typically in a white blouse and plunging neckline. No one seemed to notice the hypocrisy there either.[832]

Trump could have responded by pointing out this was ancient history, maybe issuing some sort of belated apology, and counterpunching by reminding voters of Bill Clinton's lifetime achievement award from the National Association of Philanderers. Instead, Trump sank even lower. The fact was, if you're going to be in a Miss Universe contest, or if you're going to be Miss Universe, then weight is an issue. It simply is. American football players can't be skinny and play the game. Beauty contest winners can't gain much weight and still stay in character. Trump pointed this out and got slammed, again.

Then he upped the game by tweeting at three in the morning, attacking the media for how it "made up lies." At this point, the facts didn't matter, and Clinton counterpunched effectively by asking the rather sensible question, "By the way, who gets up at 3 in the morning to launch a Twitter attack on Miss Universe?" Fair question.

Then the *New York Times* got into the act by publishing some of Trump's old New York, New Jersey, and Connecticut state income tax returns.[833] According to the *Times*, reporter Susanne Craig just found Trump's old tax returns in her mailbox. Imagine that. Nothing unusual there; we've all gone to our mailbox occasionally and found some billionaire's tax returns.

Then in violation of Federal and state laws, the *Times* published the first pages of all three returns. As it was all for a good cause, there was never any suggestion the *Times* would be prosecuted. No one in America is above the law, except of course the media when they deem themselves on a righteous cause.

Trump's tax returns just happen to end up in the hands of his enemies, and the media were just delighted. And what a year for Trump's returns! Trump had suffered a string of bad business losses resulting in $916 million in tax losses. Even for a multibillionaire, losing nearly a billion dollars had to get Trump's attention. Ergo these weren't just any Trump tax returns. Whoever had stolen them took enough time to sort through to find some incendiary, juicy choices.

While the pilfering and printing of the tax returns was grossly inappropriate, not to mention illegal, the information was now public. It was fair to wonder how Mr. Brilliant Businessman had lost nearly a billion dollars. The simple answer Trump was never able to give is—that's business. You lose $1 billion. You make $2 or $3 billion. Indeed, Trump's real estate development business relied heavily on medium-term debt finance. It was high-stakes stuff, and betting wrong is commonplace. Recall, four of Trump's operations had declared bankruptcy over the years. But on net, Trump had made a lot of money for himself and his partners. This was hard for the general public to grasp and accept as reality. The press knew it and so ran with it.

Much the same was true of the tax side to the issue. The deal with an income tax is the government is effectively a passive partner in the business. When the business turns a profit, the government gets its full cut, but the government also has a limited exposure when the business takes a loss. Typically, the business can take the loss against a handful of prior years' profits, thus lowering prior years' reported profits relative to what the tax returns originally showed. As the business had previously paid tax according to the higher previous profit levels, the business can file for a refund on past taxes paid—this is one way government shares in the loss.

In this case, Trump hadn't made enough profit in the years immediately preceding 1995 to apply the loss fully, so he carried the excess into the future. If Trump made a profit in 1996, he could use some of the leftover 1995 losses to reduce or eliminate 1996's taxable profit, and so on for later years until all the 1995 loss had been charged against later profits. This also meant Trump paid no income tax until those 1995 losses were exhausted.

Many of Trump's critics went into high dudgeon, as though Trump had done something exceptional, if not illegal. The *Times* went on to assert Trump used the tax code as a giant tax shelter.[834]

In fact, Trump had done nothing unusual. What he did, in fact, was perfectly legal, normal, and proper for any business taking a loss and so commonplace that despite having decades' worth of opportunities to correct the tax code if something was amiss, neither Congress nor Pres. Obama had raised an objection. The Congress just ending had seen not one bill introduced to stop future businesses from doing exactly what Trump had done. Neither Congress's Joint Tax Committee nor Obama's Treasury Department had in their respective lists of tax loopholes ever listed the provisions Trump used.

Why not, if what Trump did was obviously so wrong? Because it wasn't wrong. It was, in fact, how a business income tax is supposed to work, so much so both Clinton and the *New York Times* itself had used the same or similar provisions in the past to reduce their own tax liabilities.[835] Surprising no one, the *Times* proved once again its hypocrisy and willingness to shill for Hillary Clinton knew no limits.

Because Trump's team either didn't know how to respond or didn't see a need to do so, these events all piled on to force his campaign on the defensive. Rather than respond with facts and arguments, he responded with anger and vitriol. For the moment, Trump was off his game.

Catching Up with "Third Party" Candidates

The media focused so intensely on defeating Donald Trump and protecting Hillary Clinton it became easy for casual observers to fail to see that Jill Stein was waging a feisty campaign as America's leading socialist greenie. Despite the mainstream media's concentrated disinterest, the Far Left press continued to talk up Stein as either a solid protest vote or a way to keep the Sanders movement alive.

It was almost as easy to fail to see Libertarian Gary Johnson have a few very good moments and some very bad ones. Johnson was a nice guy, and a funny guy. Eschewing both Clinton and Trump, the *Chicago Tribune* added its name to a growing list of major newspapers endorsing Johnson.[836] The *Detroit News* endorsed Johnson the day before. He had also been endorsed by the *Manchester Union Leader*, the *Richmond Times-Dispatch*, and the *Winston-Salem Journal*, but the *Chicago Trib* was the big dog in the lot so far.

Johnson could usually provide cogent arguments on domestic policy often cutting across typical ideological lines, but he got into real trouble in foreign policy. As his attitude generally was one of benign neglect when it came to foreign affairs, and to avoid wars and similar foreign entanglements at all cost, his perspective was both natural and highly unsettling to the intelligentsia. In a television interview, he was asked what he would do about Aleppo. Johnson's response: What's Aleppo?

Aleppo, of course, was previously the largest city in Syria and was then partly a rebel stronghold where Russian and Syrian aircraft were bombing the town to rubble while those civilians not killed by air raids and artillery or caught in murderous cross fires were simply wiped out by starvation and a lack of potable water.

Johnson went on *MSNBC*, where he was asked to name a foreign leader he admired. He couldn't think of one and so finally said, "I guess I'm having an Aleppo moment."[837] That was Gary Johnson.

Trump Foundation Foibles

The Clinton Foundation had been at the center of many recent scandals dogging Clinton's campaign. It had also been at the center of the Clintons' prosperity since it served as the focus for much of the Clinton family's well-oiled payola machinery. One particularly curious item coming to light was that Qatar had offered Bill Clinton $1 million for a five-minute talk—$200,000 a minute is great work if you can get it.[838]

One way to deflect attention from the many Clinton Foundation-associated improprieties was to hammer away at Trump's Foundation. It, too, proved a target rich if substantially smaller environment.

The Trump Foundation, established in 1987, received contributions almost solely from Donald Trump through 2006. Beginning in 2007, Trump's contributions essentially stopped even as total contributions spiked to $4 million. That's right. A $4 million year was a big year for the Trump Foundation, exceeding by a factor of about five the largest donations it had received previously.

The press tried to blow this shift in funding sources into a big deal. "Trump had found a way to give away somebody else's money and claim credit for himself."[839] This was, of course, no different than what the Clintons had done, accepting contributions from individuals, corporations, and foreign governments all to give it away or spend it on others' behalf. The one big difference was the Clinton Foundation measured contributions in the hundreds of millions.

The Trump Foundation issues served as fodder for his enemies in the press and in the Clinton campaign to deflect attention away from the Clinton Foundation. These issues also pointed out another dimension crucial to the campaign—Trump had very few auxiliaries willing to join him in pushing back on a story.

When a problem arose for the Clinton campaign, she could mobilize small armies of able surrogates each carefully screened to respond most effectively, to shift, recast, or deny the issue as needed. She had scores of senators and congressmen who were adept at this game. She had former associates like Lanny Davis who excelled at this game. She could rely on her press allies to repeat and amplify her counter message, thus minimizing the damage.

Trump had Rudy Giuliani and one or two others capable of engaging in this sport. Aside from Alabama's Jeff Sessions, no senators or congressmen were ready and able to stand for him. A great weakness of building an entire campaign around the force of one person is Trump was often left just hanging in the wind. Maybe he didn't know how to respond. Maybe he did and refused. Maybe there were just too many incoming missiles to swat them all away. Trump was an Army of One, up against an army of thousands. Do the math.

BILL C: IT'S THE CRAZIEST THING IN THE WORLD

Bill Clinton had a few weaknesses to go along with his many strengths. One area presenting both weakness and strength was health care policy. During his presidency and ever since, Bill Clinton had been a student of health care policy. His weakness arose because sometimes his familiarity with and concern for health care policy ran so strong it overwhelmed his political judgment. It happened again.

The setting was a campaign rally in Michigan. Apparently, Bill had just been briefed on Michigan health care particulars, most notably the expected 17% increase in health care premiums. Bill just couldn't contain himself. "You've got this crazy system where all of a sudden 25 million more people have health care [insurance] and then the people who are out there busting it, sometimes 60 hours a week, wind up with their premiums doubled and their benefits cut in half. It's the craziest thing in the world."[840]

Welcome to Obamacare reality, Billy Boy.

To be sure, Obamacare resulted in 20 million or so newly insured Americans. It also made it nearly impossible to deny coverage on the basis of preexisting conditions. It also led to the creation of some state exchanges and the Federal exchange, thus taking an enormous step toward making insurance more widely available to those without government- or employer-sponsored health insurance.

There was also no denying Obamacare was sold on a mixture of dreams and falsehoods, the most famous of the latter being that about keeping one's insurance if one liked one's insurance. Obamacare also seemed to accelerate the rise in health care premiums. The program had so many problems even Obama acknowledged it needed substantial reforms. But so far among Democrats, only Bill Clinton had been stung hard enough with the truth bug to call the resulting system "crazy."

White House press secretary Josh Earnest did a typically creditable job of wiggling off the hook when asked about Bill's comments, "It's not exactly clear to me what argument he [Bill Clinton] was making." This is the typical falsehood press flaks are left with when confronted with awful truths. Earnest knew exactly what argument Bill Clinton was saying. Bill was pointing out the obvious—it ain't working, folks.

Kainus Interruptus

When Virginia Sen. Tim Kaine and Indiana Gov. Mike Pence were chosen as Clinton's and Trump's vice presidential running mates, respectively, many breathed a sigh of relief. Whatever one thought of the two presidential contenders, here, at least, were two candidates of relevant experience and good repute. Here were two candidates one could like personally and who would not embarrass the nation.

On October 4, Kaine and Pence squared off at Longview University in the heart of Virginia for the vice presidential debate. Pence left the debate with his reputation intact as a sensible, capable, just plain nice guy. Kaine did not. Kaine spent ninety minutes embarrassing his Virginia neighbors, leaving them wondering, "Who is this guy? This isn't the Tim Kaine I know."

Kaine had been a solid if somewhat do-little governor. He hadn't been overly partisan and followed a fairly moderate political line. He ran for Senate as much the same—a smart, sensible, nice, moderate Democrat. At Longview, a very different Tim Kaine took the stage. The new Kaine was smart-alecky, rude, and obnoxious. In short, a perfect role model for all that Americans hate about Washington and national politics.

Nor was Kaine's behavior accidental. From the outset, his clear strategy was to attack Pence by forcing him to defend Trump, to interrupt by quip and one-liner, and harass Pence into a mistake, to get under Pence's skin. Kaine's answers to questions were a steady stream of thoroughly rehearsed snark and invective. Whenever Pence tried to speak, there was Kaine interrupting time and again. By one count, Kaine interrupted Pence more than seventy times during a ninety-minute debate. One journalist tweeted, "He needs to stop interrupting."[841] Peggy Noonan concluded, "He needed to stop being a rude little rhymes-with-witch."[842]

Through it all, Pence persevered, making his points and containing his anger at Kaine's extraordinarily low behavior, parrying Kaine's barbed thrusts like a seasoned fencer holding an Olympian's épée. To be sure, Pence had a difficult charge to carry out, addressing the many outrageous comments Trump had made and the equally outrageous distortions the media and Clinton had made of even Trump's milder outbursts.

In one sense, Kaine made Pence's job easier. By taking the low road, Kaine threw away his advantage and elevated Pence in the process. Hillary Clinton liked to quote Michelle Obama's famous assertion at the Democratic National Convention: "When they go low, we go high."[843] This time, Kaine went low, Pence went high.

By the end of the debate, one had the impression the Republican Party might have Pence on their initial shortlist for 2020 if Trump lost. One also sensed the nation would fare reasonably well if Pence ever became president, whereas Tim Kaine left the clear impression he was every bit as unlikeable as his running mate.

The Clinton campaign understood well the postdebate spin operation could be as important as the debate itself. Reactions could be shaped, enhanced, or redirected if done quickly and effectively. The Trump people either didn't understand this, or didn't care, because they didn't seem to try.

Even so, while the Clinton campaign could fairly argue Kaine had done well emphasizing Trump's multiple and manifest inconsistencies and errors, they could do nothing about Kaine's horrendous performance. The impressions were impressed too deeply. That didn't mean the Clinton team didn't try to soften the blow and really overdid the spin in the process, thus affirming their own understanding Kaine actually lost the debate. As Chris Cillizza of the *Washington Post* described it, "Here's the reality: Kaine was not so good Tuesday night. . . . I named Kaine a loser [and Pence the winner] in my post-debate winners and losers column."[844]

Cillizza went on to describe the mounting Clinton spin, "But as Wednesday morning turned into Wednesday afternoon, it became increasingly clear that Kaine's performance was coming under increasing criticism. Enter Clinton to insist Kaine was, is and always will be the greatest debater this world—and this universe—will ever see. Don't be fatuous, Hillary."

Oh, That Donald Trump

> *For they sow the wind,*
> *And reap the whirlwind.*
> —Hosea 8:9

Henny Youngman, the great post–World War II American comedian, famously interspersed hilarious one-liners with playing classical violin. In his day, he was best known for his line: "Take my wife . . . please." Later, comedians might include in their routine, "Oh, *that* Henny Youngman," as though there were another. The absurdity delivered with just the right inflection made it all quite amusing.

Many Americans were not amused to realize Donald Trump was very much a WYSIWYG kind of guy—what you see is what you get. Even so, Trump stormed through the Republican primaries and at one point had the momentum on Clinton. Then he suffered a series of self-inflicted gaffes culminating in a nasty little audiotape from 2005. Many of Trump's heretofore supporters proclaimed, "Oh, that Donald Trump!"

As previously noted, few candidates for political office were as well known to the general public as Trump. He gained initial fame as a high-profile billionaire New York real estate developer/jet-setter/playboy prone to marrying and divorcing beautiful women. He magnified his fame through his long-running reality TV show, *The Apprentice*.

Trump was also known in other circles through his many appearances on Howard Stern's gutter-bound national radio program on which Trump freely discussed his sexual preferences, conquests, and failures. Millions had heard him on the radio. Many of the radio segments could be found online and on YouTube.

No one should have been, yet many Americans apparently were still surprised when a 2005 audiotape appeared a couple of days before the second presidential debate. Obviously an "October surprise" orchestrated by the Clinton campaign, yet the contents of the tape were so outrageous the orchestration went largely unnoticed.

Among the many unsavory comments Trump made on the lengthy tape was an admission Trump had failed to seduce one particular married woman despite his best and determined efforts. At the time, Trump had been married only a few weeks to Melania. Trump quickly released a video apologizing for his comments, insisting the 2005 remarks "don't reflect who I am. I said it, I was wrong, I apologize."[845]

Trump being Trump, he spent the following days pivoting to attack Bill Clinton for his behavior and Hillary for defending Bill. Contrary to Trump's video apology, the overwhelming evidence indicated the Donald Trump on the 2005 audiotape did indeed reflect who he was in 2016.

The immediate consequences for Trump's campaign were properly devastating. In the words of Larry Kudlow, CNBC economics analyst and heretofore Trump supporter, Trump "was a stock looking for a bottom."[846] Calls for Trump to step down as Republican nominee in favor of Mike Pence grew to a thunderous crescendo. The din grew so loud Trump had to respond directly, which he did insisting, "Zero chance I will quit."[847] Once again the party luminaries checked to find there was no practical way for the party to wrest the nomination from Trump at this point.

Republicans running for office distanced themselves from Trump immediately and in droves.[848] It was not a painful separation. "I am sickened by what I heard today [on the tape]. Women are to be championed and revered, not objectified," insisted Paul Ryan just before a Wisconsin event at which Trump was supposed to appear but wisely did not.[849]

In all of this, a bizarre sense of hypocrisy mixed in with the outrage directed at Trump. While Trump was properly lambasted, Bill Clinton was lauded in polite company despite his now-admitted long-term affair with Gennifer Flowers while he was Governor of Arkansas despite his incredibly inappropriate relationship with a White House intern involving oral sex in the Oval Office, despite multiple credible accusations of rape and other unwarranted sexual advances.

The difference between Donald Trump and Bill Clinton was Clinton was a Democrat and he wasn't caught on tape, only on a dress. And not incidentally, Bill's wife who had defended him every step of the way and who famously attacked those who publicly accused Bill Clinton was now running for president.

Hillary's Open Borders

Hillary Clinton has some kind of political guardian angel. Immediately following the release of Trump's 2005 audiotape came the release of thousands of emails hacked from Clinton campaign Chairman John Podesta's computer apparently by the Russian government and released through WikiLeaks.[850] Had these emails, many of them relating to her highly paid and transcribed yet withheld Wall Street speeches, come out a couple of days before the release of the 2005 audiotape, both candidates could have faced calls to quit.

In a 2013 speech brought to light by the leaked emails, Clinton revealed her "dream is a hemispheric common market, with open trade and open borders." Previously she had called the Trans-Pacific Partnership (TPP) the "gold standard" of trade agreements. During the campaign, with the tide running strongly in opposition to free trade, she insisted she opposed the TPP.

Maybe... but since her "dream" was for hemispheric open trade, one could fairly suspect a heavy dose of disingenuousness regarding her true current attitude toward the TPP. After all, as she admitted in another speech according to the hacked emails, "you need both a public and a private position" in politics. Her public position was to firmly oppose free trade. Her private position was the full Monty of free trade and open borders.

The Clinton campaign refused to "authenticate" the emails, but didn't deny them either. Rather than deal with the issues raised by their content, the campaign tried to shift the discussion to the Russian government's hacking emails to influence the American political process. Much of the press happily went along with the diversion and then quickly pivoted back to Trump's 2005 audiotape.

Most voters likely dismissed the Clinton campaign's hacked emails story. If you hated Clinton before, then you just had a bit more reason. If you loved Hillary, you explained it away with some convenient rationalization. If you were wavering between Trump and Clinton, you just had a couple of more reasons to conclude "neither."

The one group for whom the hacked email revelations were likely to continue to matter was Bernie's Army. Bernie Sanders had pressed Hillary as a phony progressive, a phony anti–Wall Streeter, and a phony critic of free trade. The hacked emails proved Sanders was right. He was three for three. Unlike the other voter groups mentioned, Bernie's Army had a choice. Whether she knew it or not, Jill Stein, the Green Party candidate, probably just had her best day of the campaign yet.

The Second Debate: Hell Comes to St. Louis

The second presidential debate held Sunday, October 9, in St. Louis, Missouri, was simply all-around awful. Normally, the townhall format of the debate lends itself to a more congenial discussion. Not this time. This time, the town hall felt more like a full-contact karate steel cage match.

Most candidates facing Trump's audio revelations would heed the advice of Ed Rollins, who listed Trump's necessary next steps: make a sincere apology to his wife and daughters and women everywhere; treat Hillary Clinton with respect during the debate; don't mention Bill Clinton; and call Republican Party leaders to grovel as long as necessary.[851] Fat chance.

Under anything vaguely approximating normal circumstances, Rollins would have been correct. But his strategy likely meant defeat with a sliver of dignity as Trump's only hope under such a strategy rested on Clinton suffering her own catastrophe of equal or greater magnitude. Such a strategy also rested on his having a "road to Damascus" quality radical change in personality. Instead, Trump remained Trump to the core.

First, Trump insisted he made a mistake in saying what he did on the 2005 audio recordings, but passed it off as "locker room banter." Apology quality? Minimum.

The reference to "locker room banter" had the benefit of superficial plausibility but didn't detract from its vile substance. Trump surely understood at least this much. So rather than offering abject contrition head bowed and humbled, Trump attacked. He held a press conference hours before the debate with some of the women who had leveled very serious charges against Bill Clinton.

To maximize the ploy's effectiveness, Trump had Kathleen Willey, Paula Jones, and Juanita Broaddrick sit in seats reserved for Trump's people, front row at the debate. Bill Clinton was sitting close by, looking old, frail, and intensely uncomfortable as though some small forest animal had him by the gonads.

Kathleen Willey had accused Bill of aggressively assaulting her in the Oval Office when Willey had gone to Clinton for help following the death of her husband. Paula Jones had accused Bill of aggressively assaulting her years before when Clinton was Arkansas Governor. Juanita Broaddrick had accused Bill Clinton of rape and had stood firmly by her accusation for many years.

One might doubt one of these women as having some long-standing ulterior motive, but not the testimony of all three, not after Bill had already admitted a years-long affair with Gennifer Flowers; not after Bill Clinton's 1992 campaign team had famously set up a "bimbo eruption" quick-response team obviously in anticipation of real accusations coming forward; not after Bill had been exposed as having an extended affair with White House intern Monica Lewinsky including the famous Oval Office oral incident.

Herein lay the second extreme variance from normal circumstances. Clinton and her media allies would reasonably go after Trump for his awful comments and past behaviors. But she was defending a man with a record of as bad or worse behavior. Worse, she had a long-established pattern of attacking the women leveling accusations at her husband. "Mr. Trump may have said some bad words. But Bill Clinton raped me and Hillary Clinton threatened me. I don't think there's any comparison."[852] This was political mud most foul.

The lowlights of the St. Louis debate began with the two candidates refusing to shake hands at the start. Both candidates were in all-out attack mode thereafter. Trump called Clinton "the Devil" and a "liar," reprising in the latter his previous attacks on his Republican opponents. Clinton tried valiantly to maintain a more presidential demeanor while pressing her own attacks.

Perhaps the most stunning moment of the debate occurred when Trump said he would appoint a special prosecutor for Clinton to put her in prison. "If I win, I am going to instruct my Attorney General to get a special prosecutor to look into your [missing email] situation."[853]

To her credit, Clinton quickly parried. "It's just awfully good that someone with the temperament of Donald Trump is not in charge of the law in our country."

"Because you'd be in jail," Trump quickly followed. Clinton clearly lost this exchange.

The evidence was plain the FBI under Director James Comey took a powder on the Clinton email investigation. The evidence was equally plain based on other cases the FBI had prosecuted relating to the inappropriate handling of top secret information that Clinton should have been awaiting sentencing toward a lengthy stay in some Federal license plate academy.

Yet there are some places no candidate for political office can go. Trump had just gone there. Trump said he would use the powers of the Federal Government to go after his political opponent. Of course, the Obama Administration had done so repeatedly with the powers of the Internal Revenue Service in dealing with conservative-oriented nonprofit organizations, but so far, no one had been sent to jail. Trump had publicly threatened his political opponent with jail. How easy it is to creep up to the borders of the police state, and how frightening.

Throughout the debate, Clinton proved herself formidable and well-prepared, if not likeable, then at least respectable. She showed she could stand up to a bully—not that she would be likely to do so if elected president, but that she could.

While faring better than Trump, Clinton didn't emerge from the debate unscathed. She still had no credible explanation for her Iraq war vote, her role in the Benghazi episode, her email server, deleting 33,000 emails, her Foundation's payola scheme, or her recently revealed comments about having both a public and a contradictory private position. *CNN* moderator Martha Raddatz put it to her directly, asking if it was "OK for politicians to be two-faced."[854]

The issue of having a public and private position stung Clinton badly because it fit the known facts. As Clinton said of Trump's crude commentary and behavior, "This is who Donald Trump is." Well, being two-faced and inauthentic is who Hillary Clinton was.

She tried to wiggle off the hook Raddatz had set, but her explanation was lame as a three-legged horse. "As I recall, that was something I said about Abraham Lincoln after having seen the wonderful Steven Spielberg movie called Lincoln."

Trump quickly pounced, "She lied. Now she's blaming the lie on the late, great Abraham Lincoln. Honest Abe never lied. That's the big difference between Abraham Lincoln and you." Clinton had nowhere to go.

Perhaps the best aspects about the second presidential debate were that it ended, and one could at least hope the campaign wouldn't sink any lower, wouldn't embarrass the nation any more deeply. At this point, likely no one was taking odds on the campaigns not becoming even more embarrassing.

A Contrast in Reactions

Seeing a great opportunity with the coming Trumpocolypse, the Democratic Party pulled out all the stops to retake the United States Senate. After recent events up to and including the second debate, even the House of Representatives looked in play. Republicans seemed to agree and were running scared. Republican Senate Majority Leader Mitch McConnell faced the same questions about Trump and the audiotape as did Republican House Speaker Paul Ryan. McConnell repeatedly responded with "no comment" and nothing more but his famous smile/smirk.

In contrast, Paul Ryan publicly wrestled with the moment. On a conference call with House Republicans the day after the debate, Ryan let it be known he would not campaign with or support Trump, though he had not yet "un-endorsed" Trump. The schism between Trump and the Republican Party yawned.

Paul Ryan was a thoroughly decent fellow. To put it gently, presidential candidate Trump was not. In light of the audiotape, Ryan's conscience couldn't accept any association with Trump. This wasn't politics. This was personal. It was also understandable, but Ryan was conflicted. He wasn't just Paul Ryan of Wisconsin. He wasn't just another House Republican. He was the Speaker of the House, responsible to his caucus and more broadly to the Republican Party. He accepted this responsibility when he accepted the Speakership. Telling his House colleagues of his new attitude toward Trump on a conference call that would leak in nanoseconds was ill-advised, to say the least.

Naturally, Trump responded by attacking Ryan, and then John McCain, and then Republicans in general with increasingly sharp barbs as the days passed, thus sealing the break in the relationship. Conventional wisdom suggested Trump might have battled Clinton to a draw during the second debate, but the damage done to his campaign up to and including the audiotape was extensive. The prevailing view seemed to be Trump was on track for a loss of historic proportions as the Republican civil war waged on for days.

Maybe, maybe not; true, Trump had made it much harder for mainstream Republicans to vote for him, but they were still left without an alternative. They would vote for Clinton instead? Some would, but few. The Libertarian, Johnson? Again, some would, but perhaps not many.

Curiously, "values voters" and evangelicals seemed to be sticking with Trump. How could values voters support a man with little apparent morality? As nationally recognized religious conservative leader Eric Metaxas put it, "What if the other candidate has a whole basket of deplorables?" [855] Metaxas observed neither candidate is "pure evil" and that "we cannot escape the uncomfortable obligation to choose between them."

The resolution for these voters ultimately rested on two issues—abortion and the Supreme Court. Trump said he opposed abortion. Maybe he did and maybe he didn't, but there was no doubt where Clinton stood. As a self-described Bible-thumping former etiquette teacher put it, "One thing I know is that Barack Obama is as far from aligning with Christian values as any president we have ever had. And with 30 years of public service doing little for the issues Christians value, Clinton is simply more Obama."[856]

The etiquette teacher continued, "Radical change is needed to fix the problems that have crippled our country, especially in the last eight years. I believe the Republican platform, Trump, Pence and justices who know and uphold the Constitution will bring exactly that. But to make it happen, the etiquette police and evangelicals must put aside their reservations and vote—please."[857] It would take a lot more than holding their noses to make many of these voters cast a ballot for Trump. But just maybe they would.

Ditto the Supreme Court—Trump had put out two lists of possible Supreme Court nominees, one from the Federalist Society, names highly appealing to values voters and constitutionalists. Clinton had put out no list, but these voters could be fairly certain no names on Trump's list would be found on Clinton's. Thus, as Metaxas concluded, "A vote for Donald Trump is not necessarily a vote for Donald Trump himself. It is a vote for those who will be affected by the results of this election."[858] In effect, Metaxas concluded one had to vote for the lesser of two evils, and Trump was, at worst, the lesser evil.

Trump's core supporters seemed unfazed by the audiotape or by anything else Trump said or did. Maybe, unlike so many who'd pretended otherwise, they knew who Trump was all along and accepted him as he was, warts and all. It's hard to outrage people who are already thoroughly outraged, and they weren't looking for a religious leader. They were looking for someone with grit who would "Make American Great Again." For these voters, Clinton's "deplorables," Trump remained the obvious choice.

For her part, Clinton would pick up some moderate Republican voters, but she likely also lost a big chunk of Sanders's voters with her recent WikiLeaks/John Podesta emails revelations. These true believers lacked the discipline of many Democratic voters. For them, like their counterparts on the Right, policy and principle transcended the lure of immediate power.

Trump probably also enjoyed the support of a "hyuge" chunk of typically rock-solid Democrat supporters. These middle-class private-sector union voters often didn't like or trust Hillary Clinton, and their distrust was inflamed anew by the leak of Podesta's emails. These were the modern version of the old southern "yellow-dog Democrats" who would never vote for a Republican.

Except Trump wasn't a Republican. He had warred with the Republican Party throughout the primaries. He continued to war with Mitt Romney. The Bushes had let it be known they held Trump in contempt. He was now battling with the Republican House Speaker. Trump simply wasn't a Republican, so it was OK for a lifelong union card–carrying Democrat to vote for Trump, and besides, they really liked Trump.

So how did it all net out? Five reputable polls of the four-way race taken over various subperiods between October 5 and October 10 had Clinton consistently up about 6 percentage points. The first poll of 1,500 likely voters taken entirely after the bulk of the various Clinton and Trump scandal stories had broken had Trump up by 2 percentage points.

What influence from the two "third party" candidates at this point? In the four-way races, Johnson was consistently polling at about 6%, while Stein polled at about 2%, leaving about 8.5% undecided.

Out of whose hide did these third-party votes come? Out of Clinton's or Trump's, or undecided? The five four-way polls showed Clinton with an average of 45% support; Trump with 38.6%. However, in two-way polls over the same period Clinton averaged 48.4% and Trump averaged 40.6%, leaving about 11% undecided. On balance, Johnson and Stein were cutting into Clinton's margin by about 3 percentage points and into Trump's by about 2 points; not a huge difference, but possibly a decisive difference in a close election.

BY GEORGE, THEY'RE ALL CORRUPT

The WikiLeaks/Podesta email hack job blew the cover off the cozy relationship between the mainstream media and the Clinton campaign. Part of the issue for the public and the media alike is the difficulty of recognizing proper boundaries. For example, many former politicos end up as media personalities. That's fine. Many are insightful and credible. Many have experiences to fill in the blanks in events, and many are also entertaining. The news is, after all, an entertainment business.

Podesta's emails included one from CNN's Donna Brazile to Clinton campaign press director Jennifer Palmieri discussing a possible question to Clinton on the death penalty "that really worries me."[859] Surprise, surprise—the question came up at the next CNN-hosted town hall in Columbus, Ohio.

No one should be outraged at Brazile's actions. No one should be offended. Donna Brazile is an unabashed and first-rate Democratic political operative who happened to get paid to comment on television. Having a lucrative contract with CNN doesn't make her a journalist and so crosses no lines.

The real question was not about Brazile, but about CNN. How could CNN even pretend neutrality in the campaign if they allowed political operatives to participate in the preparation for a debate and to continue their political associations during these preparations? Obviously, even a perfectly impartial CNN would want Brazile's involvement, but then, involvement came with a proviso—Brazile had to suspend all political activity. A good analogy is how Congress has made it illegal for former Members of Congress and senior government employees to lobby the Congress or the Federal Government for a season after their service. If she could not accept these conditions, as seemed likely, then professional ethics dictated CNN exclude Brazile from all debate preparations or similar discussions about programming content.

Second issue: National reporters develop thoroughly proper relationships with national political figures. Whether one works in tax policy, foreign affairs, or campaigns, at some point, one has to engage with reporters. Over time, a level of respect and confidence typically develops—or animus, as the case may be. The healthier relationships are useful for the reporter because the reporter needs information to report, and building a relationship based on confidence often means more and better information.

The relationships are also useful for the source because a reporter may be heading in one direction and the source may prefer a different nuance or even a wholly different conclusion. Sometimes, the source just needs to plant a story. For example, Federal Reserve Board Chairmen always have a reporter or two able to convey a message to financial markets surreptitiously or to test the market's reaction to a policy change.

But lines no journalist (as opposed to political operative) should cross also govern, lines of appearances and lines of substance. Podesta's hacked emails showed many reporters crossing the line from familiar journalist to story participant and then to willing auxiliary. The emails also showed the practice was common and blatantly favored the Democrats.

One email sent March 21, 2015, by *Washington Post* White House Bureau Chief Juliet Eilperin was to Frank Benenati, White House Assistant Press Secretary: "I just wanted to make sure John Podesta had a heads up that his name will be in a story concerning the White House's ethics policy, which could run on Monday."[860] The story ran on Monday as "Obama promised to curb the influence of lobbyists. Has he succeeded?"[861] To be fair, one could with some effort chalk this email up as a simple courtesy. However, consider the following: Would Eilperin have sent a similar email to a Republican White House? Fat chance. Not if it mattered.

Surprising few, John Harwood of the *New York Times* and CNBC showed himself to be a card-carrying member of the DNC auxiliary media corps. A multitude of emails showed he was on especially cozy terms with John Podesta and strongly supported Clinton. He bragged about writing one story about Clinton "she wants." He offered early campaign advice, telling Podesta to "watch out" for Ben Carson because "he could give you real trouble in the general."[862]

The media worked hard to ignore these stories or to shift the narrative to one of Russian government interference, which then facilitated a most convenient barely veiled pivot to the relationship real or contrived between Vladimir Putin and Donald Trump. These latter were all relevant issues, but paled compared to the content of the emails themselves and the media's duplicity.

WikiLeaks proceeded to release a few thousand Clinton emails a day, day after day. This was a new variation on the drip, drip, drip torture Clinton's campaign had suffered for months. For the most part, nothing in the subsequent emails proved all that enlightening or shocking, but every new release led to some rehashing of the old stories for context. How much if at all this hurt the Clinton campaign was unclear, but it certainly had to be irritating and distracting, and maybe a little unnerving as one never knew if the next batch of released hacked emails would include a smoking gun. Was WikiLeaks saving the best for last?

The WaPo Comes Clean, Jenny Gets Dirty

Even as the WikiLeaks drip, drip, drip of emails continued, the *Washington Post* dropped its itty-bitty fig leaf to endorse Clinton on October 13.[863] As Gomer Pyle would say, "Surprise, surprise, surprise."

The *Washington Post* ultimately faced the same conundrum as did many Republican voters. If you find one candidate, in the *Post*'s case, Donald Trump, utterly unqualified and unfit, then for all her "genuine flaws, missteps, and weaknesses," what else could the hometown paper conclude but to back Clinton and hope for the best?

Even as WikiLeaks harassed the Clinton campaign, the Clinton campaign harassed Trump with a carefully coordinated series of October surprises. First came the tax returns, then the audiotape, then what appeared to be Trump's own Bill Clinton imitation—women coming out to say they'd been sexually harassed by Trump.

Into the mix danced Democratic Party star, former Michigan Gov. Jennifer Granholm, to complain disingenuously about the slow pace of the WikiLeaks email dump. "Why is WikiLeaks dripping this out so slowly?"[864] Granholm's reputation for political smarts certainly suffered for this obtuse poser. Why so slowly? To maximize the impact, obviously, because WikiLeaks' founder, Julian Assange, had a well-known beef with Hillary Clinton.[865]

Granholm went on to suggest the slow release "lends to the suspicion that WikiLeaks is doing some bidding on behalf of perhaps Trump through Russia, or Russia through Trump."[866] This observation fit perfectly with the Clinton campaign's preferred narrative to build a smokescreen around the emails themselves by suggesting a Putin-Trump connection. However, unwittingly, Granholm had stepped in it again. Pointing out a possible conspiracy between WikiLeaks, Putin, and Trump drew attention to the Clinton campaign's own carefully orchestrated campaign conspiracy with its media allies. Suggesting a conspiracy while part of a conspiracy was too cute by half.

Donald Trump's Dodgy History

He had lived his life as a playboy. He liked beautiful women. He liked attention. None of this was particularly newsworthy. However, it's one thing to chase after beautiful women. Sexual assault in any form is another matter. A steady stream of women came forward alleging Donald Trump had inappropriately touched or groped them, some of the allegations going back decades. Trump, of course, denied every allegation.

It was entirely possible all of these women were just looking for a few minutes of fame. That all of them just made up their stories. That Trump was entirely innocent as he insisted. Maybe, but no one believed it.

Likewise, it seemed few beside those who already hated Trump cared. After Bill Clinton's lifetime of similar escapades long excused by the mainstream media and the nation's elite, Trump's behavior seemed simultaneously wrong and unremarkable. Once again, the apparent essential reality of the Trump phenomenon came to the fore, much to the bewilderment of most observers.

His essential reality was that most of the nation, and certainly most of his supporters, had long before made their peace accepting

Trump for who and what he was. They either didn't care or accepted his failings in exchange for what he offered.

A second dimension of this story remained largely unremarked. In short, where was the 2005 audiotape during the Republican primaries? Where were all these women now making accusations against Trump? How is it they would now all come forward first one then another as though on parade? This is not to say their accusations weren't valid, only that the timing seemed remarkably suspicious. The tax returns, the audiotape, the women coming forward making credible accusations all seemed well choreographed, and it wasn't by Russia.

Clinton Continues to Wiki Leak

WikiLeaks maintained a steady outpouring of emails hacked from John Podesta's computer. Every new batch included a few tidbits of embarrassment, but nothing after the first day's release had so far been a blockbuster or game changer. The Clinton campaign remained on edge, but sensed the worst might be behind them. Not quite.

On Sunday, October 16, WikiLeaks released the transcripts from Clinton's three infamous Wall Street speeches. The media initially went nuts. The Clinton campaign again tried to divert attention to Russia's involvement in the U.S. presidential election, but the attempt was useless, serving the sole purpose of giving them something to say without addressing the issue while using up airtime.

On the other hand, transcripts in hand, one could wonder why Clinton had allowed the transcripts issue to fester in the first place. Sure, she said some things she would probably like to keep under wraps; but on balance, there were no more smoking guns, no more significantly embarrassing comments, certainly nothing on the order of her previously released "open borders" remarks. There just seemed to be no there, there, and so the media's titillation quickly subsided. But then, why did Clinton allow the Wall Street speeches transcripts issue to become a big deal? The only apparent answer was that this is what Clinton did by nature, even when she didn't have to.

Between the serial Trump allegations and the steady stream of WikiLeaks email and transcript dumps, those who cared about such things among the American people were getting very close to suffering scandal fatigue, much as the nation had suffered at the end of the Bill Clinton presidency. A certain numbness had set in; oh, another woman making some charge against Donald; oh, another lie from Hillary; oh, another impolitic remark by John Podesta; ho-hum, pass the salt.

Signs of the Times

Stephen Hiltner, staff editor for the *New York Times*, rode his motorcycle 3,000 miles on an eight-day road trip across the northern tier of the United States, traveling mostly secondary roads from Portland, Oregon, to Cleveland, Ohio.[867] While counting signs wasn't the purpose of the trip, he did notice quite a few, some very large signs. Hundreds of them, in fact, and without exception they all said, "Trump." Many of them were handmade. He had to ride 2,500 miles before he saw his first "Clinton" sign. In toto, he saw five or six Clinton signs, all of them very official looking.

Despite his flaws, Trump's support remained intense outside the big cities and the northeast conclaves of the national politico-media machine. Even in suburban Washington DC, in reliable Democrat jurisdictions, Clinton signs and bumper stickers were few where they should have been legion. Of course, Trump signs were almost nonexistent, but the lack of Clinton signs around DC was striking.

Trump seemed to have found the one political argument to which Clinton had no counter. Sher could argue fitness and experience until she was blue in the face. Her supporters would dutifully nod and applaud, but she had no response to one simple proposition. If you liked the state of the country and how we'd done for the previous eight or even twenty or thirty years, then support Clinton because you're going to get more of the same, if you were lucky. If you're dissatisfied with what the professional political class had done for and to you, then try something different. Try someone new. It's worth a shot. How much worse could Trump do, really? It wasn't a rational response. It was an emotional response, but then these were emotional times, and the essential emotion wasn't hope. The most prevailing emotions among the most relevant voting blocs were fear and anger.

Trump Unleashed

In mid-October, Trump engaged in a scorched-earth divorce from the Republican Party reminiscent in intensity of the great 1989 movie *The War of the Roses* featuring Michael Douglas and Kathleen Turner in which both husband and wife end the movie sprawled on the floor of their high-priced home's foyer, dead. Unlike the movie plot, however, much of the Republican Party seemed to accept the split with relief disguised as penance.

Trump sent a letter announcing his campaign would have no further contact with the head of the Ohio Republican Party. Trump kept up a steady drumbeat of tweets criticizing House Speaker Paul Ryan, calling Ryan a "man who doesn't know how to win" and "the Democrats have a corrupt political machine pushing crooked Hillary Clinton. We have Paul Ryan, fighting the Republican nominee."[868]

On and on it went. Trump saw conspiracies everywhere, complained of "rigged" elections at every opportunity. He even went so far as to resurrect the Hillary Clinton health question, suggesting Clinton had been on drugs at the previous debate: "I think we should take a drug test prior to the debate. We should take a drug test prior, because I don't know what's going on with her. But at the beginning of her last debate—she was all pumped up at the beginning and at the end it was like, 'Oh, take me down.' She could barely reach her car."[869]

Trump campaigned like a wild man, doing event after event, railing against Paul Ryan, Hillary Clinton, the media, the establishment, you name it. In his own words, the "shackles" had come off. The nation finally saw Trump unleashed. Trump unleashed wasn't really anything new; it was just something more, and his basic message still resonated powerfully for many Americans:

> Our movement is about replacing a failed and corrupt—now, when I say "corrupt," I'm talking about totally corrupt—political establishment, with a new government controlled by you, the American people. There is nothing the political establishment will not do – no lie that they won't tell, to hold their prestige and power at your expense. And that's what's been happening.[870]

Ironically, Trump sounded a lot like Bernie Sanders back during the primary campaign.

Where was Clinton in all this? During Trump's Republican Party bonfire, she continued to do campaign events, but largely sought to keep a low profile, adhering to the political adage—when your opponent is crashing into walls, don't get in the way.

A Campaign Dominated by Sex

Forget immigration. Forget terrorism. Forget the lagging economy. Forget America's steep decline overseas and the low esteem with which much of the world held the United States. The 2016 presidential campaign had become all about sex.

Who had Trump sexually accosted and when? How gross was he? Why did he do it? Lengthy exposé followed lengthy exposé, followed by rehash and analysis. The media worked itself into a frenzy at the jackpot of political stories.

This, of course, let the door open for all the Hillary haters to recount all of Bill Clinton's escapades, though rarely did the mainstream media even touch the subject. *Fox News* showed no such reticence. Amazingly, a taped conversation between Bill and his then-mistress Gennifer Flowers popped up after all these years with Bill talking about the many beautiful women with whom he had been rumored to have affairs while Arkansas Governor.[871]

Many of these taped conversations recorded some racy commentary. One salacious line recorded Bill bantering his admittedly credible insistence that the rumors of all his other affairs while having one with Flowers were all just fiction and fantasy concocted by his jealous enemies.

The hits just kept coming. A former Arkansas television reporter, Leslie Millwee, went on camera to describe two sexual assaults and one attempt by Bill Clinton in 1980.[872] Millwee's accusations were every bit as credible as those being leveled at Donald Trump, yet the mainstream media somehow failed to take note. One question about Millwee, however, why after all these years of Bill's "bimbo eruptions" did she come forward now? Millwee explained that at the time she had young children. She'd seen what Hillary and the Clinton machine had done to other women who'd made their own accusations. Credible intimidation is a powerful weapon.

One might reasonably ask what Bill Clinton's dalliances had to do with Hillary Clinton's candidacy. The answer would be in two parts: the media and Clinton. The media was ecstatic at being able to pound Trump with stories of his past bad behavior. To be sure, back in the day, the media had covered Bill Clinton's various "bimbo eruptions" as needed, but as of 2016, these stories were largely shelved for the good of the order. The imbalance in the media's treatment of the two men was as obvious as it was intentional.

Then there was Hillary Clinton, who attacked Trump for behaviors very similar to those of her husband whom she defended. To be fair, after all these years of embarrassment from Bill Clinton, what else could she do? She was stuck literally sleeping in the bed she'd made. What she perhaps should have done and didn't was to make one dismissive comment for the record and then shut up about Trump's sexual scandals, letting her auxiliaries have all the fun. One aspect Hillary Clinton shared with Donald Trump, however—she couldn't shut up either.

Trump's Enemies Just as Bad

One of the many dirty little secrets of the 2016 campaign was that Trump's opponents could be just as low, just as violent, just as intolerant as Trump's supporters. In Hillsboro, North Carolina, a quaint little bastion of Democratic Party power, somebody firebombed the Republican Party headquarters and a neighboring store.[873] Just to be sure Republicans got the message, the firebomber spray-painted, "NAZI REPUBLICANS LEAVE TOWN OR ELSE," complete with poorly drawn swastika. It's always a curiosity when violent fascists attack somebody else claiming the target is a Nazi.

Some such acts were random, but not all. The Democratic National Committee (DNC) was very well organized for this sort of work. A video released in mid-October had an undercover investigator talking to the "tip of the spear" for the DNC effort.[874] According to Scott Foval, "I am contracted to him [Bob Creamer], but I answer to the head of Special Events for the DNC and the head of special events and political for the campaign. The [Clinton] campaign pays the DNC, DNC pays Democracy Partners, Democracy Partners pays Foval Group, The Foval Group goes and executes the sh.t. Democracy Partners is the tip of the spear on that stuff."

Who were these guys? Bob Creamer was the founder and partner of the Democratic consulting firm Democracy Partners and husband of Chicago Congresswoman Jan Shakowsky. Scott Foval was the National Field Director for the nonprofit "Americans United for Change." In short, they were the commanding officers of the DNC dirty tricks squad.

One technique Foval described was "bird-dogging," a practice that paid big dividends when sixty-nine-year-old Shirley Teeter claimed she was assaulted at a Trump rally in North Carolina. Teeter was bird-dogging. "She was one of our activists," Foval explained.

Foval described the method: "You put people in the line, at the front which means that they have to get there at six in the morning because they have to get in front at the rally, so that when Trump comes down the rope line, they're the ones asking him the question in front of the reporter, because they're pre-placed there. To funnel that kind of operation, you have to start back with people two weeks ahead of time and train them how to ask questions. You have to train them to bird dog."

Foval continued, "I'm saying we have mentally ill people, that we pay to do sh.t, make no mistake. Over the last twenty years, I've paid off a few homeless guys to do some crazy stuff." Lest there be any doubt about Pres. Obama's involvement in all this, the records show Creamer had 342 meetings in the White House and actually met with Obama at the White House 47 times through June of 2016.[875] Barack Obama was up to his neck in the dirty-tricks business.

No doubt Republicans had their own dirty-tricks shop. This is hardly "the latest thing" in political campaigning. Yet making the Foval video so intriguing was his willingness to talk openly about it and that he was so proud of his work. It was all there on the video.

Once the story broke, it only took a couple of days for first Foval and then Creamer to realize their cover had been blown as Democratic operatives closely integrated into the Clinton campaign. On October 19, Creamer, who had previously pled guilty to tax fraud and $2.3 million in bank fraud, tried to tamp down the scandal by resigning from the campaign: "I have stepped back from my responsibilities working with the campaign."[876] No kidding.

The DNC immediately tried to turn the glare of publicity on James O'Keefe, the agent/reporter who'd gotten Foval to spill the beans on camera while Foval insisted he always did absolutely everything to the highest possible ethical standards and transparency. In this case, the intensity of the denial proxied the incredibility of the denial. Caught red-handed like a Watergate burglar, the DNC and the Clinton campaign insisted they weren't really burglars, they were a late-night cleaning service with flashlights. Sure.

Melania and Ivanka Defend Donald

When a politician gets caught misbehaving with another woman (or man), the script calls for the spouse to step up and stand by the accused. Lord knows, Hillary Clinton had a lot of painful experience in this regard. Now, it was Melania Trump's turn. Melania went on *CNN* with Anderson Cooper in one of her exceedingly rare campaign appearances.[877]

In her enchanting Slovenian accent, the former world-class model presented a remarkably credible defense of her husband, insisting Donald had been "egged on" into "boy talk" on the audio, "the boys the way they talk when they grow up and they want to sometimes show each other, 'Oh, this and that' and talking about the girls."

She also took her husband's side with respect to the various allegations, throwing doubt on the claims of the many women now making strong allegations against her husband: "This was all organized from the opposition. . . . And the details, did they ever check the backgrounds of these women? They don't have any facts."

In short, Melania Trump was very clear in her views. "I believe my husband. I believe my husband." Whatever one thought about Donald, one had to conclude he was one very lucky son of a gun as Melania Trump presented a very class act.

Ivanka Trump, Donald's daughter, had been much more engaged in the campaign than Melania. Ivanka also did an interview to defend her dad. "My father's comments [on the audio] were clearly inappropriate and offensive and I'm glad that he acknowledged this fact with an immediate apology to my family and the American people."[878]

What became clear through these interviews was the profound loyalty within the Trump family; the women in Trump's life were truly shocked by what they heard Donald say on the tape, and they just didn't believe the allegations against him. Whether these interviews ultimately made any difference or not was hard to tell as the damage was extensive.

More Rigging

Are elections in the United States rigged? To an extent, obviously they are. Some areas of the country are famous for their legions of dead voters who show up every two years, or as needed. If there's a meaningful media outlet anywhere in the country without a clear favorite and bias, it had, to date, gone undetected.

After the enormous efforts made during the campaign, voting processes were little advanced from the 1960s. The Democratic Party in particular worked very hard to create opportunities for people to vote illegally, either by voting when not registered or being registered in multiple locations. For many fairly mundane purchases, an individual is required to show a government-issued photo ID to use a credit or debit card. Check in at a hotel? Need an ID. Board a plane? Need an ID. Rent a car? Need an ID. But somehow showing the same ID while voting was labeled as an attempt to disenfranchise one group or another.

There was nothing new here, yet Trump knew his campaign was flagging so he needed another outrage to rail against. He chose the "rigged election" issue. Many of his supporters agreed.[879] Pres. Obama had a different reaction: "I'd invite Mr. Trump to stop whining."[880] Sometimes simplicity is the best oratory, yet it was easy for Obama to take the high ground as most, but certainly not all, of the voter fraud helped his side.

Trump's "rigged election" gambit suggested he thought he might lose the election, albeit through fraud. His comments upset the establishment nonetheless. Democracy is a powerful force, but it also rests on fragile propositions. One such is the willingness of voters to vote. Voter turnout even in presidential races had been worrisomely low for decades. Voter fraud by definition debases the rights of those who vote legally. Why bother if some dead person's vote will offset yours?

Another of those fragile propositions is the peaceful transfer of power from one elected official to another. Offered Mark Braden, former chief counsel to the Republican National Committee, "The most important thing in the system is that the winners win and the losers lose. Almost as important is that rational people that support the loser believe that the winner won."

Americans know some shenanigans go on during elections; nothing new there. But if Trump's "rigged election" theme really caught on, then it would debase the legitimacy of Clinton's presidency at the outset while weakening a foundational compact undergirding one of the nation's most basic political principles. On the other hand, maybe the rigging of the election would be qualitatively and quantitatively different this time. Sometimes it's not just paranoia. Sometimes they really are out to get you.

Trump's Tide Turns Tail

National polls showed that Clinton's lead over Trump had shrunk to less than 1 percentage point as of September 19. About a week later, the trend lines began to reverse again as Clinton gained, Trump weakened, and neither of Johnson's or Stein's support changed much. By October 19, the day of the final presidential food fight, a.k.a. "debate," Clinton had established a firm 6.9 percentage point lead.

Confirming Trump's outgoing tide, polls in nearly every battleground state showed Clinton either tied or ahead, sometimes by healthy margins. In Florida, Clinton was up almost 4 points; in North Carolina, 3 points. Among the battleground states, Trump led only in Ohio and by less than a point.

Trump's growing weakness also affected down-ballot races. For example, Joe Heck in Nevada had enjoyed a modest cushion over opponent Catherine Cortez Masto, but Cortez Masto seemed to close the gap and took a slight lead. Pat Toomey in Pennsylvania likewise had enjoyed a small lead, but the race was now neck and neck. New York's Chuck Schumer chances of becoming the Democrat's Senate Majority Leader increased considerably. The House seemed likely to remain Republican, but California's Nancy Pelosi could reasonably hope to hold the Speaker's gavel again.

A curious fly in the "Trump-is-toast" ointment came via oddsmaker William Hill, who observed 71% of the money bet on the election had bet on Clinton to win.[881] But 65% of the bets placed were on Trump to win. No matter how intensely one supports a candidate or opposes the other, and all voter fraud notwithstanding, one can vote only once. This pattern of the bulk of the betting money on one side and the bulk of the bettors on the other incidentally tracked the pattern just before the UK's Brexit vote to leave the EU—the money was on staying in the EU while the number of bets placed leaned toward the "Leave" vote. Leave won.

The Third Debate

On October 20, Hillary Clinton and Donald Trump met in Las Vegas, Nevada, for the third and final presidential debate. Both candidates came badly wounded, but Trump more so. Trump had his parade of sexual assault accusers and his ongoing war with his own party. Clinton had her steady drumbeat of embarrassing WikiLeaks revelations, the recent DNC dirty-tricks squad scandal, and the tricky maneuver of attacking Trump for his sexual misconduct while defending her husband against similar allegations.

Clinton's main objective was to avoid screwing up, which, given her intensive preparation and extensive experience seemed to require little more than the self-discipline for which she was renowned. Trump had to decide if he would continue his scorched-earth tactics or try demonstrating he really did have the right stuff to become President of the United States.

The candidates agreed to forgo the usual coffee-table format typical of the third debate, adopting the dual-podium approach separated by as much distance as decorum permitted. On the middle of the floor of England's House of Commons sits the "Table of the House." On either side of the Table are placed in choir arrangement the benches for Members of Her Majesty's Government and on the opposite side are placed the benches for the "loyal opposition." Across the floor run two parallel red lines behind which the respective Members for each side must remain. The distance between the red lines is equal to twice a sword's length plus one foot for safety. Neither Trump nor Clinton was expected to be armed coming to the debate except with acerbic tongues, but they still wanted to be as far apart as possible.

Chris Wallace of *Fox News* moderated, sitting at a desk front and center, the auditorium filled with supporters of the respective candidates. No fistfights in the audience were reported, but the tension was intense.

Compared to the previous primary debates, the two candidates' recent debates, and the vice presidential debate, the final debate was a mostly civil affair. Both candidates took their cheap shots and made their snide remarks, but the elementary school behavior remained at tolerable levels by modern standards. This was to be mostly about policy covering a wide range of topics, none of them fully, but all sufficient to give an attentive viewer a fair sense of the candidates' views in their own words.[882]

Once again, however, the "debate" was rarely a debate. A debate typically involves the two sides engaging with, or at least talking at, one another. Chris Wallace asked one candidate a question, then asked the other candidate the same or similar question, with frequent follow-up by both candidates, in each case engaging with Wallace as proxy for the voters' perspective. Wallace acted as observer, questioner, buffer, and occasionally, policeman.

What follows is a brief summary of the discussion, which also serves to update the state of play with respect to policy views.

Supreme Court

The first issue concerned the proper role of the Supreme Court. Clinton's response in clear and reasoned discourse indicated she believed the Court should act as a second legislature, stepping in where actual legislatures, governors, and presidents failed to advance the progressive agenda adequately.

Trump's response was nearly impossible to distill into a coherent view. He rambled on about protecting the Second Amendment, referenced his lists of Supreme Court nominees, referenced the Founding Fathers while affirming repeatedly the Supreme Court was "so important." The standard conservative "strict constructionist" view asserted that the Court's main job is to uphold the Constitution and interpret matters brought before the Court in light of the Constitution as written and in light of past precedent where appropriate. If one were strained hard enough, then one could read such a view in the entrails of Trump's rambling. No other interpretation beyond a simple lack of knowledge suggested itself.

Gun Control

Clinton atypically caught herself in a self-constructed double bind on gun control. She built the first trap when she attacked Trump for his endorsement by the National Rifle Association. Then she called herself a strong supporter of the Second Amendment protecting a citizen's right to own firearms. These positions are not necessarily in conflict, but only a lot of explaining can describe how one can despise the NRA and yet embrace the Second Amendment. Her explanations fell flat, exacerbated by her lapsing into an extended dissertation on the *Heller* decision. From a lawyer's perspective, her answer may have been brilliant, but it sounded to nonlawyers as Clintonian double-talk the sole purpose of which was to provide a filibuster smokescreen.

Clinton's declared support for the Second Amendment was itself the second trap. She could parrot the talking points about gun show background checks and all the rest, but no one who cared about the Second Amendment believed her. The firmer her assurances, the deeper the doubt. Recall, Clinton had flailed Bernie Sanders mercilessly on being weak on gun control. To those not already in the Clinton fan club, it was easy to conclude she was just flat-out lying about her Second Amendment support.

Trump's task was simple. He supported gun ownership. He had been endorsed by the NRA early on in the campaign. Next question. This was the one time when Trump was as coherent in his position as Clinton was obfuscating in hers.

The Economy

Clinton laid out a very comprehensive, detailed array of economic policies, among them K–12 education, reducing college expenses, more infrastructure, protecting the environment, and redistributionist tax policy. Setting aside for the moment whether the fiscal picture permitted such a constellation of policies, the immediate question was whether they would, on net, improve the economy.

Some of her proposals would help in the long run, of course, but the killer in the package was her nod to progressive redistributionism—higher corporate and individual tax rates and a more punitive death tax. She further rationalized her tax proposals by referencing the expected revenue gain, except that any tax or budget analyst could see the revenues raised would be dwarfed by her spending proposals. She knew this, of course. And of course, she insisted higher tax rates wouldn't matter to the economy, espousing much the same beliefs as Pres. Obama whose policies had left the economy anemic and slowing.

Trump began on a strong note by reminding everyone of the economy's poor performance under Obama. He then hit the punch line—this is Obama's economy, and Clinton's policies would give you more of the same, or worse. This point was tough to contradict.

Trump then went on at length about rewriting trade agreements. This was a politically useful tack as he hammered Clinton for her support of the North American Free Trade Agreement (NAFTA) that Pres. Bill Clinton had negotiated and signed into law. Many, perhaps even millions, of traditional Democratic Party hard-core voters despised NAFTA and blamed it for all manner of economic ills, so ripping into NAFTA meant Trump was delivering body blows as he reached for Clinton's voter base.

Trump then doubled down on Clinton's weakness by referencing the Trans-Pacific Partnership (TPP), which, he noted, Clinton had once called the "gold standard" of trade agreements. The TPP was intensely unpopular among large swathes of Clinton's core voters.

In response, Clinton insisted the TPP in theory should have been a good agreement, but as it turned out, it didn't measure up. In effect, Clinton was agreeing with Trump that Obama was a lousy trade negotiator, and consequently, she now opposed TPP and always would. However, many TPP opponents recalled the assurances of longtime Clintonista and Virginia Gov. Terry McAuliffe who insisted during the Democratic National Convention that Clinton would be reasonable and would wind up supporting the TPP. Trump hit the point hard.

Accepting Rigged Elections

Wallace asked Trump if he thought the election process was "rigged," setting questions of media bias aside. Trump wouldn't set the issue of media bias aside. In his view, the issue of the rigged election began with media bias because media bias means the media was actively trying to rig the outcome.

The rigged election theme led naturally to a question arising out of Trump's own past statements: Would he commit to accepting the outcome of the election? If he lost, would he publicly accept the loss, allowing Clinton the proper political space to go about setting up her new administration?

The politically correct answer would be, "Of course, that is the American tradition, but of course I expect to win."

Trump's Answer: I will look at it at the time.

From Trump's perspective, if rampant voter fraud influenced the outcome, then why should he go away quietly? If he fought the result in the Courts on the basis of voter fraud, who would then be the defender of the democratic process? The one fighting voter fraud, or those who insist the fraud is less important than the outcome? Why should he precommit to accepting the outcome if there was a chance he would not accept the outcome?

Clinton, of course, found Trump's answer "horrifying" and "troubling." She was joined by the entire establishment, both Republicans and Democrats, who continued to object to Trump's threats to the "system" as they'd devised it.

Immigration

Trump launched his presidential bid with building a wall along the southern border and deporting those in the country illegally. The presidential debate finally came back to Trump's starting point. Trump reiterated his basic points, but then observed one cannot have a nation without borders. He then wandered off, muddying his point by raising the issue of illegal drugs pouring into the country, especially heroin. Not that heroin or other drugs coming into the country weren't a serious problem, but drugs like heroin rarely came over the border in the knapsacks of poor Mexican immigrants seeking a better life in America.

A substantial wall already existed on long stretches of the U.S.-Mexico border. Trump advocated finishing the wall and backing it with appropriate manpower and technology. Clinton acknowledged the wall, and her support in votes taken as a United States Senator for a partial wall along some portions of the border, but did not support extending the wall, preferring instead to rely on manpower and technology to fill the gaps. As this was the system already in place, it was failing badly, and a large majority of Americans were dissatisfied with the solution; Clinton's position was as politically correct as it was untenable for those concerned with illegal immigration.

Trump pressed his case effectively, noting he'd recently been endorsed by the National Border Patrol Council representing 16,500 border patrol agents, creating a nice bookend to Trump's earlier endorsement by the nation's largest police union, the Fraternal Order of Police.[883]

Trump accused Clinton of supporting amnesty for those in the country illegally. This was a fundamental aspect of the issue and through all her humanitarian verbal gyrations in response, Clinton never denied Trump's accusation, a fact more than a few interested parties noted.

In following up with Clinton, Chris Wallace referenced the transcripts from a speech Clinton had given in which she talked about her dream of open borders. Clinton appeared off balance at this point and lacking any direct response pivoted to Trump's advocating deporting all those currently in the country illegally, clearly implying this was an utterly impractical and morally dubious policy, which of course it was. The pivot proved effective, as Wallace abandoned the "open borders" issue for his next subject.

Pay to Play

The two elephants in the room involved Trump's inappropriate behavior toward women and the Clintons' pay-to-play Foundation. On the matter of the Foundation, Clinton at first successfully pivoted to noting all the good the Foundation had done around the world. This was all well and good, but nobody disputed the Foundation had done a lot of good. The issue was whether the Clintons had used the nexus of her status as secretary of state and the Foundation's activities to make her own family and her closest friends very rich. The issue wasn't good deeds. The issue was payola. She had no defense and attempted none.

When Trump pressed the matter, calling the Foundation a "criminal enterprise," he referred to a handful of the embarrassing statements found in the WikiLeaks emails.[884] Clinton at this point bore a striking resemblance to a cornered mouse in the glare of a bright flashlight, but she recovered quickly. She went on a lengthy harangue as to how Russia had hacked these emails and was attempting to manipulate the American election, and wasn't this all just outrageous.

The pivot might have worked if this had been the first time it was used, but the Clinton campaign and their allies had tried this pivot for days to little effect. Trump nailed it, calling it a "pivot" and returning the discussion to the underlying point—the Clintons had set up a vast machine to do very well for themselves while doing some good for the world.

Clinton then tried a different tack, referencing Trump's Foundation, which had done very little, good or otherwise, punctuated with a snarky reference to a six-foot portrait of Trump paid for with Foundation funds. She was right on both scores as the portrait was absurd and Trump's Foundation in its entire history had raised less money than the Clinton Foundation did in a bad month. However, attacking the Trump Foundation for being Lilliputian compared to the Clinton's Gulliver seemed just so much more smokescreen.

The central issue was the Clinton Foundation as payola machine, yet the discussion whipped around rapidly to a number of secondary points. Chris Wallace lost the thread, failing to return to the central issue and letting the moment pass. For all her difficulties, Clinton's debating skills brought her through this tussle with far less damage than the risks suggested.

The Allegations

Wallace then turned to Trump's behavior and attitude toward women. What did Trump have to say for himself? He largely ignored the issue of the 2005 audiotape and honed in on the recent allegations, insisting on his complete innocence. He even observed he hadn't apologized to his wife for what these women were alleging because he didn't do anything. The remark was somewhat comical, but it also somehow made Trump's defenses more credible.

Likely few would have believed Trump's professions of innocence but for one thing—the recent revelations of the Clinton campaign's highly organized dirty tricks squad, a unit with deep tentacles right up through the DNC and into the Obama White House (recall the 342 White House visits, including 47 with Obama himself).

The dirty-tricks unit lent credence to Trump's claim that all these women's allegations were contrived. Some might be doing this for their fifteen minutes of fame, Trump acknowledged, but many and perhaps even all of them were setups by the Clinton campaign, he alleged. Again, normally, such a "dirty tricks" defense would have flopped badly. Yet strangely, these women and their allegations against Trump, having failed to deliver the knockout blow, quickly disappeared from the national stage, almost as though, the gambit having failed, the Clinton campaign wanted the accusers to vanish to avoid any inconvenient follow-up questioning.

Given the dirty-tricks squad, and especially in light of Melania Trump's defense of her husband, one had to wonder if Trump was innocent of the charges, after all. Melania Trump is a very smart, very strong woman. If Donald were guilty as charged, then she would know, and the best he could hope for would be a nasty and very expensive divorce.

Wallace then tried to look at the flip side of the coin, turning to Clinton in reference to her husband's noted extramarital dalliances and accusations. Clinton was having none of it and quickly went on to attack Trump at length. Given the audiotape and the allegations, if one believed them, it was not a difficult task. Through her attack and Trump's response, Wallace lost the thread again. Clinton never had to reconcile how Trump was a monster and yet she defended her husband.

Throughout the debate, both candidates had some memorable comments, but perhaps only one likely to be remembered. Curiously, the one line still resonating days later was a simple aside, a quip, from Trump during one of Clinton's many effective Trump beat downs. Trump sneered, "Nasty woman."

A few days later, Democrats were still talking about what nasty women can do. Massachusetts Sen. Elizabeth Warren speaking to a New Hampshire rally spoke for many women: "Get this, Donald. Nasty women are tough. Nasty women are smart. And nasty women vote."[885] Warren apparently was vying to chair the Senate Nasty Women Caucus in the next Congress.

Perhaps Trump's "nasty woman" comment resonated for so long because he had made it at a moment when Clinton was very effectively taking Trump down a peg or two. She wasn't being nasty. She *was* being tough. She *was* being smart. And Trump obviously didn't like it. In commenting with side snark, Trump fed his opponents even more ammunition.

At one point, Clinton presented a carefully scripted comparison of her experience through the years with Trump's experience. The comparison was brilliantly constructed and perfectly delivered. As had often been pointed out in the past, however, Clinton was top of the class when it came to experience, but Hillary's accomplishments beyond defending Bill Clinton and splendidly raising Chelsea were almost nonexistent. This is where Trump countered effectively, "For 30 years you've been in a position to help. . . . The problem is you talk, but you don't get anything done, Hillary."[886] Bull's-eye. She could only scowl back.

With so many possibilities to choose from, each candidate was responsible for one of perhaps the two most shocking statements of the final debate. Clinton in her roundabout WikiLeaks defense of her pay-to-play Foundation went on at length about Russia's meddling in the American election. At one point, she inferred Trump would be Russian Pres. Putin's "puppet." This accusation was laughable and greatly weakened her argument in consequence, though Trump gave away the advantage by countering with the schoolboy response, "You're the puppet."

This then gave way to an extensive attack by Trump on Clinton and Barack Obama as to how Putin had "outsmarted" them time and again. He hit his target so often and so effectively Clinton just looked stunned, like Joe Palooka wobbling back to his corner.

But Trump probably won the prize for most outrageous statement. After referencing Clinton's email scandal and the "disgrace" of the FBI's whitewashing investigation, Trump suddenly interjected as though the thought had just occurred to him: "She shouldn't be allowed to run. It's crooked—she's—she's guilty of a very serious crime. . . . Chris [Wallace], she should never have been allowed to run for the presidency based on what she did with the e-mails and so many other things."[887]

Declaring the opposition candidate so corrupt as to be disqualified for the Office of the President of the United States was crossing a line not seen in the history of modern American politics. But then, almost everything about the Trump campaign had never been seen before, so in this sense it was perfectly in tune with the times.

In retrospect, Chris Wallace's name must be on the shortlist for finest political debate moderator in the country. He was firm when needed, direct and clear in his questioning, and injected brief notes of humor and levity where appropriate. In some instances, Wallace let the candidates off too easily with vaporous responses, but then he also had to be mindful of the timeline and that any extended discussion on one issue might prevent adequate discussion of another.

On balance, Clinton took some lumps, but as expected handled even the most difficult moments with the skill one came to expect.

In some moments, one even sensed Hillary's human side, a sincerity and authenticity she typically kept locked deep in her soul's vault.

Donald Trump had by far his best performance. It wasn't polished by any means. It wasn't great, but he hadn't said anything too over the top, at least not anything most voters would care about. The intelligentsia had plenty to thunder about, but at this point, they only talked among themselves.

Most important, Trump hadn't been a boar toward Clinton. Though he had attacked her directly and repeatedly, he did so within what had become the accepted debased bounds of modern American political discourse. With only a little imagination, one could conclude Trump had come off as substantial and presidential. In that sense, all technical debate points aside, Trump might be considered to have won this debate and, more importantly, to have stabilized his campaign for the final stretch to come.

AFTER THE DEBATE

Following the debate, the campaign could be summed up in three simple words: Trump was losing. One might add at the end a comma and the word "big." Trump was losing, big. Trump sensed it as he remarked, "What a waste of time if we don't pull this off."[888]

Clinton sensed she had the momentum. The campaign shifted modes; many fewer events, a lot more television. This was natural, but it also had the dual advantages of reducing the physical strain on Clinton and reducing the risks she might have another deplorable "basket of deplorables" moment.

The media sensed Trump was losing as it went in for the kill. Clinton's media supporters rallied to the theme that any self-respecting Republican would repudiate Trump. As Trump was and remained the non-Republican anti-Clinton candidate, this appeared superficially reasonable. One had to wonder just how disingenuous the media could become. Typical was this paragraph in a lead op-ed in the *Washington Post* by Fred Hiatt:

> Every down-ballot Republican candidate who has endorsed Donald Trump for president, which is almost every down-ballot Republican candidate, will have to explain the stance to his or her children and grandchildren.[889]

Hiatt was right, of course. Everyone voting for Trump would have to square that vote with his or her conscience and future generations. To people like Hiatt, no possible justification seemed possible. In fact, it wouldn't be all that hard. The explanation, one apparently inconceivable to Hiatt, involved two simple words: Hillary Clinton. Clinton's supporters would have to square their support with their consciences too, and for many, the answer would be Donald Trump.

The overwhelming balance of the evidence supported the view that Trump was losing. It wasn't just the national polls. Battleground state polls showed a steady trend favoring Clinton. Clinton shifted her own campaign activities away from battleground states where her margins were growing to states that should have favored Trump and, more importantly, to support down-ballot races. A seemingly straightforward campaign pivot, this one would come back to bite Hillary, big-time.

CHAPTER 22
THE COUNTDOWN

Ever since the early days of the space age, Americans have embraced the device of a countdown. News programs included a countdown clock in the corner of the screen showing the days, hours, and minutes until Election Day. For some, the election countdown was a period of building anticipation; for others, angst. For much of the country, the countdown had a similar feel as to what a condemned man might feel on death row. One way or another, one of these two candidates would be declared the next President of the United States, and the titular if not actual "leader of the free world."

E-Day Minus 14, Tuesday, October 25: The Din Gets Louder

Three phenomena dominated the campaign environment as of Election Day minus 14 days. The first was the consensus view Donald Trump trailed Hillary Clinton by around 6 points nationally, and that it would take a miracle for him to close the gap. This belief infused almost all press coverage and much of the candidates' tactics and attitudes.

The second was the background din turned up a notch. WikiLeaks continued its daily Podesta email dumps, revealing much titillation fodder but nothing overly shocking. For example, one email between Center for American Progress Fellow John Halpin and Clinton Communications Director Jennifer Palmieri affirmed the left's generally low regard for Catholics: "Many of the most powerful elements of the conservative movement are all Catholic (many of converts) . . . They must be attracted to the systematic thought and severely backwards gender relations and must be totally unaware of Christian democracy."[890] Nice.

Another fascinating email from Brian Fallon, Clinton's press secretary, ran "DOJ folks inform me there is a status hearing in this case [regarding the public release of Clinton's State Department emails]."[891] "DOJ," of course, referred to the Department of Justice. Fallon, it should be remembered, had previously been the director of the DOJ's Office of Public Affairs. We'll likely never know the true depth of corruption and politicization of the Department of Justice under Attorney General Loretta Lynch, but conspiracy bugs will have a lot of hard evidence with which to weave their theories.

James O'Keefe of Project Veritas released his third video of former DNC dirty-tricks master Robert Creamer, some of which directly tied Clinton to Creamer. Creamer was shown on video commenting, "And, in the end, it was the candidate, Hillary Clinton, the future President of the United States, who wanted ducks on the ground and so, by God, we will get ducks on the ground. Don't repeat that to anybody."[892]

People garbed as ducks appeared at numerous Trump rallies. Typically, a sign would explain how Trump was ducking the release of his tax returns. Donald ducks. Get it?

Incidentally, care to guess which newspapers managed to avoid running any stories about Creamer and the ducks? Start with the *Washington Post* and the *New York Times*. Crickets.

The third phenomenon dominating the news was the admission by administration officials that Obamacare premiums would rise 22% on average in 2017 for the benchmark "silver" plans.[893] This, after rising about 7% the previous year. For policies on the Federal exchange, premiums would increase about 25%. The lucky residents of Arizona topped the list with a 112% increase.

The good news: About 85% of Obamacare enrollees would be substantially shielded from these increases through their Federal subsidies. The bad news: These increased subsidy payments weren't funded by some magic pot of gold. The increased subsidy payments would show up as increased Federal spending.

Finally, and symbolic of much of the campaign, Trump took time out to headline the opening ceremonies for his new luxury hotel in Washington DC. Trump insisted his new hotel was a "metaphor for what we can accomplish for this country," observing the hotel was completed "under budget and ahead of schedule."[894]

Trump's friends and foes alike could only shake their heads. Trump insisted, "As soon as we're finished cutting the ribbon, I'm off to North Carolina." In fairness, he was scheduled for five rallies in three states over the next three days.

E Minus 13—"They Wanted to Get Away with It"

"Why didn't they get this stuff out like 18 months ago? So crazy," Neera Tanden, President of the Center for American Progress, wrote Clinton campaign Chairman John Podesta in March 2015 in an email released by WikiLeaks. Tanden then answered her own question in another email, "This is a cheryl [Mills] special. Know you love her, but this stuff is like her Achilles heel (sic). Or kryptonite. she just can't say no to this sh——." [895]

Podesta responded simply, "Unbelievable."

"I guess I know the answer," Tanden wrote back. "They wanted to get away with it."

E Minus 12—Bill Clinton Inc.

There were just some names the Clinton campaign didn't want to see in print. Doug Band and Teneo were two such. WikiLeaks' steady email dump brought those names to the fore, and it was really ugly.

Band had previously served as Bill Clinton's personal aide in the White House. He and former Clinton fund-raiser Declan Kelly formed Teneo, a corporate consulting firm, to serve, in Band's words, "as the primary contact and point of management for Pres. Clinton's activities—which span from political activity (e.g., campaigning on behalf of candidates for elected office), to business activity (e.g., providing advisory services to business entities with which he has a consulting arrangement), to Foundation activity."[896]

Band was the behind-the-scenes "mover and shaker." In a thirteen-page memo to Clinton Foundation lawyers, cc'd to John Podesta, Band described in detail the seamless operations of "Bill Clinton, Inc." The lawyers had been spurred to action by Chelsea Clinton's worries about the Foundation's murky cloud of supporters/parasites.[897] The memo and the picture crystallizing from the hacked emails affirmed there really was no line between the Foundation, Secretary of State Hillary Clinton's responsibilities and office, and Bill Clinton, former president and now rapacious reaper of speaking and consulting fees.

The saving grace for Clinton was the story remained fairly complicated. While scores of questions arose, many of them suggesting improprieties and illegalities, the story had not yet gained sufficient coherence for most voters to render a judgment as to whether it mattered to Hillary's candidacy. She only had to keep it that way for twelve more days.

Writing in the lead op-ed for the *Washington Post* some days later, Ruth Marcus summarized the matter nicely:

> The Clinton Foundation did good works, but the Clinton's unseemly money chase is repulsive, and it has become clear that they cannot be trusted to appropriately navigate ethical boundaries between their private interests and public responsibilities.[898]

Marcus then referred to the "compulsive money-vacuuming, comfortable nest-feathering, mutual back-scratching operation that is 'Bill Clinton, Inc.'" Marcus went on to summarize the bill of the most serious particulars regarding the Clintons' unethical and greedy behaviors. Length alone precluded a comprehensive such list which otherwise might have filled the entire second half of the Sunday newspaper.

The only certainties were that Bill Clinton would continue to get rich and House Republican investigators would be very busy for the next couple of years, assuming Hillary Clinton won and House Republicans retained the majority. The Clinton team and the mainstream media would plead that all this questionable activity was really all perfectly legal and proper, "trust me," and anyway it occurred before she was even sworn into office. Given all the nation's problems, they would argue, shouldn't the new president be given a chance to lead?

Republicans give Clinton a pass? Not a chance. House Oversight Committee Chairman Jason Chaffetz (R-UT) commented, "Even before we get to Day One, we've got two years' worth of material already lined up."[899]

After the brutality of the campaign and after the many years of dysfunction and inactivity on the nation's many problems under Pres. Obama, one could understand the broad appeal to a Pres. Clinton starting with a clean sheet. Given the media's broad agreement with Clinton's agenda, one could understand their deep interest in trying to shame Republicans into backing off to allow Clinton that clean sheet.

From the Republicans' perspective, the hyperpoliticized Obama Department of Justice (DOJ) had repeatedly whitewashed Clinton's past sins. She could have sold the secrets of the Pentagon's cybersecurity programs to the Chinese, and the DOJ would have done nothing. Would a Clinton Justice Department suddenly get religion? Fat chance.

The Constitution vests Congress with certain judicial authorities. Under the circumstances, the House would be derelict if it did not exercise those authorities, marching in to fill the vacuum left first by the Obama and then the supposed Clinton DOJ. Would there also be a political motivation? Of course; this isn't tiddledywinks.

E Minus 11—FBI: Kaboom

Hillary Clinton and Co. thought they'd put Trump away, then the polls began to tighten again. Even the poll previously showing Clinton up 12 points reported her down to 9 points and then to just 4. Most others showed the race tighter still.

Polls often tighten as Election Day approaches. There were so many done by so many outfits—national polls, state polls of the presidential race, Senate and gubernatorial race polls—who could tell if the numbers were really moving or whether differing methodologies were generating the apparent movement. In any event, rumors of Trump's demise had been premature. If some Trump supporters were lying to the pollsters as suspected, then Trump had reason for hope and Clinton to worry.

Then Clinton suffered a bigger worry. On the twenty-eighth, the FBI announced it had found new emails from Clinton's time as secretary of state. The emails were pulled from devices the FBI had confiscated from Huma Abedin, Clinton's right-hand person, and Abedin's husband, Mr. Sexting himself, former Cong. Anthony Weiner.[900] In a letter to eight congressional committee chairmen, FBI Director Comey wrote,

> In connection with an unrelated case, the FBI has learned of the existence of emails that appear pertinent to the investigation. I am writing to inform you that the investigative team briefed me on this yesterday, and I agreed that the FBI should take appropriate investigative steps designed to allow investigators to review these emails to determine whether they contain classified information, as well as to assess their importance to our investigation.[901]

The FBI had reopened the case Comey had previously slammed shut.

Ka-Boom.

Adding irony to the story, when the news broke, the Clinton campaign team were winging to Iowa for a campaign event—on a plane without Wi-Fi. They had no idea of the storm enveloping them until the plane landed. They were immediately inundated with press and staff inquiries and news bulletins. Whatever panic and pandemonium erupted on the airplane, no one outside would be the wiser. Not to be lost in what followed, in those first few hours, Clinton and her team handled the matter as best one could, staying calm, establishing their talking points, and going about the day while preparing a brief press conference later that evening during which Clinton called for all the emails to be released immediately. Kudos to the Clinton team for their calm professionalism on this occasion.

E Minus 10—Clinton's Smart Move

And what of Huma? Huma Abedin had sworn she had given the FBI all the emails in her possession. Plus or minus a few hundred thousand, apparently, though she seemed honestly at a loss to explain how all these emails ended up on her shared laptop. No doubt she was, as otherwise she would have destroyed the laptop long before. In any event, she abandoned the campaign trail for a bunker in the Brooklyn campaign headquarters where she was left to contemplate the possibility she and especially her pervert husband had handed the election to Donald Trump on a silver platter.

Clinton's calling for all the information to come out was the natural and smart call, but it was even smarter than it might have first appeared because she knew full well the FBI could do no such thing. The emails had been found as part of one investigation. The FBI then had to go back and get a second warrant to search the laptop for matters relating to Hillary Clinton.

The laptop was now part of two and possibly three investigations—Weiner, the handling of classified materials, and the Clinton Foundation's payola scheme. The emails might contain evidence relevant to any one of these investigations and would lead to other avenues to investigate. Releasing the emails was simply out of the question, which is why demanding they be released to have everything out in the open was such an easy, smart, and empty demand.

E Minus 9—Weiner Strikes Again!

The FBI's reopening of the Clinton email investigation reverberated like the rippling aftershocks of a major earthquake. As the facts settled, Anthony Weiner was found at the epicenter. The Bureau was investigating Weiner for sexting with an underage girl. Weiner was married to but legally separated from Huma Abedin. The investigation into Weiner led the FBI to Weiner and Abedin's shared home computer and to Weiner's cell phone.

Anthony Weiner had once been a rising star in the New York State Democratic Party. More immediately prior to the new email revelation, he had been generally regarded as a raw pervert whose naked and seminaked selfies were posted on the Internet. Thanks to the FBI investigation, he was also quite possibly a future resident at a Federal prison.

Who was this Huma Abedin who'd been at Hillary Clinton's side since the early years of the Bill Clinton Administration?[902] Though she grew up in Jeddah, Saudi Arabia, the daughter of strict Muslim parents, Abedin was born in 1976 in Kalamazoo, Michigan. She returned to the United States to study at George Washington University in DC, and two years later, she was an East Wing White House intern just as Hillary was being humiliated by a West Wing White House intern, Monica Lewinsky.

Abedin was for many years combination confidante, aide, protector, and gofer for Clinton; and over time her responsibilities grew. Despite an apparent love of high fashion, Abedin shunned attention. As a strict Muslim, perhaps the oddest feature of Abedin's biography was her marriage to Anthony Weiner, a rising Jewish politician from New York City. Weiner's political career eventually flopped, and before long, he became the butt of all manner of uncomfortable jokes. Unfortunately for Abedin, and for Clinton, this latter trait is what led to the FBI's searching a laptop computer, Weiner's computer, and finding a trove of emails, Abedin's emails.

Part of the confusion surrounding the new revelations arose because three separate stories played out regarding Clinton's emails—the original Clinton server emails, the daily WikiLeaks data dumps of emails hacked from John Podesta's computer, and the new Weiner-FBI emails triggering the Bureau's resumed involvement. As so typical of Clinton world, with so many scandals and so many details swirling, keeping track of the story lines was nearly impossible.

The Clinton campaign's reaction echoed that of many Republicans—what the heck! Why is the FBI releasing this information now, only a few days before the election? The answer seemed obvious. It wasn't politics. Having promised congressional Republicans, he would inform them if any additional information came to light; FBI Director Comey didn't dare sit on the news.

But the information hadn't gotten out. Only information the FBI had more information and had reopened its investigation had gotten out. Nobody outside the Bureau had seen anything of the emails involved, rumored at this early stage to number about 1,000. The FBI itself had only begun a thorough review of the emails.

The question du jour became—what *was* in these emails? One suspected there must have been some clues of material and damaging information. As journalist Carl Bernstein of Watergate fame observed, "It is unthinkable that the Director of the FBI would take this action lightly, that he would put this letter forth to the Congress of the United States saying there is more information out there about classified e-mails and call it to the attention of Congress unless it was something requiring serious investigation."[903]

Clinton took a beating in the first hours after the FBI's revelation. There was little she could in defense. Some allies attempted a diversionary tactic of attacking the Bureau for starting this firestorm. Apparently, they would have preferred the Bureau stay quiet until after the election, hoping Clinton would win; and then if based on this new information Clinton were indicted and eventually impeached, well . . . Tim Kaine would then be president and they'd still be in power.

The reactions of the political hacks to all this was especially amusing. The Right insisted this proved Clinton was corrupt. Some, such as John Kass in the *Chicago Tribune*, even suggested she should step down as the Democratic nominee, a suggestion at this point just laugh-out-loud funny.[904] Just as amusing were the reactions on the Left, such as Eli Lake of *Bloomberg*, suggesting Clinton's chances would not be affected by the latest revelation.[905]

To be clear, whether the FBI acted properly or not, it wasn't looking to sink Clinton's candidacy. Director Comey had at best previously rewritten the law to avoid influencing the political process, or at worse ignored the letter of the law to whitewash the Clinton investigation. Ultimately, in the matter of the emails recovered from Weiner, Comey would be judged in hindsight—if the emails included nothing material, then Comey would have merely added to his dismal reputation. If the emails contained a true smoking gun, then Comey would have partly restored his reputation. It doesn't have to make sense, but that's the way it works.

As the campaigns and the punditry sought to digest the news of the Abedin emails and the renewed FBI investigation, Clinton and her media allies sought a way to pivot the story. They settled on attacking Comey personally. Instant and baseless judgments were the order of the day. One could fairly observe that Comey's actions were extraordinary, but whether they were correct or not could only be judged with perspective, and certainly not before the contents of the emails were made public.

The FBI had alerted the Justice Department that Comey would be sending the letter to the House committee chairmen. The Justice Department's lawyers tried hard to dissuade Comey, correctly observing it was highly unusual for the Bureau to comment on an ongoing investigation and against agency policy to engage in activities that could influence an election. All of which was true, and all of which just heightened the suspicion the FBI had found a real smoking gun.

That was for Clinton the second edge of this double-edged sword. Attacking Comey only reinforced the impression Clinton was in serious legal trouble. Clinton added to the bonfire that seemed likely to consume either Comey or Clinton herself, observing with a smirk, "It's pretty strange to put something like that out with such little information right before an election. In fact, it's not just strange. It's unprecedented, and it's deeply troubling."[906] Troubling? Indeed, it was. But Clinton's stiff upper lip worthy of the British Foreign Service couldn't detract from the impression her campaign was in freefall.

Even before the FBI letter, Clinton's poll numbers had been deflating if only because Trump hadn't shot himself in the foot for over a week. Absent the Abedin/FBI story, Clinton's decline in support would have leveled off at some point, but perhaps not before Trump had built a small lead. With the new revelations, a new much lower bottom for Clinton's support seemed likely. Amazingly, Trump once again seemed like he could win this thing, after all.

E Minus 8—The FBI Investigates, the DOJ Stonewalls

Now that the lid was off, stories poured out of the Bureau. FBI agents indicated they'd discovered the Weiner laptop and its trove of emails in early October, but had waited to alert Comey until two weeks before the election because standard procedure required having some knowledge of the emails' contents before briefing the Director.[907] Nonsense. Under the circumstances and given the explosive nature of the new emails, the proper procedure was obviously to alert the Director immediately. What this really suggested was that some FBI agents, angry at how the Bureau had previously whitewashed the Clinton investigation, had planned and executed their own little dirty-trick operation.

The impression of an inside job gained credence as agents increasingly spilled the beans on internal FBI tensions. In addition to its investigations into the emails and the mishandling of classified information, at least four FBI offices led by the New York office were involved in a deep investigation of the Clinton Foundation's possible financial wrongdoing. In February of 2016, the FBI presented the information to the Justice Department. "That was one of the weirdest meetings I've ever been to," one participant at the meeting commented.[908]

The Justice Department tried to squash the investigation into the Clinton Foundation, plain and simple, denying the FBI the authority to issue subpoenas and related matters. The Bureau didn't give up, however, continuing the investigation with its own inherent authorities. On August 12, a senior Justice Department official called Andrew McCabe, FBI Deputy Director, to express his displeasure at learning the Bureau was continuing its investigation.

It wasn't clear at this point what happened with the Foundation investigation. Some said McCabe had issued a "Stand Down" order. Others suggested the tensions surrounding the investigation impeded progress. In any event, the tone of the matter changed shortly thereafter with the Comey letter.

The Empire Strikes Back

The Clinton machine wasn't going down quietly. Desperately hoping to distract from the underlying story, they continued to pound Comey for sending his letter. Outgoing Senate Majority Leader Harry Reid went so far as to suggest Comey had broken Federal law, violating the Hatch Act. Reid was nothing if not bold, and disingenuous, writing,

> Your actions in recent months have demonstrated a disturbing double standard for the treatment of sensitive information, with what appears to be a clear intent to aid one political party over another. I am writing to inform you that my office has determined that these actions may violate the Hatch Act, which bars FBI officials from using their official authority to influence an election. Through your partisan actions, you may have broken the law.[909]

One presumes Reid wasn't referring to Comey's previous partisan actions in whitewashing the original investigation. House Oversight and Government Reform Committee Chairman Trey Gowdy (R-SC), who had spent six years as a Federal prosecutor prior to running for Congress, offered probably the best response to Reid's statement: "I didn't know Mormons used drugs."[910] (Harry Reid is a member of the Church of Jesus Christ of Latter-Day Saints, a.k.a. the Mormons.)

CNN Parts Company with Donna Brazile

To review the facts, Donna Brazile was a highly regarded Democratic political operative. She had been elevated to Chair of the Democratic National Committee when Democrats found they could no longer suffer Congresswoman Debbie Wasserman Schultz. Brazile was also a highly paid "consultant" for CNN and frequent "on-air" contributor.

Earlier emails released by WikiLeaks indicated Brazile received questions "from time to time" that CNN moderators or reporters intended to ask Clinton. Brazile passed the questions along to John Podesta to help Clinton prepare. Another batch of emails came out with even more evidence of Brazile supplying future questions to Clinton. CNN fired Brazile, saying it was "uncomfortable with this arrangement."[911]

Just to complete the picture, CNN acknowledged a couple of days later they'd sat on the story of Brazile's firing for two weeks. They'd actually terminated Brazile's contract on October 14, suggesting CNN might be considering a name change as the middle N in CNN previously stood for "news."

Certain scenes in American movies are so perfect their echoes are heard decades later in real life. When the Nazi Major Strasser told Vichy Captain Renault he had to shut down Rick's café in the 1942 movie *Casablanca* starring Humphrey Bogart and Ingrid Bergman, the good Captain announced he was "shocked, shocked to find that gambling is going on here," just as the croupier handed Renault his evening's winnings. Was CNN really so disingenuous as to try to argue they were unaware of Brazile's leanings and actions, or were they really so naïve as to be unaware, and surprised, she would funnel information to her Democratic allies?

To be clear, Brazile did nothing wrong here. If CNN was going to pay her to speak her mind on the air, she should take the money. If they were going to be so sloppy as to let Brazile in on future questions for Brazile's preferred candidate, that wasn't Brazile's fault. The fault lay entirely with CNN for either being as naïve as the Easter bunny or as phony as a three-dollar bill.

Mutually Very Unfavorable

One aspect both Clinton and Trump shared was that likely voters viewed neither very favorably. The difference was primarily that Trump had long been on the short end of the comparison. By late October, Clinton had bested Trump on this dubious metric. To be sure, Trump still hadn't recovered from his audiotape revelations, but Clinton had now sunk to Trump's level. One poll of likely voters taken between the twenty-sixth and the twenty-ninth and therefore mostly prior to the Comey bombshell had Clinton at a dismal minus 22.[912]

	Trump			Clinton		
	Fav.	Unfav.	Net	Fav.	Unfav.	Net
Labor Day	45	54	-9	42	56	-14
September 15	37	60	-23	42	54	-12
October 1	39	59	-20	45	54	-9
October 15	40	59	-19	47	52	-7
October 29	39	58	-19	38	60	-22

A Peak at the States

Elections are not won by national favorability ratings or polls. National elections are won state by state. At this stage, virtually all publicly released state polls of either the two- or the four-way race preceded by many days the latest batch of WikiLeaks emails or the Comey bombshell. The polls of record presented what appeared as something of a preelection high-water mark for Clinton. For example, based on these state polls the RealClearPolitics Electoral College map indicated Clinton with 263 votes to Trump's 164, with about 111 rated as toss-ups.

Many of these states, however, were just barely rated as leaning Clinton or barely as toss-ups. For example, the most recent polls had Clinton up by 5 points each in Pennsylvania and Colorado, but most of these polls were in fact not very recent. It would take only a small movement in each state to shift many of the Clinton leaners into the toss-up category while toss-ups like Ohio, where the polls showed a tie, or Florida, which had Trump up by less than a point, could move firmly into the lean Trump category.

E Minus 7, Tuesday, November 1—Clinton Sinking

Desperation, thy name was Hillary Clinton. With one week left to go, exhaustion and bad news took its toll on Clinton and her dedicated team. Clinton flew without her wingman, (wingperson?) as Huma was stuck in the Brooklyn bunker and had been demoted from best gal pal to being "one of my staffers."[913] Clinton's polls were plunging. She was campaigning hard, and her seconds were doing likewise. Tim Kaine, Bill Clinton, Joe Biden, Barack Obama occasionally, Michelle Obama frequently were out in force. On Donald Trump's side, he had himself, and Mike Pence Trump's side was more than holding its own.

The *New York Times* tried to slow Trump's momentum by regurgitating the Trump tax story, but then had to backtrack on an earlier front when reporting the FBI had found no link between Trump and Russia.[914] The *Times* had previously done everything possible to hype the alleged connection between Trump and Russia.

Clinton tried to slow Trump's momentum by harkening back to one of the ugliest moments in America's history, when John F. Kennedy ran a television commercial suggesting a Pres. Barry Goldwater would result in nuclear war, complete with mushroom cloud. "Even the prospect of an actual nuclear war doesn't seem to bother Donald Trump," Clinton told an audience at Kent State University in Ohio.[915]

The media, backed by numerous former FBI and Department of Justice officials, continued to hammer away at FBI Director Comey, all the while ignoring the critics were flying blind. Until we knew what was in those Weiner laptop emails, any judgment of Comey's actions was premature.

Meanwhile, by Tuesday, one national poll that included the post-Comey period showed Trump with a 1-point lead. The full effects of the Comey bombshell had yet to be reflected, and the WikiLeaks email outpourings would continue right to Election Day. While the odds still seemed against him, if Trump could keep from shooting himself in the foot for one more week, it increasingly seemed he might win.

E Minus 6, Wednesday, November 2—Isn't That Rich!

When the narrative focused on Donald Trump, it usually meant he had messed up again, and his poll numbers sank accordingly. When the narrative focused on Hillary Clinton, it usually meant she had messed up again, and her numbers sank. Each candidate had his or her die-hard supporters, but neither would ever rise because they became more popular or even more acceptable to the undecideds.

The ebbs and flows in the poll numbers reflected the public's relative sense of revulsion toward one or the other candidate. In these last days, the focus was entirely on Clinton and she was sinking.

As the candidates prepared for the last weekend prior to voting, their messages took on different tones. Clinton's message became primarily about how awful Trump was. Trump's message became primarily about how great America could be.

In Ohio, Clinton commented, "Imagine him plunging us into a war because someone got under his very thin skin."[916]

In Florida, "I mean, really, can we just stop for a minute and consider the absurdity of Donald Trump finding fault with Miss Universe?" Reasonable question.

Later in Florida, in an echo of her famous "deplorables" remark, "I am sick and tired of the negative, dark, divisive, dangerous visions and behaviors from people who support Donald Trump."

Of course, Clinton said a lot more during her campaign stops, comments about her policies and the needs of families, but these comments were just so much background noise. The only digs that penetrated the din were those against Trump.

Trump likewise repeated his usual riffs on immigration (build the wall), trade (tear up the trade agreements), Obamacare (it's a disaster), but what really resonated was emphasizing, "I am not a politician. My only special interest is you, the American people. The guiding rule of the political class in Washington, D.C., is that they are looking out only for themselves. They will say anything, and do anything, to cling to their power and prestige at your expense. I'm running to change and reverse decades of failure, and to work with the American people to create generations of success."[917]

Trump's message resonated broadly, not because his audiences believed he could do all that he promised, but because they understood one inescapable truth—Trump meant change from the status quo. That's what they wanted. In 2008, Pres. Obama had promised "change you can believe in" and gave the country more of the same, but worse. Trump may or not bring change, but at least he would be different.

The FBI Gets a Little Jiggy

Apparently, some at the FBI were still miffed at the agency's previous whitewashing of the Clinton email investigation. So under the Freedom of Information Act, the FBI released a report done many years earlier of one of the most unseemly moments of the Bill Clinton Administration—the Marc Rich pardon.

Marc and Denise Rich were close friends of the Clintons while Bill was president. They were also very, very rich. Marc Rich was under investigation for tax fraud and was hiding in Switzerland. On his last day in office, as almost the very last act of his presidency, Bill Clinton issued an executive pardon for Marc Rich. There was utterly no basis for the pardon. All the evidence suggested he was guilty of tax fraud, but there was likewise nothing anyone could do to vacate the pardon. Marc Rich's good buddy Billy took care of it.

The FBI initiated an investigation to see if Rich had given or promised to give the Clintons money or help in return, but of course, the Clintons were far too nimble to be easily caught so the Bureau found nothing. But there was still the report, and just coincidentally, the FBI released the report days before the election.

Part of Hillary Clinton's challenge as a candidate was to distract attention away from memories of the serial scandals suffered under Bill Clinton. This was already becoming an impossible task as by one count the Clintons or their closest aides were under five separate FBI investigations, and she hadn't even been elected yet.

George Will helped bring these matters to focus by recalling some of the other highlights from the last days of Bill Clinton's presidency:

> When the Clintons decamped from Washington in January of 2001, they took some White House furnishings that were public property. They also accepted more than $190,000 in gifts including two coffee tables and two chairs, a $7,375 gratuity from Denise Rich, whose fugitive former husband had been pardoned in Clinton's final hours. A Post editorial ("Count the Spoons") identified "the Clintons' defining characteristic: They have no capacity for embarrassment. Words like shabby and tawdry come to mind. They don't begin to do it justice."[918]

To be clear, Trump had not suddenly become an appealing candidate to those previously wavering voters who now said they would support him. Clinton just looked much worse in comparison because she was the one caught in the spotlight. Those saying they were very enthusiastic in their support of Clinton fell from 51% to 43% in just a couple days.[919] Enthusiastic voters are more likely to vote. Unenthusiastic voters are more likely to find something else to do.

Taking the Temperature

Coming into the final week, the pace of the outpouring of state polls picked up dramatically and offered a more useful picture of voter attitudes in the closing days:

	Clinton	Trump	Net	Undecided[920]
National	44	44	-	5
Traditional battleground states				
North Carolina	45	49	T 4	3
Florida	44	46	T 2	8
Ohio	47	43	T 3	5
Iowa[921]	44	44	-	7
New Hampshire	39	46	C 7	8
Key new battleground states				
Pennsylvania	47	45	C 2	6
Virginia	43	48	C 5	9
Georgia	47	43	T 4	6
Michigan	50	43	C 7	2
Colorado	45	44	C 1	3
Arizona	42	44	T 2	4
Nevada	44	45	T 1	7
New Mexico[922]	–	–	–	–

Perhaps the oddest state in the nation at this point was Utah. Yes, Utah, one of the handful of states regarded as most conservative, most Republican. Utah with its six Electoral College votes was practically a toss-up, not because Mormons had suddenly embraced crony capitalism, but because Evan McMullin, Mormon independent, was running a very effective one-state race for the presidency, pulling in around 30% of the votes, almost all of which came out of Trump's totals. How ironic would it be if, in a close election, a Mormon candidate from an ultraconservative state tipped the election in favor of an ultraprogressive Democrat?

The polls for the key Senate races:

	Leading	**Status**	**Margin**
New Hampshire	Ayotte	Incumbent R	1 point
North Carolina	Burr	Incumbent R	3 points
Florida	Rubio	Incumbent R	6 points
Pennsylvania	McGinty	Challenger D	3 points
Ohio	Portman	Incumbent R	15 points
Missouri	Blunt	Incumbent R	1 point
Illinois	Duckworth	Challenger D	13 points
Indiana	Bayh	Open Seat, D	1 point
Wisconsin	Feingold	Challenger, D	5 points
Colorado	Bennet	Incumbent D	5 points
Arizona	McCain	Incumbent R	7 points
Nevada	Heck	Open Seat, R	1 point

If these polls were to be believed and held up, Democrats were on track to pick up three Senate seats, leaving Republicans with a one-seat majority. Conventional wisdom had Democrats picking up about a dozen seats in the House, leaving the Republicans firmly in the majority.

E Minus 5, Thursday, November 3—Drip, Drip, Drip, the FBI Does the Foundation

The Chicago Cubs ended one of the longest droughts in American sports history on Wednesday night, November 2, beating the

Cleveland Indians 8 to 7 in the tenth inning of Game 7 of the World Series. Nothing beats a World Series Game 7. This was one of the best ever. Earlier in the series, Cleveland had pulled to a three-games-to-one lead, but Chicago scratched its way back for the finale. In Game 7, Chicago jumped out early with a lead-off home run. Cleveland tied the game, then Chicago jumped out to a three-run lead. The teams battled on in an epic struggle. Thanks to "the national pastime," the dismal torture that was the presidential campaign was put on hold for a few hours of pure joy, especially if you were a Cubs fan.

Curiously, Game 7 was held in Cleveland, the city that had just a little more than a year earlier hosted the first Republican debate. It probably didn't mean anything, just as the Cubs winning the World Series for the first time in eighty-nine years probably didn't suggest anything about the outcome of the presidential contest. Probably. You never know.

Just hours before the Cubs victory, Bret Baier of *Fox News* reported the FBI had a very vigorous investigation under way into the Clinton Foundation's alleged payola scheme.[923] The investigation, which had gone on quietly for more than a year while the Clinton email server/classified information investigation took the limelight, had become an agency "very high priority." One source inside the Bureau told *Fox News*, "There was an avalanche of new information every day" and referred to the agency "actively and aggressively pursuing this case."

Apparently, something in this avalanche of new information had broken an internal logjam at the FBI and the Department of Justice (DOJ). Earlier in the year, Bureau investigators thought they had solid evidence and good leads regarding the Clinton Foundation/Clinton State Department payola link, but senior FBI and DOJ officials disagreed and blocked the investigators.[924]

Something unblocked the investigators. Something changed. Some new information apparently changed minds up the chain of command. One had to consider the ugly possibility Clinton could be elected President of the United States and indicted before she was even sworn into office.

Meanwhile, the WikiLeaks email dumps continued. Every few days, some tidbit provided further insight into the Clinton Foundation/Clinton State Department funding nexus, but mostly the emails just contained little more than curiosities. Yet every new batch provided an occasion to rehash, once again, the whole sorry episode involving Clinton's private email server, the Comey FBI investigation whitewash, and now the reopened FBI investigation, and on and on. Every new batch also reminded Clinton world the next batch could contain the uncontainable explosion. The Clinton campaign couldn't worry overly about this, however. They had enough on their hands. Nothing to do but soldier on, which appeared to be what they did.

This all had to be very painful for Pres. Obama. Of course, the White House staff kept him apprised of what was really going on to the extent the DOJ was telling the White House the truth. The FBI was investigating a payola scheme, among other matters, involving *his* possible *handpicked* successor. Much worse, these events all took place while Hillary Clinton was *his* secretary of state. Everything that was happening with Clinton's investigations cast a shadow on Barack Obama's legacy.

Other than a little disingenuousness as to whether he knew about Clinton's private email server, not one scintilla of evidence or even rumor suggested Obama knew of the Clinton schemes. But it happened on *his* watch. The buck stopped at *his* desk. He had to know by now what money-grubbers Bill and Hillary Clinton were. As the *Washington Post* had written in 2001, "tawdry" and "shabby" didn't begin to describe them.

Michelle and Barack Obama had to be nauseated by what they'd learned. Barack Obama had not had an easy time of it as president. This was a helluva way to go out.

And looming over it all was the possibility Trump could still win, as Clinton sank steadily. Georgia slipped into Trump's column according to the latest polls; Ohio seemed ready to follow; Florida, Colorado, Pennsylvania, and New Hampshire all shifted into the "toss-up" category—a helluva way to go out.

E Minus 4, Friday, November 4—Clinton Holds a Lead, Barely

By the Friday before the election, Clinton's slide in the polls had run its course, leaving the race dead even according to the average of the three most recent national polls. The damage to her prospects, however, had been substantial as evidenced by the steady outpouring of state polls. Polling indicated New Hampshire gave Trump a small but sustained advantage. Clinton was forced to reengage in Virginia, a state the campaign had judged safe only a few days before.

Though Clinton's campaign was losing altitude, the broad polling evidence still suggested Trump had a substantial uphill climb to prevail and very few days in which to make that climb. Clinton basically started out with a presumed "blue wall" of about fifteen states plus the District of Columbia, giving her 221 Electoral College votes. Trump started with his own "red wall" of about nineteen states, but many of them, like Montana and Wyoming, were lightly populated, so he could count on only about 180 Electoral College votes.

New Mexico and Pennsylvania were typically heavy lifts for any Republican, so normally they would supply Clinton another 25 Electoral College votes, bringing her to 246, very close to the magical 270. This meant if she held all her base state support then Trump or any Republican nearly had to run the table to win. This was certainly possible as almost all the remaining states like Florida and Ohio and Arizona were Republican-friendly, but running the table is always a stretch. On the other hand, if Trump could pick off just one decent-sized Clinton state, most likely Pennsylvania or Michigan, then the preponderance of probabilities shifted in Trump's favor.

The dominant story lines on Friday continued to follow Clinton's many scandals. The *Washington Post* was forced by events to run a front-page story describing how the Justice Department under Loretta Lynch had repeatedly stymied the FBI's efforts to investigate the Clinton Foundation.[925]

The *Wall Street* Journal ran a similar story, but much harder hitting.[926] One email to John Podesta released by WikiLeaks had come from Peter Kadzik. Who was Peter Kadzik? In 2015 at the time of the email, Kadzik was the Assistant Attorney General. The email was sent from Kadzik's private Gmail account so as to be outside the DOJ's archival system, presumably permanently hidden from prying eyes, FBI agents, and FOIA requests. Kadzik just wanted to send a friendly "heads-up" to Podesta about a coming hearing and a recent legal filing regarding Clinton's emails.

Kadzik wasn't just the Assistant Attorney General. He was a true-blue Clinton partisan and a longtime buddy to Podesta going all the way back to Georgetown Law School. And remember Marc Rich? Rich had recruited Kadzik because of his relationship to Podesta. Remember Monica Lewinsky? Kadzik had been Podesta's attorney during that little affair. In a previous leaked email to Podesta, another Clinton staffer referenced "DOJ folks" who leaked him information; Peter Kadzik, one presumes.

It was entirely possible the DOJ, including Kadzik and Lynch, had done everything by the book evidencing complete professionalism, but that didn't at all seem to be the case; and knowing how Lynch had already demonstrated a willingness to turn over the Department to the exigencies of the campaign (remember her visit with Bill Clinton on the tarmac?), the onus definitely fell on the DOJ to prove its innocence. It wasn't succeeding.

The growing possibility Donald Trump might win created a curious tremor within Republican ranks. Defeating Clinton would be grand, of course, and Trump had his supporters, but few rank-and-file Republicans had yet to embrace Trump. This left them with some very uneasy questions. Questions like, If Trump wins, what or who is the Republican Party? If Trump lost, then the party could go back to its previous processes of self-discovery as the establishment and the Tea Party types alternately warred and tried to learn to coexist. But if Trump won, he would remain first and foremost the Chairman of the Trump Party, which frequently had little in common with either the

Republican establishment or the Tea Party elements. In the medium term, could the party lose by winning?

E Minus 3, Saturday, November 5—Not Done Yet

By Saturday, the background din had grown so loud, much of the nation so tired and disgusted by the campaigns, the consensus view seemed to be, "Oh God, let it be over."

But it wasn't over. There were still a few more days to go. Both campaigns had everyone who could draw a crowd of three or more out on the stump. Hillary Clinton tried to make the case she'd recaptured some momentum, but it was just spin. She lobbed volley after volley at Donald Trump while he talked about Clinton's corruption and possible indictment, but mostly adhered to his various themes undergirding his "Make America Great Again" campaign logo.

Just about everybody who could write a newspaper column came out to insist why one candidate or the other was an abomination while the favored candidate was just what America needed at this critical juncture. In all likelihood, none of it mattered. Even those intensely unhappy with their choices pretty much knew if they were going to vote and, if so, for whom.

The national and statewide polls all told much the same story – the election would be very close. A tie at 269 Electoral College votes seemed uncomfortably possible. To this point, the two "third-party" slates of Gary Johnson and Jill Stein had received little attention, but in such a close contest, their ability to draw handfuls of votes could decide the outcome. The Green Party's Stein consistently polled at about 1% nationally and in most states. Some of these would otherwise vote for Clinton, and maybe a very few for Trump, but as these were the extremists who generally didn't trust Clinton, the greater likelihood was they wouldn't influence the final outcome much.

The Libertarian ticket was another matter. Johnson-Weld consistently polled at around 5%, some of whom would otherwise support Trump and some wouldn't vote. What would those who would otherwise support Trump really do when it came time to vote? On every level, they had to be adamantly opposed to Hillary Clinton. Knowing how close the outcome would be, how many would still vote for the Libertarians instead of Trump? If just one out of five Johnson/Weld supporters protested Clinton by voting for Trump, this could make a Trumperian hyuge difference in the final outcome.

In the early stages of the primary season, long before anyone had yet cast a vote, the national polls were most relevant. As the Iowa caucuses and then New Hampshire primary approached, polls in these states became the more important. The general election had reached a similar stage. National polls, while interesting, mattered little. Whether Clinton received 51% of the New York State or California votes, or 99%, wouldn't change the Electoral College outcome one bit. All that mattered now were the polls in the swing states.

Virginia provided Clinton some good news as she led by 5 points. The good news for Trump is that every other swing state was either leaning in his direction already or was moving in his direction. The bad news for Trump was that despite this movement, he was still behind in many key states.

Trump expected to put Michigan in play, and he did, but Clinton still led by about 4 points. A similar story was told in Pennsylvania, where Trump was closing but still lagged by about 2 points. Ditto Colorado and Florida. If the polls were to be believed, then it appeared Clinton's slide had bottomed out, and she remained on top.

E Minus 2, Sunday, November 6—The End Is Nigh, Indeed

The Sunday newspapers poured out election stories, but there was nothing new to say. The mainstream media repeated its favorite themes as to why Hillary Clinton was the only sensible choice, and Donald Trump threatened the future of humanity. Maureen Dowd summed up nicely in a piece aptly titled "The End Is Nigh."[927] After recounting Trump's evolution as a series of characters, Dowd wrote,

> The problem with Donald Trump is: We don't know which of the characters he has created [businessman, playboy, narcissist, entertainer, attention hound, cad] he would bring to the Oval Office.

Then after recounting the many ways Clinton had demonstrated her unique blend of entitlement and paranoia, Dowd concluded,

> The trouble with Hillary Clinton is: We do know. Nobody gets less paranoid in the White House.

Trump's behaviors were ultimately easy to explain. Donald Trump thought the world of Donald Trump. He lived life large. He thrived on applause. He didn't have the very personal one-on-one need-to-be-loved persona of Bill Clinton. Trump connected with large audiences very well, but not in Bill's uniquely personal way. Trump thrived on a distant adoration, which along with his well-honed skills as an entertainer explained much of his success as a campaigner.

Hillary Clinton's paranoia stemmed from a different source. Clinton believed she was fundamentally entitled and fundamentally above the rules applicable to everyone not named Clinton. She broke rules constantly, expecting to get away with it, almost looking forward to the thrill, or at least the satisfaction, of getting away with it. But this also meant she knew she was always at risk of being caught and then at risk of not being able to use her network of protectors to escape the trap, and in the end not being able to use her own finely honed skills at evasion to wriggle out.

Clinton's past episodes left her with an army of haters, those who knew she had broken the rules and gotten away with it, time and again. Knowing she had so many enemies and knowing in fact she had broken rule after rule, and likely law after law, of course Hillary Clinton was paranoid. Imagine an active spy behind enemy lines.

Even the coolest customer in that business eventually starts jumping at shadows.

If one believed the polls, then as of Sunday, it appeared Clinton would win by about the same proportions as did Barack Obama in 2012, but then there were the late deciders. After such a long and ugly campaign, it was hard to imagine many late deciders remained. Alternatively, one could argue that with two such unpleasant options, it was easy to imagine millions of voters struggling to make a decision or opting for one candidate one day and the other candidate the next. Hanging or firing squad—not an easy choice.

One big question remained—voter turnout in the black community. Barack Obama had pushed black turnout to historic highs in 2008 and 2012. He was doing everything he could to repeat that performance for Clinton, especially in states that mattered most, like North Carolina and Michigan. On the other hand, Pres. Obama hadn't done much for the black community other than getting elected and reelected, so it wasn't clear what difference his involvement would make on the marginal voter.

The potential game changer, the dimension that could realign voting blocs in the 2016 election, was the middle-class typically middle-aged white union voter. These voters were a core component of the Democratic Party's foundation. They seemed unusually displeased with the Democratic Party.

Recall the story of the union-dominated white Cleveland neighborhood where Trump's support reigned supreme. Even the union card–carrying mayor had a Trump sign on his front lawn. *The Economist* was, like most of the mainstream media, totally in the tank for Clinton, and it remained utterly at a loss to explain how Trump could appeal to anyone not a legitimate member of the "basket of deplorables." So the magazine sent a reporter to a building site in Youngstown, Ohio, to ask a bunch of union workers, "What's going on?"[928]

Sprinkled in with much colorful language inappropriate for repetition, perhaps the nicest thing these core Democratic Party members could say about Clinton was, "She pisses me off."

Most of the union leadership remained foursquare behind Clinton's candidacy, if only because they knew their status in the Democratic Party superstructure demanded it, but the membership, especially of the private-sector unions, seemed far from convinced. These, by the way, would also likely be candidates for the status of Trump supporters who refused to tell pollsters the truth. Imagine getting a call from someone who says he's doing a presidential poll for some outfit you may or may not recognize. Is it really a pollster? Or is it the local union checking up on you? Why take a chance?

If these voters went for Trump in large numbers, then they could put a handful of medium-sized typically safe Democrat states into the Republican column. The "blue wall" could crumble, a game changer for the election, the factor that fundamentally altered the playing field for the parties. If not, then Trump was likely going to lose.

Comey's Second Letter

On the Sunday before the election, FBI Director James Comey released yet another letter to Congress. This letter essentially blared, "Never mind." After a frantic search of the Weiner laptop emails involving Huma Abedin and the Clinton campaign, the FBI concluded there was no new material information.

For the past two weeks, the Clinton campaign, their allies in Congress, and their allies in the media had excoriated Comey for his previous bombshell letter alerting Congress the FBI had reopened the investigation. Now, those same people declared once again he was Saint James.

Comey's actions also took attention away from the vigorous and ongoing investigation into the Clinton Foundation/Clinton State Department payola scandal as *Fox News* analyst Stephen F. Hayes reminded in a story the mainstream media tried hard to ignore.[929] However, as CNN's Senior Law Enforcement Analyst Tom Fuentes reported,

The FBI has an intensive investigation ongoing into the Clinton Foundation. The FBI made the determination that the investigation would go forward as a comprehensive unified case and be coordinated. So that investigation is ongoing and Huma Abedin and her role in the foundation and possible allegations concerning the activities of the secretary of state in the nature of the Foundation and possible pay-to-play, that's still being looked at.

One could be fairly sure under Comey that this investigation too would come to naught. The difference was Congress would pick up where the FBI left off.

Obama Encourages Illegal Residents to Vote

Pres. Obama did all he could for the Clinton cause, but he forgot some truths ought not be told. In a television interview on the Latin-oriented YouTube channel mitú, Obama told illegal aliens they could vote and do so without risk of getting caught.[930]

> Many of the millennials, Dreamers, undocumented citizens—and I call them citizens because they contribute to this country—are fearful of voting. So if I vote, will Immigration know where I live? Will they come for my family and deport us?
>
> Not true, and the reason is, first of all, when you vote, you are a citizen yourself. And there is not a situation where the voting rolls somehow are transferred over and people start investigating, etc. The sanctity of the vote is strictly confidential.

To recap, "undocumented" persons, who Obama preferred to call "citizens," need not fear the immigration service if they voted (of course, as illegal persons, they were not entitled to vote) because the voter rolls are never given to the immigration service. Obama had just encouraged millions of illegal aliens to break the law, putting the old debate about voter fraud in a harsh new light.

The DOJ Has a Mole

The outpouring of WikiLeaks emails no longer generated much attention for, indeed, much of it repeated the same outrages over and over. But every few days, something particularly outrageous came along. One such was an email dated May 19, 2015, from then Assistant Attorney General Peter Kadzik to Clinton campaign chairman John Podesta:

> There is a HJC [House Judiciary Committee] oversight hearing today where the head of our Civil Division will testify. Likely to get questions on State Department emails. Another filing in the FOIA case went in last night or will go in this am that indicates that it will be awhile (2016) before the State Department posts the emails.[931]

Kadzik didn't send the email on his DOJ account. As with his previous emails to Podesta, he sent it on his personal account. Why was that? To keep it out of the Department's email archival system, of course. The text of the email reaffirmed the very close relationship between the DOJ and the Clinton campaign, yet there's nothing especially outrageous in the email itself. Yet Kadzik thought the email crossed the line. How do we know? He used his private Gmail account to send it.

Neither Comey's second letter, Obama's encouraging the defilement of the democratic process, nor the revelation of the DOJ's mole would change the course of the election. But they bear noting, nonetheless, if only to remind how deep the rot of corruption had seeped into America's institutions.

E Minus One, Monday, November 7—Down to the Last

Much to her dismay, Hillary Clinton was getting most of the attention. Little of it was favorable. Amazingly, Donald Trump had managed for over two straight weeks to avoid shooting himself in the foot. However, aside from sticking with greater discipline to his standard campaign riffs, he hadn't changed. He still made absurd statements. He still had the same past littered with indiscretions and the many terrible things he'd said.

Indeed, one of the more perplexing political alliances in the 2016 campaign was between Donald Trump and the social conservative/evangelical leadership. Trump had told his supporters to "beat the crap" out of protestors at his events—and even promised to pay their legal bills. He not only was twice divorced, but commented in detail about his extramarital affairs, even with married women.

To be sure, Trump's alternative was no prize either for evangelicals or social conservatives. Just the opposite. Yet the evangelicals' support for Trump was rarely grudging. Jerry Falwell Jr., President of Liberty University, proclaimed, "Donald Trump lives a life of loving and helping others as Jesus taught in the great commandment."[932] Falwell's comments were a real headscratcher, but he wasn't alone.

Franklin Graham, son of one of America's greatest evangelists ever, the Reverend Billy Graham, embraced Trump, saying, Trump's "shaking up the Republican Party and the political process overall. And it needs shaking up." The list of major national figures in the social conservative movement backing Trump included Ralph Reed, founder of the Faith and Freedom Coalition; James Dobson, founder of Focus on the Family; and Charles Land, formerly of the Southern Baptist Convention's prestigious Ethics and Religious Liberty Commission.

To be fair, one can understand evangelicals' support for Trump following the logic of noted conservative theologian Eric Metaxas that (1) not voting for Trump was effectively voting for Clinton, (2) one could vote for Trump the movement without voting for Trump the man, and (3) if Trump loses because evangelicals don't vote, then God "will not hold us guiltless." However, there was an enormous difference between accepting what is necessary and actively championing Trump as the next David as Jerry Falwell Jr. suggested.

A. B. Stoddard summed up best the political reality regarding "evangelical voters." For 2016, at least, "they weren't really a specific voting bloc. They weren't unique in any notable way. Evangelical voters were simply Republican voters, nothing more, and nothing less."[933]

This observation brought to mind a second such development, equally strange—the total disappearance of the Tea Party. The Tea Party wing of the conservative movement entered the 2016 contest with a good many credible standard bearers. None but Marco Rubio and Ted Cruz lasted long, and in the end, they all fell by the wayside to Trump's rawer form of nationalist populism.

Even afterward, the Tea Party seemed utterly absent from any of the major Senate races. Rob Portman, Roy Blunt, and Kelly Ayotte were hardly Tea Party faves. To be sure, Republicans were running strong conservatives in a handful of Senate races, like Pat Toomey in Pennsylvania and Ron Johnson in Wisconsin, but not one was emphasized his Tea Party affiliation.

Likewise, many current Members of the House of Representatives considered themselves Tea Party adherents, but their Tea Party associations weren't especially notable even in their reelection campaigns, and the ranks of Tea Party members were unlikely to increase as a result of the election. The Tea Party movement, like its presidential candidates, appeared to have been waylaid by the more politically potent Trump movement.

CLINTON LEADS, BUT TRUMP CONTENDS

The four-way national polls had split into two identifiable camps, and no one knew which was more accurate. Two tracking polls consistently showed Donald Trump up between 2 and 5 points. All other polls showed Hillary Clinton up about 4 points nationally. Battleground state polls from Florida through Pennsylvania and Colorado showed a similar pattern—mostly slight leads for Clinton. She had grounds for optimism; Trump had grounds for hope. Everyone else had grounds for wishing it were Tuesday already, or maybe Wednesday.

Beyond the polls, almost everything about the circumstances leading up to Election Day suggested Trump should get clobbered. Only a few of the obvious external factors ran in his favor. Clinton was running on Obama's economy, which continued to underperform badly and seemed to slow further, so economic insecurity remained widespread and especially for those who felt most threatened by technology and trade.

Obamacare provided another source of anger at Democrats generally and at Pres. Obama and Clinton specifically. In state after state, insurers were pulling out, often leaving health insurance customers with a single company while insurance premiums in many states were shooting up rapidly. Minnesota Gov. Mark Dayton, a major supporter of Obamacare who voted for the bill as a United States Senator, was forced to admit "the Affordable Care Act is no longer affordable" in the face of news that premiums for many Minnesotans were about to shoot up 50% or more.[934] As Bill Clinton had observed, Obamacare was indeed "the craziest thing in the world."[935]

The economy and health care were very important, obviously, but just about everything else was going against Donald Trump, if not for Hillary Clinton. The many revelations about Trump's past behavior toward women would seem to make appealing to that half of the voting public problematic.

Further, neither in terms of training, temperament, or experience had he any apparent qualifications to be President of the United States. He didn't even qualify for "amateur status" in the industry he sought to lead.

Trump also remained a man without a party. Of course, he had never really been a Republican, but he'd managed to capture the nomination and then proceeded to brawl constantly with party leadership. The effect of the schism, most notably public in Trump's constant sniping at House Speaker Paul Ryan, was to weaken substantially the party apparatus's willingness and ability to work with the Trump campaign on such common yet essential matters as "get out the vote" drives.

What could sustain Trump's support, fierce in many areas of the country, in the face of so many flaws and problems? It was not just an almost equal antipathy toward Clinton nor attributable to her own weaknesses as a candidate. Something else seemed in play at a very fundamental level.

Like citizens in many countries, especially in Europe, a large swath of American voters were deeply angry at the establishment elites who'd ignored their concerns for years while the elites carried out their own agendas for how the citizens' cities, their states, their countries, and indeed the world should operate under the elites' careful and expert guidance. These long-ignored concerns manifested in so many ways, some local, some national.

In the 1970s, a psychological therapy called "primal scream" became momentarily popular. Proponents argued that some psychological pains become so repressed they could be brought to the surface and healed only if the individual let loose with a primal scream. Just watching someone with traffic rage rant in their car can verify the therapeutic value of a good scream in a variety of circumstances.

There were, indeed, two Americas. One America dominated the Northeast of the country, with close cousins on the West Coast, and an extended family in many of the major cities. The second America dominated everywhere else. The second America was Trump country, not because they necessarily approved of him, but because he was the first person in decades willing to shout unabashedly, repeatedly, and without reservation, "ENOUGH!" Trump had become America's primal scream, and it didn't matter in the moment whether Trump would make anything any better. The second America just had to let it out, and they didn't give a damn if the first America liked it or not.

CHAPTER 23
DECISION AT JOURNEY'S END

As Election Day dawned, the world waited anxiously to learn what American voters would decide. Most world leaders and most markets pulled for Hillary Clinton because she was the known quantity. She was establishment. She was a card-carrying member of the global "in" club. She represented continuity. Whether her presidency would be a success or failure, it would likely develop along familiar lines. She was literally "the devil you know."

Donald Trump more than anything personified protest against everything Clinton represented. He was "the great unknown" incarnate. He was chaos waiting to be let loose. He was the angry bull champing at the bit to break into the china shop. Naturally, most leaders and intelligentsia at home and abroad found Trump frightening, but to millions of American voters fed up with "more of the same," even if they disliked him personally, at least he represented a chance to let loose their own primal screams.

Sometimes, election turnout is hindered by weather. On Election Day, except for a narrow band of modest showers essentially following the course of the Mississippi River, the entire nation was bathed in seasonal sunshine. Whatever happened, it couldn't be explained away by adverse weather.

Pres. Obama had done well by this election season. His policies hadn't suddenly become popular. But the comparisons to his possible successors pushed his net approval rating to about 8 points, the highest since his reelection. When the contest began twenty-four months prior, Obama's weak numbers suggested he would be a major drag on the Democratic ticket, just as he'd been in 2014's congressional races. This didn't seem to be the case on Election Day 2016.

The national polls of a four-way race continued as they had for days, with the two tracking polls showing Trump with a 2- to 4-point lead and all the others showing Clinton with a firm lead averaging about 4 points. The polls of a two-way race showed the combination of Johnson and Stein subtracted about 2 points each from Trump and Clinton, suggesting at least at the national level the "third party" candidates were unlikely to influence the outcome.

In RealClearPolitics' (RCP) judgment, Clinton went into Election Day with a 203 to 164 Electoral College advantage, with 171 votes undecided. It appeared RCP was being very cautious, which was prudent as the margins of error were probably twice or more what the pollsters claimed. For example, RCP treated Virginia and Ohio as "undecided," whereas the polls had consistently shown Clinton with a 5-point advantage in Virginia and Trump consistently had a 3-point advantage in Ohio.

Allocating all states where one candidate or the other polled at a 3-point or better advantage, Clinton's total jumped to 239 Electoral College votes, whereas Trump's jumped to 219. With this allocation, Trump cut Clinton's advantage roughly in half but with far fewer votes remaining to distribute. The only true "undecideds" were Maine's second congressional district, Pennsylvania, North Carolina, Florida, Colorado, and Nevada, for a total of 80 votes.

If all other states voted as the polls suggested, then to prevail, Trump had to win all three of the big eastern states. Clinton led in Pennsylvania by 1.9 points. Trump led in North Carolina by 1 point and in Florida by 0.2 point.

The Senate polls demonstrated a similar pattern. On balance, they suggested Republicans would lose seats in Pennsylvania, Illinois, and Wisconsin, and come up short attempting to take one from the

Democrats in Nevada. If so, then Republicans would preserve a one-seat Senate majority to go with their House majority.

The Wait

On the day of the Super Bowl, sports stations spend hours saying pretty much nothing, but they do so enthusiastically. It's all background noise for pregame Super Bowl parties. The election-night television coverage of the 2016 election mirrored that of a Super Bowl in many ways.

Hour after hour, the TV talking heads said little or nothing new. But Americans watched anyway. They had to. There was little else one could do before the results started rolling in after the first polls closed at 7:00 p.m. Eastern time. Even then, for the first couple of hours, there was little new to say.

Time and again, the political reporters went to their "big board" depicting the states and their associated Electoral College votes to walk through scenario after scenario. If Clinton wins Florida, Trump is toast. But if Trump wins Pennsylvania and Michigan, then Clinton is toast. To have a chance, Trump has to win the big three of Florida, North Carolina, and Ohio. Which way will Virginia swing? The permutations were endless and the talking heads had little to do but keep up their excitement while walking through each and every permutation as the hours crept along.

As interlude between the permutations, the networks brought on various Republican and Democratic operatives, each of whom engaged in manic spinning as to how they were hopeful and how this county or that hadn't been heard from yet and would turn the tide. The new informational content of these discussions was nearly nil. But still, America watched because it had to.

Finally, news: Marco Rubio survived his reelection bid in Florida. Not a surprise, but it was no sure bet either.

The polls closed in Virginia at 7:00 p.m. Trump maintained a lead of about 5 percentage points for a couple of hours. Even as some of the base-case states were coming in, such as Connecticut and South

Carolina, others like Virginia, North Carolina, and Florida continued to show him winning.

The Virginia pattern in recent elections was for the Republican to jump out to an early lead as rural and southern counties reported quickly, then holding the suspense for a bit, the heavily populated and heavily Democratic counties of Northern Virginia finally report and the Democrat roars back, usually into the lead, usually for good. This pattern held true in 2016 as Clinton captured her first and, as it turns out, about her only battleground state.

Calls on other races came steadily as the night progressed and tension built. Todd Young defeated Evan Bayh for the U.S. Senate seat in Indiana. Bayh, a popular former senator, had been an early heavy favorite to win, but he had just one little problem: he didn't live in Indiana. He couldn't even remember the address of his little condominium he maintained in Indianapolis to preserve the illusion of Indiana connections. You really can't fool all the people all the time, especially if they're from Indiana.

STUNNING

By 9:00 p.m. it began to dawn on the shocked and usually appalled media heads that the races in many of these states were not playing out as anticipated. Overwhelmingly, anyone not on Donald Trump's payroll believed Hillary Clinton would win the election, either by a little or by a lot. But as the vote totals built up in Florida, North Carolina, and Ohio, the three states Trump had to win to be viable, his lead in each held firm. Could Trump really win this thing? one and all began to wonder, astonished.

Just before 11:00 p.m., the Associated Press called Florida for Trump. He had to have Florida, it seemed, so this just meant the game was still on. The media still had hope, but knuckles were getting whiter by the minute. The matter stayed largely undecided until finally Pennsylvania was declared shortly after 2:00 a.m., which meant the impossible candidate had won. Just about everybody was shocked, likely up to and including Donald Trump. Hillary Clinton called to congratulate Trump at 2:30 a.m.

Even by noon the next day, New Hampshire, Michigan, and Minnesota remained too close to call, with Trump ahead in Michigan. However, even without Michigan, Trump had secured 290 Electoral College votes to Clinton's 218. In the final count, as Michigan's results were settled, Trump claimed 306 Electoral College votes.

Final Results

Hillary Clinton won the contest in the sense she received about 1.6 million more votes overall.[936] Donald Trump won the election by winning in the Electoral College by 74 votes.

	Popular Votes	Electoral Percent	College Votes	Percent
Donald Trump	62,238,425	46.6	306	56.9
Hillary Clinton	64,156,255	48.0	232	43.1
Gary Johnson	4,274,975	3.3	0	0
Jill Stein	1,316786	1.0	0	0

One can play "what if" in many ways, but perhaps the most intuitive in 2016 is to ignore the traditional battleground states and focus on three—Pennsylvania, Wisconsin, and Michigan—formerly part of the "blue wall," states that were supposedly reliably Democratic that went for Trump. Winning any two out of three of these previously blue states gave him the election win. According to the early counts, for her to win, earning 278 Electoral College votes, she needed all of 105,330 votes across these three states for Hillary to wake up as president-elect.

The tightest race would have resulted had Pennsylvania gone for Clinton, for then Michigan and Wisconsin would have provided Trump's margin of victory with a combined 26 Electoral College votes. According to the early counts, Trump won these two states by a combined 37,094 votes, or about .03% of all votes cast nationally. As mentioned in an earlier chapter, close elections are decided by very few voters, and likely you're not one of them.

	Trump Margin	Out of Statewide	Percent	Electoral College
Pennsylvania	68,236	5,575,646	1.2%	20
Michigan	9,837	4,544,583	0.8%	16
Wisconsin	27,257	2,791,677	1.2%	10

Of course, all the other states needed to play out as they did for this particular group of voters to have the decisive say, and many of these other states were very close affairs in both directions. A quick scan, however, reveals that even among the close state races, Trump's winning margin consistently beat Clinton's. Had a total of about 73,000 Clinton voters of three states she won (New Hampshire, Minnesota, and Nevada) woke up feeling Trumpish on Election Day, Trump's Electoral College total would have reached a very impressive 326. Very small margins in a very few states make all the difference.

	Winner	Margin
North Carolina	Trump	177,529
Florida	Trump	119,770
Georgia	Trump	231,323
New Hampshire	Clinton	2,528
Minnesota	Clinton	43,785
Nevada	Clinton	26,434

TWO AMERICAS, REVISITED

Once again, the Democrat had won the popular vote and the Republican had prevailed where it mattered most—the Electoral College. Once again, in vivid blues and reds, the Electoral College state map portrayed the fundamental schism that is the modern "two Americas." The East Coast and the West Coast strongly favored

Democrats while almost every state in between the coasts favored Republicans.

Looking to individual states, whether the state leaned Republican or Democrat, nearly every state described a second "two Americas" dimension. In short, urban centers voted reliably Democratic and appeared on individual state maps as little islands of blue surrounded by an ocean of red Republican voters. This held true in Maryland, for example, a reliably blue state as the Baltimore and I-95 corridor contrasts with the heavily Republican but more lightly populated areas just to the west.

This urban versus rural schism also held true in deep red states like Missouri where St. Louis on the eastern edge and Kansas City on the western provide the bulk of Missouri's Democratic voters, along with Boone County, which neighbors the capital of Jefferson City, providing the third island in the chain. The rest of the Missouri is an ocean of deep red where Republican candidates for Congress rarely receive less than 68% of the vote.

INTO THE WEEDS A BIT

One of the media's enduring favorite themes is how Republicans have trouble attracting female voters. Somehow, the converse that Democrats have trouble attracting male voters is rarely mentioned. In this election, Clinton took the female vote 54% to 42%, but Trump took the male vote 53% to 41%. Another clear distinction was that Clinton received about 52% of the votes of those aged forty-four and under while Trump took 53% of those forty-five and older.

Other aspects of the voting immediately apparent from the exit polls:

- Trump won the white vote 58% to 37%. At 21%, Trump's margin exceeded the previous record of 20% set by Ronald Reagan in 1984 and Mitt Romney in 2012.
- Clinton would have been the first female president in history. Apparently, many women voters were unimpressed. The

percentage of women voting at 53% was down a point from Obama's tally in 2012, and her share of the women's vote was essentially unchanged from four years prior. Incredibly, despite the audiotape and all the rest, 42% of women voters still preferred Trump to the woman candidate.
- Even so, Clinton's strongest demographic was black women, where she claimed 94% of the vote.
- The vaunted surge of Hispanic voters? Didn't happen, despite Trump's caustic remarks about illegal aliens and Mexicans.
- Further evidence the "evangelical" vote had become little more than just another Republican vote, Trump at 81% did better with evangelicals than did Romney four years prior.
- The No. 1 issue for voters? The economy, and Clinton won on that score 52 to 48.[937] Go figure.
- The two figures from the exit polls probably most relevant in explaining Trump's victory were that he took 43% of union household votes and 72% of white, noncollege-educated men. How do you explain Trump's victory? He held his own base and took a big chunk out of the Democratic Party's base.

Trump's victory wasn't the only surprise of the night. Miraculously, Republicans Pat Toomey in Pennsylvania and Ron Johnson in Wisconsin held on to their Senate seats. Johnson had long been given up for dead, and Toomey had looked to be sinking prior to election night. Republicans managed to hold on to the Senate against tremendous odds given the number of high-risk seats at stake. Republicans also managed to keep their hold on the House, 241 to 194, losing only six seats. And they added 3 governorships on net, bringing their total to 33.

The electoral results and exit polls provided an enormous wealth of information on American voting patterns; data professionals would sift and parse for years to come. One aspect seemed to stand out immediately, however. The American people had elected Donald Trump as agent of change. They'd sent a similar signal in four out of the past five elections—Obama in 2008, the revolt against Obama in

2010 and 2014 benefiting Republicans, and now in 2016. The voters seemed to be saying to the governing elites, "We really mean it, dammit."

Yet looking at the results in the House of Representatives, only thirteen seats changed parties. Nine formerly Republican-held seats went to a Democrat and four formerly Democrat-held seats went to a Republican. Out of 435 races, less than 3% changed parties. Three of the biggest states—California with 52 seats, Texas with 36 seats, and New York with 27 seats—saw not one seat change hands. In the presidential election, voters seemed to be demanding change, yet in the House elections, they seemed to be saying something else entirely.

Americans certainly wanted change, but what they clearly wanted was more of their preferred change, and here the two Americas story hit hardest. Blue states wanted more blue. Red states wanted more red. Nobody, it seemed, wanted more purple. The centrifugal forces in American politics hadn't been dulled by the election; they'd increased.

Immediate Aftermath

The 2016 campaign will be rehashed for decades. How a substantially flawed and neophyte candidate, whose realistic odds of winning judged two years prior were infinitesimal, could march through a primary ordeal against sixteen mostly qualified opponents, capture the nomination of a party to which he had no particular affiliation, and go on to defeat an amazingly competent political machine backing a sufficiently capable yet flawed candidate would defy easy explanation. Anyone who writes in years to come that Trump's victory was preordained or obvious upon analysis would be just blowing smoke.

Donald Trump gave an address in which he called on the nation to unite and heal and complimented Hillary Clinton, praising especially her long service to the nation. Clinton likewise called on the nation to unite and heal, complimenting Trump on his victory and affirming her faith in the nation's future. Pres. Obama gave a superb address following the same themes and then observed he had instructed his staff to meet the high standards of George W. Bush's Administration before them, to help in any way possible to ensure Trump's success as president. For all the brutality of the campaign, decision made, all three played their roles to perfection, suggesting hope was indeed at least a little justified, that adults could still be adults.

In the election's immediate aftermath, six features stood out.

1. Trump would have his hands full. He campaigned for the job. He got it. And while the Electoral College described a respectable win, the fact remained that Clinton received more total votes. Every incoming president attempts to spin the election's results as suggesting a strong governing mandate, but Trump would have a tough time making this narrative stick, especially in the face of a mainstream media sure to turn on him full force as soon as respectable politeness permitted.
2. For all the grief pollsters suffered, the final results offered hope for the profession. The national polls had been a little too generous to Clinton, but they mostly favored her to win by a handful of points and she did, indeed, win the popular vote. State polls had shown close races where the races were close.
3. Republicans now owned it. They controlled the House. They had the majority in the Senate. They had the White House. Whatever bad, or good, happened in the economy, or in society, or in foreign policy, Republicans would own it lock, stock, and barrel.
4. Thoroughly on the outs, the Democratic Party was in disarray and in for a period of painful self-examination. Republican strength lay not in Washington, but in the governorships and state legislatures. Democrats were supposed to be the lords and masters of all things Washington DC, yet they were barely a factor except in the U.S. Senate, where the minority party has some influence.

   Would Democrats now lurch left, toward Bernie Sanders and Elizabeth Warren, believing Hillary Clinton's problem

was she had never really drunk the Kool-Aid? Or would they decide one can't win elections with only redistributionism and feel-goodism, that they would need the political center, the old Bill Clinton "third way" approach? Much of Trump's victory could be ascribed to his inroads into the Democratic base, specifically blue-collar whites, especially in the northern tier of the blue wall—Wisconsin, Michigan, and Pennsylvania. What could the Far Left offer these voters? This wasn't going to be fun, and the Far Left hardly waited for Trump's election-night confetti to hit the floor before preparing for all-out war.
5. Pres. Barack Obama had to face the reality that not only had his chosen successor failed, but the voters had given him and his policies a thorough cuffing. He had explicitly campaigned for Clinton as the preserver and extender of his legacy as president. Legacy? Fuhgetaboutut!
6. With Clinton's defeat joining Jeb Bush's early flameout, the Bush-Clinton era of American politics drew to a sputtering close. Starting with George H. W. Bush's service as Vice President, these two families had played many a starring role for three and a half decades. That was now over for good.

But what of Hillary Clinton? On the cusp of towering over an era, she had within the space of a few hours been relegated to a footnote in history.

There were so many unanswered questions at this point. There was still an open seat on the U.S. Supreme Court, and Merrick Garland's nomination was toast. What would Trump do about the Federal Reserve Chair, Janet Yellen, whose term expired in February of 2018? What would the Congress do in the coming lame-duck session to complete its work on the budget? What would Trump's initial priorities be, and could he work with Congress to bring them about? What would he do to reverse Obama's outpouring of economy-draining regulations? So many questions.

These were the deeper questions, but the immediate questions followed Washington's traditional pattern of musical chairs. Who would be the new White House Chief of Staff, or Treasury secretary, or secretary of defense? The campaign now over, Washington went back to its favorite games until the inauguration.

As often observed in this work, Americans are at heart a hopeful lot. Many even of those devastated by Hillary Clinton's loss would take an extended period to proceed through the five stages of grief and eventually come around to embracing an abiding belief in America's future; however, the nation might struggle to secure it. As so often happens in such moments, Winston Churchill speaking decades before somehow provided the suitable perspective:

> Good night, then—sleep to gather strength for the morning. For the morning will come. Brightly will it shine on the brave and true, kindly on all who suffer for the cause, glorious upon the tombs of heroes. Thus, will shine the dawn.

ENDNOTES

1 http://101sharequotes.com/quote/napoleon-bonaparte-in-politics-absurdity-is-not-a--319157.

2 Thomas B. Edsall, "The Trouble with That Revolving Door," *The New York Times*, December 18, 2011, at http://campaignstops.blogs.nytimes.com/2011/12/18/the-trouble-with-that-revolving-door/?src=tp&_r=0.

3 Estimated Cost of Election 2014, OpenSecrets, at https://www.opensecrets.org/overview/cost.php.

4 Alexander Bolton, "Reid's chief of staff stepping down," *The Hill*, January 7, 2015, at http://thehill.com/homenews/senate/228815-david-krone-to-leave-reids-staff.

5 Barry Svrluga, "For Nationals Rizzo, work is never done," *The Washington Post*, July 5, 2015, at http://www.washingtonpost.com/sports/nationals/for-mike-rizzo-a-seasons-end-means-a-seasons-beginning/2015/07/03/5dc45636-19d3-11e5-93b7-5eddc056ad8a_story.html.

6 "Romney, Bush Are Top GOP Contenders for 2016 Race, Quinnipiac University National Poll Finds; Clinton Leads, Tied with Christie or Romney," Quinnipiac University, November 26, 2014, at http://www.quinnipiac.edu/news-and-events/quinnipiac-university-poll/national/release-detail?ReleaseID=2116.

7 Avik Roy, "Contrary to White House Denials, Emails Show Jonathan Gruber Was 'Integral' to Obamacare," Forbes, June 15, 2015, at http://www.forbes.com/sites/theapothecary/2015/06/21/contrary-to-white-house-denials-emails-show-jonathan-gruber-was-integral-to-obamacare/.

8 Angie Drobnic Holan, "Lie of the Year: 'If you like your health care plan, you can keep it,'" PolitiFact, December 12, 2013, at http://www.politifact.com/truth-o-meter/article/2013/dec/12/lie-year-if-you-like-your-health-care-plan-keep-it/.

9 Shushannah Walshe, "How Little-Known MIT Professor Jonathan Gruber Shook Up Washington This Week," ABC News, November 14, 2014, at http://abcnews.go.com/Politics/obamacare-architect-jonathan-gruber-fire/story?id=26919286.

10 John Sexton, "Jonathan Gruber in 2013: States Without Exchanges Will Cost Residents," Breitbart, March 2, 2015, at http://www.breitbart.com/big-government/2015/03/02/jonathan-gruber-in-2013-states-without-exchanges-will-cost-residents/.

11 "Wheels up" is congressional staff speak for "My boss is heading out of town. Thank God."

12 Amanda Macias and Hunter Walker, "Georgetown Blames Low Turnout at

Hillary Clinton Speech on Final Exams," *Business Insider*, December 3, 2014, at http://www.businessinsider.com/hillary-clinton-spoke-at-georgetown-and-hardly-anyone-showed-up-2014-12.

13 Shushannah Walshe, "Hillary Clinton Speaks Out Against U.S. Use of Torture," *ABC News*, December 17, 2014, at http://abcnews.go.com/US/hillary-clinton-speaks-us-torture/story?id=27654296.

14 Dan Balz, "Clinton's Campaign Will Be Different From the Last One. But What About Her?" *The Washington Post*, February 7, 2015, at http://www.washingtonpost.com/politics/clinton-builds-a-different-campaign-for-2016-will-she-be-different-too/2015/02/07/280e5aac-aee7-11e4-ad71-7b9eba0f87d6_story.html.

15 George F. Will, "Immigration and Common Core stand in Jeb Bush's way," *The Washington Post*, December 29, 2014, at https://www.washingtonpost.com/opinions/george-will-immigration-and-common-core-stand-in-jeb-bushs-way/2014/12/26/622035a8-8ba6-11e4-8ff4-fb93129c9c8b_story.html.

16 Ed O'Keefe, "Struggling to make 2016 about Jeb, not Bush," *The Washington Post*, June 7, 2015, http://www.washingtonpost.com/politics/for-jeb-bush-the-challenge-remains-making-it-about-jeb-not-bush/2015/06/05/ecd087ea-0af2-11e5-9e39-0db921c47b93_story.html.

17 Ibid.

18 George F. Will, "Immigration and Common Core Stand in Jeb Bush's Way," *The Washington Post*, December 26, 2014, at https://www.washingtonpost.com/opinions/george-will-immigration-and-common-core-stand-in-jeb-bushs-way/2014/12/26/622035a8-8ba6-11e4-8ff4-fb93129c9c8b_story.html.

19 Ibid.

20 Cindy Boren, "Chris Christie's trip to Dallas on Jerry Jones' dime raises ethics concerns," *The Washington Post*, January 6, 2013, http://www.washingtonpost.com/blogs/early-lead/wp/2015/01/06/chris-christies-trip-to-dallas-on-jerry-jones-dime-raises-ethics-concerns/.

21 That's "coffee" for those who don't speak Jersey.

22 Karl Rove, "Who's Winning the GOP's Invisible Primaries?" *The Wall Street Journal*, December 4, 2014, at http://www.rove.com/articles/560.

23 Kate Zernicke, "George Washington Bridge Scandal: What You Need to Know," *The New York Times*, May 1, 2015, at http://www.nytimes.com/2015/05/02/nyregion/george-washington-bridge-scandal-what-you-need-to-know.html.

24 Unfortunately for Christie, the story continued in September of 2016 when Federal prosecutors in the trial of Christie's aides, Bridget Ann Kelly, David Wildstein, and Bill Baroni, indicated Christie knew of the lane closures, who closed the lanes and why when they occurred (not necessarily beforehand) and participated in a coverup. This was long after Christie's presidential ambitions had collapsed. Kate Zernicke, "Chris Christie Knew About Bridge

Lane Closures as They Happened, Prosecutors Say," *The New York Times*, September 20, 2016, at http://www.nytimes.com/2016/09/20/nyregion/bridgegate-trial.html

25 "AFC playoffs: Peyton Manning struggles as Broncos fall to Colts, 24-13, in divisional round," Adam Kilgore, *The Washington Post*, January 12, 2015, at http://www.washingtonpost.com/sports/afc-playoffs-peyton-manning-struggles-as-broncos-fall-to-colts-24-13-in-divisional-round/2015/01/11/8967777a-99cf-11e4-a7ee-526210d665b4_story.html.

26 Peggy Noonan, "Don't Do It, Mr. Romney," *The Wall Street Journal*, January 16, 2015, at http://www.wsj.com/articles/dont-do-it-mr-romney-1421367202.

27 Melissa Quinn, "Rand Paul on Mitt Romney's 2016 Run," *The Daily Signal*, June 14, 2015, at http://dailysignal.com/2015/01/13/rand-paul-mitt-romney-2016-run-time-fresh-blood/.

28 Dan Balz, "Can Scott Walker's unflashy style break through in the 2016 presidential race," *The Washington Post*, January 16, 2015, at http://www.washingtonpost.com/politics/can-scott-walkers-unflashy-style-break-through-in-the-2016-presidential-race/2015/01/18/892e0314-9f29-11e4-9f89-561284a573f8_story.html.

29 David A. Farenthold, "As Scott Walker mulls White House bid, questions linger over college exit," *The Washington Post*, February 11, 2015, at http://www.washingtonpost.com/politics/as-scott-walker-mulls-white-house-bid-questions-linger-over-college-exit/2015/02/11/8e17ea44-b13e-11e4-886b-c22184f27c35_story.html.

30 Shushannah Walshe, "Gov. Walker 'Punts' on Foreign Policy, Evolution Questions," ABC News, February, 11, 2015, at http://abcnews.go.com/Politics/gov-scott-walker-punts-foreign-policy-evolution-questions/story?id=28899257.

31 Scott Walker, "Unintimidated: A Governor's Story and a Nation's Challenge," Sentinel, November 13, 2013.

32 This was the same legislative train wreck with which Republican presidential aspirant and Ohio Governor John Kasich was deeply involved as Chairman of the House Budget Committee and thus Gingrich's chief budget advisor. Curiously, Kasich never mentioned his role in this disaster on the campaign trail.

33 The expression "government shutdown" is something of a misnomer. If Congress and the president fail to come to terms on a Federal appropriations spending bill before the previous bill expires, then much of the day-to-day operations of the Government continue under special authority and at the spending levels established in the then-expired spending bill. Thus, the Department of Defense continues to defend, the Treasury continues to manage the debt, and so forth. All functions necessary to ensure the safety

and security of the American people continue, but much else stops until a new spending bill is passed. Except for a few outliers, such as the national parks, few citizens actually notice anything different when a "shutdown" occurs.

34 Marina Koren, "John Boehner Is Not Budging on His DHS Funding Plan," The National Journal, http://www.nationaljournal.com/congress/john-boehner-literally-laughs-at-idea-of-passing-short-term-resolution-to-fund-dhs-20150212.

35 Cristina Marcos and Rebecca Shabad, "GOP infighting grows over Homeland Security funding," *The Hill,* February 13, 2015, at http://thehill.com/homenews/senate/232704-gop-infighting-grows-over-homeland-security-funding.

36 Basic structure in the United States Congress is the rules of the House are designed to protect the privileges of the Majority, whereas the rules in the Senate are designed to protect the rights of the Minority. Reid led the Democrats in the Minority.

37 Maggie Haberman and Nicholas Confessore, "Critics in G.O.P. Say Christie Is in a Bubble," *The New York Times,* February 19, 2015 at http://www.nytimes.com/2015/02/20/us/some-chris-christie-supporters-now-turn-their-backs.html?_r=0.

38 Dan Balz, "The CPAC faithful's big hope: A true conservative who can win in 2016," *The Washington Post,* February 26, 2015.

39 Amy Davidson, "What the Hillary Clinton Foundation Is Costing Hillary," The New Yorker, February 26, 2015, at http://www.newyorker.com/news/amy-davidson/what-the-clinton-foundation-is-costing-hillary.

40 Eugene Robinson, "Is Hillary Hiding Something," *The Washington Post*, March 10, 2015, at http://www.washingtonpost.com/opinions/new-scandals-offer-reasons-to-wonder-whether-clinton-is-hiding-something/2015/03/09/fef22b02-c693-11e4-aa1a-86135599fb0f_story.html.

41 Laura Meckler, "Bill Clinton still doesn't use email," Wall Street Journal Washington Wire, March 10, 2015, at http://blogs.wsj.com/washwire/2015/03/10/bill-clinton-still-doesnt-use-email/.

42 Amy Chozick and Michael S. Schmidt, "Hillary Clinton Tries to Quell Controversy Over Private Email," *The New York Times,* March 11, 2015, at http://www.nytimes.com/2015/03/11/us/hillary-clinton-email.html?_r=0.

43 Frank Brunni, "Hillary's Prickly Apologia," *The New York Times,* March 10, 2015, at http://www.nytimes.com/2015/03/11/opinion/frank-bruni-hillary-clinton-the-email-controversy-and-the-2016-presidential-race.html.

44 Dan Balz, "Clinton's strategy on e-mail use: 'Trust me.' But how will voters respond?" *The Washington Post,* March 11, 2015, http://www.washingtonpost.com/politics/clinton-says-trust-me-will-the-voters-reciprocate/2015/03/10/582b17f6-c74d-11e4-a199-6cb5e63819d2_story.html.

45 James Carville on ABC News, March 15, 2015, at http://www.realclearpolitics.

com/video/2015/03/15/james_carville_i_expect_hillary_didnt_want_louis_gohmert_rifling_through_her_emails_--_people_flapping_their_jaws_about_nothing.html.

46 Michael S. Schmidt and Matt Apuzzo, "Hillary Clinton Emails Said to Contain Classified Material," *The New York Times*, July 24, 2015, at http://www.nytimes.com/2015/07/25/us/politics/hillary-clinton-email-classified-information-inspector-general-intelligence-community.html?_r=0.

47 Michael Goodwin, "Hillary faces dangerous enemy in Obama administration," *The New York Post*, July 26, 2015, at http://nypost.com/2015/07/26/hillary-has-a-dangerous-enemy-in-the-obama-administration/.

48 Dylan Byers, "Trump claims $213 million payout for 'Apprentice,'" Politico, October 5, 2015, at http://www.politico.com/blogs/media/2015/07/trump-claims-213m-payout-for-apprentice-210595.

49 Amy Bingham, "Donald Trump's Companies Filed for Bankruptcy 4 Times," ABC News, retrieved October 5, 2015, http://abcnews.go.com/Politics/donald-trump-filed-bankruptcy-times/story?id=13419250.

50 Participants on the Democratic side included Reid's two contending successors – Dick Durbin of Illinois and Chuck Schumer of New York, the soon-to-be-indicted Bob Menendez of New Jersey, and Michael Bennet of Colorado. Whereas the Republicans were seeking to outflank many in their own caucus, the Democrats still following President Obama's lead presented a more united front.

51 Jim Geraghty, "Bush on Cruz: I Just Don't Like the Guy," National Review, October 20, 2015, at http://www.nationalreview.com/corner/425818/bush-cruz-i-just-dont-guy-jim-geraghty.

52 Sean Sullivan, "The biggest upset of 2012," The Washington Post, November 28, 2012, at https://www.washingtonpost.com/news/the-fix/wp/2012/11/28/the-biggest-upset-of-2012/.

53 Dylan Byers, "N.Y. Times keeps Cruz off bestseller list," Politico, July 9, 2015, http://www.politico.com/blogs/media/2015/07/ny-times-keeps-cruz-off-bestseller-list-210254.html.

54 It's called spiking because editors used to have a long needle like a knitting needle embedded on a circular base and the stories that failed to make the editor's cut ended up on the spike.

55 Charles Krauthammer, "She Rides by Van: The Hillary Clinton Launch," *The Washington Post*, April 17, 2015, http://www.washingtonpost.com/opinions/the-queen-travels-by-van/2015/04/16/4ca7c956-e46c-11e4-b510-962fcfabc310_story.html.

56 See BuzzFeed, "Hillary Clinton Wrong on Family's Immigration History, Records Show," April 15, 2015, at http://www.buzzfeed.com/andrewkaczynski/hillary-clinton-wrong-on-familys-immigration-history-records#.wbGZ4KBOm.

57 Ken McIntyre, "Here's 14 Fun Facts about Hillary Clinton's First Democratic Challenger for President," The Daily Signal, May 2, 2015, at http://dailysignal.com/2015/05/02/heres-14-fun-facts-about-hillary-clintons-first-democratic-challenger-for-president/.
58 Jennifer Jacobs, "Q&A with Bernie Sanders: What he means by socialism," *USA Today* On Politics, July 8, 2015, at http://onpolitics.usatoday.com/2015/07/08/qa-with-bernie-sanders-what-he-means-by-socialism/.
59 Charles Krauthammer, "Game Over," *The Washington Post*, October 16, 2015, at https://www.washingtonpost.com/opinions/game-over/2015/10/15/5538cb8a-7367-11e5-9cbb-790369643cf9_story.html.
60 Former Rhode Island Sen. Lincoln Chafee and former Virginia Sen. Jim Webb threw their hats in the ring, but neither met even a minimal standard for viability and their candidacies never made a ripple.
61 See "I paid for this microphone, Mr. Breen," NBC Learn K-12, at http://archives.nbclearn.com/portal/site/k-12/flatview?cuecard=4511.
62 Chris Cillizza, "For Hillary Clinton, A Trust Deficit to Surmount," *The Washington Post*, May 3, 2015, at http://www.washingtonpost.com/politics/for-clinton-a-trust-deficit-to-surmount/2015/05/03/fbd201ba-f19d-11e4-b2f3-af5479e6bbdd_story.html.
63 Ruth Marcus, "Sloppiness and Greed," *The Washington Post*, April 26, 2015, at http://www.washingtonpost.com/opinions/sloppiness-and-greed/2015/04/24/e4d53446-eaa9-11e4-aae1-d642717d8afa_story.html.
64 Nicholas Confessore and Amy Chozick, "Unease at Clinton Foundation Over Finances and Ambitions," *The New York Times*, August 13, 2013, at http://www.nytimes.com/2013/08/14/us/politics/unease-at-clinton-foundation-over-finances-and-ambitions.html?_r=0.
65 Capitol Report, "Bill Clinton defends speaking fees, 'I gotta pay our bills'," May 4, 2015, Marketwatch, at http://www.marketwatch.com/story/bill-clinton-defends-speaking-fees-i-gotta-pay-our-bills-2015-05-04.
66 Jon Greenberg, "Hillary Clinton says she and Bill were 'dead broke'," The Washington Post, June 10, 2014, at http://www.politifact.com/truth-o-meter/statements/2014/jun/10/hillary-clinton/hillary-clinton-says-she-and-bill-were-dead-broke/.
67 Amy Chozick, "New Book, 'Clinton Cash,' Questions Foreign Donations to Foundation," *The New York Times*, April 19, 2015, at http://www.nytimes.com/2015/04/20/us/politics/new-book-clinton-cash-questions-foreign-donations-to-foundation.html.
68 Jonathan Chait, "If This Is the Best Defense of the Clinton Foundation, She's in Trouble," *The New York Times* magazine, April 28, 2015, at http://nymag.com/daily/intelligencer/2015/04/clinton-foundation-needs-better-defense.html.
69 Michael Cohn, "Clinton Foundation Expected to Amend Tax Returns," April 24, 2015, Accounting Today, at http://www.accountingtoday.com/news/

tax-practice/clinton-foundation-expected-to-amend-tax-returns-74404-1.html.

70. Mike McIntire and Jo Becker, "Canadian Partnership Shielded Identities of Donors to Clinton Foundation," *The New York Times*, April 29, 2015, at http://www.nytimes.com/2015/04/30/us/politics/canadian-partnership-shielded-identities-of-donors-to-clinton-foundation.html.

71. Al Weaver, "Peggy Noonan on Hillary's Press Strategy, 'She's Running a Silent Movie of a Press Campaign'," *The Daily Caller*, May 19, 2015, at http://dailycaller.com/2015/05/17/peggy-noonan-on-hillarys-press-strategy-shes-running-a-silent-movie-of-a-campaign/.

72. Matea Gold, Rosalind S. Helderman, and Anu Narayanswamy, "Hillary Clinton was paid millions by tech industry," *The Washington Post*, May 19, 2015, at http://www.washingtonpost.com/politics/hillary-clinton-was-paid-millions-by-tech-industry-for-speeches/2015/05/18/f149d598-fd86-11e4-805c-c3f407e5a9e9_story.html.

73. "Hillary Goes Conservative on Immigration Reform," *The Washington Times*, December 13, 2004, at http://www.washingtontimes.com/news/2004/dec/13/20041213-124920-6151r/?page=all.

74. Greg Sargent, "Hillary: Minors crossing border must be sent home," *The Washington Post*, June 18, 2014, at http://www.washingtonpost.com/blogs/plum-line/wp/2014/06/18/hillary-minors-crossing-border-must-be-sent-home.

75. Frank Luntz, "Don't trust those polls," *The Washington Post*, May 10, 2015, at http://www.washingtonpost.com/opinions/dont-trust-those-polls/2015/05/08/b9f2d678-f59b-11e4-bcc4-e8141e5eb0c9_story.html.

76. William Safire, "Essay: A Blizzard of Lies," *The New York Times*, January 8, 1996, at http://www.nytimes.com/1996/01/08/opinion/essay-blizzard-of-lies.html.

77. Fox News Sunday, May 24, 2015, at http://www.foxnews.com/transcript/2015/05/24/mike-huckabee-lays-out-path-to-2016-republican-nomination-amb-john-bolton-talks/.

78. Janet Hook, "Jeb Bush Tries to End Iraq War Controversy," *The Wall Street Journal*, May 14, 2015, at http://www.wsj.com/articles/jeb-bush-tries-to-end-iraq-war-controversy-1431628650.

79. Chris Cillizza, "Who Had the Worst Week in Washington? Jeb Bush," *The Washington Post*, May 17, 2015, for this and the next two quotes.

80. "Remarks by the President and First Lady on the End of the War in Iraq," December 14, 2011, at https://www.whitehouse.gov/the-press-office/2011/12/14/remarks-president-and-first-lady-end-war-iraq.

81. Juliet Eilperin, "Despite no-shows, Obama plays host to Gulf leaders," *The Washington Post*, May 14, 2015, at http://www.washingtonpost.com/blogs/post-politics/wp/2015/05/14/despite-no-shows-obama-plays-hosts-to-gulf-leaders/.

82 Charles Krauthammer, "You want hypotheticals? Here's one." *The Washington Post*, May 22, 2015, at http://www.washingtonpost.com/opinions/you-want-hypotheticals-heres-one/2015/05/21/909713d6-ffe9-11e4-805c-c3f407e5a9e9_story.html.

83 Hugh Naylor and Mustafa Salim, "Iran-aligned Shiite militias gather to join fight against Islamic State gains," *The Washington Post*, May 18, 2015, at http://www.washingtonpost.com/world/iranian-aligned-shiite-militias-head-towards-the-is-captured-city-of-ramadi/2015/05/18/46d26210-fce1-11e4-8c77-bf274685e1df_story.html.

84 Sean Sullivan, "Does Rubio have a spending problem?" *The Washington Post*, May 20, 2015, at http://www.washingtonpost.com/politics/marco-rubios-struggles-with-money-are-back-under-the-campaign-spotlight/2015/05/20/4dec1732-fd89-11e4-8b6c-0dcce21e223d_story.html.

85 Marc Caputo, "Rubio sells his house of horrors," Politico, June 3, 2015, at http://www.politico.com/story/2015/06/marco-rubio-sells-house-of-horrors-118572.html?hp=r1_4.

86 Paul Walsh, "Overflow crowd in Minneapolis hears Bernie Sanders," *Minneapolis Star Tribune*, May 31, 2015, at http://www.duluthnewstribune.com/news/3756652-overflow-crowd-minneapolis-hears-bernie-sanders.

87 Trip Gabriel and Patrick Healy, "Challenging Hillary Clinton, Bernie Sanders Gains Momentum in Iowa," *The New York Times*, May 31, 2015, at http://www.nytimes.com/2015/06/01/us/politics/challenging-hillary-clinton-bernie-sanders-gains-momentum-in-iowa.html?_r=0.

88 Huffington Post, "Hillary Clinton Favorability Rating," June 2, 2015, at http://elections.huffingtonpost.com/pollster/hillary-clinton-favorable-rating.

89 Dan Balz and Peyton M. Craighill, "Poll: While GOP lacks a front-runner, Democrats' front-runner takes a hit," *The Washington Post*, June 3, 2015, at http://www.washingtonpost.com/politics/poll-2016-republicans-tightly-bunched-clintons-image-erodes/2015/06/01/9e9c26c6-0893-11e5-9e39-0db921c47b93_story.html.

90 Jennifer Agiesta, "Poll: New Speed Bumps for Hillary," CNN politics, June 2, 2015, at http://www.cnn.com/2015/06/02/politics/hillary-clinton-2016-poll-gop-field-close/index.html.

91 Thomas F. Schwartz, "You Can Fool All the People," Abraham Lincoln Association, at http://www.abrahamlincolnassociation.org/Newsletters/5-4.pdf.

92 Lanny Davis on the Ed Schultz show, July 23, 2015, at http://www.realclearpolitics.com/video/2015/07/23/lanny_davis_hillary_clintons_poor_trustworthy_numbers_partly_due_to_the_right-wing_conspiracy.html.

93 Dan Balz and Peyton M. Craighill, "Poll: While GOP lacks a front-runner, Democrats' front-runner takes a hit," *The Washington Post*, June 3, 2015, at http://www.washingtonpost.com/politics/poll-2016-republicans-

tightly-bunched-clintons-image-erodes/2015/06/01/9e9c26c6-0893-11e5-9e39-0db921c47b93_story.html.
94 Fox News Poll, interviews conducted May 31 – June 2, at http://www.foxnews.com/politics/interactive/2015/06/03/0603152016nsaweb/.
95 Alan Rappeport and Steve Eder, "Marco Rubio and His Wife Cited for 17 Traffic Infractions," June 5, 2015, First Draft, *The New York Times*, at http://www.nytimes.com/politics/first-draft/2015/06/05/marco-rubio-and-his-wife-cited-17-times-for-traffic-infractions-2/?_r=0.
96 Brent Scher, "Democratic Oppo Firm's Finger Prints on NYT Rubio Hit," June 5, 2015, *The Washington Free Beacon*, http://freebeacon.com/politics/democratic-oppo-firms-fingerprints-on-nyt-rubio-hit/.
97 Ed O'Keefe and Robert Costa, "Jeb Bush shakes up team ahead of campaign launch," *The Washington Post*, June 9, 2015, at http://www.washingtonpost.com/politics/jeb-bush-shakes-up-his-team-ahead-of-formal-campaign-launch/2015/06/08/857c8f80-0e08-11e5-a0dc-2b6f404ff5cf_story.html.
98 See Marc Caputo and Alex Isenstadt, "Behind the Jeb Bush campaign shake-up," Politico, June 9, 2015, at http://www.politico.com/story/2015/06/jeb-bush-campaign-shake-up-sally-bradshaw-118803.html.
99 Tim Fernholz, "Be skeptical of Jeb Bush's ability to create 4% growth in the U.S.," Quartz, June 16, 2015, at http://qz.com/429286/be-skeptical-of-jeb-bushs-promise-to-create-4-growth-in-the-us/.
100 Labor productivity growth – how much more workers produce per hour today versus yesterday – depends on the amount of productive capital available and on how efficient markets for labor, capital, goods, and services signal excess and shortage. It depends on how rapidly technology is advancing and how rapidly it can be captured in the capital stock as new machinery replaces old.

In contrast, projecting the growth in the labor force is based mostly on demographics, starting with: How fast is the population growing? This growth rate might then need to be adjusted for factors like the baby boom coming out of World War II which temporarily (for a few decades) elevated the portion of the population in the labor pool, and which is about to have the reverse effect as the baby boom becomes the senior boom, elevating the proportion of retirees relative to the population as a whole. Sometimes, cultural shifts alter the labor force growth rate, such as the relatively recent cultural shift significantly increasing the proportion of women working outside the home.

Prior to the late 2000s the workforce grew on average about 1.1 percent per year. Because of the senior boom, beginning in roughly 2008 and over the next few years that rate will to drop to around 0.5 percent a year for many years to come for about a 0.6 percentage point drop in the workforce growth rate which translates directly into a 0.6 percentage point drop in the U.S. economy's normal growth rate relative to the post-war experience.

101 Kevin Williamson, "Witless Ape Rides Escalator," *The National Review*, June 16, 2015, at http://www.nationalreview.com/article/419853/witless-ape-rides-escalator-kevin-d-williamson.

102 Jeremy Diamond, "Trump jumps in: The Donald's latest White House run is officially on," CNN politics, June 15, 2016, at http://www.cnn.com/2015/06/16/politics/donald-trump-2016-announcement-elections/, and Amy Bingham, "Donald Trump's Companies Filed for Bankruptcy 4 Times," ABC News, April 21, 2011, at http://abcnews.go.com/Politics/donald-trump-filed-bankruptcy-times/story?id=13419250.

103 Peter Roff, "The Trump Card," US News & World Report, June 29, 2015, at http://www.usnews.com/opinion/blogs/peter-roff/2015/06/29/dont-dismiss-donald-trumps-ability-to-shape-the-2016-race?int=a39d09&int=a6ea09.

104 Philip Rucker, "As Donald Trump surges in polls, Democrats cheer," July 1, 2015, *The Washington Post*, at http://www.washingtonpost.com/politics/donald-trump-surges-and-democrats-cheer/2015/07/01/895d9e9e-1f5d-11e5-84d5-eb37ee8eaa61_story.html.

105 Chris Moody and Ashley Killough, "Chris Christie launches 2016 presidential bid," June 30, 2015, CNN, at http://www.cnn.com/2015/06/30/politics/chris-christie-2016-presidential-campaign/.

106 Daniel Strauss, "Trumka: Walker 'a national disgrace'," Politico, July 14, 2015, at http://www.politico.com/story/2015/07/richard-trumka-scott-walker-2016-announcement-120025.html.

107 Dan Balz, "Walker seeks to rally the GOP on a pledge of victory with no compromise," *The Washington Post*, July 14, 2015, at http://www.washingtonpost.com/politics/walker-seeks-to-rally-gop-on-a-pledge-of-victory-with-no-compromise/2015/07/14/c30228a0-29d9-11e5-bd33-395c05608059_story.html.

108 "Editorial: Kasich a good addition to the race," *Cincinnati Enquirer* Editorial Board, July 21, 2015, at http://www.cincinnati.com/story/opinion/editorials/2015/07/21/editorial-kasich-good-addition-race/30464047/.

109 Nikki Battiste, Emily Shapiro, and Matthew Stone, "Charleston Shooting: What the Gunman Allegedly Told Churchgoers Before the Shooting," ABC News, June 18, 2015, at http://abcnews.go.com/US/charleston-shooting-gunman-allegedly-survivor-inside-church/story?id=31872085.

110 Stephen Collinson and Nia-Malika Henderson, "Why Obama's N-word was shocking," CNN Politics, June 22, 2015, at http://www.cnn.com/2015/06/22/politics/obama-n-word-race-politics/.

111 Tim Devaney and Mike Lillis, "South Carolina governor calls for the Confederate flag to be removed," *The Hill*, June 23, 2015, at http://thehill.com/blogs/blog-briefing-room/news/245750-sc-governor-calls-for-confederate-flag-to-be-removed.

112 Sarah Pulliam Bailey and Karen Tumulty, "Southern Baptist leader is surprising voice against battle flag," *The Washington Post*, June 25, 2015, at http://www.washingtonpost.com/politics/how-a-southern-baptist-leader-became-surprising-voice-on-confederate-flag/2015/06/24/33ffbde6-1a9a-11e5-bd7f-4611a60dd8e5_story.html.

113 Samantha-Jo Roth, "Ted Cruz Cracks Jokes on Gun Control Days after Charleston Shooting," *The Huffington Post*, June 21, 2015, at http://www.huffingtonpost.com/2015/06/20/ted-cruz-gun-control-charleston_n_7628960.html?utm_hp_ref=politics.

114 Jonathan Easley, "Where the GOP Field Stands on the Confederate Flag," *The Hill*, June 23, 2015, at http://thehill.com/homenews/campaign/245741-where-the-2016-gop-field-stands-on-the-confederate-flag.

115 Jonathan Easley, "Rand Paul: Confederate flag 'a symbol of human bondage and slavery'," *The Hill*, June 23, 2015, at http://thehill.com/blogs/ballot-box/245831-rand-paul-confederate-flag-a-symbol-of-human-bondage-and-slavery.

116 "'We are all sick': FBI boss says gun check breakdown allowed Dylann Roof to buy weapon," Fox News, July 10, 2015, at http://www.foxnews.com/us/2015/07/10/are-all-sick-fbi-boss-says-gun-check-breakdown-allowed-dylann-roof-to-buy/.

117 Sam Levine, "Charleston Mayor Joseph Riley: Lack of Gun Control is 'insane'," *The Huffington Post*, June 21, 2015, at http://www.huffingtonpost.com/2015/06/21/joseph-riley-gun-control_n_7631162.html.

118 Arlette Saenz, "Here's Where the 2016 Candidates Stand on the Confederate Flat Issue," ABC News, June 23, 2015, at http://abcnews.go.com/Politics/2016-candidates-stand-confederate-flag-issue/story?id=31947516.

119 Ted Cruz and Paul Ryan, "Putting Congress in Charge on Trade," *The Wall Street Journal*, April 21, 2015, at http://www.wsj.com/articles/putting-congress-in-charge-on-trade-1429659409.

120 Philip Rucker and John Wagner, "On the trail in Iowa, Clinton and Sanders make trade a hot issue," *The Washington Post*, June 14, 2015, at http://www.washingtonpost.com/politics/on-the-trail-in-iowa-clinton-and-sanders-make-trade-a-hot-issue/2015/06/14/f86c1c68-12cc-11e5-9ddc-e3353542100c_story.html.

121 Ibid.

122 Max Ehrenfreud, "Clinton takes a stand on trade," *The Washington Post*, June 19, 2015, at http://www.washingtonpost.com/blogs/wonkblog/wp/2015/06/19/wonkbook-hillary-clinton-takes-a-stand-on-trade/.

123 Domenico Montanaro, "A Timeline of Hillary Clinton's Evolution on Trade," NPR, April 21, 2015, at http://www.npr.org/sections/itsallpolitics/2015/04/21/401123124/a-timeline-of-hillary-clintons-evolution-on-trade.

124 Ariane de Vogue, Jeremy Diamond, and Deena Zaru, "'Jiggery-pokery': The

best lines from Antonin Scalia's Obamacare dissent," CNN Politics, June 25, 2015, at http://www.cnn.com/2015/06/25/politics/supreme-court-scalia-obamacare-roberts/.

125 James C. Capretta, "How Many People Will Pay the Individual Mandate Tax for 2014?" e21, May 7, 2014, at http://www.economics21.org/commentary/how-many-people-will-pay-individual-mandate-tax-2014.

126 The omission referred to was whether individuals purchasing insurance on the Federal exchange would qualify for Obamacare's subsidies.

127 Mark Sherman, "Supreme Court Extends Gay Marriage Nationwide," AP, June 26, 2015, at http://hosted.ap.org/dynamic/stories/U/US_SUPREME_COURT_GAY_MARRIAGE?SITE=AP&SECTION=HOME&TEMPLATE=DEFAULT&CTIME=2015-06-26-10-02-52.

128 Ilya Somin, "A great decision on same-sex marriage – but based on dubious reasoning," *The Washington Post*, June 26, 2015, at http://www.washingtonpost.com/news/volokh-conspiracy/wp/2015/06/26/a-great-decision-on-same-sex-marriage-but-based-on-dubious-reasoning/.

129 Brian Beutler, "Anthony Kennedy's Same-Sex Marriage Opinion Was a Logical Disaster," The New Republic, July 1, 2015, at http://www.newrepublic.com/article/122210/anthony-kennedys-same-sex-marriage-opinion-was-logical-disaster.

130 Chris Cillizza, "What Donald Trump means for 2016," *The Washington Post*, July 13, 2015, at http://www.washingtonpost.com/politics/what-donald-trump-means-to-2016/2015/07/12/5cb5f316-289d-11e5-a5ea-cf74396e59ec_story.html.

131 Ibid.

132 Ibid.

133 Dan Balz and Peyton M. Craighill, "Poll: Trump surges to big lead in GOP presidential race," *The Washington Post*, July 20, 2015, at http://www.washingtonpost.com/politics/poll-trump-surges-to-big-lead-in-gop-presidential-race/2015/07/20/efd2e0d0-2ef8-11e5-8f36-18d1d501920d_story.html?wpisrc=al_alert-politics.

134 Ben Schreckinger, "Trump attacks McCain: 'I like people who weren't captured'," Politico, July 19, 2015, at http://www.politico.com/story/2015/07/trump-attacks-mccain-i-like-people-who-werent-captured-120317.html.

135 To have a sense of what this was like, watch Paramount's "Flight of the Intruder" with Danny Glover and Willem Dafoe.

136 The Smoking Gun, "Deferments Helped Trump Avoid Vietnam," April 28, 2011, at http://www.thesmokinggun.com/documents/celebrity/deferments-helped-trump-dodge-vietnam.

137 Craig Whitlock, "Questions linger about Trump's draft deferments during Vietnam War," *The Washington Post*, July 21, 2015, at https://www.

washingtonpost.com/world/national-security/questions-linger-about-trumps-draft-deferments-during-vietnam-war/2015/07/21/257677bc-2fdd-11e5-8353-1215475949f4_story.html.

138 Doug Schoen, "Hillary Clinton's Reality Check: Her Polling Numbers," Forbes, July 23, 2015, at http://www.forbes.com/sites/dougschoen/2015/07/23/hillary-clintons-reality-check/.

139 Ben White, "Reaction to Clinton's economics speech: 'Is that it?',", Politico, July 14, 2015, at http://www.politico.com/story/2015/07/hillary-clinton-economy-speech-reaction-120033.html.

140 The Associated Press, "Sanders says spreading the wealth, not economic growth, should be priority," July 13, 2015, at http://readingeagle.com/ap/article/sanders-says-spreading-the-wealth-not-economic-growth-should-be-priority.

141 Lawrence Summers, "Incrementalism won't cure these crises," *The Washington Post*, July 12, 2015, at http://www.washingtonpost.com/opinions/incrementalism-wont-cure-these-crises/2015/07/12/30469f66-27fc-11e5-b77f-eb13a215f593_story.html.

142 Chris Cillizza, "Money talks, and this is what it says so far," *The Washington Post*, July 20, 2015, at http://www.washingtonpost.com/politics/winners-and-losers-in-2016-fundraising-race/2015/07/19/c7171316-2e1f-11e5-8353-1215475949f4_story.html.

143 A.B. Stoddard, "Clinton must be joking," *The Hill*, July 29, 2015, at http://thehill.com/opinion/ab-stoddard/249734-ab-stoddard-clinton-must-be-joking.

144 David Daley, "'Ted Cruz gives me the willies': Camille Paglia analyzes the GOP field – and takes on Hillary Clinton," Salon, July 30, 2015, at http://www.salon.com/2015/07/30/ted_cruz_gives_me_the_willies_camille_paglia_analyzes_the_gop_field_and_takes_on_hillary_clinton/.

145 United States Department of State, "Draft Supplementary Environmental Impact Statement," March 1, 2015, at http://keystonepipeline-xl.state.gov/draftseis/index.htm.

146 Dan Merica and Jeff Zeleny, "Hillary Clinton won't answer Keystone XL pipeline question," CNN, July 29, 2015, at http://www.cnn.com/2015/07/28/politics/hillary-clinton-keystone-xl-pipeline/.

147 Ruth Marcus, "Biden Can't Defeat Clinton – She Can Do That Herself," *The Washington Post*, August 5, 2015, at http://www.realclearpolitics.com/articles/2015/08/05/biden_cant_defeat_clinton_--_she_can_do_that_herself_127658.html.

148 John Hellemann, "Where Joe Biden Is Coming From," Bloomberg Politics, August 3, 2015, at http://www.bloomberg.com/politics/articles/2015-08-03/where-joe-biden-is-coming-from.

149 Dan Merica and Eric Bradner, "Clintons earned nearly $141M from 2007

to 2014, tax returns show," CNN, August 1, 2015, at http://www.cnn.com/2015/07/31/politics/hillary-clinton-tax-returns/.
150 Rebekah Metzler, "Trump: Mexico will pay for wall because I say so," CNN Politics, August 5, 2015, at http://www.cnn.com/2015/08/04/politics/donald-trump-mexico-wall-pay/.
151 In the 2004 Democratic primaries Howard Dean, former Governor of Vermont, came in third behind Sen. John Kerry and former North Carolina Gov. John Edwards in the Iowa caucuses. It had been a fierce contest and Dean became overly excited in addressing his Iowa supporters. He let loose with a primal scream that was for the times decidedly unpresidential and his campaign collapsed within days. In 2016, Dean's scream would probably have gone unnoticed. For the full story, see Blake Morrison, "Dean scream gaining cult-like status on the web," CNN, January 19, 2016, at http://usatoday30.usatoday.com/news/politicselections/nation/2004-01-22-dean-usat_x.htm.
152 Gabriel Debenedetti and Dylan Byers, "Democrats set debate schedule," Politico, August 6, 2015, at http://www.politico.com/story/2015/08/democrats-debate-schedule-nevada-october-13-121092.html.
153 Peggy Noonan, "Fireworks at the Republican Debate," *The Wall Street Journal*, August 7, 2015, at http://www.wsj.com/articles/fireworks-at-the-republican-debate-1438921640.
154 Isabelle Taft, "Donald Trump's 9 craziest comments," Politico, August 7, 2015, at http://www.politico.com/story/2015/08/donald-trump-5-craziest-comments-gop-debate-121124.html.
155 Carl M. Cannon, "10 Takeaways from the Prime-Time GOP Debate," RealClearPolitics, August 7, 2015, at http://www.realclearpolitics.com/articles/2015/08/07/10_takeaways_from_the_prime-time_gop_debate_127696.html.
156 "Republican presidential candidates' debate: Quotes of the night," *The Daily Telegraph*, August 6, 2015, at http://www.telegraph.co.uk/news/worldnews/republicans/11788975/Republican-presidential-candidates-debate-Quotes-of-the-night.html?frame=3400429.
157 Peggy Noonan, "Fireworks at the Republican Debate," *The Wall Street Journal*, August 7, 2015, at http://www.wsj.com/articles/fireworks-at-the-republican-debate-1438921640.
158 Joel Gehrke, "Fiorina Fundraising Spikes after Debate," National Review, August 9, 2015, at http://www.nationalreview.com/article/422295/fiorina-fundraising-spikes-after-debate-joel-gehrke.
159 Michael Gerson, "Donald Trump will inevitably flame out, and here's why," *The Washington Post*, August 11, 2015, at https://www.washingtonpost.com/opinions/showing-the-donald-the-door/2015/08/10/78e4bbc4-3f92-11e5-bfe3-ff1d8549bfd2_story.html.

160 Aaron Bycoffe, "Rick Perry's Low-Budget Campaign Needs Super PACs to Survive," FiveThirtyEight, August 11, 2015, at http://fivethirtyeight.com/datalab/rick-perrys-low-budget-campaign-needs-super-pacs-to-survive/.

161 Philip Rucker, Abby Livingston, and Dan Balz, "Rick Perry stops paying all of his staff as fundraising dries up," *The Washington Post*, August 11, 2015, at http://www.washingtonpost.com/news/post-politics/wp/2015/08/10/rick-perry-stops-paying-his-south-carolina-staff-as-fundraising-dries-up/.

162 "Has 'The Donald' peaked?" Rasmussen, August 11, 2015, at http://www.rasmussenreports.com/public_content/politics/elections/election_2016/has_the_donald_peaked.

163 R. Kelly Myers, Franklin Pierce/Boston Herald poll results, August 11, 2015, at http://www.bostonherald.com/sites/default/files/blog_posts/FPU-BH-0811-Rep.pdf, and Suffolk/EDU poll results, August 11, 2015, at http://www.suffolk.edu/documents/SUPRC/8_11_2015_marginals.pdf.

164 Deena Zaru, "Rapper drops Clinton for Sanders," CNN, August 10, 2015, at http://www.cnn.com/2015/08/10/politics/lil-b-based-god-black-lives-matter-clinton-sanders/.

165 Candi Peterson, "Teachers Say No Freaking Way to AFT Endorsement of Hillary Clinton," July 13, 2015, The Washington Teacher, at http://www.commondreams.org/views/2015/07/13/teachers-say-no-freaking-way-aft-endorsement-hillary-clinton.

166 Alex Seitz-Wald, "Bernie Sanders event shut down by Black Lives Matter activists," August 8, 2015, MSNBC, at http://www.msnbc.com/msnbc/bernie-sanders-event-shut-down-black-lives-matter-activists.

167 Scott Shane and Michael S. Schmidt, "Hillary Clinton Emails Take Long Path to Controversy," *The New York Times*, August 8, 2015, at http://www.nytimes.com/2015/08/09/us/hillary-clinton-emails-take-long-path-to-controversy.html?_r=0.

168 Jonathan Allen, "Hillary Clinton to give private email server to Justice Department," Reuters, August 11, 2015, at http://www.reuters.com/article/2015/08/12/us-usa-election-clinton-emails-idUSKCN0QG2DZ20150812.

169 Anita Kumar, Marisa Taylor, and Greg Gordon, "Top Secret emails found as Clinton probe expands to top aides," McClatchy DC, August 12, 2015, at http://www.mcclatchydc.com/news/nation-world/national/article30714762.html.

170 John R. Schindler, "The Spy Satellite Secrets in Hillary Clinton's Emails," *The Daily Beast*, August 12, 2015, at http://www.thedailybeast.com/articles/2015/08/12/the-spy-satellite-secrets-in-hillary-s-emails.html.

171 David Martosko, "Hillary shrugs off suggestions she 'wiped' her server clean with snarky response, 'What, with a cloth or something'," *Daily Mail*, August 18, 2015, at http://www.dailymail.co.uk/news/article-3202887/

Hillary-shrugs-question-wiped-server-clean-like-cloth-insists-did-not-send-classified-material-secret-email-account.html.

172 Maggie Haberman, "Hillary Clinton Takes 'Responsibility' for Email Use, Saying It Wasn't the Best Choice," *The New York Times*, August 26, 2015, at http://www.nytimes.com/politics/first-draft/2015/08/26/hillary-clinton-takes-responsibility-for-email-use-saying-it-wasnt-the-best-choice/?_r=0.

173 Ruth Marcus, "Stop digging that hole, Secretary Clinton," *The Washington Post*, August 21, 2015, at https://www.washingtonpost.com/opinions/stop-digging-the-hole-secretary-clinton/2015/08/21/8f40c684-4824-11e5-8ab4-c73967a143d3_story.html?utm_term=.f854ddace777.

174 Mary Dejevsky, "I'm a Hillary Clinton fan. But I hope she bows out with grace," *The Guardian*, August 17, 2015, at http://www.theguardian.com/commentisfree/2015/aug/17/hillary-clinton-white-house-too-much-baggage.

175 David A. Fahrenthold, "20 times Donald Trump has changed his mind since June," *The Washington Post*, August 18, 2015, at http://www.washingtonpost.com/news/post-politics/wp/2015/08/17/20-times-donald-trump-has-changed-his-mind-since-june/.

176 Ashley Killough and Theodore Schleifer, "Trump birthright citizenship ban splinters GOP field," CNN Politics, August 19, 2015, at http://www.cnn.com/2015/08/19/politics/john-kasich-for-birthright-citizenship/index.html.

177 Charles Krauthammer, "Donald Trump's Fantasy of Mass Deportation Is Political Poison for GOP," *The Washington Post*, August 21, 2015, at http://www.nationalreview.com/article/422864/donald-trump-deportation-republicans

178 Ed O'Keefe, "Jeb Bush: 'Anchor babies' is not offensive," *The Washington Post*, August 20, 2015, at http://www.washingtonpost.com/news/post-politics/wp/2015/08/20/jeb-bush-anchor-babies-isnt-offensive/.

179 Jose A. DelReal, "Jeb Bush: People should 'chill out' on the 'anchor baby' issue," *The Washington Post*, August 24, 2015, at http://www.washingtonpost.com/news/post-politics/wp/2015/08/24/jeb-bush-people-should-chill-out-on-the-anchor-baby-controversy/.

180 Ibid.

181 Andrew Rafferty, "Rubio: Trump's immigration plan is unworkable," MSNBC, August 18, 2015, at http://www.msnbc.com/msnbc/marco-rubio-donald-trump-immigration-plan-unworkable.

182 John Harwood, "Birthright citizenship makes the U.S. exceptional," CNBC, August 20, 2015, at http://www.cnbc.com/2015/08/20/rubio-birthright-citizenship-makes-us-exceptional.html.

183 Jenna Johnson, "On birthright citizenship, Scott Walker takes yet another stance," *The Washington Post*, August 24, 2015, at http://www.washingtonpost.com/news/post-politics/wp/2015/08/23/on-birthright-citizenship-scott-walker-takes-yet-another-stance-dont-change-the-constitution/.

184 Jose A. DelReal, "Scott Walker clarifies: His current position on birthright citizenship is no position at all," *The Washington Post*, August 21, 2015, at http://www.washingtonpost.com/news/post-politics/wp/2015/08/21/scott-walker-clarifies-his-current-position-on-birthright-citizenship-is-no-position-at-all/.

185 Matea Gold, "Possible Biden run puts Obama fundraising network on high alert," *The Washington Post*, August 27, 2015, at http://www.washingtonpost.com/politics/possible-biden-run-puts-obama-fundraising-network-on-high-alert/2015/08/26/2b9bc644-4c00-11e5-bfb9-9736d04fc8e4_story.html.

186 Jeff Zeleny and Peter Morris, "Obama gives Joe Biden 'blessing' for 2016 bid," CNN politics, August 25, 2015, at http://www.cnn.com/2015/08/24/politics/joe-biden-obama-blessing-2016/.

187 Arit John, "Biden More Competitive Than Clinton Against Leading Republicans: Poll," Bloomberg Politics, August 27, 2015, at http://www.bloomberg.com/politics/articles/2015-08-27/biden-more-competitive-than-clinton-against-leading-republicans-poll.

188 Ibid.

189 Edward-Isaac Dovere and Gabriel Debenedetti, "Elizabeth Warren backers lukewarm on Joe Biden," Politico, August 24, 2015, at http://www.politico.com/story/2015/08/elizabeth-warren-backers-lukewarm-joe-biden-2016-121688.html.

190 Nick Schwartz, "James Harrison explains why he returned his children's participation trophies," Fox Sports, March 3, 2016, at http://www.foxsports.com/nfl/story/james-harrison-steelers-participation-trophies-parenting-steve-harvey-030316.

191 Anthony Salvanto, Jennifer De Pinto, Sarah Dutton, and Fred Backus, "Battleground Tracker: Sanders Surges in IA; NH; Clinton Up in SC," CBS News, September 13, 2015, at http://www.cbsnews.com/news/battleground-tracker-sanders-surges-in-ia-nh-clintonup-in-sc/.

192 Mark Murray, "Bernie Sanders Leads Hillary Clinton by 9 Points in New Hampshire, Gains in Iowa: Poll," NBC News, September 6, 2015, at http://www.nbcnews.com/meet-the-press/bernie-sanders-leads-hillary-clinton-9-n-h-gains-iowa-n422111.

193 *The Huffington Post* at http://elections.huffingtonpost.com/pollster/hillary-clinton-favorable-rating.

194 David A. Fahrenthold, "Campaigns start too early? Well, not Jim Gilmore's," *The Washington Post*, September 7, 2015, at http://www.washingtonpost.com/politics/campaigns-start-too-early-well-not-jim-gilmores/2015/09/07/f9c3bf72-556f-11e5-8bb1-b488d231bba2_story.html.

195 Nick Gass, "Clinton: I am not a natural politician," Politico, March 16, 2016, at http://www.politico.com/blogs/2016-dem-primary-live-updates-and-re

sults/2016/03/hillary-clinton-i-am-not-a-natural-politician-220544.
196 Karen Tumulty, "Hillary Clinton tries to show that her record is more than just talk," *The Washington Post*, September 11, 2015, at http://www.washingtonpost.com/politics/in-clinton-voters-see-a-long-resume-but-a-short-list-of-accomplishments/2015/09/09/fff3fc60-573e-11e5-8bb1-b488d231bba2_story.html.
197 Rasmussen Reports, September 10, 2015, at http://www.rasmussenreports.com/public_content/politics/obama_administration/obama_approval_index_history.
198 Stephen F. Hayes, "Clinton Takes Tough Shot at Obama," The National Review, September 9, 2015, at http://www.weeklystandard.com/blogs/clinton-takes-tough-shot-obama_1027919.html.
199 Bradford Richardson, "Poll: South Carolina wants Graham to end White House run," *The Hill*, September 10, 2015, at http://thehill.com/blogs/ballot-box/gop-primaries/253077-poll-south-carolina-wants-graham-to-end-white-house-run.
200 This little paragraph in Bush's acceptance speech then gave rise to a presidential commission led by two outstanding former senators, Republican Connie Mack of Florida and Democrat John Breaux of Louisiana, and ultimately produced a first-rate report on tax reform concepts and options. These good former senators took time out from their own busy lives and businesses to serve the country diligently at the president's request, but never got the joke: From the outset everyone in the White House knew this effort had a precisely measured zero point zero chance of gaining White House backing whatever the commission produced. Washington is not a nice place and even seasoned veterans are sometimes conned.
201 Jeb Bush, "My Tax Overhaul to Unleash 4% Growth," *The Wall Street Journal*, September 8, 2015, at http://www.wsj.com/articles/my-tax-overhaul-to-unleash-4-growth-1441754195.
202 Kyle Pomerleau, "Details and Analysis of Governor Jeb Bush's Tax Plan," The Tax Foundation, September 10, 2015, at http://taxfoundation.org/article/details-and-analysis-governor-jeb-bush-s-tax-plan.
203 J.D. Foster, "The New Flat Tax: Easy as One, Two, Three," Heritage Foundation Backgrounder #2631, December 13, 2011, at http://www.heritage.org/research/reports/2011/12/the-new-flat-tax-easy-as-one-two-three.
204 Alan Cole and Scott Greenberg, "Details and Analysis of Senator Bernie Sanders's Tax Plan," Tax Foundation, January 28, 2016, at http://taxfoundation.org/article/details-and-analysis-senator-bernie-sanders-s-tax-plan.
205 Note that the candidates' tax plans often accreted additional items and details over the course of the campaign.
206 Kyle Pomerleau and Michael Schuyler, "Details and Analysis of Hillary

Clinton's Tax Plan," Tax Foundation, January 26, 2016, at http://taxfoundation.org/article/details-and-analysis-hillary-clinton-s-tax-proposals.

207 Carrie Dann, "In Another Instagram Video, Donald Trump Mocks 'Low Energy' Jeb Bush," NBC News, September 8, 2015, at http://www.nbcnews.com/politics/2016-election/another-instagram-video-trump-mocks-low-energy-bush-n423616.

208 Paul Solotaroff, "Trump Seriously: On the Trail With the GOP's Tough Guy," Rolling Stone, September 9, 2015, at http://www.rollingstone.com/politics/news/trump-seriously-20150909.

209 Jon Ward, "Jindal takes on the Trump 'carnival act' in a way Bush hasn't," Yahoo Politics, September 10, 2015, at https://www.yahoo.com/politics/jindal-takes-on-the-trump-carnival-act-in-a-way-128802124696.html.

210 Tom LoBianco, "Trump explains jab at Fiorina's face: I'm an entertainer," CNN politics, September 11, 2015, at http://www.cnn.com/2015/09/11/politics/donald-trump-carly-fiorina-entertainer/.

211 Rosalind S. Helderman, Tom Hamburger, and Carol D. Leonnig, "Tech company: No indication that Clinton's e-mail server was 'wiped'," *The Washington Post*, September 12, 2015, at https://www.washingtonpost.com/politics/tech-company-no-indication-that-clintons-e-mail-server-was-wiped/2015/09/12/10c8ce52-58c6-11e5-abe9-27d53f250b11_story.html.

212 Ruth Marcus, "Can we finally delete Clinton's e-mail issue?" *The Washington Post*, September 11, 2015, at https://www.washingtonpost.com/opinions/can-we-finally-delete-clintons-e-mail-issue/2015/09/11/95f0da9a-58a1-11e5-abe9-27d53f250b11_story.html?utm_term=.42e65bf2e6d.

213 Stephanie Marcus, "Donald Trump Says Remarks About Carly Fiorina's Face Were Made as an 'Entertainer'," Huffington Post Entertainment, September, 11, 2015, at http://www.huffingtonpost.com/entry/donald-trump-entertainer-told-you-so_55f2c7ece4b042295e35d8d5.

214 "Full Replay and Transcript of Second Republican Debate," RealClearPolitics, September 17, 2015, at http://www.realclearpolitics.com/video/2015/09/17/full_replay_and_transcript_of_second_republican_debate.html.

215 Brian Stelter, "23 million watched GOP debate, a record for CNN," CNN Money, September 17, 2015, at http://money.cnn.com/2015/09/17/media/cnn-republican-debate-ratings/index.html.

216 Transcript: Second-tier CNN Republican debate – 2015, September 16, 2015, at http://www.cbsnews.com/news/transcript-second-tier-republican-debate-2015-reagan-library/.

217 Peggy Noonan, "The Undercard and the Mane Event," The Wall Street Journal, September 17, 2015, at http://www.wsj.com/article_email/the-undercard-and-the-mane-event-1442530625-lMyQjAxMTA1ODEyODExMzgxWj.

218 CNN/ORC Poll, September 20, 2015, at http://i2.cdn.turner.com/cnn/2015/

images/09/20/rel10a.pdf.
219 Andrew Rafferty, "Fiorina: Women 'Heard Very Clearly' What Trump Said," NBC News, September 17, 2015, at http://www.nbcnews.com/politics/2016-election/fiorina-women-heard-very-clearly-what-trump-said-n428786.
220 The Tonight Show with Jimmy Fallon, "Carly Fiorina Sings Songs About Her Dogs," NBC television, September 22, 2015, at https://www.youtube.com/watch?v=1TOFdWGToKQ.
221 Maggie Haberman, "Jeb Bush Doubles Down on Defending His Brother: 'He Kept Us Safe'," September 17, 2015, at http://www.nytimes.com/politics/first-draft/2015/09/17/jeb-bush-doubles-down-in-defending-his-brother-he-kept-us-safe/.
222 Eric Bradner, Dan Merica, and Brianna Keilar, "Hillary Clinton opposes Keystone XL pipeline," CNN Politics, September 22, 2015, at http://www.cnn.com/2015/09/22/politics/hillary-clinton-opposes-keystone-xl-pipeline/.
223 Rebecca Leber, "Hillary Clinton Keeps Ducking Questions About the Keystone Pipeline," The New Republic, July 28, 2016, at http://www.newrepublic.com/article/122391/hillary-clinton-keeps-ducking-questions-about-keystone-pipeline.
224 Carol D. Leonnig and Rosalind S. Helderman, "State Department's account of e-mail request differs from Clinton's," *The Washington Post*, September 23, 2015, at http://www.washingtonpost.com/politics/state-departments-account-of-e-mail-request-differs-from-clintons/2015/09/22/54cd66bc-5ed9-11e5-8e9e-dce8a2a2a679_story.html.
225 Jennifer Jacobs, "'I can't answer' apparent email discrepancy," *The Des Moines Register* and *USA Today*, September 23, 2015, at http://www.usatoday.com/story/news/politics/elections/2015/09/22/clinton-cant-answer-apparent-email-discrepancy/72655122/.
226 Eyder Peralta, "FBI Investigators Recover Clinton Emails Thought To Have Been Lost," NPR, September 23, 2015, at http://www.npr.org/sections/thetwo-way/2015/09/23/442797133/fbi-investigators-recover-clinton-emails-thought-to-have-been-deleted.
227 Federal spending is generally grouped by category. One category is "mandatory spending," which includes entitlement spending and net interest expense on the government's debt. Only the net interest expense can be regarded as mandatory in any constitutional sense. Entitlement spending is mandatory only in the sense that under the law, the spending continues as benefits are provided as stated in the law whether Congress acts or not. "Discretionary spending" in contrast covers most of the day-to-day activities of the Federal Government and is legislated annually in the appropriations process. Discretionary spending is then divided into two general categories: defense and non-defense spending. This is done in part because defense

spending today is about half of all discretionary spending, and because defense spending levels often provide the starting point for budget fights.

228 Josh Siegel, "How House Conservatives Are Approaching Boehner's Successor Race," September 29, 2015, The Heritage Foundation, at http://dailysignal.com/2015/09/29/how-house-conservatives-are-approaching-boehners-successor-race/?utm_source=heritagefoundation&utm_medium=email&utm_campaign=morningbell&mkt_tok=3RkMMJWWfF9wsRouu6rLZKXonjHpfsX56ukoWKG1lMI%2F0ER3fOvrPUfGjI4ATcdmNK%2BTFAwTG5toziV8R7jHKM1t0sEQWBHm.

229 Manu Raju, Deirdre Walsh, and Tal Kopan, "House Republicans repudiate McCarthy comments on Benghazi probe," CNN Politics, October 1, 2015, at http://www.cnn.com/2015/09/30/politics/kevin-mccarthy-benghazi-committee-speaker/.

230 Charles Krauthammer, "Double suicide: The presidential campaign of 2015," *The Washington Post*, September 24, 2015, at https://www.washingtonpost.com/opinions/double-suicide-the-presidential-campaign-of-2015/2015/09/24/b71f332c-62e4-11e5-8e9e-dce8a2a2a679_story.html.

231 Fox News Poll, May 15, 2015, at http://www.foxnews.com/politics/interactive/2015/05/14/fox-news-poll-voters-believe-wh-incompetent-us-still-in-recession-isis-has/.

232 Alan Cole, "Details and Analysis of Donald Trump's Tax Plan," The Tax Foundation, September 29, 2015, at http://taxfoundation.org/article/details-and-analysis-donald-trump-s-tax-plan.

233 Andrew Rafferty, "NBC News/WSJ/Marist Poll Iowa, October 2015," October 5, 2015, at http://www.scribd.com/doc/283708713/NBC-News-WSJ-Marist-Poll-Iowa-Annotated-Questionnaire-October-2015.

234 PredictWise, extracted October 6, 2015, from http://www.predictwise.com/politics/2016RepNomination.

235 PredictWise, extracted October 6, 2015, from http://www.predictwise.com/politics/2016DemNomination.

236 International Trade Commission, "Trans-Pacific Partnership Agreement: Likely Impact on the U.S. Economy and on Specific Industry Sectors," May, 2016, at https://www.usitc.gov/publications/332/pub4607.pdf.

237 Patrick Howley, "Hillary Clinton Flip-Flops, Will Oppose Obamatrade," Breitbart, October 7, 2015, at http://www.breitbart.com/big-government/2015/10/07/hillary-clinton-flip-flops-will-oppose-obamatrade/.

238 CNN News, October 8, 2015, retrieved October 9, 2015, at http://www.realclearpolitics.com/video/2015/10/08/axelrod_on_clinton_tpp_clintons_biggest_liability_is_the_sense_that_shes_inauthentic.html.

239 "The CNN Democratic debate transcript, annotated," *The Washington Post*, October 13, 2015, at https://www.washingtonpost.com/news/the-fix/wp/2015/10/13/

the-oct-13-democratic-debate-who-said-what-and-what-it-means/.
240 "Frank Luntz Focus Group Agrees: Bernie Sanders Won Debate," October 13, 2015, at http://www.realclearpolitics.com/video/2015/10/13/frank_luntz_focus_group_agrees_bernie_sanders_won_debate.html.
241 David Axelrod, "The man who wasn't there: How debate affects Joe Biden," CNN, October 14, 2015, at http://www.cnn.com/2015/10/14/opinions/axelrod-democratic-debate/index.html.
242 Maureen Dowd, "The Empire Strikes Back," *The New York Times* Sunday Review, October 24, 2015, at http://www.nytimes.com/2015/10/25/opinion/sunday/the-empire-strikes-back.html?_r=1.
243 Sara Dutton, Jennifer De Pinto, Anthony Salvanto, and Fred Backus, "CBS/NYT poll: Ben Carson edges out Donald Trump," October 27, 2015, at http://www.cbsnews.com/news/cbsnyt-poll-ben-carson-edges-out-donald-trump/.
244 Henry Olsen, "Why Ben Carson Can Win," National Review, October 24, 2015, at http://www.nationalreview.com/2016-gops-four-faces/426028/why-ben-carson-can-win.
245 Brian Steinberg, "CNBC's Debate Notches 14 Million Viewers," Variety, October 29, 2015, at http://variety.com/2015/tv/news/cnbc-republican-debate-14-million-viewers-1201629722/.
246 "The third Republican debate, annotated," *The Washington Post*, October 28, 2015, at https://www.washingtonpost.com/news/the-fix/wp/2015/10/28/the-third-republican-debate-annotating-the-transcript/.
247 Denis Slattery and Adam Edelman, "Chris Christie lashes out at CNBC," *The New York Post*, October 28, 2015, at http://www.nydailynews.com/news/politics/christie-lays-cnbc-debate-hosts-fantasy-football-article-1.2415653.
248 Ben Brody, "Fiorina Super-PAC Takes Out Full-Page New York Times Ad Defending Business Record," August 27, 2015, at http://www.bloomberg.com/politics/articles/2015-08-27/fiorina-super-pac-takes-out-full-page-new-york-times-ad-defending-business-record.
249 Indeed, as WikiLeaks later revealed in the emails hacked from Clinton campaign Chairman John Podesta's computer, John Harwood was indeed a card-carrying member in good standing of the Hillary Clinton fan club.
250 Peggy Noonan, "The Not Ready for Prime Time Bush," The Wall Street Journal, October 29, 2015, at http://www.wsj.com/article_email/the-not-ready-for-prime-time-bush-1446160562-lMyQjAxMTI1NDMyMDYzNjAwWj.
251 Caitlin Huey-Burns, "Jeb 2.0: Embattled Bush Tries to Reboot," RealClearPolitics, November 2, 2015, at http://www.realclearpolitics.com/articles/2015/11/02/jeb_20_embattled_bush_tries_to_reboot_128621.html.
252 Patrick O'Connor, "Ben Carson Vaults to Lead in Latest Journal/NBC Poll," *The Wall Street Journal*, November 3, 2015, at http://www.wsj.com/article_email/ben-carson-vaults-to-lead-in-latest-journal-nbc-poll-1446507001-

lMyQjAxMTE1ODA0MzAwNTM4Wj.

253 Elias Isquith, "The meaning of Matt Bevin: Why his victory undermines a major Democratic party theory," *Salon*, November 5, 2015, at http://www.salon.com/2015/11/05/the_meaning_of_matt_bevin_why_his_victory_undermines_a_major_democratic_party_theory/.

254 Michael Barbaro, "Donald Trump Questions Ben Carson's Honesty, Despite Own Record," *The New York Times*, November 8, 2015, at http://www.nytimes.com/2015/11/09/us/politics/donald-trump-questions-ben-carsons-honesty-despite-own-record.html?_r=0.

255 Jim Sciutto, Evan Perez, Kevin Liptak, and Z. Byron Wolf, "Why did Obama declare ISIS 'contained' the day before Paris attack," CNN Politics, November 16, 2015, at http://www.cnn.com/2015/11/14/politics/paris-terror-attacks-obama-isis-contained/.

256 Ruth Marcus, "Bernie Sanders highlights a critical division within the Democratic party," *The Washington Post*, November 18, 2015, at https://www.washingtonpost.com/opinions/the-significance-of-sanders/2015/11/17/540dfe7c-8d54-11e5-acff-673ae92ddd2b_story.html.

257 Dan Balz and Scott Clement, "Trump still leads among Republicans," *The Washington Post*, November 22, 2015, at https://www.washingtonpost.com/politics/trump-leads-carson-second-as-gop-voters-favor-change-over-experience/2015/11/21/a1f05f1c-8fcb-11e5-acff-673ae92ddd2b_story.html.

258 S. V. Date, "The Many, Um, Misstatements of Donald Trump," National Journal, December 1, 2015, at http://www.nationaljournal.com/s/120388/many-um-misstatements-donald-trump.

259 ABC/Washington Post, "Trump Hits a New High in the GOP Race; Against Clinton, it's Outsider vs. Insider," December 15, 2015, at http://www.langerresearch.com/wp-content/uploads/1174a2GOPElection.pdf.

260 Donald Trump's pronunciation of the word "huge" rendered in reasonable phonetics requires some adaptation, here shown as "hyuge."

261 Matea Gold, "Jeb Bush's superpac burning through money with little to show for it," *The Washington Post*, December 9, 2015, at https://www.washingtonpost.com/politics/jeb-bushs-super-pac-burning-through-money-with-little-to-show-for-it/2015/12/09/0baaa5fe-9df8-11e5-8728-1af6af208198_story.html.

262 Carpet bombing is a term from World War II and means to use aircraft to lay down a carpet of bombs to wipe out everything and everybody in a certain area, often whole cities. Trump likely meant he would launch enormous and highly targeted bombing raids on ISIS military targets, but that's not what he said, repeatedly.

263 The "tax extenders" referred to an ever-lengthening list of tax provisions Congress enacted on a temporary basis and which Congress then "extended"

temporarily. These provisions included such popular items as the R&D tax credit and a great many far less meritorious items.

264 CBS News, December 2015 Battleground Tracker, Iowa, Dec 14-17, at http://www.scribd.com/doc/293729658/CBS-News-December-2015-Battleground-Tracker-Iowa.

265 CBS News, December 2015 Battleground Tracker, New Hampshire, Dec 14-17, at http://www.scribd.com/doc/293729829/CBS-News-December-2015-Battleground-Tracker-New-Hampshire.

266 Sean Sullivan and Karen Tumulty, "Will Rubio work hard enough to become president? Some backers are worried," *The Washington Post*, December 21, 2015, at https://www.washingtonpost.com/politics/strategic-or-overconfident-rubio-plays-hard-to-get-with-voters/2015/12/20/60b8a3e8-a5a0-11e5-9c4e-be37f66848bb_story.html.

267 CBS News, December 2015 Battleground Tracker, Iowa, Dec 14-17, at http://www.scribd.com/doc/293729658/CBS-News-December-2015-Battleground-Tracker-Iowa.

268 CBS News, December 2015 Battleground Tracker, New Hampshire, Dec 14-17, at http://www.scribd.com/doc/293729829/CBS-News-December-2015-Battleground-Tracker-New-Hampshire.

269 Robert Farley, "Did Cruz Support Legalization?" FactCheck.org, December 16, 2015, at http://www.factcheck.org/2015/12/did-cruz-support-legalization/.

270 "Without Ted Cruz, Amnesty Would Have Passed," RealClearPolitics, December 20, 2015, at http://www.realclearpolitics.com/video/2015/12/20/jeff_sessions_without_ted_cruz_amnesty_would_have_passed_in_2013.html.

271 David Weigel, "Supporters trust Ted Cruz, even when the tape says not to," *The Washington Post*, December 22, 2015, at https://www.washingtonpost.com/politics/supporters-trust-ted-cruz-even-when-the-tape-says-not-to/2015/12/22/6610205a-a811-11e5-9b92-dea7cd4b1a4d_story.html.

272 Quinnipiac University, December 22, 2015, at http://www.quinnipiac.edu/images/polling/us/us12222015_Uhkm63g.pdf.

273 Editorial Board, "A U.N. resolution on Syria is shattered – and Russia is to blame," *The Washington Post*, December 21, 2015, at https://www.washingtonpost.com/opinions/a-un-resolution-on-syria-is-shattered/2015/12/21/069c0f66-a803-11e5-9b92-dea7cd4b.

274 Louis Charbonneau, "Iran's October missile test violated U.N. ban: Expert panel," Reuters, December 16, 2015, at http://www.reuters.com/article/us-iran-missiles-un-exclusive-idUSKBN0TY1T920151216.

275 Editorial Board, "Iran provokes the world as Obama does nothing," *The Washington Post*, December 20, 2015, at https://www.washingtonpost.com/opinions/stop-iran-now/2015/12/20/07ca2936-a4f7-11e5-9c4e-be37f66848bb_

story.html.
276 Kevin Liptak, "Obama says Trump exploiting 'blue-collar' fears," CNN Politics, December 22, 2015, at http://www.cnn.com/2015/12/21/politics/barack-obama-isis-interview/.
277 Ruth Marcus, "Trump is right: Bill Clinton's sordid sexual history is fair game," *The Washington Post*, December 29, 2015, at https://www.washingtonpost.com/opinions/trump-is-right-bill-clintons-sordid-sexual-history-is-fair-game/2015/12/28/70a26bdc-ad92-11e5-b711-1998289ffcea_story.html.
278 Tony Leys, "Clinton says Trump's vulgarity doesn't shock her," *Des Moines Register*, December 23, 2015, at http://www.desmoinesregister.com/story/news/elections/presidential/candidates/2015/12/22/clinton-says-trumps-vulgarity-doesnt-shock-her/77789692/.
279 Nate Cohn, "Donald Trump's Supporters: A Certain Kind of Democrat," *The New York Times*, December 31, 2015, at http://www.nytimes.com/2015/12/31/upshot/donald-trumps-strongest-supporters-a-certain-kind-of-democrat.html?ref=todayspaper.
280 George Will, "Before the voting begins, remember when government wasn't reviled," *The Washington Post*, January 1, 2016, at https://www.washingtonpost.com/opinions/before-the-voting-begins-remember-when-government-wasn't-reviled/2016/01/01/9d8528b6-af08-11e5-b820-eea4d64be2a1_story.html.
281 Anthony Faiola and Stephanie Kirchner, "Man in failed attack on Paris police lived in German shelter for asylum seekers," *The Washington Post*, January 11, 2016, at https://www.washingtonpost.com/world/suspect-who-tried-to-attack-paris-police-station-lived-with-asylum-seekers-in-germany/2016/01/10/63ee826c-7bb7-4c6f-9b4c-7538a9c95d55_story.html.
282 BBC News, "Cologne sex attacks: Women describe 'terrible' assaults," January 7, 2016, at http://www.bbc.com/news/world-europe-35250903.
283 Ben Brumfield and Shimon Prokupecz, "Wounded Philadelphia officer shoots attacker; suspect pledges allegiance to ISIS," January 9, 2016 at http://www.cnn.com/2016/01/09/us/philadelphia-police-officer-shot/.
284 Average of Fox News and IDP/TIPP polls at http://www.foxnews.com/politics/interactive/2016/01/08/fox-news-poll-national-presidential-race-obama-ratings/ and http://news.investors.com/ibd-editorials-polls/011116-789089-hillaryclinton-lead-nearly-vanishes-among-democrats.htm.
285 NBC/WSJ/Marist poll taken January 2 to January 7 at http://maristpoll.marist.edu/110-cruz-and-trump-vie-in-ia-trump-nh-favorite-clinton-and-sanders-competitive/.
286 Average of NBC, Fox News, and PPP polls.
287 All polls for Republicans parallel those for Democrats, except in New Hampshire where a fourth poll by NH1 is included at http://www.nh1.com/

files/2016_fitn_reach_poll_1.7.16_gopund.pdf.
288 David A. Fahrenthold, "In Iowa, Clinton aims to avoid another flurry of campaign gaffes," *The Washington Post*, June 7, 2015, at https://www.washingtonpost.com/politics/in-2008-clinton-couldnt-buy-iowans-love-so-she-bought-them-snow-shovels/2015/06/06/742be0e0-07a6-11e5-95fd-d580f1c5d44e_story.html.
289 Ibid.
290 Rebecca Berg, "Scott Walker's Iowa," Politico, July 27, 2015, at http://www.realclearpolitics.com/articles/2015/07/27/scott_walkers_iowa_127549.html.
291 National Association of Manufacturers, "Manufacturing's Share of Gross State Product, 2014," at http://www.nam.org/Data-and-Reports/State-Manufacturing-Data/2014-State-Manufacturing-Data/Manufacturing-s-Share-of-Gross-State-Product---2014/.
292 Alexander Bolton, "Trump puts Cruz off balance by fanning 'birther' controversy," *The Hill*, January 12, 2015, at http://thehill.com/blogs/ballot-box/presidential-races/265496-trump-puts-cruz-off-balance-by-fanning-birther.
293 RealClearPolitics, "Ann Coulter: I was joking when I tweeted Trump should deport Haley," January 13, 2016, at http://www.realclearpolitics.com/video/2016/01/13/ann_coulter_i_was_joking_when_i_tweeted_trump_should_deport_nikki_haley.html.
294 George W. Bush acknowledged his Texas accent sometimes played havoc with the English language. He once observed, "My mouth is where words go to die." Early in his administration he tried to say the word "strategy" and it came out "strategery." Bush laughed at it afterward and the term was in frequent use internally by administration officials through the duration of his second term.
295 M.J. Lee, "Iowa Governor wants Ted Cruz defeated," CNN politics, January 19, 2016, at http://www.cnn.com/2016/01/19/politics/terry-branstad-ted-cruz-defeat/index.html.
296 John Santucci, "Donald Trump Ramps Up Attacks on Ted Cruz: Says 'He's a "Nasty Guy'," ABC News, January 17, 2016, at http://abcnews.go.com/Politics/donald-trump-ramps-attacks-ted-cruz-hes-nasty/story?id=36335768.
297 Emily Heil, "Ted Cruz's college roommate fantasy-casted the movie about their dorm years," *The Washington Post*, January 22, 2016, at https://www.washingtonpost.com/news/reliable-source/wp/2016/01/21/ted-cruzs-college-roommate-fantasy-casted-the-movie-about-their-dorm-years/.
298 Arnold Steinberg, "With Friends Like Bob Dole, Jeb Doesn't Need Any ...," *The Daily Caller*, January 22, 2016, at http://dailycaller.com/2016/01/22/with-friends-like-bob-dole-jeb-doesnt-need-any/.
299 Maggie Haberman, "Bob Dole Warns of 'Cataclysmic' Losses With Ted Cruz, and Says Donald Trump Would Do Better," *The New York Times*, January 20,

2016, at http://www.nytimes.com/politics/first-draft/2016/01/20/bob-dole-warns-of-cataclysmic-losses-with-ted-cruz-and-says-donald-trump-would-do-better/.

300 Democratic Convention Watch, April 2, 2015, at http://www.democraticconventionwatch.com/diary/3806/.

301 Mark Mazzetti, "Hillary Clinton Email Said to Include Material Exceeding 'Top Secret'," *The New York Times*, January 19, 2016, at http://www.nytimes.com/2016/01/20/us/politics/hillary-clinton-email-said-to-include-material-exceeding-top-secret.html?_r=0.

302 Laura Koran and Ariane de Vogue, "Clinton emails may be delayed due to snow, State Department tells Federal judge," CNN Politics, January 22, 2016, at http://www.cnn.com/2016/01/22/politics/hillary-clinton-emails-state-department-blizzard/index.html.

303 Jamelle Bouie, "Why Michael Bloomberg could make Donald Trump president," Slate, January 26, 2016, at http://www.slatecom/articles/news_and_politics/2016/01/michael_bloomberg_could_make_donald_trump_president.html.

304 Callum Borchers, "Fox News head lets Trump walk, keeps Megyn Kelly as moderator," *The Washington Post*, January 27, 2016, at https://www.washingtonpost/news/the-fix/wp/2016/01/26/fox-news-head-ill-let-donald-trump-walk-before-replacing-megyn-kelly-as-debate-moderator?.

305 Jonathan Easley, "Trump lands Falwell endorsement," *The Hill*, January 26, 2016, at http://thehilld/blogs/ballot-box/presidential-races/267032-trump-lands-falwell-endorsement.

306 Ken Walsh, "Daughter of 'the Duke' Backs 'the Donald'," US News and World Report, January 19, 2016, at http://www.usnews.com/news/blogs/ken-walshs-washington/2016/01/19/donald-trump-nabs-endorsement-of-john-waynes-daughter.

307 Marisa Guthrie, "TV Ratings: Fox News Rises Without Donald Trump, Hits 12.5 Million," *The Hollywood Reporter*, January 29, 2016, at http://www.hollywoodreporter.com/news/tv-ratings-fox-news-debate-860284.

308 Brian Stelter, "Who Won the Ratings Race? Fox News or Donald Trump?" CNN Money, January 29, 2016, at http://money.cnn.com/2016/01/29/media/republican-debate-ratings-donald-trump/.

309 Paola Chavez, "Best Lines of the Seventh Republican Debate," ABC News, January 29, 2016, at http://abcnews.go.com/Politics/best-lines-seventh-republican-debate/story?id=36574992.

310 Catherine Herridge and Pamela K. Browne, "Official: Withheld Clinton emails contain 'operational' intel, put lives at risk," Fox News, February 1, 2016, at http://www.foxnews.com/politics/2016/02/01/official-withheld-clinton-emails-contain-operational-intel-put-lives-at-risk.html.

311 Jeremy Diamond, "Sanders: Clinton emails 'very serious issue'," CNN, January 31, 2016, at http://www.cnn.com/2016/01/31/politics/bernie-sanders-hillary-clinton-emails-iowa/index.html.

312 Jennifer Jacobs, "A closer look at the Democrats' Iowa poll results," *The Des Moines Register*, January 30, 2016, at http://www.desmoinesregister.com/story/news/elections/presidential/caucus/2016/01/30/closer-look-democrats-iowa-poll-results/79571562/.

313 Ibid.

314 Karen Friar, "Coin toss broke 6 Clinton-Sanders deadlocks in Iowa – and Hillary won each time," Marketwatch, February 2, 2016, at http://www.marketwatch.com/story/coin-toss-broke-6-clinton-sanders-deadlocks-in-iowa-and-hillary-won-each-time-2016-02-02.

315 Philip Rucker, "In N.H., the undecideds easily can become the deciders," *The Washington Post*, February 6, 2016, at https://www.washingtonpost.com/politics/political-spotlight-swings-to-famously-slow-to-decide-independents-of-nh/2016/02/04/089a2f4a-ca96-11e5-ae11-57b6aeab993f_story.html.

316 The three polls were by Umass Lowell/7News, CNN/WMUR, and Boston Herald/FPU.

317 Jessica Taylor, "Trumpertantrum: Trump Says Cruz Cheated in Iowa, Wants Results Overturned," NPR, February 3, 2016, at http://www.npr.org/2016/02/03/465459903/trumpertantrum-trump-says-cruz-cheated-in-iowa-wants-results-overturned.

318 Robert Eno, "Are Carson's Iowa Troubles His Own Fault?" Conservative Review, February 4, 2016, at https://www.conservativereview.com/commentary/2016/02/carsons-iowa-troubles-are-his-own-fault.

319 Jason Noble, "Bush's final rally interrupted by 'seat fillers' demanding to be paid," *The Des Moines Register*, February 1, 2016, at http://www.desmoinesregister.com/story/news/politics/onpolitics/2016/02/01/bushs-final-rally-interrupted-seat-fillers-demanding-paid/79651646/.

320 Michael Isikoff, "Meet the lobbyists, donors, and bundlers behind Hillary's $157 million juggernaut," Yahoo politics, February 4, 2016, at https://www.yahoo.com/politics/hillarys-financial-armada-233033648.html.

321 Henry C. Jackson, "Whoa, whoa, whoa…wow," Politico, February 5, 2016, at http://www.politico.com/tipsheets/the-2016-blast/2016/02/whoa-whoa-whoawow-212542.

322 Daniel Halper, "Moderator Hugs Candidates After the Debate," The Weekly Standard, February 4, 2016, at http://www.weeklystandard.com/article/2000942/.

323 Theodore Schleifer, "Tony Perkins backs Ted Cruz," CNN, January 26, 2016, at http://www.cnn.com/2016/01/26/politics/ted-cruz-tony-perkins-iowa/

index.html.

324 Michelle Fields, "Sen. Mike Lee to Donald Trump: 'Ted Cruz Is My Friend'," Breitbart, February 6, 2016, at http://www.breitbart.com/big-government/2016/02/06/mike-lee-ted-cruz-is-my-friend/.

325 Fox News, "SC Senator endorses Marco 'On the Record': 'Rubio is the real deal'," February 2, 2016, at http://nation.foxnews.com/2016/02/02/sc-senator-tim-scott-endorses-marco-record-rubio-real-deal.

326 Cooper Allen and Paul Singer, "Top Takeaways from the New Hampshire Republican Debate," *USA Today*, February 7, 2016, at http://www.usatoday.com/story/news/politics/onpolitics/2016/02/07/top-takeaways-new-hampshire-republican-debate/79952722/.

327 Annie Karni, "Clinton Allies Grapple with Crushing Loss," Politico, February 10, 2016, at http://www.politico.com/story/2016/02/hillary-clinton-new-hampshire-african-americans-219039.

328 Chuck Ross, "Lots of Women Will Be Going to Hell Now, According to Clinton Supporter Madeleine Albright," Politico, February 9, 2016, at http://dailycaller.com/2016/02/09/lots-of-women-will-be-going-to-hell-now-according-to-clinton-supporter-madeleine-albright/.

329 Peter Roff, "One Odd Primary Season," US News and World Report, February 10, 2016, at http://www.usnews.com/opinion/blogs/peter-roff/articles/2016-02-10/clintons-loss-and-trumps-win-presage-an-odd-2016-race?int=a39d09&int=a6ea09.

330 MSNBC, "Andrea Mitchell: Bill Clinton 'Freaking Out.' Face Says, 'Oh My Gosh, This Is Happening Again. She's Going to Lose'," February 9, 2016, at http://www.realclearpolitics.com/video/2016/02/09/andrea_mitchell_bill_clinton_freaking_out_face_says_hillary_clinton_going_to_lose.html.

331 Fox News report, February 10, 2016, at http://www.foxnews.com/politics/elections/2016/primary-caucus-results/new-hampshire.

332 David Corn, "Here's How You Know Marco Rubio's Robot Gaffe Is Serious," Mother Jones, February 7, 2016, at http://www.motherjones.com/politics/2016/02/can-marco-rubio-reboot-after-robot-gaffe.

333 Tom LoBianco, "Sanders campaign raised $6.2 million after New Hampshire polls closed," CNN, February 10, 2016, at http://www.cnn.com/2016/02/10/politics/bernie-sanders-raises-5-2-million/.

334 Jennifer Shutt, "Axelrod Subtweets Bill and Hillary Clinton after shake-up report," Politico, February 8, 2016, at http://www.politico.com/story/2016/02/david-axelrod-clinton-shakeup-218964#ixzz3zcFCUddl.

335 David A. Fahrenthold, "Clinton's wonky policies of fine-grained complexity contrast with rivals' grandiose ideas," *The Washington Post*, May 8, 2016, at https://www.washingtonpost.com/politics/clintons-wonky-policies-of-fine-grained-complexity-contrast-with-rivals-grandiose-ideas

/2016/05/08/7a6f4b66-10a3-11e6-93ae-50921721165d_story.html.
336 Glenn Thrush and Annie Karni, "Clinton weights staff shake-up after New Hampshire," Politico, February 9, 2016, at http://www.politico.com/story/2016/02/hillary-clinton-staff-shakeup-218955.
337 Darren Samuelsohn, "Warning: The dirty tricks are about to start," Politico, February 11, 2016, at http://www.politico.com/story/2016/02/south-carolina-dirty-tricks-republicans-219116.
338 Tina Nguyen, "This Week in Shameless Ted Cruz Trickery," Vanity Fair, February 19, 2016, at http://www.vanityfair.com/news/2016/02/ted-cruz-south-carolina-dirty-tricks.
339 Vaughn Hillyard, "Ted Cruz, Ben Carson Meet Among Strained Relationship," NBC News, February 19, 2016, at http://www.nbcnews.com/politics/2016-election/ted-cruz-ben-carson-meet-amid-strained-relationship-n522056.
340 Eliza Collins and Nolan D. McCaskill, "Cruz fires top staffer for promoting false story about Rubio," Politico, February 22, 2016, at http://www.politico.com/story/2016/02/breaking-news-cruz-asks-for-national-spokesman-rick-tylers-resignation-219632.
341 Pre-New Hampshire is the average of the CBS and NBC pools. CNN/ORC poll taken February 10 through 15 was typical for the post-New Hampshire polls.
342 Tom Hamburger and Rosalind S. Helderman, "Clinton Foundation received subpoena from State Department investigators," *The Washington Post*, February 12, 2016, at https://www.washingtonpost.com/politics/clinton-foundation-received-subpoena-from-state-department-investigators/2016/02/11/ca5125b2-cce4-11e5-88ff-e2d1b4289c2f_story.html.
343 Chris Cillizza, "Hillary Clinton's week just went from bad to worse," *The Washington Post*, February 11, 2016, at https://www.washingtonpost.com/news/the-fix/wp/2016/02/11/hillary-clintons-week-just-went-from-bad-to-worse/.
344 Josh Gerstein, "Judge orders four more Hillary Clinton email releases," Politico, February 11, 2016, at http://www.politico.com/blogs/under-the-radar/2016/02/judge-orders-four-more-clinton-email-releases-219134.
345 Stephen Collinson, "Democratic debate: Clinton embraces Obama," CNN Politics, February 12, 2016, at http://www.cnn.com/2016/02/11/politics/democratic-debate-highlights/.
346 Ibid.
347 Pam Key, "Trump Battles Jeb: George W. Bush 'Lied' – He Knew There Were No WMD," Breitbart, February 13, 2016, at http://www.breitbart.com/video/2016/02/13/trump-battles-jeb-george-w-bush-lied-he-knew-there-were-no-wmd/.
348 Aaron Blake, "Schumer, McConnell or Leahy: Who flip-flopped the most

on election-year Supreme Court nominees?" *The Washington Post*, February 15, 2016, at http://www.washingtonpost.com/news/the-fix/wp/2016/02/16/schumer-mcconnell-leahy-who-flip-flopped-the-most-on-election-year-supreme-court-nominees/.

349 Charlie Spiering, "Pollster Pat Caddell: Hillary Clinton Email Scandal 'Worse Than Watergate'," Breitbart, February 13, 2016, at http://www.breitbart.com/big-government/2016/02/13/pollster-pat-caddell-hillary-clinton-e-mail-scandal-worse-than-watergate/.

350 Associated Press, "AP: Many foundation donors to Clinton Foundation met with Hillary Clinton at State Dept.," August 23, 2016, at http://www.cbsnews.com/news/ap-many-donors-to-clinton-foundation-met-with-her-at-state/.

351 Greg Sargent, "Loser Pope takes on Donald Trump, suffers massive humiliation, slinks off to Vatican," *The Washington Post*, February 18, 2016, at https://www.washingtonpost.com/blogs/plum-line/wp/2016/02/18/loser-pope-takes-on-donald-trump-suffers-massive-humiliation-slinks-off-to-vatican/.

352 Ibid.

353 Fox News, "Trump: Pope 'did not understand' illegal immigration crime problem," February 19, 2016, at http://www.foxnews.com/politics/2016/02/19/trump-pope-did-not-understand-illegal-immigration-crime-problem.html.

354 Amanda House, "JEB BUSH: 'CONSERVATISM TERMPORARILY DEAD'; POPE BORDER MASS FUELED TRUMP," Breitbart, July 12, 2016, at http://www.breitbart.com/2016-presidential-race/2016/07/11/jeb-bush-blames-pope-others-for-campaigns-failures-says-conservatism-is-temporarily-dead/.

355 Paul Demko, "Who's advising Trump on health care?" Politico, February 20, 2016, at http://www.politico.com/story/2016/02/donald-trump-health-care-plan-219533.

356 Caitlin Huey-Burns, "Cruz-Trump feud heats up ahead of S.C. vote," RealClearPolitics, February 18, 2016, at http://www.realclearpolitics.com/articles/2016/02/18/cruz-trump_feud_heats_up_ahead_of_sc_vote.html.

357 David Brody, "Brody File Exclusive: Trump on Ted Cruz: 'You don't hold up the Bible and lie'," CBS News, February 18, 2016, at http://blogs.cbn.com/thebrodyfile/archive/2016/02/18/brody-file-exclusive-donald-trump-on-ted-cruz-you-dont.aspx?mobile=false.

358 Caitlin Huey-Burns, "Cruz-Trump feud heats up ahead of S.C. vote," RealClearPolitics, February 18, 2016, at http://www.realclearpolitics.com/articles/2016/02/18/cruz-trump_feud_heats_up_ahead_of_sc_vote.html.

359 Daniel Halper, "Jeb: I Should Stop Campaigning, Maybe?" The Weekly Standard, February 17, 2016, at http://www.weeklystandard.com/jeb-i-should-stop-campaigning-maybe/article/2001128/.

360 RCP average of six polls.

361 Amie Parnes, "Dem candidates ready for Nevada caucus fight," *The Hill*, February 11, 2016, at http://thehill.com/homenews/campaign/269043-dem-candidates-ready-for-nevada-caucus-fight.
362 TD Goddard, Nevada Poll, Gravis Marketing, at http://www.scribd.com/doc/294241032/Nevada-Poll-December-28-2015-3.
363 Jon Ralston, "Poll: Sanders and Clinton in Nevada dead heat," Ralston Reports, February 12, 2016, at https://www.ralstonreports.com/blog/poll-sanders-and-clinton-nevada-dead-heat.
364 RCP average of Gravis, CNN/ORC, and TargetPoint polls taken in the second week of February.
365 Maeve Reston, "Trump scores big win in Nevada," CNN Politics, February 24, 2016, at http://www.cnn.com/2016/02/23/politics/nevada-republican-caucus-results/.
366 Elizabeth Williamson, "Cruz and Rubio Leave Trump Sputtering," *The New York Times*, February 26, 2016, at http://takingnote.blogs.nytimes.com/2016/02/26/rubio-and-cruz-leave-trump-sputtering/.
367 Tom LoBianco, "Ex-Mexican President Fox: 'I'm not going to pay for that f***ing wall'," CNN, February 25, 2016, at http://www.cnn.com/2016/02/25/politics/vicente-fox-donald-trump-wall/.
368 Ryan Teague Beckwith, "Read the Full Transcript of the Tenth Republican Debate in Texas," Time, February 26, 2016, at http://time.com/4238363/republican-debate-tenth-houston-cnn-telemundo-transcript-full-text/.
369 Ibid.
370 Alan Cole, "Details and Analysis of Donald Trump's Tax Reform Plan," Tax Foundation, September 29, 2015, at http://taxfoundation.org/article/details-and-analysis-donald-trump-s-tax-plan.
371 Pat Garofalo, "Donald Trump's Real Tax Return Problem," US News and World Report, February 26, 2016, at http://www.usnews.com/opinion/blogs/pat-garofalo/articles/2016-02-26/donald-trumps-real-tax-return-problem-at-the-gop-2016-debate.
372 Gromer Jeffers Jr. and Tristan Hallman, "Trump, Rubio hit Dallas area swinging insults," *The Dallas Morning News*, February 27, 2016, at http://www.dallasnews.com/news/politics/headlines/20160226-trump-rubio-hit-dallas-area-slinging-insults.ece.
373 Peg Brickley, "Trump Taj Mahal Settles Over Anti-Money-Laundering Charge," *The Wall Street Journal*, February 11, 2015, at http://www.wsj.com/articles/trump-taj-mahal-settles-over-anti-money-laundering-violations-1423669834.
374 Reid J. Epstein and Heather Haddon, "Christie endorses Donald Trump's bid for president," *The Wall Street Journal*, February 26, 2016, at http://www.wsj.com/articles/chris-christie-endorses-donald-trumps-bid-for-pres

ident-1456510124.

375 Spencer S. Hsu, "U.S. judge orders discovery to go forward over Clinton's private email system," *The Washington Post*, February 23, 2016, at https://www.washingtonpost.com/local/public-safety/us-judge-weighs-deeper-probe-into-clintons-private-email-system/2016/02/23/9c27412a-d997-11e5-81ae-7491b9b9e7df_story.html.

376 CBS News, "Hillary Clinton: 'I've always tried' to tell the truth," February 18, 2016, at http://www.cbsnews.com/news/campaign-2016-hillary-clinton-ive-always-tried-to-tell-the-truth/.

377 CBS News, "South Carolina Democratic Primary," February 28, 2016, at http://www.cbsnews.com/elections/2016/primaries/democrat/south-carolina/?linkId=21718299.

378 Chris Casteel, "Coburn endorses Rubio, slams Trump," NewsOK, February 29, 2016, at http://newsok.com/tom-coburn-endorses-rubio-slams-trump/article/5481917.

379 Bryan Snyder, "Congresswoman quits Democratic National Committee, endorses Bernie Sanders," Reuters, February 28, 2016, at http://www.reuters.com/article/us-usa-election-sanders-gabbard-idUSMTZSAPEC2S9JDNKG.

380 David M. Jackson, "Trump blames bad television ear piece for KKK comments," CNN, February 29, 2016, at http://www.usatoday.com/story/news/politics/onpolitics/2016/02/29/donald-trump-marco-rubio-david-duke-ku-klux-klan/81101906/.

381 Nia-Malika Henderson and David Mark, "Ben Carson doesn't 'see a political path forward'," CNN Politics, March 2, 2016, at http://www.cnn.com/2016/03/02/politics/ben-carson-doesnt-see-a-political-path-forward-wont-go-to-debate/.

382 Claire Groden, "Bernie Sanders More Than Doubles His January Fundraising Total," Forbes, March 1, 2016, at http://fortune.com/2016/03/01/bernie-sanders-february-fundraising/.

383 Gregory Krieg, "Donald Trump defends size of his penis," CNN Politics, March 4, 2016, at http://www.cnn.com/2016/03/03/politics/donald-trump-small-hands-marco-rubio/.

384 Peter Roff, "Nothing Presidential About It," US News and World Report, March 7, 2016, at http://www.usnews.com/opinion/blogs/peter-roff/articles/2016-03-07/nothing-presidential-about-donald-trumps-debate-antics?int=a39d09&int=a6ea09.

385 Michael C. Bender, "Republican Elites Harden Resolve Against Trump as Voters Flock to Him," Bloomberg Politics, March 2, 2016, at http://www.bloomberg.com/politics/articles/2016-03-02/republican-elites-harden-to-trump-as-voters-flock-to-him.

386 Ibid.

387 Adam Goldman, "Justice Dept. grants immunity to staffer who set up

Clinton email server," *The Washington Post*, March 3, 2016, at https://www.washingtonpost.com/world/national-security/in-clinton-email-investigation-justice-department-grants-immunity-to-former-state-department-staffer/2016/03/02/e421e39e-e0a0-11e5-9c36-e1902f6b6571_story.html.

388 Cassandra Vinograd, "Mitt Romney Lays Out Scathing Critique of Donald Trump," NBC News, March 3, 2016, at http://www.nbcnews.com/politics/2016-election/mitt-romney-eviscerate-donald-trump-phony-fraud-n530877.

389 Magnus Nysveen, "U.S. NOW HOLDS MORE OIL RESERVES THAN SAUDI ARABIA" Rystad Energy, July 4, 2016, at http://www.rystadenergy.com/NewsEvents/PressReleases/united-states-now-holds-more-oil-reserves-than-saudi-arabia.

390 Editorial Board, "Mr. Sanders's fractured reasoning on fracking," *The Washington Post*, March 9, 2016, at https://www.washingtonpost.com/opinions/mr-sanderss-fractured-reasoning-on-fracking/2016/03/08/938579aa-e4ab-11e5-bc08-3e03a5b41910_story.html, and Editorial Board, "More heat than light in the US fracking debate," The Financial Times, March 9, 2016, at http://www.ft.com/cms/s/0/440a959e-e529-11e5-bc31-138df2ae9ee6.html.

391 Michael R. Bloomberg, "The Risk I Will Not Take," Bloomberg View, March 7, 2016, at http://www.bloombergview.com/articles/2016-03-07/the-2016-election-risk-that-michael-bloomberg-won-t-take.

392 "Tweener Tuesday" refers to the Tuesday between Super Tuesday (March 1) and Lesser Tuesday (March 15).

393 David Sirota and Andrew Perez, "Hillary Clinton Said Outsourcing 'Benefited' America After She Criticized Bush Officials for Saying the Same Thing," *International Business Times*, March 6, 2016, at http://www.ibtimes.com/political-capital/hillary-clinton-said-outsourcing-benefited-america-after-she-criticized-bush.

394 Matt Arco, "Christie's 5-minute fiery battle with Rubio on Republican stage debate," NJ.com, February 6, 2016, at http://www.nj.com/politics/index.ssf/2016/02/christie_assails_rubio_on_the_debate_stage.html.

395 Theodore Schleifer, "Donald Trump: 'I think Islam hates us'," CNN politics, March 10, 2016, at http://www.cnn.com/2016/03/09/politics/donald-trump-islam-hates-us/.

396 Tim Hains, "Ted Cruz: Donald Trump Is Right About Trade, But 'China Bad' Is Not an Answer," RealClearPolitics, March 10, 2016, at http://www.realclearpolitics.com/video/2016/03/10/ted_cruz_donald_trump_is_right_about_trade_but_china_bad_is_not_a_solution.html.

397 Devlin Barrett, "Man Arrested for Punching Protester at Trump Rally in North Carolina," *The Wall Street Journal*, March 10, 2016, at http://blogs.wsj.com/washwire/2016/03/10/punch-of-trump-protester-in-north-carolina-

398 Todd Beamon, "Trump to St. Louis Protesters: Go Home to Mommy," Newsmax, March 13, 2016, at http://www.newsmax.com/Headline/donald-trump-taunts-protesters-stlouis/2016/03/11/id/718757/.

399 CNN Wire, "Man at Trump rally: 'We might have to kill' black lives matter protester," March 11, 2016, at http://wtvr.com/2016/03/11/man-at-trump-rally-we-might-have-to-kill-black-lives-matter-protester/#.

400 Eric Morath and Kristina Peterson, "Trump: Unrest at Rallies Due to Planted Protesters, Voters' Anger," *The Wall Street Journal*, March 13, 2016, at http://blogs.wsj.com/washwire/2016/03/13/trumpunrest0313/.

401 Lee Stranahan, "BLACK LIVES MATTER ACTIVISTS TAKE ONLINE VICTORY LAP OVER TRUMP RALLY SHUTDOWN," Breitbart News, March 11, 2016, at http://www.breitbart.com/big-government/2016/03/11/black-lives-matter-activists-take-online-victory-lap-over-trump-rally-shutdown/.

402 Jeremy Diamond, "More than two dozen 'Black Lives Matter' protesters disrupt Trump rally," CNN Politics, March 4, 2016, at http://www.cnn.com/2016/03/04/politics/donald-trump-protesters-black-lives-matter/index.html.

403 Fox News, "KASICH ON COMPANIES OUTSOURCING: 'THERE HAS TO BE A VALUE SYSTEM' BESIDES 'JUST PROFITS'," March 13, 2016, at https://grabien.com/story.php?id=50896.

404 Stuart Rothenberg, "John Kasich's Utterly Strange, Bizarre Campaign," RollCall, March 22, 2016, at http://cdn1.cq.com/rollcallpdf/20160322-rollcall-qvUTj5bDzwXGM61kcii6-9RkA_Q.pdf.

405 Dylan Byers and David Goldman, "Fox News cancels GOP debate after Donald Trump pulls out," CNN, March 16, 2016, at http://money.cnn.com/2016/03/16/media/donald-trump-republican-debate-fox/.

406 Eugene Scott, "Donald Trump on brokered convention: I think you'd have riots," CNN Politics, March 16, 2016, at http://www.cnn.com/2016/03/16/politics/donald-trump-ted-cruz-brokered-convention/.

407 Jake Sherman, "Ryan: 'I am not going to be the nominee'," Politico, March 17, 2016, at http://www.politico.com/story/2016/03/paul-ryan-not-president-gop-nominee-220869.

408 Stephen F. Hayes, "Believing the Unbelievable," The Weekly Standard, March 28, 2016, at http://www.weeklystandard.com/believing-the-unbelievable/article/2001620.

409 Nick Gass, "Donald Trump names foreign policy team members," Politico, March 21, 2016, at http://www.politico.com/blogs/2016-gop-primary-live-updates-and-results/2016/03/trump-foreign-policy-team-221049.

410 "MEMO: TED CRUZ IS THE ONLY CANDIDATE WHO CAN DEFEAT

DONALD TRUMP," Cruz campaign web site, February 22, 2016, at https://www.tedcruz.org/news/memo-ted-cruz-is-the-only-candidate-who-can-defeat-trump/.

411 Steve Peoples, "Cruz Embraces Bush's Endorsement, Says He Can Defeat Clinton," Associated Press, March 23, 2016, at http://hosted.ap.org/dynamic/stories/U/US_CAMPAIGN_2016?SITE=AP&SECTION=HOME&TEMPLATE=DEFAULT&CTIME=2016-03-23-08-21-25.

412 Juliet Eilperin and Karen DeYoung, "Obama addresses the Cuban nation: 'It is time now for us to leave the past behind'," *The Washington Post*, March 21, 2016, at https://www.washingtonpost.com/world/obama-to-address-the-cuban-nation-in-historic-havana-visit/2016/03/22/d454c642-ef9c-11e5-a2a3-d4e9697917d1_story.html.

413 Alan Gomez, "Fidel Castro to Obama: 'We don't need the empire to give us anything'," *USA Today*, March 28, 2016, at http://www.usatoday.com/story/news/2016/03/28/fidel-castro-president-obama-cuba-trip/82347680/.

414 "Wir Sind Im Krieg", Zeit Online, March 22, 2016, at http://www.zeit.de/politik/ausland/2016-03/reaktionen-bruessel-anschlaege.

415 Andrew Peek, "How terrorist attacks will finish the European Union," Daily News, March 22, 2016, at http://www.nydailynews.com/opinion/andrew-peek-terrorist-attacks-finish-e-u-article-1.2573379.

416 The Canadian Press, "Canada not at war with ISIS, Trudeau says following Brussels attacks," March 22, 2016, at http://www.ctvnews.ca/canada/canada-not-at-war-with-isis-trudeau-says-following-brussels-attacks-1.2829596.

417 The White House, "Remarks by President Obama to the People of Cuba," March 22, 2016, at https://www.whitehouse.gov/the-press-office/2016/03/22/remarks-president-obama-people-cuba.

418 Anthony Zurcher, "Brussels attacks: Cruz says police must 'secure' US muslim neighbourhoods," BBC World News, March 22, 2016, at http://www.bbc.com/news/election-us-2016-35867967.

419 Jonathan Easley, "Trump calls for Muslim patrols, torture in wake of Brussels attacks," *The Hill*, March 22, 2016, at http://thehill.com/blogs/ballot-box/273970-trump-calls-for-muslim-patrols-torture-in-wake-of-brussels-attacks.

420 Kristina Wong, "Vocal Trump critics in GOP open to supporting Clinton," *The Hill*, March 24, 2016, at http://thehill.com/policy/defense/274145-vocal-trump-critics-in-gop-open-to-supporting-clinton.

421 Greg Sargent, "GOP elites think Trump would be a disaster for the party. GOP voters disagree." *The Washington Post*, March 24, 2016, at https://www.washingtonpost.com/blogs/plum-line/wp/2016/03/24/gop-elites-think-trump-will-be-a-disaster-for-the-party-gop-voters-disagree/.

422 Theodore Schleifer and Julia Manchester, "Donald Trump makes wild threat

to 'spill the beans' on Ted Cruz's wife," CNN Politics, March 24, 2016, at http://www.cnn.com/2016/03/22/politics/ted-cruz-melania-trump-twitter-donald-trump-heidi/.

423 Theodore Schleifer, "Cruz on Trump's attacks on his wife: Leave Heidi the Hell alone," CNN Politics, March 24, 2016, at http://www.cnn.com/2016/03/24/politics/ted-cruz-donald-trump-heidi-cruz-hell-alone/index.html.

424 J.R. Taylor, "Shocking Claims: Pervy Ted Cruz Caught Cheating – With 5 Secret Mistresses," The National Enquirer, March 23, 2016, at http://www.nationalenquirer.com/celebrity/ted-cruz-sex-scandal-mistresses-cheating-claims/.

425 Manuel Roig-Franzia, "Opposing lawyer recalls startling offer by Trump," *The Washington Post*, March 26, 2016, at https://www.washingtonpost.com/politics/in-heat-of-legal-fight-lawyer-says-he-got-a-shocking-phone-call-from-donald-trump/2016/03/25/b8c8d900-e7c1-11e5-b0fd-073d5930a7b7_story.html.

426 Just to confuse matters further, Washington State Democrats also held a primary on May 24. Clinton won, but all the delegates had been awarded at the Caucuses. The purpose of the primary remains something of a mystery. See Stephen Ohlemacher, "Trump, Clinton Win Washington State's Presidential Primaries," ABC News, May 24, 2016, at http://abcnews.go.com/Politics/wireStory/trump-wins-gop-presidential-primary-washington-state-39355036.

427 Maggie Haberman, "Donald Trump, Revoking a Vow, Says He Won't Support Another G.O.P. Nominee," *The New York Times*, March 29, 2016, at http://www.nytimes.com/politics/first-draft/2016/03/29/donald-trump-says-he-no-longer-vows-to-support-the-republican-nominee/?_r=0.

428 FoxNews, "Trump campaign manager charged with battery after alleged arm grab," March 29, 2016, at http://www.foxnews.com/politics/2016/03/29/report-trump-campaign-manager-charged-with-battery-over-reporter-incident.html.

429 Note: In the end, the police dropped the charges against Lewandowski after Trump and Lewandowski shared an apology letter with the police. See Dylan Byers, Tal Kopan, and Tom LoBianco, "State will not prosecute Donald Trump's campaign manager," CNN, April 14, 2016, at http://www.cnn.com/2016/04/13/politics/corey-lewandowski-donald-trump-charges-dropped/.

430 David M. Jackson and Donovan Slack, "Wisconsin Gov. Scott Walker Endorses Ted Cruz," *USA Today*, March 29, 2016, at http://www.usatoday.com/story/news/politics/onpolitics/2016/03/29/scott-walker-ted-cruz-donald-trump-wisconsin-primary-republican-race/82373402/.

431 Peter Nicholas, "Bernie Sanders Targets Hillary Clinton's Superdelegates," *The Wall Street Journal*, March 30, 2016, at http://blogs.wsj.com/washwire/2016/03/30/bernie-sanders-targets-hillary-clintons-superdelegates/.

432 Chris Cillizza, "There are dozens of FBI agents involved in the Hillary Clinton email investigation," *The Washington Post*, March 28, 2016, at https://www.washingtonpost.com/news/the-fix/wp/2016/03/28/there-are-147-fbi-agents-involved-in-the-hillary-clinton-email-investigation/.

433 Alyssa Canobbio, "Jim Vandehei: Clinton's Biggest Problem Is That the FBI 'Dug In'," *The Washington Free Beacon*, March 30, 2016, at http://freebeacon.com/politics/jim-vandehei-clinton-biggest-problem-fbi-dug-in/.

434 Del Quentin Wilber, "Clinton email probe enters new phase as FBI interviews loom," *The Los Angeles Times*, March 27, 2016, at http://www.latimes.com/nation/la-na-clinton-email-probe-20160327-story.html.

435 In the end Comey folded like a cheap suitcase, but as the case developed it hung over Clinton like a very dark, very menacing cloud.

436 Matthew Flegenheimer and Maggie Haberman, "Donald Trump, Abortion Foe, Eyes 'Punishment' for Abortion, Then Recants," *The New York Times*, March 30, 2016, at http://www.nytimes.com/2016/03/31/us/politics/donald-trump-abortion.html.

437 Ibid.

438 Jake Miller, "Donald Trump: Don't Change Abortion Laws," CBS News, April 3, 2016, at cbsnews.com/news/donald-trump-dont-change-abortion-laws.

439 Bradford Richardson, "Clinton hit for 'unborn person' gaffe from both sides," *The Washington Times*, April 4, 2016, at http://commentators.com/hillary-clinton-unborn-person-has-no-constitutional-rights-washington-times/.

440 Angela Greiling Keane, "Obama Meets with NATO Head in Rebuke as Trump Questions Alliance," Bloomberg Politics, April 4, 2016, at http://www.bloomberg.com/politics/articles/2016-04-04/obama-meets-with-nato-head-in-rebuke-as-trump-questions-alliance.

441 Joanna Gill, "Pay up or get out: Trump blasts NATO allies and Clinton responds," Euronews, April 3, 2016, at http://www.euronews.com/2016/04/03/pay-up-or-get-out-trump-blasts-nato-allies-and-clinton-responds/.

442 RT, "We need a new 'NATO' that includes Russia to defeat ISIS," November 20, 2015, at https://www.rt.com/usa/322770-sanders-democratic-socialism-fdr/.

443 Susan Cornwell, "Trump threat to run as an independent counterproductive: party chief," Reuters, April 3, 2016, at http://www.reuters.com/article/us-usa-election-priebus-idUSKCN0X00RB.

444 Chuck Ross, "Diane Feinstein Has To Use Google To Look Up Hillary's Accomplishments," *The Daily Caller*, March 31, 2016, at http://dailycaller.com/2016/03/31/feinstein-googles-hillarys-senate-accomplishments/.

445 H.A. Goodman, "This is how the FBI destroys Hillary; The 10 questions that could end her White House dreams," Salon, April 5, 2016, at http://www.salon.com/2016/04/05/this_is_how_the_fbi_destroys_hillary_the_10_questions_that_could_end_her_white_house_dreams/.

446 Congressional Budget Office, "An Update to the Budget and Economic Projections: 2016 to 2026," August, 2016, at https://www.cbo.gov/sites/default/files/114th-congress-2015-2016/reports/51908-2016_Outlook_Update-2.pdf.
447 Juliet Eilperin and Anne Gearan, "Clinton questions whether Sanders is qualified to be president," *The Washington Post*, April 6, 2016, at https://www.washingtonpost.com/news/post-politics/wp/2016/04/06/clinton-questions-whether-sanders-is-qualified-to-be-president/.
448 Ibid.
449 Theodore Schleifer, "Bernie Sanders: Hillary Clinton is not 'qualified' to be president," CNN Politics, April 7, 2016, at http://www.cnn.com/2016/04/06/politics/bernie-sanders-hillary-clinton-qualified/.
450 Fox News, "Sanders wins Wyoming Democratic caucuses, Cruz takes Colorado delegates," April 10, 2016, at http://www.foxnews.com/politics/2016/04/10/sanders-wins-wyoming-democratic-caucuses-cruz-takes-colorado-delegates.html.
451 Editorial page, *The Washington Post*, April 10, 2016.
452 Fox News, "Sanders wins Wyoming Democratic caucuses, Cruz takes Colorado delegates," April 10, 2016, at http://www.foxnews.com/politics/2016/04/10/sanders-wins-wyoming-democratic-caucuses-cruz-takes-colorado-delegates.html.
453 Hanna Trudo, "Gardner defends Colorado from Trump," Politico, April 12, 2016 at http://www.politico.com/story/2016/04/cory-gardner-colorado-donald-trump-221821.
454 Ed O'Keefe, "Once again, Trump campaign makes mistakes trying to win delegates," *The Washington Post*, April 9, 2016, at https://www.washingtonpost.com/news/post-politics/wp/2016/04/09/once-again-trump-campaign-makes-mistakes-trying-to-win-delegates/?tid=pm_politics_pop_b.
455 Leah Barkoukis, "Trump Slams 'Totally Unfair' GOP Results After Cruz Wins Colorado Without Votes," Townhall.com, April 11, 2016, at http://townhall.com/tipsheet/leahbarkoukis/2016/04/11/trump-slams-totally-unfair-gop-results-after-cruz-wins-colorado-without-voters-n2146532.
456 Nick Gass, "Sanders picks up another Colorado delegate as party admits error," Politico, April 12, 2016, at http://www.politico.com/blogs/2016-dem-primary-live-updates-and-results/2016/04/bernie-sanders-colorado-delegate-221835.
457 Kyle Cheney, "Trump misses another shot at delegates in Nebraska," Politico, April 14, 2016, at http://www.politico.com/story/2016/04/donald-trump-nebraska-cruz-221863.
458 Travis Zimpfer, "Delegate selection leads to schism in Missouri GOP," *The Missouri Times*, April 18, 2016, at http://themissouritimes.com/28686/delegate-selection-leads-to-schism-in-missouri-gop/.

459 Greg Richtor, "Trump Aide Manafort: Cruz Using 'Gestapo' Tactics to Get Delegates," Newsmax, April 10, 2016, at http://www.newsmax.com/Politics/paul-manafort-donald-trump-convention-manager-cruz/2016/04/10/id/723131/.

460 Ed Stokols and Kenneth P. Vogel, "Donald Trump shuffles struggling campaign team," Politico, April 13, 2016, at http://www.politico.com/story/2016/04/rick-wiley-donald-trump-campaign-221909.Black Lives.

461 Kenneth P. Vogel and Ben Schreckinger, "Trump orders new campaign hierarchy, spending plan," Politico, April 20, 2016, at http://www.politico.com/story/2016/04/donald-trump-campaign-staff-222110.

462 Hayley Hoefer, "Views You Can Use: How Trump Would Build His Wall," US News and World Report, April 5, 2016, at http://www.usnews.com/opinion/articles/2016-04-05/donald-trump-would-ban-remittances-to-make-mexico-pay-for-border-wall.

463 Tom LoBianco, "Cruz stands by 'New York values' criticism," CNN Politics, April 7, 2016, at http://www.cnn.com/2016/04/07/politics/ted-cruz-new-york-values/index.html.

464 John Edwards address to the Democratic National Convention, July 28, 2004, at http://www.washingtonpost.com/wp-dyn/articles/A22230-2004Jul28.html.

465 Chad Pergram, "Speaker Ryan's rejection of presidential bid a 'Sherman esque' rejection," Fox News, April 12, 2016, at http://www.foxnews.com/politics/2016/04/12/speaker-ryans-rejection-presidential-bid-shemanesque-pledge.html.

466 Eric Bradner, "Bill Clinton spars with Black Lives Matter protesters," CNN Politics, April 8, 2016, at http://www.cnn.com/2016/04/07/politics/bill-clinton-black-lives-matter-protesters/.

467 Dan Balz, "Bill Clinton grapples uncomfortably with the then and the now," *The Washington Post*, April 13, 2016, at https://www.washingtonpost.com/politics/bill-clinton-grapples-uncomfortably-with-the-then-and-the-now/2016/04/12/0f964a0e-00bf-11e6-9203-7b8670959b88_story.html.

468 Jeanette Johnson-Jing, "Hillary Clinton in Black History," at https://www.youtube.com/watch?v=5uWu0nSsg7w&ebc=ANyPxKqS4cJLqpAw7uttMDPwJrCEbxhlS4bX51TSDlmXVfb3PXxh8WB9-NRskeJxW8MQUAKE3hqw&nohtml5=False.

469 Peter Hermann and Keith L. Alexander, "Suspect arrested in fatal stabbing at Deanwood Metro stop," *The Washington Post*, April 13, 2016, at https://www.washingtonpost.com/local/public-safety/suspect-arrested-in-fatal-stabbing-at-deanwood-metro-stop/2016/04/12/47bfe164-008e-11e6-b823-707c79ce3504_story.html.

470 Kevin B. Blackistone, "Will Smith isn't the only black male to die by the gun.

When will we take notice?" *The Washington Post*, April 14, 2016, at https://www.washingtonpost.com/sports/redskins/will-smith-isnt-the-only-black-male-to-die-by-the-gun-when-will-we-take-notice/2016/04/13/019b05c0-018c-11e6-9203-7b8670959b88_story.html.

471 Dan Balz, "Bill Clinton grapples uncomfortably with the then and the now," *The Washington Post*, April 13, 2016, at https://www.washingtonpost.com/politics/bill-clinton-grapples-uncomfortably-with-the-then-and-the-now/2016/04/12/0f964a0e-00bf-11e6-9203-7b8670959b88_story.html.

472 Amy Chozick, "Hillary Clinton Puts Racially Charged Skit on Bill de Blasio's Shoulders," *The New York Times*, April 12, 2016, at http://www.nytimes.com/politics/first-draft/2016/04/12/bill-de-blasio-hillary-clinton/.

473 Jeff Merkley, "Why I'm Supporting Bernie Sanders," *The New York Times*, April 13, 2016, at http://www.nytimes.com/2016/04/13/opinion/why-im-supporting-bernie-sanders.html.

474 Caitlin Huey-Burns, "Clinton, Sanders Let Loose in NY Debate," RealClearPolitics, April 15, 2016, at http://www.realclearpolitics.com/articles/2016/04/15/clinton_sanders_let_loose_in_new_york_debate_130295.html.

475 Lisa Riley Roche, "Poll: Utah would vote for a Democrat for President over Trump," Deseret News, March 20, 2016, at http://www.deseretnews.com/article/865650513/Poll-Utah-would-vote-for-a-Democrat-for-president-over-Trump.html?pg=all.

476 Jenna Johnson and Ed O'Keefe, "It's on: Tensions between Trump and GOP escalate in public fight," *The Washington Post*, April 15, 2016, at https://www.washingtonpost.com/politics/its-on-tensions-between-trump-and-the-gop-escalate-in-public-fight/2016/04/15/2949b1c6-031b-11e6-9d36-33d198ea26c5_story.html.

477 Donald J. Trump, "Let me ask America a question," *The Wall Street Journal*, April 14, 2016, at http://www.wsj.com/articles/let-me-ask-america-a-question-1460675882.

478 Ben Neary, "Cruz sweeps all of Wyoming's delegates at convention," April 16, 2016, *The Albuquerque Journal*, at http://www.abqjournal.com/758518/news/cru-zsweeps-all-of-wyomings-delegates-at-convention.html.

479 Kareem Abdul-Jabbar, "In this crucial election I'm endorsing Hillary Clinton," *The Washington Post*, April 15, 2016, at https://www.washingtonpost.com/opinions/kareem-abdul-jabbar-in-this-crucial-election-im-endorsing-hillary-clinton/2016/04/15/305bd5fc-0244-11e6-9203-7b8670959b88_story.html.

480 Isaac Arnsdorf, "Sanders outraises Clinton for third month in a row," Politico, April 21, 2016, at http://www.politico.com/story/2016/04/bernie-sanders-hillary-clinton-fundraising-222240.

481 Janet Hook, "Both Parties Presidential Front-Runners Increasingly Unpopular," NBC News/Wall Street Journal, April 17, 2016, at http://www.wsj.com/articles/both-parties-presidential-front-runners-increasingly-unpopular-1460898001.
482 PPP, April 19, 2016, at http://www.publicpolicypolling.com/pdf/2015/PPP_Release_MD_41916.pdf.
483 RealClearPolitics average, April 21, 2016, at http://www.realclearpolitics.com/epolls/2016/president/pa/pennsylvania_democratic_presidential_primary-4249.html.
484 Gravis, April 20, 2016, at http://gravismarketing.com/polling-and-market-research/delaware-polling/.
485 Quinnipiac, April 20, 2016, at https://www.qu.edu/images/polling/ct/ct04202016_Crbw42dm.pdf.
486 PPP, April 25, 2016, at http://www.publicpolicypolling.com/pdf/2015/April26thPrimaryPolls.pdf.
487 WSJ/NBC News poll of 1000 voters taken April 10-14, 2016, at http://www.wsj.com/articles/republicans-begin-tangling-over-convention-rules-1461281343.
488 Kyle Cheney, "Cruz crushes Trump in delegate fights over weekend," Politico, April 23, 2016, at http://www.politico.com/story/2016/04/ted-cruz-donald-trump-delegate-222354.
489 Ibid.
490 Kyle Cheney, "Trump aide antagonizes delegates he was sent to woo," Politico, April 23, 2016, at http://www.politico.com/story/2016/04/trump-aide-accused-of-bullying-delaware-gop-for-delegates-222335.
491 Heath Haussamen, "Candidates' deal to stop Trump could bring attention to New Mexico," NMPolitics.net, April 25, 2016, at http://nmpolitics.net/index/2016/04/candidates-deal-to-stop-trump-could-bring-attention-to-new-mexico/.
492 Tina Nguyen, "The Kasich-Cruz Alliance Is Already Falling Apart," Vanity Fair, April 25, 2016, at http://www.vanityfair.com/news/2016/04/kasich-cruz-alliance-broken.
493 Lee Edwards, "When Reagan Almost Won: The 1976 GOP Convention," *Daily Signal*, April 15, 2016, at http://dailysignal.com/2016/04/15/when-reagan-almost-won-the-1976-gop-convention/?utm_source=TDS_Email&utm_medium=email&utm_campaign=MorningBell&mkt_tok=eyJpIjoiTURBeU9EVXdNbUZsWlRCaCIsInQiOiJRTU9iU002cXRHMTFWQ0tJQnNicGp0K2FPUXJTSlZFc0JwNlBwWnk3dTFvMGJaQUFMaWZtd09aazdoYjJsTGFqWkpWbmRJVlZkd05EZFRUMHBOT1VWTlUydDVWblZCWlc4d1ozRllVVXQyTmpWSFREaGljRmhQZHpsd1JUMGlmUSUzRCUzRA%3D%3D.
494 Nick Gass, "Boehner: Cruz Is 'Lucifer in the Flesh,'" *Politico*, April 28, 2016, at http://www.politico.com/ story/2016/04/john-beohner-ted-cruz-lucifer-222570.

495 Allison Carter, "Cruz Calls Hoop a 'Basketball Ring' and Twitter Erupts," *IndyStar*, April 27, 2016, at http://www.indystar.com/story/sports/2016/04/26/cruz-calls-hoop-basketball-ring-and-twitter-erupts/83573574/.

496 Ian Schwartz, "Bobby Knight Endorses Trump: 'Most Prepared Man in History to Step in as President,'" *RealClearPolitics*, April 28, 2016, at http://www.realclearpolitics.com/video/2016/04/27/bobby_knight_endorses_trump_most_prepared_man_in_history_to_step_in_as_president.html.

497 *New York Times*, "Transcript: Donald Trump's Foreign Policy Speech," April 27, 2016, at http://www.nytimes.com/2016/04/28/us/politics/transcript-trump-foreign-policy.html?_r=0.

498 Ibid.

499 Bret Stephens, "The GOP Gets What It Deserves," *Wall Street Journal*, May 3, 2016, at http://www.wsj.com/articles/the-gop-gets-what-it-deserves-1462231897.

500 Reuters, "German Foreign Minister Criticizes Trump's 'America First' Foreign Policy," April 28, 2016, at https://ca.news.yahoo.com/german-foreign-minister-criticizes-trumps-america-first-oreign-102200855.html.

501 Rachel Weiner, "He Once Hoped for the GOP Nomination, Now He Can't Even Get Elected to the Convention," *Washington Post*, May 3, 2016, at https://www.washingtonpost.com/local/virginia-politics/2016/05/02/61d0e896-107e-11e6-8967-7ac733c56f12_story.html.

502 Gregory Krieg, "Trump Campaign Accuses Arizona GOP of Stealing Delegate Election," *CNN Politics*, May 1, 2016, at http://www.cnn.com/2016/05/01/politics/arizona-republican-delegates-convention-trump-cruz-brewer/.

503 Rebecca Berg, "Obscure Panel May Have Big Effect on GOP Convention," *RealClearPolitics*, May 2, 2016, at http://www.realclearpolitics.com/articles/2016/05/02/obscure_panel_may_have_big_effect_on_gop_convention_130442.html.

504 Kerry Picket, "RNC Prepares for Likely Challenges on Credentials Committee at Convention," *Daily Caller*, April 13, 2016, at http://dailycaller.com/2016/04/13/rnc-prepares-for-likely-challenges-on-credentials-committee-at-convention/.

505 Shane Goldmacher, "Trump Delegates Blocked from Key Posts in New Hampshire," *Politico*, May 2, 2016, at http://www.politico.com/story/2016/05/donald-trump-new-hampshire-delegates-blocked-222688.

506 Kimberley A. Strassel, "The Agony of a Trump Delegate," *Wall Street Journal*, April 28, 2016, at http://www.wsj.com/articles/the-agony-of-a-trump-delegate-1461884907.

507 Letter addressed to "Fellow Republican National Committee Members" from Curly Haugland, dated March 11, 2016, at http://dailycaller.com/wp-content/uploads/2016/03/CURLY_HAUGLAND.pdf.

508 Alice Gainer, "Violence, Arrests Accompany Trump Appearances in

California," *CBS New York*, April 29, 2016, at http://newyork.cbslocal.com/2016/04/29/california-anti-trump-protest/.

509 Andrew Rafferty and Phil Helsel, "Protesters and Police Face Off Outside Trump Speech in California," *NBC News*, April 30, 2016, at http://www.nbcnews.com/politics/2016-election/protesters-police-clash-outside-trump-rally-california-n564991.

510 Nolan D. McCaskill, "Trump Accuses Cruz's Father of Helping JFK's Assassin," *Politico*, May 3, 2016, at http://www.politico.com/blogs/2016-gop-primary-live-updates-and-results/2016/05/trump-ted-cruz-father-222730.

511 Louis Jacobson and Linda Qiu, "Donald Trump's Pants on Fire Claim Linking Ted Cruz's Father and JFK Assassination," *PolitiFact*, May 3, 2016, at http://www.politifact.com/truth-o-meter/statements/2016/may/03/donald-trump/donald-trumps-ridiculous-claim-linking-ted-cruzs-f/.

512 Nolan D. McCaskill, "Cruz on Trump's JFK Theory: 'This Is Nuts,'" *Politico*, May 4, 2016, at http://www.politico.com/story/2016/05/ted-cruz-jfk-assassination-trump-222736.

513 David Wright, Tal Kopan, and Julia Manchester, "Cruz Unloads with Epic Takedown of 'Pathological Liar,' 'Narcissist' Donald Trump," *CNN Politics*, May 3, 2016, at http://www.cnn.com/2016/05/03/politics/donald-trump-rafael-cruz-indiana/.

514 Jim Newell, "Ted Cruz Drops Out, and the GOP Is Donald Trump's Party Now," *Salon*, May 3, 2016, at http://www.slate.com/blogs/the_slatest/2016/05/03/ted_cruz_quits_the_presidential_race_it_s_all_over.html.

515 Julie Pace, Scott Bauer, "Trump, Sanders Win Indiana," *Tribune Star*, May 3, 2016, at http://www.tribstar.com/news/local_news/trump-wins-indiana/article_8c53f619-1b52-54dc-acfc-d3ccc9d60b33.html.

516 David Sherfinski, "Reince Priebus, RNC Chairman: 'It's Time to Unite. It's Time to Come Together,'" *Washington Times*, May 3, 2016, at http://www.washingtontimes.com/news/2016/may/4/reince-priebus-rnc-chairman-its-time-unite-its-tim/.

517 Shout-out to Paris Jacobs of Maryland for this marvelous saying.

518 Indiana exit polls, *CNN*, May 3, 2016, at http://www.cnn.com/election/primaries/polls/in/Dem.

519 Catherine Herridge, "Romanian Hacker Guccifer: I Breached Clinton Server, 'It Was Easy,'" *Fox News*, May 4, 2016, at http://www.foxnews.com/politics/2016/05/04/romanian-hacker-guccifer-breached-clinton-server-it-was-easy.html.

520 , Julian Hattem, "Federal Judge Opens the Door to Clinton Deposition in Email Case," *The Hill*, May 4, 2016, at http://thehill.com/policy/national-security/278702-judge-leaves-open-door-for-clinton-deposition-in-email-probe.

521 Josh Gerstein, "State Department Claims It Can't Find Any Clinton Texts or Email File for IT Aide," *Politico*, May 10, 2016, at http://www.politico.com/blogs/under-the-radar/2016/05/hillary-clinton-texts-bryan-paglia no-emails-222973.

522 *New Hampshire Union Leader*, "NH Sen. Ayotte will support—but not endorse—Trump," May 4, 2016, at http://www.unionleader.com/article/20160504/NEWS0605/160509712.

523 Eliza Collins, "Ryan: Trump needs to 'unify' GOP to get his backing," *USA Today*, May 5, 2016, at http://www.usatoday.com/story/news/politics/onpolitics/2016/05/05/speaker-paul-ryan-not-ready-support-trump/83983402/.

524 Joseph Gerth, "McConnell Gives Tepid Trump Endorsement. Bevin Demurs," *Courier-Journal*, May 5, 2016, at http://www.courier-journal.com/news/.

525 Alex Pappas, "Republican Senator Outlines Call for Third-Party Candidate," *Daily Caller*, May 5, 2016, at http://dailycaller.com/2016/05/05/republican-senator-outlines-call-for-third-party-candidate/.

526 Gideon Resnick, "Trump's VEEP Volunteers Could Fill a Clown Car," *Daily Beast*, May 9, 2016, at http://www.thedailybeast.com/articles/2016/05/09/trump-s-veep-volunteers-could-fill-a-clown-car.html.

527 Karl de Vries, "Sarah Palin Will Work to Defeat Ryan in Primary for Trump Stance," *CNN*, May 8, 2016, at http://www.cnn.com/2016/05/08/politics/sarah-palin-paul-ryan-paul-nehlen-endorsement/.

528 Tim Hains, "Gingrich: Paul Ryan Made a Mistake by Not Endorsing Trump, 'He Has an Obligation to Unify the Party,'" *RealClearPolitics*, May 6, 2016, at http://www.realclearpolitics.com/video/2016/05/06/newt_gingrich_paul_ryan_made_a_mistake_by_not_endorsing_trump.html.

529 Zach Carter, "Great, Donald Trump Threatened to Default on the National Debt," *Huffington Post*, May 6, 2016, at http://www.huffingtonpost.com/entry/donald-trump-default-national-debt_us_572d08e3e4b096e9f0917fac.

530 Matea Gold, "Trump now welcoming wealth donors," *Washington Post*, May 7, 2016, at http://thewashingtonpost.newspaperdirect.com/epaper/viewer.aspx.

531 Ibid.

532 Glenn Kessler, "Regardless of the Truth, Trump Repeats the Same Lines," *Washington Post*, May 8, 2016, at https://www.washingtonpost.com/politics/few-stand-in-trumps-way-as-he-piles-up-the-four-pinocchio-whoppers/2016/05/07/8cf5e16a-12ff-11e6-8967-7ac733c56f12_story.html?hpid=hp_rhp-top-table-main_factcheck-trump-whoppers-605pm%3Ahomepage%2F story.

533 Zach Carter, "Great, Donald Trump Threatened to Default on the National Debt," *Huffington Post*, May 6, 2016, at http://www.huffingtonpost.com/

entry/donald-trump-default-national-debt_us_572d08e3e4b096e9f0917fac.
534 Darren Samuelsohn and Ben White, "Trump's Empty Administration," *Politico*, May 9, 2016, at http://www.politico.com/story/2016/05/donald-trump-administration-transition-222944.
535 Reena Flores, "Donald Trump Rules Out a Democratic Running Mate," *CBS News*, May 6, 2016, at http://www.cbsnews.com/news/donald-trump-democrat-running-mate-election-2016/.
536 Nicki Rossoll, "Donald Trump Doesn't Think Republican Party 'Has To Be Unified,'" *ABC News*, May 7, 2016, at http://abcnews.go.com/Politics/donald-trump-doesnt-republican-party-unified/story?id=38955749.
537 Michael Patrick Leahy, "Hillary Clinton Promise: 'WE'RE GOING TO PUT A LOT OF COAL MINERS AND COAL COMPANIES OUT OF BUSINESS,'" *Breitbart*, March 14, 2016, at http://www.breitbart.com/big-government/2016/03/14/hillary-clinton-promise-were-going-to-put-a-lot-of-coal-companies-and-coal-miners-out-of-business/.
538 Dylan Stableford, "Hillary Clinton Says She 'Misspoke' When She Vowed to 'Put Coal Companies out of Business,'" *Yahoo News*, May 3, 2016, at https://www.yahoo.com/news/hillary-clinton-coal-miners-out-of-business-west-140835530.html.
539 Mary Jordan, "From Playboy to President? Trump's Past Crude Sex Talk Collides with His White House Bid," *Washington Post*, May 11, 2016, at https://www.washingtonpost.com/politics/from-playboy-to-president-trumps-past-behavior-collides-with-his-white-house-bid/2016/05/09/46bed6f8-12fe-11e6-93ae-50921721165d_story.html.
540 Manu Raju, "Trump, Ryan Tout Unity in Wake of Meeting," *CNN*, May 12, 2016, at http://www.cnn.com/2016/05/11/politics/paul-ryan-donald-trump-meeting/.
541 Ibid.
542 Ibid.
543 Allan Smith, "'It's None of Your Business': George Stephanopoulos and Donald Trump Have Testy Exchange on Tax Returns," *ABC News*, May 11, 2016, at http://www.businessinsider.com/donald-trump-tax-returns-2016-5.
544 Jackie Calmes, "Donald Trump Won't Alter Tax Plan, Spokeswoman Says as Confusion Reigns," *New York Times*, May 12, 2016, at http://www.nytimes.com/2016/05/13/us/politics/donald-trump-wont-alter-tax-plan-spokeswoman-says-as-confusion-reigns.html?smid=tw-share&_r=0.
545 Shane Goldmacher, "Trump Launches Tax Plan Rewrite," *Politico*, May 11, 2016, at http://www.politico.com/story/2016/05/donald-trump-taxes-tax-reform-223041.
546 Robert Strohmeyer, "The Seven Worst Tech Predictions of All Time," *PCWorld*, December 31, 2008, at http://www.pcworld.com/article/155984/

worst_tech_predictions.html.

547 James Manyika, Michael Chui, Jacques Bughin, Richard Dobbs, Peter Bisson, and Alex Marrs, "Disruptive Technologies: Advances that Will Transform Life, Business, and the Global Economy," McKinsey Global Institute, May 2013, at http://www.mckinsey.com/business-functions/business-technology/our-insights/disruptive-technologies.

548 Dustin Stockton, "MAN OF HONOR: DANA MILBANK EATS HIS WORDS PREDICTING A TRUMP DEFEAT," *Breitbart*, May 15, 2016, at http://www.breitbart.com/2016-presidential-race/2016/05/15/dana-milbank-eats-words-trump-literally/.

549 Dan Balz, "Trump's Win Is Faint, No Matter the Electoral Forecast," *Washington Post*, May 15, 2016, at http://thewashingtonpost.newspaperdirect.com/epaper/viewer.aspx?issue=105820160515000000000001001&page=2&article=5e8d584c-ea95-458c-9d5a-8b4be99d1f6c&key=UfXVwsgF98cGfGyV4Ko/ww==&feed=rss&google=1.

550 S. V. Date, "Some Republicans Hope that Trump Gets Thumped," *National Journal Daily*, May 16, 2016, at https://www.nationaljournal.com/s/626388?mref=mostread-1.

551 Anne Gearan and Dan Balz, "Even Supporters Agree: Clinton Has Weaknesses as a Candidate. What Can She Do?" *Washington Post*, May 16, 2016, at https://www.washingtonpost.com/politics/even-supporters-agree-clinton-has-weaknesses-as-a-candidate-what-can-she-do/2016/05/15/132f4d7e-1874-11e6-924d-838753295f9a_story.html?hpid=hp_hp-top-table-main_clinton-weakness-908pm%3Ahomepage%2Fstory.

552 Matt Zapotosky, "Clinton Aide Cheryl Mills Leaves FBI Interview Briefly after Being Asked about Emails," *Washington Post*, May 10, 2016, at https://www.washingtonpost.com/world/national-security/clinton-aide-leaves-interview-once-the-fbi-broaches-an-off-limits-topic/2016/05/10/cce5e0e8-161c-11e6-aa55-670cabef46e0_story.html?postshare=4851462906536261&tid=ss_tw.

553 Bob Cusack and Ian Swanson, "Hillary's Unlikely Ally in 2016: The Media," *The Hill*, May 17, 2016, at http://thehill.com/homenews/campaign/280117-hillarys-unlikely-ally-in-2016-the-media.

554 Jonathan Easley, "NYT Story on Trump's History with Women Creates Backlash," *The Hill*, May 17, 2016, at http://thehill.com/homenews/campaign/280114-nyt-story-on-trumps-history-with-women-creates-backlash.

555 Michael Barbaro and Megan Twohey, "Crossing the Line: How Donald Trump Behaved with Women in Private," *New York Times*, May 14, 2016, at http://www.nytimes.com/2016/05/15/us/politics/donald-trump-women.html?_r=0.

556 Jonathan Easley, "NYT Story on Trump's History with Women Creates Backlash," *The Hill*, May 17, 2016, at http://thehill.com/homenews/campaign/280114-nyt-story-on-trumps-history-with-women-creates-backlash.

557 Ibid.
558 Ibid.
559 James V. Grimaldi, "Clinton Charity Aided Clinton Friends," *Wall Street Journal*, May 12, 2016, at http://www.wsj.com/articles/clinton-charity-aided-clinton-friends-1463086383.
560 Joe Tacopino, "Clinton Charity Arranged $2M Pledge to Firm Owned by Bill's 'friend,'" *New York Post*, May 13, 2016, at http://nypost.com/2016/05/13/clinton-charity-arranged-2m-pledge-to-company-owned-by-bills-friend/.
561 Geoff Earle, "It's a Bombshell," *Daily Mail*, May 13, 2016, at http://www.dailymail.co.uk/news/article-3589071/It-s-bombshell-Trump-steps-row-Bill-Clinton-s-charity-helping-woman-dubbed-Energizer-cash-company.html.
562 Allan Smith, "Donald Trump Rips Hillary Clinton for Suggesting Bill Will Be in Charge of 'Revitalizing' the Economy," *Business Insider*, May 17, 2016, at http://www.businessinsider.com/donald-trump-hillary-bill-clinton-energizer-economy-2016-5.
563 Rosalind S. Helderman and Tom Hamburger, "Former Mafia-Linked Figure Describes Association with Trump," *Washington Post*, May 17, 2016, at https://www.washingtonpost.com/politics/former-mafia-linked-figure-describes-association-with-trump/2016/05/17/cec6c2c6-16d3-11e6-aa55-670cabef46e0_story.html.
564 Malia Zimmerman, "Flight Logs Show Bill Clinton Flew on Sex Offender's Jet Much More than Previously Known," *Fox News*, May 13, 2016, at http://www.foxnews.com/us/2016/05/13/flight-logs-show-bill-clinton-flew-on-sex-offenders-jet-much-more-than-previously-known.html.
565 "Donald Trump Uses the Word 'Rape' to Talk about Bill Clinton," *CBS News*, May 18, 2016, at http://www.cbsnews.com/news/donald-trump-uses-the-word-rape-to-talk-about-bill-clinton/.
566 Bethania Palma Markus, "Chaos Erupts at NV Democratic Convention amid Tensions between Clinton and Sanders Supporters," *RawStory*, May 14, 2016, at http://www.rawstory.com/2016/05/violence-erupts-at-nv-democratic-convention-amid-tensions-between-clinton-and-sanders-supporters/.
567 Gayle Brandeis, "I Watched Hillary Clinton's Forces Swipe Nevada: This Is What the Media's Not Telling You," *Salon*, May 20, 2016, at http://www.salon.com/2016/05/20/i_watched_hillary_clintons_forces_swipe_nevada_this_is_what_the_medias_not_telling_you/.
568 Lange post can be found here: https://www.dropbox.com/sh/plk8x3hugdasxl4/AABtyUqg1UXol-hVRRBVTwFFa?dl=0.
569 Alex Griswold, "Bernie Sanders Abruptly Ends Interview after Reporter Asks about Nevada Chaos," Mediaite, May 17, 2016, at http://www.mediaite.com/online/bernie-sanders-abruptly-ends-interview-after-reporter-asks-about-nevada-chaos/.

570 Chris Cillizza, "This Bernie Sanders Statement on the Nevada Convention Reads Like an Open Threat to the Democratic Establishment," *Washington Post*, May 17, 2016, at https://www.washingtonpost.com/news/the-fix/wp/2016/05/17/bernie-sanders-is-mad-as-hell-and-hes-not-going-to-take-it-anymore-at-least-in-nevada/.

571 Tom LoBianco, "DNC Chair Rips Sanders Response to Nevada Chaos," *CNN*, May 18, 2016, at http://www.cnn.com/2016/05/17/politics/bernie-sanders-nevada-democrats/.

572 Alexander Bolton, "Dems Discuss Dropping Wasserman Schultz," *The Hill*, May 24, 2016, at http://thehill.com/homenews/campaign/281147-dems-discuss-dropping-wasserman-schultz.

573 Burgess Everett, "Big-name Democrats Won't Defend Wasserman Schultz," *Politico*, May 26, 2016, at http://www.politico.com/story/2016/05/debbie-wasserman-schultz-coup-223565.

574 The video can be seen here: https://www.youtube.com/watch?v=-dY77j6uBHI.

575 Mark Sherman and Jill Colvin, "TRUMP'S SUPEREME COURT LIST UNDERSCORES ELECTION'S IMPORTANCE," Associated Press, May 19, 2016, at http://hosted.ap.org/dynamic/stories/U/US_GOP_2016_TRUMP_SUPREME_COURT?SITE=AP&SECTION=HOME&TEMPLATE=DEFAULT&CTIME=2016-05-18-14-08-40.

576 Rebecca Ballhaus, "Donald Trump, Republicans Finalize Joint Fundraising Deal," *Wall Street Journal*, May 17, 2016, at http://www.wsj.com/articles/donald-trump-republicans-finalize-joint-fundraising-deal-1463537455.

577 Kenneth P. Vogel and Ben Schreckinger, "Trump Aides' Rivalries Plague Super PACs," *Politico*, May 18, 2016, at http://www.politico.com/story/2016/05/trump-allies-rivalries-plagues-super-pacs-223300.

578 Jonathan Martin, "Sheldon Adelson Is Poised to Give Donald Trump a Big Boost," *New York Times*, May 13, 2016, at http://www.nytimes.com/2016/05/14/us/politics/sheldon-adelson-donald-trump.html?_r=0.

579 Glenn Kessler, "Yes, Clinton Laughed, but not about Lenient Sentence," *Washington Post*, May 22, 2016, at https://www.washingtonpost.com/news/fact-checker/wp/2016/05/19/did-clinton-laugh-about-a-rapists-light-sentence-and-attack-sexual-harassment-victims/.

580 Ruth Marcus, "When It Comes to Lying, Trump Is in a Class by Himself," *Washington Post*, May 20, 2016, at https://www.washingtonpost.com/opinions/when-it-comes-to-lying-trump-is-in-a-class-by-himself/2016/05/20/e7668d42-1e9a-11e6-9c81-4be1c14fb8c8_story.html, and Ruth Marcus, "Liar in chief," *The Washington Post*, May 22, 2016, at https://www.washingtonpost.com/politics/poll-election-2016-shapes-up-as-a-contest-of-negatives/2016/05/21/8d4ccfd6-1ed3-11e6-b6e0-c53b7ef63b45_story.html?hpid=hp_rhp-top-table-main_poll0522-1201am%3Ahomepage%2Fstory.

581 Dan Balz and Scott Clement, "Voters Accentuate the Negative in Poll," *Washington Post*, May 22, 2016, at https://www.washingtonpost.com/politics/poll-election-2016-shapes-up-as-a-contest-of-negatives/2016/05/21/8d4ccfd6-1ed3-11e6-b6e0-c53b7ef63b45_story.html.

582 Tom Hamburger and Anu Narayanswamy, "Clinton's Cash for Election Day Far Surpassing Her Rivals," *Washington Post*, May 22, 2016, at https://www.washingtonpost.com/news/post-politics/wp/2016/05/21/clinton-campaigns-money-machine-dominates-trump-and-sanders-in-latest-fec-reports/.

583 Rachel Bade, Josh Gerstein, and Nick Gass, "State Dept. Watchdog: Clinton Violated Email Rules," *Politico*, May 25, 2016, at http://www.politico.com/story/2016/05/hillary-clinton-email-inspector-general-report-223553#ixzz49gMq2Yo7.

584 Zachary Warmbrodt, "Warren Steps Up War on 'Insecure' Trump," *Politico*, May 26, 2016, at http://www.politico.com/story/2016/05/warren-attacks-trump-223541.

585 Jeremy Diamond, "Trump Launches All-Out Attack on the Press," *CNN*, June 1, 2016, at http://www.cnn.com/2016/05/31/politics/donald-trump-veterans-announcement/.

586 Chris Cillizza, "Donald Trump Is Dead Wrong about the 'Sleaze' Media," *Washington Post*, June 1, 2016, at https://www.washingtonpost.com/news/the-fix/wp/2016/05/31/donald-trump-is-totally-wrong-about-the-media-when-it-comes-to-his-veterans-donations/.

587 Jerry Brown, "An Open Letter to Democrats and Independents," May 31, 2016, at http://www.jerrybrown.org/an_open_letter_to_california_democrats_and_independents.

588 Maegan Vazquez, "Marco Rubio Is Turning Heads with His 180 on Endorsing Trump," *Independent Journal Review*, April, 2016, at https://www.ijreview.com/2016/04/589529-marco-rubio-donald-trump-nominee/.

589 Paul Ryan, "Donald Trump Can Help Make Reality of Bold House Policy Agenda," *Janesville Gazette*, June 2, 2016, at http://www.gazettextra.com/20160602/paul_ryan_donald_trump_can_help_make_reality_of_bold_house_policy_agenda.

590 Jonathan Easley, "Who is David French?" *The Hill*, June 2, 2016, at http://thehill.com/homenews/campaign/ 281946-kristols-third-party-pick-was-evangelical-organizer-for-romney.

591 Clare Malone, "Pay Attention to Libertarian Gary Johnson; He's Pulling 10% against Trump and Clinton," FiveThirtyEight, May 24, 2016, at http://fivethirtyeight.com/features/pay-attention-to-libertarian-gary-johnson-hes-pulling-10-vs-trump-and-clinton/.

592 Stephen Collinson and Dan Merica, "Hillary Clinton's Evisceration of Donald Trump," *CNN*, June 3 2016, at http://www.cnn.com/2016/06/02/politics/

hillary-clinton-donald-trump-foreign-policy-speech/.
593 K. T. McFarland, "Hillary's 'Major' Foreign Policy Speech Shows How Clueless She Is about Trump," Fox News Opinion, June 2, 2016, at http://www.foxnews.com/opinion/2016/06/03/hillarys-major-foreign-policy-speech-shows-how-clueless-is-about-trump.html.
594 Ethan Epstein, "San Jose Mayor Justifies Mob Violence," *The Weekly Standard*, June 3, 2016, at http://www.weeklystandard.com/article/2002680.
595 Tom Kludt and Brian Stelter, "Donald Trump Revokes Washington Post Press Credentials," *CNN*, June 14, 2016, at http://money.cnn.com/2016/06/13/media/donald-trump-washington-post-credentials/.
596 Ralph Ellis, Ashley Fantz, Faith Karimi, and Eliott C. McLaughlin, "Orlando shooting: 49 killed, shooter pledged ISIS allegiance," CNN, June 13, 2016, at http://www.cnn.com/2016/06/12/us/orlando-nightclub-shooting/.
597 *BBC News*, "French Jihadist Murders Police Couple at Magnanville," June 14, 2016, at http://www.bbc.com/news/world-europe-36524094.
598 Fox News, "FBI, DOJ Release Full Transcript of Orlando Shooter's 911 Call," June 20, 2016, at http://www.foxnews.com/us/2016/06/20/fbi-doj-release-new-full-transcript-orlando-shooters-911-call.html.
599 Spencer S. Hsu and Ann E. Marimow, "Judge Orders Videotaping of Deposition of Clinton IT Specialist to Go Forward," *Washington Post*, June 15, 2016, at https://www.washingtonpost.com/local/crime/judge-deposition-of-clinton-it-aide-will-go-forward-remain-sealed/2016/06/14/499920c6-2f38-11e6-b5db-e9bc84a2c8e4_story.html.
600 Richard Pollock, "Cryptic NY Filing Revealed Clinton Foundation Foreign Donations," *Daily Caller*, June 14, 2016, at http://dailycaller.com/2016/06/14/exclusive-cryptic-ny-filing-revealed-clinton-foundation-foreign-donations/.
601 Ellen Nakashima, "Russian Government Hackers Penetrated DNC, Stole Opposition Research on Trump," *Washington Post*, June 14, 2016, at https://www.washingtonpost.com/world/national-security/russian-government-hackers-penetrated-dnc-stole-opposition-research-on-trump/2016/06/14/cf006cb4-316e-11e6-8ff7-7b6c1998b7a0_story.html.
602 Michael Riley and Jordan Robertson, "Clinton Foundation Said To Be Breached by Russian Hackers," *Bloomberg*, June 21, 2016, at http://www.bloomberg.com/news/articles/2016-06-21/clinton-foundation-said-to-be-breached-by-russian-hackers.
603 Ryan Lizza, "Donald Trump's Hostile Takeover of the G.O.P.," *The New Yorker*, January 28, 2016, at http://www.newyorker.com/news/daily-comment/donald-trumps-hostile-takeover-of-the-g-o-p.
604 Tré Goins-Phillips, "Trump Chastises Republican Party Leadership: 'Just Please Be Quiet,'" *Blaze*, June 15, 2016, at http://www.theblaze.com/stories/2016/06/15/trump-chastises-republican-party-leadership-just-please-be-quiet/.

605 Ibid.
606 Jeremy Diamond, "Republican Maryland Gov. Hogan Says He Won't Vote for Trump," *CNN*, June 15, 2016, at http://www.cnn.com/2016/06/15/politics/larry-hogan-donald-trump/index.html.
607 Theodore Schleifer, "Clinton Burying Trump: $42 Million to $1.3 Million," *CNN*, June 21, 2016, at http://www.cnn.com/2016/06/20/politics/republicans-cash-crunch-donald-trump/.
608 Nick Gass, "Trump, in Speech, Attacks Clinton as 'World Class Liar,'" *Politico*, June 22, 2016, at http://www.politico.com/story/2016/06/trump-clinton-is-a-world-class-liar-224653.
609 Rachel Koning Beals, "Donald Trump Welcomes U.K. 'Independence', Vows Close Ties," MarketWatch, June 24, 2016, at http://www.marketwatch.com/story/donald-trump-welcomes-uk-independence-vows-close-ties-2016-06-24?mod=MW_story_latest_news.
610 Nick Corasaniti, Alexander Burns, and Binyamin Appelbaum, "Donald Trump Vows to Rip Up Trade Deals and Confront China," *New York Times*, June 28, 2016, at http://www.nytimes.com/2016/06/29/us/politics/donald-trump-trade-speech.html.
611 Ibid.
612 Ibid.
613 Select Committee on Benghazi, U.S. Congress, June 28, 2016, at https://benghazi.house.gov/NewInfo.
614 Faith Karimi, Steve Almasy, and Gul Tuysuz, "ISIS Leadership Involved in Istanbul Attack Planning, Turkish Source Says," *CNN World News*, June 30, 2016, at http://www.cnn.com/2016/06/30/europe/turkey-istanbul-ataturk-airport-attack/.
615 Gregory Korte, "Obama: Despite Attack in Turkey, Terrorists Are Losing Ground," *USA Today*, June 30, 2016, at http://www.usatoday.com/story/news/politics/2016/06/29/obama-istanbul-ottawa-islamic-state-terrorism/86516076/.
616 James Robbins, "Are We Sure ISIL Is Losing?" *USA Today*, June 30, 2016, at http://www.usatoday.com/story/opinion/columnist/2016/06/29/turkey-airport-attack-kerry-isil-losing-terrorism-column/86521154/.
617 Saagar Enjeti, "Obama Must Really Trust Putin, Because They Just Cut a Secret Deal," *Daily Caller*, June 30, 2016, at http://dailycaller.com/2016/06/30/obama-must-really-trust-putin-because-they-just-cut-a-secret-deal/.
618 Michael Biesecker, "Another 165 Pages of Clinton Emails Released, Including Some She Deleted," Associated Press, June 27, 2016, at http://www.pbs.org/newshour/rundown/another-165-pages-of-clinton-emails-released-including-some-she-deleted/.
619 Josh Gerstein, "State Department Seeks 2-Year Plus Delay in Suite for Clinton

Aides' Emails," *Politico*, June 30, 2016, at http://www.politico.com/blogs/under-the-radar/2016/06/clinton-emails-state-lawsuit-delay-request-224981.

620 Pamela Brown and Tal Kopan, "Loretta Lynch on Clinton Meeting: 'I Certainly Wouldn't Do It Again,'" *CNN*, July 1, 2016, at http://www.cnn.com/2016/07/01/politics/lynch-to-accept-guidance-from-fbi-on-clinton-email-probe/.

621 Dan Balz, "Everyone Looks Bad Because Clinton Met with Lynch," *Washington Post*, July 3, 2016, at https://www.washingtonpost.com/politics/how-everyone-looks-bad-because-bill-clinton-met-with-loretta-lynch/2016/07/02/a7807adc-3ff4-11e6-a66f-aa6c1883b6b1_story.html?tid=pm_politics_pop_b.

622 Ruth Marcus, "When the System Seems Rigged," *Washington Post*, July 3, 2016, at https://www.washingtonpost.com/opinions/bill-clinton-and-loretta-lynchs-toxic-meeting/2016/07/01/a52e2892-3fae-11e6-80bc-d06711fd2125_story.html.

623 Gregory Krieg, "FBI Boss Comey's 7 Most Damning Lines on Clinton," *CNN*, July 5, 2016, at http://www.cnn.com/2016/07/05/politics/fbi-clinton-email-server-comey-damning-lines/index.html.

624 Ben Shapiro, "FBI: Yes, Queen Hillary Broke the Law. No, She Won't Be Prosecuted," *Daily Caller*, July 5, 2016, at http://www.dailywire.com/news/7177/fbi-yes-queen-hillary-broke-law-no-she-wont-be-ben-shapiro.

625 Michael B. Mukasey, "Clinton Makes the FBI's Least-Wanted List," *Wall Street Journal*, July 6, 2016, at http://www.wsj.com/articles/clinton-makes-the-fbis-least-wanted-list-1467760857.

626 Charles Krauthammer, "Comey: A Theory," *Washington Post*, July 8, 2016, at https://www.washington post.com/opinions/comey-a-theory/2016/07/07/297f9bd0-4478-11e6-8856-f26de2537a9d_story.html.

627 Andrew P. Napolitano, "The Department of Political Justice," *Washington Times*, July 7, 2016, at http://www.washingtontimes.com/news/2016/jul/6/clintons-have-different-rules-than-the-rest-of-us/.

628 Charles Krauthammer, "Comey: A Theory," *Washington Post*, July 8, 2016, at https://www.washington post.com/opinions/comey-a-theory/2016/07/07/297f9bd0-4478-11e6-8856-f26de2537a9d_story.html.

629 Jeremy Diamond, "Trump Praises Saddam Hussein's Efficient Killing of Terrorists, Calls Today's Iraq 'Harvard for Terrorists,'" *CNN*, July 6, 2016, at http://www.cnn.com/2016/07/05/politics/donald-trump-saddam-hussein-iraq-terrorism/.

630 Ibid.

631 Jose A. Del Real, "Trump's Favorite Dictators: In Reviled Tyrants, GOP Nominee Finds Traits to Praise," *Washington Post*, July 7, 2016, at https://www.washingtonpost.com/politics/trumps-favorite-dictators-in-reviled-tyrants-gop-nominee-finds-traits-to-praise/2016/07/06/8debf792-4385-11e6-bc99-7d269f8719b1_story.html?hpid=hp_hp_top-table-main_trumpdictator

s910p%3Ahomepage%2Fstory.

632 Sarah McCammon, "Make Britain Great Again? Donald Trump's Remarkable Reaction to Brexit," *NPR*, June 24, 2016, at http://www.npr.org/2016/06/24/483353866/make-britain-great-again-donald-trumps-remarkable-reaction-to-brexit.

633 Joshua Berlinger, Catherine E. Shoichet, and Steve Almasy, "Alton Sterling Shooting: Piercing Together What Happened before the Videos," June 7, 2016, at http://www.cnn.com/2016/07/07/us/baton-rouge-alton-sterling-shooting/index.html?adkey=bn.

634 Abigail Hauslohner and Ashley Cusick, "Alton Sterling's Relatives Weather Scrutiny, Call for Justice," *Washington Post*, July 14, 2016, at https://www.washingtonpost.com/national/alton-sterlings-relatives-weather-scrutiny-call-for-justice/2016/07/13/dbf0ba60-490f-11e6-bdb9-701687974517_story.html.

635 Eliott C. McLaughlin, "Woman Streams Aftermath of Fatal Officer-Involved Shooting," *CNN*, July 8, 2016, at http://www.cnn.com/2016/07/07/us/falcon-heights-shooting-minnesota/.

636 Richard Fausset, Manny Fernandez, and Alan Blinder, "Micah Johnson, Gunman in Dallas, Honed Military Skills to a Deadly Conclusion," *New York Times*, July 9, 2016, at http://www.nytimes.com/2016/07/10/us/dallas-quiet-after-police-shooting-but-protests-flare-elsewhere.html.

637 AP, "Police: Gunman in Vehicle Shoots at Georgia Officer," July 8, 2016, at http://jacksonville.com/ news/georgia/2016-07-08/story/police-gunman-vehicle-shoots-georgia-officer.

638 AP, "AUTHORITIES: HIGHWAY GUNMAN MOTIVATED BY POLICE SHOOTINGS," July 8, 2016, at http://hosted.ap.org/dynamic/stories/U/US_HIGHWAY_SHOOTINGS?SITE=AP&SECTION=HOME&TEMPLATE=DEFAULT&CTIME=2016-07-08-14-54-28.

639 Ben Bradlee, "CHICAGO MURDERS SURGE BUT SOLVE RATE REMAINS LOW," *ABC Eyewitness News Chicago*, June 29, 2016, at http://abc7chicago.com/news/chicago-murders-surge-but-solve-rate-remains-low/1407251/.

640 Annie Sweeney and Jeremy Gorner, "10 Shootings a Day: Complex Causes of Chicago's Spiking Crime," *Chicago Tribune*, July 1, 2016, at http://www.chicagotribune.com/news/ct-chicago-shootings-violence-2016-met-20160630-story.html.

641 *Fox News*, "Trump Declares Himself the 'Law and Order Candidate,' Calls for Anti-Police 'Hostility' to Cease," July 11, 2016, at http://www.foxnews.com/politics/2016/07/11/trump-declares-himself-law-and-order-candidate-calls-for-anti-police-hostility-to-end.html.

642 Nick Gass, "Biden Laughs at Trump's 'Law and Order Candidate' Claim," *Politico*, July 12, 2016, at http://www.politico.com/story/2016/07/

joe-biden-trump-law-and-order-225402.

643 Rachel Bade, "Republicans Ask DOJ to Investigate Clinton for Perjury," *Politico*, July 12, 2016, at http://www.politico.com/story/2016/07/hillary-clinton-chaffetz-perjury-225386.

644 Josh Gerstein, "Clinton Legal Team Moves to Block Deposition in Email Lawsuit," *Politico*, July 13, 2016, at http://www.politico.com/story/2016/07/hillary-clinton-block-deposition-email-225418.

645 The Editorial Board, "Donald Trump Is Right about Justice Ruth Bader Ginsburg," *New York Times*, July 13, 2016, at http://www.nytimes.com/2016/07/13/opinion/donald-trump-is-right-about-justice-ruth-bader-ginsburg.html?ref=opinion&_r=0.

646 *Daily Telegraph*, "Nice Terror Attack," July 15, 2016, at http://www.telegraph.co.uk/news/2016/07/15/ nice-terror-attack-driver-who-killed-84-on-french-riviera-was-cr/.

647 Cassandra Vinograd, Christopher Nelson, and Kurt Chirbas, "Nice Attack: Americans Sean and Codie Copeland from Texas Killed," *NBC News*, July 15, 2016, at http://www.nbcnews.com/storyline/france-truck-attack/nice-attack-americans-sean-brodie-copeland-texas-killed-n609946.

648 Reuters, "Islamic State Supporters Celebrate Deadly Attack in France on Social Media," July 15, 2016, at http://indianexpress.com/article/world/world-news/islamic-state-supporters-twitter-celebrate-deadly-attack-bus-nice-terror-terrorist-crash-in-france-on-social-media-2914836/.

649 Sophie Tatum, "Newt Gingrich: Test Every Muslim in U.S. to See if They Believe in Sharia," *CNN*, July 15, 2016, at http://www.cnn.com/2016/07/15/politics/newt-gingrich-hannity-interview/.

650 Hans von Spakovsky, "16 Democrat AGs Begin Inquisition against 'Climate Change Disbelievers,'" *Daily Signal*, April 4, 2016, at http://dailysignal.com/2016/04/04/16-democrat-ags-begin-inquisition-against-climate-change-disbelievers/.

651 James Delingpole, "ATTORNEY GENERAL: 'WE'VE DISCUSSED' PROSECUTING CLIMATE CHANGE DENIERS," *Breitbart*, March 10, 2016, at http://www.breitbart.com/big-government/2016/03/10/us-attorney-general-we-may-prosecute-climate-change-deniers/.

652 Washington Post–ABC News Poll, July 11–14, 2016, at https://www.washingtonpost.com/page/2010-2019/WashingtonPost/2016/07/17/National-Politics/Polling/release_433.xml?tid=a_inl.

653 Alexis Levinson, "Rob Portman's Home-State Convention Bind," *National Review Online*, July 19, 2016, at http://www.nationalreview.com/article/438041/rob-portman-reelection-bid-cleveland-convention-politically-sensitive.

654 Ibid.

655 Ian Schwartz, "Melania Trump: American Citizenship 'The Greatest

Privilege on Planet Earth,'" *RealClearPolitics*, July 18, 2016, at http://www.realclearpolitics.com/video/2016/07/18/melania_trump_american_citizenship_the_greatest_privilege_on_planet_earth.html.

656 Krissah Thompson, "How Michelle Obama's Team Wrote the Speech that Sparked Melania Trump Controversy," *Washington Post*, July 20, 2016, at https://www.washingtonpost.com/news/arts-and-entertainment/wp/2016/07/19/how-the-michelle-obama-team-wrote-the-2008-speech-that-melania-trump-echoed/?hpid=hp_no-name_hp-in-the-news%3Apage%2Fin-the-news.

657 Eliza Collins and David Jackson, "Trump Campaign Denies Plagiarism in Melania's Speech, Blames Reaction on Clinton," *USA Today*, July 19, 2016, at http://www.usatoday.com/story/news/politics/onpolitics/2016/07/19/trump-campaign-denies-plagiarism-melanias-speech-blames-reaction-clinton/87282068/.

658 Ryan Teague Beckwith, "Watch Ted Cruz Fail to Endorse Donald Trump at the Republican Convention," *Time*, July 20, 2016, at http://time.com/4416396/republican-convention-ted-cruz-donald-trump-endorsement-speech-transcript-video/.

659 Michael Edison Hayden, "Trump Blasts Ted Cruz for 'Not Honoring the Pledge' after Convention Speech," *ABC News*, July 21, 2016, at http://abcnews.go.com/Politics/trump-blasts-ted-cruz-honoring-pledge-convention-speech/story?id=40758796.

660 Peggy Noonan, "Trump and the Unknowable Moment," *Wall Street Journal*, July 22, 2016, at http://www.wsj.com/articles/trump-and-the-unknowable-moment-1469162752.

661 David Sherfinski, "Ken Cuccinelli: I Helped Escort Heidi Cruz Away from the GOP Convention Floor for Her Safety," *Washington Times*, July 20, 2016, at http://www.washingtontimes.com/news/2016/jul/21/ken-cuccinelli-i-helped-escort-heidi-cruz-away-gop/.

662 Nick Gass and Matthew Nussbaum, "Pence Tries to Unify after Cruz," *Politico*, July 20, 2016, at http://www.politico.com/story/2016/07/rnc-2016-mike-pence-225921.

663 Beth Reinhard and Rebecca Ballhaus, "Billionaire Pete Thiel Speaks at GOP Convention," *Wall Street Journal*, July 21, 2016, at http://www.wsj.com/articles/billionaire-peter-thiel-speaks-at-gop-convention-1469155232.

664 Julia Prodis Sulek and Matthew Artz, "Silicon Valley's Peter Thiel Receives Standing Ovation at GOP Convention," *Mercury News*, July 21, 2016 at http://www.mercurynews.com/elections/ci_30153175/how-did-peter-thiel-silicon-valleys-libertarian-leaning.

665 Eric Bradner, "10 Takeaways from Donald Trump's Republican Convention," *CNN Politics*, July 21, 2016, at http://www.cnn.com/2016/07/22/politics/republican-convention-takeaways/.

666 Shane Goldmacher, "Trump Claims the Prize," *Politico*, July 21, 2016, at http://www.politico.com/story/2016/07/rnc-2016-donald-trump-speech-225982.

667 Peggy Noonan, "Trump and the Unknowable Moment," *Wall Street Journal*, July 22, 2016, at http://www.wsj.com/articles/trump-and-the-unknowable-moment-1469162752.

668 Ibid.

669 Tom Hamburger and Karen Tumulty, "As Democrats' Convention Nears, Hacked Emails Are Posted Online," *Washington Post*, July 23, 2016, at https://www.washingtonpost.com/politics/2016/07/22/117f0574-504f-11e6-a422-83ab49ed5e6a_story.html.

670 John Wagner, "Kaine Not Liberal Enough? Just Ask Virginians," *Washington Post*, July 25, 2016, at https://www.washingtonpost.com/politics/kaine-not-liberal-enough-just-ask-virginians/2016/07/24/ff5f6e2a-519c-11e6-bbf5-957ad17b4385_story.html.

671 Theodore Schleifer and Naomi Lim, "Labor, Abortion Rights Groups Praise Kaine Pick," *CNN*, July 23, 2016, at http://www.cnn.com/2016/07/22/politics/reactions-tim-kaine-pick/.

672 Jim Hoft, "Detailed List of Findings in Wikileaks DNC Document Dump," *Gateway Pundit*, July 24, 2016, at http://www.thegatewaypundit.com/2016/07/detailed-list-findings-wikileaks-dnc-document-dump/.

673 Chris Cillizza, "Why Debbie Wasserman Schultz Failed," *Washington Post*, July 25, 2016, at https://www.washingtonpost.com/news/the-fix/wp/2016/07/25/the-decline-and-fall-of-debbie-wasserman-schultz-explained/?hpid=hp_hp-top-table-main_fix-wasserman-740a-top%3Ahomepage%2Fstory.

674 David Catanese, "Debbie Wasserman Schultz Driven Out of Chaotic Florida Democratic Breakfast," *US News and World Report*, July 25, 2016, at http://www.usnews.com/news/articles/2016-07-25/debbie-wasserman-schultz-driven-out-of-chaotic-florida-democratic-breakfast.

675 "Unaired 60 Minute Clips with Clinton and Kaine," July 24, 2016, at http://www.cbsnews.com/news/60-minutes-overtime-hillary-clinton-tim-kaine-clips/.

676 Dana Farrington, "Michelle Obama: I Want a President 'Who Is Worthy of My Girls' Promise,'" *NPR*, July 25, 2016, at http://www.npr.org/2016/07/26/487429223/michelle-obama-i-want-a-president-who-is-worthy-of-my-girls-promise.

677 Stephen Collinson, "Bernie Sanders: 'I Am Proud to Stand with Her,'" *CNN Politics*, July 26, 2016, at http://www.cnn.com/2016/07/25/politics/bernie-sanders-democratic-national-convention-speech/.

678 Tyler Pager, "PolitiFact: Democrats Never Mentioned Terrorism on Day One of DNC," *Politico*, July 25, 2016, at http://www.politico.com/story/2016/07/did-democrats-mention-islamic-state-convention-226202?lo=ap_c3.

679 Mikhaela Singleton, "Suicide Bomber Injures 12 Near German Music

Festival," July 25, 2016, at http://wrbl.com/2016/07/25/suicide-bomber-in jures-12-near-german-music-festival/.
680 Kenya Sinclair, "Germany Suffers Multiple Attacks," *Catholic Online*, July 25, 2016, at http://www.catholic.org/news/international/europe/story.php?id=70059.
681 *Daily Mail*, July 26, 2016, at http://www.dailymail.co.uk/news/arti cle-3708394/Two-men-armed-knives-people-hostage-French-church.html.
682 Eyder Peralta, "Bill Clinton Makes the Case for the 'Best Darn Change-Maker' He Has Met," *NPR*, July 26, 2016, at http://www.npr.org/2016/07/26/487550122/bill-clinton-to-headline-second-day-of-the-democratic-national-convention.
683 Eric Bradner, "McAuliffe: Clinton Would Flip-Flop on TPP," *CNN Politics*, July 27, 2016, at http://www.cnn.com/2016/07/27/politics/hillary-clinton-trans-pacific-partnership-terry-mcauliffe/.
684 Amber Phillips, "Why Terry McAuliffe's TPP Gaffe Is So Damaging for Hil lary Clinton," *Washington Post*, July 27, 2016, at https://www.washingtonpost.com/news/the-fix/wp/2016/07/27/why-terry-mcauliffes-tpp-gaffe-is-so-dam aging-for-hillary-clinton/.
685 Grabien News, "WATCH OBAMA REFER TO HIMSELF 117 TIMES DURING HILLARY NOMINATION SPEECH," July 28, 2016, at https://news.grabien.com/story-watch-obama-refer-himself-119-times-during-hillary-nomination.
686 Chris Moody, "Memorable Lines from the DNC's Final Night," *CNN International*, July 28, 2016, at http://www.cnn.com/2016/07/28/politics/dnc-memorable-lines-night-four/index.html?eref=mrss_igoogle_politics.
687 Ashley Parker and David E. Sanger, "Donald Trump Calls on Russia to Find Hillary Clinton's Missing E-Mails," *New York Times*, July 27, 2016, at http://www.nytimes.com/2016/07/28/us/politics/donald-trump-russia-clinton-emails.html?_r=0.
688 Morgan Winsor, "Donald Trump Says He Was Being 'Sarcastic' about Wanting Russia to Find Hillary Clinton's Deleted Emails," *ABC News*, July 28, 2016, at http://abcnews.go.com/Politics/donald-trump-sarcastic-want ing-russia-find-hillary-clintons/story?id=40955437.
689 Chelsea Schneider, "Trump, Pence Appear to Differ on Russian Hacking," *Indianapolis Star*, July 27, 2016, at http://www.indystar.com/story/news/politics/2016/07/27/trump-pence-appear-differ-russia-hacking/87623232/.
690 Richard A. Oppel Jr. "In Tribute to Son, Khizr Khan Offered Citizenship Lesson at Convention," *New York Times*, July 29, 2016, at http://www.nytimes.com/2016/07/29/us/elections/khizr-humayun-khan-speech.html.
691 *BBC News*, "Fury as Trump Mocks Soldier's Mother Ghazala Khan," July 31, 2016, at http://www.bbc.com/news/election-us-2016-36935175.
692 Jason Easley, "Donald Trump Insults Vets by Claiming He Sacrifices as Much as Fallen Soldiers," *Politics USA*, July 30, 2016, at http://www.politicususa.

com/2016/07/30/trump-insults-military-claiming-sacrifices-fallen-soldiers.html.
693 Letter from President Abraham Lincoln to Mrs. Bixby, November 21, 1864, at http://www.bartleby.com /43/38.html.
694 Mike Huckabee on BrainyQuote at http://www.brainyquote.com/quotes/quotes/m/mikehuckab473375. html.
695 Louis Jacobson, "Donald Trump Gets a Full Flop on Whether He's Had a Relationship to Vladimir Putin," *PolitiFact*, August 1, 2016, at http://www.politifact.com/truth-o-meter/statements/2016/aug/01/donald-trump/donald-trump-gets-full-flop-whether-hes-had-relati/.
696 Ibid.
697 Ibid.
698 Ibid.
699 *New Jersey Star-Ledger* editorial board, "Clinton's Lies vs. Trump's Lies: Separate and Unequal," August 3, 2016, at http://www.nj.com/opinion/index.ssf/2016/08/clintons_lies_vs_trumps_lies_separate_and_unequal.html#incart_2box_opinion.
700 *Guardian*, "Obama Launches Blistering Attack on Trump—Video," August 2, 2016, at https://www.theguardian.com/us-news/video/2016/aug/02/obama-donald-trump-video.
701 Charles Hurt, "Obama Speaks of What He Knows, 'Unfit To Be President,'" *Washington Times*, August 2, 2016, at http://www.washingtontimes.com/news/2016/aug/2/obama-speaks-of-what-he-knows-being-unfit-to-be-pr/.
702 Jeremy Stahl, "Watch Obama Get Angrier about Trump than He's Ever Been," *Slate*, August 2, 2016, at http://www.slate.com/blogs/the_slatest/2016/06/14/watch_obama_get_angrier_about_trump_than_he_s_ever_been.html.
703 Emily Schultheis, "Donald Trump Won't Endorse Paul Ryan, John McCain in Primary Races," *CBS News*, August 2, 2016, at http://www.cbsnews.com/news/donald-trump-wont-endorse-paul-ryan-john-mccain-in-primary-races/.
704 Jen Lawrence, "POTENTIAL SPOILER DROPS OUT OF AZ SENATE RACE, NOW WARD VS. MCCAIN," *Breitbart News*, August 1, 2016, at http://www.breitbart.com/big-government/2016/08/01/potential-spoiler-drops-az-senate-race-setting-ward-v-mccain-showdown/.
705 In early August, Ryan stomped Nehlen, claiming over 80% of the vote, while McCain won his primary 52% to Ward's 39%.
706 AFP, "Trump Makes 'You Want to Retch' Says Hollande," *Yahoo News*, August 2, 2016, at https://www.yahoo.com/news/trump-makes-want-retch-says-hollande-022327536.html?ref=gs.
707 Rick Noack, "Nearly 90 Percent of the French Now Disapprove of Hollande," *Washington Post*, July 5, 2016, at https://www.washingtonpost.com/news/worldviews/wp/2016/07/05/nearly-90-percent-of-the-french-now-dis

approve-of-their-president/.

708 Tami Luhby, "Donald Trump Reveals His Economic Advisers," *CNN Money*, August 5, 2016, at http://money.cnn.com/2016/08/05/news/economy/donald-trump-economic-advisers/index.html.

709 Susan Collins, "Why I Cannot Support Trump," *Washington Post*, August 9, 2016, at https://www.washingtonpost.com/opinions/gop-senator-why-i-cannot-support-trump/2016/08/08/821095be-5d7e-11e6-9d2f-b1a3564181a1_story.html.

710 George Will, "The Strained Logic of Trump's Supporters," *Washington Post*, August 6, 2016, at http://www.nationalreview.com/article/438736/donald-trump-supreme-court-constitution-promises-are-fantasy.

711 Jerry Markon, "As Senator, Clinton Promised 200,000 Jobs in Upstate New York. Her Efforts Fell Flat," *Washington Post*, August 7, 2016, at https://www.washingtonpost.com/world/national-security/as-senator-clinton-promised-200000-jobs-in-upstate-new-york-her-efforts-fell-flat/2016/08/07/339d3384-58d2-11e6-831d-0324760ca856_story.html.

712 Tal Kopan, "Donald Trump: I Meant that Obama Founded ISIS, Literally," *CNN*, August 12, 2016, at http://www.cnn.com/2016/08/11/politics/donald-trump-hugh-hewitt-obama-founder-isis/.

713 Anna Palmer, "Dozens of Republicans to Urge RNC to Cut Off Funds for Trump," *Politico*, August 11, 2016, at http://www.politico.com/story/2016/08/republicans-urge-rnc-cut-funds-trump-226918.

714 Jeanne Sahadi, "Hillary Clinton's 2015 Tax Return Shows $10.6 Million in Income, 31% Rate—and Puts Pressure on Donald Trump," *CNN*, August 12, 2016, at http://money.cnn.com/2016/08/12/pf/taxes/hillary-clinton-tax-return/.

715 Steve Eder and Kitty Bennett, "Hillary Clinton and Tim Kaine Show New Tax Returns, Pressuring Donald Trump," *New York Times*, August 12, 2016, at http://www.nytimes.com/2016/08/13/us/politics/hillary-clinton-tim-kaine-taxes.html?_r=0.

716 Robert Costa and Jose A. Del Real, "Trump Shakes Up Campaign, Demotes Top Adviser," *Washington Post*, August 17, 2016, at https://www.washingtonpost.com/news/post-politics/wp/2016/08/17/trump-reshuffles-staff-in-his-own-image/.

717 Ibid.

718 Mark Landler, "F.B.I. Gives Documents Related to Hillary Clinton E-Mail Inquiry," *New York Times*, August 16, 2016, at http://www.nytimes.com/2016/08/17/us/politics/fbi-gives-congress-documents-related-to-hillary-clinton-e-mail-inquiry.html?ref=todayspaper&_r=0.

719 Chris White, "Congressman Says Some of Clinton Emails 'Classified' Simply to Avoid Embarrassment," *Law Newz*, August 22, 2016, at http://lawnewz.

com/video/congressman-claims-some-of-clinton-emails-classified-simply-to-avoid-embarrassment/.

720 Candace Smith, "Trump Apologizes for Words on Campaign Trail, Says 'I Will Never Lie to You,'" *ABC News*, August 18, 2016, at http://abcnews.go.com/Politics/trump-apologizes-words-campaign-trail-lie/story?id=41496030.

721 Fox News, "Obama Denies US Paid Iran to Release Hostages, Says ISIS Still a Threat," August 4, 2016, at http://www.foxnews.com/politics/2016/08/04/obama-denies-us-paid-iran-to-release-hostages-says-isis-still-threat.html.

722 Daniel Halper, "State Dept.: $400M to Iran Was Contingent on US Prisoners' Release," *New York Post*, August 19, 2016, at http://nypost.com/2016/08/18/state-department-400m-cash-to-iran-was-contingent-on-us-prisoners-release/.

723 Steven Lee Myers and Andrew E. Kramer, "How Paul Manafort Wielded Power in Ukraine Before Advising Donald Trump," *New York Times*, July 31, 2016, at http://www.nytimes.com/2016/08/01/us/paul-manafort-ukraine-donald-trump.html.

724 FoxNews.com, "Judge orders Clinton to Provide Answers to Written Questions on Private Email Use," August 19, 2016, at http://www.foxnews.com/politics/2016/08/19/judge-orders-clinton-to-answer-questions-on-email-use.html.

725 Spencer S. Hsu, "FBI Uncovers 14,900 More Documents in Clinton Email Probe," *Washington Post*, August 22, 2016, at https://www.washingtonpost.com/local/public-safety/fbi-uncovered-at-least-14900-more-documents-in-clinton-email-investigation/2016/08/22/36745578-6643-11e6-be4e-23fc4d4d12b4_story.html.

726 Editorial Board, "Clinton's Colin Powell Excuse," *Wall Street Journal*, August 23, 2016, at http://www.wsj.com/articles/clintons-colin-powell-excuse-1471906341.

727 Rosalind S. Helderman, Spencer S. Hsu, and Tom Hamburger, "Emails Reveal How Foundation Donors Got Access to Clinton and Her Close Allies at State Dept.," *Washington Post*, August 22, 2016, at https://www.washingtonpost.com/politics/emails-reveal-how-foundation-donors-got-access-to-clinton-and-her-close-aides-at-state-dept/2016/08/22/345b5200-6882-11e6-8225-fbb8a6fc65bc_story.html.

728 *FoxNews.com*, "Clinton Foundation Hired Cyber Security Firm after Hack Attack," August 18, 2016, at http://www.foxnews.com/politics/2016/08/18/clinton-foundation-reportedly-hired-cyber-security-firm-after-possible-hack-attack.html.

729 Amy Chozick, "If Hillary Clinton Wins, Foundation Will Stop Accepting Foreign Donations," *New York Times*, August 18, 2016, at http://www.nytimes.com/2016/08/19/us/politics/if-hillary-clinton-wins-foundation-will-stop-ac

cepting-foreign-donations.html?_r=0.
730 Austin Wright, "Clinton Campaign Manager Calls Trump a Kremlin Puppet," *Politico*, August 22, 2016, at http://www.politico.com/story/2016/08/trump-russia-mook-clinton-foundation-227237.
731 NRO Staff, "Clinton State Department Stonewalled AP for Three Years," *National Review*, August 23, 2016, at http://www.nationalreview.com/happening/439286/clinton-foundation-ap-report-meetings-delayed-three-years-state-department-associated-press.
732 Stephen Braun and Eileen Sullivan, "MANY DONORS TO CLINTON FOUNDATION MET WITH HER AT STATE," *AP*, August 23, 2016, at http://hosted.ap.org/dynamic/stories/U/US_CAMPAIGN_2016_CLINTON_FOUNDATION?SITE=AP.
733 Chris Cillizza, "Now Hillary Has a Big Clinton Foundation Problem, Too," *Washington Post*, August 24, 2016, at https://www.washingtonpost.com/news/the-fix/wp/2016/08/23/now-hillary-has-a-big-clinton-foundation-problem-too/.
734 Monica Lewinsky had kept a blue dress on which Bill Clinton had left some unique incriminating evidence, and this evidence became the hard fact Clinton couldn't explain away. See Calvin Woodward, "Monica Lewinsky Breaks Silence on Her Affair with Bill Clinton," *AOL News*, May 6, 2014, at http://www.aol.com/article/ 2014/05/06/monica-lewinsky-breaks-silence-on-affair-with-bill-clinton/20881257/.
735 Ian Schwartz, "Clinton on Foundation Accusation: 'I Know There's a Lot of Smoke and There Is No Fire,'" *CNN*, August 24, 2016, at http://www.realclearpolitics.com/video/2016/08/24/clinton_on_foundation_ accusations_i_know_theres_a_lot_of_smoke_and_there_is_no_fire.html.
736 Kimberley A. Strassel, "The U.S. Department of Clinton," *Wall Street Journal*, August 26, 2016, at http://www.wsj.com/articles/the-u-s-department-of-clinton-1472167746.
737 Robert Schlesinger, "Trump's Immigration Shruggie," *US News and World Report*, August 25, 2016, at http://www.usnews.com/opinion/articles/2016-08-25/donald-trumps-immigration-policy-waffle.
738 Ibid.
739 Oliver Darcy, "RUSH LIMBAUGH: Who Knew Donald Trump Would Be the One to Convert the Republican Base to Amnesty?" *Business Insider*, August 25, 2016, at http://www.businessinsider.com/rush-limbaugh-donald-trump-immigration-amnesty-2016-8.
740 Jessie Hellmann, "Giuliani: Trump's Immigration Shift Propelled by Christie," *The Hill*, August 26, 2016, at http://thehill.com/blogs/ballot-box/presidential-races/293436-giuliani-trumps-immigration-shift-propelled-by-christie.
741 Stephen F. Hayes, "Why Trump's Risky Trip to Mexico Paid Off,"

Weekly Standard, August 31, 2016, at http://www.weeklystandard.com/why-trumps-risky-trip-to-mexico-paid-off/article/2004094.

742 Charles Krauthammer on *Fox News*, August 31, 2016, at http://www.realclearpolitics.com/video/2016/08/31/krauthammer_trump_dominated_mexican_president_took_charge_i_think_he_really_helped_himself.html.

743 *Politico*, "Transcript: Hillary Clinton's Full Remarks in Reno, Nevada," August 25, 2016, at http://www.politico.com/story/2016/08/transcript-hillary-clinton-alt-right-reno-227419.

744 Theodore Schleifer, "Trump Defends 'Bigot' Labor for Clinton," *CNN*, August 25, 2016, at http://www.cnn.com/2016/08/25/politics/donald-trump-hillary-clinton-bigot/.

745 Noah Bierman, "Donald Trump Accuses Hillary Clinton of Calling Him and His Supporters Racist to Distract from Her Failures and Scandals," *Los Angeles Times*, August 25, 2016, at http://www.latimes.com/nation/politics/trailguide/la-na-trailguide-updates-donald-trump-accuses-hillary-clinton-of-1472152942-htmlstory.html.

746 Fox News, "Clinton Team Used Special Program to Scrub Server, Gowdy Says," August 26, 2016, at http://www.foxnews.com/politics/2016/08/26/clinton-team-used-special-program-to-scrub-server-gowdy-says.html.

747 Margaret Chadbourn, "Government Attorneys Say Recovered Clinton Emails Could Include as Many as 30 Benghazi-Related Messages," *ABC News*, August 30, 2016, at http://abcnews.go.com/Politics/government-attorneys-recovered-clinton-emails-include-30-benghazi/story?id=41748556.

748 Matea Gold and John Wagner, "Inside the Exclusive Events Helping to Fund Clinton and the Democratic Party," *Washington Post*, August 24, 2016, at https://www.washingtonpost.com/politics/inside-the-exclusive-events-helping-to-fund-clinton-and-the-democratic-party/2016/08/23/f8ef52d4-6926-11e6-8225-fbb8a6fc65bc_story.html.

749 Aaron Blake, "A Record Number of Americans Now Dislike Hillary Clinton," *Washington Post*, August 31, 2016, at https://www.washingtonpost.com/news/the-fix/wp/2016/08/31/a-record-number-of-americans-now-dislike-hillary-clinton/.

750 Jeremy Pelzer, "Democratic Group Postpones Ted Strickland Ad Buy," *Cleveland.com*, August 30, 2016, at http://www.cleveland.com/open/index.ssf/2016/08/democratic_group_postpones_ted.html.

751 The exceptions are Maine and Nebraska, which apportion their electors by the congressional district method in which one elector is allocated according to the winner of each respective congressional district, and two are allocated by statewide popular vote.

752 *New York Times*, "The F.B.I.'s Summary of Its Investigation into Hillary Clinton's Email," September 2, 2016, at http://www.nytimes.com/interactive/2016/09/02/

us/politics/document-Hillary-Clinton-FBI-Investigation.html.

753 Eric Lichtblau and Adam Goldman, "F.B.I. Papers Offer Closer Look at Hillary Clinton Email Inquiry," *New York Times*, September 2, 2016, at http://www.nytimes.com/2016/09/03/us/politics/hillary-clinton-fbi.html?_r=1.

754 Ibid.

755 FoxNews.com, "Comey Defends Clinton Private Email Server Investigation in FBI Memo," September 7, 2016, at http://www.foxnews.com/us/2016/09/07/comey-defends-clinton-private-email-server-investigation-in-fbi-memo.html.

756 Rosalind S. Helderman and Michelle Ye Hee Lee, "Inside Bill Clinton's Nearly $18 Million Job as 'Honorary Chancellor' of a For-Profit College," *Washington Post*, September 6, 2016, at https://www.washingtonpost.com/politics/inside-bill-clintons-nearly-18-million-job-as-honorary-chancellor-of-a-for-profit-college/2016/09/05/8496db42-655b-11e6-be4e-23fc4d4d12b4_story.html.

757 John Solomon and Kelly Riddell, "FLASHBACK: Bill Clinton's Foundation Cashed in as Sweden Lobbied Hillary on Iran-Related Sanctions," *Washington Times*, June 2, 2015, at http://www.washingtontimes.com/news/2015/jun/2/clinton-foundations-sweden-fundraising-arm-cashed-/.

758 Francesca Chambers, "Hillary Clinton Is Caught Up in a Marathon Coughing Fit and Struggles to Speak in Cleveland but Tries to Play It Off as an 'Allergic Reaction' to Trump," *Daily Mail*, September 5, 2016, at http://www.dailymail.co.uk/news/article-3774941/Clinton-says-coughing-fit-allergic-reaction-Trump.html.

759 See https://www.youtube.com/watch?v=apuA5CACTfs.

760 Reuters, "HILLARY CLINTON BLAMED CONCUSSION FOR MEMORY FAILURE: FBI REPORT," *Newsweek*, September 2, 2016, at http://www.newsweek.com/hillary-clinton-concussion-fbi-report-495401.

761 Tim Hains, "Hillary Clinton Leaves 9/11 Memorial Due to Health Issue," *NBC News*, September 11, 2016, at http://www.realclearpolitics.com/video/2016/09/11/hillary_clinton_left_911_memorial_service_early_because_she_felt_overheated.html.

762 Jonathan Martin and Amy Chozick, "Hillary Clinton's Doctor Says Pneumonia Led to Abrupt Exit from 9/11 Event," *New York Times*, September 11, 2016, at http://www.nytimes.com/2016/09/12/us/politics/hillary-clinton-campaign-pneumonia.html.

763 Juanita Lopez, *CNN*, September 13, 2016, at https://www.youtube.com/watch?v=pV_JcDovENQ.

764 Kyle Cheney, "Former DNC Chairman Calls for Clinton Contingency Plan," *Politico*, September 12, 2016, at http://www.politico.com/story/2016/09/hillary-clinton-health-replace-contingency-228037.

765 Ian Schwartz, "It Isn't about the Health, It's about the Stealth," *RealClearPolitics*,

September 12, 2016, at http://www.realclearpolitics.com/video/2016/09/12/maureen_dowd_on_clinton_problems_it_isnt_about_the_health_its_about_the_stealth.html.

766 Jake Sherman and Anna Palmer, "Pelosi: Democrats Could Win the House," *Politico*, September 8, 2016, at http://www.politico.com/story/2016/09/pelosi-democrats-could-take-the-house-227850.

767 To recall, relying on Democrats to pass a bill ultimately led to Boehner's ouster. Scott Wong, "Ryan Faces New Pressures from House Conservatives," *The Hill*, September 8, 2016, at http://thehill.com/homenews/house/294913-ryan-faces-new-pressures-from-house-conservatives.

768 Lauren Katzenberg, "Six WTF Moments from the Commander-in-Chief Forum," Task & Purpose, September 7, 2016, at http://taskandpurpose.com/6-wtf-moments-commander-chief-forum/.

769 The "Red Queen" is a fictional character in Lewis Carroll's *Through the Looking-Glass*. In the 2010 Tim Burton version of the movie, the Red Queen is "quick to anger if things do not go the way she wants them to. She is merciless against her enemies and those who betray her." For a description, see http://aliceinwonderland.wikia.com/ wiki/The_Red_Queen.

770 Shane Goldmacher, "Trump, Clinton Stumble in Debate Dry Run," *Politico*, September 7, 2016, at http://www.politico.com/story/2016/09/clinton-and-trump-are-not-ready-to-debate-227868.

771 Katie Reilly, "Read Hillary Clinton's 'Basket of Deplorables' Remarks about Donald Trump's Supporters," *Time*, September 10, 2016, at http://time.com/4486502/hillary-clinton-basket-of-deplorables-transcript/.

772 Chris Cillizza, "Don't Look Now, but Donald Trump Has All the Momentum in the 2016 Race," *Washington Post*, September 15, 2016, at https://www.washingtonpost.com/news/the-fix/wp/2016/09/14/dont-look-now-donald-trump-has-all-the-momentum-in-the-2016-race/.

773 Ben Kamisar, "Powell in Leaked Email Slams Bill Clinton on Continuing Affairs with 'Bimbos,'" *The Hill*, September 14, 2016, at http://thehill.com/policy/technology/295939-powell-in-leaked-email-slams-bill-clinton-on-affairs-with-bimbos.

774 Michael Finnegan, "In Ohio, Trump Tees Off on Ford's Move to Mexico, Says He'd Tax It for Making Cars outside the U.S.," *Chicago Tribune*, September 15, 2016, at http://www.chicagotribune.com/news/nationworld/ politics/trailguide/la-na-trailguide-updates-trump-tees-off-on-ford-s-move-to-1473903620-htmlstory.html.

775 Marianne Levine, "Trump Unveils Child Care Plan," *Politico*, September 145, 2016, at http://www.politico.com/tipsheets/morning-shift/2016/09/trump-unveils-child-care-plan-immigration-advocates-miss-ins-record-rise-in-incomes-could-boost-clinton-216312.

776 United States Census Bureau, Department of Commerce, "Income and Poverty in the United States: 2015," September 13, 2016, at http://www.census.gov/library/publications/2016/demo/p60-256.html.
777 The White House posted a copy of Barack Obama's birth certificate in April of 2011 at https://www.whitehouse.gov/sites/default/files/rss_viewer/birth-certificate-long-form.pdf.
778 Domenico Montanaro, "Without Apology, Trump Now Says: 'Obama Was Born in' the U.S.," *NPR*, September 16, 2016, at http://www.npr.org/2016/09/16/494231757/without-apology-trump-now-says-obama-was-born-in-the-u-s.
779 A *rickroll* is a type of Internet bait-and-switch technique using a disguised hyperlink. Cooper Allen, "Trump Birther Event Blasted as Trump Hotel 'Informercial,'" *USA Today*, September 16, 2016, at http://www.usatoday.com/story/news/politics/onpolitics/2016/09/16/trump-birther-statement-hotel-media/90495452/?hootPostID=2811bf85089fd06c647e9a612803e0dc.
780 "Grasshopper" was the nickname given to Kwai Chang Caine by the temple's Master Kan in the 1970s television hit series *Kung Fu*.
781 Pervaiz Shallwani and Devlin Barrett, "New York Bombs Filled with Explosives, Shrapnel," *Wall Street Journal*, September 18, 2016, at http://www.wsj.com/articles/new-york-explosion-caused-by-bomb-authorities-say-1474213735.
782 CBS New York, "Suspect in Chelsea, Seaside Park Explosions Captured; Investigators Say 'No Indication' of Broader Cell," September 19, 2016, at http://newyork.cbslocal.com/2016/09/19/chelsea-blast-suspect/.
783 Phil Helsel and Daniella Silva, "Nine Hurt in Minnesota Mall Attack, Suspect Killed," *NBC News*, September 19, 2016, at http://www.nbcnews.com/news/us-news/nine-people-taken-hospital-after-minnesota-mall-stabbings-n650081.
784 Dave Boyer, "Obama Marks Muslim Holy Day of Eid al-Adha with Call to Accept Refugees," *Washington Times*, September 12, 2016, at http://www.washingtontimes.com/news/2016/sep/12/obama-marks-muslim-holiday-call-accept-refugees/.
785 Reid J. Epstein and Byron Tau, "After Bombings, Clinton Calls for Vigilance, Trump for Tightening Immigration," *Wall Street Journal*, September 19, 2016, at http://www.wsj.com/articles/after-bombings-clinton-calls-for-vigilance-trump-for-tightening-immigration-1474301672.
786 Rasmussen Reports, "Election 2016: Nevada," September 20, 2016, at http://www.rasmussenreports.com/ public_content/politics/elections/election_2016/nevada/election_2016_nevada_president.
787 John Hinderaker, "HILLARY'S HEALTH AGAIN FRONT AND CENTER IN NORTH CAROLINA," Powerline, September 20, 2016, at http://www.powerlineblog.com/archives/2016/09/hillarys-health-again-front-and-cen

ter-in-north-carolina.php.

788 PPD Election Staff, "Hillary Clinton Cancels Event in California, Campaign Says Pneumonia Is Back," *People's Pundit Daily*, September 19, 2016, at https://www.peoplespunditdaily.com/news/elections/2016/09/19/hillary-clinton-cancels-event-california-campaign-says-pneumonia/.

789 Niall Stanage, "Dems Startled by Trump's Numbers with Hispanics," *The Hill*, September 20, 2016, at http://thehill.com/homenews/campaign/296747-trump-is-doing-better-with-hispanics-than-you-think.

790 MJ Lee, Dan Merica, and Jeff Zeleny, "Obama: Would Be a 'Personal Insult' to Legacy if Black Voters Don't Back Clinton," *CNN*, September 17, 2016, at http://www.cnn.com/2016/09/17/politics/obama-black-congressional-caucus/.

791 Shane Goldmacher, "Trump Shatters Republican Records with Small Donors," *Politico*, September 19, 2016, at http://www.politico.com/story/2016/09/trump-shatters-gop-records-with-small-donors-228338.

792 Chuck Todd, "First Read: Trump's Charitable Foundation Takes Another Hit," *NBC News*, September 21, 2016, at http://www.nbcnews.com/politics/first-read/first-read-trump-s-charitable-foundation-takes-another-hit-n651801.

793 Meghan Keneally, "Donald Trump Jr.'s Skittles Tweet Highlights His Key Campaign Role," *ABC News*, September 20, 2016, at http://abcnews.go.com/Politics/donald-trump-jrs-skittles-tweet-highlights-key-campaign/story?id=42218871.

794 Jacqueline Alemany, "On a Street in Ohio, Defiant Democrats Flock to Trump," *CBS News*, September 21, 2016, at http://www.cbsnews.com/news/on-a-street-in-ohio-defiant-democrats-flock-to-trump/.

795 Liam Stack, "Video Released in Terence Crutcher's Killing by Tulsa Police," *New York Times*, September 19, 2016, at http://www.nytimes.com/2016/09/20/us/video-released-in-terence-crutchers-killing-by-tulsa-police.html?_r=0.

796 Ed Lavandera, Eliott C. McLaughlin, and Holly Yan, "Charlotte Police Chief: Video Won't Be Made Public," *CNN*, September 22, 2016, at http://www.cnn.com/2016/09/22/us/charlotte-protests/.

797 Wesley Lowery and Cheryl W. Thompson, "Autopsy Shows Keith Lamont Scott Had Four Gunshot Wounds—Including One in the Back," *Washington Post*, October 13, 2016, at https://www.washingtonpost.com/news/post-nation/wp/2016/10/12/autopsy-shows-keith-lamont-scott-was-shot-four-times-by-charlotte-officer-once-in-the-back/?utm_term=.9962a3f0f860.

798 Tyler Durden, "Who Is Behind the Riots? Charlotte Police Say 70% of Arrested Protesters Had Out of State IDs," *ZeroHedge*, September 22, 2016, at http://www.zerohedge.com/news/2016-09-22/who-behind-riots-charlotte-police-says-70-arrested-protesters-had-out-state-ids.

799 Jon Schuppe, "Terence Crutcher Had PCP in System When Tulsa Police Shot Him, Toxicology Report Shows," *NBC News*, October 11, 2016, at http://www.

nbcnews.com/news/us-news/terrence-crutcher-had-pcp-system-when-tulsa-police-shot-him-n664656.

800 Justin Juozapavicius and Sean Murphy, "Tulsa, Oklahoma, Police Officer Charged in Man's Death," *AP*, September 22, 2016, at http://bigstory.ap.org/article/14ce6ee113ff47f894fb1e7e3fcb3892/tulsa-police-officer-charged-mans-death.

801 Ben White, "New Poll Shows Grim Economic Views," *Politico*, September 23, 2016, at http://www.politico.com/tipsheets/morning-money/2016/09/new-poll-shows-grim-economic-views-216479.

802 Marianne Levine, "Poll: Most Americans Think BLS is BS," *Politico*, September 23, 2016, at http://www.politico.com/tipsheets/morning-shift/2016/09/poll-most-americans-think-bls-is-bs-216491.

803 Tom DiChristopher, "Bill Clinton Supports Lower Corporate Tax Rate, Says Reasoning for TPP Clear," CNBC, September 22, 2016, at http://www.cnbc.com/2016/09/21/bill-clinton-supports-lower-corporate-tax-rate-says-reasoning-for-tpp-clear.html.

804 Richard Rubin, "Hillary Clinton Proposes 65% Top Rate for Estates," *Wall Street Journal*, September 22, 2016, at http://www.wsj.com/articles/hillary-clinton-proposes-65-tax-on-largest-estates-1474559914.

805 Catherine Rampell, "When Will Millennials Start Liking Hillary Clinton?" *Washington Post*, September 23, 2016, at https://www.washingtonpost.com/opinions/when-will-millennials-start-liking-hillary-clinton/2016/09/22/4f2e0de8-80fb-11e6-a52d-9a865a0ed0d4_story.html?utm_term=.7410629c1fce.

806 The video is here: http://www.funnyordie.com/videos/b2fc974d1d/between-two-ferns-with-zach-galifianakis-hillary-clinton?_cc=__d___&_ccid=418b3ae4-f9ee-4008-9ef9-b09058768ec5.

807 Katie Rogers, "A Deadpan Hillary Clinton Visits 'Two Ferns,'" *New York Times*, September 22, 2016 at http://www.nytimes.com/2016/09/23/us/politics/a-deadpan-hillary-clinton-visits-between-two-ferns.html?_r=0.

808 Dan Merica, "Hillary Clinton Goes between Two Ferns: 'I Really Regret Doing This,'" *CNN*, September 22, 2016, at http://www.cnn.com/2016/09/22/politics/hillary-clinton-between-two-ferns/.

809 Josh Gerstein and Nolan D. McCaskill, "Obama Used a Pseudonym in Emails with Clinton, FBI Documents Reveal," *Politico*, September 23, 2016, at http://www.politico.com/story/2016/09/hillary-clinton-emails-fbi-228607.

810 Reena Flores, "Obama Weighs In on Hillary Clinton's Private Emails," *CBS News*, March 7, 2015, at http://www.cbsnews.com/news/obama-weighs-in-hillary-clinton-private-emails/.

811 Kyle Cheney, "Clinton Aid Talked of Needing to 'Clean Up' Obama's Comments on Server," *Politico*, October 25, 2016, at http://www.politico.

com/story/2016/10/clinton-email-server-when-did-obama-know-230285.
812 Courtney Weaver, "Clinton on the Defensive Ahead of Crucial TV Debate with Trump," *Financial Times*, September 26, 2016, at http://www.ft.com/cms/s/0/2e4a7022-7907-11e6-a0c6-39e2633162d5.html#axzz4LMfThJPV.
813 Frank Luntz, "How Donald Trump Can Defeat Hillary Clinton in the First Debate," *Time*, September 26, 2016, at http://time.com/4504482/presidential-debate-how-donald-trump-defeat-hillary-clinton/?xid=homepage.
814 John King, "Sources: Clinton Admits Sexual Affair with Flowers," *CNN*, January 22, 1998, at http://www.cnn.com/ALLPOLITICS/1998/01/22/flowers.king/.
815 Eric Bradner, "Bill Clinton's alleged sexual misconduct: Who you need to know," *CNN*, January 7, 2016, at http://www.cnn.com/2016/01/07/politics/bill-clinton-history-2016-election/.
816 Aaron Blake and TEAM Fix, "The First Trump-Clinton Debate Transcript, Annotated," *Washington Post*, September 26, 2016, at https://www.washingtonpost.com/news/the-fix/wp/2016/09/26/the-first-trump-clinton-presidential-debate-transcript-annotated/.
817 Eddie Scarry, "In Debate, Clinton Gets No Follow-Up Questions, Trump Gets 6," *Washington Examiner*, September 27, 2016, at http://www.washingtonexaminer.com/in-debate-trump-gets-6-follow-up-questions-clinton-gets-none/article/2602939.
818 Phillip Stucky, "HOLT INTERRUPTED TRUMP WAY MORE THAN CLINTON IN DEBATE," *Daily Caller*, September 27, 2016, at http://dailycaller.com/2016/09/27/holt-interrupted-trump-way-more-than-clinton-in-debate/.
819 "Stop and frisk" refers to a situation where a police officer who is suspicious of an individual detains the person, questions the person, and runs his hands lightly over the suspect's outer garments to determine if the person is carrying a concealed weapon, drugs, or other contraband. Whether stop and frisk is effective in deterring crime is disputed, as is the constitutionality of the practice.
820 Timothy Williams and Monica Davey, "U.S. Murders Surged in 2015, F.B.I. Finds," *New York Times*, September 27, 2016, at http://www.nytimes.com/2016/09/27/us/murder-crime-fbi.html?_r=0.
821 Howard Fineman, "Donald Trump's Debate Performance Was the Worst Ever," *Huffington Post*, September 26, 2016, at http://www.huffingtonpost.com/entry/trump-worst-debate_us_57e9e5fce4b024a52d2a3b61.
822 Charles Hurt, "Donald Trump Won, but He Needs To Be Better on His Own Best Arguments," *Washington Examiner*, September 27, 2016, at http://www.washingtontimes.com/news/2016/sep/27/donald-trump-won-he-needs-be-better-his-own-best-a/.
823 Katie Jerkovich, "Michael Moore Says Trump 'Won' the Debate,"

Daily Caller, September 27, 2016, at http://dailycaller.com/2016/09/27/michael-moore-says-trump-won-the-debate/.

824 The ABC News poll showed Johnson/Weld with 15% and Jill Stein with 21%. Jim Hoft, "POST DEBATE POLL SHOCKER," *Gateway Pundit*, September 26, 2016, at http://www.thegatewaypundit.com/2016/09/shock-post-debate-poll-hillary-clinton-takes-4th-place-abc-news-poll-behind-jill-stein-gary-johnson/.

825 William McGurn, "The Secrets of Cheryl Mills," *Wall Street Journal*, September 27, 2016, at http://www.wsj.com/articles/the-secrets-of-cheryl-mills-1474932673.

826 Kimberley A. Strassel, "Jim Comey's Blind Eye," *Wall Street Journal*, September 30, 2016, at http://www.wsj.com/articles/jim-comeys-blind-eye-1475191703.

827 Josh Gerstein, "Comey on Clinton Email Probe: 'Don't Call Us Weasels,'" *Politico*, September 28, 2016, at http://www.politico.com/story/2016/09/james-comey-not-weasels-clinton-email-228835.

828 Robert Burns, "Officials: US to Send More Troops to Iraq to Help with Mosul," *ABC News*, September 28, 2016, at http://abcnews.go.com/Politics/wireStory/officials-us-send-troops-iraq-mosul-42415519.

829 Terence P. Jeffrey, "FLASHBACK—Obama: 'We're Leaving Behind a Sovereign, Stable, and Self-Reliant Iraq," cnsnews.com, June 12, 2014, at http://www.cnsnews.com/news/article/terence-p-jeffrey/flashback-obama-we-re-leaving-behind-sovereign-stable-and-self.

830 David M. Jackson, "Debate Commission: Trump Did Have Microphone Problems," *USA Today*, October 1, 2016, at http://www.usatoday.com/story/news/politics/onpolitics/2016/09/30/donald-trump-hillary-clinton-the-commission-on-presidential-debates/91349488/.

831 Jeremy Diamond, "Donald Trump quadruples down," CNN, October 1, 2016, at http://www.cnn.com/2016/09/30/politics/trump-overnight-media-tweets/.

832 Michael Barbaro and Megan Twohey, "Shamed and Angry: Alicia Machado, a Miss Universe Mocked by Donald Trump," *New York Times*, September 27, 2016, at http://www.nytimes.com/2016/09/28/us/politics/alicia-machado-donald-trump.html.

833 David Barstow, Susanne Craig, Russ Buettner, and Megan Twohey, "Donald Trump Tax Records Show He Could Have Avoided Taxes for Nearly Two Decades, Records Show," *New York Times*, October 1, 2016, at http://www.nytimes.com/2016/10/02/us/politics/donald-trump-taxes.html?hp&action=click&pgtype=Homepage&clickSource=story-heading&module=a-lede-package-region&region=top-news&WT.nav=top-news&_r=1.

834 James B. Stewart, "How Donald Trump Turned the Tax Code into a Giant Tax Shelter," *New York Times*, October 2, 2016, at http://www.nytimes.com/2016/10/03/business/how-donald-trump-turned-the-tax-code-into-a-

giant-tax-shelter.html.

835 Thomas Lifson, "Trump's Tax Loss Carryforward Is So Despicable that *The New York Times* and Hillary Clinton both used the same provision," *American Thinker*, October 3, 2016, at http://www.americanthinker.com/blog/2016/10/trumps_tax_loss_carry_forward_is_so_despicable_that_the_new_york_times_and_hillary_clinton_both_used_the_same_provision.html.

836 Editorial Board, *Chicago Tribune*, "A Principled Option for U.S. President: Endorsing Gary Johnson, Libertarian," September 30, 2016, at http://www.chicagotribune.com/news/opinion/editorials/ct-gary-johnson-president-endorsement-edit-1002-20160930-story.html.

837 Emma Ashford, "Gary Johnson's 'Aleppo Moments' Don't Erase His Solid Foreign-Policy Platform," *Business Insider*, October 2, 2016, at http://www.businessinsider.com/gary-johnsons-aleppo-moments-dont-erase-his-solid-foreign-policy-platform-2016-10.

838 Steve Eder, "Email about Qatari Offer Shows Thorny Ethical Issues Clinton Foundation Faced," *New York Times*, October 15, 2016, at http://www.nytimes.com/2016/10/16/us/politics/wikiLeaks-bill-clinton-foundation.html?_r=0.

839 David A. Fahrenthold, "How Donald Trump Retooled His Charity to Spend Other People's Money," *Washington Post*, September 10, 2016, at https://www.washingtonpost.com/politics/how-donald-trump-retooled-his-charity-to-spend-other-peoples-money/2016/09/10/da8cce64-75df-11e6-8149-b8d05321db62_story.html.

840 Sarah Ferris, "Bill Clinton Goes Way Off Message on ObamaCare," *The Hill*, October 6, 2016, at http://thehill.com/policy/healthcare/299314-bill-clinton-goes-way-off-message-on-obamacare.

841 Peter Schroeder, "RNC: Kaine Interrupted over 70 Times," *The Hill*, October 4, 2016, at http://thehill.com/blogs/ballot-box/presidential-races/299338-rnc-kaine-interrupted-debate-over-70-times.

842 Peggy Noonan, "The Kaine Impunity," *Wall Street Journal*, October 7, 2016, at http://www.wsj.com/articles/the-kaine-impunity-1475797041.

843 Steve Benen, "When They Go Low, We Go High," *MSNBC*, July 26, 2016, at http://www.msnbc.com/rachel-maddow-show/michelle-obama-when-they-go-low-we-go-high.

844 Chris Cillizza, "Hillary Clinton Is WAY overcompensating for Tim Kaine's Poor Debate Performance," *Washington Post*, October 5, 2016, at https://www.washingtonpost.com/news/the-fix/wp/2016/10/05/hillary-clinton-is-way-overcompensating-for-tim-kaines-poor-debate-performance/.

845 Fox News, "Trump Apologizes for Lewd Remarks in Video Statement amid GOP Uproar," at http://www.foxnews.com/politics/2016/10/08/trump-apologizes-for-lewd-remarks-in-video-statement-amid-gop-uproar.html.

846 Larry Kudlow, "Melania Trump's Making Me Take a Second Look at Donald,"

CNBC, October 19, 2016, at http://www.cnbc.com/2016/10/18/kudlow-melania-trumps-making-me-take-a-second-look-at-donald.html.

847 Monica Langley, "Donald Trump Says Campaign Not in Crisis, and There Is 'Zero Chance I Will Quit,'" *Wall Street Journal*, October 9, 2016, at http://www.wsj.com/articles/trump-tells-wsj-i-never-give-up-and-getting-unbelievable-support-1475940443.

848 Karen Tumulty, Tom Hamburger, Matea Gold, "Elephant Stampede: Many in GOP Trying to Escape Trump as Crisis Deepens," *Chicago Tribune*, October 9, 2016, at http://www.chicagotribune.com/news/nationworld/ ct-trump-tape-reaction-republicans-20161008-story.html.

849 Manu Raju, "Trump Now Too Toxic for Ryan, Hill GOP," *CNN*, October 8, 2016, at http://www.cnn.com/2016/10/07/politics/paul-ryan-donald-trump-toxic/index.html.

850 Laura Koran, Dan Merica, and Tom LoBianco, "WikiLeaks Posts Apparent Excerpts of Clinton Wall Street speeches," *CNN*, October 8, 2016, at http://www.cnn.com/2016/10/07/politics/john-podesta-emails-hacked/index.html.

851 Ed Rollins, "How Trump Can Salvage His Campaign during the Debate," *New York Post*, October 8, 2016, at http://nypost.com/2016/10/08/6-ways-donald-trump-can-turn-his-campaign-around/amp/.

852 Robert Costa and Philip Rucker, "ATTACKS, SLUTS, DOMINATE DEBATE," *Washington Post*, October 10, 2016, at https://www.washingtonpost.com/amphtml/politics/second-presidential-debate-takes-the-low-road-as-attacks-and-slurs-dominate/2016/10/09/d0ad5c3a-8e29-11e6-9c85-ac42097b8cc0_story.html.

853 Gregory Krieg, "Trump Threatens to Jail Clinton if He Wins Election," *CNN*, October 9, 2016, at http://www.cnn.com/2016/10/09/politics/eric-holder-nixon-trump-presidential-debate/index.html.

854 Liz Goodwin, "'Honest Abe Never Lied': Trump Mocks Clinton for Citing Lincoln in Debate," *Yahoo News*, October 9, 2016, at https://www.yahoo.com/news/honest-abe-never-lied-trump-mocks-clinton-for-citing-lincoln-at-debate-022803257.html.

855 Eric Metaxas, "Should Christians Vote for Trump?" *Wall Street Journal*, October 13, 2016, at http://www.wsj.com/articles/should-christians-vote-for-trump-1476294992.

856 Diann Catlin, "I'm a Bible-Thumping Etiquette Teacher for Trump," *USA Today*, October 18, 2016, at http://www.usatoday.com/story/opinion/2016/10/18/bible-thumping-etiquette-teacher-for-trump-column/92304778/.

857 Ibid.

858 Eric Metaxas, "Should Christians Vote for Trump?" *Wall Street Journal*, October 13, 2016, at http://www.wsj.com/articles/should-christians-vote-for-trump-1476294992.

859 Chuck Ross, "REVEALED: Donna Brazile Shared CNN Town Hall Questions with Clinton Camp," *Daily Caller*, October 11, 2016, at http://dailycaller.com/2016/10/11/revealed-donna-brazile-shared-cnn-town-hall-questions-with-clinton-camp/.

860 Mark Tapscott, "Washington Post Reporter Spiked Info about Podesta Conflict of Interest," *Daily Caller*, October 10, 2016, at http://dailycaller.com/2016/10/11/washington-post-reporter-spiked-info-about-podesta-conflict-of-interest/.

861 Juliet Eilperin, "Obama Promised to Curb the Influence of Lobbyists. Has He Succeeded?" *Washington Post*, March 22, 2015, at https://www.washingtonpost.com/politics/obama-promised-to-curb-the-influence-of-lobbyists-has-he-succeeded/2015/03/22/e9ec766e-ab03-11e4-abe8-e1ef60ca26de_story.html.

862 Alex Pfeiffer, "Hill's Shills: Leaks Have Exposed Journalists in Media's Corner," *Daily Caller*, October 11, 2016, at http://dailycaller.com/2016/10/11/hills-shills-leaks-have-exposed-journalists-in-clintons-corner/.

863 Editorial Board, *Washington Post*, "Hillary Clinton for President," October 13, 2016, at https://www.washingtonpost.com/opinions/hillary-clinton-for-president/2016/10/12/665f9698-8caf-11e6-bf8a-3d26847eeed4_story.html?utm_term=.551755a1e067.

864 Ian Schwartz, "Jennifer Granholm: 'Slow Drip' of WikiLeaks Release Implies They Are 'Doing Someone's Bidding,'" on Bloomberg Politics, posted on *RealClearPolitics*, October 12, 2016, at http://www.realclearpolitics.com/video/2016/10/12/jennifer_granholm_slow_drip_of_wikiLeaks_releases_implies_there_are_doing_someones_bidding.html.

865 Zack Beauchamp, "Why WikiLeaks Hates Hillary Clinton," *Vox*, October 11, 2016, at http://www.vox.com/2016/9/15/12929262/wikiLeaks-hillary-clinton-julian-assange-hate.

866 Ibid.

867 Stephen Hiltner, "Where the Trump Name Is Emblazoned Now: The Front Yard," *New York Times*, October 15, 2016, at http://www.nytimes.com/2016/10/16/us/politics/donald-trump-signs.html?_r=3.

868 Marina Fang, "Donald Trump Won't Stop Attacking Paul Ryan," *Huffington Post*, October 16, 2016, at http://www.huffingtonpost.com/entry/donald-trump-paul-ryan-twitter_us_5803fae7e4b0162c043cadfa.

869 Nancy Dillon and Stephen Rex Brown, "Donald Trump Says Hillary Clinton Was 'All Pumped Up' at the Last Debate, Insists They Should Both Take Drug Tests," *Daily News*, October 15, 2016, at http://www.nydailynews.com/news/politics/trump-insists-hillary-clinton-drug-tests-debate-article-1.2832042.

870 Jake Novak, "The Trump Dragon Has Been Unleashed Now that the 'Shackles' Are Off," *CNBC*, October 14, 2016, at http://www.cnbc.com/2016/10/14/the-trump-dragon-has-been-unleashed-now-that-the-shackles-are-off-commentary.html.

871 Aaron Klein, "Exclusive—Bill Clinton Caught on Tape . . .," *Breitbart*, October 16, 2016, at http://www.breitbart.com/big-government/2016/10/16/caught-tape-bill-clinton-equal-opportunity-fcker-ive-got-good-taste/.

872 Aaron Klein, "EXCLUSIVE VIDEO INTERVIEW: New Bill Clinton Sexual Assault Accuser Goes Public for the First Time," *Breitbart*, October 19, 2016, at http://www.breitbart.com/big-government/2016/10/19/exclusive-video-interview-new-bill-clinton-sexual-assault-accuser-goes-public-first-time/.

873 Tim Stelloh, "NC Republican Office Firebombed, 'Nazi' GOPers Threatened in Graffiti," *NBC News*, October 17, 2016, at http://www.nbcnews.com/news/us-news/nc-republican-office-firebombed-nazi-gopers-threatened-graffiti-n667316.

874 Project Veritas Action Fund, at https://d1sb17b1leotpq.cloudfront.net/rigging-election-video-i-clinton-campaign-and-dnc-incite-violence-trump-rallies.html.

875 Peter Hasson, "Dem Operative Who Oversaw Trump Rally Agitators Visited White House 342 Times," *Daily Caller*, October 18, 2016, at http://dailycaller.com/2016/10/18/exposed-dem-operative-who-oversaw-trump-rally-agitators-visited-white-house-342-times/.

876 Daniella Diaz and Drew Griffin, "Dem Operative 'Stepping Back' after Video Suggests Group Incited Violence at Trump Rallies," *CNN*, October 18, 2016, at http://www.cnn.com/2016/10/18/politics/project-veritas-action-robert-creamer-donald-trump-rallies/.

877 Eric Bradner, "Melania Trump: Donald Trump Was 'Egged On' into 'Boy Talk,'" *CNN*, October 18, 2016, at http://www.cnn.com/2016/10/17/politics/melania-trump-interview/index.html.

878 Anjali Mullany, "Ivanka Trump Doesn't Flinch," *Fast Company*, October 17, 2016, at https://www.fastcompany.com/3063963/behind-the-brand/ivanka-trump-doesnt-flinch.

879 Jenna Johnson, "Donald Trump Says the Election Is 'Rigged.' Here's What His Supporters Think He Means," *Washington Post*, October 18, 2016, at https://www.washingtonpost.com/news/post-politics/wp/2016/10/18/donald-trump-says-the-election-is-rigged-heres-what-his-supporters-think-that-means/.

880 Mark Landler and Ashley Parker, "Obama Tells Trump: Stop 'Whining' and Trying to Discredit the Election," *New York Times*, October 18, 2016, at http://www.nytimes.com/2016/10/19/us/politics/obama-donald-trump-election.html.

881 James Moore, "The Betting Pattern that Signals a Trump Presidency Isn't as Remote as the World Thinks," *Independent*, October 18, 2016, at http://www.independent.co.uk/news/world/americas/us-elections/punters-rush-to-back-trump-despite-disastrous-week-of-campaigning-a7368196.html.

882 Transcript of the third presidential debate, *Politico*, October 20, 2016, at

http://www.politico.com/story/ 2016/10/full-transcript-third-2016-presidential-debate-230063.

883 Eric Bradner, "Border Patrol Union Endorses Donald Trump," *Washington Post*, March 30, 2016, at http://www.cnn.com/2016/03/30/politics/border-patrol-union-endorses-donald-trump/index.html, and Ben Kamisar, "Nation's Largest Police Union Endorses Trump," *The Hill*, September 16, 2016, at http://thehill.com/blogs/ballot-box/presidential-races/296342-nations-largest-police-union-endorses-trump.

884 *Fox News*, "Trump Won't Commit to Accepting Election Results, at Fiery Final Debate with Clinton," October 19, 2016, at http://www.foxnews.com/politics/2016/10/19/trump-won-t-commit-to-accepting-election-results-at-fiery-final-debate-with-clinton.html.

885 Asma Khalid, "Elizabeth Warren Rallies 'Nasty Women' to Vote for Clinton," *NPR*, October 24, 2016, at http://www.npr.org/2016/10/24/499224776/elizabeth-warren-rallies-nasty-women-to-vote-for-clinton.

886 Ibid.

887 Khorri Atkinson, "Donald Trump: Hillary Clinton 'shouldn't be allowed to run'," MSNBC, October 10, 2016, at http://www.msnbc.com/msnbc/donald-trump-hillary-clinton-shouldnt-be-allowed-run.

888 Todd J. Gillman, "Trump Says 'If I Lose . . .' and Some Supporters Mull Revolt," *Dallas Morning News*, October 21, 2016, at http://www.dallasnews.com/news/politics/2016/10/21/trump-says-lose-supporters-mull-revolt.

889 Fred Hiatt, "Believe Rubio Post-Trump at Your Own Risk," *Washington Post*, October 23, 2016, at https://www.washingtonpost.com/opinions/believe-rubio-post-trump-at-your-own-risk/2016/10/23/885cd2c8-97a0-11e6-bb29-bf2701dbe0a3_story.html?utm_term=.2b31835c2b04.

890 Eliza Collins, "Four of the Juiciest Leaked Podesta Emails," *USA Today*, October 13, 2016, at http://www.usatoday.com/story/news/politics/onpolitics/2016/10/13/four-juiciest-leaked-podesta-emails/92014368/.

891 Ibid.

892 Valerie Richardson, "Democratic Operative in Undercover Video Says Clinton Wanted 'Donald Duck' to Stalk Trump," *Washington Times*, October 24, 2016, at http://www.washingtontimes.com/news/2016/oct/24/video-hillary-wanted-donald-duck-stalk-trump/.

893 Tami Luhby, "Obamacare Premiums to Soar 22%," *CNN*, October 24, 2016, at http://money.cnn.com/2016/10/24/news/economy/obamacare-premiums/.

894 Rebecca Berg, "Trump Pauses Campaign for D.C. Hotel Opening," *Politico*, October 26, 2016, at http://www.realclearpolitics.com/articles/2016/10/26/trump_pauses_campaign_for_dc_hotel_opening_132168.html.

895 Daniella Diaz, "Neera Tanden on Clinton Email Server: 'They Wanted to Get Away with It,'" *CNN International*, October 25, 2016, at http://www.cnn.

com/2016/10/25/politics/neera-tanden-john-podesta-clinton-email-server-wikileaks/index.html.

896 Editorial, *Wall Street Journal*, "The Cold Clinton Reality, Why isn't the IRS investigating the Clinton Foundation?" October 28, 2016, at http://www.wsj.com/articles/the-cold-clinton-reality-1477608696.

897 Rosalind S. Helderman and Tom Hamburger, "Top Aide's Leaked Memo Details 'Bill Clinton Inc.,'" *Washington Post*, October 27, 2016, at https://www.washingtonpost.com/politics/inside-bill-clinton-inc-hacked-memo-reveals-intersection-of-charity-and-personal-income/2016/10/26/3bf84bba-9b92-11e6-b3c9-f662adaa0048_story.html.

898 Ruth Marcus, "The Problem with Bill Clinton," *Washington Post*, October 30, 2016, at https://www.washingtonpost.com/opinions/bill-clintons-role-as-first-spouse-to-disappear/2016/10/27/2be6160a-9c8a-11e6-b3c9-f662adaa0048_story.html?utm_term=.ce207783f8bb.

899 David Weigel, "House Republicans Are Already Preparing for 'Years' of Investigations of Clinton," *Washington Post*, October 25, 2016, at https://www.washingtonpost.com/politics/house-republicans-are-already-preparing-for-years-of-investigations-of-clinton/2016/10/26/e153a714-9ac3-11e6-9980-50913d68eacb_story.html?tid=a_inl.

900 Adam Goldman, Alan Rappeport, Michael S. Schmidt, and Matt Apuzzo, "New Emails in Clinton Case Came from Anthony Weiner's Electronic Devices," *New York Times*, October 28, 2016, at http://www.nytimes.com/2016/10/29/us/politics/fbi-hillary-clinton-email.html?_r=0.

901 Evan Perez and Pamela Brown, "FBI Reviewing New Emails in Clinton Probe," *CNN*, October 28, 2016, at http://www.cnn.com/2016/10/28/politics/fbi-reviewing-new-emails-in-clinton-probe-director-tells-senate-judiciary-committee/index.html?adkey=bn.

902 Brian Snyder, "MEET HUMA ABEDIN, MYSTERIOUS CLINTON AIDE WHOSE EMAILS MAY CHANGE HISTORY," Reuters, carried by *Newsweek*, April 28, 2016, at http://www.newsweek.com/2016/05/06/ huma-abedin-hillary-clinton-anthony-weiner-453204.html.

903 Tim Hains, "Bernstein: FBI Would Not Reopen Case Unless New Evidence Was 'a Real Bombshell,'" RealClearPolitics, October 28, 2016, at http://www.realclearpolitics.com/video/2016/10/28/bernstein_fbi_would_not_reopen_case_unless_new_evidence_was_a_real_bombshell.html.

904 John Kass, "Democrats Should Ask Hillary Clinton to Step Aside," *Chicago Tribune*, October 29, 2016, at http://www.chicagotribune.com/news/columnists/kass/ct-hillary-clinton-emails-kass-1030-20161028-column.html.

905 Eli Lake, "Don't Let the FBI's E-Mail Surprise Swing the Election," *Bloomberg*, October 29, 2016, at https://www.bloomberg.com/view/articles/2016-10-28/don-t-let-the-fbi-s-e-mail-surprise-swing-the-election.

906 Reena Flores, "Hillary Clinton Blasts 'Deeply Troubling' Comey Letter to Congress on New Emails," *CBS News*, October 30, 2016, at http://www.cbsnews.com/news/hillary-clinton-blasts-deeply-troubling-comey-letter-congress-new-emails/.

907 Devlin Barrett, "FBI in Internal Feud over Hillary Clinton Probe," *Wall Street Journal*, October 30, 2016, at http://www.wsj.com/articles/laptop-may-include-thousands-of-emails-linked-to-hillary-clintons-private-server-1477854957.

908 Ibid.

909 Barney Henderson and Chris Graham, "FBI Director James Comey Accused of Breaking Law as Hillary Clinton's 12-Point Lead 'Wiped Out,'" *Telegraph*, October 31, 2016, at http://www.telegraph.co.uk/news/2016/ 10/31/fbi-obtains-warrant-to-search-emails-as-hillary-clintons-11-poin/.

910 Tim Hains, "Gowdy on Harry Reid's Statement, 'I Didn't Know Mormons Use Drugs,'" *Fox News*, October 30, 2016, at http://www.realclearpolitics.com/video/2016/10/30/gowdy_on_harry_reids_statement_i_didnt_know_mormons_use_drugs.html.

911 Michael M. Grynbaum, "CNN Parts Ways with Donna Brazile, a Hillary Clinton Supporter," *New York Times*, October 31, 2016, at http://www.nytimes.com/2016/11/01/us/politics/donna-brazile-wikileaks-cnn.html.

912 Post-ABC Tracking Poll, Oct. 26–29, at http://apps.washingtonpost.com/g/page/politics/post-abc-tracking-poll-oct-26-29/2116/.

913 Geoff Earle, "Now Huma Is Just 'One of My Staffers' after Close Aide Gets Left Behind on Ohio Campaign Trip while Hillary Keeps Up Her War on the FBI in Defiance of White House Backing for Comey," *Daily Mail*, October 31, 2016, at http://www.dailymail.co.uk/news/article-3890990/Now-Huma-just-one-staffers-close-aide-gets-left-Ohio-campaign-trip-Hillary-keeps-war-FBI-stunning-decision-emails.html/.

914 Eric Lichtblau and Steven Lee Myers, "Investigating Donald Trump, F.B.I. Sees No Link to Russia," *New York Times*, October 31, 2016, at http://www.nytimes.com/2016/11/01/us/politics/fbi-russia-election-donald-trump.html.

915 Heidi M. Przybyla, "Clinton: Private Server 'a Mistake,' but a Vote for Trump Risks Nuclear War," *USA Today*, October 31, 2016, at http://www.usatoday.com/story/news/politics/elections/2016/10/31/hillary-clinton-donald-trump-ohio/93076890/.

916 MJ Lee and Dan Merica, "Why Clinton's Closing Message Is So Somber," *CNN*, November 3, 2016, at http://www.cnn.com/2016/11/02/politics/hillary-clinton-2016-election/index.html

917 Chris Cillizza, "Donald Trump Gave a Very, Very Good Speech in Pennsylvania Today," *Washington Post*, November 1, 2016, at https://www.washingtonpost.com/news/the-fix/wp/2016/11/01/donald-trump-gave-a-very-very-

good-speech-today-in-pennsylvania/.
918 George Will, "A Fitting Finale for the Sleaze Sweepstakes," *Washington Post*, November 2, 2016, at https://www.washingtonpost.com/opinions/a-fitting-final-chapter-to-2016s-sleaze-sweepstakes/2016/11/01/ b3c724be-a05a-11e6-a44d-cc2898cfab06_story.html?utm_term=.9d84fda4fd86.
919 Emily Guskin and Scott Clement, "Post-ABC Tracking Poll: Trump 46, Clinton 45, as Democratic Enthusiasm Dips," *Washington Post*, November 1, 2016, at https://www.washingtonpost.com/news/the-fix/wp/2016/11/01/post-abc-tracking-poll-clinton-falls-behind-trump-in-enthusiasm-but-has-edge-in-early-voting/.
920 Reflects the most recent polls; "undecideds" are net of Trump, Clinton, Johnson, and Stein voters.
921 The Iowa polls were all at least a week old at this point.
922 The most recent New Mexico poll was a month old at this point.
923 Fox News, "FBI's Clinton Foundation Investigation Now a 'Very High Priority,'" November 2, 2016, at http://www.foxnews.com/politics/2016/11/02/fbis-clinton-foundation-investigation-now-very-high-priority-sources-say.html.
924 Devlin Barrett and Christopher M. Matthews, "Secret Recordings Fueled FBI Feud in Clinton Probe," *Wall Street Journal*, November 3, 2016, at http://www.wsj.com/articles/secret-recordings-fueled-fbi-feud-in-clinton-probe-1478135518.
925 Matt Zapotosky, Rosalind S. Helderman, Sari Horwitz, and Ellen Nakashima, "'He's Got to Get Control of the Ship Again': How Tensions at the FBI Will Persist after the Election," *Washington Post*, November 4, 2016, at https://www.washingtonpost.com/world/national-security/hes-got-to-get-control-of-the-ship-again-how-tensions-at-the-fbi-will-persist-after-the-election/2016/11/03/d28fc6c6-a050-11e6-8832-23a007c77bb4_story.html?hpid=hp_rhp-top-table-main_clintonfbi-850pm%3Ahomepage%2Fstory.
926 Kimberley A. Strassel, "The Clinton Campaign at Obama Justice," *Wall Street Journal*, November 4, 2016, at http://www.wsj.com/articles/the-clinton-campaign-at-obama-justice-1478216727.
927 Maureen Dowd, "The End Is Nigh," *New York Times*, November 5, 2016, at http://www.nytimes.com/ 2016/11/06/opinion/sunday/the-end-is-nigh.html?ref=opinion&_r=1.
928 *The Economist*, "What's Going On," November 5–11, 2016, at http://www.economist.com/news/united-states/21709596-support-donald-trump-working-class-whites-not-what-it-seems-whats-going.
929 Stephen F. Hayes, "Clinton Foundation Probe Continues," *The Weekly Standard*, November 6, 2016, at http://www.weeklystandard.com/clinton-foundation-probe-continues/article/2005261.
930 Joe Kovacs, "VIDEO: OBAMA 'ENCOURAGES ILLEGALS TO VOTE,'"

November 6, 2016, at http://www.wnd.com/2016/11/obama-encourages-illegal-aliens-to-vote/.
931 WikiLeaks, November 6, 2016, at https://twitter.com/wikileaks/status/793831278382428164.
932 Jonathan V. Last, "The Strangest of Bedfellows," *The Weekly Standard*, November 7, 2016, at http://www.weeklystandard.com/the-strangest-of-bedfellows/article/2005121.
933 A. B. Stoddard, "Things We Know at a Moment of Uncertainty," *The Hill*, November 6, 2016, at http://www.realclearpolitics.com/articles/2016/11/06/things_we_know_at_a_moment_of_uncertainty_132265.html.
934 Jennifer Mayerle, "Gov. Dayton Declares Affordable Care Act 'No Longer Affordable,'" *CBS Minnesota*, October 12, 2016, at http://minnesota.cbslocal.com/2016/10/12/gov-dayton-affordable-care-act/.
935 Naomi Lim, "Bill Clinton Calls Obamacare the 'Craziest Thing in the World,' Later Tries to Walk It Back," *CNN*, October 5, 2016, at http://www.cnn.com/2016/10/04/politics/bill-clinton-obamacare-craziest-thing/.
936 All figures reported here were those shown immediately after the election. Subsequent recounts and error corrections would change the totals somewhat.
937 Note: All these figures are shown here as reported immediately after the election and would likely change as new data came in and calculation and coding errors were collected.

INDEX

A

ABC News, 69, 277, 301, 509, 611, 619
Abedin, Huma, 317, 445, 467, 473, 498, 564, 610, 674–76, 697–98
abortion, 294, 391–93, 455, 568, 640
Afghanistan, 7, 25, 32, 95, 108–9, 238, 246, 480, 484, 508, 598
African American, 3, 118, 132, 307–8, 412, 448
AFT (American Federation of Teachers), 160
Alabama, 259, 265, 345, 347, 349, 355, 525
Alaska, 11, 203, 265, 345–47, 385
Alberta, 79, 148
Aleppo, 627–28
America First, 432–33
American businesses, 192, 239, 370
American Samoa, 345, 377–78
American voting patterns, 578, 711
amnesty, 568, 662
anchor babies, 172
anti-Trump forces, 341, 354, 437, 479, 481, 489
AP (Associated Press), 512, 564–66, 707
The Apprentice, 71–73, 142, 562, 633
Archer, Edward, 259
Arizona, 76, 265, 374, 377–78, 435, 499, 550, 569–70, 574, 592, 670, 687
Arkansas, 82, 84, 104, 265, 345, 347–49, 408, 462, 470, 524, 634
audiotape, 633–35, 639–41, 645, 647, 664–65, 711

B

bailouts, 179–80, 355
Baltimore, 114, 238, 308, 411, 520
Balz, Dan, 34, 69, 227, 412, 459
Band, Doug, 671–72
Bannon, Stephen, 559, 561–62
Baton Rouge, 507, 520
battleground states, 440, 592, 601, 656, 668, 707
Becker, Doug, 582
Benghazi, 108, 209, 220–22, 273, 497, 526
Bern, the (*see also* Sanders, Bernie), 160, 261, 272, 275, 304–5, 355, 372, 441, 466
biography, 80, 104, 230, 364
bird-dogging, 652
birthright citizenship, 171–72, 174–75
black communities, 26, 33, 419, 605–6, 615, 696
Black Lives Matter, 160–61, 239, 308, 367–68, 410–11, 508, 571, 606
blacks, 132, 238–39, 602. *See also* African American
Blitzer, Wolf, 335–37
BLS (Bureau of Labor Statistics), 607
borders, 169, 171–72, 204, 301, 325, 437, 494, 573, 594, 599, 638, 661–62
open, 326, 634–35, 647, 662
Boulder, 222, 238
Bradshaw, Sally, 123
Brazile, Donna, 534, 643, 681–82
Breen, John, 95
Brexit, 493, 506
Broaddrick, Juanita, 464, 613, 636–37
Brussels, 380–81

attacks, 381–82
BTT (business transfer tax), 190
budget, 61–62, 206–7, 245, 331, 375, 379, 586, 671, 714
deficits, 24, 62, 212, 271
Bush, George W., 1, 3, 7–9, 15, 39, 41–42, 94, 111, 121, 188, 202, 277, 322, 439, 451, 479, 527, 579
campaign, 123, 125, 235, 295
Bush, Jeb, 21–22, 28, 31, 36–39, 42–45, 48–49, 52, 54–56, 65, 77, 80, 108, 110–12, 118–19, 125–26, 172–74, 202, 225–26, 228, 243, 247–48, 285, 295–96, 439, 519

C

Caddell, Pat, 324–25
California, 6, 46, 92, 120, 196–97, 209, 240, 265, 359, 372, 429, 437, 470, 478, 482, 578, 613, 712
Cameron, David, 106, 493, 598
campaign team, 1, 550, 637
campaign trail, 37, 146, 226, 353, 509, 675
Canada, 79, 89, 148, 204–5, 270, 495
candidates, third party, 40, 479, 577, 627, 642, 705
Capretta, Jim, 451
Cardenas, Al, 37–38
Carson, Ben, 21–22, 74, 82, 104–5, 118–19, 153–54, 156–57, 182–84, 199, 212–13, 219, 223–24, 227–28, 230, 234–36, 283–84, 288, 290–93, 296–97, 314–15, 330, 333–35, 340–41, 347–48, 364–65
Carter, Jimmy, 49, 258, 324, 492–93
Carter, Zach, 448
Cassidy, Bill, 25, 27
Castro, Fidel, 44, 380
caucus, 128, 263–65, 267, 277–79, 290, 296–97, 304, 344–46, 404, 441, 640
CBC (Congressional Black Caucus), 317
CBS News, 321, 339, 533, 604
Chaffee, Lincoln, 103, 117, 154
Charleston, 130–31, 155, 308, 520
Chen, Lanhee, 196
Chicago, 12, 238, 240, 242, 411, 441, 507, 509, 618, 689
China, 7–8, 32, 45, 57, 91, 124, 131, 136–37, 214, 238, 252, 271, 319, 415, 433, 521, 538
Christie, Chris
campaign, 50, 248, 309
Cillizza, Chris, 96, 477, 565, 592, 632
Cleveland, 155, 243, 376, 424, 517, 523–24, 528, 530, 583, 648, 689
debate, 156–57
climate change, 147, 203, 518
Clinton, Bill, 2, 15, 26, 33, 38–39, 41–42, 49, 62, 68–69, 81, 97, 100, 254–56, 410, 444–45, 462–64, 499–500, 536–37, 613, 628–30, 634, 636–37, 650–51, 671–73, 686
Clinton, Hillary
campaign, 34, 69, 101, 145, 195, 205, 209, 215, 245, 256, 261, 272, 278, 490, 534, 610–12, 624, 628–29, 632–33, 635, 645–47, 653, 663–64, 690–91, 697
Clinton Foundation, 96, 98–99, 101, 107, 398, 486–87, 491, 551, 558, 564–66, 603, 628, 663, 672, 675, 679–80, 689, 691, 698
deplorables remark, 591, 640–41, 685
email investigation, 619, 638, 676, 678–79, 685
emails, 67–69, 84, 100, 107, 166, 186, 195, 272, 280–81, 287, 324,

486–87, 498, 502, 563, 572, 581, 645, 666
State Department, 564, 567, 583
supporters, 217, 308, 423, 668
Clinton email scandal, 69, 84, 100, 107, 166, 186, 272, 280, 287, 486, 563, 572
Clinton scandals, 99, 217, 306, 450
close elections, 577, 602, 642, 688, 709
CNBC, 179, 222, 224–25, 227–28, 230, 450, 457, 619
CNN, 170, 197, 215, 281, 284, 296, 298, 318, 334, 363, 466, 480, 489, 501, 528, 546, 556, 558, 583–84, 643, 653, 681–82
Coats, Dan, 29, 434
Colorado, 11, 29, 87, 130, 144, 240, 256, 265, 268, 344, 348–49, 404–5, 417–18, 553, 575, 578–79, 592, 601, 683, 687, 690, 702, 705
Comey bombshell, 682, 684
Communism, 45, 88
Confederate flag, 132–35
Congress, 10, 12, 15, 19–20, 22, 24, 30–31, 57, 62, 76–77, 88, 108–9, 113, 137–39, 141–42, 206, 245, 277–78, 552, 585–87, 626, 643, 677, 697–98, 714
Congressional Budget Office, 189, 212, 398
congressional districts, 208, 280, 372, 401, 406, 424, 426
Connecticut, 265, 416, 421–22, 706
conservatives, 13, 38, 41–44, 66, 80, 83, 88, 92–93, 102–3, 106, 117, 140, 190, 198, 239, 250, 276, 278, 294, 343, 368–69, 375, 451–52, 467–68, 523
Constitution, 57, 82–83, 102, 135, 137, 141, 171, 174, 322, 329, 455–56, 486, 494, 545, 641, 658

contested convention, 243, 354, 371, 409, 418–20, 425, 439
Conway, Kellyanne, 559, 562
CPAC (Conservative Political Action Committee), 65, 76
Creamer, Bob, 652–53, 670
CRomnibus, 30–31
Crutcher, Terence, 605–6
Cruz, Heidi, 383, 527
Cruz, Ted
campaign, 297, 313–14, 418, 439
supporters, 313, 406, 419, 434
Cuba, 44–46, 380

D

Dallas, 507–8
de Blasio, Bill, 412–13
Delaware, 265, 316, 416, 422, 424
Democratic convention, 18, 444, 478, 524, 531, 534–35, 543–44, 546–47, 552, 631, 660
Democratic debate, 155, 215, 227, 232, 255, 746
Democratic establishment, 117, 286, 310, 312, 324, 466, 557, 562, 605
Democratic nomination, 53, 90–91, 114, 116–17, 150, 236, 297, 374, 428, 453
Democratic Party, xix, 4, 21, 33, 85, 101, 103, 117, 144–45, 176, 195, 224, 229–30, 245, 267, 301, 352, 385, 389, 424, 427, 441, 445, 466, 696–97
Democrats, 6–7, 10–13, 27–29, 49, 63–64, 144–45, 207–10, 216–18, 229–30, 232–33, 251–54, 260–61, 266–69, 280–81, 289–90, 344–45, 348–50, 384–86, 401–2, 420–21, 440–42, 536–37, 539–41, 601–2, 709–10

Des Moines Register, 205, 255, 287–88, 744
DHS (Department of Homeland Security), 30, 61, 484
DNC (Democratic National Committee), 154–55, 215, 367, 466, 487, 530–34, 551, 584, 652–53, 664, 681
DOJ (Department of Justice), 460, 486, 670, 673, 684, 689–90, 692, 699
domestic policy, 77, 468, 627
Dowd, Maureen, 221, 585, 694–95, 794

E

Earnest, Josh, 630
economy, 9, 83, 90, 95, 123–25, 144, 178, 180, 191–92, 210–11, 214, 238, 257, 259, 271, 285–86, 336, 369, 402, 415, 462–63, 492, 522, 607–8, 659–60
Election Day, 576–77, 579, 589, 596, 669, 684, 702, 704–5
Electoral College, 4, 459, 577–80, 601, 687, 691, 693, 705, 708–9, 713
EU (European Union), 136, 493–94, 506, 521, 656
Europe, 137, 194, 380–81, 393–95, 415, 521, 703
evangelicals, 41, 104, 202, 228, 235, 247, 262, 290, 327, 329, 364–65, 640–41, 700–701, 711

F

Falwell, Jerry, Jr., 282, 700–701
Far Left, 71, 80, 85, 88, 91, 98, 114, 117, 148, 160, 177, 276, 374, 379, 532, 616, 714
Farook, Rizwan, 241, 246
Far Right, 80, 85, 207, 276
FBI (Federal Bureau of Investigation), 71, 134, 195, 205, 351, 390, 397–98, 421, 427, 445, 460, 484, 499–501, 503–4, 510, 518, 533, 580–82, 610, 619–21, 638, 674–80, 685–86, 688–90, 697–98
Feinstein, Dianne, 396, 537
Ferguson, 25–26, 33, 308, 520
Florida, 17, 28, 37, 45, 113, 121, 125, 134, 155, 183, 200, 265, 343, 346, 354, 358–59, 366, 371–73, 387, 401, 479, 577–80, 685, 690–91, 705–7
FOIA (Freedom of Information Act), 281, 390, 445, 685, 692, 699
FOIA request, 445–46, 460, 466
Ford, Gerald, 428–30, 492–93
Fourteenth Amendment, 140, 171, 174
Foval, Scott, 652–53
Fox News, 37, 104, 110, 129, 157, 209, 281, 284–85, 437, 444, 450, 463–64, 518, 548, 650, 657, 689, 697
France, 131, 231, 241, 517, 535, 600
Freedom Caucus, 207, 209, 220, 375–76

G

Galifianakis, Zach, 608–9
Georgia, 11, 265, 345, 347, 349, 394, 419, 429, 508, 592, 601, 687, 690
Germany, 259, 381, 433–34, 521, 535, 600
Gilmore, Jim, 74, 153–54, 159, 185, 291, 308, 434
Gingrich, Newt, 62, 154, 511, 517–18
Goodman, H. A., 397–98
GOP, 228, 281, 557, 759, 769. *See also* Republican Party
Gore, Al, 3, 41, 49, 145, 310, 365, 479, 579–80
government shutdown, 40, 62, 207–9, 585, 588
Graham, Lindsey, 76, 91–92, 132, 153, 159, 184, 187–88, 192, 197–98, 235–36, 252, 331

Green Party, 479, 608, 635
Gruber, Jonathan, 23–25, 139
Guccifer (Romanian hacker), 324, 444, 487

H

Haley, Nicky, 132–34, 327
Harrison, James, 177–78
Hawaii, 253, 265, 343, 357, 385, 596–97
HFC (House Freedom Caucus), 41, 220, 375–76, 586–88
Hispanics, 173, 230, 269, 308, 366, 368, 481, 573, 602
Holt, Lester, 614–15
Hoosiers, 431, 437
House Budget Committee, 129, 425
Huckabee, Mike, 104, 119, 133, 153, 159, 183, 190, 192, 198, 213, 235–36, 290, 293, 364, 546
Huffington Post, 184, 483, 618
Hussein, Saddam, 108–9, 320, 505

I

Idaho, 265, 357, 377–78
IED (improvised explosive device), 598
Illinois, 28, 210–11, 265, 269, 372–73, 575, 705
immigration, 22–23, 30, 43, 62, 80, 87, 102, 127, 169, 216, 244, 249–50, 256, 270, 301, 319, 366, 407, 454, 522, 567–70, 573, 603, 650, 661
illegal, 102, 126, 142, 170–71, 249–50, 326, 343, 363, 366, 662
Indiana, 29, 52–53, 265, 425–26, 429–33, 438–39, 441–42, 444, 519, 523, 579, 707
Indianapolis Colts, 51–52
international trade, 359, 363–64, 495, 538
Iowa, 11, 16, 49, 56, 70, 84, 87, 123, 133, 144, 183–85, 235–36, 244, 247–48, 256–58, 261–65, 267–71, 274–75, 277–78, 282, 290–93, 307, 309–10, 339–41, 579–80
caucuses, 104, 259, 273, 281–82, 285, 287, 292–93, 295–96, 304, 428, 694
Iowa and New Hampshire, 117, 146, 159, 184, 228, 247–48, 251, 268, 274, 279, 292, 307
IPC (ideological-political complex), 587–88
Iraq, 7–8, 25, 95, 109–10, 112, 238, 246, 320, 381, 402, 480, 497, 520, 544–45, 556, 621–22
Iraq War, 33, 109, 111, 125, 319–20, 450, 589, 612, 616
IRS (Internal Revenue Service), 74, 557, 616
ISIS, 7–8, 32, 91, 100, 110, 112, 169, 225, 231, 233–34, 241, 246, 259, 325, 380–81, 432, 484, 497–98, 519–20, 535, 556, 615, 622
Israel, 8, 363–65

J

Jews, 365–66, 531
Jindahl, Bobby, 118, 127, 153, 159, 173, 184, 193, 233
Jones, Paula, 464, 636–37
Judicial Watch, 389–90, 445, 466, 510, 563, 572
Justice Department, 71, 163–64, 167, 352, 421, 460, 499, 503, 563, 670, 678, 680, 689, 691

K

Kadzik, Peter, 692, 699
Kaine, Tim, 512, 530, 532–33, 546, 558, 608, 630–32, 677, 683
Kansas, 11, 265, 350, 353–54
Kelly, Megyn, 158, 282, 464

Kentucky, 11–12, 229–30, 265, 354, 424, 441, 454, 464
Kerry, John, 49, 145, 579–80
Kessler, Glenn, 449, 470–71, 765
Keystone XL pipeline, 25, 147–49, 203–5
Khans, 545–47, 549, 553
Krauthammer, Charles, 87, 112, 171, 173–74, 210, 253, 504, 570, 769
Kudlow, Larry, 457–58, 633

L

Labor Day, 175, 182–84, 403, 571–72, 574, 576–77
Landrieu, Mary, 24–25, 27
Lewinsky, Monica, 637, 676, 692
liberals, 41, 92–93, 140, 368–69, 484, 573, 588
libertarians, 11, 83, 239, 294, 479–80, 640, 694
Libya, 32, 209, 221–22, 381, 480, 497
Lincoln, Abraham, 116, 546, 639
Louisiana, 11, 13, 27, 40, 233, 256, 265, 350, 354, 400, 404, 507
Luntz, Frank, 106, 218, 613
Lynch, Loretta, 351–52, 499–501, 510, 518, 670, 691–92, 769

M

Maine, 265, 353–54, 601, 705
mainstream media, 10, 38, 50–51, 56–57, 80, 98, 176, 199, 226, 229, 294, 339, 367, 369, 440, 461, 463, 480–81, 505, 518, 597, 611, 623, 650–51, 696–97
Malik, Tashfeen, 241, 246
Manafort, Paul, 406–7, 469, 489–90, 523, 558, 561–62
Manning, Peyton, 51–52
Marcus, Ruth, 97, 149, 166–67, 195, 232, 255, 352–53, 472, 500, 672, 765, 769
Maryland, 70, 265, 268, 416, 421–22, 426, 488, 710
Massachusetts, 256, 265, 267, 344–47, 349, 476, 546
McAuliffe, Terry, 538–39, 660, 774
McCain, John, 3, 12, 15, 48, 53, 74, 76, 92, 95–96, 101, 126, 143, 216, 226–27, 276, 383, 549–50, 553, 561, 574, 578–80, 640
McConnell, Mitch, 10, 63–64, 229, 639
Merkley, Jeff, 414, 757
Metaxas, Eric, 640–41
Mexican government, 154, 156, 319, 325, 335, 569
Mexico, 154, 171, 230, 319, 325–26, 328, 335, 399, 407–8, 417, 495, 567, 569–70, 593–94
Michigan, 105, 265, 350, 355, 357, 359, 443, 514, 592, 594, 629, 676, 687, 691, 694, 696, 706, 708–9, 714
millennials, 608, 698
Mills, Cheryl, 460, 473, 499, 582, 619–21, 671
Minneapolis, 115, 507
Minnesota, 256, 265, 345–49, 507, 598–99, 708–9
Mississippi, 40, 266, 350, 357–58
Missouri, 25, 33, 266, 269, 372–73, 520, 592, 636, 710
moderates, 3, 59, 173, 264, 378–79, 429, 512, 530, 631
Mook, Robby, 34, 313, 564, 611
Moore, Steve, 457–58, 554, 618
Muslims, 419, 485, 517, 547, 549
refugees, 246, 599

N

NAFTA (North American Free Trade Agreement), 138, 495, 536, 555, 660
NAM (National Association of Manufacturers), 269
national debate, 126–27, 193, 246, 408
National Democratic Party, 27, 82
National Enquirer, 384, 438
National Republican Party, 82, 281, 447
NATO (North Atlantic Treaty Organization), 393–95, 521
NEC (National Economic Council), 188, 197, 451
Nevada, 17, 29, 155, 215, 261, 266–67, 278, 307, 310–11, 331–34, 338–40, 342, 464, 571, 579, 601, 656–57, 687, 705–6, 709
Never Trumpers, 480, 524, 532
New Hampshire, 16, 94, 144, 155, 165, 183–85, 223, 227, 229, 235–36, 244–45, 247–48, 256–57, 261, 266–67, 270, 274–75, 290–93, 299–300, 303, 307–12, 314–15, 361, 577–79, 708–9
debate, 245, 300–302, 309, 319, 337, 362
New Jersey, 50–51, 73, 119, 127, 156, 234, 266, 338, 426, 470, 482, 598–99, 625
New Mexico, 266, 425–26, 470, 482, 577, 579, 687
New Orleans, 9, 368, 411
New Republic, 140–41
New York City, 109, 147, 315–16, 408, 412, 431, 583, 589, 676
Nieto, Enrique, 549, 569–70, 613
nomination
presidential, 31, 258, 292, 488
process, 31, 142, 268, 311, 417
Noonan, Peggy, 54, 101, 156, 200, 227, 527, 529, 631

North Carolina, 16, 40, 130, 256, 266, 367, 372–73, 408, 428, 505, 577–79, 601, 605, 652, 656, 671, 687, 696, 705–7
North Vietnam, 143, 383
NRA (National Rifle Association), 355, 659
NRSC (National Republican Senatorial Committee), 470–71

O

Obama, Barack, 3–4, 6–10, 12–13, 15–16, 22–26, 30–34, 108–12, 144–45, 175–77, 185–87, 214, 231–34, 252–54, 259–61, 269–71, 321–23, 380–82, 539–40, 549, 576–79, 596–97, 599–600, 602–3, 609–11, 698–99
administration, 9, 24, 118, 138, 149, 206, 253, 485, 494, 538, 560, 638
economy, 555, 660, 702
executive orders, 22, 30, 62–63, 102, 142, 172, 299
job approval, 210, 257, 552
Justice Department, 352, 427, 499
legacy, 53, 176, 242
policies, 189, 260, 491–92, 522
pseudonym, 610–11, 620
Obama, Michelle, 525, 534–35, 540, 631, 683
Obamacare, 23–25, 40, 107, 139, 141, 229, 239, 260, 336, 537, 630, 685, 702
Ohio, 130, 155, 190, 266, 347, 357, 366, 371–73, 401, 425, 429, 443, 506, 523, 574, 577–79, 583, 592, 604, 643, 648, 656, 683–84, 690–91, 705–7
OIG (Office of Inspector General), 472–74

Oklahoma, 223, 266, 345–49, 373, 406, 605
O'Malley, Martin, 21, 70–71, 91, 114–15, 117–18, 127, 135, 154, 183, 215–17, 219, 232, 236, 248–49, 251, 260–61, 287, 289, 291–92
Oregon, 160, 240, 266, 425–26, 454, 464, 580, 648
Orlando, 479, 484, 520
Orlando shooting, 484–85, 488
Oswald, Lee Harvey, 437–38
Oval Office, 4, 39, 511, 634, 637, 695. *See also* White House

P

Pagliano, Bryan, 351, 398, 445–46, 486
Palin, Sarah, 56, 73–74, 276–77, 282, 448
Paris, 231, 233–34, 241, 259, 485
Pataki, George, 74, 153–54, 159, 235–36, 257
Paul, Rand, 22, 55, 65, 80, 82–83, 119, 133–34, 146, 153, 156, 159, 184, 193–94, 198, 213, 235–36, 285, 288–89, 291, 293–95
Pence, Mike, 82, 433–34, 512, 516–17, 519, 523, 526–28, 530, 544, 630–32, 634, 641
Pennsylvania, 28, 87, 223, 266, 416, 422, 424, 426, 429, 443, 495, 575, 592, 656, 683, 687, 690, 694, 701–2, 705–9, 711, 714
Perkins, Tom, 225–26
Perry, Rick, 73, 120–21, 125, 153, 158–59, 184, 192, 299
Philadelphia, 259, 410, 412, 530, 542
Phoenix, 499–500
Podesta, John
emails, 642–43
political campaigns, 1, 122–23, 131, 196, 243, 325, 361, 377, 554

political parties, 3, 15, 180, 316, 379, 386, 420, 542, 567, 680
polls, 11, 21, 116–17, 119–20, 141–42, 144, 152, 176, 183–84, 212–13, 260–61, 282–83, 287–88, 292–93, 332–34, 423, 469, 513–15, 552–53, 592, 607–8, 674, 682–83, 694, 705–6
exit, 306, 346, 442, 710–11
national, 126, 158, 183–84, 236, 243–44, 251, 261, 283, 416, 423, 469, 480, 656, 668, 674, 684, 694, 701, 705, 713
pre-election, 106–7
Rasmussen, 158–59
state, 423, 514, 674, 683, 687, 691, 693, 713
tracking, 623, 701, 705
Pope, 325–26, 383, 547
Portman, Rob, 28, 523, 574, 701
Powell, Colin, 109, 167, 444, 563, 593
PredictWise, 213, 574
presidential candidates, 3, 48, 56, 66, 105, 172, 204, 210, 325, 327, 471, 558, 701
presidential debate, 120, 624, 630, 633, 636, 639, 657, 661
presidential election, 5, 7, 242, 379, 469, 647, 712
Priebus, Reince, 228, 395–96, 417, 440, 448, 455
primal scream, 180, 703–4
Puerto Rico, 350, 354, 470
Putin, Vladimir, 7–8, 240, 246, 253, 282, 394, 487, 498, 543, 548, 612, 646, 666

Q

Quintanilla, Carl, 224–27

R

racism, 130, 239, 509, 571, 591
radical Islam, 380–81, 484, 599
RCP (RealClearPolitics), 235–36, 287–88, 305–6, 514, 552, 705, 747
Reagan, Ronald, 6, 15, 41, 94–95, 117, 124, 131–32, 175, 321, 379, 428–29, 710, 758
recession, 210–11, 257, 259, 399, 415–16, 614
refugees, 233, 237, 241–42, 246, 259, 535, 599, 603
Reid, Harry, 29, 31, 64, 339, 466, 575, 680–81
Republican candidates, 113, 138, 173, 283, 302, 321, 346, 364, 376, 433, 480
Republican convention, 243, 376, 423, 512, 515–16, 519, 524, 526–29, 531–32, 610
contested, 375, 400
Republican debate, 155, 170, 230, 232, 245, 273
Republican establishment, 36, 118, 127, 226, 242, 247, 278, 330, 338, 557, 560–62, 693
Republican nomination, 3, 48, 95, 353, 440, 459, 552
Republican nominee, 28, 199, 254, 267, 281, 387, 447, 478, 489, 527, 634, 649
Republican Party, 4, 13, 38–41, 85, 103, 157, 180, 194, 219, 228, 271, 350, 354, 378, 382, 395, 437, 446, 451, 453–54, 488–90, 519, 551–52, 639–40, 649
Republican president, 27, 29, 217, 267, 395, 633, 647
Republican primaries, 27, 29, 217, 267, 395, 633, 647
Republican race, 119, 276, 288–89, 388, 401
Republicans, 9–12, 27–30, 48–50, 61–64, 118, 137–38, 161–62, 197–200, 206–7, 214–15, 220–24, 251–53, 260–62, 267–69, 280–81, 344–47, 349–52, 373–77, 386–88, 413–17, 440–42, 451–52, 538–40, 595–96, 709–13
Republican voters, 187, 262, 267, 351, 373, 376, 395, 442, 447, 592–93, 645, 701
RGA (Republican Governor's Association), 49
Rhode Island, 103, 266, 416, 421–22, 426–27
Rich, Denise, 685–86
Rich, Marc, 685–86, 692
RNC (Republican National Committee), 75, 152, 375, 395–96, 440, 446, 448, 455, 468, 472, 551, 557, 655
Roberts, John, 139–40
Romney, Mitt, 12, 38, 48–49, 52–56, 196, 337, 353, 358, 376, 436, 576–78, 580, 602, 604, 711
Rove, Karl, 37, 39, 55
Russia, 8, 32, 57, 97, 246, 252, 395, 433, 480, 498, 521, 543–44, 646–47, 663, 683
Ryan, Paul, 22, 55, 138, 208–9, 220, 245, 375–76, 388, 409–10, 422, 447–48, 455–56, 478, 550, 586, 588, 639, 649, 766

S

San Bernardino, 240–41, 246
Sanders campaign, 367, 374, 405, 413, 427, 745
Santorum, Rick, 153, 159, 173, 184, 192, 235–36, 291, 293, 295

Scalia, Antonin, 140, 321–22
Schultz, Wasserman, 466, 533–34
Schweiker, Richard, 429
Second Amendment, 133, 135, 270, 485, 658–59
Senate Democrats, 25, 63, 92, 207
Senate Republicans, 27, 207, 250
Sessions, Jeff, 250, 343, 525, 629
sexism, 255–56, 298–99, 303, 461, 571, 591
Socialism, 88–90, 92–93, 114–15, 192, 194, 232, 242, 417
Social Security, 86, 191, 328, 364, 399
SOFA (Status of Forces Agreement), 622
South Carolina, 76, 91, 130, 132–34, 183, 248, 256–57, 261, 266–67, 274–75, 278, 299, 307–11, 313–14, 319, 321, 327, 329–31, 333, 338–42, 365, 408, 419
South China Sea, 521
Soviet Union, 90, 393–94
State Department, 67, 70–71, 97, 99, 149, 163, 168, 186, 205, 221, 281, 286, 317–18, 324, 339, 445–46, 460, 474, 497–98, 501, 510, 561, 563–65, 572, 582
Stein, Jill, 608, 627, 635, 642, 693, 705, 708
Sterling, Alton, 507–8
St. Louis, 367, 406, 636, 710
"Stronger Together," 590–91
superdelegates, 275, 278–80, 385–86, 389, 416, 423, 464
Super Tuesday, 16–17, 275, 310, 332, 334, 340, 342, 344, 346–50, 353, 356, 402
Super Tuesday II, 370–74
swing states, 129, 155, 202, 267, 348, 577–79, 694

Syria, 232, 237, 242, 246, 394, 480, 497–98, 627

T

Taliban, 7–8, 108, 535
TARP (Troubled Asset Relief Program), 34
Tax Foundation, 189, 192, 212, 336, 457
tax plans, 191–92, 336, 457
Tea Party, 3, 10, 40–42, 82, 85, 92, 128, 162, 179–81, 202, 229, 247, 256, 276–77, 289, 294, 299–300, 451, 481, 538, 550, 587, 693, 701
Tea Party Caucus, 41, 83, 586. *See also* HFC (House Freedom Caucus)
Tennessee, 266, 345, 347, 349, 508
Texas, 19, 37, 46, 74, 79, 94, 120, 133, 148, 223, 266, 337, 345–47, 349, 369, 379, 401, 429, 517, 578, 712
Thanksgiving, 234, 238, 243
Toomey, Pat, 28, 300, 575, 656, 701, 711
TPA (Trade Promotion Authority), 100, 137–38
TPP (Trans-Pacific Partnership), 136–37, 214–16, 238, 260, 532, 538–39, 554, 635, 660, 774
Trump, Donald, 2–4, 71–73, 118–19, 254–57, 282, 328–29, 349–53, 382–83, 385–87, 416–18, 441–43, 446–49, 453–59, 461–62, 478, 480–84, 511–12, 528–29, 541–46, 548–50, 562–64, 589–93, 632–34, 644–46, 692–95
administration, 338, 451, 468, 529
behavior, 553, 612, 616, 646, 664, 695
birther maneuver, 270
campaign, 193, 231, 238, 395, 435, 439, 457, 468, 506, 525, 558, 561–62, 572, 597, 602, 604, 633, 666, 703
candidacy, 65, 353, 569, 618
performance, 358, 360, 443

persistence, 184, 278
plan, 211, 336, 595, 599
policies, 336, 570
position, 391, 394, 567, 617
supporters, 237, 367–68, 405–6, 423, 435, 437, 450, 481, 568, 591, 603, 634, 652, 674, 697
tax, 399, 457, 625
tax plan, 328, 336
Trump, Ivanka, 528–29, 654
Trump, Melania, 383, 524–26, 633, 653–54, 664
Trump Foundation, 628, 663
TTIP (Transatlantic Trade and Investment Partnership), 136–37
Tulsa, 605–6
Tweener Tuesday, 356, 358
Tyler, Rick, 313–14

U

United Kingdom, 194, 493–94, 598
United States of America, 1–2, 7–8, 43–45, 110, 133–34, 136–37, 148, 154, 171–72, 194, 203–4, 240, 242, 246, 252, 271, 302, 324–25, 328, 355–56, 393–94, 494–500, 553–54, 593–94, 621–22
United States Senate, 4, 14, 19, 22, 26–30, 34, 55, 62–64, 77, 82–83, 88–90, 92, 103, 138, 186, 198, 206–7, 209, 277–78, 299–300, 321–23, 396, 494–95, 585–87, 713
United States Supreme Court, 23–24, 66, 79, 82, 128, 139–41, 171, 321–23, 468, 494, 530, 555, 579, 640–41, 658, 714
US News and World Report, 126, 307, 350
Utah, 77, 266–67, 374–75, 377–78, 416, 687

V

Vermont, 88–89, 103, 115, 144, 266, 308, 316, 345, 347–49
veterans, 284, 476–77, 547, 597
Virginia, 6, 10–11, 144, 185, 229, 266, 282, 345, 347–49, 419, 434, 436, 459, 512, 530, 538, 550, 578–79, 592, 630, 687, 691, 694, 705–7
vote
black, 333, 602
evangelical, 290, 711
immigrant, 172
popular, 4, 416, 436, 708–9, 713
statewide, 401
white, 442, 710
women's, 256, 306, 441, 710–11
voter fraud, 162, 655–56, 661, 699
voters
American, 24, 61–63, 80, 195, 210, 243, 432, 443, 607, 703–4
dead, 162, 654
Democratic, 251, 267, 306, 374, 443, 542, 641
Hispanic, 256, 307, 602, 711
independent, 10, 49
undecided, 4, 88, 292
voter turnout, 378, 459, 655, 696

W

Walker, Scott, 22, 49, 55–56, 58–60, 65, 77, 80, 118–19, 126–28, 133, 142, 153, 156, 159, 174–75, 182–84, 198, 201–2, 264, 388, 406, 439
Wallace, Chris, 657–58, 661–62, 664–66
Wall Street, 40, 298, 303, 402–3, 491, 554, 634, 647
Wall Street Journal, 138, 156, 418, 432, 436, 457, 462, 502, 519, 569, 692
Warren, Elizabeth, 21, 34–35, 54, 70–71, 80, 92, 175, 177, 299, 475–76, 482, 665, 713

Washington, 5, 9, 19–20, 25, 40, 49–50, 62, 66, 69, 75, 95, 100–101, 128, 140, 142, 156, 160, 179, 185, 206, 209, 228–29, 385, 685–86, 769
Weiner, Anthony, 674–76, 678
emails, 684, 697
Weingarten, Randi, 160
West Virginia, 266, 369, 447, 453–54
White House, 29, 31, 41, 51, 59, 78, 97, 108, 116, 118, 121, 126, 141–42, 193, 197, 199, 214, 219, 221, 258, 286, 352, 539, 653, 690
WikiLeaks, 531–32, 534, 543, 634, 645–47, 669, 671, 681, 692
emails, 645, 648, 663, 682, 690, 699
Wildstein, David, 50
Will, George, 44, 253, 258, 686
Willey, Kathleen, 464, 636–37
Wisconsin, 28, 59, 92, 119, 127, 155, 220, 266, 374, 388–89, 400, 410, 448, 478, 575, 580, 592, 639, 701, 705, 708–9, 711, 714
WMD (weapons of mass destruction), 108–9, 320
Womack, Steve, 524
Wyoming, 48, 266, 344–45, 366, 401, 403, 418, 691

Z

Zeitz, Glenn, 384

CPSIA information can be obtained
at www.ICGtesting.com
Printed in the USA
BVHW070709171019
561296BV00001B/6/P